SCREENING AMERICAN INDEPENDENT FILM

This indispensable collection offers 51 chapters, each focused on a distinct American independent film.

Screening American Independent Film presents these films chronologically, addressing works from across more than a century (1915–2020), emphasizing the breadth and long duration of American independent cinema. The collection includes canonical examples as well as films that push against and expand the definitions of "independence." The titles run from micro-budget films through marketing-friendly Indiewood projects, from auteur-driven films and festival darlings to B-movies, genre pics, and exploitation films. The chapters also introduce students to different approaches within film studies including historical and contextual framing, industrial and institutional analysis, politics and ideology, genre and authorship, representation, film analysis, exhibition and reception, and technology.

Written by leading international scholars and emerging talents in film studies, this volume is the first of its kind. Paying particular attention to issues of diversity and inclusion for both the participating scholars and the content and themes within the selected films, *Screening American Independent Film* is an essential resource for anyone teaching or studying American cinema.

Justin Wyatt is an Associate Professor of Communication Studies, Film/Media, and Journalism at the University of Rhode Island. He is the author of *The Virgin Suicides: Reverie, Sorrow and Young Love* (Routledge) and the co-editor of *Contemporary American Independent Film: From the Margins to the Mainstream* (Routledge). He is completing a manuscript on qualitative and quantitative market research methods in the media industries. He has published in the fields of media history, film marketing, and media industry studies.

Wyatt D. Phillips is an Associate Professor of Film and Media Studies in the English Department at Texas Tech University. His work primarily engages questions of the political economy of media production and circulation. His current book project considers the historical relationship between turn-of-the-century business culture and the significance of genre in early Hollywood. His publications include work on the economic structure and history of the American film industry, the rise of drive-in theaters, and Camp TV of the 1960s.

Screening Cinema
Series Editor: Gary Needham

Supporting the use of film screenings as a core aspect of film studies pedagogy, *Screening Cinema* fills a gap in teaching film where screenings are a core activity. Each volume of the series includes fifty essential readings on individual films specifically designed to support film screenings and to demonstrate that alternative approaches and films can exist alongside, and at no cost to, the canonical. Written by leading scholars in film studies and emerging talents specializing in film studies and cognate disciplines, *Screening Cinema* is the first series of its kind.

Screening Independent American Film
Justin Wyatt and W.D. Phillips

For more information visit: https://www.routledge.com/Screening-Cinema/book-series/SACINEMA

SCREENING AMERICAN INDEPENDENT FILM

Edited by Justin Wyatt and W.D. Phillips

LONDON AND NEW YORK

Designed cover image: Photo 12 / Alamy Stock Photo

First published 2023
by Routledge
4 Park Square, Milton Park, Abingdon, Oxon OX14 4RN

and by Routledge
605 Third Avenue, New York, NY 10158

Routledge is an imprint of the Taylor & Francis Group, an informa business

© 2023 selection and editorial matter, Justin Wyatt and W.D. Phillips; individual chapters, the contributors

The right of Justin Wyatt and W.D. Phillips to be identified as the authors of the editorial material, and of the authors for their individual chapters, has been asserted in accordance with sections 77 and 78 of the Copyright, Designs and Patents Act 1988.

All rights reserved. No part of this book may be reprinted or reproduced or utilised in any form or by any electronic, mechanical, or other means, now known or hereafter invented, including photocopying and recording, or in any information storage or retrieval system, without permission in writing from the publishers.

Trademark notice: Product or corporate names may be trademarks or registered trademarks, and are used only for identification and explanation without intent to infringe.

British Library Cataloguing-in-Publication Data
A catalogue record for this book is available from the British Library

Library of Congress Cataloging-in-Publication Data
Names: Wyatt, Justin, 1963– editor. | Phillips, W. D. (Wyatt D.), editor.
Title: Screening American independent film / Justin Wyatt, W. D. Phillips.
Description: Abingdon, Oxon; New York: Routledge, 2023. |
Series: Screening cinema | Includes bibliographical references and index.
Identifiers: LCCN 2022060495 (print) | LCCN 2022060496 (ebook) |
ISBN 9781032160603 (hardback) | ISBN 9781032160627 (paperback) |
ISBN 9781003246930 (ebook)
Subjects: LCSH: Independent films—United States—History and criticism.
Classification: LCC PN1995.9.I457 S37 2023 (print) |
LCC PN1995.9.I457 (ebook) | DDC 791.43/6—dc23/eng/20230302
LC record available at https://lccn.loc.gov/2022060495
LC ebook record available at https://lccn.loc.gov/2022060496

ISBN: 978-1-032-16060-3 (hbk)
ISBN: 978-1-032-16062-7 (pbk)
ISBN: 978-1-003-24693-0 (ebk)

DOI: 10.4324/9781003246930

Typeset in Bembo
by codeMantra

WDP: to my brother, Zack, with whom I first saw so many of these films

JW: to Joanne Yamaguchi and Audrey Joan Reynertson, my first film professors

CONTENTS

List of contributors xii
Acknowledgments xxii

Introduction: On the Sweep of American Independent Film Histories 1
W.D. Phillips and Justin Wyatt

1 *Two Knights of Vaudeville* (1915) 12
Allyson Nadia Field

2 *Safety Last!* (1923) 22
Christina G. Petersen

3 *Steamboat Bill, Jr.* (1928) 31
Peter Krämer

4 *Billy the Kid Returns* (1938) 40
W.D. Phillips

5 *Detour* (1945) 49
Todd Berliner

6 *The Hitch-Hiker* (1953) 59
Lisa Dombrowski

7   *The Man with the Golden Arm* (1955)   68
    Philip Drake and Nessa Johnston

8   *Attack of the 50 Foot Woman* (1958)   77
    Jamie Hook

9   *I Want to Live!* (1958)   87
    Peter Labuza

10 *Color Me Blood Red* (1965)   96
    Murray Leeder

11 *My Hustler* (1965)   104
    Kevin John Bozelka

12 *Portrait of Jason* (1967)   113
    James Morrison

13 *Bob & Carol & Ted & Alice* (1969)   122
    Cynthia Lucia

14 *The Learning Tree* (1969)   131
    Arthur Knight

15 *Wanda* (1970)   140
    Pamela Robertson Wojcik

16 *Billy Jack* (1971)   149
    Nicholas Godfrey

17 *Deep Throat* (1972)   158
    José B. Capino

18 *Pink Flamingos* (1972)   167
    Nathan Koob

19 *Dark Star* (1974)   176
    Nitin Govil

20 *A Very Natural Thing* (1974)   186
    Matt Connolly

21 *The Killing of a Chinese Bookie* (1976) — 195
Sam Littman

22 *Chan Is Missing* (1982) — 204
Cynthia Baron

23 *One from the Heart* (1982) — 214
Justin Wyatt

24 *Choose Me* (1984) — 223
Caryl Flinn

25 *Desert Hearts* (1986) — 233
Chelsea McCracken

26 *Down By Law* (1986) — 243
Yannis Tzioumakis

27 *She's Gotta Have It* (1986) — 252
Apryl Lewis

28 *Eight Men Out* (1988) — 261
Aaron Baker

29 *Sex, Lies, and Videotape* (1989) — 269
Michael Z. Newman

30 *Paris Is Burning* (1990) — 277
Michele Meek

31 *Teenage Mutant Ninja Turtles* (1990) — 286
Cortland Rankin

32 *My Own Private Idaho* (1991) — 295
Daniel Herbert

33 *Twin Peaks: Fire Walk with Me* (1992) — 304
Rick Warner

34 *Pulp Fiction* (1994) — 313
Scott L. Baugh

35 *Eve's Bayou* (1997) 323
   Kristi McKim

36 *Donnie Darko* (2001) 333
   Claire Parkinson

37 *The Royal Tenenbaums* (2001) 342
   Warren Buckland

38 *Stranger Inside* (2001) 351
   Kathleen McHugh

39 *Far from Heaven* (2002) 361
   Ken Feil

40 *Real Women Have Curves* (2002) 370
   Mirasol Enríquez

41 *American Splendor* (2003) 379
   Alberto Zambenedetti

42 *Paranormal Activity* (2007) 389
   Aslı Ildır

43 *The Great Flood* (2012) 398
   Dale Hudson and Patricia R. Zimmermann

44 *Before Midnight* (2013) 408
   Chuck Tryon

45 *Dallas Buyers Club* (2013) 417
   Mark Gallagher

46 *Jason and Shirley* (2015) 427
   Alexandra Juhasz

47 *The Witch* (2015) 437
   Alex Brannan

48 *1985* (2018) 447
   Daniel Humphrey

49	*First Cow* (2020) J.J. Murphy	456
50	*The Forty-Year-Old Version* (2020) Sarah E.S. Sinwell	466
51	*Nomadland* (2020) Geoff King	476

Index   *485*

CONTRIBUTORS

Aaron Baker is a Professor of Film and Media Studies at Arizona State University where he teaches courses on American film and television. His most recent book is *The Baseball Film. A Cultural and Transmedia History* (2022).

Cynthia Baron is a Professor in the Department of Theatre and Film and an affiliated faculty in the doctoral American Culture Studies Program at Bowling Green State University. She is the author of *Modern Acting: The Lost Chapter of American Film and Theatre* (2016) and *Denzel Washington* (2015). Her co-authored books include *Acting Indie: Industry, Aesthetics, and Performance* (2020), *Appetites and Anxieties: Food, Film, and the Politics of Representation* (2014), and *Reframing Screen Performance* (2008). She is the editor of the *Journal of Film and Video* and series editor for a book series in Screen Industries and Performance.

Scott L. Baugh is a Professor of English in the Film and Media Studies program at Texas Tech University (Lubbock, TX, USA), specializing in multicultural American aesthetics. His publications include *Y Tu Mamá También: Mythologies of Youth* (2019); *Born of Resistance: Cara a Cara Encounters with Chicana/o Visual Culture*, co-edited with Victor A. Sorell (2016); and *Latino American Cinema* (2012).

Todd Berliner is a Professor of Film Studies at the University of North Carolina Wilmington, teaching film aesthetics, narration and style, and American film history. He is the author of *Hollywood Aesthetic: Pleasure in American Cinema* (2017) and *Hollywood Incoherent: Narration in Seventies Cinema* (2010). He was the founding chairman of UNCW's Film Studies Department and the recipient of two Fulbright Scholar awards, including the Laszlo Orszagh Distinguished Chair in American Studies.

Kevin John Bozelka is an Assistant Professor of Communication Arts & Sciences at Bronx Community College. His research interests concern genre, popular music, the Hollywood musical, pornography, and avant-garde cinema. He has had articles published in *Porn Studies*, *Jump Cut*, and *La Furia Umana* as well as film and popular music criticism in *Village Voice*, *MTV.com*, *Dallas Morning News*, *Chicago Reader*, and a variety of other newspapers and magazines.

Alex Brannan is a PhD student at Indiana University in the Media School. He received an MA in Media Studies at the University of Texas at Austin. His work has been published in the journals *Film International* and *Flow*. His current research focuses on the distribution practices and exhibition venues for horror and exploitation cinemas, with a particular emphasis on low-budget, "low-taste" film properties.

Warren Buckland is a Reader in Film Studies at Oxford Brookes University. He is the author or editor of a number of books, including *Puzzle Films: Complex Storytelling in Contemporary Cinema* (ed., 2009), *Hollywood Puzzle Films* (ed., 2014), *Film Theory: Rational Reconstructions* (2012), and *Wes Anderson's Symbolic Storyworld* (2019).

José B. Capino is a Professor of English and Cinema and Media Studies at the University of Illinois at Urbana-Champaign. His most recent book is *Martial Law Melodrama: Lino Brocka's Cinema Politics* (2020).

Matt Connolly is an Assistant Professor of Film Studies in the Department of English at Minnesota State University, Mankato. He has published articles in *JCMS* (formerly *Cinema Journal*), *Velvet Light Trap*, and *Spectator*. He has written criticism for *Film Comment*, *Reverse Shot*, and other publications. He researches the aesthetic, industrial, and cultural histories of LGBTQ cinema in the United States. His current project analyzes directorial persona and cultural reputation in the career of John Waters.

Lisa Dombrowski is a Professor of Film Studies and Professor of East Asian Studies at Wesleyan University. She authored *The Films of Samuel Fuller: If You Die, I'll Kill You!* (2008), edited *Kazan Revisited* (2011), and co-edited *ReFocus: The Later Films and Legacy of Robert Altman* (2021). She has contributed chapters to *United Artists: Hollywood Centenary* (2020), *Independent Female Filmmakers: A Chronicle Through Interviews, Profiles, and Manifestos* (2018), *Silent Features: The Development of Silent Feature Films, 1914–1934* (2018), *Behind the Silver Screen: Cinematography* (2014), and *Widescreen Worldwide* (2010). Her articles have also appeared in *Film History*, *Film Quarterly*, *Film Comment*, *New York Times*, and the Criterion Collection.

Philip Drake is a Professor of Media and Creative Industries and the Director of Education in the Faculty of Arts and Humanities at Manchester Metropolitan

University. He has published extensively on screen industries, including film distribution, Video-on-Demand, European co-production and policy, as well as on Hollywood, independent American cinema, and screen performance. He co-edited the collection *Hollywood and the Law* (2015). He has also advised the Council of Europe on film funding and directed a research project on independent film distribution and Video-on-Demand.

Mirasol Enríquez is the Director of Moody College's Latino Media Arts and Studies program and an Assistant Professor in the Department of Radio-Television-Film at the University of Texas at Austin. Her scholarship focuses on US-based Latina filmmakers, media production culture, and representations of race and gender in media. As a film and media scholar and arts administrator, she has devoted her career to community building through film and the arts. Her scholarship has appeared in *JCMS: Journal of Cinema and Media Studies* and *Feminist Media Histories*.

Ken Feil is an Assistant Professor in Emerson College's Visual & Media Arts Department. Ken is a recipient of the National Endowment for the Humanities "Enduring Questions" grant and the author of *Rowan & Martin's Laugh-In* (2014), *Dying for a Laugh: Disaster Movies and the Camp Imagination* (2005), and numerous articles for journals and collections. Ken's newest book, *Fearless Vulgarity: Jacqueline Susann's Queer Comedy and Camp Authorship*, was published in 2022.

Allyson Nadia Field is an Associate Professor of Cinema and Media Studies at the University of Chicago. She is the author of *Uplift Cinema: The Emergence of African American Film & The Possibility of Black Modernity* (2015). She is also co-editor with Marsha Gordon of *Screening Race in American Nontheatrical Film* (2019) and co-editor with Jan-Christopher Horak and Jacqueline Stewart of *L.A. Rebellion: Creating a New Black Cinema* (2015). She was named a 2019 Academy Film Scholar by the Academy of Motion Picture Arts and Sciences and a 2020–2021 ACLS/Burkhardt Fellow.

Caryl Flinn is a Professor of Film, Television, and Media at the University of Michigan. The author of five books on film music and musicals, she is currently completing a monograph on Alan Rudolph's 1985 *Trouble in Mind*. Flinn's essays on film music and sound, feminist theory, camp, and kitsch have appeared in dozens of anthologies and journals.

Mark Gallagher is the author of *Tony Leung Chiu-Wai* (2018), *Another Steven Soderbergh Experience: Authorship and Contemporary Hollywood* (2013), and *Action Figures: Men, Action Films and Contemporary Adventure Narratives* (2006), and co-editor of *East Asian Film Noir* (2015). His current research on United States, East Asian, and global screen industries, genres, and professional cultures includes the book project *Sexy Men of the World: Acting, Stardom and Sex Appeal in Global Cinema*.

Nicholas Godfrey is a Senior Lecturer in Screen at Flinders University in South Australia. He is the author of *The Limits of Auteurism: Case Studies in the Critically Constructed New Hollywood* (2018) and has recently written book chapters on Barbra Streisand in the 1970s and United Artists in the 1980s.

Nitin Govil is an Associate Professor of Cinematic Arts at the University of Southern California. He is the author of *Orienting Hollywood: A Century of Film Culture between Los Angeles and Bombay* (2015) and one of the co-authors of *Global Hollywood* (2001) and *Global Hollywood 2* (2004).

Daniel Herbert is an Associate Professor in the Department of Film, Television, and Media at the University of Michigan. He is the author of *Videoland: Movie Culture at the American Video Store* (2014), *Film Remakes and Franchises* (2017), and the co-author of *Media Industry Studies* (2020). His monograph on New Line Cinema is set to be published in 2023.

Jamie Hook received his PhD from the Department of Communication and Culture at Indiana University, Bloomington. His research explores the intersections of adaptation, taste politics, film history, and representations of gender and sexuality. He has published work in Routledge's *Porn Studies* journal as well as in collections on adaptation, Doris Wishman, and Camp TV of the 1960s.

Dale Hudson is an Associate Professor of Film and New Media at New York University Abu Dhabi and digital curator for the Finger Lakes Environmental Film Festival. He is co-author of *Thinking through Digital Media: Transnational Environments and Locative Places* (2015), author of *Vampires, Race, and Transnational Hollywoods* (2017), and co-editor of a special double issue of *Middle East Journal of Culture and Communication* on "Film and Visual Media in the Gulf" (2021) and of *Reorienting the Middle East: Film and Digital Media Where the Persian Gulf, Arabian Sea, and Indian Ocean Meet* (2023). His essays appear *in Afterimage, Cinema Journal, Screen, Studies in Documentary Film*, and elsewhere.

Daniel Humphrey is a Professor of Performance, Visualization & Fine Arts at Texas A&M University. He is the author of *Queer Bergman: Gender, Sexuality and the European Art Film* (2013), *Archaic Modernism: Queer Poetics in the Cinema of Pier Pasolini* (2020) and articles in *Criticism, Screen, GLQ, Post Script, Invisible Culture*, and a number of anthologies. His research interests include Queer Theory and Feminist Theory, the culture and politics of the "New Left," European Art Cinema, American Independent Cinema, and the horror genre. From 1987–1998 he was a lowly but observant volunteer at the Sundance Film Festival.

Aslı Ildır is a PhD fellow in Design, Technology, and Society at Koç University and a member of the joint PhD program by the University of Antwerp, Department of Film Studies and Visual Culture. Her doctoral research explores the discourse of choice and control associated with video-on-demand platforms and the changing modes of film and TV viewership. Aslı also works as an editor and film critic for Turkey's leading film magazine, *Altyazı*.

Nessa Johnston is a Lecturer in Digital Media and Culture at the University of Liverpool. She has published widely on sound and music in screen media, is a co-investigator on the Leverhulme-funded research project *Anonymous Creativity: Library Music and Screen Cultures in the 1960s and 1970s* and author of *The Commitments: Youth Music and Authenticity in 1990s Ireland* (2021).

Alexandra Juhasz is a Distinguished Professor of Film at Brooklyn College, CUNY. She makes and studies committed media practices that contribute to political change and individual and community growth. She is the author and/or editor since 1995 of scholarly books on activist media in light of AIDS, Black lesbian and queer representation, feminism, and digital culture. Dr. Juhasz also makes videotapes on feminist issues from AIDS to teen pregnancy as well as producing the feature fakes *The Watermelon Woman* (Cheryl Dunye, 1997) and *The Owls* (Dunye, 2010).

Geoff King is a Professor of Film Studies at Brunel University London. He is the author of numerous books on American independent cinema, including *American Independent Cinema* (2005), *Indiewood, USA: Where Hollywood Meets Independent Cinema* (2009), and *Indie 2.0: Change and Continuity in Contemporary American Indie Film* (2014). His most recent books are *Positioning Art Cinema: Film and Cultural Value* (2019) and *The Cinema of Discomfort: Disquieting, Awkward and Uncomfortable Experiences in Contemporary Art and Indie Film* (2021).

Arthur Knight teaches American Studies, Film & Media Studies, and English at William & Mary. Most of his publications have focused on African American musical performance and film, including his book, *Disintegrating the Musical: Black Performance and American Musical Film* (2002), and on Black stardom. His current project focuses on the Black biopic and African American fame.

Nathan Koob is a Teaching Assistant Professor in the English Department and Film and Media Studies Program at the University of Pittsburgh. He received his PhD from the University of Michigan in 2015. His work examines the production process, authorship, and texts through their spatial and industrial contexts. He has published work in *Post Script*, *Film Criticism*, the collection *The City in American Cinema: Postindustrialism, Gentrification, and Urban Culture*, and the recent collection *ReFocus: The Later Films and Legacy of Robert Altman*.

Peter Krämer is a Senior Research Fellow in Cinema & TV at the Leicester Media School at De Montfort University (Leicester, UK). He is the author or editor of twelve academic books, including monographs on *The General* (2016) and *2001: A Space Odyssey* (2nd ed., 2020) as well as *The Silent Cinema Reader* (co-edited with Lee Grieveson, 2004).

Peter Labuza is a Researcher at the International Cinematographers Guild, IATSE Local 600. His dissertation, "When A Handshake Meant Something: Lawyers, Deal Making, and the Emergence of New Hollywood," was awarded the Society for Cinema and Media Studies prize for Best Dissertation and cited as a finalist for the Herman E. Krooss Prize for Best Dissertation in Business History. He has published in *Journal for Cinema and Media Studies*, *American Journal of Legal History*, *Film History*, *Velvet Light Trap*, and *Film Quarterly*.

Murray Leeder is an Adjunct Professor in the Department of English, Film, Theatre and Media at the University of Manitoba. He is the author of *Horror Film: A Critical Introduction* (2018), *The Modern Supernatural and the Beginnings of Cinema* (2017), and *Halloween* (2014), and editor of *Cinematic Ghosts* (2015) and *ReFocus: The Films of William Castle* (2018).

Apryl Lewis is an English Instructor at Fresno City College, having received her PhD in English from Texas Tech University in 2021. Her areas of specialization are African American literature, trauma studies, and Black Feminist studies. She has published in *Women, Gender, and Families of Color*, in *Sport in American History* and has a co-authored piece in *Spark: A 4C4Equality Journal*. Apryl has presented her work at the Futures of American Studies Institute, South Central Modern Language Association, Popular Culture Association, and the National Association of African American Studies.

Sam Littman is a PhD candidate in English (Film & Media Studies) at Texas Tech University. After receiving his MA in Film Studies from Columbia in 2015, he worked as an assistant and manager at talent agencies in Los Angeles. He has published multiple articles in *Senses of Cinema* and short pieces in the *Historical Journal of Film, Radio and Television* and *Film & History*. His dissertation considers the relationship between trauma and the cinematic long take in global art cinema.

Cynthia Lucia is a Professor of Film and Television at Rider University and is co-chair of the Columbia University Seminar on Cinema and Interdisciplinary Interpretation. Author of *Framing Female Lawyers: Women on Trial in Film* (2005), she is also co-editor of a four-volume series on the history of American film, and the two-volume pedagogically enhanced edition of that series. A *Cineaste* editor for more than three decades, she is widely published in that magazine and is co-editor of *Cineaste on Film Criticism, Programming, and Preservation in the new Millennium*. Her essays appear in a variety of edited anthologies and scholarly journals.

Chelsea McCracken is an Assistant Professor of Media Studies at SUNY Oneonta. She received her PhD from the University of Wisconsin-Madison's Department of Communication Arts. Her research often focuses on LGBTQ media, and she works to integrate studies of these media texts with broader developments in media industries and American independent cinema in particular. She has published work in *Screen*, *Media History*, and *Asian Cinema*, and is working on a book project that outlines and discusses 100 queer films since Stonewall.

Kathleen McHugh is a Professor at UCLA Departments of English and Film, Television and Digital Media. She is the author of *Jane Campion* and *American Domesticity: From How-To Manual to Hollywood Melodrama* (2007), co-edited *South Korean Golden Age Melodrama* (2005) and special issues of *Signs*, *Biography*, and *Television and New Media* on Film Feminisms, Collaborative Life Narratives, and Transnational Female Detectives, respectively. She has published on transnational film feminisms, global melodrama, experimental autobiography, domesticity, and celebrity in *Signs*, *Camera Obscura*, *Cultural Studies*, *Jump Cut*, *Screen*, *South Atlantic Quarterly*, and *Velvet Light Trap*. She is currently researching mental illness and anger in contemporary genres.

Kristi McKim is a Professor of English/Film and Media Studies at Hendrix College, where she has been honored with college-wide awards for both teaching and advising. She has published the books *Love in the Time of Cinema* (2011) and *Cinema as Weather: Stylistic Screens and Atmospheric Change* (2013) and is writing a forthcoming book that approaches *Rushmore* through a phenomenological, ecocritical, and feminist framework.

Michele Meek is an Assistant Professor in Communication Studies at Bridgewater State University in Massachusetts. She published the books *Independent Female Filmmakers: A Chronicle Through Interviews, Profiles, and Manifestos* (2019) and *Consent Culture and Teen Films: Adolescent Sexuality in US Movies* (2023). She has published numerous scholarly and industry articles, presented a TEDx talk, and serves on the board of *Short Film Studies*. She has also directed numerous award-winning short films, including *Imagine Kolle 37* (2017), and she worked as an associate producer on the documentary *Salvage* (2019), which premiered at SXSW Film Festival. For more information, see http://www.michelemeek.com.

James Morrison is a Professor of Literature and Film at Claremont McKenna College. He is the author of *Roman Polanski* (2007), *Auteur Theory and My Son John* (2018), and many other books. Most recently, with Mary Cappello and Jean Walton, he co-authored *Buffalo Trace: A Threefold Vibration* (2018), a triptych on queer educations. His current project is a study of "minor" characters and character acting in American cinema.

J.J. Murphy is a filmmaker and scholar who has written extensively on screenwriting studies, avant-garde cinema, and American independent cinema. He is the author of four major books: *Me and You and Memento and Fargo: How*

Independent Screenplays Work (2007), *The Black Hole of the Camera: The Films of Andy Warhol* (2012), *Rewriting Indie Cinema: Improvisation, Psychodrama, and the Screenplay* (2019), and *The Florida Project* (2021). Murphy is Professor Emeritus of Film at the University of Wisconsin-Madison, where he taught courses in film production, screenwriting, and cinema studies.

Michael Z. Newman is a Professor in the Department of English at the University of Wisconsin-Milwaukee, where he teaches in the programs in Media, Cinema, and Digital Studies and Film Studies. He is the author of *Indie: An American Film Culture*, *Legitimating Television: Media Convergence and Cultural Status* (co-authored with Elana Levine), *Video Revolutions: On the History of a Medium*, *Atari Age: The Emergence of Video Games in America*, and *The Media Studies Toolkit*.

Claire Parkinson is a Professor of Culture, Communication and Screen Studies at Edge Hill University. Her research interests sit at the intersections between political economy, media, film, critical animal studies, activism, and multispecies storytelling. Claire's publications include three monographs and five co-edited collections, the most recent of which are *Animals, Anthropomorphism and Mediated Encounters* (2019) and *A Critical Companion to Christopher Nolan* (2022).

Christina G. Petersen serves as Christian Nielsen Associate Professor of Film Studies at Eckerd College. She has published widely on silent cinema, including essays on the independent race film industry, the international avant-garde, and the origins of the youth film, including a monograph on Harold Lloyd's *The Freshman* published by Routledge.

Wyatt D. Phillips is an Associate Professor of Film and Media Studies in the English Department at Texas Tech University. His work primarily engages questions of the political economy of media production and circulation. His current book project considers the historical relationship between turn-of-the-century business culture and genre in early Hollywood. He is co-editor of *Camp TV of the 1960s: Reassessing the Vast Wasteland* (2023) and has published in journals such as *Film History* and *Genre: Forms of Discourse and Culture*.

Cortland Rankin is an Assistant Professor in the Department of Theatre and Film at Bowling Green State University. His research focuses primarily on cinematic representations of postindustrial urbanism and the relationship between war cinema and American cultural memory. His book *Decline and Reimagination in Cinematic New York* (2023) examines representations of New York City across mainstream, independent, documentary, and avant-garde cinema from the late 1960s through the mid-1980s. He is the author of two chapters on Korean War and Iraq War films as war memorials in *Hollywood Remembrance and American War* (2020).

Sarah E.S. Sinwell is an Associate Professor in the Department of Film and Media Arts at the University of Utah. She has published essays on *Green Porno*, *BoJack Horseman*, and *Mysterious Skin* in *Women's Studies Quarterly*, *Jump Cut*, and *Asexualities: Feminist and Queer Perspectives*. Examining shifting modes of independent film distribution and exhibition on YouTube, Hulu, Netflix, and SundanceTV, her book *Indie Cinema Online* (2020) redefines independent cinema in an era of media convergence. Sarah teaches both undergraduate and graduate courses, including Diversity in Film and Media, Women Directors, Queer Media, Independent Cinema, and Convergence Cultures.

Chuck Tryon is a Professor of English at Fayetteville State University. He is the author of three books, including *On-Demand Culture: Movies in the Age of Media Convergence* and *Political TV*. He has also published essays in the journals *Media, Culture & Society*, *Media Industries*, and *Screen*.

Yannis Tzioumakis is a Reader in Film and Media Industries at the University of Liverpool. He is the author of five books, most recently *Acting Indie: Industry, Aesthetics, and Performance* (co-authored with Cynthia Baron, 2020), and co-editor of six volumes, most recently *Indie TV: Industry, Aesthetics and Medium Specificity* (co-edited with James Lyons, 2023). Yannis is currently working on two projects: *Rock Around the Clock: Exploitation, Rock 'n' Roll and the Origins of Youth Culture* (co-authored with Siân Lincoln) and the monograph *When Hollywood Came to Greece, 1957-1967*. He also co-edits the Routledge Hollywood Centenary and the Cinema and Youth Cultures book series.

Rick Warner is an Associate Professor and Director of Film Studies in the Department of English and Comparative Literature at the University of North Carolina, Chapel Hill. He is the author of *Godard and the Essay Film: A Form That Thinks* (2018), and co-editor, with Colin MacCabe and Kathleen Murray, of *True to the Spirit: Film Adaptation and the Question of Fidelity* (2011). He is currently at work on a book that examines alternative modes of suspense that operate in slow, contemplative art cinema.

Pamela Robertson Wojcik is a Professor and Chair in the Department of Film, TV and Theatre at the University of Notre Dame and Past President of the Society for Cinema and Media Studies. She is the author of books on feminist camp, the apartment plot as genre, the urban child in cinema, and *Gidget*, as well as numerous edited collections, most recently *Media Crossroads: Intersections of Space and Identity on Screen* (2021). Supported by a Guggenheim fellowship, she is currently writing a book about mobility and placelessness in American cinema.

Justin Wyatt is an Associate Professor of Communication Studies, Film/Media, and Journalism at the University of Rhode Island. He is the author of *High Concept: Movies & Marketing in Hollywood* and *The Virgin Suicides: Reverie, Sorrow &*

Young Love and the co-editor of *Contemporary American Independent Film: From the Margins to the Mainstream* and *Refocus: The Later Films and Legacy of Robert Altman*. He is completing a manuscript on assessing qualitative and quantitative market research methods in the media industries. He has published in the fields of media history, film marketing, and media industry studies in journals such as *Film Quarterly*, *Sight and Sound*, *Journal of Film and Video*, *Media Industries*, and *Cineaste*.

Alberto Zambenedetti is an Associate Professor in the Department of Italian Studies and the Cinema Studies Institute at the University of Toronto. He is the author of *Acting Across Borders: Mobility and Identity in Italian Cinema* (2021), the editor of *World Film Locations: Florence* (2014) and *Cleveland* (2016), and co-editor of *Federico Fellini. Riprese, riletture, (re)visioni* (2016). His scholarship has appeared in journals such as *Annali d'Italianistica*, *Studies in European Cinema*, *Journal of Adaptation in Film and Performance*, *Short Film Studies*, *The Italianist*, *Quaderni d'Italianistica*, *ACME*, and *Space and Culture*.

Patricia R. Zimmermann is the Charles A. Dana Professor of Screen Studies at Ithaca College and codirector of the Finger Lakes Environmental Film Festival (FLEFF). Her most recent books include *Thinking Through Digital Media: Transnational Environments and Locative Places* (2015), *Open Spaces: Openings, Closings, and Thresholds of Independent Public Media* (2016), *The Flaherty: Decades in the Cause of Independent Film* (2017), *Open Space New Media Documentary: A Toolkit for Theory and Practice* (2018), *Documentary Across Platforms: Reverse Engineering Media, Place, and Politics* (2019), and *Flash Flaherty: Tales from a Film Seminar* (2021).

ACKNOWLEDGMENTS

To begin with, we must thank Gary Needham for initiating the Screening Cinema series and for introducing "the Wyatts." Natalie Foster has offered guidance and support throughout the project. We are grateful to Natalie, Kelly O'Brien, and the entire Routledge team for their support of this project.

Wyatt Phillips thanks Texas Tech University and the Department of English, and especially his colleagues in Film & Media Studies, for their steadfast support. He appreciates the opportunities that both Texas Tech's English and NYU's Cinema Studies departments provided to develop and teach courses in American Independent Cinema. He is very thankful for two Austin, Texas, institutions (the second now defunct) that helped foster his love and appreciation for independent cinema in the late 1990s/early 2000s: the Austin Film Society and Vulcan Video. He also thanks the Film Club at the Alamo Drafthouse Cinema in Lubbock for the programming freedom that has kept contemporary independent cinema in his purview. As always, he thanks his wife and daughters for their love and unwavering support. Finally, he thanks Justin for being a truly exceptional co-editor and also a great new friend.

Justin Wyatt would like to thank the University of Rhode Island Interim Provost Laura L. Beauvais, Dean Jeannette E. Riley, Associate Deans Nedra Reynolds and Adam Roth, Film/Media chair Rebecca Romanow, acting Communication Studies chair Kevin McClure, and Communication Studies Chair Norman Mundorf for their support of his sabbatical proposal on American independent film. In addition, Justin has benefited significantly from his discussions on independent films with his collaborator and friend Chris Holmlund. Justin owes the greatest debt to co-editor Wyatt Phillips whose intelligence, analytical skills, good humor, and discriminating mind added so much to this project. Our collaboration was fated to happen as we share the same name and the same birthday (7/7).

Both Wyatt and Justin would like to thank our amazing contributors. Working during COVID-19 and often juggling academia, family, teaching, and scholarly writing commitments like this one, this set of contributors has never failed to impress and inspire us. Their valuable insights on independent film, American film history, and a host of other media, social, and cultural topics shine through in every chapter. Thank you, wonderful contributors, one and all, for joining us on this journey.

INTRODUCTION

ON THE SWEEP OF AMERICAN INDEPENDENT FILM HISTORIES

W.D. Phillips and Justin Wyatt

The essays assembled in this volume have been designed to serve as a series of teaching and learning tools by offering critical analysis and discussion of 51 distinctive representations of "American independent film." To offer our readers a broad exploration of this field, this collection includes both well-remembered, canonical examples of independent cinema as well as lesser- or even not-very-well-known independent films from across 100+ years of American filmmaking (1915–2020).

Organized around close readings and contextual studies of individual films that exemplify but also examine, challenge, and expand our understanding of what "independence" is and how it is manifested and articulated in American cinema, each chapter is written to be accessible to a wide range of interested readers and students. At a relatively brief length of 4000 words each, these chapters have also been designed to be easily comprehensible for those new to the film, the topic, or both. As such, each chapter operates best and, in fact, was tailored to work in conjunction with an accompanying screening of the film. Our aim as editors is that through this series of paired readings/viewings, readers will become interested in and excited by the larger field of independent cinema and that these chapters will, individually and collectively, explore films that are historically consequential but also (and perhaps most importantly) challenging, provocative, and entertaining in and of themselves.

Purpose and Premise

Generally speaking, we perceive "independence" in the context of American cinema to describe those films and filmmaking practices that exist outside, or at least at the periphery, of the dominant mainstream, broadly understood to include cultural trends, aesthetic style, narrative strategies, ideological positions,

2 W.D. Phillips and Justin Wyatt

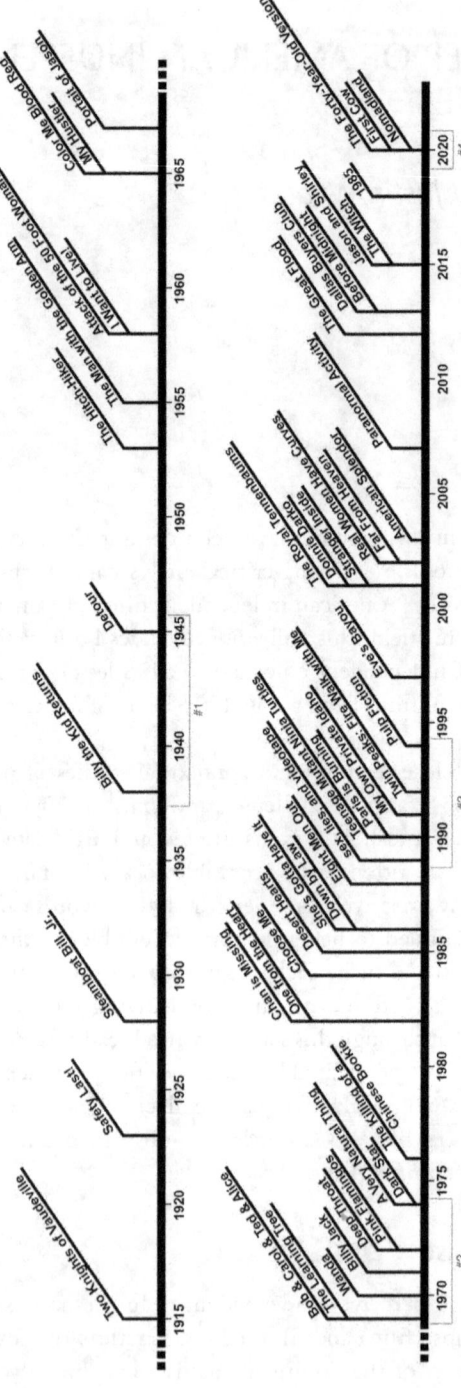

FIGURE 0.1 A timeline (1915–2020) of the American independent films addressed in this volume. The four specific periods or "moments" addressed in the Introduction have been marked and numbered here as well.

industrial structures, exhibition spaces, and standard technologies. Each author in the collection reads their chosen film within key but often unfamiliar or even forgotten contexts – historical, political, stylistic, industrial, and so on – that help us understand how and why the film was positioned, historically as well as contemporarily, as "independent." By working to realize how each film reinforces or reimagines ideas of independence within American cinema, the chapters focus their analyses on a range of critical characteristics that interconnect and, collectively, help to posit this volume of independent cinema. A brief list of these aspects would include, at least:

- Aesthetic innovation
- Narrative alternatives
- Cultural commentary/critique
- Prosocial Mission
- Business practices
- Commerce, marketing, and exploitation
- Genre/generic revision
- Authorial voice/distinct directorial vision
- Star/icon signifying and/or performing independence
- Inclusion and marginalization
- Location
- Cooptation by the mainstream
- Technology
- Audiences
- Viewing platforms

As is hopefully clear by now, this book is neither a traditional monograph on independent cinema nor an assemblage of article-length pieces that critically analyze individual American independent films in support of a larger intervention proffered by the volume as a whole. The scholarly field for these works is by now robust (see "Suggested Reading: American Independent Cinema" below) and we have not attempted to summarize that history and scholarship in this Introduction. As a result, and due as well to the nature of this volume, not every period, genre, and subfield – and certainly not every key filmmaker – relevant to the long history of American independent cinema get addressed. We have, for example, limited our choices and inclusions to those films understood to be feature-length. Other notable omissions include the first Independents of the early 1910s that challenged the Motion Pictures Patents Company (MPPC), the "race" pictures of the mid-20th century, avant-garde films, the LA Rebellion, and the first wave of digital features. These and other gaps are, however, generally given some mention and attention within one or more of the book's chapters. Taken collectively, the films and discussions included here attend to the project's intended scope. As the first volume in Routledge's new "Screening Film" series, we are pleased to be able to offer readers such a purview of American Independent Film.

Ambit of the Collection

Put simply, this collection provides a significant number of new case studies, demonstrating a wide range of approaches to studying American independent cinema. Critical lenses that readers will find employed frequently include American (and global) film history; media industry studies; cultural studies and area studies (especially in relation to historically marginalized communities); critical theory; media and entertainment studies (beyond just film); performance studies; and technology studies – to name perhaps only the most prevalent. While such breadth can be daunting, it can also be extremely enriching, bringing both new perspectives to established and canonical films as well as providing lesser-known films with a new degree of scholarly attention.

The scholars in this collection represent an intentionally wide range of identities and backgrounds with specializations inside and outside of film and media studies. One key benefit that results from this, in conjunction with the design of the collection, is that individual authors both draw on different aspects of the existing scholarship on American independent cinema and also move substantially beyond that literature, bringing their own areas of study to bear on their selected film. Our contributors, as a result, have positioned their chapters within a truly broad scope of distinct but still overlapping bodies of scholarship. Collectively, this introduces readers to a wealth of ways that contemporary scholars from across multiple fields approach, study, research, teach, and understand independent films.

At the level of individual chapters, perhaps the most significant takeaway is that no definition of "independence" is all-encompassing. Hence, definitions previously developed in reference to one historical period of the independent film are neither fully retroactive nor wholly relevant to future iterations (e.g., definitions developed in reference to the early 1990s independent boom are not comprehensive for analyzing films from the 1980s, much less the 1940s, just as they are an imperfect fit for analyzing and understanding independent films made after the turn of the millennium). This is generally clearest when the time between the film and the applied definition is great (e.g., *Steamboat Bill, Jr.* [1928] against contemporary definitions), yet it can also be true on much smaller scales. As a result, even as we offer "independent film" as a catch-all context, each film or at least each period and phase of American independent cinema traced here needs to be understood within its particular moment of "independence" and as responding (as all cultural products do) to the unique aggregation of contexts – social, cultural, industrial, or otherwise – of its own time.

The inclusion of so many films here encourages readers (and viewers!) to recognize and appreciate their similarities and hence the continuities that the field of independent cinema demonstrates. Yet it also helps to chart the changing nature of "independence" within American film and American culture (and hence the changing definition of "mainstream" as well). To that end, just as definitions of "independence" change over time, the informing contexts for those definitions (see, for example, the bulleted list above) should be understood to be in constant flux as well – not evolutionary, but certainly dynamic. Reading the chapters and viewing the films from this collection will help readers understand more fully what is intended when filmmakers, audiences, critics, and scholars apply the label "independent" but also discern the ways that both independent films and the circumstances and contexts of independent filmmaking have changed over time.

Using This Collection

Any interested American independent film fan should be able to use this book to learn more about individual films and their contexts, informing all viewers about the experience of watching films not yet seen and enriching the experience for those films already known or even known well. Certainly, readers will be able to engage with this volume in several ways. Each chapter offers a close study of an individual film, and these case studies can anchor and elaborate on the many existing scholarly overview texts on American independent cinema. Through the Works Cited in each chapter, scholars can begin further exploration of the film and its connection to other American independent films.

In addition, by its design, this volume offers a chronological survey of American independent film. The titles represent just a small sample of the larger independent cinema universe, yet we expect that the chronology will nevertheless be helpful in at least two fundamental ways. Those designing a course on American independent film can choose a number of films and chapters from this collection to paint a picture of the continuities and transformations across the field's long history, complemented we anticipate with books, articles, and chapters from other collections (that again can be gleaned from our contributors' bibliographies) that expand on key aspects of that history. This book can also be used to consider, or reconsider, sampled histories and the many smaller strands – such as the "B" film, Black filmmaking, and queer cinema – composing the category of American independent film.

Creation of Independent Cinema Moments

Fitting every film into a larger framework of a singular independent cinema history is a task that, as we have already indicated, is perhaps misleading and potentially unproductive. Rather, we feel that it can be more useful to consider snapshots of various moments within the American independent cinema timeline. We refer to these groupings as independent cinema moments and suggest that such "moments" can be another way to effectively engage the chapters in this collection. Adjacent chapters' analyses are put into a conversation to both appreciate key films from critical moments in American independent cinema and recognize the historically specific contexts which informed the choices of independent filmmakers in that period. Understanding that such cinema moments are necessarily linked to the chapters in this volume, the moments we identify are not designed to be exhaustive or comprehensive. Keep in mind, for instance, that the start and conclusion of each moment are here tied to the release dates of only the films in this book. In the independent cinema moments we describe below, the periodization cannot fully contain the relevant contexts (Poverty Row, for example, began earlier and lasted longer than the two-film periodization here would seem to indicate). Still, what may be lost in terms of temporal precision is more than made up in the breadth of contexts and correspondences such moments can illuminate.

Connecting these independent cinema moments can also yield additional insights into the category of independent film. Factors within the cinema moments resonate and echo with other elements in different moments. Looking at business practices outside the major studios, for example, is enriched by considering both the structures supporting the "B" film in the 1930s and the rise of the American independent film movement in the 1990s. Similarly, readers might associate the social inequalities reflected in American independent film in the late 1960s with those reshaping independent cinema in 2020. Readers are encouraged to seek additional independent cinema moments in the book and also uncover their own correlations, whether between well-established strands such as these or new ones of their own discovery.

As a set of illustrative examples, we briefly characterize four moments/four sets of films addressed in this collection:

1. 1938–1945: The "B" Film & Poverty Row (2 films)
2. 1969–1974: Social Change & New Markets (8 films)
3. 1989–1994: The American Independent Intervention (6 films)
4. 2020: Addressing Social Inequality & Rethinking Distribution (3 films)

1938–1945: The "B" Film & Poverty Row

The first subset of films is the two films made by Poverty Row production companies, *Billy the Kid Returns* (Republic, 1938) and *Detour* (PRC, 1945). Apart from the shared black and white photography, little else on the surface of these two films initially appears to be very similar, with one a singing cowboy picture and the other a bleak film noir. This grouping of individual case studies, however, draws forward key overlapping contexts and presents a range of options that existed for independent filmmakers and production companies in that era in terms of stories, aesthetics, and audiences. Reading these chapters, for example, one would find that both films were "B" movies, a low-budget film that was the result of the double feature program begun in the early 1930s to entice Depression-era audiences with few cheap entertainment options (pre-television) into theaters under the guise of a two-for-one deal. The first, or "A," film was understood to be the main draw, of higher quality, and almost always produced and distributed by one of the eight dominant Hollywood film companies. The

"B" film was extra and hence low risk and low reward; as a result, it was generally produced on a much lower budget.

Poverty Row films still needed though to engage and entertain the audience. These two films articulate very different approaches to doing so on equally limited budgets – one through a basic hero story with musical numbers and a clear moral coding and the other via a dark and bizarre tale of bad luck, stolen identity, and a femme fatale determined to seek justice against a supposed murderer. Both films, in their own way, offer pleasures quite distinct from those provided by the A films, which had to appeal to a mass and mainstream audience. *Detour* would have enticed a more adult audience attracted to the noir genre; *Billy the Kid Returns* was designed specifically to appeal to both juvenile and rural audiences underserved by the Hollywood "A" pictures. This imbrication of exhibition structures, production location, budget, film genre, and underserved audiences as mutually informing contexts then, while consequential to both films individually, is revealed more expressly when the two films/chapters are studied together.

1969–1974: Social Change & New Markets

At the end of the 1960s, the major film studios suffered continual financial losses. To remedy this, the studios attempted to secure a younger audience, lured in part by the greater freedom on screen with the adoption of the MPAA rating system in 1968. "The New Hollywood," as the period was tagged, also foregrounded younger filmmakers with an eye for social commentary and positive social change. These profound changes were felt within the independent cinema which, in turn, was able to create and secure new revenue through developing original distribution, marketing, and exhibition opportunities during this era.

Reflecting the progress in civil rights, American independent film offered the perspective of Black, female, and gay filmmakers, largely ignored by mainstream Hollywood filmmaking. Gordon Parks's *The Learning Tree* (1969), although set in the 1920s, sketches a picture of racial discrimination and exclusion that spoke to so much of the contemporary struggles for Black rights. With Barbara Loden directing and starring in the film, *Wanda* (1970) plays as an anti-genre low stakes heist film, confounding viewer expectations and repositioning the tale from a feminist perspective. *A Very Natural Thing* (1974) similarly depends on presenting a different point of view. Following a gay man through daily life, the film simply states that it is most certainly a very natural thing to love.

The American independent film companies of this period created business practices in contexts outside those of the traditional Hollywood studios, distributors, and exhibitors. More specifically, the cult and midnight movies, the adult soft/hardcore film, and the four-wall feature, mostly untouched by Hollywood, became viable commercial alternatives. Both John Waters's *Pink Flamingos* (1972) and John Carpenter's *Dark Star* (1974) enjoy a cult following, with *Pink Flamingos* helping to create the midnight movie category. Carpenter's film inflects a popular film genre with countercultural influences; Waters pushes even further, with a film dedicated to finding the filthiest person alive.

Sexuality was approached in many ways by the independent film during this period. Falling somewhere between satire and romantic comedy, *Bob & Carol & Ted & Alice* (1969) lampoons the opportunities for an open marriage, even while it titillates with potential wife-swapping and free sexual expression. With the MPAA ratings system allowing a self-imposed X rating, the period of porno chic was ushered in by *Deep Throat* (1972). Four-wall features, in which independent distributors rented a theater outright and saturated the airwaves with television advertising, proved to be phenomenally successful for Tom McLaughlin's *Billy Jack* (1971). Aspects of the four-wall release, such as heavy television promotion, were soon adopted by the major studios. This period, therefore, embraced both more permissive screen content and the means to present film outside the traditional methods of marketing, distribution, and exhibition.

1989–1994: The American Independent Intervention

The 1990s were a time in which American independent filmmaking made a sizable intervention in culture: the commercial and social impact of independent film was the focus of much press coverage along with academic and popular criticism. This era is marked by two signposts, both winners of the Palme d'Or at the Cannes Film Festival: *sex, lies, and videotape* (1989) and *Pulp Fiction* (1994). Between these two films, American independent films flourished at Cannes, with David Lynch's *Wild at Heart* (1990) and the low-budget Coen brothers' film, *Barton Fink* (1991), released by Fox, also winning the Palme d'Or.

Steven Soderbergh's *sex, lies, and videotape* matched its examination of fidelity, intimacy, and videotaped sexual discussions with energy, sardonic humor, and unexpected Southern charm. The film's commercial success ($25 million domestically against a $1.2 million budget) heralded a new focus on independent cinema, proving to be of interest to many viewers beyond the traditional art house space. Independent companies, like New Line Cinema, began to target more marketing-friendly properties. *Teenage Mutant Ninja Turtles* (1990) transferred the comic book and animated series to a live-action martial arts turtle extravaganza, pitched so its hipness could appeal to both children and adults (and grossed more than $200 million globally). Certainly, authorial voices, like David Lynch in *Twin Peaks: Fire Walk with Me* (1992), continued to have a strong presence as well in the independent landscape.

With the HIV/AIDS epidemic making visibility and recognition crucial, queer filmmakers added to the independent film world with content, style, and messages that provoked, startled, and entertained viewers. Jennie Livingston's 1990 documentary *Paris Is Burning* offered a fascinating portrait of drag ball culture in New York City, populated by many Black, Latinx, queer, and trans people. Livingston's documentary highlighted those almost always ignored by mainstream media and often by independent film too. Gus Van Sant's meditation, *My Own Private Idaho* (1991), blended Shakespeare's *Henry IV* with a narcoleptic gay hustler, his best friend, and a sensibility embracing queerness in form and content. Both Livingston and Van Sant anticipated critic B. Ruby Rich proclaiming the New Queer Cinema in 1992.

Five years after Soderbergh, another American independent film won the Palme d'Or: Quentin Tarantino's *Pulp Fiction*. While Soderbergh's film helped initiate a shift toward commercial reward in independent film, *Pulp Fiction*, grossing $108 million domestically, set a whole new standard. And, along the way, the film reminded us that independent film could be the space for bold experiments in storytelling, self-conscious engagements with narrative, and evocations of dismissed and disgraced content. Appropriately, the marketing of *Pulp Fiction* by Miramax Films focused on the intersection between its critical acclaim (the Palme d'Or) and the tawdry subject matter. If commercial and marketing imperatives appeared ever-present by the mid-1990s, the merger between independent film and the larger media conglomerates (e.g., Miramax with Disney in 1993, New Line with Turner in 1994) could be supported as a key contributing factor. The independence of the films was a brand to be highlighted in marketing. The intervention of independent film became an illusion just as the public started to label independent film as a highly desirable media category.

2020: Addressing Social Inequality & Rethinking Distribution

The last set of films we are using to demonstrate this type of localized contextual analysis is the final group of three from 2020: *First Cow*, *The Forty-Year-Old Version*, and *Nomadland*. The first thing to notice is that all three are directed by women filmmakers. Moreover, all three films are socially conscious works that, at least in part, tell their stories to raise awareness of issues of social inequality and the conditions that create it, with two of the three films centered around female protagonists. Such similarities then may be understood within both the long history of independent cinema as a venue for a range of socially marginalized voices, but also in relation to the #MeToo movement which rose to the fore in 2017.

In addition, the industrial location of the three is telling in terms of post-Indiewood American independent film, with the three films all acquired for distribution separately from their production financing and by three distributors representing an array of histories and approaches: for *Nomadland* it was the still extant Indiewood/major specialty division Searchlight Pictures (previously Fox Searchlight [1994–2020], now under Disney); for *First Cow*, a relatively recent standalone specialty film company in A24 (2012–); and with *The Forty-Year-Old Version* a streaming service in Netflix that primarily distributes but also (since 2015) produces films. With an established independent distributor (owned by a media conglomerate), a thriving independent company, and a streaming service, the diversity of the current industrial situation in American independent cinema can be fully appreciated.

Notably, all three films were released in a period that was heavily transformed by nationwide theater closures due to COVID-19. After a successful festival run that included Telluride, the New York Film Fest, and Berlin, *First Cow* was designated by its distributor to receive a relatively standard platform release and placed in select theaters in March 2020 with the intention of expanding before A24 was forced to pull it due to COVID-19 closures. Initially intending to re-release it again theatrically, it was ultimately released to VOD (video-on-demand) later that year. *Nomadland* also played key film fests in 2020 including Venice and Toronto to initiate positive buzz and was then, in anticipation of an awards-season push, given a hybrid release, distributed both in a limited fashion to theaters and simultaneously streaming on Hulu (Disney, the corporate parent of Searchlight, also owns a majority stake in Hulu). Finally, *The Forty-Year-Old Version* was purchased by Netflix after its successful premiere at the Sundance Film Festival and released directly (and only) on that service, bypassing any theatrical distribution whatsoever. The distribution histories of these three films then collectively indicate the continuing critical relevance of film fests and awards for garnering attention in a crowded field of visual content, the current state of media conglomeration, and, perhaps, the future of distribution and exhibition for American independent cinema.

Final Words

Screening American Independent Film exhibits how independence has been articulated in American cinema and sheds light on past and current trends in the scholarship on American independent cinema. At the same time, the collection illuminates new areas for growth, research, and ways to understand these films and the field of American independent cinema. We encourage students, teachers, fans, and other readers to take advantage of the flexibility and range offered by this collection of more than 50 films and chapters.

We do have a final comment or rather a hope. One strain connecting many of the chapters in this book is a focus on those who are often marginalized or simply forgotten by the mainstream media. In this book, we hope that you will discover voices, stories, and lives that are different from your own, but that speak to the abundance of the American and, moreover, the human experience. Independent film benefits substantially from diverse voices and from the accompanying rich texture of life. Our hope moving forward is that this book can be another point of departure for understanding and appreciating our differences, with independent film as one means to foster this dialogue.

Suggested Reading: American Independent Cinema

Monographs

Baron, Cynthia, and Yannis Tzioumakis. *Acting Indie: Industry, Aesthetics, and Performance.* Palgrave Macmillan, 2020.

King, Geoff. *American Independent Cinema*. Indiana University Press, 2005.
———. *Indiewood, USA: Where Hollywood Meets Independent Cinema*. I.B. Tauris, 2009.
———. *Indie 2.0: Change and Continuity in Contemporary American Indie Film*. Columbia University Press, 2014.
Mann, Denise. *Hollywood Independents: The Postwar Talent Takeover*. University of Minnesota Press, 2008.
Murphy, J.J. *Me and You and Memento and Fargo: How Independent Screenplays Work*. Bloomsbury, 2007.
Murray, Rona. *Studying American Independent Cinema*. Liverpool University Press, 2010.
Newman, Michael Z. *Indie: An American Film Culture*. Columbia University Press, 2011.
Perren, Alisa. *Indie, Inc.: Miramax and the Transformation of Hollywood in the 1990s*. University of Texas Press, 2012.
Sinwell, Sarah E.S. *Indie Cinema Online*. Rutgers University Press, 2020.
Tzioumakis, Yannis. *Hollywood's Indies: Classics Divisions, Specialty Labels and American Independent Cinema*. Edinburgh University Press, 2012.
———. *American Independent Cinema: An Introduction*. 2nd ed., Edinburgh University Press, 2017.
Wilkins, Kim. *American Eccentric Cinema*. Bloomsbury, 2019.

Edited Collections

Badley, Linda, Claire Perkins, and Michele Schreiber, editors. *Indie Reframed: Women's Filmmaking and Contemporary American Independent Cinema*. Edinburgh University Press, 2016.
Holmlund, Chris, and Justin Wyatt, editors. *Contemporary American Independent Film: From the Margins to the Mainstream*. Routledge, 2005.
King, Geoff, editor. *A Companion to American Indie Film*. Wiley-Blackwell, 2016.
King, Geoff, Claire Molloy, and Yannis Tzioumakis, editors. *American Independent Cinema: Indie, Indiewood and Beyond*. Routledge, 2012.
Perkins, Claire, and Constantine Verevis, editors. *US Independent Films After 1989: Possible Films*. Edinburgh University Press, 2015.

1

TWO KNIGHTS OF VAUDEVILLE (1915)

Allyson Nadia Field

From campaigns waged by the NAACP in the 1940s against Hollywood studios' perpetuation of racist stereotypes to the hashtag #OscarsSoWhite, created by April Reign in 2015, calls for diversity and inclusion in the American film industry have attempted to respond to its pervasive history of exclusion, marginalization, and misrepresentation of nonwhite people. And yet, outside of the Hollywood studio system, independent filmmaking has long provided a means for filmmakers to explore more nuanced and complex depictions of African Americans. These independent spaces encompass a range of practices, from nontheatrical films made for purposes other than theatrical entertainment, such as sponsored films, educational films, and home movies, to documentary films that explore underrepresented communities. Independent filmmaking has also provided a space for African American fiction filmmakers to assert an image of Black life that refutes the misrepresentations, whether egregious stereotypes or racist by elision, that were a predominant feature of the studio era.

Within the history of American independent filmmaking, there is a subset of films made for African American audiences. Known as race films, they featured primarily Black casts and were produced by Black, white, and interracially run film companies whose target audiences were de facto (and in many places de jure) segregated African American moviegoers.[1] This industry, active from the early 1910s to the early 1950s, constituted an independent enterprise on a double order – independent from mainstream film production, distribution, and exhibition, and independent from white hegemonic structures governing films' content, production, and intended audience.

Race films were often made solely for Black audiences, but not always. For example, Chicagoan William Foster – considered the first African American to

FIGURE 1.1 Frank Montgomery, Florence McClain, and Bert Murphy enjoying a vaudeville show in *Two Knights of Vaudeville*. Visual artifacts such as the white vertical line are vestiges of the surviving 35mm print.

own and manage a film company in the 1910s – made films for Black audiences while also seeking out screening opportunities in theaters catering to predominantly white audiences. Foster was invested in a dual-uplift project: to promote African American advancement through filmic self-fashioning against racist white misrepresentation and to promote the film industry as a viable economic venture for Black entrepreneurs and investors.

For some white-owned film companies, segregation presented a business opportunity they were eager to exploit, imagining a ready audience in Black theaters in addition to their primary market in white-catering theaters. These producers were not always attuned to the differences in film reception among their audiences and did not always anticipate African American moviegoers to be savvy spectators alert to pejorative forms of Black representation that stemmed from traditions of minstrelsy and that posited race as fodder for comedic vignettes. This was the case with the Historical Feature Film Company that produced *Two Knights of Vaudeville*, a short comedy with a predominantly Black cast about sites of performance and spectatorship. A kind of inverse of William Foster's strategy, Historical was a venture primarily interested in producing Black-cast comedies for white audiences that also sought to capitalize on the segregated Black audience. That makes these companies – Foster and Historical – distinct from other producers of Black-cast films who were targeting Black audiences almost exclusively, such as African American film pioneer Oscar Micheaux and race filmmaker Richard Norman, the white owner of the Norman Film Manufacturing Company.[2]

Foster's films do not survive, and *Two Knights* is the only film produced by the Historical Feature Film Company known to be extant. The absence of surviving exemplars of race film's earliest years is a challenge for film historians and it makes a unique survivor like *Two Knights* all the more significant. The film was recently released on Blu-ray and DVD by Kino Classics as part of the *Pioneers of African-American Cinema* set curated by film scholars Charles Musser and Jacqueline Najuma Stewart. This important collection includes silent and sound films made by Micheaux over his extensive filmmaking career that spanned 1919–1948, sound films made by Black filmmaker Spencer Williams in a range of genres in the 1930s and 1940s, and a Black cast western featuring a singing cowboy played by Herb Jeffries, a famed race film actor of the late 1930s. The collection provides a significant sampling of independent films that responded to, in varying degrees, the exclusion of Black voices and subjects in the mainstream film industry. *Two Knights'* inclusion in this set – and the earliest film in the collection – affords it a privileged position. But, as with most films of its time, its meanings are not self-evident. Here, I aim to provide context for the film to help understand its assumptions and appeals, its significance as an artifact of American independent cinema, and to offer the necessary background to inform contemporary viewers who might be confused by the film's curious representational politics.

I see *Two Knights* as reflecting the influence of the popular live performance landscape on early film production, where Black actors found success performing in predominantly white venues, or venues with segregated seating for Black patrons, as well as in theaters serving an African American clientele. Here, I argue that in thematizing independent production, *Two Knights* effectively stages its own tenuous position, straddling exhibition sites between mainstream (majority-white) spaces and the intraracial space of all-Black theaters. In doing so, the film enacts a major tension of race film as a category: the contested forms of exhibition, its sites, audiences, and the risks attendant to Black representation in comedy shorts of the 1910s.

Two Knights of Vaudeville

Two Knights of Vaudeville is a comedy consisting of two parts of equal length. The first part opens with a well-dressed white man accidentally dropping a set of tickets as he exits an upscale vaudeville theater. The tickets are picked up by two Black men (Frank Montgomery and Bert Murphy) who invite a third friend (Florence McClain) to attend that evening's vaudeville show, a spectacle consisting of a series of unrelated acts brought together on a common bill. The friends are seated in exclusive box seats overlooking the stage where they watch the acts – a singer, acrobat, and juggler – and applaud and even mimic the performers by attempting their feats. In doing so, they ultimately disrupt the performance and get expelled from the theater.

The film's second half involves the friends resolving to put on their own ersatz vaudeville show for an all-Black audience. The makeshift performance begins with a singer followed by acrobats – Murphy and Montgomery – who perform approximate acrobatic feats. As Murphy performs a set of somersaults, the audience responds by throwing objects at him and the film ends with slapstick pandemonium. A dialogue intertitle reads in presumed "Black" dialect: "'Jest all time messin' up somethin'. That's all. Nevah agin.'"

How should we understand this film, its comedy, and the tensions it enacts? Is the film mocking its Black performers and is the comedy predicated on racist presumptions? Or is it showcasing the talent and range of its vaudeville stars? How should we receive it in the 21st century? What frameworks do we need to understand its operations without perpetuating the anti-Black context of its production and exhibition? In what follows, I offer a historically grounded analysis of the film and attempt to give the reader the necessary context in which to approach the film and come to their own informed conclusions.

The Performers

The three principal actors in the film, Bert Murphy, Florence McClain, and Frank Montgomery, were celebrated vaudeville performers who achieved success in theaters soliciting predominantly white audiences, as well as theaters catering to Black patrons. A key component of the film's significance as a historical artifact is in how it showcases its performers as they appeared in vaudeville and Black musical theater, serving as an extension of the performance personae they developed for the stage. In doing so, the film preserves the otherwise ephemeral performance of its stars, albeit without sound, giving us a rare glimpse into American popular theater of the 1910s.

Murphy was known as a unique comedian with a very physical dancing style that "no one could ever imitate without fear of injuring themselves," according to a theater reviewer for the African American newspaper the Indianapolis *Freeman*, who also noted his expressive and humorous facial expressions (Sampson 189–190). The dog in *Two Knights* likely belonged to Murphy who was known for performing with "his canine comedian" (Dope).

As a vaudeville actor, McClain was known for her beauty and versatility. Nicknamed "Dainty Florence" for her diminutive stature, she played a range of roles, specializing in swapping between gender masquerade in male roles and hyper-feminized performances in which she sang attired in stylish gowns (Owsley, "Montgomery and McClain"). The male characters she played on the vaudeville stage – for example, a sheriff, tramp, and soldier – led the Black press to comment, "O, what a pretty boy she makes" (Owsley, "Frank Montgomery"). *Two Knights* shows off her range as well as the variety of costumes for which she was known, from mannish suits to elaborate gowns to boyish garb.

McClain and her husband and performing partner Frank Montgomery shared the stage with white performers, often the only "colored" act on the bill, performing in predominantly white theatrical spaces as well as for Black audiences in theaters catering exclusively to segregated audiences on the Colored Consolidated Time, a circuit of vaudeville theaters. At these theaters, they were tremendously popular and would break box office records; in the intraracial, all-Black performance space, they were stars and their act was celebrated as "elegant in stage effect" and "artistically aristocratic" (Meadows).

Despite their fame, audiences did not always know they were African American actors. Murphy and Montgomery would perform in blackface makeup, a convention of minstrelsy adopted by some Black performers, and McClain, being a "colored strawberry blonde," led to audience confusion (Russell 1913). As one Black theater critic noted of Montgomery and McClain, "the audience did not know the team was colored" (Russell, "An Excellent Bill"). This confusion extends to current viewers who may misread McClain as a white woman, presuming the film to be promoting a transgressive portrayal of interracial social intimacy. Charles Musser has even suggested that the supporting actors who are playing the "white" vaudevillians are actually Black actors performing in a racial masquerade that subverts and reverses the conventions of white performers playing Black characters in blackface makeup (Musser 8). However, without credits, a verified cast list, or positive identification of the supporting actors, this would be tricky (and inadvisable) to determine. The film's play with performance, masquerade, mimicry, and parody is certainly augmented by the racial indeterminacies that attended its cast.

Another aspect of Montgomery and McClain's vaudeville act that informs how we might understand *Two Knights* is in their blurring of the distinction between the stage and the space of the theater. Their autumn 1914 act, for example, opened with an announcement that the pair would not be appearing due to an unavoidable delay, but then Montgomery would burst down the aisle insisting that the announcement was wrong and that the duo was ready to perform (Owsley, "Montgomery and McClain"). During this tour, Montgomery and McClain performed at the Grand, a Chicago theater catering to Black patrons, on the same bill as their films. Thus, the confusion of spaces that opened their act – the inversion of the space of the theater with the orchestra aisle becoming the site of spectacle as Montgomery rushed in – would have been echoed by the play with performance space and sites of spectatorship narrativized in *Two Knights*. This resonance would have then functioned as another layer of comedy for the live audiences at the Grand.

Historical Feature Film Co. and Ebony Film Co.

Little is known about the production history of *Two Knights of Vaudeville* or about the company that made it, but given the echoes between the film and the stage personae of its lead actors, the performers might have had a hand in the scenario or perhaps the scenario was written for them. They performed in their own costumes, showcasing aspects of their stage personae for which they were best known.

In 1914, the Historical Feature Film Co. was founded in Chicago, up-dating the former studio space of French magician and early pioneer of trick films Georges Méliès with new equipment. Aiming for novelty, the company set out to make animated cartoons and comedies, including four "Black and White Comedies" with Murphy, Montgomery, and McClain, as well as fellow Black stage performers Jimmy Marshall and Sam Gaines: *The Shooting Star, Money Talks in Darktown, Aladdin Jones,* and *Two Knights of Vaudeville*. These were likely filmed at the same time and released in October and November 1914. In September 1914, Murphy, Montgomery, McClain, and Marshall were appearing on stage in Chicago in "The Two Detectives," a "farce comedy song review" produced by Martin Klein, the manager of the New Monogram, along with Murphy and Montgomery (Russell 1914). This production was likely underway or in rehearsals when the performers shot the film as part of Historical's series of "Black and White" comedies. As producers of an actual review show, Murphy and Montgomery's appearance in *Two Knights* serves as an in-joke. Indeed, their interpretation of incompetent performance seems especially lighthearted and ironic.

From descriptions of the lost Historical productions, *Two Knights* seems quite distinct from the other comedies, especially in the ways in which the film reflected – and showcased – its stars' vaudeville talents, albeit adapted for the silent medium. For example, it is the only one of that set of films to directly reference performance and exhibition spaces. And yet there is no record of the initial release of *Two Knights* and no clear explanation of this choice. It is possible that the set of "Black and White Comedies" were not released together, or that Historical went bankrupt before *Two Knights* could be commercially released, a failure common among early independent film producers. In any case, Historical ceased to make films and the newly formed Ebony Film Company acquired the films and re-released them, changing intertitles to include the Ebony brand, and in some cases changing film titles.

In 1917, with African American general manager Luther J. Pollard at the helm, Ebony would go on to produce comedies with other Black vaudeville actors, but Murphy, Montgomery, and McClain only appear in the films previously produced by Historical. Indeed, Ebony's reissue of the vaudevillians' films was noted in the Black press; the films were evidently not new as they were dated by the appearance of the performers who had not been in Chicago together for a few years. Further, Murphy had been sick and died in 1917, rendering his screen performance in the re-release a poignant posthumous note.

Critical Reception

The initial reception of the Historical films in the Black press was positive. Historical even marketed their films directly to Black spectators through newspaper advertisements in the Black press in December 1914: "If you want to see Your Own Race! In the finest series of Real Negro Comedies! Ever produced for moving pictures," ads implored readers to ask their local theater managers "to exhibit the Black and White Films! Produced by the Historical Feature Film Co." (Advertisement). According to records in the film industry trade press, the Historical films were officially released in February 1915 (at least to the majority white-serving theaters), so these earlier screenings might have been an attempt to dovetail with the performers' theatrical appearance as well as capitalize on their popularity with Black audiences ("Historical Feature Film Co.").

While the initial release of the films seems to have been well received by Black audiences and critics, certainly in no small part due to the popularity of their stars, upon their re-release by Ebony there was significant criticism in the Chicago *Defender*, a major African American newspaper, extending beyond the films' evident datedness. The shift in response is marked by a "letter of protest" from a *Defender* reader, Mrs. J. H., who wrote to theater editor Tony Langston about the films, naming *Aladdin Jones*, *Money Talks in Darktown*, and *Two Knights of Vaudeville* in particular: "I consider it my duty, as a member of the respectable class of theater patrons, to protest against a certain class of pictures which have been and are being shown at the theaters in this district" (Langston, "Ebony Films"). In a critique based on an investment in middle-class respectability and public comportment, Mrs. J. H. lambasts the Ebony films for their "exaggerated display of the disgraceful actions of the lowest element of the race" (ibid.). Mrs. J. H. does not question the representations or critique them as conjured by white racist fantasies of blackness, instead she objects to them on class grounds: "When the beastly actions of the degraded of our people are flaunted before our eyes in places of amusement it is high time to protest in the name of common decency" (ibid.).

Langston took up the cause and published the letter and his extensive reply, telling readers he had intervened with theater managers to prevent the further screening of the Ebony films. He writes,

> It would hardly be good policy for any theater in this district to book pictures from a company whose photoplays carry 'comedy' that causes respectable ladies and gentlemen to blush with shame and humiliation.... Anyhow, the films themselves are what is commonly called 'crap,' having been taken here over a year ago, and having failed in booking through the film company which produced them.

Langston concludes by advising readers to look out for Black theaters advertising "so-called 'all-colored comedies'" and avoid them. He exhorts: "keep your money in your pocket and save that dime as well as your self-respect." Positing the Ebony comedies against other genres, he writes, "Someday we will have race dramas which will uplift, instead of rotten stuff which degrades" (Langston, "Ebony Films"). He ends by calling on South Side Chicago theaters and managers by name. The managers responded publicly the following week, all saying they would stop showing the Ebony films, including at the Monogram and the Grand where the films had been well received on their initial run (Langston, "The Hammer").

Even a year later, the theater managers of the South Side's Black-serving theaters had not forgotten Langston's campaign. Ebony re-released *The Shooting Star* under the title *A Natural Born Shooter* and it was scheduled to be shown at the Phoenix theater in May 1917 when the *Defender* intervened and called on the theater manager to pull the film, which it quickly did. If Mrs. J. H.'s critique hinged on a form of respectability politics and a class-based concern over forms of entertainment and venues of public presentation, especially for audience members who were invested in a form of race uplift based in part on middle-class propriety, the *Defender*'s campaign against the Ebony pictures extended to the broader question of misrepresentation. On this point, Langston did not hold back:

> The moving picture business can no longer be considered in its infancy and the patrons of the modern houses should not be subjected to the humiliating experience of seeing things which lower the Race in the estimation of its own people as well as in the eyes of whatever members of the 'other' race who may happen to be in attendance.

He concludes by decrying Ebony's scenes of "moral depravity": "People who attend the theaters do so to be entertained, and not to be insulted. [...] We want clean Race pictures or none at all" (Langston, "Ebony Film Cancelled").

Scenes of "moral depravity" might have referred to the early Ebony productions released in 1917 including *Dat Blackhand Waitah Man*, *Shine Johnson and the Rabbit's Foot*, and *A Busted Romance*, none of which survive, but it is not readily apparent how this critique applies to *Two Knights of Vaudeville*. Did audiences, beyond Mrs. J. H., object to *Two Knights* as well as the other Historical/Ebony films? Or was the film swept up in the ire directed at the other productions? *Two Knights*' mockery of its characters' naiveté and inappropriate public behavior in both interracial and intraracial spaces could be read both as an insult to the Black audience or as a self-mocking of the vaudeville stars themselves – a gesture of comedic irony that gives them the last laugh. And yet, without knowing that Murphy, Montgomery, and McClain are actual vaudeville stars, does this interpretation hold? Is it contingent on an audience who would recognize and appreciate their poking fun at themselves, such as the audience at the Grand that witnessed both their stage act and the motion pictures? Perhaps Mrs. J. H. and her friends eschewed even high-class vaudeville, or perhaps moving pictures were already tinged with disreputability from a class perspective. What is clear is that most forms of comedy posed a risk to uplift ambitions that hinged on public respectability and the rejection of anything that might be interpreted as ridicule of the race. *Two Knights* might have showcased its stars' talents, but its bawdy humor, indeterminate objects of ridicule, and lack of a redeeming respectable African American figure left it open to the charge of being not just unedifying, but overtly insulting. These are the terms that Black independent filmmakers like Oscar Micheaux would have to negotiate in the coming decades.

Conclusion

Like many films of its era, *Two Knights of Vaudeville* depends on a set of associations and allusions that are context-specific and whose meanings have lost valence over time. What is clear in an otherwise ambiguous picture is how the film showcases talent that is otherwise lost due to the ephemeral nature of vaudeville and stage performance. Here we have a record of popular African American performers and a glimpse into their styles, shticks, and appeals to audiences, both humorously conjured in the narrative and invoked in the direct addresses to the filmic spectator as a surrogate theatergoer.

Yet, beyond its value as a record, how do we understand this curious film? It is hard to determine the representational stakes at play in *Two Knights*, the role of the film in the *Defender*'s critique of Ebony, and how the film fits in the broader trajectory of race filmmaking and Black independent cinema that would follow. Is it a racist mockery of Black "trespass" and mimicry of white institutions? Or is it a critique of the absurdities of segregation that relegate Black talent – and audiences – to extreme lengths to partake in modern entertainment? In depicting intraracial sites of spectatorship and discerning audiences (even if played for comedy), does the film offer an image of an audience that would reject buffoonery as spectacle? Does the film, then, anticipate its own rejection? Perhaps this is what contributed to Historical's failure, its inability to represent something that would be acceptable by those whom it thought it was representing.

Notes

1 I follow a convention of capitalization of Black when referencing people and as a social category. There are longstanding – and ongoing – debates around capitalization of "black" and "white" in reference to race. Unresolved among journalists and scholars, the vexed issue of capitalization reflects disparities in power and lived experiences, and the question of a presumed shared history and culture. Until language conventions find a way to capture the nuances of longstanding systemic racism caused by white supremacist culture, I will continue to capitalize Black and not white in reference to race.
2 For more on race filmmaking, see: Bowser et al.; Lupak, *Richard E. Norman*; Lupak, *Early Race Filmmaking in America*.

Works Cited

Advertisement. *Freeman* [Indianapolis], 26 Dec. 1914, p. 2.
Bowser, Pearl, Jane Gaines, and Charles Musser, editors. *Oscar Micheaux and His Circle: African-American Filmmaking and Race Cinema of the Silent Era*. Indiana University Press, 2001.
Dope, Real. "The Collender's Minstrels Presented by Miller & Lyles," *Freeman* [Indianapolis], 28 Aug. 1915, p. 6.
"Historical Feature Film Co.," *Moving Picture World*, 6 Feb. 1915, p. 898.
Lupak, Barbara Tepa. *Richard E. Norman and Race Filmmaking*. Indiana University Press, 2014.
———, editor. *Early Race Filmmaking in America*. Indiana University Press, 2016.
Meadows, Herbert S. "St. Louis Theater Notes," *Freeman* [Indianapolis], 25 Apr. 1914, p. 5.
Musser, Charles. "Race Cinema and the Color Line." *Pioneers of African-American Cinema: Film Notes*. Kino Classics, 2016, pp. 6–29.

Owsley, Tim E. "Frank Montgomery and Florence McClain," *Freeman* [Indianapolis], 28 Sept. 1912, p. 5.

———. "Montgomery and McClain, Susie Sutton and the Lincoln Players at the New Crown Garden Theatre," *Freeman*, 14 Nov. 1914, p. 5.

Russell, Sylvester. "An Excellent Bill at the Grand," *Freeman* [Indianapolis], 19 Oct. 1912, p. 5.

———. "Chicago Weekly Review," *Freeman* [Indianapolis], 11 Apr. 1913, p. 5.

———. "Chicago Weekly Review," *Freeman* [Indianapolis], 12 Sept. 1914, p. 5.

Langston, Tony. "Ebony Films," *Chicago Defender*, 1 July 1916, p. 4.

———. "The Hammer Misses New York," *Chicago Defender*, 8 July 1916, n.p.

———. "Ebony Film Cancelled," *Chicago Defender*, 12 May 1917, p. 4.

Sampson, Henry T. *Blacks in Blackface: A Sourcebook on Early Black Musical Shows*. 2nd ed., Scarecrow Press, 2014.

2
SAFETY LAST! (1923)

Christina G. Petersen

One of the most iconic images of silent film features a bespectacled young man (filmmaker and star Harold Lloyd) in a straw hat and three-piece suit dangling precariously from a giant clock affixed to a towering office building in downtown Los Angeles. This shot from the silent slapstick comedy *Safety Last!* (1923) captures the anxious state of those looking to achieve the 1920s American Dream in an era in which the pressure to conform to corporate interests increasingly trumped individual initiative.

In the film, Lloyd plays an unnamed small-town "Boy" who comes to the big city to make good. However, he quickly finds that his path to success lies not within the system but in clambering up its outside edges, exploiting what makes him different from the crowds who line the streets below. In this sense, *Safety Last!*'s depiction of the Boy as an ultimately successful outsider parallels Harold Lloyd's own rise to filmmaking prominence during this era. At the same time major American film studios were organizing into vertically integrated factories combining production, distribution, and exhibition to maximize profits, Lloyd garnered success by holding to the independent workshop style of production he learned during American cinema's early years.

This chapter will explore the independent silent comedy filmmaker-star's ability to draw crowds at the point in Lloyd's career in which he was transitioning from his beginnings at Rolin (later Hal Roach) Studios to the formation of his own production company (just three months after the release of *Safety Last!*). Through a discussion of the industrial context of the film, its production and aesthetics, and its place in Lloyd's career, this chapter will explore how the Boy's journey in *Safety Last!* from lowly wage worker to active producer of spectacles mirrors Lloyd's career trajectory and the basis of his appeal. While only Lloyd's fourth feature (after more than a hundred short comedies), *Safety Last!* broke records – earning over

DOI: 10.4324/9781003246930-3

FIGURE 2.1 Independent filmmaker-star Harold Lloyd dangles above busy Los Angeles streets as his character goes out on his own in *Safety Last!*

$1.5 million on a $120,000 budget – to become a top earner for 1923 (and among the top 20 highest-grossing films of the silent era), cementing Lloyd's prominence alongside fellow silent comedy stars Charlie Chaplin and Buster Keaton (Dardis 142; Ramsaye 942). As this chapter will discuss, Lloyd's character in *Safety Last!* captured the star's own attitude toward filmmaking as an independent endeavor. Like the Boy's hair-raising climb on the outside of the downtown commercial high-rise, Lloyd's success as an independent filmmaker depended on the structures of mainstream distribution and exhibition erected by the burgeoning major American film companies while his films lampooned those same structures. Although *Safety Last!* might seem to be a departure from later concepts of independent film, particularly Michael Newman's definition of the post-1978 "indie" film as a cultural phenomenon associated with opposition to mainstream Hollywood, formal play, and character-focused realism (15–16), Lloyd's film includes inklings of these aspects in its negative depiction of the factory-like department store that mirrors the 1920s film industry, playful parallels to the act of film viewing, and exploration of young white masculinity as a source of anxiety as well as empowerment. *Safety Last!*, like its title, considers how going out on one's own in the 1920s, in opposition to the dominant methods of filmmaking and industrialization, required throwing caution to the wind and taking big risks with minimal safeguards.

Act I: Independent Beginnings

Harold Lloyd was born in Nebraska in 1893, three years before Thomas Edison's vitascope premiered at Koster & Bial's New York Music Hall (Dardis 1–2; Musser 115–116). After acting in theater as a boy, Lloyd went west to San Diego, California, where he took part in local stock shows before making his film debut in an Edison film in 1912 (Lloyd 39). In 1913, Lloyd moved to Los Angeles for greater opportunities just as the American film industry was beginning the transition from single-reel films to features (Bordwell et al. 132–133). In Los Angeles, Lloyd got his start in movies by sneaking onto the lot of the recently formed Universal Film Manufacturing Company, witnessing firsthand the latest phase in the organization of the film industry. Five years before, ten film production and distribution companies, led by Edison, had formed the Motion Picture Patents Company (MPPC), a trust which sought to control the burgeoning industry by holding the rights to key patents required for the production and exhibition of motion pictures. The filmmakers working on the Universal lot in the spring of 1913 represented "unlicensed outlaws" who shot on the West Coast to avoid the long arm of the East Coast-based MPPC (Tzioumakis 22). These early independent film companies were defined not by the style or content of their films but in industrial terms, distinguished by their "position outside an established (or semi-established) industrial-economic system" (23). Although outsiders to the MPPC, early independents' working style modeled the transition from a workshop system (where each film's producers hired their own personnel, including extras like Lloyd) to the factory-like approach of film production that would become commonplace during the later studio era.

In distinction from the industry's trajectory toward the consolidation of resources and standardization of product, Lloyd's career trended in the opposite direction. As Universal transitioned to a centralized system that employed Fordist assembly-line methods and Taylorist economies of labor, Lloyd left the lot and eventually joined fellow former Universal extra Hal Roach as a featured player at Roach's self-funded Rolin Studios in 1914 (Bordwell et al. 134–136; Schickel 25–27). At Rolin, Lloyd would become famous as the Chaplinesque working-class clowns Willie Work and Lonesome Luke before lighting on the comic persona of "an average recognizable American youth" (Lloyd 59). For his "Glass character," Lloyd donned a straw hat, lensless horn-rimmed glasses, and a demeanor that was "quiet, normal, boyish, clean, sympathetic, not impossible to romance" (59). As the Glass character, Lloyd embodied the anxieties of white middle-class masculinity in an era in which urban white-collar work "was equated to imprisonment in a corporate bureaucracy that limited manly independence" and the recent influx of southern and eastern European immigrants was perceived as a threat to the hegemony of white Anglo-Saxon Protestant America (Studlar 28). Amid these societal shifts, Lloyd's Glass character offered reassurance in the power and spectacle of the white male body as a continued path to success all the while poking fun at such assumptions.

Lloyd would go on to film dozens of Glass character comedies, making the transition to feature comedies in 1921 at the same time as the American film industry was organizing into the system that would hold sway into the 1950s. This period saw the ascendance of the vertically integrated Big Five studios (Metro-Goldwyn-Mayer, 20th Century-Fox, Paramount, RKO, and Warner Bros.), which owned theaters as well as produced and distributed their own films, and the Little Three studios (Universal, Columbia, and United Artists), which were primarily organized around film production and distribution (Ward 16). While the Big Five and Little Three adopted factory-like methods of centralized leadership and resources, including increasing departmentalization of labor within managerial hierarchies, Lloyd worked within Hal Roach Studios (as Rolin was renamed in 1920) in a version of the workshop system that he had first experienced on the Universal lot (Bordwell et al. 121–124). Lloyd and his team of three "gag men" employed a process opposite to the Fordist production methods of the major studios. Rather than produce a full script before shooting, the gag men would work backward from the central conceit. In the case of *Safety Last!*, Lloyd shot the climbing sequence first and then his gag men wrote the rest of the film to lead up to the climax (Lloyd 84–87).

With little oversight in his last years at Roach, Lloyd functioned as "virtually an independent producer using Hal Roach Studios as his production facility" (Ward 44). In his final contract with Roach, signed in November 1921, Lloyd successfully negotiated for 80 percent of the net profits on his films (with Roach earning just 20 percent), exclusive use of the company's Culver City sound stage, and "first call on everything," including Roach as a producer (Ward 45; Lloyd 89). In contrast to the increasing consolidation of power in the mainstream studios in this era, Roach, as an independent producer and studio head, found his influence as well as profit margins waning over Lloyd. He even had to ask Lloyd's permission to strike the sets from *Safety Last!* once production was complete to begin work on another film (Ward 45). So when Lloyd and Roach parted ways in July 1923, it was a mutually beneficial development that would allow Roach a better return on the investment of resources and Lloyd even greater autonomy (44–45).

Act II: The Perils and Pleasures of Going Out on One's Own

In recent years, the prevalent definition of independent film has relied as much on "aesthetic and social distinctions" from Hollywood as on production outside of established studios (Newman 6). Although *Safety Last!*'s conventional three-act structure, young white male protagonist, and blockbuster success would seem to suggest that its independent status stems largely from the way in which it was made rather than its form and content, this section will explore the film's engagement with aesthetic and social difference. In its depiction of American industry and the modern city as sites of dehumanization where the only path to success is to embrace one's interchangeability with objects, *Safety Last!* casts a critical eye on Hollywood's adoption of Fordist methods of mass production and consumption. As Newman describes, the form of American independent cinema that has dominated since the decline of the Hollywood Renaissance in the late 1970s has regularly asserted the importance of the individual – in the filmmaker as an individual artist in distinction to the "soulless studio committee," in the character who represents the "uniqueness of identity positions," and in the spectator who is invited to view the film as a type of game and herself as a discrete player (34, 45). *Safety Last!* offers a much earlier exploration of these aspects, valorizing individuality and independence while also demonstrating that they can only be achieved by performance rather than inherent traits.

One hallmark of the post-1978 independent film has been its focus on characters who are so strongly identified with their lived realities that they become "emblems of their social identities," redefining community not as a celebration of a transcendent humanism but as a specific experience of difference (Newman 30, 34). *Safety Last!* begins with an early version of this by setting up youthful white masculinity as a distinct identity. The film introduces the Boy in a situation that many would recognize in 1920s America, though presented in an unfamiliar way. We meet the Boy on the cusp of leaving small-town Great Bend for a "long, long journey" into – it would seem – the afterlife, as he is framed in close-up behind a set of bars with a noose dangling in the background as if he is about to be hanged for some unnamed capital crime. The camera then tracks out to show two women – one younger and one older – crying at the Boy's situation as a man in an official-looking uniform walks up to the Boy and gestures toward the noose. A priest enters the frame and shakes the Boy's hand as the women join the rest of the characters on the other side of the bars, embracing the Boy. As the three turn away from the camera and walk into the background though, a match-on-action to the reverse angle reveals that the Boy is at a train station where he is about to take his leave for the big city, promising to marry his best girl Mildred (Mildred Davis) once he has found success there. The sequence ends with the Boy rushing to catch his train and, in his haste, mistaking a nearby baby for his suitcase. The mother runs after him, he apologizes for his error, and then he promptly makes another, mistaking a passing ice truck for his train. These opening sight gags set up the movement of the film, in which the act of leaving one's previous community and moving to the American city leads to confusion between things (movement and death, human and object) usually considered distinct. In what follows, *Safety Last!* presents the Boy's immigration from a member of a rural community to an alienated urban worker and ultimate transformation into an empowered entertainment producer as a general experience of imprisonment and objectification that culminates in liberation and independence accessible only to the young white American male.

The next sequence demonstrates the Boy's transformation into an urban dweller who now understands that being mistaken for something else is the means to achieve what he desires. When the film picks up with the Boy a few months later, he is pining for Mildred, buying her jewelry to convince her that he is successful although he must pawn his possessions to achieve this illusion. In this, the film suggests that attaining the American Dream is no longer based on hard work but on performance, and the film quickly asserts what successful performance looks like in 1920s America. When the landlady comes to collect their overdue rent, the Boy and his roommate Limpy Bill (Bill Strothers) put on their overcoats and hang from hooks on the wall, pulling their feet up and successfully fooling her into thinking that they are inanimate objects. Unlike the opening execution gag, hanging in this sequence becomes a form of empowerment as it is associated with the ability to transform into an object. As Alex Clayton notes, *Safety Last!* mines its comedy from the Boy's repeated "reduction to an object among other objects" that paralleled the realities of life in 1920s America where people were now considered as interchangeable as factory-produced goods (162–163). As the film plays out though, the Boy rises in society by accepting his newfound status as an interchangeable object.

At work at the DeVore Department Store, the Boy is objectified and disempowered until he finds an audience for whom to perform. To avoid being late to work, the Boy employs the same skill of becoming an object – this time through a form of feminization (putting on a women's hat and overcoat and pretending to be a mannequin) – to sneak in and reset the store's time clock. When he sneezes in the arms of the Black worker (uncredited) carrying him into the store, the film depicts the masquerade-as-object as productive for the young white man and traumatizing for the Black man who is confronted with the breakdown of that masquerade. The film depicts the African American worker, terrified, clutching a ladder near the ceiling, unable to go up or down (in a striking contrast to the Boy's successful climb outside of the store in the third act). While the young white male can masquerade as something else and find success, this path is not accessible to the urban Black worker, who disappears from the film after this shot. In this sense, *Safety Last!* presents young white American masculinity in the 1920s as a negotiation of difference, where the Boy can gain some measure of control by accepting that what would seem to be threats to his individual identity are the means to upward mobility in this new world.

Safety Last! further valorizes independence as a form of individual endeavor, taking aim at modern industry and the mainstream film industry similar to contemporary independent film's opposition to mainstream Hollywood and celebration of the individual filmmaker as an artist (Newman 45). The department store in *Safety Last!* is a clear allegory for the Fordist factory and, by extension, the 1920s film industry, as all three provide customers with mass-produced goods through a system where each worker is focused on their compartmentalized responsibilities and productivity is ruled by the clock. Inside the store, in addition to fears about punctuality, the Boy is presented as subject to floorwalker Stubbs's (Westcott Clarke) managerial gaze and at the beck-and-call of finicky and violent female customers, who nearly tear him asunder like one of the bolts of fabric sold at his dry-goods counter. The suggestion is that working in this fashion is dehumanizing and emasculating, rendering the Boy an object that others control.

While the Boy is just another interchangeable worker inside the big established concern, Bill, a skyscraper metalworker, offers an image of individual achievement when he climbs the outside of a multistory building to escape a policeman. Lloyd had discovered Bill Strothers in summer 1922 when he came upon a crowd who had gathered to watch Strothers scale the outside of a ten-story building in downtown Los Angeles as part of a promotional stunt. After witnessing Strothers's death-defying climb, Lloyd invited him to Roach Studios on the spot (D'Agostino Lloyd 308–309). A few months later, Strothers would feature in *Safety Last!* both as his character and as Lloyd's double for the final climb. Shown in a long shot in real time, Bill's effort on the outside of the building presents the opposite of the Boy's struggles inside. Instead of an emasculating mob of insatiable female consumers, the mixed-gender crowd (including the Boy) that gathers on the street to watch Bill's successful climb represents a means of empowerment for the individual who rises above them.

This sequence sets up *Safety Last!*'s third act, which invites the spectator into an engaged and playful relationship with the film similar to later indies' metacommentaries on the nature of cinema (Newman 37–38). After realizing that working inside an established enterprise will not bring him what he desires, the Boy proposes to "attract an enormous crowd" to the store by having Bill climb the outside of the 12-floor building for a fee. This scheme transforms the Boy into a version of Lloyd's position at Roach Studios in 1922, no longer just a salaried worker but now sharing in the profits made from the spectacles of bodies in peril. The comparison between character and filmmaker-star becomes even more apt when Bill is unable to begin the stunt and the Boy must take his place, now performing as well as producing, just like Lloyd. In addition, during the final segment, the department store shifts from a reflection of the Fordist factory to that of the 1920s movie theater, where the crowd in the film acts as a surrogate for the film's audience (Bilton 165–166). As the Boy confronts new challenges at each floor – birds landing on him, a net dropped from above, vertigo – the film's spectator is invited to respond like a member of the on-screen crowd, holding their breath and clapping as the Boy (and Lloyd) clears each new obstacle. This is due to the fact that the danger caught on camera was largely real, incorporating an actual climb by Strothers staged for the film up the side of the ten-story Los Angeles International Bank Building on 7 September 1922. The film employed long shots of Strothers with cut-ins to Lloyd produced on faux exteriors erected on the roofs of four different buildings in downtown Los Angeles, carefully working out camera angles to create the illusion of the Boy climbing a single building in a real location long before the use of green screens. The effect is like watching a live event that prompts the spectator to feel like one of the on-screen crowd but also to approach this sequence with wonder at the cinematic tricks and physical prowess required to produce this spectacle.

In this sense, *Safety Last!*'s famous shot of Lloyd hanging from the clock combines a sense of actual and social realism – an anxious feeling of being at the mercy of industrial clock time – that drew audiences in droves. In the context of the film, this sequence hearkens back to the threat of hanging (and death) associated with moving to the city in the film's opening, the Boy's reworking of this threat into an opportunity for empowerment by hanging from the coat hooks in his apartment, and his successful masquerade as an object (the mannequin) to reset the clock at work. Once again, the Boy finds a way to save himself from a potentially catastrophic situation by reworking an object (the clock) for his own ends while offering himself up as an object of the crowd's gaze. All comes to a head when the film depicts the Boy's final obstacle as a revolving wind gauge that he cannot see but that the crowd can. The gauge's movement puts him in danger while prompting his most spectacular stunt, an accidental fouling in a loose rope that leads to a balletic swing in front of the building's façade that ends in Mildred's waiting arms. An American flag featured in the background of the shot suggests that, while dangerous, going out on one's own is a realization of a new American Dream in an era of corporate assembly lines and department store counters. As the film depicts, independence as a type of upward mobility is only accessible to the young white male in this era and the film's final gag, where the Boy walks alongside his love through roof tar and loses his shoes, suggests that his new individual vantage point atop the building (and, for Lloyd, atop the film industry) is a source of anxiety as well as triumph. By exploiting his body for a dangerous spectacle, the Boy is able to move up in American society but with the potential to lose one's shirt (or shoes) in the process.

Act III: Rise to Independence

Safety Last! would go on to break box office records, earning Lloyd over $600,000 from the film's $1.5 million gross (Dardis 125–128). Lloyd would make one more film with Roach Studios – *Why Worry?* (1924) – before going fully out on his own. While made within the confines of an established independent studio, *Safety Last!* rehearses many of the ideas about independence in the film industry in the 1920s and includes early iterations of what would later become hallmarks of indie cinema. Lloyd's status as an independent filmmaker stemmed from American cinema's early definition of independence as a resistance to industrial organization and centralization; *Safety Last!* explores 1920s concerns about losing individuality in a world increasingly organized around mass production and conformity. Independence is not a carefree state though, as each step that the Boy takes outside of the established DeVore building couples greater levels of achievement with equal amounts of risk and anxiety. In comparison to subsequent understandings of independent film, *Safety Last!* might seem to be a difficult fit. Yet upon further examination, Lloyd's film engages with these later aspects in its representation of youthful white masculinity as an experience of difference, a negative depiction of the modern department store as a mirror of the

1920s mainstream film industry, and the invitation to view the film's final act as a metacommentary on film viewing itself. For both the Boy and Harold Lloyd, putting the relative safety of the established system increasingly in their rear view led to one of their greatest successes.

Works Cited

Bilton, Alan. *Silent Film Comedy and American Culture*. Palgrave Macmillan, 2013.
Bordwell, David, Janet Staiger, and Kristin Thompson. *The Classical Hollywood Cinema: Film Style & Mode of Production to 1960*. Columbia University Press, 2015.
Clayton, Alex. *The Body in Slapstick Cinema*. McFarland, 2007.
D'Agostino Lloyd, Annette. *The Harold Lloyd Encyclopedia*. McFarland, 2010.
Dardis, Tom. *Harold Lloyd: The Man on the Clock*. Penguin Books, 1984.
Lloyd, Harold. *An American Comedy*. Dover Publications, 1971.
Musser, Charles. *The Emergence of Cinema: The American Screen of 1907*. University of California Press, 1990.
Newman, Michael Z. *Indie: An American Film Culture*. Columbia University Press, 2011.
Ramsaye, Terry, ed. "The All-Time Best Sellers." *The 1937–38 International Motion Picture Almanac*. Quigley Publishing, 1937, https://archive.org/details/international193738quig.
Schickel, Richard. *Harold Lloyd: The Shape of Laughter*. New York Graphic Society, 1974.
Studlar, Gaylyn. *This Mad Masquerade: Stardom and Masculinity in the Jazz Age*. Columbia University Press, 1996.
Tzioumakis, Yannis. *American Independent Cinema: An Introduction*. 2nd ed. Edinburgh University Press, 2017.
Ward, Richard Lewis. *A History of the Hal Roach Studies*. Southern Illinois University Press, 2005.

3
STEAMBOAT BILL, JR. (1928)

Peter Krämer

Steamboat Bill, Jr. (1928) is a classic of silent cinema.[1] The film was made by Buster Keaton – widely regarded at the time as one of the three top comedians (the other two being Charles Chaplin and Harold Lloyd) – at the studio carrying his name. He had produced nine previous features at Buster Keaton Productions, beginning in 1923, and before that numerous shorts. A former child star on the vaudeville stage who, at the age of 21, got his start in movies in 1917 as a sidekick to leading slapstick comedian Roscoe "Fatty" Arbuckle, Keaton was not only the star of the shorts and features made at his studio but also, often uncredited, their co-writer and (co-)director. *Steamboat Bill, Jr.* was released in May 1928 by United Artists (UA), a distribution company originally set up in 1919 by four of Hollywood's leading stars and filmmakers – Chaplin, Douglas Fairbanks, Mary Pickford, and D.W. Griffith – so as to gain more control over, and more profits from, the release of their movies.

Steamboat Bill, Jr. is usually characterized as Keaton's last independent movie.[2] Four months before the film's release he had signed an employment contract with Loew's Inc./Metro-Goldwyn-Mayer (MGM), one of the vertically integrated major studios that dominated the American film industry by combining a huge production facility in California with an international distribution network and a large movie theater chain headquartered in New York. From 1928 to 1933 Keaton was a contract star (but no longer a writer or director) at a film "factory" employing hundreds of people to get a new feature ready for release almost every single week. Compared with his work at Buster Keaton Productions, at MGM Keaton had much less, and eventually no, influence on the overall shape of the movies he starred in; his initial input into story development, directing, and editing gradually vanished.[3] At the same time, Keaton's MGM films lost some of the thematic and stylistic characteristics of his earlier features.[4]

DOI: 10.4324/9781003246930-4

FIGURE 3.1 Buster Keaton's world goes to pieces, giving rise to his most spectacular and dangerous stunt.

My examination of *Steamboat Bill, Jr.* in the first section of this chapter foregrounds some of the characteristics of Keaton's work, with reference to his earlier career and also to the circumstances of the film's production. This is followed by a more general account of his film work from the 1910s to the 1930s which situates it in a dynamic film industrial context characterized by changing configurations of vertically integrated major studios and independent filmmaking, and also by differing stylistic regimes. This should deepen our understanding of what "independence" meant during this period in Hollywood history.

1

Because of extensive location shooting, the staging of large-scale action (often featuring massive sets, huge vehicles, and lots of extras) and the cost of running a fully equipped and fully staffed studio, the features made at Buster Keaton Productions were expensive as was their distribution into movie theaters. Keaton's films had to generate substantial income at the box office so that both Buster Keaton Productions and the distributor could recover their expenditures and make a profit. When Keaton's first film for UA, the particularly expensive and thematically ambitious civil war comedy *The General* (released in February 1927) flopped at the box office (and also with many critics), and its successor, the contemporary comedy *College* (September 1927), performed badly as well, it became clear that the film Keaton had started working on in the summer of 1927, *Steamboat Bill, Jr.*, would be his last for UA and for Buster Keaton Productions (Krämer, "One of the United Artists").

Arguably, at one of the major studios the production of *Steamboat Bill, Jr.* would not have gone ahead because the film was going to be very expensive and, dealing with a devastating natural disaster, it failed to take into account the lessons to be learned from the failure of *The General*. Some critics and audiences objected to deadly serious subject matter in a comedy, and the staging of large-scale action was not always conducive to the generation of the kind of uproarious laughter cinemagoers were led to expect from a Keaton comedy.[5] At Buster Keaton Productions, the filmmaker was able to go ahead with *Steamboat Bill, Jr.*, perhaps driven to extremes (in terms of the level of destruction being staged and the danger of his stunts) by his sense of an ending.

The film's title was derived from a popular 1910 song called "Steamboat Bill," a macabre ditty telling the story of a steamboat captain who is ordered to break a speed record and blows up his vessel in the process. The film developed the song's climactic catastrophe into a natural disaster devastating a whole town.[6] The opening sequence of *Steamboat Bill, Jr.* signals the film's scale and ambitiousness by putting a mighty river and two steamboats on display as well as featuring a large crowd of extras and the massive set of the fictional Mississippi town of River Junction. The story starts out as a drama about an old-fashioned steamboat captain – William Canfield, known as Steamboat Bill and owner of the Stonewall Jackson – fighting for his livelihood in the face of aggressive competition from powerful local businessman J.J. King.

The story thus sets a small, independent business against a huge corporation that tries to monopolize the market, which echoes the contrast between Buster Keaton Productions and MGM. When, later on in the story, a storm hits the town, all of King's enterprises, including his steamboat, are destroyed, but the old Stonewall Jackson remains intact and can be used to save King and his daughter Kitty. King and Steamboat Bill make their peace with each other; perhaps they – and also Jr. – will work *together* from now on, in the same way that Keaton probably hoped that he would be able to work *with* (not just *for*) MGM.

The opening sequence ends with a telegram from Steamboat Bill's son, in which a tragic backstory is briefly evoked. Bill and his wife must have separated when their son was a baby, and Bill has not seen him since. Now the mother is dead, and it was perhaps on her deathbed that she asked Jr. to visit his father.[7] Steamboat Bill imagines his son to be the kind of young man who could perhaps help him with his failing business. Judging by several of Keaton's previous features, viewers could expect that Jr. will initially disappoint his father. In his biggest hit *Battling Butler* (1926), for example, Keaton had played a pampered, rich weakling whom his father sends out camping – with disastrous results when this weakling finds himself impersonating a famous boxer to impress the father of the girl he has fallen for. In other films such as *Sherlock Jr.* (1924) and *The General*, it is his girlfriend's father whom the Keaton character manages to disappoint early on.

After seven and a half minutes (of the film's 70-minute running time), Keaton, playing a dandified college boy who would surely feel much more at home in a campus comedy like *College*, finally wanders into this drama about rival steamboat operators. Through his presence, the film is transformed into a comedy, and also into a romance, because he soon bumps into Kitty, who he knows from college. Both King and Steamboat Bill strongly object to their union. Thus, *two* fathers stand in the way of the young people's romance, as do misunderstandings between the youngsters and their inability to take decisive action (another familiar theme from Keaton's earlier features). Jr. also turns out to be worse than useless when it comes to handling the steamboat, and his attempts to meet up with Kitty result in fights between his father and King. Eventually, Steamboat Bill orders Jr. to leave, yet when Jr. witnesses his father being arrested after an altercation with King, he decides to stay and free him. In a rather roundabout way Jr. manages to do so, but gets himself knocked out by the town's sheriff in the process and ends up in the hospital.

By this point, it is already clear that a big storm is brewing. Fifty-six minutes into the film, the storm sequence begins in earnest, showing the impact of ferocious winds on people, vehicles, and buildings. After two minutes of this, the scene shifts to the hospital where Jr., still suffering from his recent head trauma, is trying to make sense of what is going on around him before he starts wandering, all on his own, across a wind-battered, shapeshifting, dangerous town- and landscape. In typical Keaton fashion (employing long-shot long takes), the subsequent destruction of River Junction is staged for real: What one sees are *not* tiny models, but huge sets. Houses, vehicles, and trees go to pieces or get blown away. And the house front falling on Jr., who happens to stand exactly where the opening of the attic window lands, just misses Keaton's head (this being an extravagant variant of a gag appearing in several earlier Arbuckle and Keaton films such as *Back Stage* [1919] and *One Week* [1920]).

The shots that show Jr. clinging to a tree and flying with it through the air are not only amazing in their own right but also resonate with the publicity that had surrounded Keaton ever since he had become a child star. In the early 1900s, his father had told the press many, largely made-up stories about the adventures of his little boy; in one of these, he was blown into the air by a cyclone and then safely deposited on the ground again. Later publications retold this story about "the cyclone baby" (the title of an article in the fan magazine *Photoplay* from May 1927), which the filmmaker reenacted in *Steamboat Bill, Jr.* The storm sequence also includes a brief scene in an abandoned theater, involving a ventriloquist's dummy, a magical disappearing act, a stage backdrop for a sketch, and many other things evoking Keaton's vaudeville days.

The climactic sequence takes on a new quality after Jr. has been dumped into the river where he makes his way to his father's boat. The storm pushes buildings into the water, which echoes earlier Keaton films featuring open water and ships of various sizes, ranging from the homemade vehicle in *The Boat* (1921) to the ocean liner in *The Navigator* (1924). These scenes also expand the film's references to real-life storm and flood disasters, of which there had been many in the United States in preceding years. *Steamboat Bill, Jr.* deals head-on with the danger of being crushed by the debris blown around in a storm or drowning in a flooded house.

While Jr. for the longest time is just trying to avoid getting injured or killed, the final minutes of the film – as was usual in Keaton's features – show him taking control of the situation, mastering his father's steamboat, and rescuing Steamboat Bill, Kitty, and her father. He then jumps into the water as if he wants to escape from the romantic relationship that is about to be confirmed and also from the business partnership that appears to be formed by Steamboat Bill and King. As it turns out, he is just eager to retrieve a pastor from the river who can sanctify his union with Kitty. Most of Keaton's previous features – from *Sherlock Jr.* to *College* – had similarly twisty endings, which both subvert and adhere to the conventional happy end.

All this leaves the impression that, at the conclusion of an important phase in his career, Keaton saw *Steamboat Bill, Jr.* as an opportunity not only to review his life and career up to this point but also to stage the most amazing spectacle imaginable (taking up a fifth of the film's running time), a spectacle so destructive and of such Biblical dimensions that it could serve to wipe the slate clean for a new beginning, or, alternatively, to signify the very end of the world, or at least of *his* familiar, "independent" world.

2

I have offered an analysis of *Steamboat Bill, Jr.* as a deeply personal movie, and in doing so I have referred to the differences between the operations of major studios such as MGM and those of smaller companies such as Buster Keaton Productions and UA. Both at the time and later, such smaller companies have been labeled "independent," a term that, in recent decades, has had some connotations that do not apply in the 1920s.[8]

Far from being at the margins of the commercial operations of the American film industry (already known at that time as "Hollywood"), in the 1920s UA and most of the production companies whose output UA distributed were specializing in big-budget and prestige productions designed to reach the largest possible audiences, and indeed dominating box office charts in the United States.[9] The stars, filmmakers, and producers associated with UA were among the most successful and powerful people in Hollywood. While this last statement does not apply to Keaton, it characterizes Joseph Schenck who was the co-owner and president of both Buster Keaton Productions and UA. Importantly for understanding an industry often built on family connections, Schenck also was Keaton's brother-in-law.

Keaton owned no shares in "his" studio, and his employment contract at Buster Keaton Productions was not so different from the one he signed with MGM in January 1928: he was paid for his work as an actor. That Schenck gave

Keaton and the team he had assembled the opportunity to co-write and (co-) direct his films at Buster Keaton Productions with relatively little supervision and interference from senior management was not contractually guaranteed, but, in a sense, a personal *favor*, which made perfect *business* sense as long as the output of the studio was commercially successful. The first seven features produced by Buster Keaton Productions before its deal with UA had been on an upward curve in terms of their box office performance, but when the first two UA releases were commercial disappointments, Schenck decided to close the studio after the third, handing Keaton over, on a very lucrative employment contract, to MGM, the parent company of which (Loew's Inc.) was run by Nicholas Schenck, Joe's brother.

Before releasing through UA, Buster Keaton Productions had distribution deals with Metro and its successor companies (Metro-Goldwyn and MGM). Owned by the Loew's theater chain, these were all fully vertically integrated major studios, which in addition to their in-house productions also released films by small "independent" studios. This means that while Buster Keaton Productions was involved in independent *production*, its output was *not distributed* independently, as distribution was handled by a major studio. When Schenck switched the distribution to UA, this famous "independent" distributor was in fact on the verge of turning into one of the majors. With the exception of Chaplin, the owners of UA also owned a theater chain and production companies; this came very close to vertical integration, except for the fact that the other companies were not actual subsidiaries of UA.

More generally, from the outset of Keaton's film career, he had been in the orbit of the vertically integrated major studios of the day. The Arbuckle films in which Keaton started out in 1917 were independently produced at the Comique Film Corporation, a small studio owned by Joseph Schenck and Arbuckle, but distributed by Paramount, the dominant film company of the late 1910s. In 1920, Keaton made his feature film debut – as an actor, but not as a writer/director – in an in-house Metro production (*The Saphead*), which, among other things, served to promote Keaton as a star in his own right. Metro also initially distributed the short films Keaton made – as actor, co-writer, and (co-)director – at Comique, the company being reorganized as Buster Keaton Productions in 1922. At that time, distribution of the shorts shifted to First National, another of the major studios, before Schenck switched back to Metro for Keaton's initial features.

All of the above reflections concern industrial definitions of "independence." But what can one say about textual definitions, for example with regard to departures from Hollywood conventions of the day? Keaton's most striking departure was his extremely reduced use of facial muscles, that is his trademark "frozen face" or "stoneface." As a child on the vaudeville stage he had been very expressive, and in the Arbuckle films he can be seen laughing and crying in an exaggerated fashion. But in *The Saphead* and the short films he made in 1920 Keaton adopted his stoneface, which he presented from then on both on screen and in off-screen publicity. Despite the fact that, with regards to *The Saphead* and the features he made at Buster Keaton Productions, there were numerous complaints about his facial inexpressiveness from critics (whereas this comic mask seemed perfectly acceptable in the shorts), he never relented. During his employment at MGM from 1928 to 1933 much changed in his performance, but not his deadpan (Krämer, "Battered Child"; Krämer, "Comic Star").

Keaton's reliance on long-shot long takes was also at odds with what has been called the classical Hollywood style, which in turn is closely linked to Hollywood's mode of production (as per the title of Bordwell, Staiger, and Thompson's groundbreaking study), whereby detailed division of labor in the production process is connected to detailed shooting scripts (which were not being used at Buster Keaton Productions) and particular ways of dissecting individual scenes (an establishing long shot being followed by a medium shot, close-up shot/reverse shots, etc.). It is difficult to know whether, among the thousands of films made in-house by the major studios, there are any that use long-shot long takes as extensively as Keaton does, but it seems unlikely. The films Keaton starred in at MGM from 1928 to 1933 certainly did not maintain this approach.

It must be noted, though, that the classical style did not characterize all of the major studios' output. For example, short films ranging from animation and slapstick to newsreels and musical numbers were put together according to different principles (Krämer, "Comic Star"; Wolfe, "Vitaphone Shorts"). Also, with the introduction of pre-recorded synchronized sound in the late 1920s, various forms of all-talking, all-singing, all-dancing musical films and what Henry Jenkins has termed "anarchistic comedies" became very prominent in the output of the major studios and indeed in box office charts; such films often departed quite drastically from classical norms. Consequently, the most radical changes in the style and content of the films Keaton appeared in did not concern his move from Buster Keaton Productions to MGM, but his moves from shorts to features in 1923, and from silent movies to sound films at MGM in 1929/1930 (Krämer, "Derailing" 114–115).

Finally, in terms of their focus on romance and spectacular action, the features made at Buster Keaton Productions were perfectly aligned with the major studios' output in the 1920s. But Keaton's obsessive concern with father-son relationships stood out. It went back all the way to his vaudeville act which focused on acrobatic, mock-violent interaction between he and his father, and characterized many of his short films, also the reworking of a familiar stage play for *The Saphead*, and then most of the features made at Buster Keaton Productions. While a focus on the relationship between adult men and father figures was not unheard of in the output of the major studios, it was absent from the films Keaton made as a contract star at MGM.

In conclusion, then, as the last film made at Buster Keaton Productions, *Steamboat Bill, Jr.* can be understood as the culmination of various strands of Keaton's previous stage and film work, a movie that self-consciously reflected on his career up to this point and marked a spectacular endpoint. Keaton had spent his whole film career under the wings of Joseph Schenck, one of the film industry's most powerful men, who was able to negotiate with the major studios from a position of strength (and indeed worked hard to transform the independent distributor United Artists into a major).

Schenck provided Keaton with considerable resources (including a self-contained studio, highly qualified staff, and production funds) and granted him unusual levels of control over his work. In this context, Keaton developed a distinctive approach to his physical performance, to the shooting and editing of his films, and to their stories and themes. But Schenck was not willing to continue with this very expensive arrangement when Buster Keaton Productions started to turn out box office flops. During his subsequent employment at MGM from 1928 to 1933, Keaton's creative control vanished and, apart from his deadpan performance, so did the distinctive qualities of his filmmaking.

Notes

1. I have been working on Keaton for over 35 years. So as not to clutter the text with too many references, I often refer to my own publications which in turn contain references to numerous primary and secondary sources. Further detailed information on Keaton's life and career can be found in several biographies (see especially Curtis). For Keaton's own account of his life, see his autobiography (Keaton with Samuels) and his interviews (many of them collected in Sweeney).
2. For a particularly poignant discussion which overlaps considerably with the ground I cover in this chapter, see Stevens 231–258.
3. On Keaton's employment at MGM, see Neibaur 11–74, in addition to the sources listed above.
4. For systematic studies of the style, form, and themes of the ten features Keaton made at Buster Keaton Productions, see especially Moews and Carroll. Analyses of his later work at MGM have been much less systematic.
5. On the marketing and reception of *The General* and other Keaton films in the 1920s, see Krämer, *The General*; Wolfe, "Buster Keaton"; and Gehring.
6. There are numerous discussions of *Steamboat Bill, Jr.* in the rapidly expanding scholarly literature on Keaton. For a recent analysis that focuses on the natural disaster in the film, see Fay 23–58.
7. All of this is quite similar to *Our Hospitality* (1923), which also delays Keaton's first appearance so as to relate a melodramatic backstory.
8. For more on the changing contexts of independence within American cinema, see the introduction to this volume.
9. This paragraph and the next three are based on Krämer, "One of the United Artists."

Works Cited

Bordwell, David, Janet Staiger, and Kristin Thompson. *The Classical Hollywood Cinema: Film Style & Mode of Production to 1960*. Routledge, 1985.

Carroll, Noël. *Comedy Incarnate: Buster Keaton, Physical Humor, and Bodily Coping*. Blackwell, 2007.

Curtis, James. *Buster Keaton: A Filmmaker's Life*. Alfred A. Knopf, 2022.

Fay, Jennifer. *Inhospitable World: Cinema in the Time of the Anthropocene*. Oxford University Press, 2018.

Gehring, Wes D. *Buster Keaton in His Own Time: What the Responses of 1920s Critics Reveal*. McFarland, 2018.
Jenkins, Henry. *What Made Pistachio Nuts? Early Sound Comedy and the Vaudeville Aesthetic*. Columbia University Press, 1992.
Keaton, Buster, with Charles Samuels. *My Wonderful World of Slapstick*. Doubleday, 1960.
Krämer, Peter. "Derailing the Honeymoon Express: Comicality and Narrative Closure in Buster Keaton's *The Blacksmith*." *The Velvet Light Trap*, no. 23, 1989, pp. 101–116.
———. "The Making of a Comic Star: Buster Keaton and *The Saphead*." *Classical Hollywood Comedy*, edited by Kristine Brunovska Karnick and Henry Jenkins. Routledge, 1995, pp. 190–210.
———. "Battered Child: Buster Keaton's Stage Performance and Vaudeville Stardom in the early 1900s." *New Review of Film and Television Studies*, vol. 5, no. 3, 2007, pp. 253–267.
———. *The General*. BFI, 2016.
———. "'One of the United Artists': Buster Keaton, Joseph Schenck and UA." *United Artists*, edited by Peter Krämer et al. Routledge, 2020, pp. 19–37.
Moews, Daniel. *Keaton: The Silent Features Close Up*. University of California Press, 1977.
Neibaur, James L. *The Fall of Buster Keaton: His Films for MGM, Educational Pictures, and Columbia*. The Scarecrow Press, 2010.
Stevens, Dana. *Camera Man: Buster Keaton, the Dawn of Cinema, and the Invention of the Twentieth Century*. Atria Books, 2022.
Sweeney, Kevin W., editor. *Buster Keaton: Interviews*. University Press of Mississippi, 2007.
Wolfe, Charles. "Vitaphone Shorts and *The Jazz Singer*." *Wide Angle*, vol. 12, no. 3, 1990, pp. 58–78.
———. "Buster Keaton: Comic Invention and the Art of Moving Pictures." *Idols of Modernity: Movie Stars of the 1920s*, edited by Patrice Petro. Rutgers University Press, 2010, pp. 41–64.

4
BILLY THE KID RETURNS (1938)

W.D. Phillips

In his 1974 reflective ballad, "Hoppy, Gene and Me," Roy Rogers addressed his primary, but now nostalgically invoked, silver-screen audience when he sang: "It seems like only yesterday that we rode the range together." Continuing, he pined, "Then you grew up and drifted on but I know that you remember/When you were a saddle pal to Hoppy, Gene and Me." Roy Rogers, Gene Autry, and William Boyd (Hopalong Cassidy, or "Hoppy"), each referred to directly in Roger's song, were exceedingly popular in American movie theaters in the 1930s and 1940s, as were a bevy of other cowboy picture and singing cowboy stars, including Bob Steele, Tex Ritter, Wild Bill Elliot, Charles Starrett, Tim Holt, and Lash La Rue.

These performers and the recurring western film series they starred in were designed to appeal to juvenile audiences as well as rural and working-class viewers through an action-packed story, a simplistic moral code with clear heroes and villains, and, especially, the range of spectacles that they offered. *Billy the Kid Returns*, a "B" film starring Roy Rogers that was released in the fall of 1938, is simply one example of hundreds and perhaps thousands of similar films (Rogers alone starred in over 80 such films between 1938 and 1951). Produced by Republic Pictures, a low-budget, independent, "Poverty Row" film company on the fringes of Hollywood, the film represents a form of production that responded to market needs unfulfilled by the main studios of the era such as Paramount, 20th Century Fox, and Warner Bros.[1] Popular particularly with rural audiences and in neighborhood movie houses rather than the grand downtown urban theaters commonly owned by the major film studios, *Billy the Kid Returns* played primarily within a system of independent exhibitors caught between the industrial mechanisms of Hollywood and local audiences with tastes often distinct from those of Hollywood's target audience. This chapter will consider the film in relation to these overlapping contexts, all of which impinge on our understanding of

FIGURE 4.1 Roy Rogers, posing as Billy the Kid, defends the town's new general store from the villainous rancher and his men.

the film as "independent." In doing so, the industrial conditions that facilitated such films and the aesthetic and narrative characteristics of the B movies – and more specifically the B western and singing cowboy pictures – that corresponded to these economic and institutional imperatives will be addressed. In addition, this chapter will consider the exhibitors and audiences who, while still a part of Hollywood's mass audience, were ignored to a significant degree by its "A" pictures, but whose fondness for the films considered here and fandom for their stars propelled (Hoppy, Gene, and) Roy to mid-century fame.

In contrast with the majority of films included in this collection, *Billy the Kid Returns* is an interesting but generally unremarkable film, notable principally for what it shares with a large number of films from the mid-1930s to the late-1940s. Roy Rogers, in just his second starring role, plays both the famous outlaw Billy the Kid and "Roy Rogers," a deputy sheriff from Texas headed west looking for work. Billy is killed by Pat Garrett (Wade Boteler) within the first few minutes but then Rogers is confused for Billy not just in his physical appearance but also his Robin Hood-like behavior when he chases off several cowboys hired by a powerful local rancher who are trying to burn out a family of settlers. Garrett and the local US Marshal (Joseph Crehan) see the value in having Rogers continue to pose as Billy: "You mean have Rogers help the homesteaders by doing the things Billy did?" the Marshal is asked. "Yeah," he replies, "but not the bad ones."[2] Rogers proceeds to help the process of civilization by protecting the town's new shopkeeper and impeding the efforts of the "bad guys" – while also courting the shopkeeper's daughter (Mary Hart). As local law is limited in its efficacy against the rancher's actions, Roy tricks him into stealing US Army horses, a federal offense. When the villain is caught, Rogers saves the homesteaders and wins the day.

The subgenre of the singing cowboy film derived from the popular western genre films, or "cowboy pictures," at the end of the silent era (mid-to-late 1920s) that also mapped directly onto the formula for the broader category of the B westerns of the 1930s and 1940s. Set in the late 19th century in the American West during the period of national expansion after the American Civil War, these films – like much of the western genre in early 20th-century pulp fiction – involved a cowboy hero set against a perceived impediment to civilization, be it outlaws, indigenous peoples, greedy ranchers, spoiling Eastern influences, or the harshness of the wilderness itself.[3] A romantic subplot was frequent but not necessary. Singing cowboy stories replicated this formula but were often even more specifically built around a basic oppositional plot with "[b]ad guys…trying to cheat or strong-arm some nice, ordinary folks" and the (singing) cowboy hero "eventually defeating the villain with a combination of ingenuity, good sense, and a little forceful physicality" (Buscombe, "Gene Autry" 37).

As with all cinematic action genres, forms of spectacle complemented these narrative tropes, with scholars noting that "the basic structure of the shoot-'em-ups…usually included several chases on horseback, extended fight scenes, sensational and realistic stunt work, [and] rugged scenery" (Smith 193). Distinguishing between A and B westerns, film genre scholars such as Edward Buscombe and Steve Neale have built on the general differentiation of A and B pictures (budget, stars, aesthetic quality, etc. – more on this later) to note the A westerns' inclination toward "large-scale historical and political themes," its use of western tropes to tell stories more aligned with the melodramatic conventions and dramatic range of major Hollywood films, and efforts of the A westerns' filmmakers to appeal to metropolitan audiences and a general "rather than a specifically rural" female viewership (Neale 139; Buscombe, *BFI Companion* 33–35, 43–45).

Historians such as Douglas Green and Peter Stanfield, who have focused specifically on the singing cowboy films, trace the origin of this subgenre of the western to the earliest sound films (the late 1920s) and performers such as Ken Maynard; though westerns were already one of the cheapest genres to produce due to their reliance on exterior locations rather than sound stages (which required additional time to properly light and which independent production companies generally had to rent), producers found this new subgenre even more economically viable, as "singing numbers were cheaper to stage and film than fights and brawls that involved stunt work" (Agnew 140). Hence, much like the backstage musical, interludes of song (and sometimes dance) interrupt the narrative – here that of the B western – with the (cowboy) hero also a guitar-playing balladeer. The popular success that this unique form enjoyed for nearly two decades is almost always credited initially to Gene Autry, who "took the formula Western… and grafted other forms of entertainment onto it. A typical film included musical entertainment, good stuntwork which gave an implausible plot flavor and excitement, and a sub-heroic sidekick…who provided comic relief" (Walle 195).[4] *Billy the Kid Returns* meets the expectations of both the B westerns and the singing cowboy pictures, with six set pieces of various western action, including gunplay, horse riding, fist fights, and even a horse-and-rider cliff jump, as well as seven musical interludes – five songs by Rogers, one music and dance sequence, and one song by Smiley Burnette (in the comedic sidekick role). As such, the film serves as representative of a range of American cinematic categories – cowboy pictures and the particular variation of singing cowboy films, but also (and perhaps especially) B movies – and, at the same time, exhibits notable connections to independent cinema.

The term "B movie" immediately carries with it insinuations of quality – or lack thereof – based on the hierarchy implied in the name. Though these implications of quality have always been attached, the term itself was primarily intended to demarcate the order of screening in a "double feature," a screening format that rose to prominence in the early 1930s as movie theaters during the Great Depression sought ways to offer additional value to cash-strapped consumers. Double features paired two films on the same bill so that one ticket purchased a seat for both the first, or "A," film and the second – the "B" film (Taves 316). According to Yannis Tzioumakis, the A film "was normally a well-made, standard studio production…[while] the film that received the bottom billing…was normally a low-budget picture made by specific [major] studio units specializing in efficient, no-frills production or a low-budget film made by an independent company with no corporate ties to the studios" (60). Introduced in the early 1930s, by 1935 approximately 85 percent of all American theaters employed this double-feature format, with only the most prestigious downtown urban theaters staying with the single-film bill (Davis 3; Tzioumakis 60–61).

Not surprisingly, the disparity in budget between the A and B production models was significant. The average A film's budget in the late 1930s was around $350,000 (Taves 314). Contrastingly, based on interviews with Joseph Kane, the director of *Billy the Kid Returns* (and a regular director at Republic for many years), as well as known budgets for other comparable singing cowboy pictures, we can estimate the budget of Rogers's 1930s films, including *Returns*, to be around $20,000 (McCarthy and Flynn 320; Taves 323).[5] With such disparity in budgets,[6] one might assume the hierarchy to be absolute. But as Lea Jacobs notes, "if the distinction between A and B films was relatively well fixed within the system of distribution, the status of any individual film within this system was open to negotiation" (8–9). *Billy the Kid Returns* demonstrated such flexibility between A and B programming upon its release in September 1938. It played, for example, as the second film at the Broadway Theatre in Santa Ana, California (behind Warner's *Four Daughters* [1938]), and the Capitol Theatre in Salt Lake City, Utah (following Fox's *Gateway* [1938]). However, it also played in the "A" slot at a number of theaters across the country, including the New Liberty in Fort Worth, Texas, and the Robertsdale Theatre in Robertsdale, Alabama. Finally, it even played as a solo feature in several places, including the State Theater in Scranton, Pennsylvania, and the Palace in Mexia, Texas.[7]

As this list of playdates indicates, Rogers's film was programmed in its first month of release in independent theaters across the country, not only targeting cities with concentrated populations but also a wide range of rural communities. "The success of program westerns," Western film historian Andrew Brodie Smith informs us, "depended on their wide distribution to small-town and neighborhood houses," particularly across the American Midwest, South, and Southwest (189–190), with western stars "[e]specially popular in municipalities with populations under 5,000" such as Mexia and Robertsdale (Loy 22). In addition, these examples of exhibition locations are indicative of a flexibility based largely on market placement: a film like *Billy the Kid Returns* could be a clear B in urban theaters but an A film in rural markets, or play as the B in the important weekend evening slot but be elevated to an A position for the mid-week program (Jacobs 3; Taves 317). Singing cowboy pictures and the B westerns both were also generally perceived as targeting a juvenile population, primarily of boys, that attended the Saturday matinees (Rogers's lyrics cited earlier resonate here again). According to Smith, "whatever the actual demographic for program westerns, studios made and promoted these films with children in mind," and he recognizes the emphasis on male-driven action and the frequent promotion of the horse, kid, or comedic buddy characters over the leading lady as indications of such. Moreover, "knowing boys were put off by kissing scenes, producers of program westerns kept romantic material to a minimum" (194). Though Rogers's character in the film engages in a bit of courtship, including dancing and serenading, the film sets up but then avoids a final kiss, diverting the attention to a comedic bit by the sidekick, Burnette. The shift of westerns toward younger audiences which took place in the 1920s is generally attributed to Tom Mix, whose films took on the nature of morality plays with a Manichaean moral code where "villains are villains and heroes are heroes, and there is no mistaking it after the first 500 feet [roughly five minutes]" (Taves 333–334, citing a 1937 *New York Times* article).[8] Aside from Rogers's early portrayal of Billy the Kid in *Returns* (a character that was, again, given the Robin Hood treatment), such simplistic coding is fully on display in his character and, more broadly, the film.

While the western action was largely targeting the audience of juvenile males, the inclusion of western music as well as the series star's "flamboyant costumes of tailored cowboy suits" helped the films draw both young women and the family audience (Stanfield 5, 103). In addition, the character of the singing cowboy – Rogers and others – reached beyond the juvenile audience by acting as both a representative and a hero to a segment of the American populace in the 1930s that mainstream Hollywood rarely addressed directly: the Southern, rural, and agricultural viewers (and urban working-class families recently relocated from such) who had experienced not just the economic hardships but also the fears and tears of foreclosure, dispossession, and displacement as a result of the Great Depression (1–3).[9] Reflecting on the plot of *Billy the Kid Returns*, we can see a clear allegory in the way that the villainous rancher is stealing the homesteaders' horses and running off their livestock so that the "nesters" cannot "break sod" and will hence default on their homestead contract and be evicted. Rogers, as noted already, saves the day and Depression-era viewers were thus able to find solace in a story of good triumphing over a form of evil for which they were all too familiar while simultaneously engaging in a bit of cinematic escapism.

Such escapism was, of course, foundational in the development of American cinema and, despite the bifurcation into As and Bs at the beginning of the 1930s with the rise of the double feature, Hollywood had long engaged in producing cinematic entertainment at a broad range of budget levels. Still, the principal economic model developed by the eight principal film companies was one of high risk/high reward. Their movies required high production values to appeal to a broad range of viewers and succeed in a highly competitive market. These A pictures thus emphasized individual product (film) differentiation. To maximize box office returns for their popular titles, distributors required exhibitors to share a percentage – often 60 percent – of the ticket sales (Davis 7). The B films, however, worked on a different model. Since audiences and exhibitors viewed the second film as extra incentive but not the true draw, it was not necessary to differentiate the films significantly and they were understood as a different type of sellable good and rented on a flat-fee basis rather than on a percentage of the box office take.

Since Bs were sold largely on the quality of the brand (either the production company or the star/series) and not on the quality of the individual film (as with the As), Bs relied – as we have noted in relation to the B westerns – more heavily on established genre conventions (Smith 187). In addition, the companies only needed to distinguish their program westerns from those of other companies (or their other series) and, as such, popular (B film) performers/personas became a key approach (Smith 202; Agnew 137).[10] This was true to the degree that Roy Rogers (and others), like Gene Autry before him, used his "real" name for the characters he played.[11] The low-risk/low-reward economic model that Poverty Row studios like Republic, Monogram, Grand National, and Producers Releasing Corporation (PRC) were forced to adopt had the distinct potential to produce dependable, if relatively small, profits when production costs were determined around expected rentals – a generally predictable figure for the B films due to the stability of that market. This was even more true if studios could rent them out to exhibitors in a group – such as a series of films all starring the same popular singing cowboy star – rather than individually, and the "block-booking" practices developed by the major Hollywood studios were employed as well by the more successful and stable Poverty Row studios, including Republic. Block booking allowed producers to pre-sell a large group of as-yet-unmade films on the strength of just a small subset so that exhibitors had to accept the un- or less-desirable films to get those that they expected to appeal specifically to their local audiences (Buscombe, *BFI Companion* 37; Jacobs 3). While westerns were certainly not the only genre to be sold as such, series westerns such as those with Hoppy, Gene, and Roy Rogers were especially popular.

With the quick ascendance of television after World War II and the erosion of the studio system in the wake of the US Supreme Court's 1948 antitrust decision against Hollywood's eight key companies, both the singing cowboy pictures and the B westerns rode off into the sunset – at least on the silver screen. Roy Rogers references this passing as well in that 1974 ballad: "Just stories from the silver screen, now most of them forgotten/Double feature Saturdays with Hoppy, Gene and me." However, leveraging the success he had achieved in the Republic series films, Rogers (like Hopalong Cassidy, Gene Autry, and the western genre more generally) found a new home on television. From 1951 – the last year he appeared in a Republic picture – to 1957, he produced and starred in *The Roy Rogers Show*, which played Sunday evenings on NBC (and then continued in syndication, primarily on Saturday mornings, through 1964) (Phillips 111).

B movies like *Billy the Kid Returns* and others made by Republic Pictures and the Poverty Row producers in the 1930s and 1940s were distinctly "independent" in that they were made outside the Hollywood studio system and appealed to viewers that were part of communities and taste cultures that were generally underserved by Hollywood films. As this chapter has demonstrated, the four analytical areas of 1930s American independent cinema surveyed here – production, narrative and aesthetic conventions, exhibition, and audiences – were not distinct but rather bound up in a symbiotic system of interdependence. Even so, these films and companies were clearly dependent on, and indeed built on, the industrial premises of Hollywood filmmaking; they followed both the industrial practices and institutional policies set by the oligopolistic power players and were never completely separate from Hollywood. Nonetheless, they also demonstrated that it was possible to have a successful film industry operating alongside Hollywood that offered an alternative product for an alternative audience using production techniques modified for lower budgets and with genres, stars, and filmic conventions related to but also distinct from mainstream films.

Notes

1 Hollywood's eight-company oligopoly was formed by what were known as the "five majors" and "three minors": the major studios were Warner Bros., 20th Century Fox, Paramount, RKO, and MGM – all of which were fully vertically integrated (these companies were involved in all three sectors of the industry – production, distribution, and exhibition); the minor studios were Universal and Columbia – both of which had production and distribution arms, and United Artists, a distributor. Republic Pictures was founded in 1935 by Herbert J. Yates by acquiring and merging five small, independent film production companies (Hurst 1–2; Tzioumakis 63).
2 Billy the Kid was a notorious outlaw and gunfighter killed by Pat Garrett in 1881 at the age of 21. He fought in New Mexico's Lincoln County Wars and his exploits have been romanticized in pulp fiction accounts ever since.
3 The literature on the western film genre is expansive. For more on the conventions of the A and B westerns in this period, see Agnew; Buscombe, *BFI Companion*; and Loy.
4 Audience response was instant and from 1937 to 1942 Autry topped *Motion Picture Herald*'s list of top money-making western stars. In 1943 Rogers assumed the top spot, which he then held for over a decade (Buscombe, *BFI Companion* 38). The popularity was further marked by fan mail: by 1945 Rogers was receiving an average of 35,000 letters a month (Loy 9).

5 To meet such budgets, Kane further states that the films were shot in just six days and each film was made (from scripting through editing) in approximately six weeks, so that eight films could be made in a year (McCarthy and Flynn 320). This, in small part, was helped by the shorter run times of B films, which usually fell between 55 and 70 minutes. *Variety* lists the original release of *Billy the Kid Returns* at 56 minutes; when Republic sold their catalog of B westerns to television in the 1950s, most of the films were cut to fit that medium's hour-long slot that included commercials.
6 Using an inflation calculator, the budget for A films in 1938 would have been $7.25M in 2022; for Rogers's late-1930s Republic singing-cowboy B pictures, approximately $415,000.
7 These playdates and locations were found in archived local newspapers (included in Works Cited) accessed via newspapers.com.
8 This clear moral coding, while true of the B westerns, was not true of all B films. For more on other aspects of the B film, refer to Todd Berliner's study of *Detour* (1945) in the next chapter.
9 More broadly, the B westerns in general "contained a wide opening for a key social theme of the 1930s, the loss of farms to foreclosure during economic hard times" (Taves 335).
10 According to Smith:

> In marketing their shoot-'em-ups, studios tried to get fans invested in the small differences among the various cowboy stars…Yet for all the minor differences… the studios, in attempting to portray an ideal of western heroism acceptable to American boys and small-town audiences, had created very similar characters…all white men more or less the same age.
>
> (202–203)

11 Rogers birth name was Leonard Slye; Republic first changed his name to Dick Weston for two films before changing it again to Roy Rogers when he was given his first starring role, in *Under Western Stars* (1938).

Works Cited

Advertisement. *Foley* [Alabama] *Onlooker*, 22 Sept. 1938, p. 6.
Advertisement. *Mexia Weekly Herald*, 16 Sept. 1938, p. 2.
Advertisement. *Santa Ana Daily Register*, 12 Sept. 1938 (evening ed.), p. 11.
Agnew, Jeremy. *The Creation of the Cowboy Hero: Fiction, Film and Fact*. McFarland, 2014.
Buscombe, Edward. *The BFI Companion to the Western*. New ed., BFI, 1993.
———. "Gene Autry and Roy Rogers: The Light of Western Stars." *What Dreams Were Made Of: Movie Stars of the 1940s*, edited by Sean Griffin. Rutgers University Press, 2011, pp. 33–49.
Davis, Blair. *The Battle for the Bs: 1950s Hollywood and the Rebirth of Low-Budget Cinema*. Rutgers University Press, 2012.
"Film Booking Chart." *Variety*, 21 Sept. 1938, p. 14.
Green, Douglas B. *Singing in the Saddle: The History of the Singing Cowboy*. Vanderbilt University Press, 2002.
Hurst, Richard Maurice. *Republic Studios: Between Poverty Row and the Majors*. Scarecrow Press, 1979.
Jacobs, Lea. "The B Film and the Problem of Cultural Distinction." *Screen*, vol. 33, no. 1, 1992, pp. 1–13.
Loy, R. Philip. *Westerns and American Culture, 1930–1955*. McFarland, 2001.
McCarthy, Todd, and Charles Flynn. Interview with Joseph Kane. *Kings of the Bs: Working Within the Hollywood System*. E. P. Dutton & Co., 1975, pp. 313–324.

"Movie Attractions." *Scranton Times*, 6 Sept. 1938, p. 5.

Neale, Steve. *Genre and Hollywood*. Routledge, 2000.

"Now Playing at Salt Lake Theaters." *Salt Lake Tribune*, 30 Sept. 1938 (morning ed.), p.14.

Phillips, Robert W. *Roy Rogers: A Biography, Radio History, Television Career Chronicle, Discography, Filmography, Comicography, Merchandising and Advertising History, Collectibles Description, Bibliography and Index*. McFarland, 1995.

Rogers, Roy. "Hoppy, Gene and Me." Written by Snuff Garrett, Stephen Hartley Dorff, and Milton Brown. 20th Century Records, 1974. Vinyl single.

Smith, Andrew Brodie. *Shooting Cowboys and Indians: Silent Western Films, American Culture, and the Birth of Hollywood*. University Press of Colorado, 2003.

Stanfield, Peter. *Horse Opera: The Strange History of the 1930s Singing Cowboy*. University of Illinois Press, 2002.

Taves, Brian. "The B Film: Hollywood's Other Half." *Hollywood as a Modern Business Enterprise, 1930–1939*, by Tino Balio. University of California Press, 1993.

Tzioumakis, Yannis. "Independent Filmmaking in the Studio Era: The Poverty Row Studios and beyond (1930s to 1950s)." *American Independent Cinema: An Introduction*. 2nd ed., Edinburgh University Press, 2017, pp. 58–91.

Walle, Alf. H. "The Juvenile Cowboy Hero: Mass Media, Role Models, and Marketing." *Proceedings of the Biennial Conference on Historical Analysis and Research in Marketing* (CHARM), edited by Terrence Witkowski et al. Vol. 11, 2003, pp. 191–200, https://ojs.library.carleton.ca/index.php/pcharm/issue/view/104.

"Week's Film Calendar." *Fort Worth Star-Telegram*, 18 Sept. 1938, p. 9.

5
DETOUR (1945)

Todd Berliner

If the low-budget independent filmmaking economy of the 1940s produced any masterpieces, then *Detour* (1945) certainly counts among them – a bleak and sometimes bizarre film, nightmarish, unpredictable, visually inventive, an object of curiosity. It could only have come out of Poverty Row, a set of independent film production companies located in Los Angeles along Gower Street and Sunset Blvd. Unlike their studio counterparts, Poverty Row filmmakers worked under loose supervision, targeted smaller audiences, and did not worry about glamorizing actors. They also had the freedom to experiment within their tiny budgets. Poverty Row films did not have to be good to obtain distribution, but they did not have to be bad, either. They just had to be moderately engaging and 55–70 minutes long.

The independent filmmaking economy of the 1940s offered creative possibilities unavailable to studio filmmakers. We can think of creativity as finding solutions to problems. With its constant struggles to churn out something with almost nothing, Poverty Row was a ghetto of filmmaking creativity. Budget constraints determined film style, forcing compromises and unorthodox solutions to economic challenges. Poverty Row filmmakers sought creative ways to tell stories with little time for production and little money for sets, locations, and actors. In this environment, *Detour* is not so much an outlier as an exemplar of what could be achieved within the low-budget independent filmmaking apparatus of the studio era. The film takes some characteristic traits of the "B-movie" style of the period – a compact and meandering plot, unglamorous actors and unusual characters, barren sets, and a generally minimalist visual style – and, through subtlety and directorial experimentation, transforms them into aesthetic virtues unavailable within the stylish style of studio production.

DOI: 10.4324/9781003246930-6

FIGURE 5.1 *Detour* uses props and lighting effects that create a surreal mood and compensate for the barren sets.

But to understand what makes *Detour* exemplary, we need to take our own detour through the filmmaking economy that produced it.

Independent Filmmaking in the Studio Era and the Rise of the B-Film

The studio era (roughly the 1920s through the 1950s) saw three economic tiers of independent production firms – independent, that is, of any corporate relationship with the eight major Hollywood studios. At the high end, David O. Selznick, Walter Wanger, and other elite independent producers made mainstream films indistinguishable from those coming out of the majors (Tzioumakis 4). Least expensive, so-called ethnic films – geared to African Americans, Yiddish speakers, or other niche audiences – portrayed people and issues "ignored by mainstream studio films" (Tzioumakis 5). In between those extremes were Poverty Row pictures like *Detour*, cheap "B-movies" serving the second-run theaters, which exhibited films outside of the major downtown entertainment districts and comprised the majority of theaters in the 1930s and 1940s.

During the studio era, a so-called B-movie served an important industry function. The term did not just mean "low budget movie." Rather, it referred to the second half of a double bill. From 1935 through the 1940s, most exhibitors in the United States screened two movies for one admission price – an A-film and a B-film – to encourage theater attendance. The two types of films came out of entirely different economic and production systems. The A-films had A-budgets, A-directors, A-actors, and so on, and the profits of A-films depended on box office receipts; more popular films made more money. The B-economy worked differently. B-films were rented for a flat rate of $100–$200 (Naremore 140). Since the public went to the movies primarily to see the A-film – and regarded the B-film as merely a free added attraction, along with newsreels, cartoons, serials, and trailers – exhibitors had no way to calculate the value of any particular B-film to the lineup. They rented B-films merely to fill out the three hours of entertainment promised to the public.

That's where Poverty Row came in.

Poverty Row studios had existed since the 1920s, but because of the voracious demand for B-films in the 1930s and 1940s, exhibitors relied increasingly on Poverty Row to supply the bottom half of the double bill, enabling the independent firms to ride the coattails of the studio monopoly on A-film production. "B's almost never lost money," according to historian Brian Taves (315). Consequently, the 1930s and 1940s saw dozens of independent production companies churning out cheap B-films. The three most enduring Poverty Row companies were Republic Pictures, Monogram Pictures, and Producer's Releasing Corporation (PRC), where Edgar G. Ulmer directed *Detour* and many other films.

PRC was the smallest of the three. It operated from 1939 to 1948, a peak time for movie attendance generally and, because of the popularity of the double bill, for low-end independent film production specifically. The studio worked on the cheap, with profit margins of about $1750 per picture (Dixon viii). Whereas an A-film might have a two-month shooting schedule and a budget of at least $500,000, PRC's films had an average shooting schedule of five days and a budget of at least $5,000, averaging about $18,000 per film (Taves 325; Rogers 144). Because of product shortages, the B-movie economy virtually ensured a profit, provided the films stayed on budget.

Detour's Low Budget Aesthetic

One of the triumphs of Poverty Row filmmaking, *Detour* is so strange and exhilarating that it has inspired filmmakers looking to make lasting cinema with almost no money. UCLA, in a 1983 Ulmer retrospective titled "King of the

B's," featured *Detour* as the opening-night screening. In the late 1980s, Richard Linklater named his production company after the film. "What he could do with nothing," Peter Bogdanovich wrote in an admiring interview with Ulmer, "remains an object lesson for those directors, myself included, who complain about tight budgets and schedules" (558). Indeed, it is admirable that any B-films of the studio era are any good since they had so few resources, and guaranteed distribution created few financial incentives to make good B-movies. But there were other incentives to make good B-movies, and we should acknowledge three of the key reasons since they help us understand how a film as good as *Detour* got made at all.

First, a strong B-production could sometimes graduate to A-film status and thereby obtain A-film rental rates. In its 1942–1943 season, PRC began to make "programmers," which cost about $150,000 and could be distributed as either As or Bs (Jacobs 3; Rogers 144–148). With a budget somewhere between $30,000 and $117,226.80 (accounts differ widely), *Detour* may have fallen into the intermediate programmer category, provided PRC could convince some exhibitors to screen it as an "A."[1]

Second, filmmakers working on B-films typically wanted to work on A-films, where they could earn more money and prestige and work under better conditions (more time, bigger budgets, and better films). So B-filmmakers were often trying to impress studio executives who could advance their careers. Director Anthony Mann and cinematographer John Alton did some of their most brilliant work on low-budget crime films – such as *T-Men* (1947) and *Raw Deal* (1948) – for the independent Eagle Lion before advancing to studio films in 1949 (Keating 257). Ulmer found his home at PRC, but he worked on A-films too, including *The Black Cat* (1934) for Universal and *The Strange Woman* (1946) for United Artists.

Finally, the low budgets did not just constrain B-filmmakers, it liberated them to do what they wanted. It takes artists even to make B-movies; technicians alone cannot make them. Although A-filmmakers, to rationalize the huge cost of production, needed to ensure mass appeal, B-filmmakers could take creative chances. Ulmer said that at PRC he could work without "too much interference – if there *was* interference, it was only that we had no money" (Bogdanovich 593). Because of the low budgets and guaranteed distribution, we find in Poverty Row films like *Detour* artistic devices absent from the commercial, glamorous, tightly knit films coming out of the major studios (see Taves 331–342). Indeed, we can see in *Detour*'s inventive narrative and stylistic properties traces of the B-movie system that produced it: the film's unorthodox plotting, unfamiliar characterizations, and bizarre imagery spring from creative efforts to accommodate the economic constraints.

The filmmakers designed *Detour*'s narrative for a quick shoot – between six days, according to Ulmer, and 14 days, according to PRC records, both of which could be wrong – and relied on stock footage and repeated footage when they could. The plot of Martin Goldsmith's source novel had to be adjusted and truncated for the short schedule, limiting the number of characters, scenes, sets, and locations. Most location scenes take place along a desert road 15 miles from PRC's lot, and the main sets are two diners, a nightclub, an apartment, and a car. The many car scenes relied on rear projection, a cheap technology that PRC used extensively (Dixon ix). Because people sitting in cars face the same direction, the scenes required few set-ups.

The narrative is compact, characteristic of B-films of the period (Taves 334), with twists coming every ten minutes or so. The fact that it begins and ends in a diner, with a flashback narrative in between, gives the film a classical unity typical of crime films of the forties. Still, compared to studio films, *Detour* is strangely meandering, periodically introducing storylines that fall by the wayside. Those storylines do not so much build on as *replace* one another. At first, the plot seems to concern the romance between Al Roberts and his fiancée, Sue, and his plan, initiated 13 minutes into the movie, to hitchhike to Los Angeles to join her. The narrative really launches when Roberts gets picked up by Charles Haskell, who dies unexpectedly on the drive. Roberts, thinking he has inadvertently killed Haskell, takes on the man's identity, the first twist in the plot (around minute 25). He then meets Vera hitchhiking by the road (33 minutes in).[2] The narration shifts to Vera's scheme to sell Haskell's car (around 41 minutes), then her scheme to defraud Haskell's family (57 minutes). Roberts accidentally kills Vera and flees the scene (66 minutes), initiating a new set of narrative expectations. When the movie abruptly ends two minutes after the scene of Vera's murder, the plot feels like it is still getting started.

None of the initiated storylines comes to fruition. Roberts never resolves things with Sue; he never discovers whether he really killed Haskell; Vera and Roberts never sell Haskell's car; and the plot to swindle the Haskell family just evaporates – after much argument about whether the family would recognize Roberts posing as Haskell, we never even meet the family (it would have cost money to film their part of the story). The murder of Vera, it turns out, did not start a new story for Roberts but *ended* his story, wiping out previous plot lines. The very end of the film is curiously unfinished: when we see the police stop Roberts in the film's final shot, we do not know whether the event is really happening or represents his imagination since he describes the scene hypothetically as we see it play out ("Someday a car will stop to pick me up that I never thumbed"). Most Hollywood movies feel like they are heading in a particular direction, but you can never quite tell where *Detour* is going. In that way, *Detour* is a bit like a work by David Lynch or another surrealist – plot lines get started, we think they're going to matter, but the narration moves on to something else. These subtle plot incoherencies differentiate the film from the tightly constructed narratives that the Hollywood studio system had perfected (Berliner 52–55). *Detour* poses intriguing challenges to those trying to make sense of the film's form and meaning. Consequently, it rewards repeat viewings for curious spectators investigating the film with the hope of better understanding it.

The narrative meandering also gives the film a nightmarish quality. Everything grows increasingly worse for Roberts. The moment he escapes one predicament, he finds himself in another. This nightmare quality comes also from several bizarre events in the narrative, especially Haskell's death and the accidental killing of Vera with a phone cord. Consider Vera's first scene in the car with Roberts: Vera suddenly pops out of her sleep and accuses him, "Where did you leave his body?" The accusation is completely shocking and abrupt. How does she know about Haskell's death? Roberts was just talking in voiceover about impersonating Haskell, but that was in his mind. Is she clairvoyant? There is something surreal, even absurd, about the way bad things in this movie come out of nowhere.

The filmmakers' decision to use extensive voiceover narration presumably resulted from an effort to conserve production costs. Indeed, the film stages much of the action in Roberts's head as he takes us through the story, filling in expositional details that would consume resources to depict visually. For instance, "I was in Bakersfield before I read that Vera's body was discovered and that the police were looking for Haskell in connection with his wife's murder." It is much cheaper to have actor Tom Neal voice those events than to film them. Much of the movie consists of close-ups of Roberts pondering his bad luck.

The voiceover, however, serves aesthetic as well as economic functions, focalizing the film in an unusual way and, unlike the novel, training our attention on Roberts's psychology and manner of storytelling. Voiceover is a notoriously uncinematic device, so how can filmmakers make it interesting? *By making it unreliable.* Astute viewers will notice that Roberts's narration periodically differs from the movie's narration, a difference that viewers likely attribute to Roberts's misjudgments and defeatism. For instance, when he describes his former life in New York as a piano player alongside Sue, we can note subtle inconsistencies between Roberts's description and what we witness. He says that he had "a good job as jobs went in those days. Then, too, there was Sue, who made working there a little like working in heaven." He describes their former relationship as "the most wonderful thing in the world." But when we see the two of them together in the very scene he is narrating, Roberts seems bitter about his job and harsh with Sue, who seems more concerned with her career as a singer than marrying him. They have "all the time in the world to settle down," she says. Such subtle differences between Roberts's understanding of his life and the film's depiction of it complicate his characterization. We have to be cautious with him. He may not understand his own story.

The central event of Roberts's story is Haskell's death, but the movie signals that Roberts may misunderstand that event, too. Roberts thinks he inadvertently killed Haskell when opening the car door and the sleeping Haskell fell out and hit his head on a rock; however, the movie implies that Haskell might already have died *before* he fell from the car. We saw Haskell taking pills, suggesting a heart condition, and Haskell already looked lifeless before Roberts ever opened the car door. Roberts just assumes he killed Haskell, an attitude consistent with his generally pessimistic worldview.

Finally, Roberts misunderstands us, the people he is apparently addressing in voiceover. "Start your sermon. I'll listen to it. But I know what you're going to hand me even before you open your mouths. You're gonna tell me you don't believe my story of how Haskell died and give me that 'Don't make me laugh' expression on your smug faces." Roberts, who has a charming flair with words, generally comes across sympathetically, a man cursed by poverty, bad luck, and a few self-delusions, but he talks to us as though we are deeply suspicious and unfeeling, cold-hearted judges of his doomed predicament. Forced into using extensive voiceover by the economics of B-film production, the filmmakers have exploited the device's potential to enrich characterization.

The filmmakers have also taken pains to enrich the character of Vera, played by actress Ann Savage. The character is something of a femme fatale, a wily woman who traps Roberts in a doomed plot. But Vera behaves like no other femme fatale in cinema. A stock character in forties crime films, the femme fatale, by convention, ensnares our protagonist by seducing him. But *Detour* refuses to make Vera seductive. When we meet her, she has dark circles under her eyes, her hair untamed and grimy. According to Savage, Ulmer had make-up artists put dirty-brown toner on her face and cold cream in her hair (Isenberg 48). The major studios needed to protect their investment in female actors by idealizing their feminine appearance. By contrast, *Detour* makes Vera look *interesting*, not glamorous. Roberts says she has "a beauty that's almost homely because it's so real," an apt description of Savage herself. James Naremore says that the actors in *Detour* "seem to belong to the same marginal world as the characters they play" (149).

Ulmer coached Savage to deliver her lines with intense velocity (Isenberg 48). She hurls them at Roberts in a rat-a-tat-tat that is aggressive and frightening. "Shut up," she snaps, "You're a cheap crook and you killed him. For two cents, I'd change my mind and turn you in. I don't *like* you." There is a vulgar intensity in her lines, each word enunciated but few pauses between them, rapid jabs of vitriol. She grimaces when she reaches the word "like" in "I don't *like* you." She projects insults – "You sap!" – as though she is spitting at him. Vera is an odd deviation from the femme fatale stereotype, and there is nothing like her hostility and charisma in any studio crime film. She takes over every scene. You have to watch her.

We find nuance in her character, too. The movie elicits sympathy for Vera, hinting at emotional damage and a past filled with hardship. Vera looks desperate when trying to convince Roberts to swindle Haskell's family: "No sweating, scheming, wondering where your next meal's coming from." Coughing at times, she might have tuberculosis. "There's plenty of people dying this minute that would give anything to trade places with you," she says to Roberts, "I know what I'm talking about." She says those lines breathily, holding his arm, and periodically seeks to touch him, softening her otherwise belligerent tone. Her constant scheming comes off as an effort to keep him around. She says some lines seductively – "I'm first in the bathtub," "I'm going to bed" – and when he misses her flirtations or, worse, recoils from them, she lashes out. All in all, we get the impression of a defensive woman who wants affection but who responds to every rejection with vitriol and hardness.

So far, we have examined *Detour*'s unusual plotting and characterizations, but its visual style also rejects some time-honored conventions of studio filmmaking, which regularly invested in elaborate decoration (Berliner 95–100). With little money for sets and props, *Detour*'s filmmakers adopt a minimalist style that looks vaguely like reality but has little realistic detail. New York is a foggy street and part of a nightclub. Los Angeles is a used car lot and a bare one-bedroom apartment. The entire country in between is just desert and highways spotted with diners. The film also depicts those spaces surrealistically. It presents New York as a hazy world with indistinct background features (upper left figure). Fog mostly hides a set that is barely there. Fog also enabled Ulmer to turn a small backlot into a series of dream-like New York streets.

Ulmer used lights, cinematography, and props to create a variety of distorted images, such as a mirrored reflection of Roberts standing over Vera's dead body (upper right figure), an oversized model of a coffee cup for the opening diner scene (bottom left figure), and ominous lighting effects, including spotlights on Roberts's eyes and face (middle-row figures). When Roberts imagines Sue "shooting to the top," we see her, as though in a dream, in a barren setting with a canted camera, singing before musicians represented only as shadows (bottom right figure). His voiceover suggests a happy fantasy, but the image is surreal, unbalanced, and unsettling.

Perhaps the film's most inventive low-budget visual effect comes immediately after Roberts kills Vera. In a minute-long tracking shot, the camera trains on nine successive objects in the apartment as Roberts mulls his fate and the evidence that incriminates him. The objects (a jacket, a comb, and so on) come in and out of focus as the camera settles on each one, suggesting Roberts's state of shock as he scans his memory for traces of his time with Vera, unable to focus on anything for more than an instant. As the camera moves around the room, we attempt to identify each object as it comes into focus and see strangely indistinct and abstract imagery every time the cinematography grows blurry again and moves on to the next. It is an effective, economical use of the camera that accomplishes multiple narrative and stylistic functions: it suggests Roberts's traumatized mental state, generates viewer curiosity, introduces another series of graphic abstractions, and adds one last stylistic flourish to the film's visual patterning.

Dead End

You can literally see *Detour*'s low budget in the barren sets and locations, limited set-ups, and the absence of stars – characteristic features of B-film production in the 1930s and 1940s. But the filmmakers have clearly spent creative resources on many subtleties in the storytelling and flourishes in the visual style, finding creative solutions to the financial constraints forced upon them by the independent filmmaking economy of the period.

In terms of volume, though perhaps not quality, the 1930s and 1940s were a golden age of independent filmmaking, with dozens of independent studios making hundreds of films each year. According to Taves, "never before or since has low-budget filmmaking been so integral to the Hollywood industry" (313). Three years after *Detour*'s release, however, PRC would stop making films altogether, a casualty of the studio system's collapse. The Consent Decrees of the 1940s, a set of agreements between the Justice Department and the studios, ended forced distribution and other monopolistic practices by the major studios. Films could no longer be sold in blocks. Instead, each film would be sold based on its individual profit potential, making double bills less profitable. The required industry restructuring after the Consent Decrees left no guaranteed market for B-films. B-films *had* no individual profit potential. Their value came from their pairing with an A-film as part of a full evening of entertainment. The studio system had propped up the B-film economy by ensuring a steady stream of A-films for the top half of the double bill. And when the double bill died out in the 1950s, Poverty Row died with it.

The B-film economy, while it lasted, led to a distinct film style that permeated second-run theaters in the 1940s. *Detour* shows us what the low-budget independent filmmaking apparatus could, for a brief time, achieve within that style. With *Detour*, we see what talented American filmmakers of the 1940s could accomplish when disburdened of glamor, stars, and money.

Notes

1 Tzioumakis and others list *Detour*'s budget as $30,000 (18), whereas Isenberg prices the film at $117,226.80, based on PRC documents (39).
2 Because the film never provides her last name, I refer to her simply as Vera.

Works Cited

Berliner, Todd. *Hollywood Aesthetic: Pleasure in American Cinema*. Oxford University Press, 2017.
Bogdanovich, Peter. *Who the Devil Made It*. Alfred A. Knopf, 1977.
Dixon, Wheeler, editor. *Producers Releasing Corporation: A Comprehensive Filmography and History*. McFarland & Company, 1986.
Isenberg, Noah. *Detour*. BFI, 2008.
Jacobs, Lea. "The B Film and the Problem of Cultural Distinction." *Screen*, vol. 33, no.1, 1992, pp. 1–13.
Keating, Patrick. *Hollywood Lighting from the Silent Era to Film Noir*. Columbia University Press, 2009.
Naremore, James. *More Than Night: Film Noir in Its Contexts*. University of California Press, 1998.

Rogers, Maureen. "Remaking the B Film in 1940s Hollywood: Producers Releasing Corporation and the Poverty Row Programmer." *Film History*, vol. 29, no.2, 2017, pp. 138–164.
Taves, Brian. "The B Film: Hollywood's Other Half." *Grand Design: Hollywood as a Modern Business Enterprise, 1930–1939*, edited by Tino Balio. Scribner, 1993, pp. 313–350.
Tzioumakis, Yannis. "Edgar G. Ulmer: The Low-end Independent Filmmaker *Par Excellence.*" *Edgar G Ulmer: Detour on Poverty Row*, edited by Gary D. Rhodes. Lexington Books, 2008, pp. 3–23.

6
THE HITCH-HIKER (1953)

Lisa Dombrowski

A scrappy, low-budget thriller selected for preservation by the United States National Film Registry in 1998, *The Hitch-Hiker* is championed as the first American film noir helmed by a woman and one of director Ida Lupino's most accomplished efforts. Born into an English theatrical dynasty and encouraged to embrace acting, Lupino made her screen debut at the age of 13. After a stint at Paramount playing blonde ingénues, she garnered acclaim at Warner Bros. in Raoul Walsh's gritty thrillers *They Drive by Night* (1940) and *High Sierra* (1941). Yet Lupino always felt limited by the roles she was offered and her reputation in Hollywood as "a poor man's Bette Davis." After co-founding the independent production company The Filmakers in 1949, Lupino expanded her creative labor into screenwriting, directing, and producing, becoming the only woman to direct in Hollywood during the 1950s. Lupino's work with The Filmakers is marked by an investment in realism and an interest in exploring difficult social problems, often through the stories of characters suddenly cut off from "normal" society and unsure of how to move forward (Scheib 55). While her first films as a director found her tackling women's pictures, *The Hitch-Hiker* is an all-male affair in the semi-documentary and action melodrama modes. The story concerns two war buddies, Roy Collins (Edmond O'Brien) and Gil Bowen (Frank Lovejoy), whose fishing trip derails after they unwittingly pick up a hitch-hiking serial killer, Emmet Myers (William Talman). *The Hitch-Hiker*'s significance lies in its relation to postwar independent production trends, to Lupino's embrace of realism and genre hybridity, and to her interest in revealing the double bind of postwar gender norms.

Industrial Context

The Hitch-Hiker was made in the midst of a seismic shift in the American film industry away from studio-based production and toward independent filmmaking.

DOI: 10.4324/9781003246930-7

FIGURE 6.1   Cinematographer Nicholas Musuraca utilized the hard shadows of high-contrast lighting associated with film noir to heighten the suspense.

Lupino's efforts to expand her professional work beyond acting coincided with and are illustrative of this transition. Independent production began to increase in the United States following the 1940 consent decree in the Paramount antitrust case, when the major studios agreed to distribute films in blocks of no more than five. The limitations in block booking minimized the major studios' incentive to produce lots of inexpensive films to be sold in packages with desirable big-budget pictures, leading to a reduction in studio output and opening the door for independent producers to fill exhibitors' screens. Following the US entry into World War II, attendance at movies skyrocketed along with per-picture profits, providing more capital and lowering the risk of financing independent production. At the same time, stratospheric personal income tax rates encouraged top-tier talent to incorporate as independent production companies to receive their pay as profit participation and thus be taxed through lower-rate capital gains.

The trend toward increased independent production further accelerated at the end of the 1940s and became the norm in the 1950s. Postwar declines in attendance and surging production and operating costs prompted the major studios to cut back on overhead and reduce their payroll, freeing actors, directors, writers, and craftspeople from their contracts. Studio offloading prompted more and more above-the-line talent to create their own production companies and become "hyphenates," combining their prior professional work with producing and thereby expanding their creative possibilities. Long dissatisfied with the limited opportunities provided to her as an actress in the studio system, Lupino expressed in interviews as early as 1942 that she was "tired of acting" and would "prefer the producing and writing end" of Hollywood ("Ida Wants to Be Herself"). The changing structure of the American film industry gave her a chance to enact this goal. But while many actors became producers, also becoming a director was less common – Paul Henreid, Robert Montgomery, and Dick Powell were among the few studio-era actors to make the leap. In this rarified group, Ida Lupino was the only woman. As Therese Grisham and Julie Grossman highlight, Lupino thus operated in the postwar American film industry as both an insider and an outsider – an insider with an expansive professional network and deep experience as an acclaimed actress, but also the sole woman then working as a film director in Hollywood (6–7).

Lupino's move into independent production was a collaborative effort with clearly defined aims that enabled her to expand and vary her creative contributions. Following her marriage to Columbia Pictures production executive Collier Young in 1948, Lupino and Young formed Emerald Pictures with Anson Bond, the heir to a national chain of clothing stores who was eager to get into writing and producing. Yet the partnership was short-lived. In less than a year Bond fell out with his colleagues and sold his share of the firm to screenwriter Malvin Wald. Lupino, Young, and Wald then rechristened the company The Filmakers, and together the three produced nine feature films over the next five years. Lupino formally or informally produced all nine, directed five, wrote four, and acted in four – modeling, as she did so, an approach to authorship rooted in collaboration (Grisham and Grossman 36). In interviews, the Filmakers team described their desire to make high-quality but low-cost films with provocative subject matter and to develop new acting and technical talent rather than rely on established stars. After a socially critical but unprofitable initial release (*Never Fear*, 1950), the company came to the attention of mogul Howard Hughes, who had recently purchased RKO and was hunting for low-budget producers to fill out his distribution slate. As part of a negative pickup deal, Hughes agreed to distribute The Filmakers' next three pictures through RKO and to provide financing of $250,000 per film (Dixon par. 19). The Filmakers thus developed *The Hitch-Hiker* with the assurance of advanced financing and guaranteed distribution – helpful resources when preparing a controversial project.

The origins of *The Hitch-Hiker* script lay in sources both fictional and real, and its references to an actual crime raised the hackles of industry regulators. The foundation of the screenplay originated in a story penned by Robert Joseph and based on the latter part of Daniel Manwaring's 1946 novel *Build My Gallows High* (itself adapted into a film in the noir style by Jacques Tourneur as *Out of the Past*, 1947). Lupino and Young then reworked Joseph's tale of two former army buddies on a fishing trip to Mexico who pick up a sketchy hitchhiker and integrated an unnerving real-life parallel: the murder spree of serial killer William "Billy" Cook, Jr. For 19 days beginning in late December 1950, Cook roamed between Missouri and California, kidnapping three people at gunpoint and killing six others, including a family of five and their dog. After forcing two men on a hunting trip to drive him across the Mexican border to Santa Rosalia, Cook was arrested by local police. The American media widely covered the manhunt for Cook, his capture, and his eventual execution later in 1951, including articles and photo spreads in *Time* and *Life* magazines – material

The Filmakers quickly recognized as ripe for exploitation. In early February 1951, Hollywood gossip columnist Hedda Hopper reported that Lupino had met with one of the hunters forced by Cook to drive to Santa Rosalia, and The Filmakers planned to make a film about the serial killer and his two captives. Lupino subsequently went to San Quentin "with special permission from my buddies at the FBI" to visit Cook and obtain a release for the rights to his life story (qtd. in Anderson 18). After The Filmakers submitted the script to the Production Code Administration, the blowback was fierce. The Department of Justice alleged The Filmakers had damaged the case against Cook, as legal proceedings were still underway, while the PCA declared the film in violation of the section of the Code written to prevent the exploitation of notorious real-life criminal activity (Grisham and Grossman 25–26). Only after fictionalizing the script's crime spree and assuring both institutions that the film did not glorify Cook's exploits did The Filmakers receive PCA approval and move forward with production – while still retaining "easter egg" references to the actual case that could be recognized by avid news-hounds.

Genre and Form

Lupino's aesthetic approach to *The Hitch-Hiker* was firmly rooted in Hollywood's postwar embrace of realism, expressed physically in the film through semi-documentary location shooting, structurally through references to Cook's crimes and the plot patterns of the crime melodrama, and psychologically through noir elements of story and style. While realism had long been one of the primary functions of classical Hollywood filmmaking, the lingering influence of wartime newsreels and documentary combat films as well as recent technological advances expanded the stylistic choices available to postwar Filmakers seeking a realistic effect. The development of lightweight cameras, new camera supports, and portable light units in the late 1940s particularly encouraged lower-budget Filmakers to shoot on location with smaller crews and a simplified approach to lighting (Dombrowski 67–68). While Grisham and Grossman make a case for Italian neo-realism as an influence on Lupino's embrace of realist filmmaking (50–52), a more proximate inspiration was the late 1940s semi-documentary production cycle which Lupino repeatedly referenced in interviews. Anchored by a series of films set in motion at Twentieth Century-Fox by veteran newsreel producer Louis de Rochemont beginning with *The House on 92nd Street* (1945) and reaching its apex with *The Naked City* (1948) – penned by Lupino's partner at The Filmakers, Malvin Wald – semi-documentaries were investigative dramas based on real stories and featuring an objective voiceover narration, selective use of non-actors, little or no score, and at least partial location shooting. While *The Hitch-Hiker* did not feature voiceover narration, non-professional actors, or an absent score, the film's basis in true-life crime and liberal use of location shooting near Lone Pine, California display the fingerprints of the semi-documentary.

Location shooting heightens the specificity in how *The Hitch-Hiker* presents space, language, and lived experience, adding low-cost production values to the budget picture while amplifying its appeals to authenticity. Much of the film's visual organization involves cutting between extreme wide shots of the protagonists' car racing through the desert landscape and tighter framings in the car interior of the killer and his two hostages. Lupino adopts a range of strategies in the location sequences outside of the car to duplicate the feeling of confinement within while simultaneously highlighting the texture and distinctiveness of the environment. During nighttime scenes when the men stop for meals and sleep, cinematographer Nicholas Musuraca utilizes low-key, high-contrast directed light to isolate the men's faces in the frame, drawing attention to the vulnerable anxiety of Roy and Gil and recreating the visual entrapment of the car interiors. In daytime scenes when the men stop for food or gas, wider framing and high-key lighting open the visual field. While the contrast with the car interiors may initially promise an emotional release, every interaction with locals raises the stakes, as each shop owner or bystander has the potential to be not only a witness for the police but also Myers's latest victim. In addition, Lupino opts not to subtitle conversations between Mexican characters or between locals and Gil (who speaks Spanish), adding another layer of geographic and cultural particularity. By the final act of the film, when the three men have abandoned the car and trudge across the rocky desert with vultures and search planes circling above – doubling Gil and Roy's vulnerability – the inhospitable expanse visualizes the reality understood by the hostages: there really is no escape now, as the landscape is just as unforgiving and deadly as Myers himself. Lupino further accentuates the toll captivity has taken on the two friends through costuming, hair, and makeup, as sweat, dirt, blood, and a slow in-growth of beard adorn the protagonists in a deglamorized form of naturalism.

Real-life details and narrational conventions characteristic of the crime melodrama further contribute to *The Hitch-Hiker*'s evocation of realism and the development of suspense. While Lupino and her colleagues at The Filmakers removed any overt mention of Billy Cook, Jr.'s killing spree from the film, plot details alluding to his actual crimes provide an "intertextual framework" that undergirds the fictionalized portion of the film, endowing the experiences of Gil and Roy with a heightened degree of verisimilitude (Rabinowitz 95). For example, in the opening scene depicting Myers's initial hitch-hiking murder, an Illinois license plate recalls the residency of the family Cook murdered – a fact widely covered in the press. The array of newspaper headlines trumpeting Myers's crimes – a generic trope in crime pictures – here becomes more reflexive, as contemporary viewers would likely recognize the "Nationwide Search for Hitch Hike Slayer" as an illusion to Cook, increasing their propensity to conflate the real-life serial killer with the fictional representation. Furthermore, as Gil and Roy drive Myers to Santa Rosalia under gunpoint, the characters traverse the same geographic locations as Cook and his two hostages. A barking dog Myers shoots at a gas station recalls the dog Cook shot along with its owners, while a water well in which Myers threatens to bury Gil and Roy reminds knowing viewers of the Missouri mine shaft in which Cook dumped the bodies of the family he murdered. These fictional/actual overlaps enable Lupino to exploit the Cook case in a manner unanticipated by the PCA, providing moments of recognition, shaping narrative expectations, and heightening the sense that *The Hitch-Hiker* is a semi-documentary recreation.

The Hitch-Hiker's selective use of narrative and stylistic elements characteristic of film noir further develops the picture's psychological realism and suspense, complementing its semi-documentary realism. Film noir is a term created by French critics to retroactively describe a wave of downbeat postwar American movies infused with claustrophobic shadows and a mood of self-defeat. As a range of authors have noted, *The Hitch-Hiker* is not a typical noir: there are no femme fatales leading the protagonists to destroy their mundane former lives; no criss-crosses or betrayals; no flashbacks or play with time and memory; and the presence of a serial killer and large numbers of scenes shot in broad daylight in an open desert are highly unusual for noir. Yet the film does explore in tremendous detail what Foster Hirsch describes as "the noir victim": "middle-class family men; steady, likable fellows who happen to be in the wrong place at the wrong time" (12–13). In addition, cinematographer Nicholas Musuraca photographed *The Hitch-Hiker* using lighting conventions that critics associated with the noir style. In his study of studio-era lighting, Patrick Keating notes that noir lighting was "marked by a tension between its equally palpable realist and expressionist impulses" (245). As most noirs were, in the industry parlance of the time, melodramas – designed to produce thrills and suspense – "cinematographers lit them the way they had been lighting melodramas for years: with low-placed key-lights, strong contrasts, and hard cast shadows" (245–246).

The opening sequences in *The Hitch-Hiker* are excellent examples of how low-key, high-contrast lighting can efficiently and inexpensively direct the eye while also shaping how the viewer responds to the action. Lupino presents Myers's initial killings in a fragmented and elliptical fashion, shrouding the murders in the shadows of night and utilizing car headlamps and a police officer's flashlight as single light sources to direct viewer attention to details of the crime scenes. Viewers are cued to imagine that which they cannot see, communicating "violence more violent than if viewers saw complete gore, rife with bloody bodies" (Sipiora 194). Depicting Myers's face only in the pages of a newspaper, Lupino withholds the reveal of the killer until he is in Roy and Gil's car. First his gun tilts up into the frame from the darkness of the back seat, fill light bouncing off the barrel, then the camera pushes in between Roy and Gil to reveal Myers as he leans into a single low-angle light source, his face only partially emerging from a sea of black. The high-contrast lighting emphasizes only the most pertinent information – there is a man with a gun in the back seat – while associating Myers with darkness itself. Although later nighttime scenes feature more carefully modulated lighting with less contrast and gobos used to suggest moonlight filtering through trees, Musuraca returns to a high-contrast lighting set-up in the climax of the film, when Myers has forced Roy to change clothes with him in case of a police ambush. The noir-style lighting is a tool Lupino uses to conceal and reveal information and heighten suspense, as viewers know more than either the police hiding in wait or the men cautiously approaching them. As cinematographer and noir specialist John Alton wrote, "In the dark there is mystery" (Alton 44). Yet as we have already seen, Alton's corollary, "Where there is light, there is hope…Daylight brings relief" (56) does not hold true in *The Hitch-Hiker*. Throughout the film, Roy and Gil are as trapped in the daylight as they are in the dark.

Themes

As *The Hitch-Hiker* tightens the screws on its two everyman protagonists, leaving the viewer in a state of suspense regarding their possible fate, it also prompts reflection regarding who they are and how they respond to their forced powerlessness. As such, the picture becomes "an investigation into the tensions of masculinity in postwar America" (Rabinowitz 96). In the 1950s, white middle-class men were expected to define their maturity through a commitment to marriage, fatherhood, and their role as the family breadwinner, yet sociologists and psychologists found such men also chafed against the dullness of conformity (Grisham and Grossman 41). *The Hitch-Hiker* introduces this psychological conflict through the characters of Gil and Roy in the first scene following the prologue depicting Myers's killings. Before the two men pick up Myers, they converse about where they should go on their trip. Rather than driving to the Chocolate Mountains in Arizona – where they told their spouses they were going – they decide to cross the border into Mexico to go to San Felipe; on the way, Roy suggests stopping in Mexicali for a night on the town. Gil reflects, "Except for the war, this is the first time I've been away from Maudie and the kids…Mexicali is starting to sound good." Yet when Roy drives into the neon-filled border town, Gil pretends to be asleep, prompting Roy to leave in disappointment. A two-shot then reveals Gil opening his eyes and furtively glancing at Roy – suggesting to the viewer that Gil had unspoken second thoughts. While the introduction of Gil and Roy highlights that they are similar in their "flight from their family responsibilities" (Rabinowitz 95), it also suggests an important difference – namely, that Gil is more likely to control his impulses.

After the men pick up Myers, the reveal of the gun in the back seat of Roy's car instantly upends the men's control over their own lives and places them in a position of forced passivity, a narrative signature in Lupino's directorial work that links the all-male *The Hitch-Hiker* to her women's pictures (Scheib 54). As Myers peppers the men with orders, taunts, and tests of their obedience, the expanding divergence in their responses despite their parallel situation cues the viewer to compare and contrast their personalities and actions. Gil, a white-collar draftsman, swallows his fear and frustration and adopts a strategic stoicism, telling Roy: "As long as he needs us, we're safe. When he tries to get us, we'll get him." Roy, on the other hand, increasingly loses control over his emotions, lashes out at Myers, and becomes obsessed with escape. Scheib highlights the effects of Roy's inability to deal with his feelings of helplessness: "[Roy] O'Brien, a mechanic who owns his own garage and controls his own labor, goes almost mad under another's power" (63). Crucially, both men take active steps to regain control over their fates, but only one is effective. Gil is acquiescent when Myers is paying attention but leaves his wedding ring on a gas pump when Myers is distracted, providing authorities with a clue regarding their whereabouts. Roy, on the other hand, mounts a futile escape that leads to him injuring his ankle, and when the car is leaking oil, he knowingly chooses not to fix it. As a result, the men are forced to march across the desert on foot – further exacerbating Roy's injury. Argues Rabinowitz, "Only Gil is coded as the 'adequately' masculine hero of the film" (97).

While *The Hitch-Hiker* is formally structured to encourage the comparison of Gil and Roy – and thus of two different performances of masculinity – the picture also asks the viewer to consider how their manhood is defined in relation to that of Myers. At the opening of the film, the juxtaposition between the introduction of Myers and the introduction of Gil and Roy suggests the contrast between the men is quite stark – one is a thief and a killer, living outside the law and normative society, while the others are middle-class veterans and family men, multiply rooted in society. Yet Gil and Roy's alteration of their original plans and flirtation with a night in Mexicali suggests they, too, might like to break the rules sometimes – as Myers highlights when he discovers their detour from the Chocolate Mountains: "And then you came to Mexico. What for? Dames? You guys ought to be ashamed of yourselves, causing all that trouble, telling lies." Myers's bullying and taunting of Gil and Roy form one of the narrative patterns that structure the plot, repeatedly contrasting the killer's power and freedom to do as he pleases against the men's helplessness and confinement. Myers rubs their noses in the difference, claiming their choices make them lesser men: "You guys are soft. You're suckers! You're up to your necks in IOUs. You're scared to go out on your own." Wielding the ultimate masculine tool, a gun, Myers appears as "a figure of 'deviant' manhood, masculinity run amok" (Rabinowitz 96). But as Roy rebels against Myers's sadistic games, he increasingly becomes a mirror of the killer, desperately searching for the ability to act as he pleases – to have the same power Myers wields at the handle of a gun. In the end, it is Gil who knocks the gun out of Myers's hand, thereby allowing the police to handcuff him – definitively turning the tables on the killer and placing *him* in a position of confinement and helplessness. But even after Roy finally relieves his fear and frustration by pummeling Myers, only to be pulled off by Gil, who tells him, "It's all right now. It's all right," the sudden ending of the film leaves a note of ambiguity. Are Gil and Roy *really* all right? Roy's desperate cry to the police before Gil subdues Myers still rings in viewers' ears: "I'm not Myers! I'm not Myers!" As with so many of Lupino's protagonists, Gil and Roy end the film far less confident than when they began, now "shell-shocked victims who wonder if they can ever go home again" (Scheib 57). By establishing a parallel between not only Gil and Roy but also Myers and Roy, Lupino expands potential thematic readings of the film, encouraging viewers to assess a spectrum of masculine performance and the strain of postwar America's rigidly defined gender norms. As with so many pictures in the noir style, *The Hitch-Hiker* steeps the viewer in the dark side of the American dream.

The author would like to thank Claire Moskowitz for research assistance.

Works Cited

Alton, John. *Painting with Light*. University of California Press, 1995.
Anderson, Mary Ann. *The Making of The Hitch-Hiker, Illustrated*. BearManor Media, 2013.
Dixon, Wheeler Winston. "Ida Lupino." *Senses of Cinema*, Apr. 2009, https://www.sensesofcinema.com/2009/great-directors/ida-lupino/.
Dombrowski, Lisa. "Postwar Hollywood, 1947–1967." *Cinematography*, edited by Patrick Keating. Rutgers University Press, 2014, pp. 60–83.
Grisham, Therese, and Julie Grossman. *Ida Lupino, Director: Her Art and Resilience in Times of Transition*. Rutgers University Press, 2017.
Hirsch, Foster. *Film Noir: The Dark Side of the Screen*. Da Capo Press, 1981.
Hopper, Hedda. "Drama: Story of Captives Stirs Ida Lupino." *Los Angeles Times*, 2 Feb. 1951, p. A6.
"Ida Wants to Be Herself." Warner Bros. Studio Publicity Materials, ca. 1942. Margaret Herrick Library, Academy of Motion Pictures Arts and Sciences, Beverly Hills, CA.
Keating, Patrick. *Hollywood Lighting: From the Silent Era to Film Noir*. Columbia University Press, 2010.
Rabinovitz, Lauren. "*The Hitch-Hiker* (1953)." *Queen of the 'B's: Ida Lupino Behind the Camera*, edited by Annette Kuhn. Praeger, 1995, pp. 90–102.
Scheib, Ronnie. "Ida Lupino: Auteuress." *Film Comment*, Jan./Feb. 1980, pp. 54–64.
Sipiora, Philip. "Ida Lupino, Hitchhiking into Darkness." *Ida Lupino, Filmmaker*, edited by Sipiora. Bloomsburg, 2021, pp. 193–212.

7

THE MAN WITH THE GOLDEN ARM (1955)

Philip Drake and Nessa Johnston

The Man with the Golden Arm, released by United Artists in 1955, is a film that bridges studio-era and independent Hollywood. Adapted from Nelson Algren's award-winning novel about a veteran's struggles with drug addiction, it presents a taboo-breaking portrayal of drug use. Hollywood's Production Code, enforced from the 1930s up until 1968 by the Motion Picture Association of America, operated as a form of industry self-regulation of contentious content, and at this time prohibited depiction of illegal drug use or trafficking. The film stars Frank Sinatra as Frankie Machine, a reformed heroin addict, poker dealer, and aspiring jazz drummer who struggles to stay clean. Although its depiction of addiction might seem uncontroversial by today's standards, at the time the film was ground-breaking and was released in defiance of the MPAA and its Production Code Administration (PCA). Furthermore, casting a music star of the fame of Sinatra as a drug addict in a downbeat issue-driven movie seems bold for the time, with rising Hollywood star Kim Novak as his extra-marital love interest. In this chapter, we revisit the film, its themes and stylistic elements, alongside its publicity, marketing, and controversy, to examine what elements of a recognizably independent sensibility are in operation throughout the film and its reception.

United Artists and Otto Preminger

As a United Artists release, the identity of the film was already distinctive. Founded by Charles Chaplin, Mary Pickford, Douglas Fairbanks, and D.W. Griffith in 1919, United Artists (UA) was formed to offer major Hollywood stars greater creative control and autonomy. *The Man with the Golden Arm* was released in UA's second phase of existence, after acquisition by former financiers turned independent producers Arthur B. Krim and Robert Benjamin during a

FIGURE 7.1 Sinatra's expressive performance of drug addiction and withdrawal.

challenging period for the studios. This is usually attributed to the impact and structural changes to the industry in the wake of the 1948 Paramount Decree that dismantled the vertical integration of the studios. However, it also reflected challenges brought about by wider cultural changes in US audiences in the post-war period, the emergence of television as a major rival for cinema, and the rise of independent production companies and freelance stars that ultimately ended exclusive studio talent contracts (Carman and Drake). Krim and Benjamin took operating control "offering to run the company for ten years on the condition that if the company turned a profit in any one of the first three years, they would be able to acquire half ownership of the company at a nominal cost" (Balio, "Introduction" 5). By 1955, they owned the company outright, buying it out from the remaining founders, Chaplin, and Pickford (5).

The restructuring of UA's operations continued to distinguish it from the other studios. As the smallest of the eight Hollywood studios, Balio argues that UA operated as an independent distributor:

> selectively providing financing to a host of projects that were being submitted to it by agents, producers, and entrepreneurs of all kinds, UA played the role of a maverick by starting trends, by taking on the forces of repression in Hollywood, and by investing in some offbeat pictures.
>
> *(Balio,* United Artists *49)*

Krim and Benjamin maintained UA's reputation for quality, offering financing, complete creative control, and a share of profits to producers, in exchange for distribution rights (Balio 42). The producer had final cut, and contracts were non-exclusive, with UA operating in a more independent manner than other studios at this time.

Golden Arm was therefore an offbeat, maverick picture, and a product of several distinct personalities and creative identities. Its director-producer Otto Preminger was signed from 20th Century Fox, having made his name in the 1930s and 1940s, notably with *Laura* (1944). At UA, Preminger's first project was *The Moon Is Blue* (1953), a commercial success (15th in *Variety*'s year-end box office chart with a domestic gross of $3.5 million [Fujiwara 287] against a budget of $500,000 [Balio, *United Artists* 71]) due to controversy generated by its defiance of PCA restrictions prohibiting the comic treatment of its seduction theme. Despite being refused a PCA seal, hitherto a prerequisite to assure a film was suitable for general audiences, exhibitors still booked the film. This led to UA temporarily resigning from the MPAA, with the commercial success of the film bolstering its anti-censorship position. Hence, by the time of *Golden Arm,* Preminger was known as a figure willing to challenge censorship. He was supported by risk-taking UA executives, unafraid of another run-in with the MPAA; and despite wanting a Code seal, intended distributing the film regardless of the PCA's decision (Simmons 44). Preminger also enlisted graphic designer Saul Bass's innovative and striking visual sensibility for the film's title sequence, and a hip jazzy score by a then little-known Elmer Bernstein, whose work had been restricted to low-budget independent productions, having been "graylisted" for having left-wing sympathies (Miller). This consolidated the film as a creative, independent, and exciting production.

Sinatra's Stardom and Performance

The risk-taking of United Artists and Preminger was also apparent in the casting of hugely successful music star Frank Sinatra. Sinatra, having been out of favor in Hollywood for several years, was in the process of making a comeback with *From Here to Eternity* (1953), a role for which he had to fight, having lost out to Marlon Brando to star in *On the Waterfront* (1954). The casting of Sinatra can be seen as part of a Hollywood tradition of stars crossing over from music to film, with examples including Paul Robeson, Bing Crosby, Harry Belafonte, Elvis Presley, and Doris Day. However, Sinatra's performance of the drug-addicted Frankie is different from earlier musical performances in films such as *On the Town* (1949), and his transition in the 1950s from "bobbysoxer" heartthrob to washed-up, drug-addicted veteran is worth noting. At the time of its release, Sinatra was in a transition period for his star image. His career had risen through the 1940s, becoming a globally successful singer with a string of hit records, touring to massive audiences. However, by the later 1940s Sinatra's success had waned: he was divorced, a resident performer in Las Vegas associating with figureheads in organized crime, and in a highly public extra-marital affair with Ava Gardner (whom he married in 1951 before separating around the time of *Golden Arm*'s production). Yet the 1950s eventually emerged as Sinatra's most critically well-received period, due to his acclaimed recordings with Capitol Records and his prolific work across music, film, and television. In *From Here to Eternity*

(1953) Sinatra won an Academy Award for best supporting actor, one of the eight Awards the film garnered. For *Golden Arm*, the casting of Sinatra (who seized the opportunity, beating competition from his rival, Marlon Brando [Fujiwara 361]) was a timely masterstroke. Sinatra's working-class background and street authenticity underpins his star performance, allowing him to convincingly play characters rebelling against authority and societal injustice, even if, in the film, he aspires for more (as a jazz drummer he wants to take a "real class" stage name, Jack Duvall).

Sinatra's performance drives the film's narrative, supported by newcomer Kim Novak as Molly, and Eleanor Parker as his wife Zosh. For Glenn, Sinatra's ability to play the underdog was key to his appeal. She notes how in the 1950s he performed roles where he is "victimized or caught in a system or situation in which he has no agency" (476). In *Golden Arm*, Frankie is a returning veteran, and vulnerable, attempting to escape his limited options. Frankie is trapped in multiple ways – through drug addiction, needing to deal cards to earn money, and through a marriage arranged as penance for his drunk driving, trapped by guilt. Frankie's plan to better himself is to get a job as a musician, yet his ability to escape – to become a jazz drummer, to be with Molly – is continually thwarted by his drug addiction. The elliptical dialogue of the film never includes the word heroin and relies instead on implied meanings and connotations (although it does use the words "fix" and "junkie").

All of this is played out through Sinatra's complex, detailed performance. A line he repeats throughout the film: "Here we go, down and dirty" – used in the card dealing scenes and Frankie's attempt to go "cold turkey" to escape addiction – aptly describes Sinatra's appeal in the film. He presents a tormented, working-class masculinity, seemingly powerless to escape from his situation, which he refers to as the "monkey on my back." The camerawork draws attention to the details of his performance as a man struggling, using close-ups of his facial twitching and eyes blinking. In an effort to circumvent Production Code censorship, the drug use sequences themselves cut away from the needle injecting to show Sinatra's reaction instead. Drug injection occurs beyond the frame, moving to a close-up of Frankie's face, then just his eyes, his pupils dilated – the performance via close-ups functioning as a visual synecdoche for the drug's effects. The lengthy card game sequence with Frankie dealing while craving a fix, deprived of sleep, again highlights Sinatra's physical performance (rubbing his face, hands shaking, eyes twitching) to represent both physical cravings and psychological conflict. This culminates in a painfully awkward scene where, desperately needing a fix and deprived of sleep, Frankie attends a band audition and disastrously fails to keep time to the beat due to his shaking hands.

Sinatra's performance drives the melodramatic narrative logic of the film throughout. For Frankie, gambling and heroin are inextricably linked, as intimated in a line to Molly preceding a revealing speech about how he got hooked: "I'm quitting the game. I'm quitting a couple of things." The celebrated cold turkey scene in the film places the performance of Sinatra in a confined space, performing his withdrawal through turbulent, agonized physical outbursts, involuntary expressive behavior, movement, and violent tics with Frankie curling up into a ball, clutching his stomach and crying out in pain (Drake 89). Remarkable for the time, these sequences established Sinatra and UA as willing to take risks on screen. Alongside Sinatra, Kim Novak presents a strikingly modern, understated performance as Molly – assertive, cool, glamorous, and independent, offering a counterpoint to Eleanor Parker's performance of Zosh as melodramatic, histrionic, and needy. Grounding these and lightening the tone of the film, as a counterpoint to Sinatra, are the supporting comedic turns of character actors such as Arnold Stang as Sparrow and Doro Merande as Vi.

Aesthetics and Style

Alongside Sinatra's performance and the film's daring drug theme, *The Man with the Golden Arm*'s aesthetics further underlines its offbeat, independent sensibility. The film was shot in black and white and in 1.85 to 1 ratio, rather than opting for the color ultra-widescreen aesthetic favored by the mid-1950s, with Preminger waiving his Cinemascope and Technicolor commitments ("UA's Product" 21). These aesthetic choices were appropriate for the film's dark subject matter, although Preminger's initial choice of location shooting in Chicago in a bid toward greater realism was not realized. Instead, the film was shot on an RKO Pictures lot, using sets (McNally 38), which gives the film a stagy rather than naturalistic feel – with over-lit exterior street scenes. Though not strictly a *film noir*, the film has noir-ish visual touches. These are most noticeable during the illegal card game scenes – set in a smoke-filled room with high contrast, low key lighting – with Frankie's celebrated "golden arm" dealing cards. The spatial logic of the film means that locations are just steps away from each other, with exterior scenes just as claustrophobic as interiors. Domestic spaces are cramped and restricted, while the only means of temporary escape, Antec's tavern and the Safari Lounge, offer not only temporary alcohol-fueled conviviality but also pathos, as seen when a blind panhandler desperately gathers spare change from the other drinkers for a beer. As Molly puts it, in defense of her drunk boyfriend, "Everybody's a habitual somethin'. With him it's liquor, is all."

Perhaps the most distinctive independent aesthetic sensibilities in the film are manifested by Bernstein's score and Saul Bass's title sequence. Bernstein's jazz style was unusual given that more classically influenced scores that still dominated Hollywood. *Golden Arm* innovated by integrating jazz into the score, with the collaboration of jazz musicians Shorty Rogers and Shelly Manne (Hubbert 178). Rogers and Manne even play themselves in Frankie's disastrous audition scene. In a major promotional effort by UA in the run-up to the film's release, the film's theme tune received widespread radio play across the US and was a big hit, with several versions covered by different artists all charting in the top 20 in the US ("'Golden Arm' Tune"). The commercial success of Bernstein's theme removed him from the "gray list" and made him a sought-after movie composer, later collaborating with other notable directors including Martin Scorsese and John Landis, and writing memorable scores for *The Magnificent Seven* (1960), *The Great Escape* (1963), and *Ghostbusters* (1984), among others.

Saul Bass's modernist title sequence, alongside the bold, jazzy score, provides a dramatic and memorable opening for the film. Bass worked regularly with Preminger and with Alfred Hitchcock, delivering ground-breaking title sequences for *Vertigo* (1958) and *Psycho* (1960). Bass's animated sequence was an artistic departure from the typically functional form of title and credits, a striking display of white bars appearing and disappearing on a black background, in time with the beat of the jazz, coalescing on a stylized motif of a tense, twisted arm. For maximum impact, Preminger made sure that a note accompanied prints sent to theaters instructing the projectionist to run the start of the film only after the curtains were fully open (Bass and Kirkham 116); hence the title sequence became part of the film as a cinematic event.

These striking visual elements were incorporated into the film's promotional materials for a comprehensive and heavily funded advertising campaign. At the center of the posters and magazine ads was the stylized arm motif, abstract art meets corporate brand, and unusually eschewed prominent images of the film's stars, Sinatra and Novak; indeed, the arm symbol alone was used on the marquee at the film's New York opening (Bass and Kirkham 120). Bass also designed album covers in 1956 for both Elmer Bernstein's *Blues and Brass,* and Sinatra's *Frank Sinatra Conducts Tone Poems of Color,* consolidating the links between his modernist, abstract visual sensibility and the musical endeavors of *Golden Arm*'s two key musical artists. Hence, *Golden Arm* can be understood as using distinct artistic sensibilities and personalities as marketable elements, in a manner that prefigures later independent cinema (Wyatt 122).

Censorship: Challenges and Creative Constraints

Despite its reputation for challenging censorship, paradoxically, *The Man with the Golden Arm* engaged in substantial self-censorship. The film was dogged by controversy throughout its production, with Harry Anslinger, commissioner of the Federal Bureau of Narcotics, condemning the film even before it was completed, believing it was impossible to represent drug use in movies without glamorizing it ("Dope…" 23). This is despite the fact that drug crime was covered in the news and contemporaneous TV shows such as NBC's *Dragnet* (1951–1959). As Preminger derisively put it, "why […] should movies be treated like a stepchild with no brains? Television deals with it. I've seen two or three shows where narcotics were important," viewing Anslinger's influence on the PCA as *de facto* federal government censorship ("Hollywood Scene").

UA, with the support of some members of the PCA including its president Geoffrey Shurlock, hoped that the film's serious approach to the issue of heroin addiction could be used as a test case to grant a special one-off exemption or precipitate a revision of the Production Code (Simmons 41). It was, therefore, decided that the film should not violate the Code in any other respect, so Preminger worked closely with Shurlock to avoid any additional grounds for rejection (42). Sexual or violent content was toned down; for instance, in the Club Safari scenes, where Molly works as a dancer, Preminger was advised to avoid "any strip-teasing or bumps and grinds," and told Novak could not be shown wearing anything less than a slip (42). Similarly, a scene showing Frankie being kicked for cheating at cards was cut on the grounds that it was "unacceptably brutal" – instead he is repeatedly slapped across the face – and the scene of Zosh's suicide had to be presented as an accident, as the Code prohibited suicide as a means of escape from the law (42).

Self-censorship also contributes to the film's elliptical treatment of drug use. Over the course of the film, the theme tune shifts to signify the craving taking over Frankie, with the discordant jazz of the music building as Frankie succumbs to addiction. Dialogue relies on metaphor, referring to the "monkey on your back," or when Louie talks about attempting to kick a craving for candy in an effort to push Frankie to purchase another fix. When the action shifts to Louie's apartment's interior, we are spared much visual detail of drug-taking activity, although we see Frankie roll up his shirt sleeve in anticipation, then Louie's readying of drug paraphernalia is punctuated on the soundtrack by brass and drum stingers. The efforts to placate the Production Code Administration by deglamorizing the film's themes and settings meant that the music, title sequence, and visual marketing are central to its appeal, with jazz denoting metropolitan cool, and Saul Bass's semi-abstract motif of the stylized arm functions to "distance the image from the harsh realities of shooting up, although they are implicit in the (dis)figuration" (Bass and Kirkham 116).

In spite of all of this, efforts at self-censorship were for naught, as the PCA denied *Golden Arm* a seal because of its portrayal of drug addiction, and refused an exemption or to consider revising the Code. UA's presumptuous attitude backfired, exemplified by a press release the PCA slammed as "premature," as well as their decision to rush the release in time for Oscars season (Simmons 42–43). Following the board's decision, UA announced its resignation from the MPAA, a repetition of the fallout from *The Moon Is Blue*. However, the publicity surrounding the PCA's controversial decision, along with favorable reviews, meant that *Golden Arm* was even more successful than *The Moon Is Blue*, grossing $4,350,000 in US and Canada against an estimated budget of $1,000,000 (Balio, *United Artists* 71), ranking 13th in Variety's list of top-grossing films of 1956 (Fujiwara 374) and breaking box office records on its opening in New York (Simmons 45). And in a surprise move, the Catholic pressure group Legion of Decency rated the film B ("morally objectionable") rather than C ("condemned"); which meant that the usual effect of denying a PCA seal was neutralized, and exhibitors could book and show the film without fear of protests from religious organizations (Simmons 45). The film then received three Academy Award nominations, for Bernstein's score, Sinatra's performance, and Joseph C. Wright and Darrell Silvera's art direction, further undermining the PCA and reflecting the distance between the Production Code and the critics by the 1950s.

Conclusion

The Man with the Golden Arm represents an important film in understanding both the relationship between Hollywood cinema and censorship, and Hollywood's relationship with independent production and aesthetics, paving the way for wider changes to follow in the 1960s and 1970s. In its presentation of gritty subject matter and drug use, the casting and performance of Sinatra, and its modern jazz score and title design, the film presents a distinctive, offbeat, independent sensibility. *Golden Arm* also illustrates the gamble that UA was willing to take, showing how Hollywood cinema could successfully represent hitherto prohibited social issues, prefiguring later taboo-breaking in the 1960s and 1970s. As a risk-taking film, it was cited during a 1956 United States Senate Hearing in a dispute between distributors and exhibitors over their respective share of box office receipts, with each side arguing they were underwriting the substantial risks of film releases (United States Senate). Through its controversy and the publicity it gained, the film prefigures later independent cinema not just in exploring previously taboo issues but also exploiting the publicity from doing so, using its risk-taking subject as a marketing hook to attract audiences.

Previously, the fact that exhibitors would refuse to book a film without a PCA seal had motivated compliance with the Production Code. With major cinema exhibition chains booking *Golden Arm,* this triggered a decision in January 1956 to carry out a major reassessment of the Code for the first time since 1930 (Simmons 46). It was revised later that year, allowing "careful treatment" of several previously prohibited themes, including drugs, abortion, and kidnapping, and with the PCA permitted to be more liberal in its interpretation (Balio, *United Artists* 72). As a result, *A Hatful of Rain* (1957) just two years later became the first film with a drugs theme to receive a PCA seal (Simmons 47). Unaltered versions of both *Golden Arm* and *The Moon is Blue* were quietly granted seals just a few years later in 1961 (Schumach 14), as Hollywood entered a new decade of social and industrial change. As such, *Golden Arm* represents an important staging post on the journey from studio-era Hollywood to independent-era Hollywood, demonstrating a gradual shift in the balance of power from studios to independent producers, talent, and distributors, and the increased appetite to produce and market films with controversial social issues that came to characterize Hollywood cinema from the 1960s.

Works Cited

Balio, Tino. *United Artists: The Company that Changed the Film Industry: Volume 2, 1951–1978.* University of Wisconsin Press, 2009.

———. "Introduction: United Artists in Film History." *United Artists*, edited by Peter Krämer et al. Routledge, 2020, pp. 1–14.

Bass, Jennifer, and Pat Kirkham. *Saul Bass: A Life in Film & Design.* Laurence King, 2011.

Carman, Emily, and Philip Drake. "Doing the Deal: Talent Contracts and Hollywood" *Hollywood and the Law*, edited by Paul McDonald et al. BFI Palgrave, 2015, pp. 209–234.

"Dope... and the Movies." *Film Bulletin*, 26 Dec. 1955, pp. 13, 23, https://archive.org/details/filmbulletin195523film/page/12

Drake, Philip. "Reconceptualizing Screen Performance." *Journal of Film and Video*, vol. 58, nos. 1–2, 2006, pp. 84–94.

Fujiwara, Chris. *The World and its Double: The Life and Work of Otto Preminger*. Farrar, Straus and Giroux, 2008.

Glenn, Colleen. "A Real Swinger of a Nightmare: Frank Sinatra and the Grim Side of the WWII Veteran's Story." *Quarterly Review of Film and Video*, vol. 36, no. 6, 2019, pp. 470–497.

"'Golden Arm' Tune Gets Big Play." *Film Bulletin*, 12 Dec. 1955, p. 32, https://archive.org/details/filmbulletin195523film/

"Hollywood Scene: Preminger Presents Case for His 'Man With the Golden Arm' – Other Items." *New York Times*, 2 Oct. 1955, p. 7, https://timesmachine.nytimes.com/timesmachine/1955/10/02/issue.html

Hubbert, Julie. *Celluloid Symphonies: Texts and Contexts in Film Music History*. University of California Press, 2011.

McNally, Karen. *When Frankie Went to Hollywood: Frank Sinatra and American Male Identity*. University of Illinois Press, 2008.

Miller, Cynthia. "Guardian Interviews at the BFI: Elmer Bernstein." *Guardian*, 6 Oct. 2002, https://www.theguardian.com/film/2002/oct/06/guardianinterviewsatbfisouthbank1

Schumach, Murray. "Censors Reverse Old Ban on Films." *New York Times*, 31 July 1961, p. 14, https://timesmachine.nytimes.com/timesmachine/1961/07/31/97683515.html?page Number=14

Simmons, Jerrold. "Challenging the Production Code: *The Man with the Golden Arm*." *Journal of Popular Film and Television*, vol. 33, no. 1, 2005, pp. 39–48, DOI: 10.3200/JPFT.33.1.39-48

"UA's Product Farflung: Preminger Readying Hot One." *Film Bulletin*, 5 Sept. 1955, pp. 21–22, https://archive.org/details/filmbulletin195523film/

United States Senate. *Motion-picture Distribution Trade Practices, Hearings Before a Subcommittee of the Select Committee on Small Business*, Eighty-fourth Congress, Second Session, on the Problems of Independent Motion-picture Exhibitors. U.S. Government Printing Office, 1956.

Wyatt, Justin. *High Concept: Movies and Marketing in Hollywood*. University of Texas Press, 1994.

8

ATTACK OF THE 50 FOOT WOMAN (1958)

Jamie Hook

She was preceded by apes, crabs, and ants. She would be followed by leeches, shrews, and tomatoes. The generic worlds of science fiction and fantasy cinema have long been populated by creatures disproportionate in size and scale to the landscapes surrounding them. In 1958, one such oversized being was a woman. Nancy Archer, née Fowler (Allison Hayes), a socialite-turned-giantess and the eponymous character of *Attack of the 50 Foot Woman* (hereafter *Attack*), embodies a series of contradictions that exerted special ideological weight within the rapidly reorganizing cultural politics of those years spanning the election of Eisenhower and the explosion of the sexual revolution.

Even before her vertical expansion two-thirds of the way through the film, Nancy threatens several patriarchal pillars of the postwar American status quo: she is financially independent and she confronts her gold-digging spouse point blank about his extramarital affair rather than suffer this sexual double standard in silence. For all this, as the film's theatrical trailer bluntly describes her, she is "the most grotesque monstrosity of all."[1] Her monstrous sexuality is crystalized in the heavily circulated and recreated image (memorably illustrated on the film's famous poster) of the enlarged Nancy arrayed only in her once-bedclothes as makeshift lingerie. They are not nearly enough to cover her 50-foot frame and therein lies the point: the "grotesque monstrosity" is simultaneously a sexual spectacle. These various contradictions – she is economically self-reliant and emotionally dependent, victimized and villainous, beautiful and bestial – manifested themselves through a series of generic codes and conventions associated with Hollywood, its influential reach extending to independent film production of the time.

In what follows I am interested in thinking beyond the potential symbolism of Nancy herself to consider the broader generic contexts in which the film situates her unruly body.[2] This chapter will then explore how genre conventions inform

DOI: 10.4324/9781003246930-9

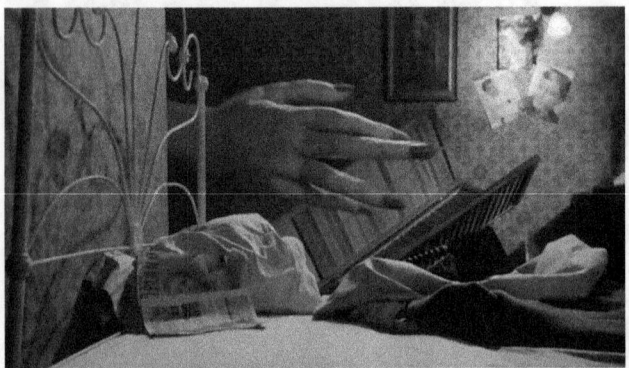

FIGURE 8.1 Beauty becomes the beast as Nancy (here represented by a patently artificial hand) searches for Harry in a shot that visually recalls *King Kong* (1933).

gender representation within a text that exemplifies independent exploitation at a transitional moment in 20th-century film history. Specifically, I argue the film owes as much to the then-current or recently passed articulations of Hollywood genres – particularly melodrama and noir – as it does to those sci-fi, exploitation, and "weirdie" contemporaries alongside which it is most commonly viewed and discussed.

Independent/Exploitation

With a great deal of interpenetration (although far from synonymous), both independent and exploitation cinemas are routinely defined by their distances – industrial/economic, aesthetic/technical, and social/political – from Hollywood. Nevertheless, unlike the largely episodic or situational sex-hygiene and nudist films of the preceding years, historian Eric Schaefer describes late-1950s films produced and distributed by the likes of Allied Artists Pictures Corp. and American International Pictures as "narratives in the strict classical Hollywood cinema mode, eschewing the educational or titillating spectacle that had differentiated classical exploitation from Hollywood product" (331). This points to a structuring facet of the indie-exploitation film as it existed during this transitory moment between the studio era and New Hollywood: namely, the extent to which the weird, independent, and exploitative are frequently imbued with intertexts from mainstream genres.

Even a cursory account of *Attack*'s production history illustrates the economic realities of much independent filmmaking of the era: it was shot over eight days (Weaver, *Science Fiction Stars* 375) for a reported budget of $65,000 (Swires 56) at a moment when, say, Hitchcock's *Vertigo* (also released in 1958) took twice the time on its San Francisco location shooting alone, which would then be followed by another two months of studio work, all for an estimated two-and-a-half million dollars. Cinematographer Jacques Marquette credits the project as the brainchild of producer Bernard Woolner (Weaver, *Attack* 201). Produced by Woolner Bros. Pictures and distributed by Allied Artists, the film's budgetary-induced constraints rankled director Nathan Juran, credited under the pseudonym Nathan Hertz. "The script was so dreadful, and the schedule was so tight, that the film had all these strikes against it right from the start," he later recalled, going on to declare, "Woolner wasn't a moviemaker...He didn't care about the script. He was only interested in making money" (Swires 56). Clearly sympathetic to Woolner, cinematographer Marquette took the opposite line against Juran, casting him as "another one of those directors...who don't give a goddamn about your budget" (Weaver, *Attack* 202).

Out of these conflicting values emerged a film routinely identified as an example of "bad" filmmaking, the adjective signaling either reproach or appeal depending on the reading formation through which the text is negotiated. Jeffrey Sconce describes the "ironic reading strategies honed by the badfilm community through countless hours of derisive interaction with late-night science fiction" (373), a viewing context surely hospitable to *Attack*, which has been remembered as showing two or three times a week on television in the 1970s.[3] While the film might very well typify B-grade sci-fi, this alone does not adequately summarize the cinematic influences through which certain aspects of its story and style are most legible, at least as they serve to condition its gender representations.

Genre theorists have long sought to dispel the notion that "[g]enres have clear, stable identities and borders" (Altman 16). Rather, they are discursively constituted and historically situated. At its moment of release, *Attack* was dismissed by trade publication *Variety* as "[m]inor science fiction" (16), a designation fortified by its initial double-billing with independent maverick Roger Corman's space saga *War of the Satellites* (1958). Later, film historian Thomas Doherty would include it as one of the "weirdies," an "inexact nomenclature for an offbeat science fiction, fantasy, monster, zombie, and/or shock film, usually of marginal financing, fantastic content, and ridiculous title" (146). While *Attack* indeed checks all of these boxes, the film remains equally allied to genre norms more associated with other films born within the very studio system from which it is ostensibly independent.

Generic Dependencies 1 – Melodrama

Clearly, as Barry Keith Grant reminds us, "genre movies have always been hybrid, combinative in practice" (23). Moreover, *Attack*'s long valuation as a cult film may find some explanation in such generic hybridity; as Ernest Mathijs and Xavier Mendik argue, cult texts frequently "blur and push the generic conventions they are supposed to respect" (2). Hardly independent in this sense, it is *Attack*'s very dependence on other traditions operative behind its sci-fi veneer through which certain genre-based understandings of its central characters are activated: from this perspective, Nancy epitomizes the melodramatic woman, while her husband Harry (William Hudson) and his lover, Honey Parker (Yvette Vickers), embody noir's morally flawed man and femme fatale respectively.

While melodrama is a representational mode to which any other genre might turn, it also maintains a distinct generic valence particularly in the social and industrial context of the 1950s as manifested through glossy, emotionally driven films set in domestic milieus and oriented around the subjectivities of women. In their study of science fiction cinema, Geoff King and Tanya Krzywinska specifically note the subgenre of "altered human scale" (27) as carrying "potential for forays into the world of domestic politics" (29), something Cyndy Hendershot also nods to when she writes of *Attack* and *I Married a Monster from Outer Space* (1958) as "unique within a body of [sci-fi] paranoiac films of the 1950s in presenting the paranoia which begins in the domestic realm" (84). Much of *Attack* takes place in the Archers' upper-class home – replete with pool and loyal butler – within whose walls Nancy battles, not menaces from space, but the all too earthbound demons of alcoholism and adultery.

The film then takes up not only the tone or style of melodrama but also certain thematic hallmarks. In terms of Nancy's fragile emotional state, one has only to think of, say, the female protagonists of Douglas Sirk's filmography of this same period to uncover a roster of other such maladies originating "in the domestic realm": the Thoreauvian "quiet desperation" of widowed mother Cary Scott (Jane Wyman) in *All That Heaven Allows* (1955), for instance. The decidedly non-maternal Nancy Archer perhaps shares the closest kinship with *Written on the Wind*'s (1956) sexually frustrated Marylee Hadley (Dorothy Malone), a character read "as a symbol for the return of the repressed and the revenge that repressed desire turned perverse exacts on the agents of repression" (Orr 384). The return of the repressed marks a central tenet of horror, while the idea of female sexuality as an excessive, vengeful force is concretized in the very title of *Attack*.

Nancy's embodiment of excess – which will become literal with respect to the term's spatial connotations only at the film's climax – is presaged by her introduction. She is first seen barreling down an isolated desert road in her sports car and spinning out of control as an otherworldly orb descends from overhead. It is here that Nancy experiences her first sighting of the supersized space creature (Michael Ross) who will later catalyze her eponymous condition. The "hysteria" engendered by this encounter is weighed against the unruffled demeanor of the local sheriff (George Douglas) when Nancy reports what she has seen. Nancy is thus framed within the diegesis as a melodramatic woman, an archetypical positioning that emerges with greater force as the film continues and her latent alcoholism rears its head.

Nancy's firsthand knowledge of the space creature is chauvinistically dismissed in realms both public (the exchange with the sheriff) and private, as Harry plans to weaponize her declarations of what she has seen against her with reference to her recent release from a sanitarium. This narrative thread relates to another branch of melodrama: the paranoia often felt by the victim-protagonists of domestic thrillers as in the paradigmatic *Gaslight* (1944). As a woman who knows too much, it is Nancy who has seen the alien and even chooses to seek it out a second time to prove its existence in the face of disbelief. Her "cracking up" and "seeing things" – as Harry chides her in a cruel monologue – anticipate a newly archetypal female role that would emerge two decades later (in a new mutation of indie-exploitation film production) as the Final Girl of the slasher film who is defined precisely by her vision and the (often unbelievable) knowledge attending it.[4]

Later, having been "contaminated" as a direct result of this knowledge, Nancy becomes an object of medico-patriarchal control. This recalls another subset of 1940s women's films in which, as Mary Ann Doane describes, "[a]lways on the verge of hysteria, the female character…is placed under the care and constraint of a medical gaze" (69). First confined to bed under the auspices of care, after her extraordinary growth, Nancy will be physically restrained there by enormous chains à la Kong, beauty having become the beast in a recollection and reversal of Cooper and Schoedsack's seminal 1933 work of American screen fantasy (which will be visually recalled at least twice in moments leading up to and at the film's climax).

Generic Dependencies 2 – Noir

Geoff King describes how within much independent cinema (including "many productions at the exploitation end of the independent spectrum") the expectations through which we define and experience genres "are not entirely thwarted…but neither are they entirely realized, creating the often-characteristic indie quality of existing in the space between familiar convention and more radical departure" (166–167). While the appearance of noir iconography within an ostensible sci-fi film may not have had a strong precedent at this time, neither is it entirely surprising to see a noir sensibility within an independent film like *Attack*. Indeed, many now-classic *films noirs* were themselves exactly this; as James Naremore posits in his pivotal study *More Than Night*, "most of the respected examples of classic noir belong not to Poverty Row but to an ambiguous middle range of the industry" (139). *Attack* emerged from a similarly liminal space insofar as the mid-1950s marked something of an economic-industrial crossroads for distributor Allied Artists. As Blair Davis recounts, they remained "the marketplace's primary source of B-movies" while simultaneously attempting to enhance this image by adding several A-pictures, such as Billy Wilder's *Love in the Afternoon* (1957), to their production schedule (61).

Naremore also acknowledges noir's encroachment on (or absorption of) sci-fi when he invites readers to imagine

> a large video store where examples of [noir] would be shelved somewhere between gothic horror and dystopian science fiction: in the center would be *Double Indemnity* [1944], and at either extreme *Cat People* [1942] and *Invasion of the Body Snatchers* [1956].
>
> *(9)*

His examples prove serendipitously perceptive in thinking about these particular generic influences on *Attack*. Like *Cat People*, the film's uncanny horror is born out of a male inability to control a metamorphosing, destructive female body.

Like *Invasion of the Body Snatchers*, also released by Allied Artists just two years earlier, a naturally frenzied reaction to a threat from outer space is met with skepticism and the threat of hospitalization. Finally, the melodramatic narrative maneuvers of *Attack* involve an extramarital love affair whose participants plot the murder of the "inconvenient" spouse, a noir formula perhaps perfected in Billy Wilder's quintessential *Double Indemnity*.

To this end, the beats, cadences, and patois of noir dialogue are unmistakable in the initial exchanges between Harry and Honey:

HONEY: Play the husband right to the end. Once she's in the booby hatch, throw the key away. That'll put you in the driver's seat. You'd make a wild driver, Harry, with 50-million bucks.

Honey here epitomizes the femme fatale, oozing sex appeal as she exerts her sway over the duplicitous and impressionable Harry by promising to restore his masculine agency (putting him rightfully back "in the driver's seat," which is even a continuation of *Double Indemnity*'s – and noir's more generally – fascination with and metaphoric use of the automobile).[5] When such generically evocative language recurs, Nancy is not just an object of the unscrupulous pair's annoyance but now their intended target for murder:

HONEY: There is a way out, if you've got the nerve...Have you got the nerve?
HARRY: Read the morning papers.

Out of this hardboiled dialogue arises a plot to eradicate Nancy as she sleeps by way of an overdose.

During the scene of the attempted murder, noir comes to permeate the film's visual style, too. Chiaroscuro lighting spotlights Harry and Nancy's sleeping nurse (Eileene Stevens) as the former looms in the living room doorway before slipping away to steal the fatal serum unobserved. A low-angle shot of Harry surveying the medical paraphernalia spread out on a tray that dominates the foreground disturbs the proportions of the mise-en-scène, a clear example of noir's penchant for disorienting composition. The double-dealing Harry is then framed on either side by his own two shadows as he ascends the stairs to Nancy's bedroom. Noir aesthetics and narrative merge in this sequence. They are both abruptly derailed, however, as the film's sci-fi imperative intervenes with the revelation of Nancy's gargantuan hand when the now alert nurse switches on the light just as Harry has entered the room to deliver the lethal dose.[6]

Generic Convergences

The following scene details the gathering of chains, meat hooks, and a morphine-filled elephant syringe to both physically and pharmaceutically restrain the 50-foot Nancy, now an object of scientific interest as Dr. Heinrich Von Loeb (Otto

Waldis) arrives to examine her. If sci-fi provides the symptom (i.e., Nancy's impossible size), melodrama is offered up as its cause: "Her health seemed to rise and fall with the tide of her emotions," Dr. Cushing (Roy Gordon), the family physician surmises. "When women reach the age of maturity, Mother Nature sometimes overworks their frustration to a point of irrationalism," corroborates Von Loeb.

The question, then, of how to control and manage a woman's psyche is hashed out in the conversation that directly precedes Nancy's escape, the moment when the masculinized loss of control over her body – and most pointedly her emotions – becomes literalized, externalized, and spectacularized through the generic iconography of disaster endemic within, if not exclusively belonging to, sci-fi. Nancy's emancipation is represented through time-honored cinematic tropes of destruction: shaky camera work, lots of dust, falling beams, debris, and so on. If the film's first two acts veered between melodrama and noir with periodic eruptions of sci-fi, in the last act it is the latter – the *announced* – genre that finally takes center stage.

Even still, everything that happens in these climactic moments is predicated on the noir and melodramatic plotting that leads up to them. Nancy's first true target of public destruction (after demolishing the home that once contained her – a suitably flamboyant rendition of the melodramatic woman fighting to break free of her limiting domestic space) is, none too subtly, the hotel sign that marks the site of Harry's marital transgressions. In terms of noir characterization, the would-be victim is now the aggressor who must fight back and is prepared to do so with a lethal vengeance (shades again too of the Final Girl) as, say, Myra Hudson (Joan Crawford) does in *Sudden Fear* (1952) after discovering she is (as here) the target of her wayward husband and his mistress.

Significantly, despite what the film's title and poster imagery – which depicts Nancy straddling a freeway strewn with wrecked cars, one of which she grips in her hand – might suggest to the uninitiated viewer, she is no Godzilla destroying for the sake of destruction.[7] Rather, her Kong-like pursuit is oriented toward one very specific, emotionally charged object. This is emphasized visually through images that evoke *King Kong*: a shot taken from within the hotel reveals Nancy's colossal face outside the room, perfectly framed in its window and, later, her arm enters the bar where terrified patrons run to and fro until it emerges with Harry in her grasp. Thus the moment of high horror – the victim falling into the monster's clutches – here flips the gender script such that a man is now rendered impotent in the grip of a woman.

In its final minutes, the film's title fails to function. As battle-ready police forces mobilize to waylay Nancy, the attack *of* the 50-foot woman becomes an attack *on* the 50-foot woman. And, right to the end, Nancy's monstrosity is explained with reference to her emotionality: "She'll kill me, she's crazy," Harry shouts, referencing his longstanding perception of Nancy's mental state – rather than her newfound proportions – as the problem at (pun intended) hand. And recalling the earlier conversation with Von Loeb, upon Nancy's destruction – she is electrocuted when the sheriff shoots a nearby power line – Dr. Cushing glibly ascribes her motivation: "She finally got Harry all to herself."

Conclusion

Attack of the 50 Foot Woman is often held as representative of filmmaking at the crossroads of exploitation, science fiction, and independent production of the late-1950s. This chapter has argued, however, that the film is additionally informed by genre conventions of Hollywood, particularly noir and melodrama. Further, these genres and their archetypes provide legible reference points for the film's central characters to a far greater extent than sci-fi's more typical roster of scientist heroes and otherworldly creatures.[8] The argument is not that the specific resonances I have discussed above were necessarily deliberate intertextual citations but, rather, that they are indicative of broader generic intertextualities that circulated freely within independent and exploitation storytelling economies in this particular moment.

In this way, a film like *Attack* illustrates the idea that independence from the studio system and its attendant resources (as well as constraints) does not foreclose a kind of indebtedness to its visual styles and narrative vocabularies that, at least in this specific instance, becomes part and parcel of the film's postulation as to "what it is about woman that is shocking, terrifying, horrific, abject" (Creed 1). Such influence, far from being derivative, finds dynamic license, which is perhaps easier to see in the independent context, made as it is to function and play at a certain level of budgetary and narrative frugality. This may be one reason for *Attack*'s continued cult appeal. Creative influence pays far less regard to the genre- and taste-based boundaries observed by some critics who work to chart its course; similar to a 50-foot woman, it refuses to be contained.

Notes

1 In this way, Nancy is an early exemplar of Barbara Creed's conception of the monstrous-feminine. More than the plain reversal implied by "female monster," Creed specifies that

> [t]he reasons why the monstrous-feminine horrifies her audience are quite different from the reasons why the male monster horrifies his audience…As with all other stereotypes of the feminine, from virgin to whore, she is defined in terms of her sexuality.
>
> (3)

2 The place of Nancy's body in the film that – just like the small California town in which it is set – struggles to contain it has been read by scholars in various ways: as "a complex image of frightening matriarchal power and atomic mutation" (Hendershot 83) and the central conceit of what is possibly "an early feminist flick" that "is, more likely, an expression of a 1950s fear of women who do not know their place" (Everman 21), among others.

3 Warner Archive DVD Commentary.

4 Theorist Carol J. Clover could be writing about Nancy when she describes the Final Girl as "the first character to sense something amiss…the only one, in other words, whose perspective approaches our own privileged understanding of the situation" (44).
5 "How fast was I going, officer?" Walter Neff (Fred MacMurray) famously asks Phyllis Dietrichson (Barbara Stanwyck) in one of that film's many celebrated innuendo-laden exchanges.
6 For a film often discussed as naïve in its construction, this marks a perceptible point of dramatic parallelism as, at the film's conclusion, Harry will find himself crushed within this giant hand, first revealed here at the exact moment *his* attempt at murder falters.
7 Given that *Gojira* (1954) was widely released in the United States in 1956 (as the heavily reedited *Godzilla, King of the Monsters!*), the iconic beast would certainly have been available as a point of reference for *Attack*'s audiences in 1958.
8 While an alien of course appears in *Attack*, like the Hitchockian Macguffin, it is quite easy to imagine something else as the cause of Nancy's growth that would not alter the plot mechanics in any significant way.

Works Cited

Altman, Rick. *Film/Genre*. Palgrave Macmillan, 1999.
Clover, Carol J. *Men, Women, and Chain Saws: Gender in the Modern Horror Film*. Princeton University Press, 1992.
Creed, Barbara. *The Monstrous-Feminine: Film, Feminism, Psychoanalysis*. Routledge, 1993.
Davis, Blair. *The Battle for the Bs: 1950s Hollywood and the Rebirth of Low-Budget Cinema*. Rutgers University Press, 2012.
Doane, Mary Ann. *The Desire to Desire: The Woman's Film of the 1940s*. Indiana University Press, 1987.
Doherty, Thomas. *Teenagers & Teenpics: The Juvenilization of American Movies in the 1950s*. Unwin Hyman, 1988.
Everman, Welch. *Cult Horror Films: From "Attack of the 50 Foot Woman" to "Zombies of Mora Tatu."* Carol Publishing Group, 1993.
Grant, Barry Keith. *Film Genre: From Iconography to Ideology*. Wallflower, 2007.
Hendershot, Cyndy. "Feminine Paranoia and Secrecy: *I Married a Monster From Outer Space* and *Attack of the 50 Ft. Woman*." *Readerly/Writerly Texts*, vol. 4, no. 2, 1997, pp. 71–86.
King, Geoff. *American Independent Cinema*. Indiana University Press, 2005.
King, Geoff, and Tanya Krzywinska. *Science Fiction Cinema: From Outerspace to Cyberspace*. Wallflower, 2000.
Mathijs, Ernest, and Xavier Mendik. "Editorial Introduction: What Is Cult Film?" *The Cult Film Reader*, edited by Ernest Mathijs and Xavier Mendik. Open University Press, 2008, pp. 1–11.
Naremore, James. *More Than Night: Film Noir in Its Contexts*. Updated and expanded ed., University of California Press, 2008.
Orr, Christopher. "Closure and Containment: Marylee Hadley in *Written on the Wind*." *Imitations of Life: A Reader on Film & Television Melodrama*, edited by Marcia Landy. Wayne State University Press, 1991, pp. 380–387.
Review: *Attack of the 50 Foot Woman*, directed by Nathan Hertz. *Variety*, 14 May 1958, p. 16.
Schaefer, Eric. *"Bold! Daring! Shocking! True!": A History of Exploitation Films, 1919–1959*. Duke University Press, 1999.

Sconce, Jeffrey. "'Trashing' the Academy: Taste, Excess, and an Emerging Politics of Cinematic Style." *Screen*, vol. 36, no. 4, 1995, pp. 371–393.

Swires, Steve. "Nathan Juran: The Fantastic Film Voyages of Jerry the Giant Killer." *Starlog*, May 1989, pp. 55–59, 62.

Weaver, Tom. *Science Fiction Stars and Horror Heroes: Interviews with Actors, Directors, Producers and Writers of the 1940s through 1960s*. McFarland & Company, 1991.

———. *Attack of the Monster Movie Makers: Interviews with 20 Genre Giants*. McFarland & Company, 1994.

9

I WANT TO LIVE! (1958)

Peter Labuza

Most films aim for box office receipts. The producers of *I Want to Live!* (1958) wanted to end capital punishment. Studio veterans Joseph L. Mankiewicz and Walter Wanger created a film examining the life of Barbara Graham, who was sent to the gas chamber in 1953 after allegedly pistol-whipping an elderly woman to death in her home during a robbery. Made during a wave of independent films financed by studios addressing social problems, Susan Hayward portrayed Graham through a series of vignettes following her interactions with various criminals, though never the particular crime that led to her death. A media witch-hunt – complete with newspapers nicknaming her "Bloody Babs" – and a prosecution-friendly trial put her on death row. One of the most stringent reporters, Edward Montgomery (Simon Oakland), regrets his reporting and works to prove her innocence to no avail.[1] The film ends with what was the most accurate depiction of the death penalty on screen at the time. By pushing an agenda aimed at depicting capital punishment with accuracy, the film made numerous narrative and stylistic decisions to break from the traditional mode of Hollywood filmmaking.

I Want to Live! was also a product of an era of a transformative Hollywood moving toward independence for above-the-line talent like writers, directors, and stars. Two critical court decisions – *De Havilland v. Warner Bros.* (1944) and *United States v. Paramount* (1948) – as well as changes in tax laws created more opportunities for these top artists to form their own production companies. Studios like the newly reenergized United Artists (UA) offered more flexibility and creativity to independent producers in exchange for full distribution rights (Balio 2). UA specifically made a deal in 1953 with Mankiewicz, a successful writer and director at 20th Century Fox known for hits like *A Letter to Three Wives* (1948) and *All About Eve* (1950), among similar deals with Otto Preminger, Stanley

FIGURE 9.1 The press looks on as the state executes Barbara Graham (Susan Hayward) via the gas chamber.

Kramer, Burt Lancaster, and Kirk Douglas. After the success of *The Barefoot Contessa* (1954), Mankiewicz and UA would renegotiate their deal to produce nine pictures under his company, Figaro, Inc. ("Financing Agreement").[2] *I Want to Live!* entered production with Wanger as producer in 1958 with a modest budget of just over $1.25 million (Bernstein 329).

Though the film would be directed by Robert Wise, many of the creative decisions around the film would be shaped through its deal negotiation. Mankiewicz, Wanger, and Hayward – though more often their business associates – sent memos and telegrams throughout production and beyond to control the film and its release. This dealmaking background represents the transitions in between the Classical Hollywood studio system and what scholars call New Hollywood that emerged in the late 1960s with independent creatives now fighting about much more than simply where to put the camera. This chapter balances an analysis of the film's aesthetic and narrative choices, made to help support its liberal cause to end capital punishment, with its unique production as an independent film navigating an era where deals often meant more than the movies themselves.

A Cry for Change

In an early memo on the film, Wanger declared the film "should be as far from the Hollywood pattern as possible… semi-documentary, episodic, realistic, emotional, powerful, no usual construction, no characters going all the way through, no expensive cast of names except Susan" (Wanger to Mankiewicz). This was of course more ambition than reality, but Wanger understood that a film that made the issue come alive would require a break from the traditional Hollywood style.

I Want to Live! thus deviates from the classical style in three notable ways: narrative construction, star performance, and its appeals to realism.

Hayward's Barbara Graham presents an enigmatic protagonist whose lack of narrative agency continually shifts the film's plot. When the film begins, she is half-naked in a sleazy motel above a jazz club with her latest client, drenched in shadow and smoking a cigarette. She performs a small act of grace when a cop busts in to threaten the gentlemen with a felony for violating the Mann Act; Graham claims she paid for the room and takes the misdemeanor instead.

But what does Barbara want? In the opening sequence, she glances longingly at a family photo in her caller's wallet, but the film rarely emphasizes her actual goals. Instead, it takes the audience through a series of vignettes into her life where she simply follows her whims into trouble. At a party sequence, the film sets up a possible romantic interest for the central character before her friend literally interrupts the frame to let Barbara know about two former friends who have arrived. The potential partner disappears from the film as Barbara agrees to lie to federal prosecutors for her companions' alibi. After she enraptures the party with a dance to some bongos, the film employs a graphic match from the bang of the drum to the bang of the gavel as she's sentenced to a year in prison for perjury. Later in the film, she suddenly announces that she has decided to marry a bartender; at the end of that scene, the film cuts from a close-up of a house of cards falling down to a crying baby in what turns out to be the last scene of their relationship. Although the film establishes a causal link between these events, it lacks a traditional three-act structure. Most notably, the supposed crime that resulted in her death penalty conviction is neither seen nor referenced until she is charged. Only once it is clear she will be put in the gas chamber does the film find a conflict for its protagonist.

In creating what often feels like a plotless narrative, Wise often emphasizes the milieu of the world Graham inhabits. This kind of construction became common in the postwar social problem genre, where films often defied traditional Hollywood storytelling. As Chris Cagle notes, films made in this genre often prioritized "location shooting, contemporary settings, and social critique" (22). Especially after the success of *Marty* (1955), which received the Palme d'Or at the Cannes Film Festival and several Academy Awards on a $350,000 budget, films like *I Want to Live!* forwent certain narrative conventions in favor of creating atmospheres to understand working class (and sometimes criminal) behavior. Wise follows this trend by presenting the social milieu by filming the jazz club above where Barbara works through a series of canted angle shots as Johnny Mandel's jazz score blasts on the soundtrack.[3] Many of the choices in make-up and clothes were deliberately taken from what Graham often wore, while the sets were constructed accurately based on interviews with prison guards and photos taken by Gordon Parks (Rich 136). Because of its dedication to being true-to-life, the film eschews traditional narrative construction to emphasize these unique locales where the audiences can view her as a product of a system that pushed her into the gas chamber.

To create a center for this non-traditional narrative, *I Want to Live!* highlights Susan Hayward's characterization and performance. As Dennis Bingham notes, "There is a decided lack of naturalism in Hayward's performance, which, although it contrasts with the film's 'realism,' seems part of a careful strategy worked out with Wanger and Wise and prepared for in the screenplay" (14). Hayward is often hoarse in her voice, bombastic in her emotions, and sarcastic toward everyone around her. Whether someone shows emotion or indifference to her, Graham treats it like a battleground. Hayward was not associated with the Method Acting movement that had become part and parcel of many independent films of this era, but much of the design of her performance in *I Want to Live!* clearly reflects those trends. As Keri Walsh has noted about Method actresses, they "pushed to allow more of women's ordinary lives on screen," often "through conscious engagement with [certain] pejoratives" used to describe non-conforming women (3, 6). Hayward's performance dares the audience to find the character unappealing, though one critic noted that "the preview audience was literally shouting for her," suggesting the unexpected joy created by her performance (Young 48).

But the critical aspect that shocked audiences was to present capital punishment through both psychological and documentary realism. Wanger had made his career on socially conscious films – including the independent drama *Riot in Cell Block 13* (1953) – but wanted to go further in his critique of the system. He consulted with the attorney general of California (Bingham 20), who had actually worked to free Graham (and would soon be elected governor of the state with an anti-death penalty agenda), to help understand her ordeal (Cairns 72, 126).

I Want to Live! differs from earlier films about capital punishment by explicitly making its case through the experience of the person waiting to die. The night and morning of the execution take over a quarter of the film's run time. Although the film attempts to create suspense over the possibility of a final stay of execution, it is always clear to the audience what will happen. The film thus mines Graham's psychological feelings, filling the soundtrack with the ticking of clocks and muffled voices over the phone that never grant her the freedom she desires. Perhaps the most revealing aspect is when the film shows Graham walking toward the gas chamber, the Mandel score pulsating, only for the telephone to ring and announce a short stay and sending her back to her cell – twice. Hayward plays these moments not as relief, but as exhausting, demonstrating the psychological trauma inflicted by this process. More so, Wise concurrently reveals the procedure with documentary-like accuracy, emphasizing each meter, screw, and lever of this process to make sure the audience can hear the horror as much as see it on screen.

Though these elements make the film feel untraditional, *I Want to Live!* remains clearly associated with the Classical Hollywood continuity. A veteran of the studio system, Wise finds a few unique aesthetic gambits – the beforementioned graphic matches and framing the film in mise en abyme to depict how the media represented Graham on television – but otherwise relies on studio-style shooting to make the narrative accessible and coherent. Instead, the film's realism and commitment to portraying its social issue transformed how the film would be received; the California State Assembly even held a hearing on Graham's case in 1960 (Cairns 125). By taking liberties with the construction of the film's Hollywood narrative, the independents behind *I Want to Live!* made a splash in public debate as well as the box office.

"In The Sole Interest of Figaro"

As much as one can weigh the film's independence from Hollywood through an analysis of the film's construction, equally important was how the deal came together through lawyers, agents, and other businessmen. As noted in a memo, Wanger became increasingly frustrated by the changes in Hollywood where "the producer no longer deals with the creative talent," instead spending their energies on the management of the deals that would become essential for these production contexts (Lantz to Mankiewicz).

Mankiewicz's production company, Figaro, Inc., was one of many companies created by former studio stars and directors. But it relied on several administrators to function. At its core was Robert Lantz, a German ex-pat turned talent agent who worked under Bert Allenberg, Mankiewicz's agent. To represent the corporation's interests, they hired Abraham Bienstock as counsel. As Jeff Menne has written, this process of self-incorporation allowed creatives to not only escape the frustrations of contract employment but also "project their personhood onto the firms' corporate agencies" (21).

Like other independent companies that had a long-term deal with UA, Mankiewicz's Figaro decided to balance films he directed with additional, lower budget films to fulfill the contract.[4] The East Coaster Mankiewicz imagined that a seasoned veteran producer like Wanger, who had put together films like *Stagecoach* (1939), *Foreign Correspondent* (1940), and *Scarlet Street* (1945), could help expand Figaro's operations in Los Angeles (Bernstein 318). But tensions arose between Wanger and the company. Matthew Bernstein notes that the producer tossed countless ideas at the team and felt frustrated when they rejected his proposals; he "could not begin new projects until Lantz obtained the okay of Mankiewicz, Allenberg, and United Artists executives," whom he often referred to as "the United Nations" (322). When Wanger discovered the Graham story, he did not wait for such approval. Instead, he bought the story and life rights for the project under his own production company in 1956 while also convincing Hayward to star (325).[5] Though he had yet to even propose the project to Figaro or UA, he promised Hayward 37.5% profit participation for the film (LaGuardia and Arceri 133).

Immediately, Wanger's decision to push this project on his own caused chaos since he had ignored the procedures of Figaro's UA contract. As Lantz told Allenberg, "Arthur [Krim, UA's chairman] was under the impression that Figaro and Walter Wanger were one and the same thing in respect of the ownership and the basic property" (Lantz to Allenberg). Wanger tried to play hardball as he set up the deal; he told his business manager he wanted to make the film with UA and Mankiewicz but with complete control. This only put the project in a precarious spot, and eventually led the producer to apologize to the parties and explain to UA that Figaro was ultimately still in control.

Wanger, however, had a point. Mankiewicz was in Vietnam shooting *The Quiet American* (1958) while he was stuck waiting and following the orders of Figaro's administrators. Lantz and Allenberg were hardly averse to creativity, but they were making decisions that Mankiewicz usually controlled. Figaro's head found this delegation of power equally frustrating. When Wanger and Lantz approved of Wise for the director, Mankiewicz asked his administrators, "Is not the executive producer usually consulted about the choice of director?" (Mankiewicz to Lantz, 13 June 1957). As these tensions rose, the producer wrote a long letter explaining his grievances:

> If it is true – as seems to be indicated – that films can be conceived and commitments made, about everything from the name of the writer and director to the starting date and budget through the sole efforts of agents and lawyers and executives without the active consultation and participation of those responsible for the actual production of the picture, then never have I been more wrong. And this is no longer a profession in which I can play any part as a serious film director.
>
> *(Mankiewicz to Lantz et al., 25 June 1957)*

Allenberg replied, trying to explain the situation:

> I have…done things that either you or Robbie Lantz would normally be expected to do as the only way to put this project together, hold it together, and bring it to fruition, and if you disapprove of any of my decisions or counsel or comments, you will know that what I have done and what I discuss is in the sole interests of Figaro.
>
> *(Allenberg to Mankiewicz)*

Eventually, Mankiewicz realized that being independent from the studios never meant complete independence; power had to be delegated just as those in the studio system had done.

More so, simply completing the film was not the end of the story, evidenced by Mankiewicz's frustrations over the film's release. His anger came to a head as UA sought the possibility of an Academy Award for Hayward's performance, which required spending out of the film's profits. Though the Oscars had been largely symbolic since their inauguration in 1927, winners like *Marty* gained huge returns at the box office through their campaigns. As Hayward's attorney, Martin Gang, told UA's Max Youngstein, everyone involved "should be concerned that the picture takes advantage of this golden opportunity because an Academy Award will add a great deal of money to the gross" (Gang to Youngstein).

But Mankiewicz ordered cuts from their paper advertising and their tour budget (Rothenberg to Mankiewicz). This came as the director discovered what "net profits" – as opposed to a share of the gross – really meant for independent producers like him. He was getting the last share while Gang had negotiated with UA to make sure that Hayward got paid first (Reiss to Shemel).[6] For a six-week engagement at one Chicago theater, *I Want to Live!* grossed a substantial $143,000. But after the theater expenses, the fees for UA as the distributor, and the costs of advertising, Figaro received just $340 in profit. An LA theater fared even worse; while UA and Hayward saw large payouts, Figaro actually owed the distributor $17,000. As Mankiewicz's CPA reminded, "It is one thing to distribute the picture with the highest gross in mind, and another to distribute it to earn the largest net profit" (Lefkowitz to Mankiewicz).

Tensions rose as to whose money was being spent and what profits would be achieved. UA's Max Youngstein noted in a memo that "the refusal to approve additional advertising and prints is nothing short of suicidal, and will be so detrimental as to affect the gross of this picture by at least half a million dollars" (Youngstein to Weshner). But as Mankiewicz wrote to Gang, the reason UA could so freely spend and promote the film was the fact "their objectives are remote from the sordid ones of profit" (Mankiewicz to Gang). Independent film contracts were now designed in a way where studios – as distributors – could freely spend to their advantage, while creative producers like Mankiewicz had to worry more about money.

Mankiewicz eventually deferred and the bet paid off. UA increased its advertising budget to $500,000, which pushed Hayward to Oscar gold and the film to a notable $3.5 million gross. This was enough to cover any losses Figaro had managed to accrue during the company's short run.

In *The Barefoot Contessa*, the film director, played by Humphrey Bogart, describes the financier for an independent production as someone who has "as much in common with anything creative as I have with nuclear physics." For Mankiewicz, independent producing took him away from what he cared about in his creative ventures, working and handling administrative issues rather than artistic ones. It was no surprise that Figaro began closing shop after his experience with *I Want to Live!* and would not produce another film.

Conclusion

Watching *I Want to Live!* demonstrates some of the unique directions that independent film strived toward through the 1950s. Its stripped-down realism, brazen method acting, and social consciousness suggested that even top Hollywood creatives desired to make something entirely different. By centering a social cause, the filmmakers broke from traditional Hollywood molds so they could further elucidate their point.

But the stories behind the scenes of *I Want to Live!* reveal how much independent production depended on an administrative state to make such films even possible. This was not the story of a single individual breaking out against the studio system, but operators writing telegrams and negotiating contract stipulations to align the needs of the financial and creative imperatives that define independent film. As Denise Mann has noted, "successful independent producers who prospered in the 1950s learned to balance their liberal views and desire for artistic freedom with the cutthroat commercial instincts of the studios upon which they relied (as independent producers still do today)" (211). Integrating the social cause with the financial constraints became critical to the film's success.

As the "New Hollywood" emerged, the dichotomies of art and business would further break, as creative impulses diverged from studio style while deal-making became more central to financial success. In the 1930s, studios often just told the director that all they needed to know was where to put the camera. As Mankiewicz noted, this new era meant they also should be "aware of the provisions of [the] Financing and Distribution Agreement" (Mankiewicz to Reiss).

Notes

1. Montgomery also participated in the production, providing a title card statement that both opens and closes the film.
2. While UA's contract claimed to have no artistic input, it could at any time instigate concerns about cost or budget decisions, not to mention "avoiding the production of salacious stories" as dictated by the Production Code ("Distribution Agreement").
3. Although crime films throughout the 1940s and 1950s had featured jazz, Mandel's score for the film was one of the first to be featured throughout the entire film (Butler), and one of the first to find success as a standalone soundtrack released by the studio (Bundy 12).
4. One of the controversies over *I Want to Live!* was Mankiewicz felt that although he was not directing, his contributions and the film's pedigree should elevate its status (and thus his own fees) as an A-list film within the nine-film contract (Reiss to Mankiewicz).
5. Wanger had played a central role in developing Hayward into a star at 20th Century Fox, but he also had few others he could turn to. MCA, the industry's largest and most powerful talent agency, had essentially blacklisted all clients from working with him after a notorious incident where he shot agent Leyland Jennings ("I Want to Live!").
6. Gang had previously been Mankiewicz's attorney, which may have added to his frustrations that his new attorney was not performing to the same level.

Works Cited

Allenberg, Bert. "Letter to Joseph Mankiewicz," 28 June 1957. Joseph L. Mankiewicz Papers: Margaret Herrick Library, Academy of Motion Picture Arts and Sciences. [From herein JLM Papers, AMPAS]

Balio, Tino. *United Artists: Volume 2, 1951–1978 the Company That Changed the Film Industry*. University of Wisconsin Press, 2009.

Bernstein, Matthew. *Walter Wanger, Hollywood Independent*. University of Minnesota Press, 2000.

Bundy, June. "Pic Tune Tie-Ups Spark UA Sales." *Billboard*, 23 May 1960, pp. 4, 12.

Butler, David. *Jazz Noir: Listening to Music from Phantom Lady to the Last Seduction*. Praeger, 2002.

Cagle, Chris. *Sociology on Film: Postwar Hollywood's Prestige Commodity*. Rutgers University Press, 2016.

Cairns, Kathleen A. *Proof of Guilt: Barbara Graham and the Politics of Executing Women in America*. University of Nebraska Press, 2013.

"Distribution Agreement between Figaro Incorporated and United Artists Corporation," 1 Dec. 1955. JLM Papers, AMPAS.

"Financing Agreement between Figaro Incorporated and United Artists Corporation," 22 Dec. 1955. JLM Papers, AMPAS.

Gang, Martin. "Letter to Max E. Youngstein," 8 Jan. 1959. JLM Papers, AMPAS.

"I Want to Live!" *Love is a Crime* (episode 8) from *Vanity Fair* and Cadence 13 (Karina Longworth and Vanessa Hope), 5 Oct. 2021, https://podcast.app/love-is-a-crime-p2415752/.

LaGuardia, Robert, and Gene Arceri. *Red: The Tempestuous Life of Susan Hayward*. Robson, 1990.

Lantz, Robert. "Memorandum to Joseph Mankiewicz and Walter Wanger," 16 Apr. 1957. Walter F. Wanger Papers, 1908–1967, US Mss 136AN – Box 50, Folder 6, Wisconsin Center for Film and Theater Research [WFWP, WCFTR].

———. "Letter to Bert Allenberg," 16 July 1957. JLM Papers, AMPAS.

Lefkowitz, Julius. "Letter to Joseph Mankiewicz," 12 Jan. 1959. JLM Papers, AMPAS.

Mankiewicz, Joseph L., "Inter-Office Communication to Robert Lantz," 13 June 1957. JLM Papers, AMPAS.

———. "Inter Office Communication to Robert Lantz, Bert Allenberg, and Abraham Bienstock," 25 June 1957. JLM Papers, AMPAS.

———. "Memorandum to Richard Reiss," 27 Oct. 1958. JLM Papers, AMPAS.

———. "Letter to Martin Gang," 16 Jan. 1959. JLM Papers, AMPAS.

Mann, Denise. *Hollywood Independents: The Postwar Talent Takeover*. University of Minnesota Press, 2007.

Menne, Jeff. *Post-Fordist Cinema: Hollywood Auteurs and the Corporate Counterculture*. Columbia University Press, 2019.

Reiss, Richard. "Letter to Sidney Shemel," 30 Apr. 1958. JLM Papers, AMPAS.

———. "Letter to Joseph Mankiewicz," 24 Oct. 1958. JLM Papers, AMPAS.

Rich, Aaron. *The Hollywood Research Library: Visual Knowledge in the Republic of Images*. 2020. University of Southern California, PhD dissertation.

Rothenberg, Jack. "Letter to Joseph Mankiewicz," 13 Oct. 1958. JLM Papers, AMPAS.

Wanger, Walter, "Letter to Joseph L. Mankiewicz," 29 Oct. 1957. WFWP, WCFTR.

Walsh, Keri. *Women, Method Acting, and the Hollywood Film*. Routledge, 2021.

Youngstein, Max. "Letter to David E. Weshner," 30 Dec. 1958. JLM Papers, AMPAS.

Young, Colin. "Home Before Dark and I Want to Live." *Film Quarterly*, vol. 12, no. 2, 1958, pp. 46–49.

10
COLOR ME BLOOD RED (1965)

Murray Leeder

Herschell Gordon Lewis is a name well known to horror film fans and generally unknown beyond them, except perhaps among those deeply invested in his second career in direct marketing. Though Lewis only worked in filmmaking for roughly 12 of his 90 years (he passed in 2016), he left a distinct mark on independent horror cinema and on independent filmmaking more broadly.

Interviewed in 1973, Lewis articulated clear ideas about making a product distinct from the Hollywood studios. He said:

> When one makes independent film product, there is only one criterion to be used for the production of films, and this is where so many producers waste so much money and then wonder why no one will play their films. The only film that an independent can make and survive with is a film that the major producers cannot or will not make. I regard that as a physical law. I don't regard it as a theory… So I said to myself, what kind of film is there that the majors are not making?
>
> *(McCarthy and Flynn 351–352)*

In Lewis's case, this "physical law" led him to become the "Godfather of Gore," the sole and singular pioneer of the underground gore film. He is celebrated – and reviled – as the man who, in the words of one scholar, took the horror film "as low as it can go" (Crane 163), and he did it all not out of perversity or a desire to challenge genre norms, but simply because it allowed him to access the filmgoing public in a new way. Terms like "underground," "independent," "exploitation," and "cult" all circulate around Lewis and cannot always be meaningfully disentangled. Covering both Lewis's career and his reception within cinephile and academic audiences, this chapter looks closely at *Color Me Blood*

Color Me Blood Red (1965) **97**

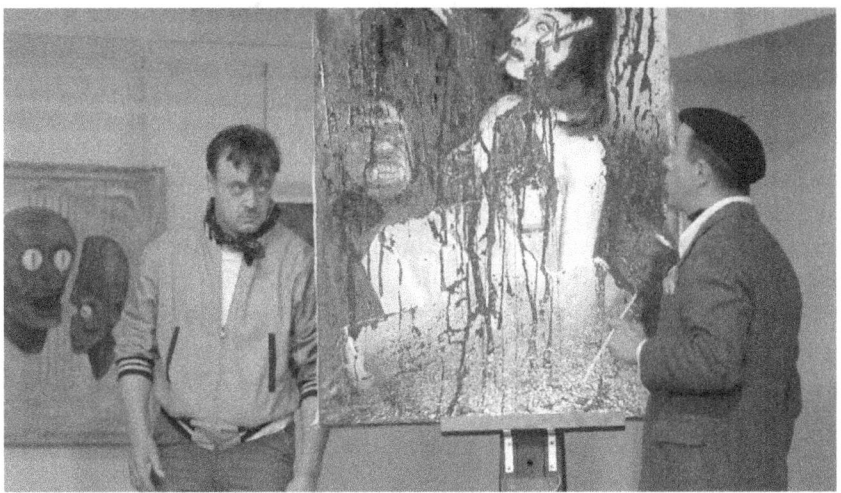

FIGURE 10.1 Murderous artist Adam Sorg (Gordon Oas-Heim) displays his blood-splattered painting.

Red (1965), which, as a pointedly artless film about art, is potentially the most reflexive Lewis film.

Color Me Blood Red is the third of the so-called "Blood Trilogy" (also including *Blood Feast* [1963] and *Two Thousand Maniacs!* [1964]), probably the films on which Lewis's reputation most rests. All three contain brutal, protracted sequences of murder, torture, and gore, surrounded by extremely dull, haphazardly staged filler. Long before the Joker (Jack Nicholson) declared himself to be "the world's first fully functioning homicidal artist" in Tim Burton's *Batman* (1989), Lewis gave us *Color Me Blood Red*'s Adam Sorg (Gordon Oas-Heim), who literally kills to cover his canvases with blood. Perhaps the character was inspired by other homicidal artists in relatively recent horror films, both high budget (*House of Wax* [1953]) and low (Roger Corman's *A Bucket of Blood* [1959]), but he is the most brutal, and Oas-Heim makes for interesting casting thanks to his thuggish presence: an aesthete with the bearing of a heavy.

To say the least, Lewis himself was no Adam Sorg. Born in Pittsburgh in 1926, Lewis was raised largely in Chicago. He earned undergraduate and graduate degrees in journalism at Northwestern University – sources differ about whether or not he earned a Ph.D. – and went to teach communications at the University of Mississippi. Lewis left academia to work in radio and then started directing commercials and industrial films, and from there moved on to exploitation filmmaking. His first feature was the rock 'n' roll-themed *The Prime Time* (1959), and he would make 34 features between 1960 and 1972 (six in 1967 alone). For the first part of that period, Lewis joined forces with David F. Friedman, and together they made nudist films with such lascivious titles as *Bell, Bare and Beautiful* (1962), *Goldilocks and the Three Bares* (1963), and the onomatopoeic *B-O-I-N-N-G!* (1963). The "nudie" had a history going back to the 1930s and was given new prominence by Russ Meyer's *The Immoral Mr. Teas* (1959) (Schaefer esp. 290–303). But Lewis intuited that the increased presence of nudity in major studio releases meant that the market would swiftly evaporate, and, in his telling, he asked himself, "what kind of film is there that the majors are not making?" (McCarthy and Flynn 352). He and Friedman transitioned into horror, first with *Blood Feast* in 1963. Almost certainly the goriest film ever made up to that time, *Blood Feast* is a deeply tasteless film about a serial killer who dismembers women in an attempt to recreate an ancient Egyptian cannibal feast and includes such shocking images as a tongue being sliced off. Danny Peary writes:

> It opened in Peoria, and by the second day there were overflowing crowds despite torrential downpours. It then went on to do astronomical business in drive-ins and grind houses throughout the country... this set the trend for future Lewis films.
>
> *(26)*[1]

It earned a reported $4 million dollars off of a budget under $25,000. But if the gore film was where Lewis left the biggest mark, it was not his sole output: he made redneck films, biker films, and other exploitation quickies, and even made children's films like *Jimmy the Boy Wonder* (1966). He also pseudonymously directed a few outright pornographic films in the late 1960s and early 1970s.[2]

Lewis's career arrived just when a major shift in the history of exploitation cinema was unfolding; indeed, one history of exploitation filmmaking ends in 1959 (Schaefer) and another begins with it (Waddell). For the most part, the exploitation label was then no longer applied to films that thinly presented themselves as educational, in the manner of 1930s exploitation items like *Freaks* (1932), *Reefer Madness* (1936), and *Maniac* (1934) – all of which were rediscovered by a fresh audience in the 1960s – and the films of Kroger Babb, Friedman's mentor. Rather, "exploitation" now referred to low-budget films that operated outside of Hollywood institutionally, aesthetically, and thematically, and which were often sold with lurid and melodramatic advertising promising taboo and transgressive contents, all of which describe Lewis's films perfectly. In addition, Lewis operated away from Hollywood geographically, initially being based in Chicago and releasing his films state-by-state to avoid running afoul of local censorship laws, sometimes unsuccessfully; on at least one occasion, in Philadelphia, an exhibitor was fined for showing *Blood Feast* on the basis that it was "obscene, sadistic and perverted" (Davis 211). Lewis repeatedly noted that the American South was his most reliable market and described his average viewer as male, lower income, and uneducated. In 1973 he estimated that half of his business was done in drive-ins (McCarthy and Flynn 357).

If Lewis is often conceptually paired with desperately low-budget "badfilm" directors like Edward D. Wood Jr. and Ray Dennis Steckler, he was arguably a good deal more professional – or at least professional*ized* – than either of them.

Lewis is also frequently mentioned in the same breath as Italian gore maestro Lucio Fulci; Roger Ebert once described Fulci as "sort of an Italian Hershell [sic] Gordon Lewis," not in praise of either director. It makes as much and perhaps more sense to bracket Lewis with American sexploitation filmmakers who emerged in the early 1960s like Meyer and Doris Wishman, though both Meyer and Wishman's films are considerably more buoyant and fun than Lewis's, which often demonstrate a palpable sense of nihilism and emptiness.

Costing a reported $50,000, *Color Me Blood Red* was shot for six days in Sarasota, Florida. It attempts to hybridize the gore film and the beach movie, with extended segments given over to young people frolicking on the beach. Beach movies were of course a trend in the early 1960s (*Where the Boys Are* [1960], *Beach Party* [1963], *Beach Blanket Bingo* [1965]), and while there were other attempts to meld its formula with horror (*The Horror of Party Beach* [1964], *The Beach Girls and the Monster* [1965]), no other example is as gory and unpleasant as *Color Me Blood Red*. In Lewis's film, the beachgoers provide eye candy and the tedious scenes of them driving, walking, and frolicking help extend the film to feature length; on the DVD commentary track for the film, Lewis openly describes these scenes as "padding." More than padding, the beach movie-style stretches play almost like wallpaper, perhaps as intervals between killings where drive-in viewers can safely look away from the screen and turn to more amorous activities or run to the concession stand. Still, the scenes do play a minor narrative function in furnishing victims for the film's monstrous artist. Adam, who lives in an isolated beach house, is henpecked by his girlfriend Gigi (Elyn Warner), who – reminiscent of Vera (Ann Savage) in *Detour* (1945) – constantly pelts him with insults, mocking him as both a man and an artist. Unable to sell his art to a local gallery because his works "lack color," Adam discovers that the missing ingredient is blood, and he develops an aesthetic where the paintings, much like the film, are splattered with it. When Gigi balks at his attempts to use her as his source of blood, Adam uses his own blood instead. Jean-Luc Godard famously described his own film, *Pierrot le Fou* (1965), as showing "not blood, red" (217), and the same year, Adam Song reversed the formulation.

In an extended sequence, Adam defiles his canvas, wielding his index finger like a paintbrush. The film goes out of focus to both signal the passage of time and represent Adam's increasing wooziness, one of Lewis's few clever uses of film form. But Adam lacks sufficient blood to finish the artwork. The deeply unpleasant Gigi confronts him with a mix of criticism ("What kind of vampire are you anyway, painting with blood? Are you a painter or a butcher?") and praise ("It is a great painting, though. You know, it doesn't speak well for you, Adam, that you can do a better job with blood than you can with paint"). Her provocations lead him to stab her in the cheek and then he literally rubs her bloody face against the canvas, converting her corpse into an instrument of his art. The painting itself not only results from his crime but portrays it: it depicts a woman being stabbed in the face.

This sequence illustrates something typical of Lewis's gore films: despite their name, the gore is poorly done. If the phrases "splatter" or "gore film" might draw to mind later horror auteurs like David Cronenberg, Clive Barker, Stuart Gordon, or Sam Raimi, or even cultish slasher films like *Maniac* (1980), there is an important difference to be drawn. Lewis's films are not works of technical virtuosity by any stretch of the imagination, and the gore scenes do not lend themselves a sense of viewer connoisseurship, where the audience is invited to admire the intricacy of the effects even while recoiling in horror. Lewis's effects, like the films in which they are contained, are crude, direct, and basic, with human gore "played" by some unidentifiable animal meat.

Within *Color Me Blood Red,* Adam's bloody painting pleases the arbiters of the local art scene, placing Adam in need of more blood and thus more victims. To satisfy demand, he murders a couple of young beachgoers, spearing them with a harpoon. He hangs a young female victim on his wall, her arms outstretched cruciform and her gut sliced open, and harvests blood for his art by milking an exposed intestine like a cow's udder. It is telling that one of the most striking compositions in the film – an image used on the cover of one VHS release – is also one of the goriest, and potentially the most pornographic, providing the film its bloodiest "money shot."

At the film's climax, Adam prepares to murder one of the beachgoers, young proto-Final Girl April Carter (Candi Conder), whom he has convinced to model for him. Meanwhile, April's friends stumble upon the discarded corpse of one of Adam's prior victims, poorly hidden under the sand. Appropriate to Lewis's style, this scene delivers both a hilariously goofy line reading of "Holy bananas, it's a girl's leg!" and then perhaps *Color Me Blood Red*'s most gratuitous moment (though there are plenty of other candidates): a lingering close up of the corpse's face crawling with worms. Confronted by one of the beachgoers, Adam delivers a monologue defending his murders on aesthetic grounds, and though Oas-Heim is unnervingly convincing, the shot is out of focus. It is difficult to say if this is an aesthetic choice to underscore his madness or a simple technical defect.

This standoff ends with one of April's friends shooting Adam in the face with a rifle. Adam stumbles around bloodily and eventually stumbles into the blank canvas. The camera, again distinctly out of focus, lingers on his life dripping away into the whiteness; this ending possibly echoes the close of *A Bucket of Blood* wherein the murderous artist Walter (Dick Miller) transforms himself into an artwork through suicide. But even the dramatic impact of this scene is casually, cynically tossed away, as one of April's friends gets the comic curtain line: "I guess I won't take up painting for a while."

The film is framed by the image of the gallery owner Mr. Farnsworth (Scott H. Hall) solemnly removing a Sorg painting from his gallery and lighting it on fire, only for blood to exude out of it. It ends with these lines between Farnsworth and the bereted art critic Gregorovich (Bill Harris):

GREGOROVICH: It takes courage, my friend, to destroy a painting worth thousands.
FARNSWORTH: Mr. Gregorovich, I'm not burning a painting. I'm lighting Adam Sorg's funeral pyre.
GREGOROVICH: You could've at least saved the frame.

This exchange sums up a lot of the tone of *Color Me Blood Red*, and Lewis's style more broadly: mock-profundity and classic exploitation film-style cod moralizing swiftly undercut with a deadpan gag, all delivered over a canvas of bubbling blood. There might be some tendency to read the film reflexively, with Adam, the tortured artist driven to violence and gore by an unfriendly market, as a stand-in for Lewis. But there is little evidence that Lewis thought of himself as any kind of subversive artist. *Color Me Blood Red* treats the myth of the suffering artist as a joke, but it is no more positive about the art market itself, presenting its exhibitors, critics, and collectors as vacant and pretentious. It is typical of Lewis's oeuvre, where no one is especially likable and nothing particularly matters.

Despite his own academic training, Lewis was a decidedly anti-intellectual director, borderline contemptuous of interpretations of his works. Trumpeting his distance from mainstream cinema, he said, "I am beyond critics… if I were to make a picture for critics, the public would not go. That is because most critics look for elements about which they can write and show off their interpretative skills" (qtd. in Mendik 191). Reveling in his status as an independent filmmaker forever focused on the bottom line, he opined that good reviews are impossible for him: "I can't expect a critic to understand the laws of economics in my films" (McCarthy and Flynn 358). On the commentary track for *Color Me Blood Red*, Lewis laughs off the suggestion that he is an artist: "Have you seen these movies?" And from his interview with Charles Flynn and Todd McCarthy comes this gem of self-deprecation:

TM AND CF: You know, you were also included in the *Cahiers du Cinéma* issue 150, the big issue on American cinema. You were classified as a subject for further research…
HGL: Well, they also say that about cancer. *(360)*

Unkind things were said of Lewis's audience as well; in 1983, Danny Peary borrowed a line from *Blood Feast* – "How could… people belong to such a vile cult?" (27) – to criticize Lewis's followers. Today, however, Lewis's main audience is aficionados of the films of the "so bad it's good" sort, or of what Jeffrey Sconce calls "paracinema."[3] Celebratory accounts of Lewis, as Mark Jancovich notes, tend to treat him as a hack "who had little sense of what [he was] doing, but whose lifestyle and adventures are almost heroically outrageous, if completely 'cuckoo'" (314) – mostly as a cultural hero for the "gorehound" audience. While some low-budget exploitation horror films have been reconsidered as covertly avant-garde (see Hawkins), this has not been the case with Lewis. It seems hard to configure him into a Roger Corman-style figure working hard at maximizing the artistic potential of the low-budget milieu, and while Lewis is a legitimately transgressive figure in some senses, his films do not seem to subvert mainstream Hollywood conventions so much as exist apart from them. Most often, Lewis was celebrated as an influence: his obituaries frequently mentioned admirers like Quentin Tarantino, Robert Rodriguez, and John Waters (e.g., Grimes). Waters has been especially vocal about the influence of Lewis, and named his film *Multiple Maniacs* (1970) after Lewis's *Two Thousand Maniacs!* (1964). Lewis's work has seen relatively lavish DVD sets released by cult specialists like Arrow Video, Vinegar Syndrome, and Something Weird Entertainment, the name of which was taken from a 1967 Lewis film. This is quite a legacy for a director whose films are often as tedious as they are titillating.

After 1972's *The Gore Gore Girls*, Lewis vanished from filmmaking to write books like *The Businessman's Guide to Advertising and Sales Promotion* (1974), *Sales Letters That Sizzle* (1994), and *How to Make Your Advertising Twice as Effective at Half the Cost* (1990). He belatedly and briefly returned to filmmaking in 2002 with *Blood Flesh 2: All U Can Eat*,[4] and in his last decades proved a lively presence at many horror conventions, often expressing surprise that films that were designed as transient products proved to be of such lasting interest.[5] Lewis's pose was self-deprecatory, freely and gleefully acknowledging that his films were terrible, but he also actively positioned himself as a DIY alternative to Hollywood's expensive excesses and art cinema's pretensions.

Lewis received a prominent citation in a successful independent film of a very different sort: *Juno* (2007). Throughout the film, Juno's (Elliot Page) quirkiness and precocity are displayed in her command of retro cultural references. She meets her match, however, in aging hipster Mark (Jason Bateman), who keeps a VHS copy of a Lewis film on his coffee table.[6] When Juno makes note of it, this exchange follows:

MARK: It's Herschell Gordon Lewis. He's the ultimate master of horror.
JUNO: [Pshaw] Please. Dario Argento is so the ultimate master of horror.
MARK: Argento? He's all right. But Lewis is completely demented. We're talking about buckets of goo. I mean, there's red corn syrup all over the place. There's fake brains coming out the yin-yang.

Juno is unconvinced so Mark silences Juno's skepticism by playing an extreme gore sequence. Juno concedes, "This *is* even better than *Suspiria* [1977]," deferring to Mark's cinephile capital. It seems hard to dispute that Lewis's films are gorier than Argento's; they are also considerably less European, "arty," and aestheticized, and an underground "authenticity" arguably emerges from that griminess. But to call Lewis "completely demented," as if he were himself a soul brother to Adam Sorg or Montag (Ray Sager) in *The Wizard of Gore,* is in its own way to accept an auteurist narrative which belies how calculated – well outside of the mainstream and yet in their own independent way still fully market-driven ("economical," as he put it) – Lewis's filmmaking truly was.

Notes

1 "Grind house" or "grindhouse" was an American term for independent theaters that charged low admissions, frequently for salacious low-budget films.
2 These can be viewed through Vinegar Syndrome's boxed set *The Lost Films of Herschell Gordon Lewis* (2016).
3 See also Hunter, esp. 494–495.
4 He also acted in Canadian director Lee Demarbre's reflexive slasher film *Smash Cut* (2009).
5 Perhaps the character Sam Sylvia (Marc Maron) on the Netflix series *GLOW* (2017–2019) is inspired by this aspect of Lewis's career, as he is shocked to learn that his underground films have gained interest among young cinephiles.
6 To be precise, *The Wizard of Gore* (1970).

Works Cited

Crane, Jonathan Lake. "Scraping Bottom: Splatter and the Herschell Gordon Lewis Oeuvre." *The Horror Film*, edited by Stephen Prince. Rutgers, 2004, pp. 150–166.
Davis, Blair. *The Battle for the Bs: Hollywood and the Rebirth of Low-Budget Cinema*. Rutgers University Press, 2012.
Ebert, Roger. "The Beyond." *RogerEbert.com*. https://www.rogerebert.com/reviews/-the-beyond-1998. Accessed 3 Dec. 2021.
Friedman, David F., and Herschell Gordon Lewis. Audio Commentary. *Color Me Blood Red* [DVD], Something Weird Entertainment, 2011.
Godard, Jean-Luc. "Let's Talk About Pierrot." *Godard on Godard*, edited by Tom Milne. Da Capo Press, 1986, pp. 215–234.
Grimes, William. "Herschell Gordon Lewis." *New York Times*. 29 Sept. 2016, p. A-24.
Hawkins, Joan. *Cutting Edge: Art-Horror and the Horrific Avant-Garde*. University of Minnesota Press, 2000.
Hunter, I.Q. "Trash Horror and the Cult of the Bad Film." *A Companion to the Horror Film*, edited by Harry M. Benshoff. Wiley-Blackwell, 2014, pp. 483–500.
Jancovich, Mark. "Cult Fictions: Cult Movies, Subcultural Capital and the Production of Cultural Distinctions." *Cultural Studies*, vol. 16, no. 2, 2003, pp. 306–322.
McCarthy, Todd, and Charles Flynn. Interview with Herschell Gordon Lewis. *Kings of the Bs: Working within the Hollywood System: An Anthology of Film History and Criticism*. E.P. Dutton & Co., 1975, pp. 347–360.
Mendik, Xavier. "'Gouts of Blood': The Colourful Underground Universe of Herschell Gordon Lewis." *Underground U.S.A.: Filmmaking Beyond the Hollywood Canon*, edited by Xavier Mendik and Stephen Jay Schneider. Wallflower, 2002, pp. 188–198.
Peary, Danny. *Cult Movies 2: 50 More of the Classics, the Sleepers, the Weird, and the Wonderful*. Delta, 1983.
Schaefer, Eric. *"Bold! Daring! Shocking! True!": A History of Exploitation Films, 1919–1959*. Duke University Press, 1999.
Sconce, Jeffrey. "'Trashing' the Academy: Taste, Excess, and an Emerging Politics of Cinematic Style." *Screen*, vol. 36, no. 4, 1995, pp. 371–393.
Waddell, Calum. *The Style of Sleaze: The American Exploitation Film, 1959–1977*. Edinburgh University Press, 2018.

11
MY HUSTLER (1965)

Kevin John Bozelka

It would seem that the most obvious way to approach Andy Warhol's film *My Hustler* is to contrast it with the operations of Hollywood cinema. Indeed, *My Hustler* is so rigidly focused on gay male desire that one might conceive of the film as a correction to decades of limited cinematic visibility of homosexuality.

Such an analysis is not altogether fair to how classical Hollywood cinema (roughly, 1917–1960) operated. Even after the Production Code of self-censorship guidelines went into effect in 1934, forbidding "sex perversion or any inference of it," Hollywood films featured plenty of characters and storylines that code as gay (Noriega 22).[1] Still, one could claim that only a perverse, ungeneralizable decoding process would be required to arrive at just such a conclusion, especially in the absence of openly gay characters or any other hardcore evidence of homosexuality.[2] By contrast, *My Hustler* provides a showcase for unapologetically, even screamingly gay characters. Only a perverse reading could deny that homosexuality forms the nucleus of the film.

However, Warhol did not aim to correct the putative oversights of Hollywood cinema by inserting gay characters into a traditional narrative. Instead of utilizing a three-act structure wherein the last act provides resolution to all conflicts, he structured the film around two rambling conversations that keep tension in play at the end of the film. Furthermore, Warhol did not concern himself with creating positive representations of gay men in a pro-social effort. Quite to the contrary, the dominant voice in the first half of the film belongs to a bitchy, ruthlessly transactional queen. Most importantly, the gay characters compete for dominance of the look with not only one another but also two women as well with none the victor. In short, *My Hustler* is a structurally queer film in that Warhol queers the operations of mainstream narrative cinema. In what follows, then, I will provide a brief overview of Warhol's film career before embarking on

DOI: 10.4324/9781003246930-12

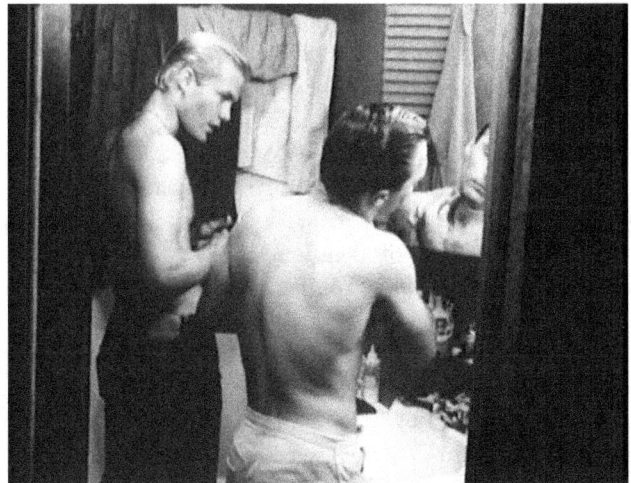

FIGURE 11.1 Paul America (left) and Joe Campbell discuss the logistics of hustling while primping in the mirror in *My Hustler*.

an analysis of how *My Hustler* rejects the architecture of more traditional Hollywood narrative films, whether pre-or post-Code. Instead of allowing for power differentials between characters, Warhol parades his cast before us as equal items in a buffet, available as figures of identification or types to ignore depending on the whim of the viewer. In this respect, Warhol's cinema was flamingly independent, blithely indifferent to the demands of storytelling and the economic imperatives of Hollywood's assembly-line production.

Overview

After achieving success in advertising and renown as one of the chief architects of Pop Art, Andy Warhol began making films in 1963. But he did not arrive at filmmaking in a vacuum. By the early 1960s, a radical scene in New York City crystallized under the aegis of the New American Cinema Group (later, the Film-Makers' Cooperative), a membership co-op dedicated to the distribution of independent cinema. The group published a manifesto in 1961 lambasting "Product Films": "The very slickness of their execution has become a perversion covering the falsity of their themes, their lack of sensitivity, their lack of style" ("First Statement" 131). As an avid filmgoer and inveterate scenester, Warhol orbited this group including its co-founder, filmmaker Jonas Mekas, and incorporated their prohibition against slickness into his filmmaking. His earliest titles betray an amateur experimenting with a Bolex camera to find his own filmmaking voice, sometimes leaving under/overexposed or out-of-focus shots into the final work such as *Tom*, his first film, or *Untitled (John in Country)* (both 1963). But he quickly developed a cinema that served as an unlikely counterpart to the cinema of the 1890s, beyond which contemporary Hollywood had long since "matured," in that many of his films were content to show objects or menial activities with no concern for encasing them in a narrative.

For instance, *Sleep* (1963) contains various shots of poet John Giorno sleeping for almost five and a half hours. *Eat* (1964) shows artist Robert Indiana eating a mushroom for 45 minutes. *Empire* (1964) focuses on the Empire State Building for slightly over eight hours. And, perhaps most redolently in relation to *My Hustler*, *Blow Job* (1964) consists of 33 minutes of a man in close-up purportedly receiving fellatio. All of these films are in black and white and silent. They are not continuous shots since cameras of the period could not allow for unbroken shots over such an extended period, something more easily achieved with digital cameras today. Instead, they are reels edited together in a raw fashion. The film will flare up toward the end of the reel and become consumed in whiteness. Then the next reel will start up with the image coming into clarity after more flare-ups and punch-code markings. Warhol spliced the reels together whereas most filmmakers, even those of the avant-garde persuasion, would have edited out the flare-ups and punch codes. I mention this aspect of Warhol's early films since many commentators, who likely have never seen the films, describe them as just one shot of the Empire State Building or a man sleeping, etc. This will become important in the discussion of *My Hustler* below since the film is edited in a similar way even though it gravitates toward narrative.

In 1964, Warhol's films began to scrape toward narrative when he adopted an Auricon camera to capture sync sound and hence dialogue. In some respects, his filmmaking practices at this time were not entirely devoid of the hallmarks of Hollywood. He moved his studio to a loft in midtown Manhattan that became known as the Factory. As Bruce Jenkins notes, "the Factory served for Warhol's cinema in much the same way that such production facilities did for the Hollywood film industry, namely as the site for principal photography" (Jenkins 132). Many Warhol titles between 1964 and 1967 were shot at the Factory which functioned as a sort of assembly line for independent filmmaking. There was even a star system at the Factory in the form of Superstars, the hipsters, beautiful people, and hangers-on who installed themselves at the Factory. Edie Sedgwick, Ondine, Brigid Berlin, and others became underground celebrities due to their appearance in Warhol films. Warhol also used scenario writers and his battalion of Superstars would improvise within (or in spite of) them. Ronald Tavel provided the scenarios for many classic Warhol films in this era including *The Life of Juanita Castro*, *Horse*, and *Vinyl* (all 1965). Later in 1965, Warhol brought Chuck Wein on board to shape subsequent films leading to the genesis of *My Hustler*. Wein is credited as co-director of the film according to many filmographies.[3]

My Hustler was shot over Labor Day weekend, 1965, in Fire Island Pines. Exploiting the Auricon camera's 1200' reels, more than ten times the Bolex's capacity, Warhol and company created the film from two black-and-white reels of slightly over 30 minutes each. There are several strobe cuts throughout, brief but jarring flashes of light (often with an accompanying "bloop" sound) created by quickly turning the camera off and then back on. But most of the film's duration consists of extremely long takes with the camera panning and zooming at various points and sync-sound dialogue on the soundtrack. This refusal to engage with the more analytical editing characteristic of mainstream cinema, breaking up scenes into constituent shots to help propel the story forward, places *My Hustler* firmly within the traditions of independent filmmaking of the time. In Tom Kalin's words,

> Warhol's explorations of the technical capacities of the Auricon resulted in a series of films that were particularly resistant to the expectations of audiences who had long been accustomed to the well-lit, well-acted films with coherent narratives turned out by Hollywood.
>
> *(Kalin 276)*

The Queerness of *My Hustler*

Much of the queerness of *My Hustler* lies in the difficulty of assigning even basic characteristics to the film. On many levels, it functions as a documentary. The characters use their real names and are essentially playing themselves. Joe Campbell portrays an aging hustler, a brutal reality of the profession since he was only 28 years old at the time of filming. In his teens, Campbell hustled on a beach in Queens where he met and began a seven-year relationship with future gay icon Harvey Milk. Paul America stars as the titular Adonis whose dyed-blond locks and chiseled body elicit fierce competition among the characters, a situation mirrored by the men and women in Warhol's cohort (including Wein himself) who lusted after America when he was introduced to them a few months before filming (Watson 234). Wein worked with no screenplay or even a scenario. Instead, he based the concept for the film on the many conversations he had with friends Ed Hood and Genevieve Charbin whose wit and extemporaneous skills carry the first reel. And while the lines between documentary and fiction become blurred in the film, so do those between pornography and the avant-garde. Given the fact that Warhol was indifferent to resolving the narrative tensions in *My Hustler*, it is no surprise that the film premiered in January 1966 at the Film-Makers' Cinematheque, a program of avant-garde/experimental cinema under the direction of Jonas Mekas, which attracted a crowd interested in challenging art. With new footage added, however, the film opened the following summer at the Hudson Theatre in Times Square, a venue exhibiting sexploitation films (the trashy precursors to hardcore pornography) at the time, occasioning reviews in the *New York Times* and the *Village Voice*. As this antithetical exhibition history demonstrates, the film exists in a variety of registers depending on which aspect is brought to the fore: the nudity and filthy dialogue; the home-movie-like long takes; the lopsided and truncated story; and so on. A queer thing, *My Hustler* lies in explicit contrast to heavily controlled Hollywood product that seeks out more rigid genres borders and predictable audience responses.

My Hustler takes place on Fire Island which for decades has provided an oasis of public queerness, even well before the Stonewall era marking the birth of the modern gay rights movement in the late 1960s.[4] The film opens with Ed (Ed Hood), a balding, campy gay man sitting on the patio of his beachfront property. He berates his servant Kali (J.D. McDermott), criticizing his shabby outfit and barking orders at him. After the reprimanding, Ed draws his attention to Paul (Paul America) whom we later discover was purchased by Ed using a Dial-A-Hustler service. As Ed talks, the camera pans over to Paul walking to the beach, taking his shirt off, and applying suntan lotion to his arms and legs.

At this early stage of the film, Ed dominates and even directs the vision. Kali poses no threat to him. Indeed, he barely exists in the film, disappearing entirely in the second reel. Paul is too far away to serve any antagonistic function. He would have to shout in order for Ed (or the film's audience) to hear him and remains unaware or unconcerned that the camera has zoomed in on him from a distance. It appears, then, that *My Hustler* will tell Ed's story and keep him in control of maintaining the gaze. Stephen Koch, an early chronicler of Warhol's cinema, arrives at just such a conclusion. In his analysis of the film, he aligns the camera with the "worrisome, watchful voyeuristic eyes of Ed Hood" (Koch 81). But closer inspection reveals that the camera is cleaved from Ed's vision. Filming from the end of the patio, it stands closer to Ed than Paul. But the editing does not engage any of the patterns (shot/reverse shots, glance-object cuts, point-of-view shots, matches on action, etc.) that would suture Ed (or the viewer) into the diegesis and kick-start an identification process. Even before many characters are introduced, they are all placed on an even playing field by the indifferent, observational camera. After all, the first camera movement of the film is a zoom-in on Ed and Kali so they are as much objects of vision as Paul.

A swish pan back to the patio shows Ed losing sight of Paul for a moment, yet another example of how no character possesses the look for too long. Seconds later, Ed's friend and neighbor Genevieve (Genevieve Charbin) arrives. She immediately signals her interest in Paul and the two engage in increasingly catty competition over him. Their dialogue highlights both the attempt to control the look and the unapologetic queerness of the proceedings. Calling Genevieve a "fag hag" or blithely disregarding heterosexual hegemony, Ed marks off a legible queer culture developing outside the purview of mainstream society. But Genevieve matches Ed's bitchiness line for line and shows no evidence of backing down in her quest for Paul.

Most of their conversation takes place over almost eight minutes of an unbroken shot of Paul killing time on the beach. Another man then enters the frame and sits next to Paul. The two chat with one another but we can hear only the continuation of the conversation between Genevieve and Ed on the soundtrack. Genevieve calls the new guy up to the house. As he gets closer, Ed realizes he knows him as "The Sugarplum Fairy." It turns out to be Joe (Joseph Campbell), an older hustler who also takes an interest in Paul. Joe joins Ed and Genevieve and the competition for Paul becomes even more fierce.

After about seven minutes of the conversation, the camera pans slowly away from the trio. It seems unrushed by the exigency of centering on any of the characters, zooming in on some sand, and taking a full minute to finally rest on Paul. In this laconic move, the camera unmoors itself from the looking of the trio and accrues an enunciative intelligence of its own. It has the effect of becoming yet another entity to compete for the attention of Paul. And it is during this pan that the trio makes a bet to determine who will wind up coupled with Paul, the closest the film comes to instigating a goal-oriented plot. Genevieve inches toward that goal when she leaves the patio to join Paul on the beach. While the camera shows them swimming, Joe and Ed engage in an increasingly hostile conversation.

While the long take and queer subject matter mark *My Hustler* as an unconventional film, the panning back and forth between the patio and the beach at the very least emulates the more conventional cutting of a Hollywood film. However, there is then a cut to the more extreme second reel. Joe and Paul are in a bathroom, presumably in Ed's house. Unlike the first reel, the camera stays motionless just outside the bathroom door. There are no obvious markers of how much time has passed. On the surface, not much happens in this scene. This is the first time we hear Paul speak but the conversation he has with Joe is a rather banal one. Gone is the sassiness of the first reel replaced by two working-class men discussing how much money can be made hustling. Both men shower and we see each in various stages of undress. They primp in the mirror for an absurdly long time. But underneath all this endless preening and chatter is a palpable tension. Joe clearly wants to have sex with Paul but must play it cool (and avoid Ed's style of campy banter) in order not to turn him off. Meanwhile, Paul may be playing naïve to get the information on the hustling life that he wants from Paul. Or perhaps he is well aware of Joe's intentions but feigns innocence to avoid anything beyond a business relationship. The language of seduction hangs in the air but it is impossible to determine who is hustling whom. As Thomas Waugh puts it, this "constellation of look, tease, and consummation enters…a post-Stonewall regime of flux," a particularly vanguard development since the film was shot almost four years before Stonewall (Waugh 58).

Both men push the blasé attitude close to a breaking point. They have been nude in front of one another. They have primped in the mirror with one another. They have discussed sex with johns in explicit detail. Paul has urinated in the toilet next to Joe. But they both grow irritated with one another and the time has come for something to happen. Joe rubs Noxzema on Paul's back but this time, he is more diligent about it. He takes his time and hugs him from behind, almost resting his cheek on his back.

At this point, five minutes before the end of the film, Genevieve steps into the doorway. Joe is frustrated at this coitus interruptus and retreats to the back of the bathroom out of frame. Genevieve offers Paul the opportunity to go away with her. Paul says nothing and she leaves. A few moments later, Ed arrives. He brandishes cash from his wallet. He offers him money, cars, girls, and travel. But Paul ignores him too and Ed leaves. Most strikingly, a woman we have never seen before (Dorothy Dean) steps into the doorway. While disinterestedly applying lipstick, she says she can offer him an education and yet Paul still says nothing. The surprise introduction of a character at the very end of the film suggests that any character with the look can have it snatched away from them at random by the camera if not by another competitor. Thus, Warhol does not provide a mere queer-positive inversion of Laura Mulvey's famous contention that in classical Hollywood cinema, men look while women are looked at; he fashions a buffet of looks that retards narrative progression due to the non-hierarchical antagonism on display.

In the middle of Dean's speech, the film stops because the reel runs out. "Stops" is the correct word here instead of "ends." As David Bordwell and Kristin Thompson note about narrative cinema, "a film doesn't simply stop; it *ends*." (Bordwell and Thompson 88). But *My Hustler* flips this tenet. This is an important distinction to make because the shape of the film is determined not by narrative exigency but rather by the indifferent length of the reel. In place of a forward-focused plot, a queer insouciance structures the film. There is no formation of the heterosexual couple (or, indeed, any couple) at the end. A dénouement showcasing a homosexual coupling would merely reverse the operations of mainstream Hollywood cinema rather than create new pleasures and ways of seeing. *My Hustler* strands the viewer in a state of unresolved, but not necessarily unpleasurable, tension. As with so many Warhol films, a space in which nothing happens becomes a field of possibilities replete with meaning, for the viewer as much as for any of the characters. Douglas Crimp highlights this aspect of Warhol's cinema as the key challenge to Hollywood modes of representation. The unblinking, immobile camera allows Crimp/the viewer to scan the bathroom and arrive at a much more active rapport with the screen than is afforded by more mainstream cinema: "In here, you can continue to play around in the space of *not coupling*, a space that hasn't been much explored in the movies – or anywhere else, for that matter" (Crimp 94).

This is why *My Hustler* works equally well in an art cinema or at a porn theater. Where the former venue elicits a cerebral, contemplative gaze, a porn theater beckons a distracted patron, one who will glance at the film in the midst of performing sexual acts in public.[5] For R. Bruce Brasell, *My Hustler*'s construction of a subject position conducive to glancing aligns that position with the specifics of gay male life, particularly the activity of cruising. Especially at the time of the film's release, cruising was a crucial gay male activity if only because a more overt expression of homosexual desire might result in violence. Therefore, there is a great deal of pleasure taken in the cruise itself rather than the actual consummation of the relation: "Though we can cruise the screen back, participate in the process, we can never consummate the cruise if consummation is defined in terms of sexual climax" (Brasell 63).

Warhol achieves this state of erotic itchiness not only by refusing to relinquish the look to any one character but also by abjuring any sense of a narrative climax.

At the point when the film stops, no one has won the bet (including Dean's character who was not even in on it in the first place) and Paul's mute response gives no clue as to who might be in the lead, if anyone, Joe included. It is in this abdication of any responsibility to conventional cinematic storytelling that Warhol spoke to an increasingly self-actualized gay audience in the mid-1960s and created a queer cinematic milestone in the process. "As a remedy to Hollywood films' focus on love that was not only stereotypical and idealized but also heterosexual," to borrow Jonathan Flatley's words, *My Hustler* offered the gay men lucky to have seen it the opportunity to imagine a variety of possibilities for living – coupling, sure, if you longed for such a thing, but also bitchiness, lust, fabulousness, etc. (Flatley 401).

If indeed these aspects of the film elicit a cruisy mode of spectatorship, however, it need not be aligned solely with gay male viewers. Despite the viciousness on display, *My Hustler* is a radically democratic film, one that never forces a subject position. We can gaze at it intently and become hypnotized by its challenge to the goal-oriented, gaze-centered machinery of mainstream cinema. Or we can barely watch it at all, catching a mere hint of it as we cruise on to other vistas.

Notes

1 For a superb analysis of the queerness of classical Hollywood cinema, see White 1999, particularly her chapter on the Production Code and *These Three* (1936).
2 See Miller for a difficult but rewarding essay on how the requiring of evidence of homosexuality functions as an insidious form of homophobia.
3 The extent of Warhol's involvement in the films and even artwork that bear his name has long been a point of contention. Along with Dorothy Dean, Wein came up with the idea for the film while Paul Morrissey, director of such Warhol films in name only as *Heat* (1972), *Flesh for Frankenstein* (1973), and *Blood for Dracula* (1974), operated the camera.
4 For a queer history of Fire Island, see Newton 2014.
5 See Capino and Champagne for more on the different subject positions and modes of viewing in porn theaters.

Works Cited

Bordwell, David, and Kristin Thompson. *Film Art: An Introduction*. 8th ed., McGraw-Hill, 2008.
Brasell, R. Bruce. "*My Hustler*: Gay Spectatorship as Cruising." *Wide Angle*, vol. 14, no. 2, 1992, pp. 54–64.
Capino, José B. "Homologies of Space: Text and Spectatorship in All-Male Adult Theaters." *Cinema Journal*, vol. 45, no. 1, 2005, pp. 50–65.
Champagne, John. "Stop Reading Films! Film Studies, Close Analysis, and Gay Pornography." *Cinema Journal*, vol. 36, no. 4, 1997, pp. 76–97.
Crimp, Douglas. *"Our Kind of Movie": The Films of Andy Warhol*. MIT Press, 2012.
"The First Statement of the New American Cinema Group." *Film Culture*, nos. 22–23, Summer 1961, pp. 131–133.
Flatley, Jonathan. "*My Hustler*, 1965." Handhardt, pp. 398–420.
Hanhardt, John G., editor. *The Films of Andy Warhol – Catalogue Raisonné: 1963–1965*. Yale University Press, 2021.

Jenkins, Bruce. "1964: Introduction." Hanhardt, pp. 132–135.
Kalin, Tom. "1965: Introduction." Hanhardt, pp. 276–281.
Koch, Stephen. *Stargazer: Andy Warhol's World and His Films*. Praeger, 1973.
Miller, D.A. "Anal *Rope*." *Inside/Out: Lesbian Theories, Gay Theories*, edited by Diana Fuss. Routledge, 1991, pp. 118–142.
Mulvey, Laura. "Visual Pleasure and Narrative Cinema." *Screen*, vol. 16, no. 3, 1975, pp. 6–18.
Newton, Esther. *Cherry Grove, Fire Island: Sixty Years in America's First Gay and Lesbian Town*. Duke University Press, 2014.
Noriega, Chon. "'Something's Missing Here!': Homosexuality and Film Reviews During the Production Code Era, 1934–1962." *Cinema Journal*, vol. 30, no. 1, 1990, pp. 20–41.
Watson, Steve. *Factory Made: Warhol and the Sixties*. Pantheon, 2003.
Waugh, Thomas. "Cocktease." *Pop Out: Queer Warhol*, edited by Jennifer Doyle, et al. Duke University Press, 1996, pp. 51–77.
White, Patricia. *Uninvited: Classical Hollywood Cinema and Lesbian Representability*. Indiana University Press, 1999.

12

PORTRAIT OF JASON (1967)

James Morrison

Portrait of Jason, the 1967 film by Shirley Clarke, is a difficult work to place. Chronicling a sprawling unscripted monologue by a 43-year-old gay Black man, Jason Holliday, over a single night in Clarke's New York City apartment, the film is even generically elusive. Is it a documentary? The record of an improvised performance piece? A home movie? It was certainly among the defining films of the New American Cinema, a vanguard movement based largely in New York in the 1960s, but its position in that canon could be said to render problems of definition around the film even more pressing, given the movement's rejection of cinematic conventions and its increasingly complex evolution.

An offshoot of the independent cinemas emerging in the United States following World War II, the New American Cinema did not just declare its sovereignty from Hollywood, as most branches defined themselves by doing. It claimed a more radical dimension, deriving from avant-garde aesthetics, beginning with a promise to rediscover a more authentic cinema by eschewing commercial motives in favor of personal expression, but its own capacious self-definition ultimately signaled a greater affinity to other cinematic forms than its early partisans acknowledged, incorporating documentary, modernist experimentation, countercultural politics, and an irreverent attitude toward genre and narrative.

In keeping with this hybrid model and with independent cinema's greater freedom of subject matter, *Portrait of Jason* is also a milestone of queer filmmaking, though its director was a heterosexual woman, and subsequent commentary has raised the question of whether she was abetting, promoting, or exploiting her subject. Of course, the problems of a "problem" text are usually just what give it its value and distinction. In this case, the shifty relation to prevailing terms and categories has everything to do with the presence and comportment of the film's main and only visible personage, as Jason variously presents himself as part

FIGURE 12.1 Performing Queer Selfhood: Jason with his boa in *Portrait of Jason*. (Image courtesy of PHOTOFEST.)

houseboy – mock-subservient and real-defiant – part hustler, part "superstar," all queer, sometimes con artist, sometimes raconteur, part self-melodramatizing pity-case, with nearly equal dollops of bold truth-teller, eccentric outsider, mischievous trickster and playful jokester, oracular dispenser of wit and wisdom, and even in small part just "ordinary" guy like anyone else, trying to get through the night.

A central dynamic of the film is a kind of push-pull between the film's determination to forge its "portrait" and Jason's undertaking to present himself on his own terms. These aspirations are not entirely at odds. The film subverts its own relation to documentary tradition through a series of self-reflexive strategies, constantly revealing the presence of the filmmakers behind the camera through their voices (without ever showing them) and making its own technique overt in its use of zooms, focal derangements, or sudden, disorienting cuts. Such subversions became a convention of its own at the time as documentarians widely disavowed any "neutral" or "objective" foundation of the genre as erroneous and naïve. Though these strategies encourage viewers' awareness of the filmmakers as interested parties, not just "making" the film but actively manipulating the material in that process, the film remains at pains to foreground its own open approach, recording long stretches of Jason's monologue without interruption or punctuation as he speaks steadily and confidently for himself.

As a branch of the US avant-garde, the New American Cinema was a phenomenon distinct to the 1960s. Its main spokesperson, Jonas Mekas, elaborated on its developing aesthetic in a series of columns in the *Village Voice* throughout the decade. The main distinction Mekas draws between avant-garde forerunners of the 1940s and 1950s – figures like Kenneth Anger or Maya Deren – is to claim a more expansive reach for the 1960s variant, encompassing a greater range of forms and styles by contrast to the prior strain's dominant predilection for dream films or surrealist escapades. Especially significant to *Portrait of Jason* is the admission of a quasi-documentary mode, albeit released from the traditional documentary's allegiance to social research or received ideas of the "true" or the "real." In the examples Mekas prizes most highly, a "new spiritualized reality of motion and light is created on the screen" (144).

That "spiritualized reality" lies somewhere at the crux of the movement, but the general aesthetic, not to mention the transgressive content, undermines any theological connotations. The films might be more comfortably aligned with an existentialist ethos. As Mekas declares, the New American Cinema answers the needs of the "new American man, lost and shaky, searching, fragile, groping in an uncertain moral landscape" (27). Though sometimes inaptly conflated with the so-called "New Hollywood" of the late 1960s, it fiercely rejects the slick professionalism of commercial cinema, not only that of Hollywood but also of other profit-minded filmmaking, however nominally independent of Hollywood it may claim to be. In line with this repudiation, the movement seeks a new, radical spontaneity, "a complete derangement of the official cinematic senses" (199). Clarke's earlier feature, *The Connection* (1961), a Beckettian drama about a group of junkies awaiting the long-delayed arrival of their dealer, received special praise for its reflection of "the uncertainty of man" and its refusal of "fake external dramatic clashes," capturing "the essence of our life today only because it is about nothing" (69).

Flouting the cultural mainstream, the New American Cinema founded key supporting institutions of its own, most of them Mekas-driven. These included *Film Culture* (1954–1996), a journal of vanguard criticism founded and edited by Mekas (with his brother Adolfas), and the Film-Makers' Cooperative, a distribution company (also known by its legal title, New American Cinema Group, Inc.). Anthology Film Archives, a venue for the exhibition and preservation of films of the movement and adjacent lines of work, was established in 1970 (and, like Film-Makers' Cooperative, remains active). A widely noted book, *The New American Cinema*, appeared in 1967 from a mainstream New York publisher (Dutton), an anthology of manifestos, interviews, and critical treatises, including work by the ever-present Mekas, who had begun to establish himself as a filmmaker in his own right by then, and other filmmakers of the movement like Charles Boultenhouse, Stan Vanderbeek, Gregory Markopoulos, and Stan Brakhage. It also featured overtly hostile takes by critics like Parker Tyler and Dwight Macdonald, who saw it as voguish and empty, as well as pieces like Susan Sontag's well-known celebration of Jack Smith's notorious *Flaming Creatures* (1963), a frenetic, ebullient film of a queer orgy – a film Mekas and others were arrested for screening publicly, subsequently standing trial for obscenity. Taken together, these contributions pointed to a canon-in-the-making comprising the filmmakers named in addition to such figures as Ken Jacobs, Ken Kelman, Harry Smith, as well as (albeit more marginally) John Cassavetes, Robert Frank, and Andy Warhol.

By the time Anthology Film Archives was established, the movement exhibited fault lines that portended its dissolution, becoming indeed more an archival phenomenon than a living, united front. Rifts had been visible almost from the first, as might be expected of an aesthetic so categorical despite its theoretical inclusiveness. Mekas had announced the movement's start on the appearance of two films from 1959, *Pull My Daisy* (Robert Frank and Alfred Leslie), a freewheeling paean to the Beat Generation, and *Shadows*, Cassavetes's impromptu variations on racial and other themes. Only a year later, Mekas sharply rescinded his praise for the latter when Cassavetes presented a more polished, reedited version that Mekas found to be "just another Hollywood film" (10).

Through the 1960s, Mekas maintained a nonnegotiable line between movement films and movies from outside the Hollywood system that claimed an "independent" mantle despite their more conventional narrative or thematic bearings, from *David and Lisa* (Frank Perry, 1962) to *Nothing but a Man* (Michael Roemer, 1964) (Mekas 199–201). His objection to the reedited *Shadows* was precisely that it blurred this line, compromising its independence from the mainstream and betraying its vanguard potential. Perhaps responding to auteurist revaluations of Hollywood cinema in the 1950s and 1960s, however, Mekas gradually admitted that the work of even such commercial filmmakers as Samuel Fuller or Alfred Hitchcock could make legitimate claims to some "independent" status due to their own more modified subversions of cinematic convention. Grudging as this concession was initially, by the end of the decade Mekas was handing out full endorsements to items like Sam Peckinpah's *The Wild Bunch*, Hitchcock's *Topaz*, or Sergio Leone's *Once Upon a Time in the West* (all 1969). Especially in light of Mekas's earlier writings or the absolutist manifestos in *The New American Cinema*, a canon this flexible, for all intents and purposes, ceased to be a canon at all.

This gradual unwinding was all to the good in revealing the place *Portrait of Jason* ultimately holds in the New American Cinema. Clarke's own position in the movement was a central one by any measure; even apart from her films, she was the author of the launching manifesto "Statement for a New American Cinema" and co-founder of the Film-Makers' Cooperative alongside Mekas, Brakhage, Markopoulos, and other men. The exclusion of women filmmakers from Hollywood was an impetus to the development of alternative cinemas, where many women thrived; the New American Cinema was receptive in its way to women's filmmaking, with Maya Deren hovering as its patron saint and filmmakers like Clarke, Marie Menken, and Yvonne Rainer in the mix. Yet a certain exclusionism was never entirely absent in the movement's canon-making gestures: recall Mekas's target audience of the "new American *man*." Clarke's foundational manifesto is curiously missing from *The New American Cinema*, and she and Menken are mentioned only in passing there. Though Rainer receives marginal pride-of-place with a still from one of her films reproduced in the book, her name is omitted from the index. Like Cassavetes's *Shadows*, meanwhile, Clarke's films were implicitly or explicitly devalued for their inclinations toward more narratively-oriented filmmaking, as when erstwhile supporter Andrew Sarris placed them in a moribund tradition of "socially conscious" cinema including "a great deal of conventional propaganda," citing, in particular, the "concern with Negroes" (Battcock 53) in Clarke's *The Connection* and *The Cool World*, her 1964 depiction of life in Harlem, made in collaboration with her African-American lover Carl Lee. For many in the movement, these elements made her work too dependent on social commentary and content as opposed to form. For his part, echoing Mekas on Cassavetes, Brakhage absurdly dismissed Clarke outright as "no more than a commercial filmmaker" (qtd. in Rabinovitz 134).

The centrality of gay sensibilities in the New American Cinema – Anger, Boultenhouse, Markopoulos, Jack Smith, Warhol, and others – was also a factor of ambivalence in the movement's establishment. As early as *Pull My Daisy*, a nexus between the downgrading of women's roles and the diminishment of queer presence appears in the story of a husband rejecting his wife's entreaties toward respectability to go off carousing with his unruly buddies, a cadre including high-profile homosexuals Allen Ginsberg and Peter Orlovsky whose queerness, however, dissolves cheerfully in the wash of boyish bonhomie. Despite Mekas's courageous backing of *Flaming Creatures*, his writing exhibits more than a little standard-issue homophobia, 1960s-bohemian-style. In one of his first columns, he regrets how a growing openness in representing homosexuality threatens to eclipse "any other kind of friendship between two men," a circumstance he deems "pitiable" (12). Elsewhere, he numbers gays alongside prostitutes and drug addicts as abject types that movement films present in admirably nonjudgmental ways, though gays in particular are said to inhabit the "sad world" of homosexuality (179). Meanwhile, Sarris has no compunction in referring to the "perverts and prostitutes of Warhol's world" who, on the plus side, are said to be "no less real and sensitive for improperly flaunting their fey fantasies" (Battcock 53).

Yet key aspects of the New American Cinema prefigure the New Queer Cinema of the 1980s and 1990s, with *Portrait of Jason* as a main exhibit. Abjection figures in Jason's monologue, but self-determination is its guiding theme. In the first scene, Jason pronounces his preferred name, then counters it with his given name, establishing a discord between a version of his identity as homegrown and fostered by familial influences – "Aaron Payne" – and one he has chosen, crafted, created for himself: "Jason." "What do you mean, 'Aaron Payne?'" Clarke asks from behind the camera, with a note of suspicion. Not batting an eye, Jason launches into an excursus on his time in San Francisco among a vaguely specified group that believed in changing one's name to suit one's personality. Meanwhile, the camera has rendered him out of focus, as if to suggest a murky dimension to this persona distinct from Jason's own self-image.

Traces of dejection return when Jason talks about his family life again later at the filmmakers' insistence. His circumstances include familiar variables: a sympathetic but ineffectual mother, an abusive father, and a hostile community rife with bigotry. Like every other chapter of his story, however, this one is overwhelmed by Jason's multifaceted humor. By no means are these recollections framed as some sort of "origin" narrative or trauma-bait; there is no semblance of a "coming-out" in this personal history. As Jason recounts it, even as Aaron Payne, he was incorrigibly himself, haunting illicit dives, seeking gay sex despite the certain consequence of violent punishment. "I balled my way from Maine to Mexico," he announces proudly, turning an advertising ditty of the time ("We are the men of Texaco, we work from Maine to Mexico") to his own subversive purposes.

In its free-associational flight path, Jason's narrative balances his makeshift strategies of survival with his guilt-free quests for pleasure. The main goal, quite by contrast to the pledge from the Men of Texaco, was to avoid the scourge of work, a category in which Jason seems to include anything other than the autonomy and freedom he covets. His life as a "houseboy" merges with his exploits as a hustler with the lone distinction between his rank ineptitude as a domestic and his happily self-professed skill in the art of "balling." Meanwhile, tales of his aspirations to show biz appear in the form of a cabaret act from which he gamely, and brilliantly, performs Camp standards from Mae West and Butterfly McQueen to Vivien Leigh, *Carmen Jones*, and *Funny Girl*.

Even an episode in the psychiatric ward at Bellevue is set forth without temporizing, minus reproach or self-reproach. Jason recounts his interactions with officials in a tone of rueful bafflement, the same nonplussed attitude he brings to any reflection on external authority, all too conscious of this power yet puzzled and dispirited by its execution. This is how Jason acknowledges racism as a ubiquitous force. Tellingly, in footage excised from the film, he refers to the filmmakers as tantamount to "cops." Throughout, he shows both an acute awareness of how others perceive him and a strategic indifference to it, including the filmmakers' pestering tendencies to patrol his act. Notably, his demeanor becomes neither guarded nor defiant in response. He rejects maudlin vantage points on the bleaker parts of his tale, ridiculing the rhetoric of drummed-up pathos: "People just love to see you suffer!" he mock-laments in faux-diva mode. Only in the film's final section, when the filmmakers begin to challenge Jason on several fronts from behind the camera, does his waggish – albeit drunken – equanimity falter. Even then, as an underlying sadness that is perceptible throughout comes to the surface, his candor and lack of self-consciousness persist.

The view of Jason advanced here may strike some as unduly positive in light of the film's allegedly "negative" images. Contemporary reviews expressed degrees of sympathy and affection for the film's "star," surprising for that pre-Stonewall era, especially from the pens of straight critics (see Callenbach; Hatch; Kronsky). The "negative images" view of the film, also surprisingly, emerges more recently, largely from viewers touting queer and race-conscious perspectives, such as Jim Hubbard and Sarah Schulman, co-founders of New York's Lesbian and Gay Experimental Film Festival. As administrators at that event, in a state of outrage at the film, they interrupted their own exhibition of *Portrait of Jason* at a 1990 screening by turning off the projector in the middle, declaring the film "profoundly racist" and "homophobic" (Jusick 50). These charges were apparently based on casting Jason as an example of the "Black maid" trope and conceiving Clarke's having given Jason this platform as manipulative and exploitative. In a perceptive analysis of the film as an entry in the screen-test-as-genre à la Warhol, Irene Gustafson similarly finds that "Jason's laughter…betrays how not funny his story really is" (Gustafson 16). Such responses approach the film as Clarke's in the first instance – the work of a white straight upper-middle-class woman "portraying" or exhibiting her subject through an othering, ethnographic lens.

The rejoinder that the film simply shows Jason as he "really is" hardly answers the case. For one thing, such a claim lends itself to legitimate charges of naivety, committing that cardinal sin of equating or conflating a film's representations with its anterior realities. In some interviews, Clarke claims that the film was shot in real-time, with pauses only for changing the film magazine every ten minutes (qtd. in Gustafson 12–13). Elsewhere, in keeping with what we know of the production history and see enacted on-screen, she describes a more complex process of giving up "my intense control" and starting to "trust Jason" while understanding that Jason's "lack of know-how of the filmmaking process would prevent him from being able to control his own image" (Mekas 289–291). The presumption of Jason's vulnerability thus becomes a condition of the project. By no means does Jason ever conceal this vulnerability; in the end, he airs it at agonizing length, even while maintaining some reserve of will and pride. At the same time, his heavily performative presence challenges received ideas about truth and falsehood, artifice, and authenticity.

In that last section, an off-screen voice accuses Jason of lying, insisting that he finally own up to unspecified offenses and start to "tell the truth." Viewers' responses to this wheedling are crucial to their overall reading of the film. I experience it as unjust and infuriating, the culmination of an increasingly truculent onslaught, a calling to account entirely out of sync with Jason's pleasure in the account of himself he has already given, a chiding especially disproportionate following such an extended bravura display. It is as if the voice of the film's critics had suddenly risen within the film, attacking Jason head-on for his performance of himself. Jason's response is telling: almost at once, he begins to weep openly and assert his love for the unseen bearer of this hostile, intransigent voice. He does not apologize and does not pledge to do better, because the point of what he's been saying the whole time is that, on the one hand, he cannot but be "himself" and, on the other – for someone rendered doubly invisible in the culture at large as a gay Black man whose very existence has been subject to intense question yet whose self-respect is somehow intact, someone who has been provided an opportunity to become "visible" in some unknown and possibly futile way – the performative *is* the real. Peripheral as it is, Jason's sadness is mainly that of being unrecognized, an experience with which he appears fully conversant despite his uninhibited personality. Most striking about this final section is that Jason seems not in the least surprised to find himself so deeply misunderstood by his beloved friend.

As it happens, the off-screen voice belongs to Carl Lee, Clarke's lover and collaborator as well as Jason's long-time friend. In Clarke's words, she and Lee had both for years "suffered from [Jason's] endless machinations as well as enjoyed his fun and games" (Mekas 291). In the end, disbanding the "fun and games," Lee demands that Jason expose and renounce his "machinations." In effect, he wants to see Jason perform the role of the pathetic and self-hating gay man instead of the exuberant alternative Jason has offered. Lee's antagonism implies a more wholesale rejection of Jason's particular variant of masculinity. This is one Black man "calling out" another, an ostensibly straight man "calling out" a gay man, at worst recalling the belligerent, homophobic exhortations of a figure such as Eldridge Cleaver (nine years Jason's junior and already famous when Jason merely longed to be) for heterosexual masculinity as the only proper Black manhood. Is this what Jason is being called to account for? For not being proper? For being effeminate, a "queen," for being promiscuous, for fetishizing cute white guys? For "suffering," like Lee "suffered" Jason – or for not suffering enough? For expressing a transient desire to be white or straight amid his overarching acceptance, against all odds, in 1967, of who he was? For being too gay, for telling tall tales, for smoking pot, for alcoholism and public drunkenness, for laughing virtually nonstop? For not being Black right? Some or all of these wrongs might well be condemned, depending on where one sits. In 1967, in independent cinemas or any other, Jason was literally without precedent – the first gay person and the first Black man to speak at length on his own behalf in a feature film, the first of either and, especially, the first of both. If in 2020 (or 1990) he must now take his place in the ranks of the too-familiar as a pitiful stereotype, this may only reveal a certain complacency on the matter of what we think we know too well. It does not deny the damage done by stereotypes to suggest that their critique can also function tacitly to authorize expressions of social or moral disapproval for certain kinds of people.

One could, like Gustafson, certainly hear Jason's laughter as a sad denial of his own suffering. For him, though, it seems to have a liberating force, enabling a way of thinking about his own narrative that places it somewhere beyond that "sad world of homosexuality" he must have known too well himself and learned so much about from the Jonas Mekases and Carl Lees in his orbit, with its predicates of closets and its rituals of coming-out, of seeking acceptance from the straight world and moving through cycles of abuse and forgiveness, ready-made suffering and prefab redemption. As he appears in the film, Jason's lack of apology for himself may be his defining trait; it is central to what permits us, if we can, to see the film, in great part, as his. As visual evidence, his tears near film's end may certify the reality of his sadness, perhaps accounting for why some viewers see them as uniquely defining, even though he cries only briefly but laughs throughout, and even though that reaction repeats the naïve truth claims those same viewers would likely censure. Equally real, his laughter is the key to the film. It does not "betray" hidden sadness, because the sadness is not hidden. It only happens to coexist with its opposite, something irrepressibly buoyant.

Jason's laughter is itself betrayed, when unheard. More than once, it verges on the joyous. To hear it, one could conclude that this film, whatever else it thinks it is doing, was the American screen's first sustained image of a *happy* gay person, even if one thought he should not have been happy or believed he really could not be. We know what *he* thinks because he says it in the movie. He wants to make "one beautiful thing that's my own." And he does.

Works Cited

Battcock, Gregory, editor. *The New American Cinema: A Critical Anthology*. E.P. Dutton, 1967.

Callenbach, Ernest. Review of *Portrait of Jason*. *Film Quarterly*, vol. 22, no. 1, 1968, pp. 75–77.

Gustafson, Irene. "Putting Things to the Test: Reconsidering *Portrait of Jason*." *Camera Obscura*, vol. 26, no. 2, 2011, pp. 1–31.

Hatch, Robert. Review of *Portrait of Jason*. *The Nation*, 30 Oct. 1967, p. 23.

Jusick, Steven Kent. "Gay Art Guerillas: Interview with Jim Hubbard and Sarah Schulman." *That's Revolting: Queer Strategies for Resisting Assimilation*, edited by Mattilda Bernstein Sycamore. Soft Skull Press, 2004, pp. 39–58.

Kronsky, Betty. "Jason Outjason's All Reviewers – Including This One." *Village Voice*, 13 Oct. 1967, p. 13.

Mekas, Jonas. *Movie Journal: The Rise of a New American Cinema, 1959–1971*. Macmillan, 1972.

Rabinovitz, Lauren. *Points of Resistance: Women, Power, and Politics in the New York Avant-garde Cinema, 1943–1971*. 2nd ed., University of Illinois Press, 2003.

13

BOB & CAROL & TED & ALICE (1969)

Cynthia Lucia

By 1969, when Paul Mazursky's directorial debut appeared in movie theaters, almost every "Hollywood" movie was "independent" to some degree. The studios had gradually transitioned from mogul-driven production/distribution/exhibition monopolies to primarily distribution entities in charge of promoting independently packaged, agent-driven productions. *Bob & Carol & Ted & Alice* [*BCTA*], co-written by Mazursky and Larry Tucker, although distributed by the Frankovich division of Columbia Pictures, typifies one of several approaches to this, by then, a common brand of what Geoff King has termed "package system" independence (5).

BCTA – with its $2 million budget, nearly $32 million box office gross, and critical acclaim – assured Mazursky a fruitful filmmaking career to follow. *BCTA* introduced three additional newcomers to the big screen: stage actor Elliot Gould, nominated for a Best Supporting Actor Oscar as Ted; TV actor Robert Culp as Bob; and TV actor Dyan Cannon in her first major film role, also nominated for Best Supporting Actress as Alice. Mazursky and Tucker were Oscar-nominated as writers, along with Hollywood veteran Charles Lang as cinematographer.

Natalie Wood – a well-established studio star since her childhood – became the requisite ribbon to tie the production package together. Producer Mike Frankovich – who started at Republic Pictures in the 1930s, advanced to Columbia's First Vice President in charge of production by the mid-1960s, and, in 1967, traded in that title to form the semi-independent Frankovich Productions – suggested (or more likely insisted) that Wood be cast as Carol to ensure Columbia's support – with Wood's agent Freddie Fields also playing a key role in the process. Frankovich suggested that Wood could be gotten at "a reasonable price," given her several-years' hiatus from screen acting (Wasson 36), along with her desire to gain recognition as an actress of relevance in this "new" industry and

DOI: 10.4324/9781003246930-14

FIGURE 13.1 Although Natalie Wood resisted this shot as "upstaging" her star status, Mazursky prevailed, clearly aware of its comic (and satiric) impact.

transforming culture (Lucia 54–55). Indeed, Wood agreed to work for an upfront fee of $250,000, well below her usual $750,000.[1]

Enter Paul Mazursky. After having been turned down by National General Pictures (NGP)[2] because his *BCTA* story about a potential sexual foursome was "too dirty," he submitted the script to Frankovich, who quickly green-lighted the project, agreeing to allow novice Mazursky to direct (Wasson 36). An actor himself, Mazursky proved to be an actors' director, with Natalie Wood ranking him in the same league as method-acting proponent Nicholas Ray, with whom she had worked on *Rebel Without a Cause* (1955), and Actors Studio co-founder Elia Kazan, with whom she worked on *Splendor in the Grass* (1961) (Wood). While having had his own initial misgivings about casting Wood because he "worried about her ability to handle the satire" (Mazursky 154), Mazursky came to realize that her absence of irony was "a stroke of luck. Her adorable sincerity about the business of being 'open' was perfect for Carol" (159). The filmmaker credits Frankovich also for suggesting actors Culp, Cannon, and Gould – an electrifying ensemble (156–158).

Like Mike Nichols's *The Graduate* (1967), *BCTA*, is set within the southern Californian world of upper-middle-class white privilege, addressing a similar audience. While *The Graduate*'s Benjamin Braddock struggles to carve out a purpose and find meaning in his parents' world of stifling material acquisition and hypocrisy, it is the parents of young children in *BCTA* who struggle to maintain honesty as the turned-on, tuned-in culture surrounding them questions so many traditional sexual and institutional values. But there are no villains here, in contrast with the Robinsons, actively, and the Braddocks, more passively, in *The Graduate*. In Mazursky's film, the two married couples are also friends who love their spouses and each other. Yet they feel naggingly curious and secretly covetous of hip credentials (Bob and Carol – note Bob's wardrobe)[3], while reluctantly self-conscious and uneasily repressed (Ted and Alice) about the *au courant* sexual experimentation surrounding them.

In content and style *BCTA* forged patterns of independence, both consistent with its time and uniquely influential on films (and television shows) to follow.[4] The film's satirically comic commentary on both middle-class sexual mores and alternative lifestyles, its reflexivity, improvisatory feel, and loosely structured narrative, along with its joining relative newcomers with a veteran star under so modest a budget arguably attest to its New Hollywood independent credentials. Just as Murray Smith refers to the "uncertain, countercultural, and marginal protagonists" of the period (10), devoid of those desires or goals that drive the classical narrative forward, scholars Dominic Lennard, R. Barton Palmer, and Murray Pomerance define New Hollywood protagonists "as failing agents of their own destinies" (20), capturing "surprising reflexes of political conflict, cultural transformation, and uncertainty about national purpose" (3). Mazursky was happy to "embrace[s] his loners and swingers, hustlers and changers, as crazily wonderful characters whose idiosyncrasies are a precious natural resource," leading film critic Richard Corliss further to claim that his work "serve[s] as a paradigm of the New Hollywood" (n.p.). This New Hollywood strand of independence is both delightfully evident and self-consciously reflective in *BCTA*. In *BCTA*, indeed, the characters' search for enlightenment and honesty requires complicated degrees of self-deception – a fascinating paradox that sharpens the film's gently satirical edge.

Sexual Curiosities and Contingencies

BCTA's narrative is a loosely structured series of vignettes, most of which are satirically charged confessionals centered on marital infidelities and repressed desires – Bob to Carol about his having had a business-trip affair; Carol to Bob, when he unexpectedly returns home to find Carol's tennis coach in their bedroom; Ted to Bob about his ostensible desire for sexual fidelity in his marriage with Alice; Alice to her psychiatrist about her feelings of repressed anger and insecurity; and Ted to Alice when, with a mouthful of peanuts, he confesses to his own business-trip affair (on which the film remains ambiguous – did it really happen or is this a fantasy he would have had trouble fulfilling?).

The film's promotional tagline, "Consider the Possibilities," ironically comments on "the plight of middle-class… white characters who must wade through a sea of new realities," as Lester Friedman observes. Similar to so many other Mazursky characters, Bob, Carol, Ted, and Alice must engage in "a full-blown reassessment of their lives… that challenges their financially comfortable, cocooned existence" (211). A weekend Esalen-style retreat provides the catalyst for this reassessment, prompting Bob and Carol to confront the contradictions that "openness" and "honesty" pose within their lives of marriage and monogamy.[5]

To the "jazzed up" accompaniment of Handel's "Hallelujah Chorus" – arranged by composer Quincy Jones (Wasson 40) – pre-credit aerial shots follow Bob and Carol's Jaguar convertible along winding mountain roads to the "Institute" retreat that Bob is visiting as a documentary filmmaker to "do research," he tells the group. Carol, introducing herself as "Bob's wife," says simply yet tellingly, "I came because Bob came." Informed audiences of the day would have recognized the ironic reference to Betty Friedan's popular treatise, *The Feminine Mystique* (1963), which identified and diagnosed the "problem" of the suburban housewife whose identity was subsumed by husband and children. Music lends an ironic tone, when "I Know That My Redeemer Liveth" accompanies the slow, balletic movements of a tai-chi class and one man coaching another in primal scream therapy. The sound-image interplay "becomes... a plaintiff, diffuse plea for a panacea in a modern context that has lost the religious dimension," as Robert Detweiler sees it (293), and brings to mind more sobering connotations of the film's tagline, which David Desser and Lester Friedman read, variously, as "an invitation (think how things could be better if you did this); a warning (you'd better contemplate the consequences before you do this); a dare (challenge yourself to do this); and a directive (you must think about doing this)" (240).

The convoluted mental, emotional, and verbal gymnastics that their newfound dedication to openness and honesty requires is no more apparent than when Bob returns home from a business trip. As he and Carol begin to make love, he loses his erection and bluntly confesses: "I had an affair in San Francisco," only to immediately revise his language: "Affair is the wrong word. We had intercourse. That's what we had" – the "fallibility" of words on self-conscious display, as Detweiler observes (294). The harsh light of a bedside reading lamp creates a chiaroscuro interrogation-like effect, as Bob counters Carol's response – "I don't feel upset....I don't feel jealous" – insisting that she "must feel jealous," to which she protests, "I don't see how I can feel jealous about a purely physical thing you had with some dumb blonde." As dialogue and emotions run in tightly-wound hermetic patterns, she reassures him, much to his chagrin that "You told me about it. If you hadn't had told me, then that would have been cheating."

When Bob moves into the adjoining bathroom, Carol, reflected in the vanity mirror, appears boxed-in. He endorses "openness" and "honesty," yet remains blind to his clearly controlling nature. Proclaiming how close she feels to him in light of his confession, Carol holds his head firmly to her breast and, in a maternally patronizing tone, assures him that he "didn't do anything wrong." Now *she* is controlling a confused and infantilized Bob. As she pulls him to the bathroom floor exhorting him to "show me" what happened with the other woman, the camera momentarily remains overhead and satirically distant, inviting viewers to chuckle and scrutinize whether Carol's actions belie her proclaimed absence of jealousy. Returning to floor level, Mazursky's camera also invites us to recognize the couple's struggle in confronting the emotionally treacherous minefields they now find themselves traversing. Do they feel genuine desire, or are they playing out newly prescribed (or formerly proscribed) roles? Although "it does not sound like intentional irony when Bob and Carol excuse their affairs by describing them as purely physical, with no love involved," it is, nevertheless, "an irony basic to the movie" (Detweiler 297), which camera work here implicitly conveys.

When Carol ecstatically discloses Bob's affair to Ted and Alice, asserting how "beautiful" it is that he shared it, Alice feels suddenly ill, while a bemused Ted ("I thought she was gonna tell us she was pregnant or something") is turned on. The film's most remarked upon and the remarkably funny yet nuanced sequence follows in their bedroom, as Alice and Ted struggle to process this new knowledge in light of their own marriage and their friendship with Bob and Carol. Mise-en-scène and shot composition contribute deliciously contradictory details to this beautifully choreographed set piece. As she aggressively removes her make-up sitting before a vanity mirror, Alice declares her "hostility" toward Bob, while Ted, in pajamas behind her, vigorously jogs in place – his nightly exercise ritual now, humorously, an attempt to release newly sparked sexual verve. "You are shaking the whole house," Alice complains – and viewers cannot help but chuckle or even laugh out loud. "I don't know why he told her... it's not the most intelligent thing to do," Ted blurts out, inadvertently adding fuel to Alice's anger. "The point is not that he told her. The point is that he did it. That he cheated on his wife," Alice insists. Thinking like the lawyer he is, Ted's retort backfires as he attempts to come on to Alice: "That's bad, but I think you'll agree with me that if he hadn't told her, there'd be no problem." A decidedly turned-off Alice responds equally strategically: "Ted, do you want me to do something against my will? Now do you really want to do it like that, with no feeling on my part?" Ted's face, in close-up with side-lighting, captures his conflicting desires, as he delivers the hilarious yet disturbing punchline, "Yeah." Carol turns passively prone on the bed, "Go ahead, do what you want," she sighs, as Ted protests, "Alice, you're making it very cheap." The circular push-and-pull creates a more fully comic – yet more intimately moving version – of the earlier power struggle in Bob and Carol's bedroom. Mazursky points out that the ten-minute duration of the scene, "gives you a series of behavioral moments that build on each other and that's what makes it funnier." Expressing his embrace of New Hollywood aesthetics as influenced by the European art cinema of Fellini and Truffaut, Mazursky explains, "... you're seeing *real* life. You're seeing a couple in *real* time" (Wasson 46).

The humor and satire in this and so many other moments emerge from Mazursky's long take shot composition that reveals incongruities as time unfolds, as it does when Alice visits a psychiatrist and addresses the camera: "I am a very happy person, most of the time," again inviting viewer scrutiny. Referring to Bob and Carol's, obsession with "sex, sex, sex," she asks, "It can't be a very good thing, can it?" hinting at her own repressed desires. When, in a satirically obvious Freudian slip, she refers to "Bob" instead of "Ted," she wonders, "Maybe I don't trust Ted. Is that possible?"

Another "confession" occurs at Bob's poolside, where Ted muses that "there's a double standard operating here. I am not going to do anything that I don't want my wife to do," in turn challenging Bob: "I don't believe that you could handle it if Carol had an affair." Bob insists, "I could handle it." An abrupt cut to Ted's slow-motion sexual fantasy involving a beautiful brunette across the aisle from him on a flight to Miami bluntly exposes his own self-deception, as does Bob's initial fury when he discovers tennis coach Horst (Horst Ebersberg) in his bedroom – "I'll kill him. I'll kill the son-of-a-bitch."

In another paradoxical lob of openness played against self-deception, Carol claims of her affair that, "I didn't do it because you did it... I did it because I wanted to do it." Yet her challenge to Bob about his own behavior reveals otherwise: "This is the man who... said to me that we should be open with each other?" Contemporaneous audiences, here, would perhaps have recognized an indirect reference to Helen Gurley Brown's 1962 best-seller, *Sex and the Single Girl*, the entertainingly witty call to liberate women from the culture's sexual double standard, declaring it "complete lunacy" for a woman to remain virginal until marriage (28). The Horst scene ends with Bob suddenly proclaiming an "insight," as the film recalls and sends up its opening "Institute" sequences. "Lights are going on in my head," he rather cluelessly claims, now praising Carol's "courage" in having brought Horst into their home rather than doing it "in a cheap hotel room," as he had in San Francisco. He invites the terrified Horst for a drink reassuring him, "There isn't going to be any hitting. We don't do that in this house. It's a nonviolent household. We don't even allow any war toys..." With his characteristic affection and humor, Mazursky satirizes Bob's smug self-assurance in parroting – and trivializing – the genuinely activist anti-war mantra of the day.

When the couples end up in a Las Vegas hotel suite together, ostensibly to see a Tony Bennett performance, their mutual desires, jealousies, and insecurities erupt, along with the potentially liberating possibility of a foursome. Upon hearing about Carol's affair with Horst and Ted's blurting out his own confession of an affair (real or imagined), Alice begins undressing in a move that is absurdly honest and dishonest – as much about anger and aggression as it is about desire. She declares: "I feel like doing what we all came up to here to do... Orgy. Have an orgy." The others entreat Alice to "relax" and "get dressed." But as Alice persists, Carol shifts from her initial stance – "You're just getting even with Ted" and "Ted is like my family... It would be incestuous" – to "Alice is right. This is where we are at," cajoling the reluctant Ted with, "It's physical fun. It's just sex." Deep focus shot composition and intricate choreography of character movement electrify the scene with satiric humor as characters argue with each other and themselves; they want to be "open," yet they "perform" what they *think* they *should* desire. Mazursky insisted on the comic juxtaposition of one shot that Natalie Wood initially rejected as undermining her star status. Carol and Ted occupy the deep space of the frame as Carol attempts to convince Ted that "it's all right," with Bob undressing in the foreground next to Alice. The four do end up in a king-sized bed together, in what would become the film's most iconic image.

But they do not have sex. That this visually titillating moment remains unconsummated led some critics to call it a "cop-out," while Mazursky argued its consistency: "...I didn't think they *could* do it." (Wasson 39). As critic Foster Hirsch observed, "They are people trying to adopt a life style [sic.] for which they are not prepared... It's a very wise and even moving conclusion" (62). And *Positif* critic Michel Cieutat declared that *BCTA* "beautifully exploited one of the most provocative aspects of the mid-sixties sexual revolution (swingism), while showing its moral limits" (n.p.).

The pattern of cross-cutting – between a reluctant, self-conscious Ted in the bathroom gargling mouthwash and applying deodorant, to Bob, Carol, and Alice in a slow-motion overhead shot ecstatically embracing on the bed – is, for Detweiler, the point when "realism fades, and the movie degenerates suddenly into marital farce" (295). But I would argue that the point precisely and self-reflexively *IS* that realism momentarily fades – these characters are embarking on a fantasy they cannot bring to fruition (much as Ted's slow-motion airplane fantasy arguably confirms). When Ted enters the bedroom, the effect is of a jarring jump cut – the other three are suddenly and shockingly no longer erotically entangled but are now sitting upright, side-by-side, and shot from a level distance. The fantasy of joy and abandon is now supplanted by a more sober reality. Bob and Ted make small talk about the stock market before kissing their best friends' wives, with initial passion fading to jolting self-awareness as eyes begin to flicker open. Bob stops kissing Alice and looks directly into the camera in a self-reflexively revealing and uncomfortably lingering close-up. As Ted and Carol kiss, he slowly pulls away; Bob looks over at them; Alice adjusts her bra strap; Bob gets up from the bed. This silent tableau captures the most genuinely open "insight" each character has experienced.

Sadder Yet Stronger

An abrupt cut to the hotel hallway reveals all four emerging fully clothed with sadder but wiser expressions that very gradually brighten as they walk through the hotel casino to the parking lot outside. There, they are joined by others – including Mazursky, Tucker, and other cast and crew members. In a reflexive Felliniesque moment of communal friendship and unity, they parade hand-in-hand as Jackie DeShannon's voice fills the soundtrack with the 1965 Burt Bacharach/Hal David hit, "What the World Needs Now Is Love." Mazursky's admiration of European art cinema, as likewise felt in so many American independent films of the period, again is on display in this ironic but nonetheless effective sound-image combination. Ironically book-ending an earlier Institute exercise, the characters make direct eye contact with the camera as Culp, Wood, Gould, and Cannon seem to shed their eponymous movie roles and interact as the real people they are. In the earlier Institute sequence participants are encouraged to look deeply into each other's eyes and faces. As they circulate around the room, so does the camera, capturing penetrating looks that discordantly break the fourth wall. "Show the other person what you feel," they are instructed. Casting the viewer as the "other" other person, the camera simultaneously captures a sincere longing for connection yet a sense that "the new 'honesty' potentially leads to further fragmentation," as Detweiler aptly observes (297). The reflexivity of this final moment, as players no longer appear to be performing, implies that they and their characters have come to embrace greater wisdom.

BCTA ends on a note of hope, even with the uncertainties that have addled its characters. While it remains true that "all of Mazursky's characters struggle in the midst of transition, wandering, as Matthew Arnold puts it, 'between two worlds, one dead/The other powerless to be born,'" as Desser and Friedman claim (236), Mazursky's ending pays homage not only to *8 ½* but also to Fellini's affection for his humanly flawed characters and the actors who embody them. As they face each other and the camera, their love and friendship intact, Bob, Carol, Ted, and Alice convey a stronger, more centered – however, perhaps, fleeting – knowledge of themselves and each other.

"No other work evokes the sexual discomfort of the late sixties as comprehensively," Wasson arguably claims, observing that *BCTA* "more than predicted the seventies, it practically invented them," through its incisive look at the so-called "Me Generation" (47–48). What is inarguable is that Mazursky's film occupies a crucially important place among the "packaged" independents of the New Hollywood.

Notes

1 See Wasson (36) and Bowman (276).
2 In existence from 1951 to 1974, NGP was originally and primarily a distribution company, though between 1967 and 1973 the company also produced nine films.
3 Actor Robert Culp wore his own personal super-hip wardrobe (see Wasson).
4 *BCTA* appears influential upon Cassavetes's *Woman Under the Influence* (1974), while earlier Cassavetes films certainly informed Mazursky. *NY Times* critic Elvis Mitchell observes that such television shows as *My So-Called Life* (1994–1995), *Once and Again* (1999–2002), *Felicity* (1998–2002), and *The Sopranos* (1999–2007) owe something, if not directly to *BCTA* then certainly to Mazursky's oeuvre in general (E3). To that list I would also add *Seinfeld* (1989–1998).
5 Located in California's Big Sur, the Esalen Institute conducted exercises and encounter sessions designed to promote emotional honesty and openness with self and others. In the 1960s, Esalen was a crucial part of the Human Potential Movement. Muzursky's visit there, with his wife, inspired the screenplay (Wasson 35). In *BCTA* Angela's Crest stands-in for Esalen, where Mazursky was denied permission to shoot.

Works Cited

Bowman, Manoah, with Natasha Gregson Wagner. *Natalie Wood: Reflections on a Legendary Life*. Running Press, 2016.

Cieutat, Michel, "Hommage Paul Mazursky 1930–2014: Le chanter du désenchantement." *Positif* no. 644, Oct. 2014, p. 75. Trans. Proquest. https://www-proquest-com.exproxy.cul.columbia.edu/docview/1621441978?pqorigsite=summon&accountif=10336. Accessed 19 Aug. 2021.

Corliss, Richard. "Paul Mazursky: The Horace with a Heart of Gold." *Film Comment*, vol. 11, no. 2, 1975, pp. 40–41. https://www.proquest.com/printviewfils?accountid=3785. Accessed 19 Aug. 2021.

Desser, David, and Lester D. Friedman. *American Jewish Filmmakers*. 2nd ed., University of Illinois Press, 2004.

Detweiler, Robert. "The Moral Failure of *Bob and Carol and Ted and Alice*." *Journal of Popular Culture*, vol. 4, no. 1, 1970, pp. 292–298.

Friedman, Lester D. "Paul Mazursky: The New Hollywood's Forgotten Man." *The Other Hollywood Renaissance*, edited by Dominic Lennard et al. Edinburgh University Press, 2020, pp. 204–221.

Grimes, William. "Mike Frankovich, 82, a Producer, Studio Executive and Civic Leader." Obituary. *New York Times*. 4 Jan. 1992. https://www.nytimes.com/1992/01/04/arts/mike-frankovich-film-producer-82-and-a-civic-leader.html. Accessed 12 Aug. 2021.

Hirsch, Foster. "Short Notices: *Bob and Carol and Ted and Alice*." Film Review. *Film Quarterly*, vol. 23, no. 2, 1969–1970, p. 62.

King, Geoff. *American Independent Cinema*. Indiana University Press, 2005.

Lennard, Dominic, R. Barton Palmer, and Murray Pomerance, "The Other Picture Show: An Introduction." *The Other Hollywood Renaissance*, edited by Lennard et al. Edinburgh University Press, 2020, pp. 1–25.

Lucia, Cynthia. "Natalie Wood: Studio Stardom and Hollywood in Transition." *The Wiley Blackwell History of American Film: Volume III, 1946 to 1975*, edited by Cynthia Lucia, Roy Grundmann, and Art Simon. Wiley Blackwell, 2012, pp. 26–61.

Mazursky, Paul. *Show Me the Magic*. Simon & Schuster, 1999.

Mitchell, Elvis. "Critics Notebook: Doing Justice to Mazursky, Long Bypassed." *New York Times*, 30 Aug. 2001, pp. E1+.

Oliver, Myrna. "Noted Movie Producer Mike Frankovich Dies." Obituary. *Los Angeles Times*, 3 Jan. 1992. https://www.latimes.com/archives/la-xpm-1992-01-03-me-5675-story.html. Accessed 12 Aug. 2021.

Smith, Murray. "Theses on the Philosophy of Hollywood History." *Contemporary Hollywood Cinema*, edited by Steve Neale and Murray Smith. Routledge, 1998, pp. 3–20.

Wasson, Sam. *Paul on Mazursky*. Wesleyan University Press, 2011.

Wood, Natalie. Interview. The American Film Institute and Screen Actors Guild Seminar. Center for Advanced Film Studies: 10 Aug. 1979. Transcript. 1–63. 20 Nov. 2015. Bonhams New York Auction House.

14
THE LEARNING TREE (1969)

Arthur Knight

The Learning Tree is *not* an independent film. In fact, it was important to its makers – Gordon Parks, its writer-director, and Warner Bros.-Seven Arts (hereafter W7), the Hollywood studio that funded and distributed it – that *The Learning Tree* be seen as an American-film-industry-*dependent* work, one crafted and positioned to reach a broad audience: a Hollywood movie.

At the same time, both the makers and audiences of *The Learning Tree* also understood it to be different from *all* previous Hollywood movies: Gordon Parks was Black, the first African American to direct a Hollywood film. This fact complicated the provenance of *The Learning Tree*, making it also important that the movie be understood simultaneously as W7's *and* as Gordon Parks's, as a white, Hollywood movie and as a film created by an autonomous Black artist.

Critics, filmmakers, and scholars have long debated what constitutes "Black film." A frequent assumption in such debates is that "independence" is vital to anything that can be thus labeled. However, as scholars like Tommy Lott, Terri Francis, and Lars Lierow have pointed out, "independence" is left underarticulated in these definitional debates, especially when they focus on feature-length narrative films and the entanglement of Black voice and vision with "white money" (Rhines). Analyzing the genesis of *The Learning Tree* provides a clearer sense of how freighted and elusive the idea of independent film – and of expressive "independence" more generally – becomes when it intersects regimes of race in US cinema culture.

Race and anti-Black racism were inescapable topics in the US in 1968 when the making of *The Learning Tree* was put in motion. The *New York Times* reported that W7 had contracted with Gordon Parks on 2 April 1968 – two days before the murder of Martin Luther King, Jr. ("Author" 51). *The Learning Tree* is set in the 1920s and in rural Kansas, far in both time and space from the urban "ghettos"

FIGURE 14.1 Four African American characters merge into two black silhouettes in an image that recalls the iconography of the Western.

most associated with racial unrest in the 1960s, but it reflects the historical foundations and pervasiveness of Black experiences with and responses to racism. *The Learning Tree* uses its story and imagery to thematize – and probe the possibilities and limits of – independent, expressive selfhood for its young main character, Newt Winger. Newt is a direct avatar of his creator, Gordon Parks, who as a renowned photographer and writer had been using his (still) camera as his "weapon of choice" in his decade's long fight to be valued as an individual person (Parks, *Choice*) – a fight Parks saw as both wholly his and as integral to the Civil Rights struggle he had documented in iconic, documentary images. With his film, he brought this individual and collective struggle into American movies.

The Learning Tree covers a pivotal year in Newt Winger's life. Over the film's course, Newt negotiates his first year of high school, struggles in both ordinary and extraordinarily dramatic ways with everyday racism and injustice, and loses his mother to a sudden illness. At the film's conclusion, Newt stands ready to leave his father and older brother in his lifelong home of Cherokee Flats, Kansas, to emigrate to Chicago to live with an older sister. Though the film does not note it explicitly, Newt is about to join the first "great migration" of African Americans to the urban north in search of safety, opportunity, and liberty. Also left implicit is that Newt is the progeny of "Exodusters," African Americans who migrated west in the 1870s from the post-Civil War south in search of the freedoms denied the formerly enslaved. Newt's story is at once a simple one – a young person grows, a boy struggles toward becoming a man – and a complex one shaped by national and even world-historical forces.

To suggest this complexity behind simplicity – the large socio-cultural forces that envelope Black individuality – *The Learning Tree* makes subtle use of genre and color cinematography. It intertwines a coming-of-age story, a family drama, and a racial social problem film. In doing so, *The Learning Tree* resists becoming a simplified "melodrama of black and white," even as it parries with that engrained American generic and racial-moral tradition (Williams).

As my selected still from *The Learning Tree* suggests, the Western provides the weft for the film's weave of genres. Iconography and ideas from that fundamentally American genre are crucial to the film's intricate balance. Western props, settings, actions, and thematic interest in individuality, property, justice, and (or versus) the law swirl around Newt: his brother and father are cowboys. There are no "Indians," but the town name of Cherokee Flats recalls the people who used to live there before being dispossessed. Revolvers appear at key moments in the plot to un/settle questions of justice. And, as the story climaxes, Newt displays extraordinary individual courage by testifying in a racialized murder trial, trying to wring complex justice out of a social and legal system that he has experienced as flawed in ways that too often yield deadly outcomes for Black people. Because of Newt's courage, the trial turns into a sort of displaced lynching. The "right thing" is done to semi-right – but also violently wrong – effect. At the liminal, unsettled conclusion of *The Learning Tree*, Newt is not satisfied with life as it is in America, but he may also sense that through acts like his and continued, long struggle, life in America might be made more perfect.

The Learning Tree is clearly a film about race. But it also uses color cinematography – an element of the film directly tied to its status as a Hollywood-dependent work, as I will explain below – to complicate the dualism that has characterized US racism. At a level easy to neglect a half-century later, the film works to represent the full range of skin tones that "race" collapses into "black" and "white," a range that film stocks throughout the 20th century made challenging to photograph (see Roth). In this sense, *The Learning Tree* might be called "realistic" and revolutionary – and in a way that could be connected to writer-director Parks's career as a photojournalist.

But if *The Learning Tree* is realistic in its representation of race in color, it is equally committed to using color evocatively. The film favors a subdued color scheme in tracking Newt's year, but it threads red throughout. While clearly invoking the Western, my chosen still from the end of the film's opening sequence introduces this thread of red in spectacular fashion, contrasting the blackness of shadow with the blazing red-orange of the setting sun to load a "simple" image with complexity: this image represents a moment of family and community bonding through a rescue of Newt who was caught and injured in a sudden storm. What we see in the still appears to be two characters, but it is in fact four characters – Newt's father and brother, a local woman who sheltered Newt, and Newt – who have been fused by the composition and color. Here red is associated with community and family ("blood" in positive senses). As the story unfolds from this opening moment, this positive sense will not only continue but also gain associations with danger, violence, and race (for which "blood" often serves as a metonym): the woman will unwittingly betray Newt, leading him to shed actual blood, the final red we see in the film. And those cowboys, Newt's father and brother, who unflinchingly rode into danger to save him will turn out to be – fully understandably – somewhat cowed by the racist violence they know their white neighbors are capable of, fearing the blood of racist slaughter.

When he signed his contract with W7 in 1968, Gordon Parks well understood the complex negotiation of individual, expressive autonomy in relation to established social norms and institutions. Parks had lived many versions of such negotiations. Arguably, he had accomplished such a negotiation simply by surviving as a poor African American boy from rural Fort Scott, Kansas, through the height of the Jim Crow era and then as a young man in the urban north. Famously, by the time he came to Hollywood's attention, Parks had experienced such individual-to-institution negotiation by becoming in 1948 a staff photographer for *Life* magazine, a Black "first" and a position he maintained, to world renown, as he did his work as Hollywood's first Black director. Parks's "life story" – as a general concept, as well as in some of its key specifics – is inescapably relevant for any analysis of *The Learning Tree*'s in/dependence.

The Learning Tree adapts Parks's 1963 novel of the same title, and that novel was marketed from its inception as autobiographical. Promoting Parks's book, *Life* published a photo essay by Parks, "How It Feels to be Black," which the magazine described this way: "In a novel *based on his real-life story* [which the essay excerpted] and in *his own* photographs, Gordon Parks tells of the Negro's long search for pride" ("Contents" 3, my emphasis). *The Learning Tree*'s protagonist is not named Gordon Parks, but the photo essay and the publicity for the novel emphasize that Newt Winger should be seen as the teen version of Parks and the day-to-day elements of Newt's story seen as Parks's lived experiences.

Hollywood's first movie by an African American, then, was an autobiographical film. As with the novel, publicity and reviews for the film from its announcement to its release emphasized this, particularly noting that Fort Scott served as the film's location. This discourse emphatically links the film to Parks, making this Hollywood movie *his* in the sense of being Parks's (dramatized) life story set in the places his life had unfolded four decades earlier. But autobiographicalness also links *The Learning Tree* to two important American and African American intellectual trends – one going back more than 100 years, the other much newer – bearing on questions of expressive independence in American filmmaking.

The newer idea was "auteurism," which by the time Parks contracted for *The Learning Tree* was an important concept in American film culture. Auteurism championed "the distinguishable personality of the director" and "the vision of the world the director projects" as key "criteria of value" and argued that movies could be – and at their best, always were – an "individualistic" art form, even if they emerged from an impersonal cultural-industrial system (Sarris 662–663). While auteurism did not require personal, individualistic films to be explicitly autobiographical, logically an autobiography would be fundamentally personal and, thus, unquestionably auteurist, at least in the sense of being rooted in a conceptually "independent" source – even if the resulting movie was also the product of a Hollywood studio. Reviewers of *The Learning Tree* certainly saw the film in these terms (see Champlain).

In the US system of categorizing people, however, there were many contexts in which Gordon Parks would not be seen as an individual but as a "Negro," one whose race occluded his individuality. "I am 50 now, but I still get called 'boy' and I know some whites will call me 'boy' until I am 100 years old," Parks wrote in "How It Feels to be Black" (87). Many scholars of African American literature and culture argue that the autobiographical "slave narratives," the predominant mode of writing by Black authors in the 18th and 19th centuries, form a foundation of African American expressive culture (see Gates). The genre's writers presented themselves both as individuals *and* as representatives of a group of people (a "race") who had to fight to be acknowledged as humans rather than as property in America. These autobiographers negotiated their senses of the individual self in relation to their sense of enforced collective identity – dramatically and obviously by making themselves free, no longer property, and then by using their stories to argue that others like them should also be free individuals.

By the time Parks began doing his multi-media autobiographical work, defining freedom was less clear-cut than escaping enslavement. But Parks was clear that defining Black freedom required self *and* collective knowledge and expressive action:

> How often have I heard a white man suggest, 'I know the Negro'. Nobody knows the Negro, not even the Negro. Because all our lives we have cloaked our feelings, bided our time, waited for the month, the day and the hour when we could do, at last, what we are doing now – looking our white oppressors squarely in the eye and telling them exactly what we think, what we want and what we intend to get.
>
> *("How" 87)*

In 1968, Hollywood's "new" Black director was 56 years old. Parks had "bided his time" and cultivated himself as a photographer, writer, and composer. He had never made a movie when he undertook *The Learning Tree*, but an unnamed (and rare) Black film industry worker quoted in a *Hollywood Reporter* article on W7 signing Parks argued, "[Parks] comes in with a package to Warners, a best-selling book, a score and lots of publicity behind him as a *Life* photographer. They couldn't turn that down if it were handed to them by a two-headed, one-legged Martian" (Hull). Parks was uniquely positioned, in this argument, to ensure that he be seen as an artist, an *auteur* making *his* personal film – his *individual* film. Which would also be Black. And Hollywood.

Gordon Parks told the story of how *The Learning Tree* came to be many times in interviews and his autobiographies, most explicitly in *To Smile in Autumn: A Memoir*:

> Two Time[-*Life*]-Incorporated employees, Alan Martin and Enfield Ford, having arranged for an option on the book's rights, spearheaded the attempt [to make *The Learning Tree*]. They met with one failure after another....

> They had selected me as director; and perhaps this was their undoing. No major Hollywood studio had ever taken on a black director and it was generally assumed they never would.... After two or more years of disparaging effort, Martin and Ford threw in the towel and I tossed mine in as well.

Some later "nibbles" followed from Hollywood producers, but they were "incredible" in their demands: all the characters should be white, or "Gloria Swanson should play the part of my mother." On these demands, Parks is succinct: "I refused" (213). Parks's implication is clear: Hollywood was racist, and to make his book into a film *dependent* on Hollywood would be impossible.[1]

Fortunately, Gordon Parks kept extensive papers that help flesh out *The Learning Tree*'s developmental period, revealing how much Parks and his first collaborators thought about in/dependence in relation to their prospective project. In early October 1964, Alan Martin wrote Parks a nine-page memo "review[ing] the past 10 months of activity so we all know where we stand." He begins: "Originally... we saw *The Learning Tree* as a film produced independently of Hollywood. This, we felt, would allow the greatest creative freedom for you and avoid the typical studio approach to making a film" (4).

Martin's memo makes clear the priorities of The Learning Tree, Inc., the company he and Enfield Ford had formed. First, Parks was to have creative freedom and control: "The way you want to do this film has always been our major consideration" (4). The second set of priorities was aesthetic: *The Learning Tree* collaborators wanted to maintain the fullness and complexity of the novel, which they felt needed a running time of more than 90 minutes, and to shoot the film in color. Given these aesthetic priorities, independent producers they consulted all thought that "while the approach [keeping the film free of Hollywood] was sound, we would be unwise to proceed with anything until there was some assurance of a release for the picture" (1). In the memo, Martin has clearly come to believe, based on the research the collaborators had done both among independent producer-financiers and in Hollywood, that their first and second priorities conflicted in the practical terms of film finance and distribution: "The film we all want to make should have original and unique qualities most Hollywood films don't have – but at the same time have technical excellence that doesn't come cheaply" (3).

In Martin's account, race is bound up in this conflict of priorities. Many potential financiers "were sympathetic toward the film, liked the book and screenplay but found the 'risk' too great" for three reasons: a new, inexperienced director, "no stars," and a story and cast that would be "predominantly Negro" (2). The last of these risks is explicitly about race, with "predominantly Negro" suggesting the film would be "non-commercial" (1). The other two risks are implicitly about race, since Hollywood had developed no Black stars (Sidney Poitier was just becoming a headlining star in 1964) and had given no African Americans opportunities to direct.

Martin also found advisors and potential backers "typing" *The Learning Tree* as "another *David & Lisa* [1962], *Nothing But a Man* [1964], *Lilies of the Field* [1963], etc." (3). These films were financed independently and the first two were also independently distributed to "art cinemas"; all had socially marginal protagonists – a white character struggling with mental illness in *David & Lisa* and working-class African American men in *Nothing But a Man* and *Lilies of the Field*; and all three shared an aesthetic of black and white, low budget realism and running times of 90 minutes. For Martin, these films were "the wrong yardstick – and the wrong category." "Our measure," he suggested, "is closer to [British two-hour, color period comedy and literary adaptation] *Tom Jones* [1963]" (3).

The Learning Tree, Inc. team, then, was imagining the film they would make as a departure from what they saw as a restrictive aesthetic of presentist social realism applied to African American characters and stories. Representing his sense of Parks's desires and ambitions, Martin envisions a film less *black and white*, both in the figurative sense of "more subtle" and in the literal sense of hue: "I think we all agree that the way you employ color is the greatest asset we have – and will be the one element that will most set this film apart from any ever done before. This is the single most exciting feature of this project" (3, punctuation simplified). Parks would add "color" – dimension, subtlety, his expressive, artistic individuality, and style – to the US cinema's generic black-and-white understanding and depiction of race. To do this he needed independence. And money: this "single most exciting feature" is also "the one that makes the cost so high" (3).

After the Martin memo, there is no mention in Parks's papers of film rights until the W7 contract appears in mid-April 1968. The catalyst for the sudden shift was actor-director John Cassavetes, a successful Hollywood actor who was also a pioneer of filmmaking conceived as fundamentally autonomous from Hollywood. When Cassavetes was championing Parks, he had just been featured in the hit film *The Dirty Dozen* (1967), which had been conceived and initiated by the independent-but-Hollywood-aligned Seven Arts Productions and financed and distributed by MGM. When Seven Arts bought out Warner Bros., forming W7, *The Dirty Dozen*'s producer, Kenneth Hyman, became W7's head of production, allowing Cassavetes to connect Parks with Hollywood power (*Smile* 213–214).

According to Parks, the initial deal was done "in less than five minutes." Recalling his conversation with Hyman, Parks also recalled his thoughts as asides: "(Was this guy kidding me?)... (This is crazy)." In subsequent meetings, Hyman "decided" Parks should also write the screenplay, compose the score, and produce in order "to keep [Parks in] control" (214–215). Parks records himself as enthusiastic *and* ambivalent, even paranoid:

> After strapping me with the extra burdens, Kenny Hyman very simply explained the challenge. "The only two directors I recall taking on similar responsibilities," he said, "were Orson Welles and Charlie Chaplin." Then he gave me a mischievous smile.... Joel Freeman, a [producer] buddy of Hyman's, chuckled and quipped, "Kenny is a very sweet and generous

> man. He's gonna hand you the knife and let you slit your own throat, then you blacks can't say we bigots didn't give you a chance out here." We laughed, but a slight touch of paranoia set in, and for a moment I couldn't help but wonder about how much truth there was in Joel's remark.
>
> *(215–216)*

Parks's interviews from 1969 and his memoirs make clear he enjoyed making *The Learning Tree*, and that "Hyman was solidly behind me" (216). The control Hyman engineered, alongside the budget and resources of a Hollywood studio, allowed Parks to adapt his autobiographical novel into a two-hour film that many critics saw as impressively "personal." It allowed Parks to shoot the film in color, conveying the importance of the natural world to Newt Winger and subtly expanding the visual aesthetic Hollywood typically drew on for stories of African Americans. It allowed Parks, as he often noted, to hire Black technicians for his crew and an African American publicist for the film, an unprecedented behind-the-scenes "integration" that put several Black film workers on the path to craft union memberships. And it allowed Parks to return to Fort Scott, Kansas, to expressively represent and reflect on his midwestern home ground – to both celebrate and critique elements of its shaping force in his life and to give the town (and, in Parks's view, the nation) an example of how facing its racist past could be productive, albeit not magically healing, in the present and future.

In 1989, *The Learning Tree* was in the inaugural group of films selected for the Library of Congress's National Film Registry alongside Charlie Chaplin's *Modern Times* (1936) and Orson Welles's *Citizen Kane* (1941) – so Parks and his film ended up in the auteurist company Kenneth Hyman put him in. Still, in 1979 reflecting on his brief Hollywood career in *To Smile in Autumn* and on the collapse of Hollywood support for Black filmmakers after the "blaxploitation" boom of the early 1970s (which Parks's second movie, *Shaft* [1971], helped initiate), Parks returned to familiar themes:

> There was, and still is, much controversy about who was to blame – the black filmmakers or the studios. The situation is hardly arguable. The studios put up the money; the studios also decided what films should be made, but critics, both black and white, seemed to ignore that fact. Unfortunately… money was the only thing that could have given black filmmakers the independence to make better pictures.
>
> *(229)*

Note

1 For Parks's first accounts of *The Learning Tree*'s genesis, see interviews in "Scrapbook 3."

Works Cited

"Author is Chosen to Make Movie of *Learning Tree*." *New York Times*, 2 Apr. 1968, p. 51.

Champlain, Charles. "A Negro Looks at His Past in *Learning Tree*." *Los Angeles Times*, 20 Aug. 1969, p. E-1, 16.

"Contents." *Life*, 16 Aug. 1963, p. 3.

Francis, Terri Simone. "Flickers of the Spirit: 'Black Independent Film,' Reflexive Reception, and the Blues Cinema Sublime." *Black Camera*, vol. 1, no. 2, 2010, pp. 7–24.

Gates, Henry Louis, Jr. "Introduction." *The Classic Slave Narratives*, edited by Henry Louis Gates, Jr. Mentor, 1978, pp. ix–xviii.

Hull, Bob. "Use of Negroes in Industry Just Tokenism." *Hollywood Reporter*, 2 May 1968, p. 8.

Lierow, Lars. "The 'Black Man's Vision of the World': Rediscovering Black Arts Filmmaking and the Struggle for a Black Cinematic Aesthetic." *Black Camera*, vol. 4, no. 2, 2013, pp. 3–21.

Lott, Tommy L. "No-Theory Theory of Contemporary Black Cinema." *African American Review*, vol. 25, no. 2, 1991. pp. 221–236.

Martin, Alan R. Untitled memo to Gordon Parks, 7 Oct. 1964. Gordon Parks Papers, Library of Congress, Box 6 (The Learning Tree).

———. Untitled memo appendix ("Companies and individuals approached on *The Learning Tree*"). Gordon Parks Papers, Library of Congress, Box 24 (Correspondence 1963–1969).

Parks, Gordon. "How it Feels to be Black." *Life*, 16 Aug. 1963, pp. 72–84, 87.

———. *A Choice of Weapons*. Harper & Row, 1966.

———. *To Smile in Autumn: A Memoir* 1979. University of Minnesota Press, 2009.

Rhines, Jesse Algeron. *Black Film/White Money*. Rutgers University Press, 1996.

Roth, Lorna. "Looking at Shirley, the Ultimate Norm: Colour Balance, Image Technologies, and Cognitive Equity." *Canadian Journal of Communication*, vol. 34, 2009, pp. 111–136.

Sarris, Andrew. "Notes on the Auteur Theory in 1962." *Film Theory and Criticism*, 2nd ed., edited by Gerald Mast and Marshall Cohen. Oxford University Press, 1979, pp. 650–665.

"Scrapbook 3 (*The Learning Tree* 1969)." Gordon Parks Papers, Wichita State University Special Collections, https://cdm15942.contentdm.oclc.org/digital/collection/p15942coll8/id/405/rec/25.

Williams, Linda. *Playing the Race Card: Melodramas of Black and White from Uncle Tom to O.J. Simpson*. Princeton University Press, 2001.

15

WANDA (1970)

Pamela Robertson Wojcik

Near the end of Barbara Loden's 1970 film *Wanda*, Wanda Goronski, played by Loden, attempts a bank robbery at the behest of her recent lover, whom she calls Mr. Dennis (Michael Higgins). They kidnap a bank manager, Mr. Anderson (Jack Ford) from his home, leaving his wife and two daughters booby-trapped with a fake bomb set to go off in a little over an hour, thus creating a deadline for the manager's safe return.

Dennis and Anderson get into Anderson's blue wood-paneled station wagon to drive to the bank. Wanda gets into a pale blue Chrysler sedan but realizes she has no key. She hops out and gets the key from Dennis, who tells her, in a rare moment of appreciation, "You did good. You're really something." Wanda gets into her car and follows the station wagon. We see Wanda driving, a subtle proud smile on her face, in alternation with point-of-view shots that show the station wagon just ahead of her. But a car gets between Wanda and Dennis, and then a second car cuts into the lane. We cut to a shot of Dennis in the passenger seat of Anderson's car and lose sight of Wanda, the camera withholding her location. The station wagon pulls over to wait for Wanda, but she does not show. Eventually, we see Wanda making a U-turn and getting pulled over by a traffic cop. As Wanda frantically fumbles for her identification and registration, the film crosscuts between shots of her with the policeman and scenes of Dennis robbing the bank. We then see Wanda driving nervously as Anderson opens the vault, and we, but not Dennis, hear an alarm that goes off because the vault is opening at 8:23 AM, too early. Tension mounts as we cut among the three spaces of the alarm company, police cars arriving at the bank, and Dennis inside. As police surround Dennis inside the bank, he pulls a gun and we hear a shot and then cut to Wanda trotting along the sidewalk. She is stopped outside by a police barrier, one of a crowd of spectators, helpless and stuck.

FIGURE 15.1 Wanda's "too late" arrival at the bank robbery.

This key scene in *Wanda* displays "the 'too late' narrative device" (Gaines 331) generally associated with melodrama – the character's arrival "too late" at self-recognition, knowledge, a rescue, or other forms of belatedness that would normally produce tears for "what might have been" and "what can never be." At the same time, the robbery's failure and Dennis's subsequent death depend upon the logic of "too soon" – the vault opened before 8:30 AM – another variant of melodrama's "wrong time" (331). However, *Wanda* is not stylistically melodramatic, but resolutely realist. While Linda Williams's expanded definition of a melodramatic modality as "the basic vernacular of American moving pictures" (58) would seemingly encompass such scenes of suspenseful crosscutting, *Wanda* teases but frustrates the promise of melodrama. The "too late" device here does not lead to pathos or tears – the side of melodrama Williams aligns with the woman's film or "weepie." Nor does the film offer recognition of the "character's moral value" that Williams affiliates with melodramatic action cinemas, such as the Western (58). Instead, *Wanda* resists both the tears and the "moral legibility" (53) of melodrama. Without ever bringing Wanda back into Dennis's sphere of action, or offering the melodramatic hope for "a better tomorrow" (Gaines 332), the film shows Wanda in a bar, being picked up by another man, a repetition of what Elena Gorfinkel refers to as her "aimless search for attachment... driven by transactional needs" (35) – for food, a roof over her head, and company – that led her to Dennis in the first place.

Rather than contain *Wanda* within a recognizable generic framework, the "too late" device here underscores the film's preoccupation with belatedness. Before this scene, we see Wanda fired for being "too slow" for a factory job; arriving late to a divorce and custody hearing in court; waking up almost too late to stop a one-night stand from ditching her in a motel. In tandem with showing the character's slowness, the film's aesthetics also display a preoccupation with slowness. Despite the one suspenseful bank robbery sequence, most of the film consists of long takes or episodic scenes that have the slow pace of life unfolding, rather than suspenseful action, which fit with Matthew Flanagan's characterization of slow cinema as exemplified by "the employment of (often extremely) long takes, de-centred and understated modes of storytelling, and a pronounced emphasis on quietude and the everyday." Things happen in *Wanda*: However, events feel quotidian and small because the film's aesthetic – its alternately slow and elliptical pacing, lack of musical score, low-key performances, and improvised feel – counteracts modalities of spectacle and action. "I like slow paced films" (Madison 69), Loden says, as she excoriates what she calls "slick pictures":

> They're too perfect to be believable. I don't mean just in the look. I mean in the rhythm, in the cutting, the music – everything. The slicker the technique is, the slicker the content becomes, until everything turns into Formica, including the people.
>
> *(Phillips)*

Beyond its investigation of belatedness within the narrative, and its slow aesthetic, belatedness also defines the film's reception as an overdue entry into the canon of independent American cinema and as a feminist film. The film's belated recognition depends ironically upon its appearance "too soon." *Wanda* appeared to be a minor marginal film amidst the cultural fascination with masculinist fantasies of freedom such as *Easy Rider* (1969) and mainstream Hollywood films like *Bonnie and Clyde* (1967) that examined "the undersides of the American experience" with glossy big stars (Reynaud 224). It was a woman-directed, woman-centered film that arrived just on the cusp of the women's movement, when it did not "quite fit in with the feminism of its day" (Hastie 83) and was ignored in most academic accounts of new women's cinema and feminist film theory (Reynaud 225). However, in the five decades since its initial release, *Wanda* has come to be recognized as "premature post-feminism" (Kehr) and as a significant independent film.

I am invoking the "wrong time" of melodrama and the conventions of the weepie not only as the road not taken by *Wanda* – modes that the film specifically resists – but as a way of thinking about the temporality of the film itself and the story of its reception and repeated rediscoveries. Jane Gaines suggests that melodrama teaches us that "the past, the present, and the future are in circular relation such that we invariably understand each one in terms of the others," understanding that "the present... is always modified by the past and the future, just as the past is modified by the present" (329–330). Without claiming *Wanda* as melodrama, I would suggest that a logic of what Gaines refers to as *melodramatic time* structures its reception. Rather than "the stubborn unidirectionality of historical time" (Gaines 329), the film's history needs to be understood as a "too late" recognition that revises our understanding of the past – "what might have been" – as it refigures our understanding of the present; *Wanda*'s "moral value" can then be recognized as a "too soon" forerunner in imagining a different feminine temporality, one that averts the constraints of linear time via tardiness, dawdling, drift, and the character's withdrawal from the demands of domestic and maternal labor.

Beginnings

Barbara Loden's career as a director itself has the feel of "wrong time," as it began relatively late and ended much too early. Born in 1932 in Asheville, North Carolina, and raised in rural Marion, North Carolina, by her religious grandparents, Loden went to New York at age 16 and began work as a model, pin-up, and nightclub dancer at the Copacabana. In 1956, she was hired as a regular on the *Ernie Kovacs Show* (1952–1956). She began working as an actress on Broadway in the 1957 production of *Compulsion* and then made her film debut in Elia Kazan's *Wild River* (1960). She followed this with a small, compelling role in Kazan's *Splendor in the Grass* (1961). In 1964, Loden won a Tony for her Kazan-directed performance as the thinly veiled Marilyn Monroe character, Maggie, in Arthur Miller's play *After the Fall*. She had an affair with Kazan and eventually married him in 1967. She was divorcing him at the time of her death from breast cancer in 1980 at the age of 48.

Wanda was inspired by a newspaper story Loden read about a woman who was an unwitting accomplice in a bank robbery and who, after getting a sentence of 20 years, thanked the judge.[1] Loden became fascinated with this woman: "It was a relief. She wanted an institution to supervise her and regulate her. But why did she get into that state where she thought it would be a good thing to be sent to jail?" (Thomas G17). In *Wanda*, Loden imagines this woman's state of being, locating her in the bleak landscape of Pennsylvania coal country.

Despite Loden having worked in Hollywood herself, "the film was made in express rejection of Hollywood techniques" (Phillips). Loden secured the film's modest budget of $115,000 from a friend, producer Harry Shuster. The film was shot over a period of six to ten weeks (depending on whose account you read) in Connecticut and Pennsylvania. Loden had a very small crew. She hired Nicholas Proferes, a cameraman and editor who had worked with pioneers of Direct Cinema such as Richard Leacock and the Maysles brothers; Lars Hedman, a lighting and sound technician; and "a fellow who ran errands," Christopher Cromin (acc. to Loden in Madison 68). With such a small crew, Loden described her role in making the film, somewhat ironically given the subject matter, as being "like a housewife" because "you do everything" (Thomas G17).

Loden was influenced by underground filmmaking, like that of Jonas Mekas, Andy Warhol, and Shirley Clarke, as well as by the French New Wave (Thomas G17). The film was shot on 16mm, using a hand-held camera and without much additional lighting, and was then enlarged to 35mm for screening. Loden employed mostly non-actors, many from the region, except for the professional actor Michael Higgins who plays Mr. Dennis. According to Bérénice Reynaud,

Loden and Proferes did not create storyboards or rehearse scenes, and, despite the existence of a script, the film was largely improvised in front of the camera (232). *Wanda* won the International Critics' Prize at the Venice Film Festival in 1970 and was selected for Director's Week at Cannes in 1971. It was, as Reynaud says, "a 'critical hit,' but primarily in the New York daily papers" (223).[2]

The film's opening scenes provide a snapshot of the film's style as well as Wanda's character and her environment. The film begins with shots of black rolling coal fields as a few trucks work to dig and move the coal, then a small wooden house with rugs drying on the front porch. We hear ambient sound but no music. Inside the house, we see shots of an older woman doing her rosary, a toddler who climbs into her lap, and a woman who wakes as we hear a baby crying off-screen. As the woman gets breakfast in a dingy kitchen strewn with beer bottles, a man enters the kitchen without speaking a word, and then leaves the house, slamming the door. His exit reveals a figure shrouded in a sheet, asleep on the couch. As she wakes and lifts her head, we see Loden as Wanda, her blonde hair messy and tied in a topknot. "He's mad cuz I'm here," she says, a sentence that encapsulates Wanda's relationship with men across the film.

In the next scene, an extreme long shot shows a tiny figure in white walking across paths in the dark black coal fields. The sound of a dog barking off-screen dominates then disappears as we focus in near silence on the figure walking, virtually swallowed by the landscape in a nearly two-minute long take. Eventually, we cut to a closer shot and see Wanda, impractically dressed in white sneakers and white pants, her hair in curlers wrapped in a scarf. After getting on a bus, Wanda arrives at court, late, after her husband tells the judge, "She couldn't even care enough to come to court … She doesn't care about anything … never took care of us." Accused of deserting her husband and two children, Wanda offers no objection and tells the judge, "If he wants a divorce, just give it to him," and says that her children would be "better off with him."

These opening scenes provide a sense of Wanda as a character trapped in poverty and an unwanted role as mother and wife, but never articulates her feelings or reasons for her actions. The refusal to explain shows the influence of key film movements of the late 1960s and early 1970s such as direct cinema and art cinema in its attempt to capture characters without commenting on the action and its ambiguity of meaning.

Wanda and Women's Liberation

As Victoria Hesford argues, 1970 was the "watershed" year when Women's Liberation became "a nationally mediated event" (3–5); and the film was seen, from the start, as being in conversation with women's liberation. John Crittenden, for example, wrote in his review of the film that

> it is hard to view *Wanda*… without thinking also about women's lib and sexism. It is, after all, a film directed by a woman from her own script (she

also stars) and tells the story of a woman who is the victim – in one way or another – of almost every man she meets.

Crittenden's parsing of the interest of women's lib in *Wanda* as, on the one hand, a film directed by a woman, and, on the other, about a woman oppressed by men, encapsulates the main ways the film was received.

While Loden is celebrated as a woman director, her writing and directing are taken to be autobiographical. For example, McCandlish Phillips writes that "More than merely a film she has made, Wanda is the woman Miss Loden might have become, before she discovered who she was." Loden herself frequently references her identification with the character of Wanda. She describes how in her previous career she slipped into being a "dumb blonde – sort of an object" (Phillips) and says that similar to Wanda, "I had no identity of my own. I just became whatever I thought people wanted me to become. Like Wanda, I had no focal point in my life" (Thomas G17). This reading continues today: in her recent book-length meditation on Loden, Nathalie Léger views the film as "a woman telling her own story through that of another woman" (11).

Because Loden was married to the famous director Elia Kazan, critics frequently question his role or influence on the film, undercutting somewhat her role as a female director. On an episode of *The Mike Douglas Show* (1961–1982), curated by John Lennon and Yoko Ono, for example, Douglas asks how much help Kazan provided, while John and Yoko suggest that they can identify with the woman's work being obscured or denigrated by her affiliation with the successful husband.[3] Loden claims that Kazan encouraged her and gave her confidence, but she asserts that he did not shape the film in any way (Madison 68). In his glowing review of the film, Vincent Canby says that it is impossible not to wonder what kind of help Loden got from Kazan, but, he says, "it does not have the look of a Kazan film. It looks like an original" (176).[4]

Mostly, critics question the film's feminist bonafides in regard to the film's subject matter and realist style. As Gorfinkel suggests, the film sits at "an uneasy angle to the discourse of women's liberation of its time as well as to the demand for 'positive' representations" (270). At the First International Festival of Women's Films, where *Wanda* screened in 1972, women critics made clear that they "did not want to be like the stereotypes they saw in Hollywood movies – sex objects, bitches, aggressive castrators, passive idiots, masochists and losers"; and Gloria Steinem articulated the desire for "a new kind of film in which women are shown as 'strong, compassionate, and beautiful – inside'" (Lester 26). Rather than a positive role model, reviews of the film frequently describe Wanda as "a classic loser" (Dietrich), a "passive, rather stupid young woman" (Greenspun), a "schlemiel with low self-esteem and mental limitations" (Lester 27), or, in Pauline Kael's famously vicious review, "a sad, ignorant slut" (138). While these reviews reveal second-wave feminism's limitations with regard to class – Wanda is not a "positive role model" because she is not educated – they also evince frustration with Loden's minimalist style and refusal to articulate a feminist message.

Of course, some reviews valued *Wanda* precisely because it did not come with a "message." Canby, for example, praises the film for not aligning itself with any political stance or obvious ideology. He describes Wanda as "stupid and, for the most part, without ordinary feeling" but he finds that "no special alibis are offered, at least none that can easily be laid at the feet of Society or Environment" (176). In a different vein, Marion Meade claims that it "shows what happens to a woman who rejects the traditional feminine role of wife and mother." For her, the film stages a feminist existential crisis: "Loden arrives at the crux of the problem, which is, where do you go after you reject the only life society permits? And once a woman gains her freedom, what can she do with it? The answers: no where and nothing." While these existential questions could similarly apply to other films of the period such as *Two Lane Blacktop* (1971) or *Five Easy Pieces* (1970), *Wanda* stands out as staging them in relation to societal roles proscribed to women rather than having the woman serve as a prop to the man's crisis. By 1974, the Madison Women's Collective felt a need to re-examine *Wanda* "in light of the attention of the women's movement" (67). As they acknowledge critiques of the film as too pessimistic, they state: "It matters little if *Wanda* complies with bourgeois values of success and accomplishment. What seems more relevant is that Loden as a feminist artist explores the situation of women who are suffocated and destroyed, the true 'Silent Americans'" (Madison 67).

Wanda Returns

In her crucial essay on *Wanda*, Bérénice Reynaud says that "Loden's voice seemed doomed to historical erasure" (Reynaud 223). However, *Wanda* and Loden have been undergoing a decades-long rediscovery. It was released on DVD in 2006 after Isabelle Huppert bought the rights to the film, then the UCLA film archive restored a print in 2011. In 2017 it was selected by the United States Library of Congress National Film Registry for being "culturally, historically, or aesthetically significant." Janus films released the film in 2018 and a Criterion DVD came out in March 2019.

In its rediscovery, *Wanda* has been claimed as a feminist film, in part due to its naturalist style. Gorfinkel sees the film's aesthetic as articulating "the politics of acute description as a tool of exposure, exposing without exposition" (40). For her, the film's "aesthetic of passivity and failure" (28) translates into "an acute observational precision" (36) that marks not only Wanda's oppression but also "the absence of that voice that could or would narrate its self-recognition" (37).

In opposition to complaints that Wanda was not a positive feminist role model – ambitious, successful, strong – contemporary critics underscore that neither is she a conventional housewife, and they value the film as evincing a feminist politics of refusal. Rather than rooted in domesticity, Wanda is a "woman who simply doesn't fit within her environment, doesn't belong anywhere (she's *never* shown as having a home of her own)" (Reynaud 234). Moreover, as Gorfinkel elegantly suggests, Wanda's temporality – her slowness – can be seen as a refusal of the demands of housewifery and "outside a recognizable zone of reproductive labor" (31). Anna Backman Rogers argues that the film "radically rejects the entire enterprise of liberal humanism as a positivist form of teleology" and "refuses the notion... that we are all going somewhere" (34).

Returning to the notion of *melodramatic time*, we can see that *Wanda* did not arrive too late, or too soon, but just in time. *Wanda* provided an alternative model for what feminism could be; one that was attentive to class and spoke to and for women for whom the discourse of women's liberation was not yet available but who, nonetheless, felt the stirrings of dissatisfaction identified by feminists and forged a different path; one not dictated by the forward march of positive representation and ambition but by a form of drift and withdrawal that pushed back against conventional gender roles. At the same time, *Wanda* provided a model for what independent cinema could be, offering an aesthetic and ethos that resisted easy assurances in favor of the messiness of everyday life.

Notes

1 Nathalie Léger (72–73) tracked down the original article about Alma Malone: "The Bank Robber Who Played a Dangerous Game," *Sunday Daily News*, 27 Mar. 1960.
2 Outside New York, the film was reviewed in the *Louisville Courier-Journal*, *The Hackensack Record*, *Seventeen* magazine, and the *Los Angeles Times*, but it did not gain broad attention or distribution on its release.
3 Douglas admits that he has not seen the film (season 11, episode 122, 15 February 1972).
4 In 1980, after Loden died, Kazan tried to take credit for the film's screenplay, even as he allowed that "it ended up being her screenplay instead of mine" (Duras and Kazan).

Works Cited

Backman Rogers, Anna. *Still Life: Notes on Barbara Loden's* Wanda *(1970)*. Punctum Books, 2021.
Canby, Vincent. "*Wanda*'s a Wow, So's *THX*." *New York Times*, 21 Mar. 1971, pp. 166, 176.
Crittenden. John. "Film on Born Loser May Not Pay Off." *The Record* (Hackensack, NJ), 1 Mar. 1971, p. 16.
Duras, Marguerite, and Elia Kazan. "Conversation on *Wanda* by Barbara Loden." *Comparative Cinema*, vol. 4, no. 8, 2016, pp. 12–13, http://www.ocec.eu/cinemacomparativecinema/index.php/en/33-n-8-english/446-conversation-on-wanda-by-barbara-loden. Accessed 11 Sept. 2021.
Flanagan, Matthew. "Towards an Aesthetic of Slow in Contemporary Cinema." *16:9*, vol. 6, no. 29, Nov. 2008, http://www.16-9.dk/2008-11/side11_inenglish.htm. Accessed 3 Dec. 2021.
Gaines, Jane. "Even More Tears: The *Historical Time* Theory of Melodrama." *Melodrama Unbound: Across History, Media, and National Cultures*, edited by Christine Gledhill and Linda Williams. Columbia University Press, 2018, pp. 325–339.
Gorfinkel, Elena. "Wanda's Slowness: Enduring Insignificance." *On Women's Films Across Worlds and Generations*, edited by Ivone Margulies. Bloomsbury Academic, 2019, pp. 27–48.

Greenspun, Roger. "Young Wife Fulfills Herself as a Robber: Barbara Loden's Film Opens at Cinema II: *Wanda* Improves with its Turn to Action." *New York Times*, 1 Mar. 1971, p. 22.

Hastie, Amelie. "Against Nostalgia." *Film Quarterly*, vol. 72, no. 2, pp. 81–84.

Hesford, Victoria. *Feeling Women's Liberation*. Duke University Press, 2013.

Kael, Pauline. "The Current Cinema: Eric Rohmer's Refinement." *The New Yorker*, 21 Mar. 1971, pp. 136–140.

Kehr, Dave. "New DVD's: 'Wanda.'" *New York Times*, 12 Sept. 2006, p. E2.

Léger, Nathalie. *Suite for Barbara Loden*. Translated from the French by Natasha Lehrer and Cécile Menon. Dorothy Project, 2016.

Lester, Elenore. "At Last: A Festival of Women's Films," *Ms. Magazine*, vol. 1, no. 4, Oct. 1972, pp. 25–27, 30. A reprint of "Every Day Was Ladies Day." *New York Times*, 2 July 1972, pp. 20, 22.

Madison Women's Collective. "Barbara Loden Revisited." *Women and Film*, vol. 1, no. 5–6, 1974, pp. 67–70.

Meade, Marion. "Lights! Camera! Women!" *New York Times*, 25 Apr. 1971, p. D11.

Phillips, McCandlish. "Barbara Loden Speaks of the World of 'Wanda.'" *New York Times*, 11 Mar. 1971, p. 32.

Reynaud, Bérénice. "For Wanda." *The Last Great American Picture Show: New Hollywood Cinema in the 1970s*, edited by Thomas Elsaesser et al. Amsterdam University Press, 2004, pp. 223–248.

Thomas, Kevin. "Miss Loden's 'Wanda' – 'It's Very Much Me.'" *Los Angeles Times*, 8 Apr. 1971, pp. G1, 17.

Williams, Linda. "Melodrama Revised." *Refiguring American Film Genres: History and Theory*, edited by Nick Browne. University of California Press, 1998, pp. 42–88.

16
BILLY JACK (1971)
Nicholas Godfrey

The tale of *Billy Jack* is one of the most unusual in the history of Hollywood: an unorthodox smash hit released at a moment when the lines between independent and studio films were blurring, *Billy Jack* paved the way for new distribution and marketing strategies that would become dominant in the following decades. In the film's journey to the screen, writer/director/star Tom Laughlin and co-writer/executive producer/star Delores Taylor challenged two major studios – Fox and Warner Bros. – through a series of convoluted legal battles. In regaining control of the film's distribution, Laughlin experimented with elaborate, targeted marketing campaigns, and innovations in four-walling – the process by which a movie theater is rented for a flat fee. While Laughlin cultivated his status as an outsider challenging the studio system, *Billy Jack* transcended its origins in independent exploitation cinema. Yet rather than rebuking the studio system, *Billy Jack* helped to reshape it, as Hollywood entered the age of the blockbuster.

Billy Jack's titular protagonist (played by Laughlin) is a Native American Vietnam veteran living an isolated life in Arizona. In episodic fashion, Billy Jack uses his martial arts expertise to defend the Freedom School, an alternative education and community center, including the Native American Martin (Stan Rice) and pregnant runaway teen Barbara (Julie Webb). The school's director, Jean Roberts (Delores Taylor), preaches a message of tolerance, which stands in contrast to the bigotry and violence of the decidedly monocultural local townsfolk, notably corrupt official Stuart Posner (Bert Freed) and his son Bernard (David Roya). Bernard perpetrates an escalating pattern of deviance, culminating in his raping Jean and murdering Billy Jack's protégé Martin. Billy Jack responds by killing Bernard and shooting a police officer, prompting a siege when police surround him at an abandoned Church. While Billy Jack is prepared to die in a violent confrontation, Jean persuades him to surrender by sharing her own experiences

DOI: 10.4324/9781003246930-17

FIGURE 16.1 Billy Jack leaves the town's ice cream parlor, having defended the Freedom School youth from Bernard's assaults.

of victimhood. Billy Jack brokers a truce, ensuring that the Freedom School will be allowed to continue without interference. The film ends with the local young folk standing in solidarity with him as he is led away in handcuffs.

In terms of its plot and its cinematic style, *Billy Jack* shares characteristics with many contemporaneous New Hollywood youth films that had proved commercially successful in the late 1960s: anti-authoritarian themes (Billy Jack's clashes with the local establishment), contemporary resonance (the film indirectly invokes the Red Power movement for Native American land rights and political self-determination, which was gaining prominence through protest movements including the occupation of Alcatraz from 1969 to 1971), use of location shooting (expansive Arizonan exteriors featured throughout), a soundtrack tie-in (Coven vocalist Jinx Dawson's cover of "One Tin Soldier" functions as the film's theme song), pseudo-documentary sequences (the lengthy improvisatory passages at the Freedom School), its downbeat ending (Billy Jack's gesture of self-sacrifice), and a prominent auteur – Laughlin, credited pseudonymously for his direction as T.C. Frank, yet inescapable in every aspect of the film. Despite his visibility, Laughlin disavowed the auteur mantle to an extent, and positioned his filmmaking as a highly collaborative process and a family enterprise, co-writing with and starring alongside wife Delores Taylor, with both masking their identities via various pseudonyms – T.C. Frank, Teresa and Frank Christina – while their children also appear in the film.

While Hollywood was appropriating exploitation tropes in its pursuit of the youth audience in the early 1970s, *Billy Jack* offered a unique mishmash of elements, blending aspects of the recent outlaw biker film cycle, western signifiers, eastern mysticism, and Native American ritual. The film's narrative treads some familiar cinematic terrain: the rape which motivates its main narrative conflict and transforms Billy Jack into an avenging figure is familiar grindhouse fare.[1] It has something of the exploitation "torn from the headlines" quality, transplanting its western iconography to contemporary settings and touching on some hot-button political issues of the day, including indigenous land rights and American imperialism abroad in Vietnam. The film coincides with a time when Hollywood was beginning to obliquely comment on such matters allegorically in violent historical westerns like *Soldier Blue* (1970) and *Little Big Man* (1970) which, like *Billy Jack*, were both independent productions.

Billy Jack's narrative works through a series of thematic oppositions that are the bedrock of the western genre: wilderness versus civilization, and natural justice versus the law (Kitses 11). Contemporary reception for the film tended to offer interpretations along these lines: Maurice Yacowar in the *Journal of Popular Film* dubbed Billy Jack "a new Western hero for contemporary America" (201). Laughlin himself acknowledged in a later interview that, "the western is built upon two archetypes in the American psyche: the rich cattle baron who buys off the law, and the sheepherder or common guy who rises up and fights back" (Walker 29).

More recent scholarship has focused on the film's representation of Native American characters and Vietnam veterans (Church; Lyons; Dixon), along with its general standing within an industry undergoing a dramatic transformation in the early 1970s (Cook; Rogers; Church). The character of Billy Jack reflects both tendencies: his violent resistance to police oppression is complicated by the character's Native American heritage, while Laughlin's own lack of indigenous ancestry could lead one to interpret the film's Native American cultural content, including its sensational snake ritual, as a gesture of exploitation in its own right. The film was released at a time when Hollywood's major studios were looking to innovations in the independent and exploitation sectors for solutions to worsening economic woes. But *Billy Jack*'s lasting legacy has been in establishing the template through which Hollywood would transcend the youth-baiting exploitation of the early New Hollywood period and establish a more stable economic footing by the mid-1970s.

The industrial and demographic changes that were afoot within Hollywood in the late 1960s have been well documented. The 1948 United States Supreme Court Paramount Decrees brought about the end of the vertical integration of production-distribution-exhibition, destabilizing the practices of the major motion picture companies and creating new opportunities within the independent sector. Small-time distributors like American International Pictures (AIP) managed to carve out a niche foothold, supplying cut-rate programmers at a prolific rate. The repeal of the Motion Picture Production Code and the introduction of the MPAA's film ratings in 1968 provided new opportunities for filmmakers to court the attention of young moviegoers with increasingly lurid subject matter, previously the province of the independent exploitation circuit.

Billy Jack arrived toward the end of the independent biker exploitation film cycle, which Peter Stanfield numbers at 40 films released between 1966 and 1972 (2). *Billy Jack* is a direct descendant of AIP's earlier *The Born Losers* (1967), which introduced Laughlin's Billy Jack character, a Vietnam veteran who avenges the rape of two young women by members of a violent outlaw motorcycle gang. Laughlin decided to revive his Billy Jack character for a sequel, which arrived in 1971, a year marked by Hollywood's lowest-ever weekly theater admission rate (Cook 133). In response to the manifest economic challenges of the preceding years, major motion picture companies sought to offset their liabilities through the acquisition of relatively low-risk independent, low-budget productions in the hope that they would successfully replicate the box office success of the likes of *The Graduate* (1967) and *Easy Rider* (1969), with the independent producers carrying much of the risk. Laughlin, however, challenged such arrangements from the outset with *Billy Jack*. While the film was initially financed by AIP for Laughlin's production company, National Student Film Corp. Laughlin became unhappy with perceived interference from AIP and raised sufficient financing to regain control of the picture and complete its production (Siminoski 36; AFI). Laughlin subsequently secured distribution with Twentieth Century Fox, but when Laughlin began to suspect that studio head Richard Zanuck may exert his control over the film's postproduction, Laughlin terminated the deal (AFI). He later claimed to have stolen the film's soundtrack so that the film could not be completed, and "more or less blackmailed" Fox into allowing him to buy back the film, a gesture emblematic of the iconoclastic mythology which Laughlin cultivated around himself and *Billy Jack* (Walker 25).

After shopping the film to various distributors after the Fox deal collapsed, Laughlin secured a deal with Warner Bros. The film performed respectably, particularly on the drive-in circuit and in small towns. Reviews were generally unfavorable: *Variety* labeled it an "overlength treatise on plight of American Indian" (Whit 22). Laughlin felt that Warner Bros. had not sufficiently promoted the film, particularly in major cities, and took the drastic step of suing his distributor for $34 million in damages, with the lawsuit announced in *Variety* on 9 February 1972, at a time when 300 prints remained in circulation ("Laughlin Pair" 15). Thus, the legal action provided publicity for the film while it remained in release, as did Laughlin's further promotional blitz, taking out ad space in trade papers to launch polemics against the major studios and extol his vision for a new independent film industry ("Laughlin Booklet" 4). Furthermore, Laughlin sought to expand his position in direct competition to established distributors, as *Variety* also announced in March 1972 that Taylor-Laughlin intended to fund up to eight productions per year for distribution, with Laughlin assuring filmmakers that they would have significant input into distribution and advertising arrangements ("Tom Laughlin, Fugitive" 4).[2] Laughlin's public promises of such an unusual degree of autonomy covertly bolstered the claims of his lawsuit. The publicity war played out in the trade papers throughout 1972, and Laughlin consciously positioned himself as an oppositional figure in a series of provocative interviews.

Part self-promotion, part self-mythologization, and part call for future investors, Laughlin continued to establish his iconoclastic credentials through public exposure while litigating against his distributor.

The lawsuit alleged that Warner Bros. (WB) did not fulfill its commercial obligations to the film's producers by mismanaging distribution and promotion and that the studio violated antitrust laws in restraining Laughlin's trade by controlling not only the film's distribution rights but the rights to subsequent markets and sequels. Furthermore, the lawsuit "alleged that WB used *Billy Jack* as a basis to increase its revenue from other productions 'to the detriment of the commercial and economic success of *Jack*'" ("Laughlin Pair" 15). In essence, the charge amounted to an accusation of

> monopolistic block booking… a practice in which the studio rented his film for a low fee in order to entice the exhibitor to book other Warners' films… in which the studio either had a higher front-money investment, or was to receive a higher share of the receipts.
>
> (Siminoski 36–37)

If substantiated, this charge would leave Warner Bros. in violation of the 1948 antitrust ruling that had fundamentally reshaped Hollywood's corporate structure. Perhaps fearing a precedent that would undermine the common post-divorcement practice of major studios acquiring independent productions for distribution – not to mention the possibility that any dissatisfied producer could sue a distributor for commercial misrepresentation in the event of an unsuccessful theatrical run – the suit was settled out of court. In the process, Warner Bros. returned ownership of the film, its marketing, and its distribution to the newly created Laughlin-Taylor Productions. Furthermore, Warner Bros. agreed to a 50/50 split of marketing costs and share of profits with Laughlin-Taylor for a theatrical re-release (Siminoski 37). Having retained control of the film, Laughlin now had a considerable interest in ensuring its commercial success and embarked on an auspicious promotion and re-release strategy.

Billy Jack's 1972 re-release proved unorthodox in two key regards: in the use of four-wall distribution and the deployment of saturation advertising. Four-wall distribution bypasses the normal process of distribution by renting the venue for a flat fee and enables the producer to take all of the profits from the house, cutting out the usual distribution fee – assuming, of course, that the cost of the venue is covered by the takings. David Cook notes that "combined with local television and ad campaigns, four-wall distribution allows a distributor to completely dominate a regional market for a weekend or two, generating enormous profits" (40). Frederick Wasser notes that in the 1970s, independent four-wall distributors typically operated in states like Utah, Oregon, and Florida, "demonstrat[ing] that the major studios had allowed several gaps to open up in the national audience," and suggesting that new modes of distribution may more effectively target increasingly fragmented moviegoing sectors (53). The cinemas selected for bookings for *Billy Jack*'s subsequent run were carefully chosen, typically overlooking major chains and instead contracting with second-run, independent, and neighborhood cinemas, which provided greater latitude when negotiating the terms of the rental. Theaters were selected through a meticulous process of market research: in a contemporary profile, *Variety* recounts the "Taylor-Laughlin offices in New York and Los Angeles are festooned with demographic maps and charts; heavy tomes profiling population density, transportation, facilities, age groups, income levels…" (Albarino 63).

Geographical and demographic research into screening venues was accompanied by extensive advertising campaigns, which particularly targeted local television. TV spots were stratified to reach different demographic sectors within geographic locations, showcasing various elements of the film: its martial arts action, its counterculture credentials, its romance, or the sheer novelty of its commercial success as a got-to-see factor. Within targeted areas, the advertisements were seemingly inescapable, running prominently during ad breaks. *Variety* observed, "so heavy is the campaign that it verges on the coercive – in Gotham, it is difficult to escape the *Billy Jack* message and at times during the first week it seemed that it was the only film playing the territory" (Albarino 1). In contrast to the New York example, the volume of advertising was typically affordable given that small markets were targeted (Wasser 57). The intention of these saturation campaigns, according to Taylor-Laughlin executives quoted in *Variety*, was to "make it easy and convenient to see the movie. A filmgoer should be able, after being dunned relentlessly by the campaign, to fall out of bed and find a theater where *Billy Jack* is playing" (Albarino 1, 63). *Variety* labeled the strategy "one of the boldest gambles in industry history"; in the same profile, Taylor-Laughlin executives noted that "all it took was money and nerve" – the former supplied via the coffers of Warner Bros. (1).

While the strategy directly challenged the conventional wisdom around the gatekeeping of distribution, only a major studio such as Warner Bros. had the financial wherewithal to persist with long runs and extended four-wall bookings, allowing word-of-mouth to benefit the film and maximizing repeat customers. *Billy Jack* did good business in the major cities: *Variety* reported solid takings in New York, Chicago, and Los Angeles, while the film proved particularly popular in Southern California and the Southwest. Maureen Rogers states that "*Billy Jack* accomplished what previous rural-oriented independent films could not, which was to show the profitability of regionally-distributed low-budget independent films" and, as such, argues that *Billy Jack* is a key example of the shifting boundaries between independent and studio films, and exploitation cinema in the 1970s (266).

The unorthodox *Billy Jack* strategy caught the attention of many Hollywood insiders, who were intrigued to gauge the effectiveness of the risky gambit. Of course, Laughlin had placed a target on himself with his provocative advertisements in the trades, attacking what he perceived as the greed and corruption of major motion picture companies. As *Easy Rider*'s imitators failed to land at the box office, *Billy Jack* was a rare example of a commercially successful youth film in the early 1970s, as cinema admissions reached their nadir. On the significance of *Billy Jack*'s release strategy, *Variety* wrote that "in an era when the industry is experimenting with marketing and distribution approaches in an effort to find a better way, the anatomy of *Billy Jack*'s smash is being examined with more than the usual interest" (Albarino 1). Hollywood would heed these lessons.

Billy Jack was an exercise in exploitation, not least by tapping the resources of Warner Bros. to pursue its atypical marketing and distribution strategy. Earlier variations on commercial exploitation had proved lucrative with the youth audience for major studios: violence (*Bonnie and Clyde* [1967]), sex (*The Graduate*, *Bob & Carol & Ted & Alice* [1969]) and now, the counter-cultural trappings of *Billy Jack*. Warner Bros. incorporated aspects of *Billy Jack*'s marketing and distribution strategy into its release of *The Exorcist* (1973): that film elevated the previously disreputable horror genre into a new realm of commercial viability; unlike the rough-hewn *Billy Jack*, *The Exorcist* was gilded with prestige production values and the Oscar glow of director William Friedkin, hot from *The French Connection* (1971). Its marketing campaign promised unthinkable horrors while shrouding them in mystery. As Rogers points out, it also four-walled its New York release, allowing word-of-mouth to carry the film's success, a feat earlier achieved by *Billy Jack*. In the same year, Universal also orchestrated a four-wall release for *Westworld*; in combination with *The Exorcist*, this prompted the National Association of Theater Owners to pursue a violation of the 1948 consent degrees, resulting in a ten-year moratorium on four-walling declared in 1976 (Cook 40). *Billy Jack* had wielded an unexpected influence on the major studios' marketing and distribution strategies, to the chagrin of exhibitors themselves.

Laughlin, for his part, reinvested the *Billy Jack* profits back into Taylor-Laughlin, expanding the company and subsequent productions, including its sequel *The Trial of Billy Jack* (1974). Wasser writes of the "interesting irony" in Laughlin "abandon[ing] four walling for his sequel because he could make more money demanding high up-front guarantees from the theatre owners" (57). Having established the commercial value of the *Billy Jack* product, Laughlin no longer needed to gamble with four-walling and could pursue more consistently favorable agreements with exhibitors for its sequel. The film was once again accompanied by a series of inflammatory print advertisements, this time targeting film critics (*"Billy Jack* vs. Critics"). However, it broke with Hollywood convention, pursuing a saturation release or wide opening, rather than a traditional, phased roll-out. Universal subsequently employed a similar strategy, along with a *Billy Jack*-style saturation marketing campaign, with the release of its prestige monster movie *Jaws* (1975), a film which in turn is widely regarded as establishing the contemporary blockbuster mode. *Jaws*, like *Billy Jack* and *The Godfather* (1972) before it, would yield a number of sequels, while Laughlin's *The Master Gunfighter* (1975) and subsequent *Billy Jack Goes to Washington* (1977) failed to reproduce the commercial success of the earlier installments. In the age of *Star Wars* (1977) and *Jaws 2* (1978), the increasingly sprawling and didactic *Billy Jack* sequels were highly incongruous.

Writing in *The Velvet Light Trap* in 1974, Ted Siminoski speculated on the possibility that *Billy Jack*'s distribution might fundamentally reconfigure Hollywood's power structure, concluding that

> Laughlin's approach is an attack on the studio-distributor power block. Yet, the ultimate goal is something of a throw-back to the years when a studio could produce, distribute, and exhibit films in its own theatres. If "Four-Walling" can be seen as a temporary purchase of a theatre, then Laughlin is in a position to produce, distribute, and exhibit films in his own theatres, with his own controls, and according to conditions he alone must set. As long as he has the capital to produce what he wants and distribute it as he wants, Tom Laughlin will be in an enviable, and hopefully, emulatable position.
>
> *(39)*

With the success of *Billy Jack*'s re-release, and Taylor-Laughlin's stated intent to move into the production and distribution of other projects, it did appear for a brief moment that a new, independent player might emerge as a significant challenger to the established Hollywood studio system. In analyzing experimentation with different distribution and exhibition patterns in the tumultuous 1970s, Justin Wyatt forecast that "independent film should also be searching for new ways to enter the marketplace, challenging business norms just as much as aesthetic and social ones. Only through such an agenda will independent cinema have long-lasting commercial impact" (243). In 1972, with the re-released *Billy Jack* topping the weekly box office charts, new possibilities did seem at hand.

As it stands, the legacy of *Billy Jack*'s success did not sustain Laughlin's continued filmmaking career. He cultivated his image as an outsider prepared to stand up to the greed of the Hollywood system with socially engaged filmmaking in the exploitation mode, while experimenting with novel innovations in four-wall distribution and elaborate, targeted marketing campaigns. However, despite Laughlin's wherewithal, *Billy Jack*'s success remained contingent on Warner Bros.' established power base. The film is a testament to the independent sector's capacity to produce innovation, and the major studios' equal tendency to rapidly subsume these new modes of operation to ensure continued collective control of the process of distribution.

Notes

1. Grindhouse both refers to the venues which exhibited exploitation films and functions as a discursive categorization for such films themselves.
2. A note on nomenclature: Siminoski states that at the time of *Billy Jack*'s re-release, Laughlin "set up a mini-conglomerate (Laughlin-Taylor Productions), consisting of Billy Jack Productions, Delores Taylor Productions[…], Taylor-Laughlin Distribution

Company, Billy Jack Records, and Billy Jack Television Productions" (37). Most trade sources from the time simply refer to Taylor-Laughlin, rather than the overarching Laughlin-Taylor conglomerate.

Works Cited

Albarino, Richard. "*Billy Jack* Hits Reissue Jackpot." *Variety*, 7 Nov. 1973, pp. 1, 63.
"Billy Jack." *AFI Catalog of Feature Films: The First 100 Years 1893–1993.* https://catalog.afi.com/Film/54033-BILLY-JACK?sid=d48845ea-e484-423b-be22-ec433f31cc2e&sr=10.560346&cp=1&pos=0.
"*Billy Jack* vs. Critics." *Variety*, 30 Apr. 1975, p. 5.
Church, David. "Red Power, White Movies: *Billy Jack*, *Johnny Firecloud*, and the Cultural Politics of the 'Indiansploitation' Cycle." *Grindhouse: Cultural Exchange on 42nd Street, and Beyond*, edited by Austin Fisher and Johnny Walker. Bloomsbury, 2016, pp. 197–215.
Cook, David. *Lost Illusions: American Cinema in the Shadow of Watergate and Vietnam 1970–1979.* University of California Press, 2000.
Dixon, Chris. "'No Fortunate Son': *Billy Jack* and Images of Vietnam Veterans, 1967–1977." *When the Soldiers Return: November 2007 Conference Proceedings*, University of Queensland, 2009, pp. 97–104.
Kitses, Jim. *Horizons West*. BFI, 1969.
"Laughlin Booklet Warns Investors of Film Dangers." *Variety*, 15 Mar. 1971, p. 4.
"Laughlin Pair Sue Over *Billy Jack*." *Variety*, 9 Feb. 1972, p. 15.
Lyons, Scott Richards. "*Billy Jack*." *Seeing Red – Hollywood's Pixeled Skins: American Indians and Film*, edited by LeAnne Howe et al. Michigan State University Press, 2013, pp. 158–163.
Rogers, Maureen. "Getting in on the Act: How Exploitation Cinema Remade the New Hollywood (And Vice Versa)." 2020. University of Wisconsin-Madison, PhD dissertation.
Siminoski, Ted. "The *Billy Jack* Phenomenon: Filmmaking with Independence and Control." *The Velvet Light Trap*, no. 13, Fall 1974, pp. 36–39.
Stanfield, Peter. *Hoodlum Movies: Seriality and the Outlaw Biker Film Cycle, 1966–1972.* Rutgers University Press, 2018.
"Tom Laughlin, Fugitive From WB, In N.Y. to Set Own Distribution; He's the Indie Producer at Bay." *Variety*, 15 Mar. 1971, pp. 4, 30.
Walker, Beverly. "Billy Jack vs. Hollywood." *Film Comment*, vol. 13, no. 4, July/Aug. 1977, pp. 24–30.
Wasser, Frederick. "Four Walling Exhibition: Regional Resistance to the Hollywood Film Industry." *Cinema Journal*, vol. 34, no. 2, 1995, pp. 51–65.
Whit. "Film Reviews: *Billy Jack*." *Variety*, 5 May 1971, p. 22.
Wyatt, Justin. "Revisiting 1970s' Independent Distribution and Marketing Strategies." *Contemporary American Independent Film: From the Margins to the Mainstream*, edited by Chris Holmlund and Justin Wyatt. Routledge, 2005, pp. 229–244.
Yacowar, Maurice. "Private and Public Visions: *Zabriskie Point* and *Billy Jack*." *Journal of Popular Film*, vol. 1, no. 3, 1972, pp. 197–207.

17

DEEP THROAT (1972)

José B. Capino

Deep Throat is a landmark of US independent cinema for several reasons. Half a century after its June 1972 premiere, it is still believed to be one of the most profitable US films released in theaters. Made on a budget of between $25,000 and 40,000 (Ephron 14) by a hairdresser-turned-porn filmmaker named Gerard Damiano (credited as Jerry Gerard), *Deep Throat* made $30,000 during opening week in a single theater, beating all Hollywood films shown in New York's Broadway area ("Pictures Grosses").

The New Yorker's Ralph Blumenthal, whose article "Porno Chic" gave a name to the epoch of trendy adult films in the United States, reported that *Deep Throat* brought in an average of 5000 patrons a week in that one cinema. *Variety* noted that the audience was "made up of off-duty policemen, judges and United Nations employees, many of them repeaters" ("UN & Show Types Dig 'Deep Throat'"). *Time* magazine related that the movie had already played in 60 US cities by January 1973, roughly six months after its premiere. Estimates of *Deep Throat's* lifetime worldwide revenue vary, ranging from $50 million to a dubious $600 million (Stoltenberg; Hiltzik).

Just as remarkable as its strong box office showing, Damiano's pornographic film was caught up in national politics. An editor at *The Washington Post* famously used the film's title as a pseudonym for the FBI official who leaked information that led to President Richard M. Nixon's downfall. The moniker was not assigned due to the intelligence officer's sexual conduct but because he provided the damning information on 'deep background,' a journalistic term meaning that information can be used but no source would be identified (Woodward and Bernstein 4). Decades after the incident, the film's producer recalled that the White House borrowed a print "for a private screening" by Nixon (Weiner 6).

Historians and critics exclude hardcore adult movies from accounts of independent filmmaking for several reasons, including a moralistic bias against erotic

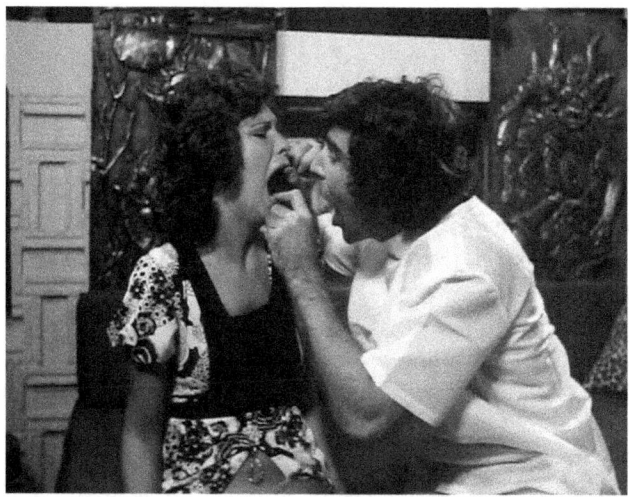

FIGURE 17.1 Dr. Young examines Linda and identifies the source of her trouble in *Deep Throat*.

content. The truth is that the overwhelming majority of hardcore pornography in the 1970s and early 1980s was made outside the so-called studio system and the conglomerate-owned entertainment behemoths of the era, thus satisfying the most basic criterion of independence in the movie industry. Though a handful of adult film studios operated in the 1970s – such as Jaguar Productions, an outfit that produced and distributed all-male adult films to "a fixed circuit of twenty-two theaters" (Turan and Zito 193) – they were also not part of Hollywood's financing and distribution arms. *Deep Throat* did not originate in adult movie studios either, but with Damiano's outfit and Bryanston Distributing, a firm with ties to organized crime and which counted releasing a 1970 documentary on Muhammad Ali among its few credits.

Deep Throat's phenomenal box office success came unexpectedly, in part because Damiano's film was no more explicit than the erotic movies that preceded or played alongside it. Hardcore film pornography had already been around in the United States since about 1915–1917, the period when a short film known as *A Free Ride* – which reportedly depicted fellatio and group sex, among others – was believed to have been made (Lewis 196). Hardcore films circulated in the ensuing decades through mail-order sales, private screenings, and in peep shows (single-person viewing booths) at adult bookstores. At the end of the 1960s, film exhibitors began showing hardcore pornography in major cities such as San Francisco, New York, and Dallas (Turan and Zito 80). Advertising materials often touted the films' self-imposed X rating (or the made-up XXX rating) to lure viewers with the promise of salacious content.[1]

Some of the earliest hardcore fare exhibited in cinemas included short films made by theater owners themselves while others were packaged as sex education (aka "marriage manual") films or documentaries about sexual subcultures. The documentary pretense was employed both to circumvent anti-obscenity laws and shield viewers from the stigma of watching pornography. Damiano made two such films before *Deep Throat*, including *Sex USA* (1971). In 1971, two hardcore films with fictional narratives resoundingly affirmed the viability of feature-length adult films: Bill Osco's *Mona, The Virgin Nymph* (1970), the hardcore feature that the makers of *Deep Throat* purportedly sought to emulate, and Wakefield Poole's *Boys in the Sand* (1971), a feature-length trilogy of gay hardcore shorts that drew sell-out crowds and received attention from alternative and mainstream press outlets.

Deep Throat brought unprecedented cultural visibility to pornography. Though the sexual revolution was already a decade old in the United States, Damiano's film caused an uproar among moral conservatives who turned it – and pornographic movies more generally – into a new front in the nation's ongoing culture wars. In Milwaukee, anti-porn protesters tried to repel Chicagoans flocking to see the film after it was banned in Illinois. The protesters slowed down admissions by paying for tickets in pennies or $100 bills (Smith 14). In Michigan, a garbage collector refused service to a cinema screening the film (Turan and Zito 143).

The film's visibility inspired numerous lawsuits, including 11 obscenity cases. The US Department of Justice (DOJ) brought the costliest suit, taking legal action against five corporations and a dozen individuals involved in federal transportation and conspiracy statutes against the interstate shipment of obscene materials. Pandering to Christian conservatives, the DOJ filed its case in the Bible Belt and designated an outspoken church elder, Assistant US Attorney Larry Parrish, as a prosecutor. Parrish reportedly told a witness for the prosecution that he "would rather see dope flowing in the streets of this country than see a sexually-oriented movie" (Brescia 6). He also indicted leading man Harry Reems even though the performer was paid only $250 for the film and was not involved in its distribution ("Pictures" 32).

One can only speculate on what made the otherwise slight 62-minute piece of filmed erotica a breakthrough success, why it gained such notoriety, and why it continues to hold cultural significance in the wake of so many far more gimmicky, explicit, technically polished, and even artistically successful porn films. Consider, for instance, that Damiano's follow-up film, *The Devil in Miss Jones* (1973), fetched $7.7 million at the box office, surpassing the $4.6 million gross reported at that time by *Deep Throat* (Wyatt 253). *Devil* also received glowing reviews from mainstream publications like *Variety,* which made the grandiose claim that with Damiano's sophomore erotic narrative, "the hardcore porno feature approaches an 'art form'" (Verrill, "The Devil" 18). To be sure, the outsize publicity given by the press, the lawsuits, and protesters helped make *Deep Throat* an unlikely cultural phenomenon. The editor of *Screw*, a popular magazine covering New York's sexual subcultures, grabbed some credit for the film's success, specifically for hyping up the "porno" with a 100% score on its "Peter

Meter" ratings scheme and feeding stories about Lovelace to the publication's hundred thousand readers. The film's visual and narrative centering of oral sex – a subject that the public was evidently curious about – might have helped as well, reinforced as it was by numerous references in reviews and articles to Lovelace's eye-popping renditions of the titular erotic act.

Big Screen Appeal

One of the keys to understanding the success that *Deep Throat* enjoyed despite the cultural stigma of its content is through an appreciation of the film's generic composition. Film scholar Linda Williams has compared feature-length porn films to musicals, "with sexual number[s] taking the place of musical number[s]" (Williams 124). While this notion is useful in apprehending the hidden structure of adult films, many feature-length hardcore porn in the 1970s and 1980s overtly followed the conventions of other, more popular genres in mainstream filmmaking, resulting in such hybrids as science fiction porn, porn Westerns, and horror porn. *Deep Throat* contains elements of drama and romance, but it is primarily a comedy, a genre that might have made the film seem more legitimate to the viewing public. Indeed, Nora Ephron, then a popular columnist in *Esquire*, recalled hearing that *Deep Throat* was "not only the best film of its kind but actually funny" (Ephron 14).

From start to finish, *Deep Throat* is replete with all kinds of humor. Following a laughable disclaimer tacked on to the beginning of the film that posits what follows as an illustration of Sigmund Freud's notion of the oral stage in human psychosexual development, *Deep Throat* begins with a serio-comic prelude about the ennui gripping the protagonist Linda (Linda Lovelace), an attractive woman who is seen traveling around Southeast Florida with a pensive expression. During conversations with her housemate Helen (Dolly Sharp), Linda bemoans that she has "never gotten off" with men despite her promiscuity. "There should be bells ringing, dams bursting, bombs going off…something!" she says exasperatedly.

If narratives that make light of erotic frustration seem familiar, it is because they are a perennial feature of sex comedies (McDonald 49). The dogged quest for successful coupling drives many sex comedies (Krutnik and Neale 170). Ludicrously enough, *Deep Throat's* heroine can only conceive of erotic fulfillment in ultra-violent metaphors. She also illustrates a facile gloss on another Freudian notion, specifically illustrating that women do not know what they really want.

As in other sex comedies, a series of amusing misadventures ensues as Helen assists Linda in seeking sexual gratification. Helen fills their house with random men who will take turns trying to please Linda. One of the would-be lovers is played by Damiano who lisps his way through a non-sexual cameo appearance. Following the event, Linda declares that while she entertained 14 men and "got off…a hundred times… [it was still] not real" because of the absence of the bells, dams bursting, and bombs during coitus. Helen gives another zinger of a comeback, asking Linda if she was hoping to level a town instead of getting off.

During another brainstorming session, Helen encourages Linda to see a psychiatrist named Dr. Young, adding that he is "really horny." The introduction of Dr. Young registers both a conspicuous shift to a wackier comedic tone and a self-conscious parody of clichés in pornography. The tone shifts with the use of zany sound effects, whimsical props, and broader comedic acting in scenes at the doctor's clinic. Dr. Young affects a phony British accent and brazenly engages in sexual acts with his nurse (played by Carol Connors) and patients. Following a clumsy "internal examination" of Linda, he declares that her sexual woes are not psychological but rather due to the fact that her clitoris has been misplaced by nature from her vagina to somewhere "deep down in the bottom of your throat." The abnormally located sex organ is a sly reference to the ancient notion of the "wandering womb" or uterus, thought to be the cause of hysteria, a spurious malady invoked to control female sexuality and behavior.

As for the trope of lecherous physicians like Dr. Young, it was already trite when *Deep Throat* was released, having been the subject of numerous stag and sexploitation films from earlier decades (Lauro and Rabkin 93). Viewed in a fittingly generous light, Damiano self-consciously recycles this cliché to poke fun not only at unethical medical professionals but also at unimaginatively crass and sometimes clever movie pornographers. Damiano casts Dr. Young as a quack from the character's initial appearance in the film. The physician inexplicably blows soap bubbles while seeing a patient and then uses the plastic bubble wand as a substitute for an ophthalmoscope. The film employs cartoonishly loud sound effects to accompany the appearance of bubbles. Synthesized electronic music with an Alberti bass pattern reminiscent of sitcom themes plays loudly under the dialogue to add wackiness.[2] The film makes its parody of Dr. Young's fraudulence more laughable by showing that his silly remedies end up working anyway. For instance, he guides Helen on how to achieve orgasm by choosing well-endowed men (such as himself) and then asking her to perform oral sex in a manner suggested by the film's title. Linda takes in the full length of Dr. Young's member and finally experiences sexual bliss.

Deep Throat uses a slyly cinematic orchestration of visuals, narrative clichés, sound effects, and music to represent Linda's sexual fulfillment. As the erotic therapy intensifies, Damiano (who also edited and scripted the film) crosscuts images of Helen and Dr. Young's oral coitus with archival footage and synchronized sound effects of bells being rung by mechanical figurines, fireworks exploding in the night sky, and a space rocket taking off. The rhythm of the intercutting drastically quickens as Dr. Young reaches sexual climax and Linda achieves fulfillment. A catchy theme song, along with nonsensical lyrics reminiscent of Dadaist poetry, enhances the humor in the sequence.

In interviews about the film, Damiano took pride in the oft-mentioned montage, relating that he chose to "fly down to Washington, go to the National Archives" to "get [footage of] rocket flights" (Smith 51). He fails to take credit, however, for reflexively drawing attention to the mechanics of representing erotic pleasure through cinematic means in adult movies. During the montage, the crescendo of sound and images suggests Linda and Dr. Young's sense of disorientation at reaching climax. Damiano moves the camera in a frenzy between faces and body parts, zooms in and out of the archival footage, and layers the various sound effects in such a way that the sound of ringing bells temporally and synesthetically matches images of exploding fireworks.

The success of Dr. Young's "cure" farcically turns into a big problem both for him and his patient. Linda offers to be a bride or sex slave to the doctor just to get regular access to his penis. Yet again, Dr. Young engages in medical malpractice by sending Linda to "treat" a fellow patient named Wilbur Wang (William Love), a socially awkward man obsessed with fantasies of robbing and assaulting women.

As usual, Dr. Young's quackery inexplicably produces favorable results. Linda initially rejects Wilbur's flaccid penis because she does not think it would grow to nine inches, the length she believes is necessary to please her. As it turns out, Mr. Wang is even more physically gifted than Dr. Young, ostensibly packing a 13-inch member. The orgasm montage of fellatio, fireworks, bells, and launching rockets recurs as Linda sexually climaxes anew.

Comedic and Cinematic

Deep Throat employs several other elements found in sex comedies, including making fun of awkward erotic situations and generating humor with crude jokes and explicit sight gags. The film often pushes these elements to the extreme, taking full advantage of the expressive freedom created by the growing tolerance of pornography in the United States at that time. As well, the film seems to be exploring how to turn pornography into comedy or to create a superior amalgam of both genres, optimizing the pornographic film's capacity not just to arouse viewers but generate distinctly cinematic sexual humor as well. Apart from enhancing popular appeal and entertainment value, the infusion of comedy broadens the adult film's expressive possibilities.

A particularly memorable scene shows Linda walking in on her roommate as she sits atop their kitchen table with her legs spread wide while a man performs oral service. Completely unfazed by Linda's presence, Helen interrupts the man – apparently the grocer's delivery person – and, with a deadpan expression, inquires "Mind if I smoke…while you eat?" As soon as the man nods, she shoves his face back into her genitals. Apart from the sight gag, wordplay, and better-than-usual comedic acting, this scene draws laughter for depicting the savage erotic hunger of a divorcee who stayed too long in an unsatisfying marriage.

Several moments in *Deep Throat* offer even more outrageous renditions of comedic pornography, combining bawdier verbal humor, depictions of genital activity, and music than featured earlier in the film. For instance, a raunchy but narratively superfluous episode depicts one of Linda's sex therapy patients inserting a hollow glass dildo into her vagina, filling it alternately with wine and Coke, and then sipping them with a transparent tube. A modified version of the soft drinks' 1970s jingle, with the famous slogan "it's the real thing," plays on the soundtrack. The explicit gag associates an iconic American product with perverse eroticism in addition to showcasing an unusual sexual kink. This example illustrates how *Deep Throat* uses not only sound design but slapstick – a mode of comedy centered on physical humor (Krutnik and Neale 21) – to devise novel fusions of comedy and pornography. Such grotesquely hilarious combinations of graphic nudity, sexual scenarios, and showy filmmaking have since become prevalent in adult movies, suggesting *Deep Throat's* enduring influence.

The film's abundant use of comedy fittingly became one of the focal points of publicity and debates around the film. *Screw* praised the film "not only for its raging raunch, but more startlingly for its wit, wild humor, fine acting and hilarious story" (Smith 31). A reviewer from *Variety* wrote approvingly of the "tongue-in-cheek approach to conventional hetero hardcore" and the "dishing out [of] enough laughs with the main course" (Verrill, "Deep Throat").

Damiano grabbed credit for putting humorous erotica on screen, claiming that

> Up until *Throat*, the worst thing you could do in sex film was comedy... The minute you get away from eroticism or make fun of it, you lose it, and that's why it was death to try and do it prior to this.
>
> *(Smith 43)*

He was misinformed, however. Blending comedy and sex had already been a winning formula since the late 1950s for Russ Meyer, a former still photographer for *Playboy* magazine who made a string of humorous films with plenty of female nudity. Capitalizing on a 1957 court ruling in New York that helped end the ban on screen nudity there and elsewhere, Meyer made *The Immoral Mr. Teas* (1959), a comedic "nudie" film about a dentist who suffers a head injury and thinks he has suddenly acquired the ability to mentally strip women of their clothing (Lewis 199). The hit spawned over a hundred imitations, indicating the effectiveness of using comedy both to reduce the social stigma of prurient content and enhance its commercial prospects (Turan and Zito 13). Among those who also found success making independently produced comedies (and other genre films) that were replete with nudity was Doris Wishman, one of the few female directors in the United States at that time.

The defenders of *Deep Throat* also invoked its characterization as a comedy to fight the DOJ's obscenity case. Since the law defined obscenity in terms of an utter lack of redeeming social purpose, defense attorneys and witnesses cited the film's humor as an indicator of its "artistic value." In his opening remarks, the chief defense counsel contended that *Deep Throat* "was a comedy, [a] satire on psychiatrists based on their patients' dealing[s] with sexual problems of individuals and the solution of those sex problems" ("'Deep Throat's' Defense: It's Art" 7). Interestingly, Judge Joel Tyler, the New York Criminal Court magistrate who was the first to rule against *Deep Throat* in an obscenity case, expressed a diametrically opposed view of the film's comedic elements. Criticizing the "ebullience and gusto" with which the sex acts were performed, he wrote that the "alleged 'humor' of the film is sick" (Smith 182). The scene involving the sex toy and Coke, he groaned, was a "clinical example of extraordinary perversion, degeneracy and possible amentia."

In 1979, appeals to the DOJ's case against *Deep Throat* were finally decided, resulting in acquittal or lighter sentences for the film's distributor and other defendants. The following year, Lovelace published a memoir titled *Ordeal* in which she alleged that her former husband and manager, J.R. Traynor, beat her up after the first day of shooting in a fit of jealousy over her interactions with Reems and other men on set.[3] She wrote "If you saw the movie, you must have seen the huge black-and-blue marks on my thighs and legs" (Lovelace and McGrady 133). Indeed, around 58 minutes into the film, Wilbur caresses an area of Linda's leg with large bruises inadequately concealed with make-up. *Ordeal* served as the basis of a Hollywood film called *Lovelace* (2013) that brought her story and that of *Deep Throat* to a new generation of viewers more than a decade after she died of injuries from a car accident.

Lovelace's criticism of *Deep Throat* was preceded by others. The film became a lightning rod for the feminist backlash against pornography upon its release. Amid the 1960s–1970s struggle for equal rights and social advancement known as "women's liberation," writers and activists decried the film's portrayal of women and the exploitation of females in pornography more generally. Ephron narrated her reaction after seeing the film with friends: "'Demeaning to women,' I wailed as we walked away from the theater" (Ephron 20).

Criticism of the film's depiction of women did not fall clearly along the lines of gender identity and political beliefs, however. For instance, Judge Tyler sounded much like a liberal feminist when he opined that *Deep Throat* "denigrates the integrity of man and particularly, woman...objectifying and insulting woman" (Smith 283).

The divergent responses to the film's treatment of women's sexuality are not surprising, however, if only because pornography is a transgressive form of social fantasy that does not lend itself to simplistic moral judgments and sweeping claims about its effects on individuals and society. As regards sexual politics and social relevance, smut is often as incoherent as it is offensive. Ellen Willis was thus right to blast *Deep Throat's* "most grotesque premise" (219), its absurdist fantasy of women designed by nature to please men constantly through oral sex. As well, Ephron and Judge Tyler – strange bedfellows – both had good reasons to question the film's seemingly progressive depiction of female sexual agency when so much of the narrative is patently chauvinistic.

Notes

1 The voluntary film rating system adopted by the MPPA in 1968 allowed producers, distributors and exhibitors to assign an X rating to their productions. Unlike other

ratings such as G, PG, and R, X did not come with an MPPA production seal, forcing distributors "to seek a payoff on parallel, limited theatrical circuit" instead of being able to play in most movie theaters (Lewis 189).
2 Thanks to Jonathon Smith for helping me describe the music.
3 During a 1983 hearing for a Minneapolis ordinance that aimed to ban pornography, Lovelace famously pronounced that "Every time someone sees 'Deep Throat,' they're seeing me being raped" (Allen 16).

Works Cited

Allen, Martha. "Hearing on Pornography Law Stirs Voices, But No Consensus." *Minneapolis Star and Tribune*, 13 Dec. 1983, p. 16.

Brescia, Matty. "Background Revelations Emerge At Memphis Trial Re 'Throat.'" *Variety*, Mar. 1976, pp. 6, 32.

"'Deep Throat's' Defense: It's Art." *Variety*, 10 Mar. 1976.

Di Lauro, Al, and Gerald Rabkin. *Dirty Movies: An Illustrated History of the Stag Film, 1915–1970*. Chelsea House, 1976.

Ephron, Nora. "Women." *Esquire*, Feb. 1973, pp. 14, 20, 22.

Hiltzik, Michael. "'Deep Throat' Numbers Just Don't Add Up." *Los Angeles Times*, 24 Feb. 2005.

Krutnik, Frank, and Steve Neale. *Popular Film and Television Comedy*. Routledge, 2006.

Lewis, Jon. *Hollywood v. Hard Core: How the Struggle Over Censorship Created the Modern Film Industry*. NYU Press, 2002.

Lovelace, Linda, and Mike McGrady. *Ordeal*. Citadel Press, 1980.

McDonald, Tamar Jeffers. *Romantic Comedy: Boy Meets Girl Meets Genre*. Wallflower, 2007.

"Pictures Grosses: N.Y. Wet Weekend, Over-Showcased; 'Great Dictator' $26,844, Top Chaplin; Deep Throat' 30G: 'Fillmore' $21,500…" *Variety*, June 1972, pp. 8, 14.

Smith, Richard. *Getting Into Deep Throat*. Playboy Press, 1973.

Stolenberg, John. "Anti-Porn Forces Call For Deep Throat Boycott." *Gay Community News*, June 1980, p. 1.

Turan, Kenneth, and Stephen Zito. *Sinema: American Pornographic Films and The People Who Make Them*. Praeger, 1974.

"UN & Show Types Dig 'Deep Throat.'" *Variety*, Aug. 1972, pp. 1, 62.

Verrill, Addison. "Film Reviews: Deep Throat." *Variety*, June 1972, p. 26.

———. "Film Reviews: The Devil in Miss Jones." *Variety*, Feb. 1973, pp. 18, 24.

Weiner, Rex. "Lost & Found: Sore from 'Throat.'" *Variety*, Aug. 1997, p. 6.

Williams, Linda. *Hard Core: Power, Pleasure, and the "Frenzy of the Visible."* Expanded ed., University of California Press, 1999.

Willis, Ellen. "Hard to Swallow." *New York Review of Books*, Jan. 1973, pp. 216–220.

Woodward, Bob, and Carl Bernstein. *The Secret Man: The Story of Watergate's Deep Throat*. Simon & Schuster, 2005.

Wyatt, Justin. "The Stigma of X: Adult Cinema and the Institution of the MPAA Ratings System." *Controlling Hollywood: Censorship and Regulation in the Studio Era*, edited by Matthew Bernstein. Rutgers University Press, 1999, pp. 238–264.

18

PINK FLAMINGOS (1972)

Nathan Koob

As a filmmaker who has only written and directed his own original screenplays while filming only in his hometown of Baltimore, Maryland, across a decades-long career, it would be difficult to think of John Waters as anything but an independent American filmmaker. His career path was also an unusual one coming not from film school, television, music videos, or even industrial filmmaking, but instead from midnight movies. Midnight movies, when defined as unusual films with highly active audiences that were exhibited around midnight, are often studied as a genre. They are perhaps more strikingly, though, a clear set of exhibition practices designed to market exclusivity to promote new content to a wider audience. It was this "business" side of midnight that most attracted John Waters and the strategies that defined his career. Waters is the only major midnight movie director who claims to have made a film specifically *for* the midnight movie circuit so he could craft the film for an existing and profitable audience (*Midnight Movies*). Beginning with self-assigned "shock value" to attract attention, Waters's early films were constructed around a clear set of marketing strategies designed to appeal to burgeoning untapped audiences. *Pink Flamingos* (1972) was a call to those who had the type of spectatorial awareness that had been cultivated by the midnight movies, namely an interest in "bad taste" that eschewed the more pretentious connotations of contemporary art house theaters. Analyzing *Pink Flamingos*'s release as a midnight movie reveals the strategies that midnight movie exhibition uses to negotiate audiences' interest in more "outsider" content within a more popular filmgoing context, making midnight movies a place for both new filmmakers and new audiences.

Pink Flamingos is certainly an independent film, though perhaps it does not fit as neatly into the connotations of the term during the early 1970s. Emanuel Levy notes, "in the past, the tag 'independent' was applied to low-budget pictures

FIGURE 18.1 "Filth are my politics" proclaims Divine (Glenn Milstead) in a scene near the end of *Pink Flamingos*.

that played for a week in the local art houses. Referring to nonstudio [sic], low-budget movies, distributed by a maverick company, the label had clearer meaning" (3). Waters self-financed his early films (through borrowing money largely from his father), learned filmmaking on his own, acted in multiple film crew roles, served as his own publicist, and distributed his films by driving around with prints in the back of his car.[1] Despite all these connections, given Waters's shocking content, it is quite difficult to place Waters among Levy's lofty "art houses." Also not particularly fitting art house cinema of the period is the fact that Waters presents unusual content in particularly standard narrative structures. As Matthew Tinkcom has argued,

> Waters' cinema is unwaveringly a narrative one and demonstrates a commitment to reaching audiences more customarily alienated from avant-garde practices and more oriented toward feature films; although his films offer strong story lines and distinct characters (hallmarks of the dominant practices of Hollywood studio productions), Waters has over the longer duration of his cinema imported nondominant artistic visual forms and forms of intellectual investments into his movies, all the while producing cinematic narrative.
>
> *(158)*

While Waters's content clearly pushes normative boundaries, his cinematic form and mode of narrative address distinctly engage with popular Hollywood conventions. This potential discrepancy aligns very well when viewing Waters as an adept self-promoter interested in a career as a filmmaker – he provides new content with a more accessible mode of address.

Due to this combination of elements, it is difficult to look at *Pink Flamingos* and envision it playing to a standard art house theater audience. The plot is a glorification of bad taste. The narrative of the film involves two Baltimore matriarchs fighting over who is the filthiest person alive in a fairly simple three-act structure. The problem between the matriarchs is introduced, the group in power shifts hands midway through the film, and our protagonists ultimately win the day. The film contains a female protagonist played by a man (Divine) dressed in what Waters has frequently referred to as "drag terrorism," a simulated sex scene wherein a live chicken is killed, an incestual act, a forced pregnancy business, a man who makes his anus sing, and of course the ever-famous finale in which lead character Divine watches a dog defecate and then eats the feces all in one continuous take.[2]

The extremity of Waters's content elements often acts as a parody of traditional normative structures, such as a love scene that comments on the strange nature of Hollywood love scenes. *Pink Flamingos* contains a scene where Connie Marvell (Mink Stole) and Raymond Marvell (David Lochary) suck on each other's toes in an extended 180-degree position – an act that Waters refers to as "shrimping." While the scene does contain both male and female full-frontal nudity, it is not particularly pornographic in that attention is specifically drawn *away* from genitalia. Connie and Raymond remain in long shot, both having the entire length of their absurdly flailing bodies in the frame for the entirety of the scene, thus muting the impact of the explicit nudity which appears only incidental to their seemingly unclassifiable activity. At one point Connie exclaims, "I want to finish you off!" which signifies that some form of sexual climax can be reached in this act. The absurdity of the scene easily suggests that whether the act is kissing, hugging, sex, or toe sucking, they all involve mashing various body parts together for pleasure, which, when thought of in those terms, makes almost all erotic encounters, and love scenes, seem rather ridiculous.

While art house theaters were in many ways the place to screen independent cinema at the time, *Pink Flamingos*'s content was likely far too lowbrow to speak to art house film audiences at large. Regarding the art house theater exhibition, media historian Barbara Wilinsky states "Art houses offered an image of a more intellectual filmgoing experience. Attached to this image were notions of high culture, art, and prestige" (3). While art houses were certainly offering a "different" experience, Waters's films do not scream "high culture" or "prestige" but instead very much scream at those concepts. The ways in which art house theaters positioned themselves as offering alternative content to the mainstream, however, was certainly a tactic that could benefit independent filmmakers who fit into an alternative niche. Rather than adjust his tastes to those of the established art houses, Waters sought out other avenues of independence. He made a "commercial" film in the sense that its purpose was to make money and get people into the theater. With a tiny budget of only $10,000, shock value was the quickest way he found to do that. In fact, he has described *Pink Flamingos* as the most commercial film ever made: "It had the showmanship, it was made to pack in an audience" (Ives 19). Waters's own cinephilic knowledge combined with his talents at self-promotion and business savvy made him realize that the burgeoning trend of midnight movies was where he belonged.

Understanding how Waters fits into this trend requires some attention to the development of midnight movies as an exhibition strategy. In 1970, with *El Topo*, Ben Barenholtz, theater manager for the Elgin Cinema in New York's Chelsea District, became the widely cited father of midnight movies. He thought he could take further advantage of the 24-hour day and market more unusual independent films to a wider audience by making the screenings solely in the late-night hour. Despite only doing one show per night around midnight with minimal advertisement Barenholtz found, "By the end of the first week, we were selling out every seat in the theater – 600 seats – every night and it lasted more than a year" (Strauss). Barenholtz's strategy proved not only sensible but also popular. In this format, audiences showed great interest in a diverse range of content such as through the reggae soundtrack of *The Harder They Come* (1972), the experimental narrative of *Eraserhead* (1977), or the drug-induced violence of *El Topo*. These screenings also fostered lively audience participation involving yelling and throwing things at the screen. With the aberrant content found in many of these films, Barenholtz showed that a certain cultural understanding of bad taste was very marketable if made exclusive to the right crowd.

Midnight movies' popularity came in part through a constructed veil of exclusivity onto the event of watching new content, allowing discerning audiences to revel in so-called "bad taste" in new ways. John Waters outlines this approach:

> To me, bad taste is what entertainment is all about...but one must remember that there is such a thing as good bad taste and bad bad taste...I could make a ninety-minute film of people getting their limbs hacked off, but this would only be bad bad taste and not very stylish or original. To understand bad taste one must have very good taste.
>
> (Waters, Shock Value 2)

Waters repackage bad taste as something that can be special and rewarding. By anticipating the reactions and word-of-mouth following the shock of ending his film with Divine eating actual dog feces, Waters constructed a form of bad taste that would both extend into the cultural consciousness and promote his film. Audiences could not believe what they were seeing at these exclusive screenings and wanted to share that "secret" experience with others. Midnight movies became both a place and a mode to support the kind of audience appreciation that Waters looked to cultivate into a filmmaking career.

This midnight movie strategy also has important connections to the earlier Underground Cinema movement of the 1960s which firmly connected non-mainstream cinema content with more exclusive screenings. The Underground film movement – including such filmmakers as Kenneth Anger, Rosa Von Praunheim, The Kuchar Brothers, and Jack Smith – was often defined by films that acted as a celebration of then-perceived "abnormal" lifestyles which craft a space positioned as inside (or underneath) the public sphere. J. Hoberman and Jonathan Rosenbaum write about the movement as a sort of beacon to independent and alternative filmmaking stating: "the underground invented a grassroots alternative to 'straight' movies, television, and theater" (73). Homosexual culture and desire, male and female nudity, violence, and gore were all frequently featured in Underground cinema. Largely due to these content choices, Underground films had a number of problems with legality, censorship, and distribution. Therefore, it behooved Underground cinema screenings to occur late at night when the concerned and "impressionable" public was most likely asleep. This practice of exclusive screenings ensured those who were not "in the know" would not be aware of them. Their alternative content also began speaking to an audience who was ready to engage with things considered too outside popular culture yet could still be appreciated by select audiences. This is precisely the connection midnight movies exploited.

When midnight movies arrived in the early 1970s, they did not have the same legal restrictions on their content due to the intervening switch from the Production Code to the rating system in 1968 and the development of the X-rating. As Justin Wyatt notes, the X-rating could be self-applied and left the door open to much broader content as well as the distribution of independent films (238). Now any film could be screened under the X-rating as long as the filmmaker or distributor could find a theater that would exhibit it. The X-rating helped to move films with so-called aberrant content out of the Underground, opening up the possibility for them to screen openly, theatrically, and perhaps even profitably. Connotations of pornography followed quickly, but this was something that midnight movies also functioned to redefine. Waters recalls, "Even though *Pink Flamingos* has a self-imposed X-rating, it is hardly a sex movie. The 'raincoat brigade' always stomps out of the theater when they discover the X is for hideousness rather than dirtiness" (*Shock Value* 14–15). This framing of X as something other than sexual titillation is a key strategy for midnight movies which showed many unrated or X-rated films that would be difficult to classify as pornography. It is thus the X-rating that most directly opened the door to the legal exhibition of alternative film content and gave these films the freedom to exhibit in independent theaters across the country.

It is in this context and history that *Pink Flamingos* was deftly inserted. The initial release by New Line severely mis-characterized the film by not putting it out as a midnight movie which is surprising in that New Line had recently found success with re-releasing *Reefer Madness* (1936) on a midnight movie-style exhibition circuit (Samuels 101). Waters recalls,

> I knew the film would work on a national level…I contacted New Line Cinema, a New York firm that had previously turned [me] down…but had encouraged me to come back when I had something 'more polished.' I had followed New Line's history in *Variety* and liked the offbeat selection

> of films they distributed...New Line agreed to take on the film but was unsure of how to market it. They tried it in a gay porno house in Boston... David Lochary went to spy and reported that 'there was more action in the bathrooms than in the theater.'
>
> *(Shock Value 20–21)*

Waters, who was aware of midnight movies and their burgeoning success with alternative audiences, knew this was the wrong choice of venue. "After many frantic fraudulent credit-card phone calls to New Line," he recalled, "I convinced them to open it at midnight at the Elgin Theater, the most popular film-buff hangout in Manhattan" (*Shock Value* 21).

In its advertising, *Pink Flamingos* did not receive much fanfare, which was typical for midnight movies at the Elgin. Whereas the premiere midnight movie hit *El Topo* had a tiny one-line notice tacked onto the regular daily theater listing in the *New York Times*, *Pink Flamingos* received only a one-time one-line notice in the *Village Voice*. As Stuart Samuels explains, Barenholtz was in part trying to circumvent bad critical reviews, which might keep audiences away while simultaneously banking on good word-of-mouth reviews (27–28). Word-of-mouth advertising quickly became a defining feature of the midnight movie. Films such as *Night of the Living Dead* (1968) and *The Rocky Horror Picture Show* (1975), which had earlier experienced failed or mediocre runs in more traditional theaters under more standard release strategies, were wildly successful as movies on the midnight circuit. Keeping the film playing only late at night with minimal-to-no advertising clearly created that 'in the know' appeal and fostered word-of-mouth as there was really no other way for such large audiences to hear about these films. Once this turned into sellout crowds, it was all the more important to rely primarily on word-of-mouth and the midnight screening time to keep the veneer of exclusivity.

Pink Flamingos had two things going for it: the audiences flocking to midnight movies and John Waters as a promoter. Waters talked approximately a hundred people into attending the first screening at the Elgin on 16 February 1973, convincing the Elgin to try it again the next weekend. When reminiscing about this night Waters recounts, "As I nervously approached the Elgin the following weekend, I was startled and thrilled to see a huge line wrapped around the block... word of mouth did it all" (*Shock Value* 21). To be a true success, though, *Pink Flamingos* needed to work at more than one theater and, beyond the Elgin, word-of-mouth advertising did not do it all.

Prints of midnight movie films would travel around and play at small venues, usually near college campuses, to audiences who were intrigued by the edgier content and participatory screenings. The films could stay for many weeks, or even just play at a one-night festival before moving on to another town. Once a given midnight movie proved to be a success in New York it would branch out to Los Angeles and Washington DC (Samuels 11). After a decent run in these three cities, it typically had created enough buzz in factions of the popular press to instill some curiosity in other parts of the country. A successful midnight movie would then expand further across the United States and often even in Europe on a theatrical run (Welling; Waller). The theatrical exhibition of midnight movies has certain significance in that exhibitors often advertised the films in local newspapers and these advertisements reveal some of the negotiations midnight movies had to make to appeal to local audiences.

Newspaper advertisements for *Pink Flamingos* outside of the Elgin usually took Waters's lead and sold the film as a new and entertaining form of bad taste. The most common version of this was just a printing of the film's main tagline "an exercise in poor taste." Some theaters offered specific warnings to patrons such as in *The New Mexican* which reads, "This film has been called an exercise in bad taste, and fully deserves this reputation. If you offend easily, don't come!" Bad taste, then, clearly acts as a marker being redefined by these theaters as a particular type of unique draw to audiences.

Presumably, due to the X-rating already gaining a strong connection to adult film, *Pink Flamingos*, was most often advertised on pages of city papers where adult film theaters also advertised. At the time, many theaters were unsure how to advertise X-rated content (Wyatt 248). However, even when the page was strongly adult-film oriented, the advertising strategy of theaters shows an aversion to connect *Pink Flamingos* with pornography. After all, the type of bad taste in *Pink Flamingos* and the type represented by pornography were not the same thing. An ad in the *Albuquerque Journal*, for instance, noted "Free KRST Barf Bags" for attendees of Waters's film.

A series of ads in *The Albuquerque Tribune* for the Pyramid Theater, which ran from 28 August to 14 September 1974, show interesting shifts in marketing strategies. The first ads in this period look very much like a non-professional advertisement. Several features look as though they have been unevenly scratched onto the image. In all versions, the ad most prominently displays the title in its common cursive font and underneath keeps the tagline, "an exercise in poor taste" in a slightly smaller font. Notably, the theater states at the very bottom of the ad, "No one will be admitted in the last 7 minutes of Pink Flamingos" thus creating both a feeling of exclusivity as well as a mystery of what could be so important during the last seven minutes. Near the bottom, in all capitalized letters providing significant emphasis, the ad states, "Warhol Tells Fellini. 'You Must See Pink Flamingos.'" The idea that Warhol, an Underground artist, feels that Fellini, a European artist, would like this film makes *Pink Flamingos* a sort of bridge between these two types of audiences. Both of these connections seem particularly out of place in the midst of pornography ads and are clearly trying to sell this film by making unusual associations.

The advertisement also works to create a sort of re-inventing of connotations of the X-rating. Just above the Warhol quote, looking very uneven and possibly scratched into the ad, reads, "Rated XXXX." The use of four X's is of course a rating that does not officially exist. In terms of the MPAA, any rating involving more than one X does not exist. While three X's has become a recognized rating for adult films to suggest even more explicit content, four X's does not really mean anything except something *other than* three X's. Finally, and of particular interest, the top border of the ad contains a row of small X's, further connecting this film to the idea of an extremely restricted, potentially depraved, rating and as something unique. It also seems to act almost as a border to the ad directly on top of this one, which was unmistakably for an adult film theater, thus clearly separating them. Overall ads for the film follow the outline set by Waters and midnight movies in general in repackaging "bad taste" as an exclusive cinema for more popular audiences.

Pink Flamingos ran steadily around the country throughout most of the 1970s and made millions.[3] As his career progressed, Waters recognized that once the age of videotape arrived the distribution model changed enough that the films which initially garnered him fame and recognition could not have the same effect.

> Midnight movies were over, you know? I'd be a fool to make a midnight movie now... Video is midnight movies now... I know the business well enough now to know that that would be like saying I want to make an underground movie. You know, the times are different.
>
> *(Stevenson 80)*

At this point, Waters goes on to further success with still quirky but ultimately also more conventional films such as *Hairspray* (1988) and *Serial Mom* (1994). Looking back, on paper, there was little about *Pink Flamingos* that would seem saleable within more traditional exhibition strategies, but the veneer of exclusivity cultivated by the midnight movies created an environment where more fringe films like *Pink Flamingos* could have a chance at success. Due to this, the intersection of John Waters and midnight movie exhibition strategies are a key moment in the transformation and expansion of American independent cinema.

Notes

1 Waters outlines these early days of his career in great detail in *Shock Value*. See also Maier, *Low Budget Hell*.
2 There is too much to say about Divine for this chapter, but I do want to note that Waters has routinely stated that Glenn Milstead, the actor who played Divine, did not think of himself as female. Waters asserts that while Divine is a female character, and the professional name he was best known by, Divine ultimately was both a character name and acting persona for Glenn Milstead.
3 Some estimates put it around $7 million, but given its itinerant nature exact numbers are difficult to track.

Works Cited

Advertisement. *The Albuquerque Tribune* (Albuquerque, NM), 6 Sept. 1974, p. C8.
Advertisement. *The Albuquerque Tribune* (Albuquerque, NM), 10 Sept. 1974, p. C7.

Advertisement. *Albuquerque Journal* (Albuquerque, NM), 22 Oct. 1976, p. C9.
Advertisement. *The New Mexican* (Santa Fe, NM), 13 Apr. 1977, p. A15.
Austin, Bruce A. "Portrait of a Cult Film Audience." *Journal of Communication*, vol. 31, no. 2, 1981, pp. 43–54.
Hoberman, J. and Jonathan Rosenbaum. *Midnight Movies*. Harper and Row, 1983.
Ives, John G. *American Originals: John Waters*. Thunder's Mouth Press, 1992.
Levy, Emanuel. *Cinema of Outsiders*. NYU Press, 1990.
Maier, Robert. *Low Budget Hell*. Full Page Publishing, 2011.
Samuels, Stuart. *Midnight Movies*. Collier, 1983.
Stevenson, Jack. *Desperate Visions*. Creation Books, 1996.
Strauss, Neil. "It Must Be Midnight and It Must be Weird." *New York Times*, 7 July 1995, p. C1.
Strout, Andrea. "In the Midnight Hour." *American Film*, vol. 6, no. 4, 1981, pp. 34–37, 72–73.
Tinkcom, Matthew. *Working Like a Homosexual*. Duke University Press, 2002.
Waller, Gregory A. "Midnight Movies." *The Cult Film Experience: Beyond All Reason*, edited by J.P. Telotte. University of Texas Press, 1991, pp. 167–186.
Waters, John. *Crackpot: The Obsessions of John Waters*. 9th ed., Scribner, 2003.
———. *Shock Value*. 3rd ed., Thunder's Mouth Press, 2005.
Welling, David. *Cinema Houston*. University of Texas Press, 2007.
Wilinsky, Barbara. *Sure Seaters: The Emergence of Art House Cinema*. University of Minnesota Press, 2001.
Wyatt, Justin. "The Stigma of X: Adult Cinema and the Institution of the MPAA Ratings System." *Controlling Hollywood: Censorship and Regulation in the Studio Era*, edited by Matthew Bernstein. Rutgers University Press, 1999, pp. 238–263.

19

DARK STAR (1974)

Nitin Govil

A rare combination of relativity physics and country and western music, *Dark Star*'s "Benson, Arizona" theme meditates on the romantic possibilities of time dilation. The lyrics also reverberate with our cultish attachments to privileged cinematic moments and events:

> Now the years pull us apart
> I am young and now you're old
> But you're still in my heart
> And the memory won't grow cold.

Perhaps we too can shuttle back and forth across spacetime, exploring *Dark Star*'s passionate claim on that which endures – in this case, the persistence of independent artistry in an otherwise inhospitable universe governed by mainstream commercial and industrial priorities.

[Interstellar Space, 18 Parsecs from Earth – c. 2250]

The scout ship *Dark Star* and its crew of four have spent 20 years bombing unstable planets to clear the way for human colonization. Back on Earth, mission control has lost interest and has informed the crew that their request for safety shielding has been denied due to government cutbacks. Human fodder for the mission, they have been forced to sleep in the food-storage facility. They have also run out of toilet paper. With their semi-conscious commander in cryogenic suspension and integral ship systems failing, the remaining crew yearns to be free from their bleak routine and participate in something more meaningful.

After a series of malfunctions compromise *Dark Star*'s weapon systems, Lieutenant Doolittle engages one of the sentient bombs in a phenomenological debate

FIGURE 19.1 *Dark Star*'s quarters, anticipating the "lived-in" aesthetics of science fiction dystopias to come.

on the nature of existence, convincing the weapon to deactivate itself. His colleague Talby is accidentally ejected into space and Doolittle goes after him while the bomb, in a fit of pique, reconsiders its decision and decides to detonate itself, destroying the ship and killing the remaining crewmembers. Talby survives, joining with an orbiting asteroid swarm on a trillion-year communion around the cosmos. Doolittle fashions a surfboard from *Dark Star*'s debris and joyfully skims the atmosphere of a nearby planet to the tune of "Benson, Arizona," before wiping out, vaporizing in the glorious blaze of reentry.

[Earth – Present Day]

The closing scenes of *Dark Star* imagine a creative liberation. This freedom from a restrictive, industrialized monotony cleverly invokes the film's production history and the independent spirit of youthful aspiration. In other words, *Dark Star* is something of a student film, albeit one stitched unevenly into a feature. Its constructed nature is a consequence of its origins as a partially completed University of Southern California (USC) thesis project, subsequently expanded to an 80-minute film. Its unfinished edges mark the audacity of filmmakers aiming higher than their humble budget, an ambition evidenced by the film's remarkable production design and special effects. The enterprising, bricoleur sensibility of John Carpenter and Dan O'Bannon, the film's co-creators, has earned *Dark Star*'s a vaulted status as an enduring cult favorite.

Like many other cult films, *Dark Star* is celebrated for its excesses and incoherencies, while its roughness belies a surprising emotional subtlety, which is not surprising given how personal a vision the film is. *Dark Star* is a celebration of artistic ingenuity under intense administrative and budgetary constraints: a testimony to seeing things through. While *Dark Star*'s on-screen crew suffers from a lack of motivation, the film's stewards held onto their creation with an unrelenting determination. "Fortunately, both Dan and I believed in the film so much that we weren't going to let it die – ever," notes Carpenter, adding that, "we did everything we could do to keep it alive" (Crawley 29).

Dark Star was shot over four years, beginning its journey in 1970 as a "thesis film for a degree [Carpenter] never got" (McCarthy 22). At the time, USC's ownership of student work meant that the fiercely independent creators had to pilfer the footage from their film school overlords, expanding *Dark Star*'s initial "truck drivers in space" idea into the full-length picture and launching the careers of many of the most significant figures in the new Hollywood. The film's tightly knit group of collaborators included the cartoonist Ron Cobb, whose design for the exterior of the spaceship propelled him to design aliens for *Star Wars*'s cantina sequence, produce concept artwork for *Alien* (1979), and devise the mothership for the Special Edition of *Close Encounters of the Third Kind* (1979). None benefited more from *Dark Star* than its creators. Dan O'Bannon, who co-wrote, designed, edited, and starred (as Pinback) in the film, followed up *Dark Star* by designing the special effects for Alejandro Jodorowsky's ultimately unsuccessful adaptation of *Dune*. Soon afterward, George Lucas approached O'Bannon to do effects work for *Star Wars*. O'Bannon would go on to reimagine *Dark Star* as a horror film by co-creating the original story for *Alien*. Notably, Pinback's encounters with *Dark Star*'s beachball extraterrestrial, who taunts its human handler in slapstick fashion, would serve as the basis for *Alien*'s terrifying confrontation with the monster in the spaceship's air ducts. O'Bannon also created other enduring works in the genre, including writing for the animated anthology film *Heavy Metal* (1981), launching a franchise by writing and directing *The Return of The Living Dead* (1985), and adapting a Philip K. Dick short story for *Total Recall* (1990).

When it comes to the career of director John Carpenter, *Dark Star* is often criticized in terms of the more commercially successful films that followed it. Carpenter's second feature, the remarkable genre pastiche *Assault on Precinct 13* (1976) is sometimes seen as his "proper" first film, especially after its success on the festival circuit in the United Kingdom. The monumental success of his third film, *Halloween* (1978), has come to symbolize the commercial potential of independent genre filmmaking. In the wake of these successes, *Dark Star* was re-released and seen widely in the late 1970s and during the ensuing home video boom, leading Carpenter to speak wistfully of its delayed recognition, commenting that "I thought that as soon as it came out, everyone was going to know what a talented and wonderful person I am. Naturally, that didn't happen" (Walker 13). Twenty years after that comment, critic Kent Jones would claim, "Carpenter stands alone as the last great genre filmmaker in America" (Jones 26).

Genre is crucial to understanding *Dark Star*. O'Bannon touted it as "an absurdist comedy within the science fiction genre, sort of a *Waiting for Godot* in outer space," adding that the film intended to capture "the free-thinking sense of wonder" of classic 1950s science fiction cinema while retaining the sophistication of contemporary SF without "the sterility" (Winogura 4–7). By invoking the metaphor of a coldly antiseptic and mainstream art, O'Bannon is targeting *2001: A Space Odyssey* (1968), one of two references to Stanley Kubrick's work in the 1975 US poster for *Dark Star*, which called the film "The Spaced Out Odyssey" and "The Mission of the Strangelove Generation." The second reference, to *Dr. Strangelove or: How I Learned to Stop Worrying and Love the Bomb* (1964), offers a more charitable recognition of the lineage of *Dark Star*'s bleak comedy, as well as a nod to Kubrick's interest in documenting humankind's desire to break free of a machinic, clockwork existence. However, *Dark Star*'s fantasy of independence from the doldrums of everyday subservience seems hard to reconcile with Carpenter's professed desire for the opportunities and guarantees of the mainstream studio system.

Admiring those directors – Howard Hawks above all – who "loved the process," Carpenter insists that "being independent and having control of your movie as a director is the biggest issue there is; all other issues pale in comparison with that" (Borst 171). For Carpenter, genre offers a solution to the creative problem of imitation and innovation and *Dark Star* marks an entry point into filmmaking under financial and logistical constraints. In many subsequent films, Carpenter has embraced a lauded budgetary restraint, creatively repurposing locations and objects in the service of efficiency. He has also resourcefully used set design and music (often his own synthesizer compositions) to create an ambient sense of atmosphere: a mood that suffuses the dramatic moral universe of the "genre filmmaker" – an appellation that remains a badge of honor for the director. As Anne Billson astutely observes, Carpenter has remained within the genre frameworks laid out in his earliest work, marking a distinctively different trajectory from other filmmakers of his generation like Francis Ford Coppola and Martin Scorsese, who moved on from early forays in genre pictures (18). Carpenter has also rejected the occasional genre revisionism of his new Hollywood compatriots, perhaps less unnerved by convention and willing to play within genre boundaries through a sly subtlety rather than overt rejection. As Carpenter puts it, "it's accepted wisdom that the minute you have the chance, you get out of the genre you came in. I don't think that's right" (Billson 19).

In terms of what *Dark Star* represented for its creators, the aspiration seems to have been modeled, in part, on the career trajectory of another filmmaker on the rise. George Lucas's 1967 short film, *THX 1138 4EB*, was a low-budget science fiction dystopia made while he was a student at USC. Winning awards at a national student film competition garnered attention not only from the mainstream press but also from Hollywood as well, leading to a feature deal at Warner Bros. and American Zoetrope. The 1971 feature release, *THX 1138*, launched Lucas's storied career. Carpenter and O'Bannon, who knew Lucas socially, wanted *their* student project to open the doors to a filmmaking career (Zinoman 54–55). Comparisons between the two films and their creators have provided some animated critical debate. Notably, the British film periodical *Sight and Sound* made some sharp distinctions as *Dark Star* began to be seen more widely in the late 1970s:

> Unlike Lucas, Carpenter seems less concerned with updating the old Hollywood ways than with trying to prove that nothing in his best of all possible worlds need ever have changed; and the difference between their respective first features, *THX 1138* and *Dark Star*, is very marked, notably by a rather strained quest for significance on the part of Lucas, and a steely determination in Carpenter to have no truck with messages.
>
> *(Milne and Combs 94)*

[Los Angeles, University of Southern California – c.1970s]

Transplanted to Los Angeles from Kentucky and Missouri, USC film school students John Carpenter and Dan O'Bannon were opposites in terms of personality. Yet, they shared tastes in film and literature, especially lowbrow 1950s genre pictures and H.P. Lovecraft stories of weird horror and fantasy. Beginning in July 1970, the two USC students collaborated on a 40-page script for Carpenter's thesis film, followed by two years of intermittent shooting whenever limited funds permitted. Usually on weekends, along with friends and fellow film school students and graduates, the team shot in and around USC, including on the film school soundstage and in a student union closet. After several name changes, including *The Electric Dutchman*, *Dark Star* was agreed upon as the title for the project.

Fans of classic science fiction cinema, *Dark Star*'s co-creators recognized the aesthetic achievements of recent additions to the canon. However, they remained, as O'Bannon put it, "contemptuous of pomposity," endeavoring to create a work that was "equally a sly deadpan mockery of sci-fi traditions and a put down of corny or heroic values" (148). This dual purpose is especially clear in O'Bannon's contributions to the film, which combined makeshift, often comedic allusions to higher-budgeted projects with a radically inventive spirit. O'Bannon worked extensively in designing and fabricating *Dark Star*'s sets, costumes, paintings, miniatures, and props, including the five-foot diameter beach ball alien. He fashioned spacesuits from vacuum cleaner hoses, cupcake tins, ice cube trays, air-conditioning insulation, and Styrofoam packaging liberated from LA's garbage dumpsters. O'Bannon's curation of *Dark Star*'s speculative junk vibe helped to further codify the "used future" look popularized by Lucas's *THX-1138*, inspiring science fiction film aesthetics for decades to come.

While economic necessity helped to guide *Dark Star*'s aesthetic and design innovations, the film's navigation of the vagaries of independent production was less certain. Over the course of a few years, the *Dark Star* team had accumulated 16mm footage without a commercial release in mind at a cost of $6000 to the director. Desiring to escape what he called USC's "exploitative" ownership of student work," Carpenter and his lawyers took the film away from the school. Having paid for equipment, stock, and processing, the school could only voice its displeasure publicly, complaining that the director had engaged in "a rip-off, pure and simple" (Fox 7). Now in full possession of a 45-minute film, too long for the festival circuit, Carpenter and O'Bannon worked on expanding it to an 80-minute feature, aided in 1972 by a $10,000 investment from Jack Murphy, a Canadian producer. Looking back on this frenetic period, O'Bannon reminisced:

> we only had one option – go ahead and shoot some extra scenes. Expanding it meant we were going to have to shoot a lot of scenes that were filler, and that would lessen the tightness of the story and make it into an episodic film. It was kind of disappointing, because that meant we had to go from the most-impressive student film ever made to one of the cheapest features in history.
> *(Gaspard 81)*

Dark Star's creators were also able to blow the film up to 35mm when independent producer Jack H. Harris, who had financed the horror classic *The Blob* (1958), agreed to provide finishing funds and buy the film outright. With added sequences, reshoots, animation, mixing, and music – including Carpenter's country music score, a swipe at *2001*'s extensive use of classical music – the final cost for *Dark Star* came to $60,000. Carpenter spent over $10,000 of his own money and he and O'Bannon were paid only $5000 for their efforts on the film. When Jack Harris ran into unforeseen financial setbacks, he sold the film to Bryanston Distributors, which had just successfully released *The Texas Chain Saw Massacre* (1974). *Dark Star* was released in a few dozen theaters in Los Angeles in January 1975, marketed unsuccessfully to a counterculture audience assumed to identify with the anti-establishment, hippie demeanor of the film's protagonists. The film's marketing and distribution were not at all helped by Bryanston's ongoing legal difficulties around its distribution of *Deep Throat* (1972), which led to the distributor filing for bankruptcy.

Dark Star remained hard to see until 1977, when it won 5th place at the Los Angeles International Filmex festival and was re-released in 16mm for Christmas 1977, in the wake of the success of *Star Wars*. This prompted some observers to hope that "the best sf film of 1974" would "now be recognized for the major achievement that it is" (Brosnan 229–230). Attuned to its parodic sensibilities, the venerable British satire magazine, *Punch*, called *Dark Star* "twenty times the intellectual superior of *Star Wars* or *Close Encounters*" (Took 448). With the festival success of Carpenter's *Assault on Precinct '13* and the commercial success of *Halloween* in the late 1970s, excitement around the director's debut feature would continue to grow. "Bombed Out in Space with a Spaced-Out Bomb!" exclaimed noted artist Tom Chantrell's poster for *Dark Star*'s initial release in the United Kingdom in 1978.

[Earth – Present Day]

When *Dark Star*'s crew finally receives a message back from the Earth, their supercilious military control officer announces that their mission has been getting "good reviews in the trades." *Dark Star* sardonically adds film criticism to its long list of institutional targets, anticipating its belated recognition in the mainstream press. Even before its completion, however, the film was recognized by genre fandom's cult audience. No publication has sustained the film with greater fanfare than *Cinefantastique*, the venerated monster film magazine, which has lionized *Dark Star* over the years. In a 1973 issue, its first engagement with the film as a 40-minute rough cut, *Cinefantastique* celebrated its professional production design and special effects, eagerly anticipating its release (Winogura 4–7). The magazine returned to the film in many subsequent interviews with its principals over the years, repeatedly celebrating both O'Bannon and Carpenter, who had published his own fanzine, *Fantastic Films Illustrated*, as a 16-year-old in 1965. In its first review of the film, *Cinefantastique* noted:

> On the surface, *Dark Star* is a terribly funny satire on spacemen, space movies, companionship, and steely nerves under pressure. In other words, all eventually goes haywire. Underneath the amazingly slick, professional exterior is a very messy movie, messy by choice and not by default. There is a casual charm to the film's variety of invention, punctuated by moments of pure and spontaneous laughter that make it an instant camp classic of sorts. Although much of the visual humor is organic to the structure, the feeling is still one of a pasted together comic book that's mockingly sophisticated, with sloppy, pointless continuity.
>
> *(Winogura 40)*

The magazine smartly captures the deliberate wildness of *Dark Star*, asserting its immediate relevance as an "instant camp classic." This appraisal supports Umberto Eco's argument about the "glorious incoherence" of cult film. "To become cult," Eco insists, "a movie should not display a central idea but many" (4). However, while cult films are a "hodgepodge of sensational scenes strung together implausibly" (1), Eco maintains the "organic" nature of cult film imperfection. This is illustrated by *Dark Star*'s marshaling of an insular address that enables the cult film's select rather than mass audience. The film accomplishes this in multiple ways: through a "sustained parody" (Sobchack 165) that serves to frame and connect otherwise farfetched scenarios; and, in its violation of slick aesthetic and narrative norms, a clearly avowed resistance to the techno-optimism of its generic predecessors.

Watching *Dark Star* with the hindsight of history, one is struck by how the film's "slapstick and stoner chic" (Brookes) taps into the generalized apathy of its time. While its creators explicitly rejected the socio-political determinism of "message movies," the crew's fantasy about escaping the button-pushing pointlessness of their mission can be situated within broader contexts. The ennui of the film's on-screen principals taps into a public indifference to the space program, with 1972's Apollo 17 serving as the final manned lunar landing to date. More significantly, the film reflects a growing lack of faith in American institutions during the height of the Watergate affair. Furthermore, *Dark Star* is positioned within an erosion of national confidence during a sustained political and military crisis, with the deterioration of the crew mirrored by the deterioration of the ship's governing systems. As Jason Zinoman suggests, the film's representations of aimlessness echoes "some of the reports coming back from Vietnam of military operations that go bad due to tedium" (55).

In the film, *Dark Star*'s crew broods over their lack of motivation, imploring their handlers to just give "them something to blow up!" Their only sense of purpose seems to be in collective response to their masculine alienation (O'Bannon 148), signified by the production design of the crew's quarters, which resemble a cramped military barracks, filthy university dorm room, and cluttered fraternity house, personalized with pin-up girls and graffiti (see Figure 19.1). Here, the crew revels in the spirit of nonconformity, inaugurating an independent sense of institutional critique that would emerge as a significant theme in Carpenter's future work. John Thonen notes:

> Beyond reinforcing Carpenter's theme of isolation, Dark Star also introduces another element of the director's oeuvre: the sure and certain failure of civilization's most revered institutions. Over the course of his career, Carpenter will repeatedly skewer the very cornerstones of civilization: in the John Carpenter universe, man's modern icons – religion, science, law, government – are all destined to fail or betray us.
>
> *(65)*

While touching on political commentary, *Dark Star* is also defined by the intense circumstances of its creation, especially the relationship between O'Bannon and Carpenter, who squabbled for years after the film's release, arguing over credit for its accomplishments. Both saw themselves reflected in the film. Bemoaning its commercial failure, Carpenter said that the film was "youthful, naïve, and innocent. It was exactly what I was" (Peary 54). O'Bannon claimed that the alienated, slacker sensibility of the film derived from the "loneliness, the hassles, the poverty of [his] student life" at USC (Mancini 54).

Yet we should not fully embrace this collapse between the filmmakers and their characters. In form and substance, *Dark Star* is an independent film about independent artistry thwarting the forces of mundane, institutionalized professionalism. The film stages an allegorical conflict between the prerogatives of mission command and the imaginative desires of the crew to escape the gloom of a routinized bureaucratic existence. Decades into his now-legendary career, Carpenter would speak of filmmaking as "the endless confrontation between management and creativity" (Taub 84). That tension is present in his first film. Ultimately, Doolittle and Talby's fantasies and realization of escape are that of the independent artist, burning brightly beyond the administrative mandates of authority.

[School of Cinematic Arts, USC – 2023]

George Lucas's name is emblazoned over the entrance of one of the two buildings where I work at USC. He has given a huge amount to his alma mater, including $175 million for the new cinematic arts complex in 2006. The other building is named for Steven Spielberg, who was denied admission by the film school on three occasions. He has also donated prodigiously and serves as a university trustee.

Cinema students often meet in the courtyard between these two buildings named for the school's most famous graduate and its most famous reject. Though they are surrounded by monuments to institutionalized film industry glory, I imagine that more than a few enterprising students identify with the rebelliously independent spirit of those that blazed away on a different path, particularly the director who dropped out and the hijacked film that enabled his escape 50 years ago. If Lucas and Spielberg represent the mainstream glow of Hollywood, Carpenter and O'Bannon's film surely remains its darker star, shining with an alternate luminosity.

Works Cited

Billson, Anne. *The Thing*. BFI, 1997.
Borst, Ronald V. "An Interview with John Carpenter." *The Cinema of John Carpenter: The Technique of Terror*, edited by Ian Conrich and David Woods. Wallflower, 2004, pp. 167–179.
Brookes, Lawrence. "Looking Back at John Carpenter's Dark Star." *Den of Geek* [online], 19 June 2011, https://www.denofgeek.com/movies/looking-back-at-john-carpenters-dark-star/.
Brosnan, John. *Future Tense: The Cinema of Science Fiction*. St. Martin's Press, 1978.
Crawley, Tony. "*Dark Star* Interview: The Film that Refused to Die." *Starburst*, vol. 1, no. 5, Dec. 1978, pp. 28–31.
Eco, Umberto. "'Casablanca': Cult Movies and Intertextual Collage." *SubStance*, vol. 14, no. 2, 1985, pp. 3–12.
Fox, Jordan. "Carpenter: Riding High on Horror." *Cinefantastique*, vol. 10, no. 1, 1980, pp. 40–42.
Gaspard, John. *Fast, Cheap & Under Control: Lessons Learned from the Greatest Low-budget Movies of All Time*. Michael Wiese Productions, 2006.
Jones, Kent. "American Movie Classic." *Film Comment*, vol. 35, no. 1, Jan./Feb. 1999, pp. 26–31.
Mancini, Marc. "Thunder and Lightning." *Film Comment*, vol. 19, no. 4, July 1983, pp. 52–55.
McCarthy, Todd. "Trick or Treat." *Film Comment*, vol. 16, no. 1, Jan. 1980, pp. 22–24.
Milne, Tom, and Richard Combs. "The Man in the Cryogenic Freezer." *Sight and Sound*, vol. 47, no. 2, Spring 1978, pp. 94–98.
O'Bannon, Dan. "The Remaking of Dark Star." *Omni's Screen Flights, Screen Fantasies: The Future According to Science Fiction Cinema*, edited by Danny Peary. Dolphin, 1984, pp. 147–151.
Peary, Danny. *Cult Movies 2*. Delta, 1983.

Sobchack, Vivian. *The Limits of Infinity: The American Science Film*. A.S. Barnes, 1980.
Taub, Eric. *Gaffers, Grips, and Best Boys*. St. Martin's Press, 1994.
Thonen, John. "John Carpenter: Cinema of Isolation." *Cinefantastique*, vol. 30, no. 7/8, Oct. 1998, pp. 64–73.
Took, Barry. "Watch This Space." *Punch*, 15 Mar. 1978, p. 448.
Walker, Jeff. "The Man Who Eyed Laura Mars has a Happy 'Halloween.'" *Feature*, Jan. 1979, p. 12.
Winogura, Dale. "Dark Star." *Cinefantastique*, vol. 2, no. 3, 1973, pp. 4–7.
———. "Dark Star." Film review. *Cinefantastique*, vol. 3, no. 4, 1974, p. 40.
Yager, John. "Benson, Arizona." Lyrics by Bill Taylor, music by John Carpenter. *Dark Star: Original Motion Picture Soundtrack*. Citadel, 1980. Vinyl LP.
Zinoman, Jason. *Shock Value: How a Few Eccentric Outsiders Gave Us Nightmares, Conquered Hollywood, and Invented Modern Horror*. Penguin, 2011.

20

A VERY NATURAL THING (1974)

Matt Connolly

"When is someone going to make a good gay film?" Such was the question posed by Chuck Ortleb in his review of a movie that purported to answer that call (19). *A Very Natural Thing*, Christopher Larkin's drama about a gay man navigating the complexities of romantic coupledom in post-Stonewall New York City, was (as noted with winking hyperbole by gay critic and activist Vito Russo) "expected to rival *Gone with the Wind* in scope and popularity and solve the problem of oppression in the bargain" when it premiered in June 1974 (207). His citing of both the film's hoped for "popularity" and ambitions to "solve the problem of oppression" highlights the ambiguities of what constituted a "good gay film" in the mid-1970s.

Did the "goodness" of *A Very Natural Thing* rest on its ability to transcend decades of cinematic stereotypes and reflect the sexual, ideological, and social realities of LGBTQ life? Or was the film to be judged as a "good" commercial object, a film that could show the economic viability of queer filmmaking to the power players of the American film industry? That both *A Very Natural Thing*'s representational and commercial reputations proved more equivocal than any constituency had hoped for offers a window into the tensions, limitations, and possibilities that shaped queer filmmaking in the gay and lesbian liberation era.

A Very Natural Thing follows David (Robert Joel), a former monk who has begun a new career as a high school English teacher in New York City. He has also recently come out of the closet. While out at a gay bar, David meets Mark (Curt Gareth), a hunky and self-possessed business executive. David and Mark go home together and soon begin dating. Even during the couple's honeymoon period (captured via a montage of strolls through Central Park and weekends reading the *New York Times*), tensions emerge. David longs for a committed partnership, while Mark embraces libidinal freedom within the city's gay social scene. Moving in together exacerbates these conflicts and eventually, the couple

DOI: 10.4324/9781003246930-21

FIGURE 20.1 David (Robert Joel) and Mark (Curt Gareth) contemplate domestic life in *A Very Natural Thing*.

breaks up. David drifts in a post-relationship malaise before stumbling onto the 1973 Christopher Street Gay Pride March, where he meets Jason (Bo White), a recently divorced photographer. It is now David who resists Jason's desire to quickly cohabitate and asks for a compromise between emotional commitment and individual exploration. The film concludes with David and Jason running naked along an empty Provincetown beach in an image of sexual freedom and romantic tenderness.

Scholarship on *A Very Natural Thing* foregrounds its attempt to balance acknowledgment of erotic openness with the representation of more "conventional" gay coupledom, a theme that is crucial if not unique to Larkin's film. As Cüneyt Çakırlar and Gary Needham note, "post-Stonewall gay cinema has frequently explored this tension between the monogamous and the promiscuous in non-pornographic films" (405). Early writings by Russo and Thomas Waugh highlight this negotiation between radical possibilities and romantic traditionalism, with Waugh arguing that *A Very Natural Thing* approaches "a recognition of the inadequacy of traditional romantic patterns for gay lifestyles" which "is ultimately undercut by the sun, the sand, and the pair of gleaming asses in the waves" highlighted in the film's final images (21–22). Subsequent mentions within broader histories of LGBTQ cinema – first by Richard Dyer and later by Harry M. Benshoff and Sean Griffin – similarly point to this representational ambivalence. Most recently, Ryan Powell observes that both of David's forays into public or group sex become defined by discordant music, ominously crowded images, and the othering appearances of people of color in a film whose narrative is focused almost exclusively on white characters. Powell sees these scenes as not merely pathologizing gay sexual cultures but indicative of the film's larger hostility toward queer community, positioning "gay collectivity and sociality as a distasteful cesspool that can be overcome with effort" (161).

Such critiques speak to the complex and at times contradictory aesthetic and ideological character of *A Very Natural Thing*, one that arose partly from the discourses and debates within the early gay and lesbian liberation movement itself. Following the Stonewall uprisings that began in New York City on 28 June 1969, a new generation of gay activism flowered, as seen in both the protests of governmental, medical, legal, and cultural entities for their entrenched homophobia and the cultivation of social spaces that celebrated LGBTQ identity, history, and politics (Cruikshank). In response to the misrepresentations seen in Hollywood products, LGBTQ-produced films made throughout the 1970s created the types of images lacking in mainstream American cinema – from continuations of 60s-era Underground filmmaking to lesbian experimental works, from hardcore gay male pornography to affirmative documentaries about LGBTQ experience (Benshoff and Griffin 153–176). Of particular importance to *A Very Natural Thing* were narrative features like *The Boys in the Band* (1970), *Sticks and Stones* (1970), and *Some of My Best Friends Are...*(1971) in which "gay life is presented as a domain made up of specific kinds of groups, cultural experiences, problems, and solutions" (Powell 120). These films' attempts to author a new type of representation for LGBTQ people that affirmed their existence, asserted their value, and revealed their lived realities also exposed disagreements among queer viewers as to what exactly constituted a "positive image" (Dyer 274).

Much like his eventual protagonist, Christopher Larkin transitioned from life in a monastery to live as an out gay man, one who saw filmmaking as a means to create an alternative to what he viewed as two malignant cinematic trends. *A Very Natural Thing*, Larkin wrote

> came out of my own personal reaction, on the one hand, to the mindless, sex-obsessed image of the homosexual prevalent in gay porno films and, on the other hand, to the debasing caricatures and slurs about gay people and gay life coming out of the vast majority of commercially oriented films.
>
> (qtd. in Russo 207)

As told to Harold Fairbanks in a 14 August 1974 profile in the gay newspaper *The Advocate*, this ambition led him to enroll in the New York Institute of Photography where he earned a certificate in the fundamentals of filmmaking. He worked on the script for what would become *A Very Natural Thing* with co-screenwriter Joseph Coencas, a graduate of NYU film school who (according to Fairbanks) "also wrote much of the actual dialog, culled from taped conversations between Larkin and his lover" (38). In both his goals of combating pernicious representation and his unorthodox path to the director's chair, Larkin embodied the do-it-yourself ethos of early gay liberation-inspired filmmakers.

The production of *A Very Natural Thing* illuminated both the specific challenges of casting and shooting a gay-themed feature in the mid-1970s and the budgetary and scheduling difficulties that marked independent cinema more generally. Larkin told Fairbanks that despite his clear intention to produce a non-pornographic love story between two men, he had to repeatedly assure leads Robert Joel and Curt Gareth that he was not secretly making a hardcore film (38). Scouting certain shooting locations proved complicated as well, most notably the school building within which David needed to be seen teaching English. Only through personal connections and a discreet approach to discussing the film's subject matter was Larkin able to find a school to film in (Fairbanks, "Naturally," 39). To secure financing, meanwhile, Larkin employed a production strategy later used by such American independent cinema luminaries as Jim Jarmusch and Spike Lee. He filmed a 10–12 minute iteration of the aforementioned "honeymoon" montage in September and October 1972 as a "pilot episode" that he could then screen to potential backers to fund the remainder of the production. Filming continued on-and-off over the next nine months. This extended schedule proved helpful, as it allowed Larkin to shoot footage at the 1973 Christopher Street Gay Pride March that would prove crucial to the film's overall structure. *A Very Natural Thing* gained further ties to the gay liberation movement through the casting of known activists in bit roles, including Arnie Kantrowitz (vice president of the pioneering Gay Activists Alliance) and Vito Russo, who became aware of the project after watching the "pilot" short while on assignment for *GAY* magazine (Schiavi 132). Principal photography wrapped by August 1973, with Larkin completing the film for around $100,000.

Before exploring how the film's ambitions as a commercially viable gay romance aligned with industrial realities, it is worth considering a bit further how Larkin translated his liberationist-inflected ideas about both gay relationships and LGBTQ politics to the screen. If *A Very Natural Thing*'s vision of sexuality feels bifurcated between (at best) ambivalent depictions of promiscuity and ennobled portrayals of sex within committed relationships, Larkin uses key stylistic decisions to underline the tangled processes by which gay men craft love and intimacy within a heteronormative society. Early in the film, David and Mark attend the wedding of David's former roommate Gary (Anthony McKay) and his girlfriend Valerie (Marilyn Meyers). The men stand side by side in the church pew in a manner that visually echoes Gary and Valerie at the altar. The priest speaks of the solemnity of the marital sacrament, which the viewer continues to hear as Larkin cuts to later shots of David and Mark moving in together. The juxtaposition of sound and image underscores David and Mark's exclusion from the institution of marriage while intimating how societal norms of monogamous coupledom and domesticity nevertheless shape the course of their relationship.

Larkin blended different modes of imagery to weave gay liberation ideals into the film as well. *A Very Natural Thing* features on-the-street conversations from the 1973 Christopher Street Gay Pride March in which actual participants and observers sound off on their own coming out journeys and the role of gay liberation in everyday life. These documentary clips open the film and are crosscut with glimpses of David's final days as a monk. His "brotherly" embrace of a handsome fellow friar becomes infused with homoerotic undercurrents when placed alongside the parade-goers' confident public proclamations. The bulk of this nonfiction material arrives later in the film, when (recalling the blurring of fiction and documentary seen in such films as Haskell Wexler's *Medium Cool* [1969]), a despondent David wanders into the real-life Pride March. The individuals interviewed in the roughly five-minute sequence reflect a greater diversity of personal identities than otherwise seen in the film as well as a broader range of views, from an apolitical celebration of togetherness to calls for a radical reconceptualization of social roles. Having this footage hover around the central story allows robust space for iconography and concepts from the gay liberation movement without necessarily integrating them completely into the film's narrative arc.

This engaged-but-tempered approach to liberationist thought might have helped to attract New Line Cinema, the independent distributor who picked up the film for distribution in May 1974 ("New Line Pick-Ups"). Founded in 1967 at a time when several smaller companies sought to fill the market gap created as major studios reduced their overall output, New Line initially focused on non-theatrical screenings at college campuses (Cook 322–334, Tzioumakis 180–182). The company offered a calculatedly eclectic mix of titles that Justin Wyatt characterizes as a mélange of "foreign, sexploitation, gay cinema, rock documentaries and 'midnight specials'" (76). The company's early forays into "gay cinema" emphasized the outré and included both Steven Arnold's psychedelic, drag-infused *Luminous Procuress* (1971) and the scabrously campy midnight-movie sensation *Pink Flamingos* (1972), whose success began a long relationship between New Line and the film's writer-director, John Waters. Throughout the early 1970s, company head Robert Shaye began moving New Line toward greater investment in the non-university filmic marketplace, culminating in the opening of a theatrical distribution arm in 1973 (Wyatt 76). The films that New Line would be seeking out in the mid-1970s, then, would need to appeal to the niche audiences (on campus and off) that drove their business while offering a broad enough attraction to justify their presence within commercial theaters.

A Very Natural Thing seemed poised to do both, a film with a strong built-in viewership of LGBTQ viewers that positioned its queer content within the inviting frames of aesthetic naturalism and liberal humanism. New Line stressed these qualities in their selling of the film to the general public. The centerpiece image of a 28 June 1974 ad in the *New York Times*, for instance, comes from the movie's final shots. Robert Joel's David moves to embrace Bo White's Jason as they romp in the water, White's hair whipping in the wind and face expressing joyful release. If the visuals showcase a fairly unambiguous moment of queer abandon, the surrounding text encases it within a universalizing structure. "David & Jason's relationship...it's the same only different" reads the tagline, a phrase that both underscores the uniqueness of gay male attraction on screen and positions said attraction within the realm of a "relationship" based on commonly understood emotional connection (25).

Indeed, once New Line released *A Very Natural Thing* on 16 June 1974, reviews frequently focused on the film's links to the conventions of typical romantic drama. Critics in the gay press, in particular, wrestled with the value of placing queer characters within types of storytelling most often utilized to tell tales of heterosexual love. While some reviewers applauded the sheer fact of same-sex intimacy on screen, *The Body Politic*'s Gerald Hannon argued that the film just replaced the gender of one character in an otherwise normative romance, "and in the final analysis the value system it both assumes and endorses is a dangerous one" (21). Even gay critics who appreciated the intent behind *A Very Natural Thing*'s co-opting of the dominant narrative still wrestled with the ultimate purpose of the project. "Is gay consciousness simply twin to a straight outlook on life? Couldn't free gay creativity produce some newer, original art forms and variations than those which straight society has produced?" asked Joe Paradin in *The Gay Alternative* (16–17). Such comments reflect the era's larger discussions linking alternative representations of marginalized subjects with reconceptualized formal modes, from Laura Mulvey advocating a cinema of "passionate detachment" that disrupts the objectification of women built into Hollywood's visual grammar (39) to the LA Rebellion directors making films "more firmly grounded in Black aesthetic traditions and less dependent on white models" (Field, Horak, and Stewart 4).

New Line and Larkin both sought to position *A Very Natural Thing* outside the circuit of gay pornography and insist upon its status as a "reputable" title. The apex of this effort occurred on 19 September 1974 when the film had its West Coast premiere at Westwood's Picwood Theatre in Los Angeles. The event was sponsored by the San Francisco-based gay social services organization the Whitman-Radclyffe Foundation and featured a post-screening panel discussion including not just Larkin but the Reverend Troy Perry (founder of the gay-affirming Metropolitan Community Church) and a psychiatrist from the University of California Medical Center (Fairbanks, "It's a Very Natural"; Barney). Framing *A Very Natural Thing* within the realm of civic engagement and social respectability assuredly helped persuade some of the exhibitors who eventually screened it. According to a 7 May 1975 *Variety* advertisement, the film played over 20 cities across the United States and Canada within one year of its release (114). Its reputation, though, ultimately became that of a box office disappointment, as seen as early as November 1974 when the *Advocate* wondered why *A Very Natural Thing* did so "poorly" in the New York market (Mark). (Expectations notwithstanding, it is worth noting that a tally of the film's box office returns from the first six weeks of its New York City run – as seen in the pages of *Variety* – totals roughly $100,000, the equivalent of *A Very Natural Thing*'s reported production budget.)

Perhaps the film's ambivalent commercial status rests partly on the stigmas that marked portions of its exhibition and reception. The film left the screens of the Paris West Cinema in West Springfield, Massachusetts after only two days when detectives from the local police department thought the film was "a little obscene" and suggested removing it (Nyland). Local gay activists had to threaten a protest demonstration before the *Los Angeles Times* would run an advertisement for the film ("Dispute"). Even when *A Very Natural Thing* appeared without legal blockages or attempts at censorship, the titles that it was paired with or the manner in which it was advertised could intimate something illicit. A 26 October 1974 listing in the *Tucson Daily Citizen* showed the film screening at the Cineworld 4 Cinemas alongside Russ Meyer's 1968 sexploitation title *Finders Keepers, Lovers Weepers!*, a double feature that local film critic Micheline Keating deemed "a duo of sexploiters" (12). The Marina Cinemas in Chicago screened *A Very Natural Thing* and *Shampoo* (1975) on 14 May 1975. Despite both films earning an "R" rating, only *A Very Natural Thing* was labeled with the designation "adults only." Ironically, one could open the *Courier-Journal* in Louisville, Kentucky roughly two weeks later and read a review of Larkin's film by critic William Mootz which asserted that "if you're looking for shocks, there's more mind-blowing stuff in a current hit like 'Shampoo' than there is in 'A Very Natural Thing'" (A17).

A Very Natural Thing did not prove to be the runaway popular success that some backers had hoped for, but it did become a permanent fixture in the growing ecosystem of gay film festivals, pride days, and LGBTQ campus events that emerged across the 1970s. A one-month stretch in early 1976, for example, found the film featured within a "Gay Awareness Symposium" in Bellingham, Washington put on by the Gay People's Alliance ("Gay Awareness Week"); shown with post-film discussion in the MCC Center in Hartford, Connecticut ("Announcements"); and co-programmed with a Columbia Broadcasting System (CBS) special on Walt Whitman by the Carolina Gay Association on the University of North Carolina at Chapel Hill campus ("Campus Calendar"). Larkin also toured college campuses with the film at roughly the same time that Vito Russo was traveling around the country presenting his "Celluloid Closet" lecture on the history of LGBTQ representation in Hollywood – lectures that would form the basis of his groundbreaking 1981 book of the same name ("Director of Gay Film"). Archival documents from the Foster Gunnison Papers at the University of Connecticut reveal the industrial strategy behind this pairing: a promotional letter from New Line noting the availability of Russo (a member of the company's special events division, New Line Presentations) for speaking engagements; and a 1976 flyer advertising both Larkin's film and Russo's lecture as among the "timely programs on the Gay Experience in America" offered by the company ("New Line Press Kit"). That by 1976 *A Very Natural Thing* could be referred to as a "gay cult film" within the pages of the *Advocate* reflects its established place within the growing firmament of LGBTQ film and culture in the decade of gay liberation ("A 'Natural' Star" 38).

A Very Natural Thing's influence on later queer filmmaking, meanwhile, illustrates the oft-delayed results of early trailblazing efforts. Larkin modeled a type of cinema that became increasingly common: observational stories of urban gay men navigating the intersections of public queer identity and personal fulfillment. While not without its formal limitations and ideological blind spots, this mode of filmmaking has been skillfully and empathetically used in a number of works addressing the early years of the HIV/AIDS epidemic – *Parting Glances* (Bill Sherwood, 1986), *Longtime Companion* (Norman René, 1989), *Jeffrey* (Christopher Ashley, 1995) – as well as in titles that grapple more generally with shifting norms of gay eroticism, sociality, and political engagement, including the cinematic and televisual titles of Andrew Haigh (*Weekend* [2011], *Looking* [2014–2015]). Some contemporary writers have also come to admire Larkin's film on its own terms. Writing for *Film Comment* in 2018, critic Michael Koresky observes that, "though undoubtedly of primary interest to many as a time capsule, Larkin's noticeably but elegantly low-budget film has an economical beauty and a purposeful freedom of form that give it a lasting sprightliness." *A Very Natural Thing* may never (perhaps could never) have offered the answer to what exactly makes a "good" gay film, but its poignant, searching sincerity and potent cultural legacy reveal how enduring and vital the question remains.

Works Cited

"A 'Natural' Star Does Meyer's Thing." *The Advocate*, 10 Mar. 1976, pp. 38–39.
Advertisement for *A Very Natural Thing*, *New York Times*, 28 June 1974, p. 25.
Advertisement for *A Very Natural Thing*, *Variety*, 7 May 1975, p. 114.
Advertisement for Marina Cinemas, *Chicago Tribune*, 14 May 1975, Sec. 4, p. 6.
Announcements for MCC Center, *Hartford Courant*, 24 Feb. 1976, p. 35.
Barney, Jeanne. "'Very Natural Thing' Has Nice, Natural Premiere." *The Advocate*, 23 Oct. 1974, p. 11.
Benshoff, Harry M., and Sean Griffin. *Queer Images: A History of Gay and Lesbian Film in America*. Rowman & Littlefield, 2006.
Çakırlar, Cüneyt, and Gary Needham. "The Monogamous/Promiscuous Optics in Contemporary Gay Film: Registering the Amorous Couple in *Weekend* (2011) and *Paris 05:59: Théo & Hugo* (2016)." *New Review of Film and Televisions Studies*, vol. 18, no. 4, 2020, pp. 402–430.
"Campus Calendar." *Daily Tar Heel*, 4 Mar. 1976, p. 5.
Cook, David A. *Lost Illusions: American Cinema in the Shadow of Watergate and Vietnam, 1970–1979*. University of California Press, 2000.
Cruikshank, Margaret. *The Gay and Lesbian Liberation Movement*. Routledge, 1992.
"Director of Gay Film Touring U.S. Colleges with Compilations." *Variety*, 2 June 1976, p. 7.
"Dispute over *Times* Ad Ends in Compromise." *The Advocate*, 9 Oct. 1974, p. 24.
Dyer, Richard. *Now You See It: Studies on Lesbian and Gay Film*. Routledge, 1990.
Fairbanks, Harold. "It's a Very Natural Opening for *A Very Natural Thing*." *The Advocate*, 11 Sept. 1974, p. 31.
Fairbanks, Harold. "Naturally, Larkin Does His Thing." *The Advocate*, 14 Aug. 1974, pp. 38–39.
Field, Allyson Nadia, Jan-Christopher Horak, and Jacqueline Najuma Stewart. "Emancipating the Image: The L.A. Rebellion of Black Filmmakers," *L.A. Rebellion: Creating a New Black Cinema*, edited by Field et al. University of California Press, 2015, pp. 1–53.

"Gay Awareness Week Planned." *Pandora*, Jan. 1976, p. 5.

Hannon, Gerald. "A Very Natural Thing." Review of *A Very Natural Thing*, directed by Christopher Larkin. *The Body Politic*, Oct. 1975, p. 21.

Keating, Micheline. "Easy Riders Days Over." *Tucson Daily Citizen*, 26 Oct. 1974, p. 12.

Koresky, Michael. "Queer & Now & Then: 1974." *Film Comment*, 6 June 2018, https://www.filmcomment.com/blog/queer-now-1974/. Accessed 1 Oct. 2021.

Mark, Julian. "New York Notes." *The Advocate*, 6 Nov. 1974, p. 34.

Mootz, William. "'A Very Natural Thing' Makes Plea for Tolerance Toward Homosexuals." Review of *A Very Natural Thing*, directed by Christopher Larkin. *Courier-Journal* [Louisville, KY], 27 May 1975, p. A17.

Mulvey, Laura. "Visual Pleasure and Narrative Cinema." *Issues in Feminist Film Criticism*, edited by Patricia Erens, Indiana University Press, 1990, pp. 28–40.

"New Line Pick-Ups." *Variety*, 24 May 1974, p. 5.

New Like Press Kit A Very Natural Thing, Foster Gunnison Papers, University of Connecticut, Box 46, Folder 438.

Nyland, Thom. "A Very Natural Raid." *Gay Community News*, 24 Aug. 1974, pp. 1–2.

Ortleb, Chuck. "A Very Natural Thing." Review of *A Very Natural Thing*, directed by Christopher Larkin. *Out*, Apr. 1974, pp. 19–21.

Paradin, Joe. "'A Very Natural Thing': Trapped in This Unnatural Thing." Review of *A Very Natural Thing*, directed by Christopher Larkin. *The Gay Alternative*, Sept. 1974, pp. 16–17.

Powell, Ryan. *Coming Together: The Cinematic Elaboration of Gay Male Life, 1945–1979*. University of Chicago Press, 2019.

Russo, Vito. *The Celluloid Closet: Homosexuality in the Movies*. Harper & Row, 1981.

Schiavi, Michael. *Celluloid Activist: The Life and Times of Vito Russo*. University of Wisconsin Press, 2011.

Tzioumakis, Yannis. *American Independent Cinema: An Introduction*. 2nd ed., Edinburgh University Press, 2017.

Waugh, Thomas. "Films by Gays for Gays: *A Very Natural Thing*, *Word is Out*, and *The Naked Civil Servant*." *The Fruit Machine: Twenty Years of Writing on Queer Cinema*. Duke University Press, 2000, pp. 14–33.

Wyatt, Justin. "The Formation of the 'Major Independent': Miramax, New Line, and the New Hollywood." *Contemporary Hollywood Cinema*, edited by Steve Neale and Murray Smith, Routledge, 1998, pp. 74–90.

21
THE KILLING OF A CHINESE BOOKIE (1976)

Sam Littman

John Cassavetes's *The Killing of a Chinese Bookie* (1976) marked the director's first foray into genre filmmaking. Cassavetes's works prior to *The Killing of a Chinese Bookie* centered on upper-middle-class characters struggling to navigate failing relationships, marriages, and mid-life crises. With *Bookie*, Cassavetes shed the bourgeois sheen of *Faces* (1968), *Husbands* (1970), *Minnie and Moskowitz* (1971), and *A Woman Under the Influence* (1975) for a seedy, nocturnal setting populated by hustlers and gangsters. The story centers on Cosmo Vitelli (Ben Gazzara), a degenerate gambler and the owner of the Crazy Horse West, a cabaret strip joint on the Sunset Strip in Los Angeles. After accruing insurmountable losses at the poker table in a mafia-run game, he has no choice but to pull off an improbable murder of the organization's chief competitors to clear his debt.

The perpetually restless Cassavetes approached the film as an "intellectual experiment," stating:

> It's interesting to me to see how other people live in our society, to look at them and ask myself, 'Why do they do it? And how do they do it?'... The fun and challenge of the film was to imagine a self-contained world different from the one I live in: to move into it and live in it.
>
> *(Carney 375)*

This "intellectual experiment" requires contextualization in the realm of independent cinema to properly assess and appreciate the filmmaker's choices as distinct from Hollywood practices. In keeping with his previous two projects, Cassavetes financed the film himself through his income as an actor and the profits that his directorial efforts generated to restrict input from outsiders with a stake in the project. Unconstrained by Hollywood's rigid insistence on airtight causal linkages

FIGURE 21.1   Cosmo Vitelli (Ben Gazzara) stands, surrounded by the "Delovlies," in his cabaret strip joint, Crazy Horse West.

and more traditional fast pacing, Cassavetes's crime film unfolds contemplatively and generates a hypnotic effect that flew in the face of the fast-paced crime films that Hollywood churned out for the masses. In this chapter, I will demonstrate how Cassavetes upended deeply encoded expectations of genre films, narratively and aesthetically, with one of the most innovative "neo-noir" films of the 1970s. I will also analyze the production and reception of the film as an instructive example of the struggles faced by filmmakers operating outside the Hollywood system. Finally, I will dissect the allegory of Cosmo as a double of Cassavetes that renders *The Killing of a Chinese Bookie* a characteristically personal film within this independent writer-director's body of work, despite his insistence to the contrary.

The story is set in motion when Cosmo ventures to a trendy Los Angeles restaurant to pay off a seven-year gambling debt. That very night Cosmo returns to his poker haunt and exceeds the credit limit at the establishment with a disastrous $23,000 loss. The boss of the racket overseeing the operation, Mort Weil (Seymour Cassel), demands that Cosmo murder a rival bookie to pay off the exorbitant sum. Cosmo improbably manages to fatally shoot the bookie, whose lavish compound suggests he was not as "low-level" as Mort claimed in the meeting. Cosmo returns to Crazy Horse West only to be whisked away by one of Mort's henchmen to meet with Mort in a nearby parking garage. Gunfire from the henchmen then rains down on Cosmo, but he seemingly escapes the shots and kills Mort as he flees the scene. Upon returning to the club, he buys his performers some time by going up on stage and offering everyone a free drink. He is greeted with applause for his graciousness, exits the stage, and stumbles outside. In the final shot of the film, the camera follows Cosmo as he gathers himself on the street, blood dripping from his suit jacket as he observes the heavy traffic on the Sunset Strip.

In the decades since its theatrical release, *Bookie* has become regarded as one of Cassavetes's finest achievements, reassessed and widely treasured for its eccentric deviations from crime genre conventions. When *Sight & Sound* conducted its decennial poll of the greatest films of all time in 2012, directors ranked the film in the top 100. Cassavetes's independence from Hollywood enabled him to construct a genre film that drastically dials down quintessential Hollywood crime film features such as suspense, action, and romance in favor of the filmmaker's signature focus on dailiness, loneliness, and extended naturalistic conversation sequences that rarely advance the story. One of the film's most ardent supporters since its release, Jonathan Rosenbaum refers to *Bookie* as a "post-noir masterpiece," providing a sturdy entry point for assessing the features of the film that qualify it as a unique, essential, and influential contribution to the neo-noir genre that burgeoned in the late 1960s. Quintessential features of film noirs, generally considered to have flourished between roughly 1941 and 1959, that distinguish them from typical crime films include psychological centering on an obsessive hero; expressionistic, shadowy lighting; and prioritization of feelings of moral ambiguity, frustration, and disillusionment over suspense (Gross 44). The features of the neo-noir were first identified by Larry Gross in his influential essay, "Film Après Noir," notably published the same year Cassavetes's film was first released. *The Killing of a Chinese Bookie* is not part of Gross's discussion, but they arguably work through different media to establish similar parameters of the genre. Gross demonstrated how neo-noirs

> emphasize the reality of Form itself, attempting to shift from a psychological to a sociological analysis, and to aggress against Hollywood narrative convention.... By turning the thematic materials of film noir into forms, they all force the attentive viewer into a contemplation of his own expectations, demands, assumptions, his own complicity with a kind of "entertainment" that obscures the real character of contemporary life.
>
> *(44–45)*

My analysis of the film will be guided by Gross's claim that neo-noirs "aggress against Hollywood narrative convention" in the context of Cassavetes's artistic independence. His formal and narrative innovations in the genre figure prominently among the qualities of the film that distinguish it as an essential deconstruction of mainstream genre filmmaking.

Bookie is in every sense a noir but labeling it as such necessitates consideration and appreciation of how Cassavetes's infusion of his primary characteristics as an auteur radically reshaped the genre. In the most expansive study of *The Killing of a Chinese Bookie* to date, George Kouvaros draws on Gilles Deleuze's conception of "white events" to demonstrate how Cassavetes quite intentionally grinds the guiding action to a halt throughout the film in flagrant disregard of Hollywood noirs' dedication to airtight causal linkages in the structuring and execution of the crime narrative. Deleuze considered "white events" to be idle periods and event delays that distract from the overarching action propelling the plot forward. The effect of Cassavetes's frequent digressions throughout the film and typical preoccupation with orienting his narratives around white events generates a distinct sense of soporific bewilderment in the context of the genre in which it is operating. Kouvaros observes that the film provides us with an experience of time that is more elusive yet also more abrupt and that instead of giving us a series of defining actions, the film focuses on the interval between actions (168). The film's prioritization of "white events" over escalating action aggressively contradicts Hollywood's mandate that every scene in a crime film must advance the plot.

Cosmo's winding, borderline absurdist journey from the Sunset Strip to Chinatown to assassinate the bookie is the best example of Cassavetes's innovative insertion of white events into the film noir as he eats up 20 minutes of precious screen time with comical and heartfelt digressions that serve primarily to distract from the task at hand. In perhaps the most iconic scene in the film, Cosmo stops his first of many cabs en route to the bookie's compound to call the Crazy Horse West from a payphone. When the manager of the club cannot identify the number currently being performed on stage, Cosmo becomes incensed and – in an endearing display of his dedication to the artistic integrity of the club – passionately sings the opening lyrics to Dorothy Fields's "I Can't Give You Anything but Love, Baby" to ensure that his employees know how to arrange the act. Cosmo then hops in a different cab and heads toward a diner to purchase a dozen hamburgers to distract the gangsters' guard dogs. The weight of the titular assassination takes a backseat to Cosmo's follies as he struggles to explain to the waitress why he does not care that the burgers are not individually wrapped: "You can't put 12 hamburgers in a brown paper bag, you're gonna ruin it," she insists, to Cosmo's exhausted chagrin. Cosmo's journey to and from the club over the final 45 minutes of the film following the murder of the bookie contains only one scene – the parking garage shootout – that bears directly on the central crime narrative. Phillip Lopate reminds us that "Cassavetes was always trying to break away from the formulas of Hollywood narrative to uncover some fugitive truth about the way people behave." He further argues that *Bookie*'s enduring power is generated by the emphasis on subtle details of character and setting that play as inertial counterpoints to obligatorily propulsive scenes such as the shootout. *Bookie* is a noir that depends not on strict adherence to causality but on the creative possibilities and potential for generic revision opened up by defying the constraints of causality. Geoff King adds that in *Bookie,* the crime film is given "generically unconventional Cassavetes-style treatment. The film is very low-key, in most cases lacking the usual markers of heightened melodrama and suspense" (194). Crucially, King points to the absence of a musical score in *Bookie* that would "mark" moments of melodrama and suspense for the viewer (King 194). Music is an integral element of Hollywood productions as it reflects the feelings and emotions of the characters and possesses the capacity to manipulate viewers' emotions. A Hollywood film devoid of a soundtrack is an unfathomable concept. In an independent film such as *Bookie*, the absence of musical cues throughout generates a mark of distinction against Hollywood material.

The trancelike nature of the deliberately meandering narrative is augmented by the director's aesthetic strategies. Cassavetes is rarely discussed in terms of aesthetics due to his philosophy that cinematography should never distract the viewer from his actors' performances. Cassavetes instructed his directors of photography to follow the actors' cues in each shot, occasionally leading the camera to abruptly pan and tilt in a manner that could appear clunky and unpolished. Cassavetes also preferred high-key lighting and an undecorated aesthetic to train the viewer's focus on the features and gestures of the performances (Carney 116). *Bookie* is a singular exception in his filmography. The interior shots in *Bookie* are elaborately composed and often emphasize the environment over the character. Cosmo is frequently soaked in neon lighting typified by the deep red and blue hues of the interior of Crazy Horse West or fully encased in the darkness of the Los Angeles night in a manner that routinely diminishes his prominence in the image. Throughout the film, Cosmo oscillates between the ravishingly lighted and eminently cozy club that he designed himself and the blaring urban jungle of Los Angeles that tends to only introduce problems for the protagonist, visually extending the metaphor of the club as Cosmo's artistic haven and the outside world as a gangster-owned space of disillusionment. Classical film noirs are defined by consistently shadowy cinematography, but Cassavetes's take on the genre draws a clear aesthetic distinction between the world of the club and the world that exists outside the club. The colorful, expressionistic lighting of Crazy Horse West reflects his conception of it as an inspiring, creativity-inducing atmosphere for the artist. Cassavetes, in fact, insisted the nightclub scenes be shot through gels to create pools of red or blue light for the star of the Crazy Horse West to walk through (Lopate). We can read the oppressively lighted city in relation to the developing aesthetics in neo-noir (though I will also argue that it has an allegorical connotation). The supersaturation of both environments generates a psychedelic haze that reimagines the consistent, manicured, chiaroscuro fashioning of the classical noir as constantly disconcerting and ultimately kaleidoscopic. With *Bookie*, Cassavetes generates an entrancing effect from the stark juxtaposition of psychedelic lighting and lusterless lighting in a manner that a Hollywood production would rarely, if ever condone. Although Hollywood cinematography ensures that principal characters are always sufficiently illuminated and prominently displayed in the frame, Cassavetes routinely diminishes Cosmo's presence in the image through underexposure in scenes set at night or in the cabaret, the vast majority of scenes in the film.

Perhaps because of its significant deviation from genre expectations, *The Killing of a Chinese Bookie* was panned by every major critic upon its initial theatrical release in 1976 and bombed at the box office, grossing a mere $11,456 on its nearly $2 million budget (Box Office Mojo). Cassavetes was so devastated by the universally negative reviews that he returned to it following its disastrous theatrical release with the intention of re-releasing the film, again through his Faces

Distribution. Cassavetes cut 27 minutes from the original version, consolidated much of the action, and re-released the film in 1978. The version of the film that is more widely circulated today (on 35mm, Digital projection/DCP, DVD and Blu-ray, and streaming platforms) and analyzed in this chapter is the re-cut 1978 version.

Cassavetes was a remarkably savvy businessman as well as an innovative filmmaker. He self-financed his directorial debut, *Shadows* (1959), as well as his most acclaimed film of the 1960s, *Faces* (1968). He was able to consistently maintain strict creative control of the films that he wrote and directed by putting up the entire budget himself, with occasional help from the actors that he regularly collaborated with such as Peter Falk, Seymour Cassel, Timothy Carey, Gazzara, and Gena Rowlands, his wife. As the financier of all but two of the films that he directed, Cassavetes reaped a significant portion of the revenue. *The Killing of a Chinese Bookie* is an exception. Following successful collaborations with powerful Hollywood distributors such as Columbia (*Husbands*, 1970) and Universal (*Minnie and Moskowitz*, 1971) on his self-financed directorial efforts, Cassavetes decided to self-distribute his films through his Faces Distribution label. King points out that "One of the numerous ways John Cassavetes marked his status as a hero to later independents was his move into the distribution of his own films" (26). Given that the first film he released through Faces Distribution, *A Woman Under the Influence,* generated millions in profits despite being a lengthy, grueling drama about mental illness, he was justifiably confident that his "gangster film" possessed the potential to reach a much wider audience. Cassavetes conceived the film under the spell of the historic financial success of Francis Ford Coppola's *The Godfather* (1972) and *The Godfather Part II* (1974) – even though, according to Ray Carney, "Cassavetes not only did not have a very high opinion of the genre but didn't think of gangsters themselves as being very interesting" (377). Cassavetes intended to make an entirely different kind of gangster film than Coppola, inspired by Arthur Penn's surreal *Mickey One* (1965) and the TV movie *The Family Rico* (1972), starring Gazzara (Carney 381). As Cassavetes developed the screenplay, the gangsters receded to the margins of the story and became a parable of the forces in the film industry that Cassavetes spent his career eliding by financing his directorial projects himself.

Cassavetes never considered fielding offers from distributors for the film and endeavored to finance the publicity and marketing for the film entirely on his own. He hired a part-time post-production staff that nearly matched the size of the credited crew on the film's four-month shoot to manufacture thousands of press kits and posters and coordinate north of 100 bookings, starting with theaters in New York and LA. By the time the prints were ready to be shipped to theaters, Cassavetes had spent approximately $1.5 million out of his own pocket on shooting, editing, promoting, and preparing to distribute the film (Carney 384). In marketing the film to theaters, Cassavetes emphasized the inclusion of genre tropes such as extortion, an organized criminal enterprise presiding over the protagonist, double-crossings, and shootouts. In actuality, and unbeknownst to the theater owners who consented to screen the film based on his reputation, these commercial properties of the production were overwhelmingly drowned out by the filmmaker's acute interest in how a character like Cosmo would behave *in between* the action sequences and melodramatic scenarios that the successful gangster pictures of the period treated with mythic importance.

Audiences were not just disappointed with Cassavetes's rendition of the gangster film but were seemingly appalled, and the few published reviews of the film ranged narrowly from dismissive to degrading. Vincent Canby of the *New York Times* proclaimed the film "bland" and "sloppily edited" (Canby). Canby took issue with Cassavetes's amateurish staging of action sequences and condescendingly remarked, "In the trade this is known as an action sequence, and it quickly becomes rather too existential if you can't figure out who is stalking whom, or why." Canby praised Gazzara's "thoughtful, intelligent interpretation of the role," but bemoaned that the supporting cast was hamstrung by Cassavetes's depiction of gangsters as one-dimensional caricatures. Similarly, Charles Champlin of the *Los Angeles Times* remarked,

> It may be that Gazzara is too intelligent for the character Cassavetes intended him to create...The characters, you might say, tell even less about themselves than they know, leaving us in the dark to no point whatsoever. It's a disappointment from a man whose work has so often carried such urgency or such powerful emotions.

Cassavetes had not only failed to deliver entertainment on the level of the gangster films whose coattails he aspired to ride to box office glory, but critics and patrons also apparently felt downright deceived by the moody, existential, and discombobulated character study that bore no resemblance to the rip-roaring crime drama that the advertising had promised. *Bookie* played for just two weeks before Cassavetes pulled the film from theaters and canceled the long-planned expansion to dozens of others.

A variety of factors likely contributed to audiences and critics misunderstanding the film in its initial theatrical run. As already noted, Cassavetes marketed *Bookie* as a thrilling gangster epic, but the film was less akin to *The Godfather* than the gritty, existential crime films that emerged in the early 1970s and deromanticized the genre by focusing acutely on dailiness and loneliness as opposed to propulsive storytelling. Audiences in the early 1970s had clearly developed a fascination with dynamic, sympathetic depictions of underworld figures, as evidenced by *The Godfather*'s historic $133.6 million haul despite its prohibitive R rating. Yet Cassavetes grew increasingly hellbent on eschewing features of the gangster genre that audiences craved despite conceiving *Bookie* as a distinctly commercial endeavor. Cassavetes was renowned for his intimate, probing depictions of men and women suffering relatable crises and moral dilemmas but influential critics such as Canby spoke for audiences when he lamented that *Bookie* lacked the nuance and complexity expected from his characters. For audiences, the original version of *Bookie* lacked both the writer-director's signature as an auteur as well as the requisite action and thrills to suit the gangster genre. Cassavetes marketed his first genre film as bankable entertainment intended for a wide audience, but the 135-minute product featured only two action sequences and unfolded at a much slower pace than audiences were conditioned to expect from a gangster film. In re-editing the film, Cassavetes principally sought to address the issue of the slow pacing by cutting 27 minutes of the film, shedding extended portions set in Crazy Horse West that distracted from both the study of Cosmo and the storyline. The version that he re-edited and re-released was tighter, flowed more engagingly, and crucially refocused attention on Cosmo's interior strife.

While Cassavetes insists that *Bookie* was a distinctly commercial endeavor that enabled him to explore a world he was entirely unfamiliar with as an "intellectual experiment," considerable evidence suggests that the film was a much more personal work than he let on. Relatively recent interviews with friends and collaborators reveal that Cassavetes crafted Cosmo as his double, an allegory for his philosophy of artistic freedom and expression in the face of so much pressure and constraint from the Hollywood powers-that-be. When we first meet him in the Crazy Horse West, he takes over the PA system and announces to his patrons, "My name is Cosmo Vitelli. I'm the owner of this joint. I choose the numbers, I direct them, I arrange them. You have any complaints, you just come to me and I'll throw you right out on your ass." In the original version, this sequence occurs 14 minutes into the film. In the 1978 version, Cassavetes rearranges the groundwork for interpreting Cosmo as his double by situating the scene in which Cosmo makes this announcement as the *opening* of the film. Cassavetes is keen to instill in his audience that the artistically principled Cosmo is the double of one of the most uncompromising independent filmmakers in the history of American cinema. Carney was the first to pick up on the similarities between Cassavetes and Cosmo through his extensive interviews with Cassavetes, published in the book *Cassavetes on Cassavetes*. Gazzara offered evidence that reaffirms Carney's insight, testifying: "The gangsters were a metaphor, and Cosmo was John, certainly" (Charity 122). As additional evidence of Cassavetes's affection for the character, he adopted a dog, "whom he dearly loved," two years after the re-release of *Bookie* and named him Cosmo (Carney 384). The brunt of critical discussion of *The Killing of a Chinese Bookie*, which has ramped up considerably over the last decade, has centered on the portrait of the artist in Gazzara's character and performance. With *Bookie*, Cassavetes not only aggressed against narrative and generic convention but also those in charge of enforcing those conventions.

Works Cited

Box Office Mojo: *The Killing of a Chinese Bookie*. https://www.boxofficemojo.com/title/tt0074749/credits/?ref_=bo_tt_tab.

Canby, Vincent. "Screen: 'Chinese Bookie:' Cassavetes is Director of Bland Effort." *New York Times*, 16 Feb. 1976, p. D13.

Carney, Ray. *Cassavetes on Cassavetes*. Farrar, Strauss and Giroux, 2001.
Champlin, Charles. "Against the Gangster Grain." *New York Times*, 17 Feb. 1976, p. E4.
Charity, Tom. *John Cassavetes: Lifeworks*. Omnibus Press, 2012.
Gross, Larry. "Après Film Noir." *Film Comment*, vol. 12, no. 4, 1976, pp. 44–49.
King, Geoff. *American Independent Cinema*. Indiana University Press, 2005.
Kouvaros, George. "'I Don't Know What To Do With My Hands': John Cassavetes' *The Killing of a Chinese Bookie*." *When the Movies Mattered: The New Hollywood Revisited*, edited by Jonathan Kirschner and Jon Lewis. Cornell University Press, 2019, pp. 160–179.
Lopate, Phillip. "'The Killing of a Chinese Bookie': The Raw and the Cooked." *Criterion*, 24 Oct. 2013, https://www.criterion.com/current/posts/577-the-killing-of-a-chinese-bookie-the-raw-and-the-cooked.
Rosenbaum, Jonathan. "The Killing of a Chinese Bookie." *Chicago Reader*, 27 Sept. 1991, p. 47.

22
CHAN IS MISSING (1982)

Cynthia Baron

Chan Is Missing represents a milestone in both American independent film and Asian American cinema. Produced, directed, edited, and co-written by Wayne Wang, the film exemplifies independence. It vividly displays the artist's creative vision and the work of a committed local cast and crew that produced the 16mm black-and-white film on a $22,500 grant-funded budget (Liu 107).

The film's detailed and compassionate exploration of San Francisco's Chinatown reflects Wang's longstanding collaborations with Bay Area Asian American community groups and illustrates the regional emphasis of independent film in the 1980s (Mark 103–105). Created entirely outside the studio system, *Chan Is Missing* is one of many productions that benefited from the independent network of Asian American theater companies, media art centers, professional organizations, and film and video festivals that emerged in the 1960s and 1970s.

Notably, *Chan Is Missing* represents the first feature film made by Asian Americans to secure theatrical distribution. Demonstrating that Asian American production teams could create work that appealed to wider audiences, Wang's micro-budget film grossed more than $1.5 million following its opening on 4 June 1982 (Liu 107). Established (white) critics immediately recognized the significance *Chan Is Missing* held for American film history (Mark 4). As Roger Ebert argued at the time, mainstream film and television had long offered depictions of Chinese Americans distorted by "filters and fictions," whereas *Chan Is Missing* conveyed the range and complexity of Chinese American identities, so that by "sharing its characters" with non-Asian audiences, the film illuminated "a part of America." Wang's independent film not only offered "an oblique, ironic response to dominant cinema" (Mimura xv), its "unforced, affectionate sense of humor about its characters" skillfully deflected and tacitly defied the wave of anti-Asian sentiment that had accompanied the loss of US manufacturing jobs in the 1970s and 1980s (Ebert). Wang's groundbreaking and socially

FIGURE 22.1 Steve (Marc Hayashi) and Jo (Wood Moy) give expression to conflicting perspectives in Asian American society.

relevant film thus became "important to the Asian American community as well as to the burgeoning independent film scene" (Okada 30–31).

To show how *Chan Is Missing* encapsulates the independent cinema of its historical moment, the chapter identifies its relationships to other 1980s independent films, traces cinematic and cultural influences that led the grant- and community-supported project to become a critical success, and describes the burgeoning, sometimes culturally specific infrastructure that supported the era's independent productions. In addition, the chapter explores the aesthetic and cultural influences that shaped the film's emphasis on the authenticity of ordinary people and highlights ways that Wang's film challenged media stereotypes of Asian Americans and Chinatowns across the United States. The chapter shows that through its focus on Chinese characters, concerns, and locales, Wang's imaginative film demonstrated that minority perspectives are an important part of American independent cinema and American life.

An Icon of 1980s Independent Cinema

Chan Is Missing follows two Chinese American cab drivers, Jo (Wood Moy) and his nephew Steve (Marc Hayashi), as they visit Chinatown residences, institutions, and businesses in search of their friend, Chan Hung (never shown), to whom they have given $4000 to secure a taxi cab license. Jo and Steve look for

Chan "more out of curiosity than vengeance; they don't really think he intended to steal the money, but they can't figure out why he would have disappeared" without returning their money or using it to purchase the license (Ebert). Chan's daughter, Jenny (Emily Yamasaki), eventually returns the $4000, but Jo and Steve never find Chan. Instead, they discover that everyone they speak with sees the first-generation Taiwanese immigrant in a different light. Lending richness to the simple story, the search for Chan deftly illuminates the unique personalities in, and myriad distinctions among, Chinatown's inhabitants. Some scenes illustrate generational differences or distinctions between "FOB" (fresh off the boat) and "ABC" (American-born Chinese) perspectives (terms that characters in the film employ). Some shed light on intermittent social friction in Chinatown caused by the ongoing political tensions between Taiwan and the People's Republic of China. Other scenes, such as the one featuring dancers and a romantic bolero ballad at the Filipino senior center, invite audiences to reflect on what it means to be Asian American, an identity that obscures people's cultural heritages but can foster community strength in white-dominated America (Feng, "Being Chinese American" 190).

Chan Is Missing helped define 1980s independent filmmaking as a low-budget, culturally engaged alternative to Hollywood movies (Tzioumakis 1). During this period, independent filmmakers often secured support from federally funded arts programs established in response to civil rights activism, which included the efforts of Asian Americans, who had been "demanding greater access to funding, the means of production, and screening venues" (Liu 93). The new institutional support for Wang's independent film and other Asian American projects coincided with the rising mainstream awareness of Asians and Asian Americans (93). Films such as *Fist of Fury* (1972) made Bruce Lee an international star, fostered a wave of martial arts films, and prompted scores of Americans to take up martial arts. At the same time, the dominant culture's entrenched hostility toward Asian Americans had reignited when companies like Ford, General Motors, and Chrysler lost ground to Toyota, Honda, and Nissan in the late 1970s. This resentment was expressed in virulent form when two white men attacked Chinese American Vincent Chin on 19 June 1982, in the Detroit metropolitan area. Chin died four days later; the well-publicized case, which led to only small fines for the two men, sparked civil rights efforts to strengthen hate crime legislation and enforcement (Brockell). Wang's film references these divergent trends through background images of Bruce Lee posters and stark photos of the International Hotel, home to elderly Chinese and Filipino tenants who had lost a decade-long battle against developer-initiated, government-backed eviction in 1977.

Like some independent films in the 1980s, *Chan Is Missing* reflects disparate influences. Its *cinema vérité* approach thoughtfully depicts Chinatown settings and regular people going about their lives. Its film noir strategies often enhance audience engagement, with Jo's wry voiceover conveying Jo and Steve's amateur-detective mission as well as Jo's insights about Chan Hung, Chinese Americans, white tourists, and the various people he and Steve meet in Chinatown. Yet sometimes the film's experimental, self-reflexive deployment of noir tropes disrupts the narrative; the excessively heightened music cues when Jo discovers the gun in Chan's cab or thinks he is being followed on a busy street combine with framing and editing choices to playfully comment on mystery storytelling. *Chan Is Missing* thus ingeniously blends the documentary and experimental trends in Asian American film and video in the late 1970s and early 1980s.

Wang's inventive combination of aesthetic influences also illuminates key trajectories in 1980s independent cinema. *Chan Is Missing* shares common ground with Gregory Nava's naturalistic epic *El Norte* (1983), Lizzie Borden's modernist production *Born in Flames* (1983), and even *Blood Simple* (1984), Joel and Ethan Coen's droll, postmodern neo-noir. Wang's film shares the social engagement underlying the visibly different aesthetics of *El Norte* and *Born in Flames*. Wang's inventive use of noir conventions parallels the ironic approach in *Blood Simple,* but his nuanced exploration of San Francisco's Chinatown contrasts sharply with the Coen brothers' apolitical stance; departing from dominant norms, Wang deploys noir tropes to deconstruct stereotypes of Asian Americans in much the same way *The Brother from Another Planet* (1984) mobilizes science fiction tropes to criticize racism in America. Notably, *Chan Is Missing* exemplifies the era's independent filmmaking in its casting choices (little-known actors and first-time performers), character design (characters as both individuals and social types), and style of performance details (naturalistic physical/vocal expression). *Chan Is Missing* also reflects the DIY independent spirit that infused the entire production. Emphasizing that "strong creative ideas" provided the basis for the film, Wang explains that he and his collaborators found creative ways to work with the "roughness" of their low-budget project, which depended on their commitment "to just do it" (qtd. in Mark 108).

An Independent Production and Distribution Journey

Born in the British protectorate Hong Kong (1841–1997), Wang moved to the San Francisco Bay Area in the late 1960s. He earned a Bachelor of Fine Arts in Painting and a Master of Fine Arts in Film and Television from the California College of Arts and Crafts (CCAC), known for its rich tradition of experimental filmmaking (Ferncase 30; Liu 93). Following his collaboration with Rick Schmidt to make an avant-garde gangster film in 1972, Wang worked in Hong Kong television for two years and returned to the Bay Area due to his disinterest in commercial TV and "the whole film *business*" (qtd. in Mark 104). Subsequent experiences unrelated to film became essential influences for Wang and *Chan Is Missing*. Upon seeing Chinatown community members "not only economically depressed, but psychologically and emotionally, too," Wang began teaching English courses to help people secure jobs, and he became active in Xin Feng She (New Wind), a Chinese cultural and community organization (qtd. in Mark 103). Aside from making an avant-garde film titled *New Relationships* (1977), Wang focused on community-based projects. He served as the producer-director of *Wah Kue: The Chinese in America*, a bilingual public affairs program for San Francisco PBS affiliate KRON, and worked on *Bean*

Sprouts (1977), a five-part children's series on multicultural identity that independent filmmaker and media activist Loni Ding created for KRON (Mark 104). Wang also invested time "writing science curriculum for kids," which influenced his approach to *Chan Is Missing*; as he explains, learning to communicate "abstract, intellectual ideas... at a very broad level" fostered his interest in reaching an audience beyond devotees of experimental cinema (qtd. in Mark 105).

The project that became *Chan Is Missing* began as a short documentary about cab drivers. In 1979, Wang secured a $10,000 American Film Institute grant to develop that non-fiction film. However, with those funds in hand, he decided to make *Fire Over Water*, an experimental feature about two cab driver characters (Ferncase 31; Mark 104). The film was shot on weekends over the course of roughly ten weeks with support from the Asian American Theater Company, Asian Bilingual Cross-Cultural-Materials Development Center, Association of Chinese Teachers, Chinatown Neighborhood Improvement Resource Center, Chinatown Resources Development Center, Kearny Street Workshop, and Manilatown Senior Center. In 1981, a $12,500 grant from the National Endowment for the Arts allowed Wang to complete that experimental film, which reflected the DIY aesthetic of punk music and performance art along with Wang's interest in Chinese calligraphy and Sergei Eisenstein's ideas about intellectual montage (Eagan 773). *Fire Over Water* premiered at the 1981 Asian American International Film Festival in New York.

Due to his dissatisfaction with the film and based on input from his collaborators, Wang decided to rewrite and reedit *Fire Over Water* to create *Chan Is Missing*. As Wang explains, Danny Yung, co-founder of Asian CineVision, had worked on the "more structural version" of the film, but Terrel Seltzer, who wrote the scripted elements of Wang's *Dim Sum: A Little Bit of Heart* (1985), "worked on the next version, which was much more narrative and story-oriented" (qtd. in Mark 107). For *Chan Is Missing*, Wang also wrote Jo's voiceover narration in collaboration with Isaac Cronin, a filmmaking colleague of Seltzer. *Chan Is Missing* premiered at the Pacific Film Archive in Berkeley, had a three-day run at the Roxie Theater in San Francisco, and was shown at the 1982 Asian American International Film Festival and the Berlin International Film Festival. Screenings at FILMEX and the New Directors/New Films series, organized by the New York Museum of Modern Art, prompted acclaim in the mainstream press. The reviews led to a distribution deal with New Yorker Films, which paid for the film's music rights and its transfer to 35mm (Ferncase 31). The successful art house release included screenings in Boston, Chicago, Los Angeles, and San Francisco, and a five-month run in New York. *Chan Is Missing* became "one of the first 'no-budget' films to grace many of the year's ten-best lists" (30), an accomplishment that makes it a key work of American independent cinema.

The Independent Film's Cultural and Institutional Context

Illustrating its era's progressive priorities, *Chan Is Missing* reflects "the increasing importance of new social identities" (Suárez 4). Following World War II, independence movements in colonial nations across the globe inspired marginalized people worldwide to search for aesthetic expression grounded in culturally specific traditions. In the United States, the civil rights movement of the 1950s and 1960s prompted artists in marginalized groups to "make their own films, representing themselves, their own communities, their own histories" (James 297). In New York, the infrastructure that supported emerging independent filmmaking included not just Amos Vogel's Cinema 16 film society (1947–1963) and the New York Film Festival established in 1963, it also depended on institutions such as Asian CineVision (ACV), the community-based media center founded in 1975. ACV produced Chinese-language television programs and soon turned to producing, exhibiting, and providing support for Asian American film and media productions. In 1978, ACV organized the Asian American International Film Festival, the first devoted to Asian American productions.

In Los Angeles, independent filmmakers often allied themselves with public television station KCET, labor and community groups, or the Ethno-Communications Program at UCLA, which "became the chief crucible for the new ethnic cinemas" (James 304), providing training and support for Asian Americans, Native Americans, African Americans, and Latinos during and after their time as students. UCLA was home to Latino filmmaker Gregory Nava and Black filmmakers such as Charles Burnett, Julie Dash, and Haile Gerima. In the 1970s, Robert Nakamura, Duane Kubo, Eddie Wong, and Alan Ohashi created Visual Communications (VC), which was an outgrowth of the UCLA program. VC produced documentaries about the lives of Asian immigrants and the US internment of Japanese Americans. It also produced *Hito Hata: Raise the Banner* (1980), co-directed by Duane Kubo and Robert A. Nakamura, the first feature film "made by and about Asian Americans" (James 343; see Okada 31).

In the Bay Area, experimental filmmaker Bruce Baillie established the filmmaking collective Canyon Cinema in 1961. That same year, Baillie and avant-garde feminist filmmaker Chick Strand founded the San Francisco Cinematheque film society. Independents affiliated with Canyon Cinema developed an experimental aesthetic that incorporated "old serials, foreign films, and local Surrealist and funk traditions" (James 358). In 1980, media activists created the National Asian American Telecommunications Association (NAATA), which "programmed documentaries to air on national public television" (Okada 12–13). In 1982, filmmakers started the San Francisco International Asian American Film Festival. *Chan Is Missing* reflects Bay Area mediamaking's interest in both documentary work and experimental collage techniques. As the film's performances illustrate, it also reveals Wang's commitment to exploring the social identities of its central characters and the array of everyday people that they encounter.

Independent Performances

The Asian American Theater Company, established by playwright Frank Chin in San Francisco in 1973, proved to be an invaluable resource for *Chan Is Missing*.

Wood Moy (Jo), Marc Hayashi (Steve), Emily Yamasaki (Chan's daughter, Jenny), and Judi Nihei (Chan's lawyer) were all members of the Asian American Theater Workshop. Notably, Moy and Hayashi "played important roles not only in the film itself, but in the synergistic process of fleshing out the drama, based on their senses of character and plot action" (Mark 5). In the film, Wood and Hayashi seamlessly keep the improvised scenes on track as they interact with the first-time actors who embody the rich diversity of Chinatown residents. The gentle expressiveness and wry humor that colors Moy's voiceover give warmth and humanity to the accompanying *vérité* images of shops, streets, and ordinary people waiting for buses and visiting markets.

The unvarnished qualities of the central and peripheral characterizations in *Chan Is Missing* reflect Wang's attempt to strip away artifice to render an authentic lived experience. In the 1960s, video art, installation pieces, and unscripted performance art projects had challenged aesthetic hierarchies. In the new aesthetic scheme, "the performing body [became] the prime vehicle of signification" (Johnson 6). Avant-garde artists rejected the conventional process of portraying scripted characters in productions orchestrated by directors, seeking instead to put (trained and non-professional) performers at the center of performances that "fit the politics of the time" (Russell vii). Performance art pieces not only "surfed in on the wave of Punk Music in the late seventies, [the] liberation of women, blacks, Hispanics, gay men and women, and so many other marginalized cultures [also] brought wider concerns to the national debate" (vii). These developments strongly influenced the aesthetic approach to performances in *Chan Is Missing*.

Performance art's emphasis on unpolished authenticity carried into Asian American and other threads of independent cinema, making performers' physical appearances and normal speaking voices significant components of a film. Andrew Higson's "Film Acting and Independent Cinema" clarifies this point. Higson explains that "the facial, the gestural, the corporeal (or postural), and the vocal" in independent films are not simply the "material sites" of "acting signs" in an abstract story (159). Instead, they register with audiences largely because a performer's "physical type (e.g., long face, large body, high-pitched voice...) [calls] up specific cultural connotations" (159). The physical appearances of Wood Moy, who is short and middle-aged, and Marc Hayashi, who is tall, lanky, and young, are essential components of their socially grounded portrayals. The amusing image created by the physiognomies of the unlikely pair also sets the tone for their leisurely, often self-deprecating detective adventure, and it underscores "the heterogeneity of Chinese American subjectivities" depicted in the film (Feng, "Being Chinese" 189). In addition, *Chan Is Missing* employs multiple registers of performance, sometimes within a single scene. When Jo and Steve meet Henry (Taiwanese actor Peter Wang), a cook at the Golden Dragon restaurant, the film presents three types of "performances." Jo's sardonic voiceover gently mediates Peter Wang's colorful improvisation, explaining that Henry "wears a samurai-night-fever shirt, drinks milk, chain smokes, and sings 'fry me to the moon' all while he's cooking up five orders of sweet and sour pork."

Meanwhile, *vérité* images of ordinary people dining at the restaurant create a counterpoint to Peter Wang's showy performance. Later, he uses another type of performance in the scene that features Wang in a business suit, spelling out his thoughts in crisp, detached terms.

The film is sustained by the pleasant banter between Jo/Moy and Steve/Hayashi, which eventually culminates in their argument on the pier as Jo defends and sympathizes with Chan, while Steve's frustration with the unsuccessful search for Chan ignites the underlying anger he feels about his place in society. The handheld camera in this key scene "underlines the tension" of the conversation (Ferncase 35). Sometimes seen as "the true core of the film," the debate between Jo and Steve exposes "the central conflicts between their generations" (Eagan 773). A few days before shooting the scene, Wang gave Moy and Hayashi a rough script that identified the main points of the characters' interaction (Mark 106). Then, without rehearsal, Wang and cinematographer Michael Chin did a few takes of the entire scene to allow for intercutting, as Moy and Hayashi improvised the lines and the behavior that communicated their characters' anger, frustration, and desire to communicate and be understood. Thus, the scene represents not only the film's narrative climax but also its allegiance to independent film principles, which foster and depend on the collaboration of creative artists.

Conclusion: *Chan Is Missing* and Independent Filmmaking

Chan Is Missing exemplifies the independent path of casting little-known actors and non-professionals to illuminate the complexities of social types. The film's cultural engagement and aesthetic priorities (ordinary people, raw/authentic performance) carry into subsequent iterations of both independent and Asian American filmmaking. Wang's commitment to making art despite financial barriers anticipates Asian American filmmaker Gregg Araki, whose punk-influenced, DIY contributions to New Queer Cinema also explore race and social identity. Wang's film foreshadows *Slacker* (1990), another micro-budget production that uses performances by non-professionals to create a composite portrait of a locale. *Chan Is Missing* predates Ang Lee's *Pushing Hands* (1991) by almost a decade, another independent film that explores tensions between traditional Chinese ideas and those shaped by individualist American life.

The acclaim *Chan Is Missing* received foreshadows accolades for other independent Asian American films; in 1989, "three Asian American-directed films were nominated for Oscars: Renee Tajima and Christine Choy's *Who Killed Vincent Chin?*, Lise Yasui's *Family Gathering*, and Mira Nair's *Salaam Bombay*" (Xing 16). *Chan Is Missing* also launched Wang's fruitful career as an independent and mainstream director. *Dim Sum: A Little Bit of Heart*, was produced with profits from *Chan Is Missing* and funds from American Playhouse (Liu 93). Wang's *The Joy Luck Club* (1993) and Lee's *The Wedding Banquet* (1993) were the first major releases since *Flower Drum Song* (1961) to have majority Asian casts and represent steps toward a film such as *Crazy Rich Asians* (2018).

Chan Is Missing exemplifies independent, global majority filmmaking that aims to "challenge, reimagine, and advance the existing terms of cultural representation" (Mimura xiv). As Wang explains, the film's unresolved mystery is a "direct contradiction to the Charlie Chan mode, where there's always a solution" (qtd. in Mark 112). It offers something other than the "easy answers" in commercial films because, in his view, "people can be more creative in their ways of finding answers" (qtd. in Mark 112). From D.W. Griffith's *Broken Blossoms* (1919) through Roman Polanski's *Chinatown* (1974), mainstream features had presented "Chinatown" as a space marked by vice and treachery. In comparison, *Chan Is Missing* offers audiences "a slice of American life" set inside Chinatown restaurants, apartments, kitchens, and community centers (Mark 6). The film welcomes white audiences, who lack first-hand experience, and "Asian American viewers, who find a realistic portrait of themselves" (6), including the reality that Asian American identities span a "wide range of Asian ethnicities and cultures, different histories in the United States, and different removes from Asia" (Feng, *Identities in Motion* 167). With its authentic expression of the "collision of cultures" that Wang experienced as he moved between Chinese and American worlds in the 1980s (qtd. in Ferncase 31), *Chan Is Missing* made a valuable contribution to Asian American cinema and confirmed the importance of minority voices in American independent filmmaking.

Works Cited

Brockell, Gillian. "The Long, Ugly History of Anti-Asian Racism and Violence in the U.S." *Washington Post*, 21 Mar. 2021. https://www.washingtonpost.com/history/2021/03/18/history-anti-asian-violence-racism/

Eagan, Daniel. *America's Film Legacy: The Authoritative Guide to the Landmark Movies in the National Film Registry*. Continuum, 2010.

Ebert, Roger. "*Chan Is Missing*." RogerEbert.com, 1 Jan. 1982. https://www.rogerebert.com/reviews/chan-is-missing-1982.

Feng, Peter X. "Being Chinese American, Becoming Asian American: *Chan Is Missing*." *Screening Asian Americans*, edited by Peter X. Feng. Rutgers University Press, 2002, pp. 185–216.

———. *Identities in Motion: Asian American Film and Video*. Duke University Press, 2002.

Ferncase, Richard K. *Outsider Features: American Independent Films of the 1980s*. Greenwood Press, 1996.

Higson, Andrew. "Film Acting and Independent Cinema." *Star Texts: Image and Performance in Film and Television*, edited by Jeremy G. Butler. Wayne State University Press, 1991, pp. 155–181.

James, David E. *The Most Typical Avant-Garde: History and Geography of Minor Cinemas in Los Angeles*. University of California Press, 2005.

Johnson, Dominic. *The Art of Living: An Oral History of Performance Art*. Palgrave Macmillan, 2015.

Liu, Sandra. "Negotiating the Meaning of Access: Wayne Wang's Contingent Film Practice." *Countervisions: Asian American Film Criticism*, edited by Darrell Y. Hamamoto and Sandra Liu. Temple University Press, 2000, pp. 90–111.

Mark, Diane Mei Lin. *Chan Is Missing: A Film by Wayne Wang*. Bamboo Ridge Press, 1984.

Mimura, Glen M. *Ghostlife of Third Cinema: Asian American Film and Video*. University of Minnesota Press, 2009.

Okada, Jun. *Making Asian American Film and Video: History, Institutions, Movements*. Rutgers University Press, 2015.

Russell, Mark. "Foreword." *Out of Character: Rants, Raves, and Monologues from Today's Top Performance Artists*, edited by Mark Russell. Bantam Books, 1997, pp. vii–xiv.

Suárez, Juan A. *Jim Jarmusch*. University of Illinois Press, 2007.

Tzioumakis, Yannis. *American Independent Cinema: An Introduction*. 2nd ed., Edinburgh University Press, 2017.

Xing, Jun. *Asian America Through the Lens: History, Representations and Identity*. AltaMira Press, 1998.

23
ONE FROM THE HEART (1982)

Justin Wyatt

To appreciate the larger industrial and commercial filmmaking landscape for *One from the Heart*, you must look back to the era of the New Hollywood. Set against a period of significant social and political change with mainstream filmmaking failing to connect with the moviegoing public, the Hollywood studios of the late-1960s were searching for ways to become more relevant to their audience. With legacy Hollywood not meeting the needs of the audience, other – generally younger – creatives in Hollywood began to consider some alternatives, aesthetically and industrially.

New Hollywood ushered in more experimental films in both form and content, often guided by the vision of a Hollywood auteur, such as Martin Scorsese, Brian DePalma, Steven Spielberg, and Francis Coppola. By aligning with the auteur theory and the model of the European art cinema, these directors sought to create a new model for mainstream filmmaking, morphing the visual style of classical Hollywood cinema and the means of creating and producing films. The freedoms associated with the New Hollywood auteurs on a creative level allowed for an independent vision to appear on screen. As Yannis Tzioumakis notes, though, these directors still needed a distribution apparatus, located mainly within the Hollywood studios (168). Independent film is often linked to low budgets and a separation from the Hollywood studios. This tendency is contradicted by the "independent" films of the New Hollywood auteurs. Francis Coppola's audacious romance *One from the Heart* illustrates how a New Hollywood director could exact a creative and aesthetically groundbreaking independent film with little interference from the studios or larger commercial forces.

Critic Kent Jones speaks of "the lunatic gorgeousness of the reviled but hypnotic *One from the Heart*" in an apt summary of the film's original reception (30). At the exorbitant cost – for 1982 – of $27 million, director Francis Coppola created a highly stylized replica of Las Vegas within his Zoetrope Studios. Set against a song

FIGURE 23.1 Frannie (Teri Garr) searches for Ray on the neon-drenched Las Vegas Strip.

score by Tom Waits, Hank (Frederic Forrest), the taciturn co-owner of the Reality Wrecking junkyard, breaks up with his live-in girlfriend of five years, Frannie (Teri Garr), a vaguely dissatisfied travel agent. Over the course of one weekend, each partner has a brief affair: Hank with the circus girl Laila (Nastassja Kinski) and Frannie with the lounge piano player/waiter Ray (Raul Julia). Frannie and Ray leave on a trip to Bora Bora, with Hank left all alone in a rain-soaked Las Vegas. *One from the Heart* concludes though with Frannie returning home to Hank soon after her departure, realizing that she does, in fact, love him and their life together. This simple tale of love momentarily lost then found again allows Coppola to make an intervention in the world of independent filmmaking through aesthetics, technology, and industrial structure. Although Coppola's heady dream of rethinking Hollywood moviemaking was short-lived, this chapter illustrates how independent film and innovation can intersect, artistically and commercially.

Aesthetics: Theatrical Realism & Cinematic Style

Armyan Bernstein's original script was set in Chicago, but, with Coppola's involvement, this location was soon changed to Las Vegas. This shift facilitated a parallel Coppola wanted to make between gambling in life and gambling in love. Both Hank and Frannie are rolling the dice for romance, looking for love and long-term security. As Tom Waits's song "Once Upon a Town" makes clear, Vegas is central to the film's vision. The first end credit even lists "Filmed entirely on the stages of Zoetrope Studios." This is most appropriate as the film's aesthetics are guided by the recreation of Las Vegas within the studio's soundstages. From a block of the Vegas strip to a two-level department store and McCarran airport, every image within the film is built either full-size, or, as in the opening credits, as a miniature. Coppola creates a "Las Vegas of the mind," a neon-streaked city of fun and excitement untarnished by any real-world troubles. This is manifested in two ways: through fantastic and magical sets and images, such as Laila dancing in a life-size neon martini glass, and through creating in the studio realistic sets similar to Hank and Frannie's home.

As Kristin Thompson notes, realism is "an affect created by the artwork through the use of conventional devices" (197). Viewers navigate their path through a film by responding to cues linking what they see and hear on screen to their experience of the real world. We become connected to characters and the storyline, in part, through this construction of reality. *One from the Heart*, however, operates in a much different fashion. Carrie Rickey describes Coppola's film as an example of theatrical realism. Theatrical realism calls attention to the theatricality of creating a cinematic world. As Rickey describes the aesthetic, "its self-consciousness acknowledges that, though a given set captures the distorted and exaggerated vistas of lived experience, it is unquestionably the work of artificers" (32). Coppola describes his vision for the film as a juxtaposition of the real and the artificial:

> I never wanted the décor to look artificial as such. I wanted it to be built up in sections, but still it should be as real as possible, even if you know it isn't real. My story lies at the heart of this contradiction.
>
> *(Cowie 156)*

One from the Heart alternates between wildly imaginative creative flourishes, such as disco lights embedded in the intersection of a Las Vegas street or a full-scale replica of a travel agency's window display of Bora Bora come to life, with the mundane, like Hank's junkyard office or a middle-class suburban street. All these environments though are clearly artificial. Even the suburban street betrays the elements of matte painting and smaller models in forced perspective. In this way, theatrical realism draws the viewer's attention to the constructed nature of reality. The movement between the fantastic and the quotidian emphasizes that our lives are built through this combination. Coppola's film underlines this theme, alerting us that our everyday lives can be morphed in an instant through creativity, imagination, and dreams. While *One from the Heart* portrays the banality of our everyday lives, the film champions the transcendent moments when our fantasies come true.

The theatrical realism is evident in many stylistic decisions made by Coppola. This can be appreciated in the cinematography, production design, and music during the sequence of Hank being comforted by his best friend Moe (Harry Dean Stanton) and Sally by her friend Maggie (Lainie Kazan). The scene starts in Moe's apartment as Hank arrives to discuss his break-up. Throughout the scene, Coppola utilizes the Steadicam, a camera stabilizer mount that allows the cinematographer to walk through the scene with smooth coverage rather than irregular camera movements. Garrett Brown, the Steadicam inventor, describes how it was incorporated by Coppola and cinematographer Vittorio Storaro:

the Steadicam could be used to the best advantage in the picture to photograph scenes in which Hank (Fred Forrest) and Franny [sic] (Teri Garr) were together, during which their relationship was either breaking up or breaking up again. These emotional conflicts needed to be covered closely, moving with the energy, flowing with as little interruption as possible; and since their arguments and reunions usually took place on the move up and down stairs and in and out of doors around their house, the Steadicam was highly useful.

(85)

In this specific sequence, as the dialogue between the friends continues, the camera simply follows the characters as they move throughout the space. No cuts are evident. Eventually Hank and Moe sit on the sofa as Hank finally becomes emotional in talking about the break-up. At this moment, the wall behind the sofa is revealed to be a scrim. The light goes up behind the scrim, you can see through it, and Frannie and Maggie are shown talking in Maggie's apartment. David Bordwell describes this key stylistic device: "Hank has broken up with Franny [sic], but Coppola violates realism to keep them bound together, making far-flung locales adjacent through depth compositions" (261). The camera now follows the two women as they move throughout the apartment. The scene ends with the song "Old Boyfriends," sung by Crystal Gayle, as Frannie wanders aimlessly through Maggie's apartment.

With no cutting at all during the lengthy scene, Coppola's use of theatrical realism becomes clear. The lack of editing lends an element of realism as the actors are followed documentary-style throughout the set. These elements lean toward realism, but at the same time, there is a strong theatricality to the scene. The use of the scrim to connect two spaces comes directly from the theater. In addition, the physical connection of the two apartments echoes the same emotional beats for each pair, with Coppola connecting the physical space to emphasize the common dramatic action enacted in the two apartments. Shifting lighting at the source to show change in time and to draw the viewer's attention is another theatrical device used by Coppola in the scene. Finally, the "Old Boyfriends" song, dealing with the issue of breaking up and past relationships, is a direct commentary on the dramatic action at that moment in the story. In sum, the scene combines elements of realism and theatricality to create an emotional effect on the viewer. Theatrical realism becomes a distinguishing feature of *One from the Heart,* and a means to set it apart from other films addressing the highs and lows of romantic love.

Theatrical realism infuses another core element of the film, the song score by Tom Waits, sung by Waits and Crystal Gayle. The film features a complete set of ten songs that were nominated for the Best Music/Original Song Score Academy Award. In the typical musical, characters express their feelings (and move the plot forward) through song and dance, either contained within a realistic setting, like the club in *Cabaret* (1972), or simply breaking through the realistic world, like the musical numbers in *La La Land* (2016). Coppola offers a unique variant on the musical. First, he aligns the fictional characters, Hank and Frannie, with the singers, Waits and Gayle. The contrast between the two voices is stark: Waits, known for jazz, blues, and rock music, has a gravelly, seasoned voice (think of someone who has been drinking whisky and smoking all night), while Gayle's country music voice is pristine and capable of an incredible range. The songs are used either to offer commentary on the narrative action or to represent, and sometimes to replace, the characters' emotions and feelings. Breaking with the convention of the musical, Frannie and Hank are mostly cut off from song and dance, with the exceptions of Frannie dancing a single tango with Ray and Hank offering one off-key verse of "You Are My Sunshine" to woo back his girlfriend.

Nevertheless, the songs are an integral part of the film's design and help to define the characters, their dilemmas, and their opportunities. Consider "Picking Up After You," set against Hank and Frannie returning home on the night of their anniversary. The song mirrors the dramatic action: Frannie has dropped groceries as she entered the house, and Hank is picking them up on his way in. This dull domestic scene is placed next to Waits's lyrics which push much further to show the discord between the two characters: the lines "Looks like you spent the night in a trench/And how long have you been combing your hair with a wrench?" illustrate the hostility of Hank to Frannie, for instance. Waits's vivid descriptions and visual metaphors help the viewer to appreciate the central conflict of the film. Similarly, other songs, such as "You Can't Unring a Bell," and "This One's from the Heart" present ways to interpret the characters' actions, almost a meta-dialogue on the cinematic narrative. At several other times, the songs are used to express the characters' feelings, giving the inarticulate pair a more imaginative and poetic way to show their emotions. The back-to-back pairing of "Old Boyfriends" and "Broken Bicycles" describes Frannie's and then Hank's view of the break-up. For Frannie, she has just grown apart from Hank ("He fell in love, you see/With someone that I used to be"); Hank believes there is still love between them ("Summer is gone/But our love will remain/Like old broken bicycles/Left out in the rain"). In the finale, the embracing couple are silent while Crystal Gale's "Take Me Home" perfectly captures what Frannie might be saying to Hank ("I'm so sorry that I broke your heart/Please don't leave my side/Take me home, you silly boy/Because I'm still in love with you"). In Coppola's unusual version of the musical, the soundtrack score carries much of the narrative, shaping the characters and reflecting their moods, emotions, and actions. With these stylistic choices, an independent vision for the romantic movie musical is presented by Coppola.

Technology: The Dawn of Electronic Cinema

The effects of theatrical realism were aided considerably by the larger technological innovations adopted by Coppola. The film was released more than two decades before digital cinema and CGI were the norm in Hollywood filmmaking.

Starting with *One from the Heart,* Coppola was fascinated with electronic cinema, essentially any electronic means that could enhance or facilitate filmmaking from pre-production through post-production. *One from the Heart* was the first test case for Coppola's new electronic exploration. The film helped Coppola launch these technological innovations which would eventually become commonplace in the digital media landscape. In the first set of electronic tools, Coppola was able to "pre-visualize" *One from the Heart* before production even began. This process started with Coppola's electronic storyboard. A static storyboard offers mini-frames illustrating the action and dialogue at key moments in the film. Directors typically use a storyboard to develop their choices of camera placement and composition in anticipation of filming. Coppola began with 1800 frame sketches for *One from the Heart*, which were placed on cork boards, hung on the walls of his office, and photographed with a video camera and stored electronically. As planning progressed, actors recorded a "radio play" version of the script. This audio track was then connected to the visual frames yielding a very rough sense of the film. The drawn sketches of the shots and scenes were eventually replaced by photos of the actors, videotaped footage of the actors in rehearsal, or test footage from the special effects unit. The special effects unit was responsible for combining foreground and background elements using blue-screen technology (predecessor of green-screen). As the sets were constructed, these rehearsals were moved to take place on set, giving a closer approximation of the scene. The result was a visual and audio electronic document that gave the director and his creative crew a good sense of the action, flow, and development of the film even before one frame was shot. Coppola used this electronic storyboard to aid in his decision on what was working and what needed to be improved or eliminated in the film and later claimed that $2 million in set construction was ultimately saved through this new technology (Fielding 45).

Once shooting began, Coppola continued the electronic experiments, largely from his control center van located within the studio. The van allowed Coppola to record what was being filmed in studio on half-inch videotape (compared with a standard quarter-inch VHS tape) with the capacity of recording three separate images from three cameras at a time. As a result, Coppola could immediately cut the scene or sequence on videotape rather than wait for the shoot's dailies to be developed and printed on film (as was standard practice). Merging components from the previsualization with the video tape from the shooting, Coppola was able to hold a sneak preview of the film in Seattle on 15 March 1981, even though the film had a month left to shoot (Bygrave and Goodman 43)! Footage only on video tape was blown up to 35mm film and edited into the print used in the test screening and missing elements were replaced by rehearsal footage or the audio-enhanced storyboard elements. Feedback from the Seattle screening was used by Coppola to make changes in the structure, dialogue, and editing of the finished film (Fielding 48).

Unfortunately, Coppola's experiences of previewing *One from the Heart* were not all successful. An additional screening for exhibitors of a rough cut had a large and negative impact on the film's reception. Motion pictures exhibitors in certain states are allowed to view a film before making bids on showing it. To accommodate this regulation, *One from the Heart* was screened for exhibitors in August 1981. At that time, the Tom Waits/Crystal Gayle song score, along with certain transitional effects and special effects, had not yet been included. For a film that relies heavily on style to tell the story, these omissions were significant. The reaction from the exhibitors was negative, impacting not only word-of-mouth but also Coppola's relationship with Paramount Pictures which had contracted to release the film (Lewis 63). These factors led to Coppola previewing the film, at his own expense, for the public at Radio City Music Hall in New York on 15 January 1982. The goal again was to reverse the soft buzz on the film generated by the earlier exhibitor screening and the negative coverage of the film's expanding budget (given a preliminary budget of $15 million, the film eventually was completed for just under $27 million) (Lewis 57). Unfortunately, the reaction to the Radio City Music Hall screenings was again soft overall. Paramount withdrew their offer of distribution for *One from the Heart*.

Industry: The New Hollywood Auteur & Independent Filmmaking

During the 1970s, Coppola became known as an auteur with both public and critical appeal. Coppola enjoyed huge commercial and critical success in this period with *The Godfather* (1972) and *The Godfather Part II* (1974) and strong reviews for *The Conversation* (1974). Coppola's Vietnam epic *Apocalypse Now*, released in 1979, was marked by a troubled production history, a lengthy and extended shooting schedule, and more than enough (negative) publicity surrounding the film (from star Harvey Keitel being replaced by Martin Sheen, Martin Sheen's heart attack during shooting, the loan of helicopters from the Philippines army, and so on). The financial risk for that film was largely shouldered by Coppola, who presold certain foreign distribution rights to raise money, rather than by distributor United Artists. As a result, the narrative of the film's production became tied to Coppola as the manic genius guiding a picture budgeted at $12 million to a cost well over $30 million (Biskind 375). Despite running over its budget by a large margin, the film ended up being popular both with the public (a worldwide gross of over $100 million) and critics (eight Academy Award nominations, including Best Picture). *Apocalypse Now* appeared to underline the idea that Coppola could produce great art with considerable appeal to the moviegoing public.

The successes in the 1970s and the recent ability of *Apocalypse Now* to succeed, despite years of negative publicity, left Coppola emboldened to think about film production on a larger scale. In his most audacious move to date, Coppola purchased Hollywood General Studios in 1980 and launched Zoetrope Studios. With nine sound stages, 34 editing rooms and ten acres, Coppola built a team of senior advisers, including British filmmaker Michael Powell, and a repertory company of actors including Forrest, Garr, Julia, and Kinski from *One from the Heart* (Bygrave and Goodman 41). *One from the Heart* was scheduled as an initial production for the new studio, along with *Hammett* (1982) and *The Escape Artist* (1982). Coppola built ties to well-known European directors, such as Wim Wenders, Nicolas Roeg, and Jean-Luc Godard, and planned projects with them at Zoetrope Studios. Given Coppola as the director, *One from the Heart* received the most attention from the press. This film would be the first example of how Zoetrope Studios operated using Coppola's guidance and his vision of electronic cinema.

The financial history of *One from the Heart* dovetails with the fate of Zoetrope Studios. As with *Apocalypse Now*, Coppola maintained artistic and financial control over the film. Coppola contracted with Paramount Pictures, but only to distribute and market the film (with a promised $4 million advertising budget) (Lewis 56). Since they were not producing, Paramount's financial commitment was minimal. The production budget for *One from the Heart* ballooned during shooting. Coppola raised funds through foreign presales and loans from Chase Manhattan Bank and other banks, and, most curiously, from a Canadian real estate tycoon, Jack Singer (Lewis 57–58). Production was delayed by expensive decisions like a $4 million opening titles sequence, all done in miniatures of the land leading up to Las Vegas. While the experiments with electronic cinema were garnering press coverage, they were also leading to higher costs for the film. The competing Hollywood studios were uninterested in partnering with Coppola on the film. Jon Lewis sums up the issue in terms of mainstream Hollywood becoming less enamored with the independent auteur:

> Coppola's hype that *One from the Heart* was a kind of trial run for *his* new technology just made matters worse. No studio wanted to fund Zoetrope's research and development without a stake in the technologies' future use and revenues.
>
> *(56)*

After Paramount dropped out as the distributor, Coppola forged a new distribution deal with Columbia Pictures. Columbia employed a market research consulting firm to brainstorm ways to position the film in the marketplace. Three pitches were proposed: using Coppola's name recognition, emphasizing the innovative nature of the film, and treating it as a love story "captured by the extraordinary atmosphere of fantasy-photography, scenery, lighting and music" (Lewis 68). Curiously, none of these approaches was adopted; instead, Columbia, mirroring their successful campaign for Roman Polanski's *Tess* (1979), marketed *One from the Heart* as an art film with the potential for a wider audience. A limited release pattern failed to generate even modest public interest, and the film grossed less than $1 million domestically. Chase Manhattan and other creditors demanded repayment soon after the release, and Coppola was forced to sell Zoetrope Studios to one of his financiers, Jack Singer, in February 1984 (Cowie 152).

One from the Heart became a signpost for the demise of the New Hollywood era. It was another example of an independent auteur using a large budget to create their personal vision on film. By the early 1980s, many of the New Hollywood auteurs failed to connect with audiences, including Spielberg with *1941* (1979), Scorsese with *The King of Comedy* (1982), and DePalma with *Blow Out* (1981). Film critic David Ehrenstein identifies several traits associated with auteur-driven films of this period: big budget, extravagantly designed but with a thin script. He concludes that each film was "an Art Film aimed at a mass audience" (45). Many examples are cited: *Heaven's Gate* (1980), *Pennies from Heaven* (1981), *Honky Tonk Freeway* (1981), *Cannery Row* (1982), *Tempest* (1982), and *One from the Heart*. To Ehrenstein, these films fail due to their quest for cultural respectability, linked to the hubris of the director and their desire to make a "major statement" (47).

Partly as a result of such failures, the landscape for American filmmaking began to shift more toward marketing-friendly films and away from auteur filmmaking. The era of the high concept film, with an emphasis on marketability and visual style, would become a dominant factor in Hollywood filmmaking in the 1980s and beyond (Wyatt 20). Certainly, *One from the Heart* would be classified as a failure, critically and commercially. Nonetheless, Coppola's singular vision and his experiments with storytelling and technology created an independent film on a grand scale. A leading independent filmmaker of the 1970s, Coppola hoped, as he moved into the 1980s, to remake the contemporary studio and filmmaking through his own principles; we are left, however, with a film of epic ambition and creativity marking the end of the New Hollywood era.

Works Cited

Biskind, Peter. *Easy Riders, Raging Bulls: How the Sex-Drugs-and-Rock 'N' Roll Generation Saved Hollywood*. Simon and Schuster, 1999.

Bordwell, David. *On the History of Film Style*. Harvard University Press, 1997.

Brown, Garrett. "The Steadicam and *One from the Heart*." *American Cinematographer*, Jan. 1982, pp. 44–45, 82–87.

Bygrave, Mike, and Joan Goodman. "Meet Me in Las Vegas." *American Film*, Oct. 1981, pp. 38–43.

Cowie, Peter. *Coppola*. Applause Theatre & Cinema Books, 2014.

Ehrenstein, David. "The Aesthetics of Failure." *Film Comment*, vol. 19, no. 3, 1983, pp. 44–47.

Fielding, Raymond. "Recent Electronic Innovations in Professional Motion Picture Production." *Journal of Film and Video*, vol. 36, no. 2, 1984, pp. 43–49, 72.

Jones, Kent. "Mythmaker Francis Ford Coppola: The Great Conductor of American Cinema." *Film Comment*, vol. 38, no. 3, 2002, pp. 30–36.

Lewis, Jon. *Whom God Wishes to Destroy: Francis Coppola and the New Hollywood*. Duke University Press, 1995.

Rickey, Carrie. "Theatrical Realism." *Film Comment*, vol. 18, no. 1, 1982, pp. 32–33.

Thompson, Kristin. *Breaking the Glass Armor: Neoformalist Film Analysis*. Princeton University Press, 1988.

Tzioumakis, Yannis. *American Independent Cinema*. 2nd ed., Edinburgh University Press, 2017.

Wyatt, Justin. *High Concept: Movies and Marketing in Hollywood*. University of Texas Press, 1994.

24
CHOOSE ME (1984)
Caryl Flinn

Alan Rudolph, known for his appreciation of actors, has directed a stunning array of 20th- and 21st-century talent, among them Geraldine Chaplin, Julie Christie, Bruce Willis, Jennifer Jason-Leigh, and Albert Finney. He has helmed projects with Alice Cooper, Alberta Hunter, and Willy Nelson, and engaged cultural icons no less than Timothy Leary, Kurt Vonnegut, and Divine (in male drag, no less). In 1995, Leonard Maltin referred to him as an "important independent filmmaker whose eccentric tastes have not endeared him to the filmgoing masses." Rudolph concurs, "I want to reach the individual and let the masses take care of themselves" (Carroll 20).

But he has made a massive number of them: 22 as of this writing, from *Premonition* in 1972 to *Ray Meets Helen* in 2017, most of which he wrote. Despite having never made a legitimate genre picture, he has worked in rom-coms (*Ray Meets Helen*), horror (*Nightmare Circus* [1974]), biopics (*Mrs. Parker and the Vicious Circle* [1994]), rock and roll (*Roadie* [1980]), film noir (*Trouble in Mind* [1985]), the woman's film (*Remember My Name* [1978]), thrillers (*Mortal Thoughts* [1991]) and dramas about political corruption (*Trixie* [2000]), infidelity (*Secret Lives of Dentists* [2002]), and bereavement (*Afterglow* [1997]).

A wide sweep for any director, such diversity and scale have not, unfortunately, translated into sustained success or even recognition for Rudolph, particularly within the histories of American Independent Cinema. Not only does an American cinema of the 1980s anthology fail to include a chapter on him, but Rudolph doesn't even appear in its index (Prince). When his name *is* mentioned – whether in scholarship, criticism, or informal conversation – it is usually followed by, "Robert Altman's protégé." Rudolph's career took off while working as an AD with Altman, whom he always acknowledges (he'd say that from his father on studio sets he learned about movies, and from Altman, he learned about films).[1] Reducing Rudolph to protégé, however, is an altogether different matter. Yes, he

FIGURE 24.1 Filming *Choose Me*'s climatic rooftop scene (photo credit: Joyce Rudolph. Photo courtesy of the Alan and Joyce Rudolph Papers, University of Michigan Library, Special Collections Research Center).

shares with Altman the penchant for ensemble casts; certain actors (Keith Carradine, most notably); an outsized sense of irony. But the film worlds they construct could not be more different. For Tom Charity,

> Rudolph['s]…distinctive comic universe…is nearly as populous but more romantic and artificial than Altman's: his playful, poetic scripts glisten with puns, surreal non sequiturs and arch literary conceits. Borrowing ingredients from farce – amorous doublings, mistaken identities and coincidences – Rudolph nevertheless steers his films towards melancholy and regret.

Choose Me, Rudolph's most well-known film, shows these traits in abundance, with its sensuous, dreamlike, offbeat world. The 1984 film enjoyed international critical acclaim and received, for example, the International Critics' Award at the Toronto Film Festival; it was also a rare commercial success for the director, readily recouping its $800,000 production costs and smoothing the path for his 1985 film, *Trouble in Mind*. These successes are reason enough for *Choose Me* to introduce a new generation of viewers and readers interested in Independent Filmmaking. It is compelling for other reasons: on the one hand, *Choose Me* refuses to behave as if it were fully "independent" from Hollywood, borrowing its character types, quoting iconic scenes, and even hanging studio posters. On the other, it keeps Hollywood at a purposeful distance – its playful, heightened sense of style impedes any link to Hollywood's invisible style or naturalism – and in this way too goes against many American "independent films" of the 70s and 80s. Yet, on the third hand, Rudolph's commitment to atmospheric mood places him within the realm of European art cinema, with its more irregular narrative adventures and poetic style.

This essay examines *Choose Me* across that three-way intersection. Despite many substantial nods to Hollywood, the film is nearly devoid of naturalism – although no attempt is made to use style for style's sake, as some art and experimental films do. Elaborated through pithy bits of dialogue, music, and color – its style presents a set of emotional "realities," realities that invite us to connect to it, realities that show the same respect for characters that Rudolph imparts to his actors. This vibrant emotionality infuses sound- and image tracks alike, but any diegesis that explains or responds directly to their feelings or that situates them within logical, ill-fitting plotlines, is elusive. Vincent Canby characterized *Choose Me* and Rudolph's other work as "adult fairy tales," a description that encapsulates their cynicism, hope, and sense of romance.

The Story

Choose Me's opening image immediately blasts you into a space of irreality: after a screen filled with nothing but porn-pink, the credits begin and the camera moves, slowly pulling back to reveal the neon lights of Eve's Lounge where sex workers waft around street corners, couples pour out of night clubs and dives, making out, and making deals. It is very noir and stagey. Eve's Lounge anchors what one critic labels the film's "placeless setting" (Combs) and its eponymous owner (Lesley Ann Warren), we learn, is the second Eve to run the bar – her predecessor may have killed herself for love. Warren's highly sensuous Eve might be on the same path: her love life is s a casting call of failures. She's seeing a married man, Zack; engaged in one-night stands, and is instantly fascinated with newcomer Mickey (Keith Carradine, an Altman and Rudolph regular), who walks into Eve's bar like a hero from a western who left the map behind. Mickey chats up barfly-poet Pearl (Zack's abused wife, played by Rae Dawn Chong) to whom he enumerates a list of improbable pasts: multiply-married ("I'd still be married if something hadn't happened each time"), a military pilot stationed in Germany, a spy arrested by Russians, a Yale poetry teacher, an award-winning photographer, and someone who tells any woman he kisses that he wants to marry her.

Eve's home provides the film's second key setting (the third is Dr. Love's radio studio). Its hip, decorative glamor is on par with Eve's rich sartorial ones, though in contrast to the bar, it is brightly lit; even night scenes appear to be bathed in the light of day. Not unlike *The Moderns* (1988), large, abstract paintings cover the walls, many depicting anguished women in love (one, has a knife plunged into a man's chest, states "A recurring image I often thought of killing him," indicative of Eve's perspective on love). Like the bar, Eve's home is a transfer station in which characters have sex, talk, or try to kill each other in unexpected encounters. After the opening street scene, we see Eve at home on the phone, where she is a disguised guest caller to "The Love Line," a radio show in which hyper-repressed "Dr. Nancy Love"/Ann (Geneviève Bujold) dispenses advice to the lovelorn. As they chat, Rudolph briefly injects a shot of Dr. Love standing behind Eve, telegraphing the above-mentioned function of Eve's spaces – along with Love's telephone lines – of *connecting people* with disregard for spatial verisimilitude.

In contrast to the steamy sensuality of the bar, Eve's home brims with comic, farcical interactions. After brawling with Zack, Mickey goes to Eve's house to rest, and he intrigues roommate Ann/Doctor Love who lets him in. Her detached character shifts, babbling and speculating about Dr. Love in the third person to a disinterested Mickey, who has never heard of her. But Mickey responds to her as an outcast with a poorly concealed desire to experience passion and gives this to her. From here, a series of character shifts, chance encounters, and misunderstandings further the plot (critics make comparisons to *La Ronde* [1950]). As Ann sheds her repressed detachments, Eve, upset that the church mouse of a roommate has slept with Mickey, throws her hands up while angrily acknowledging that "[Mickey] is not mine, and no man owns me." But she is doubly disappointed, for she also believes Mickey to be the culprit behind bruised Pearl's eye (it is Zack). Despairing, she ends up on the roof – an elevated stage on top of the already stagy streets, replete with an audience of onlookers. She threatens self-harm, and when Mickey scrambles up to join her, he does too. As the pair talk and scream, Rudolph's camera closes in, their bodies come together, and their visual setting becomes irrelevant. *Choose Me*'s last scene occurs at the back of a bus where Mickey and Eve explain to a neighbor that they are heading to Las Vegas for their honeymoon. Little more is said, a clear tip of the hat to *The Graduate* (1967), but with less self-doubt on the couple's faces.[2]

Hollywood

Rudolph calls *Choose Me* a love triangle with five edges that doesn't renounce Hollywood love stories so much as re-work them. A love triangle this cumbersome surely must include some jealousy and retaliation, which dutifully erupt in small clichés. Their prime host is Zack, who feels that he must defend his honor constantly and pugnaciously, first going after Mickey over the latter's winnings in a card game; later, for Mickey's having slept with Pearl – and for his interest in Eve. Played by Patrick Bauchau, Zack is the film's most overt stereotype; the cheaply-staged brawls between Zack and Mickey are almost slapstick, and Bauchau's performance topples any cosmopolitanism his French-speaking character might have offered. Such a caricature of male buffoonery – not uncommon in Rudolph's work – was, and arguably remains, a rarity on the silver screen, especially at the time of *Choose Me*'s release, when Hollywood was awash in the sympathetic depictions of threatened white, straight, middle-aged men of means – think of anything starring Michael Douglas or Clint Eastwood. Independent cinema – a movement largely dominated by men – scarcely attended to them either; there, most male downfalls would be attributed to narrative or diegetic circumstance rather than to character traits. Art cinema seemed readier to take them on, but again, with tragedy in the air rather than the gentle irreverence of Rudolph. Zack is the figurative corollary to Rudolph's description of his work: "My goal was to make American films like European art films, but with an American sense of humor" (Rudolph, [Loose]).

Pearl is another member of Rudolph's overpopulated love triangle. Like her husband, her views of romance are a cliched by-product of American movies. A veritable prison house of cinema, the walls of Pearl's bedroom are smothered by Hollywood movie posters such as *The Man I Married* (1940); *The Man I Love* (1946); the best is *Don't Bother to Knock* (1952), positioned behind the door through which Mickey and Zack each enter without knocking. So cinematized is Pearl's conception of love and romance that she interprets Zack's beatings as signs of attentiveness, and in her worldview, he's not the problem, it is Eve, whom he has seduced. Pearl's remarks on their marriage offer a delectable example of Rudolph's commentary on mass-made fantasy, "we had sex and more sex. It was great; then we started to talk, and it stopped working." The competing décor of Pearl and Eve's domestic spaces comically opposes *Choose Me*'s pivots between Hollywood films to independent, aesthetically oriented cinema. Pearl and Zack's lurid movie posters seem to duke it out with the oversized, abstract paintings of women on Eve's walls. (Interestingly, the lessons on Eve's canvases are no less destructive to women than Pearl's mass-marketed images.)

Eve, in fact, filters a less comic rendering of the story's overheated love triangle. She is worn down by love, while still craving deeper engagement with it. Believing that her hopes for Mickey had been misplaced, Eve is despondent to the point of stagy, furious threats of suicide, sentiments worked out in the stylistically and emotionally charged rooftop scene culminating the film. For as over-the-top as her reactions may be, it is noteworthy that they are transmitted with sympathy – and with full-on artifice.

Scholars rightly characterize classical cinema by its emotional appeal: we engage with lead characters, root for them, or hate them, and their goals guide us through causal chains that occur in legible temporal and spatial worlds. Emotionalism rules the day in *Choose Me,* but it results in narrative zig-zags, unsteady truths, and abstract space, closer to its paths in "real" life. The anti-naturalism of art and independent cinemas is more prominent. If Rudolph lets style do the talking, it doesn't know how to pin down truthful plot points any more than Mickey does. For Mickey "tells stories" just like a screenwriter or filmmaker does. Indeed, at the outset of the film, we see Mickey leaving a psychiatric facility, where the doctors say, "There's nothing that's wrong with him, he just lies," and the film does nothing to clarify his mental condition. Later, Ann, intrigued, sifts covertly through Mickey's notebook and finds photos, magazine covers, and newspaper articles whose headlines are facsimiles of his accounts of his past. Despite the physical heft of its contents, however, its authority is weightless, evidence without any proof (Ironically, "M.E.W.'s notebook is one of the few props that survive of the film).

Independent Filmmaking

Rudolph's film work, robust from the 1970s through 1990s, more sporadic in the 2000s, follows the high and low arcs of American independent cinema. As other chapters in this anthology note, however, "independent film" is not a linear phenomenon, and as a category, it is at once leaky and restrictive. To an extent, it is an auteur- and market-making machine whose aims aren't that distinct from commercial studio cinema. Says Rudolph, "independent is such a loaded term. Every filmmaker is *dependent* on the financing" (Rudolph, Personal interview). Indeed, *Choose Me* cannot be fully framed by the bounds of independent filmmaking. For the sake of this chapter, though, I take several features to exemplify its independent status and consider its stylistic traits – including the mood that these sounds and images evoke – as part of the tradition of art cinema. But these are arbitrary distinctions.

First, its production history. Rudolph had relatively free reign making *Choose Me*, thanks to the support of the newly formed Island Alive for having come in on time and under budget with his previous film, *Return Engagement* (1983). Island Alive was burnished with the hipness and "independence" of its parent company, Island Records, which represented rock and roll stars and introduced reggae to the world in the 1970s; it also preceded Miramax and Fine Line.

Rudolph again kept his expenses down with *Choose Me:* his costume designer, Tracy Tynan, bought outfits at going out-of-business sales and secondhand shops and even shared pieces from her personal wardrobe with Bujold. (Warren wore much of her own clothing). Rudolph blocked and improvised the opening scene in 30 minutes; Eve's home was a three-week rental found while driving around. Efficiency even marked the script, which Rudolph wrote in two weeks.

Casting furthered the sense of *Choose Me*'s independent status, particularly with Carradine, a staple in indies by Robert Altman and others. His Mickey is built out of multiple male movie character fragments, mainstream *and* independent, including his own image. Attracted to three women, proposing to all of them, *Choose Me* seems to give Carradine the opportunity to hop beds as he had in *Welcome to LA* or in Altman's *Nashville,* but his sexual wanderings here are different, lacking a sense of conquest or even of initiative agency. In *Choose Me* he is a lost soul rather than a lecherous lothario. Charming but aimless, he is a little damaged, like Eve, if more hopeful. In a nice touch, Rudolph has him articulate his hopes for the future backward: first, get married; *then*, go to Vegas.

Choose Me's "placeless" space also keeps it adrift from Hollywood. Indeed, the situational rather than geographical notion of its narrative world is what's stressed. One of the few setting details that Rudolph provides is signs for Garden and Adam Streets in the vicinity of Eve's Lounge. Rather than situating audiences spatially – or biblically – it raises another primal question of Warren's Eve and the original, undepicted Eve being in repeat rotation, as if the two businesswomen were interchangeable, which they might well be. Not for nothing does the action surrounding "our" Eve occurs in front of a huge billboard for Coca-Cola – a quick nod to capital and its own circular patterns of exchange.

Art Cinema

It is the *degree* of Rudolph's break with cinematic conventions that aligns *Choose Me* and his work in general against classical cinema and closer to American independent and European art cinema. The opening bright pink shot makes short work of this project. Even as the camera moves, tilting down to the street near Eve's, that inaugural image works like an anti-establishing shot, producing colors rather than a location. Its resting place, moreover, is a stagy setting reminiscent of another important independent film of the 1980s, Coppola's *One From the Heart* (1982). There, any real Las Vegas setting utterly recedes as the Zoetrope Studios set comes into play (this is where *its* lead couple attempt to live out a happy ending, just as Mickey wants to). Critics actually assumed *Choose Me* was really shot in Vegas, though knowing that Rudolph shot *Choose Me* in LA ultimately counts for little: Locations matter insofar as they stage, not place. The text produces the impression that all that matters are affective experiences that, of course, cannot be summed up: sweet, ironic, sad, impassioned, hopeful, aimless, conveyed through the cross-wired experiences of its misfit figures (how can they be otherwise, with each having so many identities and influences?). In both sound and image, *Choose Me* pairs deep sensuality and feeling with an artifice so spirited and flighty that any stabilizing facts of space, character backstories, or even narrative events are rendered even more moot.

Rudolph's visual style is recognizably distinctive yet hard to describe. Functionally, it helps keep audiences from falling into any "lies" of realism or its enablers. In a discerning turn of phrase, Tom Milne influentially calls *Choose Me* "as suggestive as a neon orchid." Colors fly throughout the film: Warren is dressed with flair: costumer Tynan deliberately outfitted her in red, matched with lipstick and cut flowers, generating a saturated artifice that screams sensuality and affect but provides no roadmap for how to read it. Along with her black and red work outfit, and her long, body-conforming night-robe, Eve wears the sartorial equivalent of the neon signs and flashes of color created by cars driving by, saturating *Choose Me* with a sensuality that feels ready for release. The explosiveness of her and Mickey's situations, and perhaps one of their pasts, erupts in a repeated dream fragment of a handgun going off with a flash of red filters, edited in such a way that prevents us from attributing it definitively to one or the other of them. At one point, Mickey has said that he killed a man; Eve's predecessor at her bar purportedly shot herself over a man, a threat "our" Eve also seems willing to repeat.

The soundtrack is critical in producing *Choose Me*'s special style and in detaching it from standard Hollywood fare. A small tinkling of a bell, for instance, tends to sound in scenes with Ann/Nancy; it even opens the film, suggesting that Love "might be in the air" before we even meet Bujold's character, an impatient sound pre-lap connecting us to her as Eve's environs are established. Even more abstract is the music. Few scores are as memorable as *Choose Me*'s. The director spells out its function, calling music, "film's great illuminator, a direct bridge to an audience's emotional reservoir" (Rudolph, Personal correspondence).

It started with singer Teddy Pendergrass sending some demos to Island Records. Producer Carolyn Pfeiffer recalls that an entire soundtrack by Pendergrass eventually proved too costly, but Rudolph took one of the songs, "Choose Me (You're My Choice Tonight),"[3] and based his picture on it. Its import is irrefutable: parts of it introduce the film, appear throughout, and give it its title (two other films have songs for names: *Remember My Name* [1977] and *Trouble in Mind* [1985]). Pendergrass's soulful voice makes it very difficult not to get the sense of desire awash in romantic possibilities. Background vocals appear in whispered, pleading phrases, "Choose Me/I'm your choice tonight," "feels so right/what delight," a Greek chorus of soul.

Other kinds of music occur (jazz and blues instrumentals among others) to produce a score that is unified in tone, atmosphere, and feeling. Notably, and like classical cinema, this unity is created from fragments, since existing compositions are rarely played out in full, so as not to take time or focus away from the storytelling. *Choose Me* leans on that tradition even harder, presenting tiny snippets of songs that dart across scenes, irradiating them. In that regard, the music is *unlike* conventional film music: impossible to put into the background, more a storytelling device getting us to root for characters and lose ourselves in the flow.

It can also be said that the songs and music speak – in fits and starts – for the feelings, hopes and emotional baggage carried around by the film's fable-weary characters. This runs through Rudolph's other work, as Steven Rybin argues about the eponymous song in *Welcome to LA:* "Rudolph's characters offer their inner lives to the world. That these emotional lives have been received, at least, in the performance of a song…suggests that there may be a hope for Rudolph's romantics…" (303).

Coda

At once an example of independent, art cinema, and (anti) Hollywood, *Choose Me* defies the rules. Even as an "adult fairytale," *Choose Me* unsettles generic expectations, since it lacks their usual moral instruction: if those Hollywood posters in Pearl's bedroom schooled her in the lessons of romance, for instance, her black eye shows the downside of taking its fables to heart. And so Hollywood, while present in *Choose Me*, does not help its internal world – just as it did not help Rudolph outside of it. The film is more concerned with human connections and longings. Conveyed through style, they produce a dialectic of hope and disillusionment in a text filled with affectionate, if sardonically rendered, references to various cinematic practices. For these and other reasons, *Choose Me* is distinctive enough to free Rudolph from the protégé label. Rudolph believes in second chances, in love in its many goofy forms; no one in their right mind would depict Altman that way. That he presents that through an emotionalized visual and acoustic style – along with character illogic – makes Rudolph truly independent. Bathed in a sensuous fog of mood and fantastic "realities," *Choose Me* makes specifics indeterminate – and unimportant. It is the irrational, impassioned pathways of desires and yearnings that move where they may: whether whirring across Dr. Love's phone lines or in the vocals of Pendergrass. That *Choose Me*'s feelings roam so freely between its quirky characters and its audience viewers is testimony to Rudolph's skill and to the Independence of his vision.

Acknowledgments

My thanks to Gabby Dias, Phil Hallman, Carolyn Pfeiffer, and Alan Rudolph.

Notes

1 Rudolph's career took off in the 1970s working with Altman; his father, Oscar Rudolph, enjoyed a career that ran the gamut of acting in silent pictures by Cecil B. de Mille, to working as cinematographer and assistant director in the major studios, to directing television shows in the 1950s – a personal embodiment of the Hollywood studio era.
2 Ness's reading of the film stresses the scene's homage to *It Happened One Night* (1934)
3 Rudolph further saved money by using songs in the public domain, such as the blues number "Trouble in Mind," or pieces from the Island Records catalog, such as the reggae song "King Tubby Meets the Rockers Uptown."

Works Cited

Canby, Vincent. "Alan Rudolph Finds His Upbeat Style." *New York Times*, 13 Jan. 1985. https://nyti.ms/29CT0Hk.
Carroll, Tomm. "Sir Alan and the Days of the Round Table." *DGA News*, Oct./Nov. 1994, pp. 20–24, 34.
Charity, Tom. *The Rough Guide to Film 1*. Rough Guides, 2007. Qtd. in https://www.theyshootpictures.com/rudolphalan.htm.
Combs, Richard. 28 May 1985. Unpublished interview questions sent in advance of the BFI's *Monthly Film Bulletin,* July 1985. University of Michigan Library Special Collections, Alan and Joyce Rudolph Collection, Correspondence, personal 1973–2002 and undated, Box 1.1d
Maltin, Leonard. *Leonard Maltin's Movie Encyclopedia*, Plume, 1995. Qtd. in https://www.theyshootpictures.com/rudolphalan.htm.
Milne, Tom. "As Suggestive as a Neon Orchid." *Sight and Sound*, Summer 1985, pp. 214–216.
Ness, Richard. *Alan Rudolph*. Twayne Press, 1996.
Prince, Stephen, editor. *American Cinema of the 1980s*. Rutgers University Press, 2007.
Rudolph, Alan. [Loose page of quotations]. University of Michigan Library Special Collections, Alan and Joyce Rudolph Collection.

———. Personal interview, August 2020.
———. Personal correspondence, October 2021.
Rybin, Steven. "We've Never Danced: Alan Rudolph's *Welcome to LA* and *Remember My Name.*" *The Other Hollywood Renaissance,* edited by Dominic Lennard et al. Edinburgh University Press, 2020, pp. 296–307.

25

DESERT HEARTS (1986)

Chelsea McCracken

In a media landscape where streaming services offer a range of LGBTQ content, it might be hard to imagine a time when there were almost no depictions of same-sex love between women. Those fleeting images that did make their way to screens concluded with women entering into relationships with men, dying, or being otherwise punished for their "unspeakable acts."[1] This was the world in which *Desert Hearts* emerged, a beloved film that told a sincere story of two women falling in love without a tragic ending.

The film worked to fill a conspicuous absence of mainstream, positive lesbian representation.[2] This chapter explores *Desert Hearts*'s trailblazing status, its struggles, and its complex reception. Director Donna Deitch fought for years to see her vision on the big screen. What made *Desert Hearts* groundbreaking was, ironically, its simple adherence to conventions of the romance genre. This was a story that had not been told on screen, with this level of production value and mainstream appeal. Given the conservative hesitations of Hollywood in the 1980s, *Desert Hearts* could only have been made independently, and it needed to be made, to show future producers and distributors that there is an audience for films with lesbian content.

Blazing a Trail

The film *Desert Hearts* begins and ends at a train station. Among the disembarking passengers in the opening scene is a tense, modestly dressed woman in her thirties. Vivian Bell (Helen Shaver), a reserved and unassuming east coast college professor, traveled to Reno, Nevada to divorce her husband, who is never seen on screen. A Reno divorce was a relatively quick option in 1959 when the movie takes place. This process, however, required that the divorcee establish residency in the state, which involved living in Nevada for at least six weeks. This context

FIGURE 25.1 The rugged Nevada landscape serves as a backdrop to Vivian and Cay's budding romance.

provides the background for Vivian's lengthy stay at Frances Parker's "divorce ranch," a homestead for women who were awaiting divorce proceedings. Vivian sparks the interest of Reno local Cay Rivvers (Patricia Charbonneau). Frances (Audra Lindley) was the longtime mistress of Cay's father, and they have a complex stepmother/daughter relationship. Cay is introduced as she recklessly drives backward down an open desert highway, immediately signifying her wild, free spirit that provides a perfect romantic coupling for Vivian's timid restraint. As Vivian and Cay grow closer and eventually consummate their budding romance, they face the disapproval of Frances (a stand-in for conservative society) and their own internalized hesitations. Despite setbacks, the film ends with Vivian and Cay boarding a train together. Their future is uncertain, but *Desert Hearts* leaves audiences with the promise of more. The possibility of happiness for these women, while it might seem trite for today's audiences, was a remarkable achievement in 1986.

Deitch's film is a loose adaptation of Jane Rule's acclaimed 1964 novel, *Desert of the Heart*. The novel created a stir when it was published, due to its frank and controversial depiction of love between two women. Rule was writing at a time when homosexuality was criminalized, and many were outraged by the book's matter-of-fact, positive depiction of the romantic relationship. Others embraced the novel, and it became a much-loved cult text, shared between friends and read repeatedly. The novel gained enough of a following that Hollywood studios became interested in optioning the film rights. Rule declined because she feared studios would mishandle her work and alter the core of her book. She was then approached by Deitch, who loved the novel and made an impassioned pitch to make a film version. Rule sold the rights to Deitch, and the long journey to produce *Desert Hearts* took its first steps. Deitch initially looked into acquiring funding from a studio, but after a few meetings, it was clear that she would not be able to make the film her way from within the confines of studio production ("Director's Commentary"). Independently financing and producing the film was her only option, if she wanted to see her vision come to life.

Money is a constant, pressing challenge for independent filmmakers. Filmmaking is an expensive enterprise, with budgets in the 1980s averaging around $18 million and reaching over $60 million for expensive Hollywood films (a relatively small cost when compared with current franchise releases). Even *Desert Hearts*, a low-budget film, cost around $1.5 million. First-time directors like Deitch face further hurdles, as they do not have a proven track record with which to tempt financial backers. In addition, mainstream and even independent American companies (with some notable exceptions) were reluctant to work with gay and lesbian content for much of the 1980s. Without this support, many films lingered in development, never to be produced, and others, such as John Sayles's lesbian-themed *Lianna* (1983), were self-financed.

Desert Hearts was produced without a distributor attached, and this lack of industry support pushed Deitch to apply for grants and use grassroots fundraising techniques – raising relatively small amounts of money from a large number of people, a form of pre-internet crowdfunding. Deitch began this process in 1980, and an article in 1982 suggested that the film was "readying production" (Montgomery). Despite this optimism, it would be years before they began shooting. Deitch received support from prominent figures such as Gloria Steinem, Lily Tomlin, and Stockard Channing. These women lent their names to the fundraising efforts, assisting in the sale of "limited partnership" shares for $15,000 each (Dry). Deitch recalled that her fundraising operated

> like a Broadway backers party. When I began I didn't know anyone who had money to invest. So I reached out to all of my friends and contacts all over the country and wrote letters. This was a networking process that went on month after month and then year after year
>
> (Silverstein, "Interview")

Many investors identified as gay or lesbian and having a well-networked community, one that was passionate about the arts and creating lesbian images on film, greatly assisted in Deitch's ability to raise money. Deitch even invited some investors to be extras in the film's casino scenes. Not only did this increase her backers' enthusiasm for the project, but it also provided her with free extras.

Overcoming Production and Distribution Hurdles

Once Deitch secured enough money to move toward production, she faced her next challenge: casting. In the 1980s, there was a strong hesitation, by many actors and actresses, to portray an LGBTQ character on screen. Some were uncomfortable acting romantically toward someone of the same sex, and there was a concern that "playing gay" would materially harm their careers. Agents advised their clients not to take these roles, and some even expressed anger at being approached. Deitch noted that many actresses declined to meet about the film, and agents said they were "not interested in the subject matter" ("Director's Commentary"). Even for smaller roles, agents "felt that this was way too dangerous for any client to be in… People didn't want anything to do with this movie" (Deitch in Silverstein, "Desert Hearts"). Fortunately, Shaver and Charbonneau (both openly heterosexual actresses) were seemingly unfazed by the subject matter, had chemistry in their screentests, and accepted the roles.

Deitch and her crew shot the film in 31 days. They shot around two scenes a day, which was a very tight schedule that did not allow them to film many takes of each shot or do "pickup shots," additional footage that could enhance the final film. The production team made smart use of their limited funds, relying on natural landscapes, inexpensive locations, and cost-saving filming techniques. As characters drive down the center of Reno, for example, the camera remains focused inside the car. This allowed the production to avoid having to do a costly period setup of the downtown space.

Although Deitch worked with an extremely tight budget, she wanted to emulate Hollywood filmmaking style and accessibility, creating a film "that you could bring your mother to" (Finch). The conventional form is often brought up in discussions of the film, which note, for example, that *Desert Hearts* was "written and directed in a fairly realistic, straightforward style, not that different from Hollywood style" (Benshoff and Griffin 195). Andrea Weiss likewise argued that the film

> sits on the fence between being independent (in its means of production) and Hollywood (on whose conventions it heavily relies)… the film operates within the dominant modes of representation, with very polished, impersonal camera work and a narrative style as linear and traditional as that of any romance story.
>
> *(8)*

Deitch herself has said that her "initial intention was to tell a lesbian love story framed in a very accessible style that would appeal universally" (qtd. in Silverstein, "Desert Hearts"). Looking at the bleak lack of positive representation, Deitch sought to provide self-affirming images and a different perspective, and she reached an audience hungry for these images. As she said, "I made the movie I wanted to make, the movie I wanted to see because it hadn't been made… I wanted it to be a universal love story" (qtd. in Carlin) that would have crossover potential to "mainstream" (straight) audiences. *Desert Hearts*'s soundtrack of popular mid-century Country Western songs also played a significant role in the film's commercial feel and lent an air of authenticity to the 1959 Reno setting. As evidence of the importance of music, they spent $250,000 of their small budget on music rights ("Director's Commentary"). The songs deal largely with romantic love and heartbreak, which contributes to the film's larger themes and a connection between heterosexual romance and the experiences of two women falling in love.

Getting an independent film into theaters, especially those that cater to mainstream fare, required negotiating another set of hurdles. Deitch had trouble pre-selling the film to distributors, and she had to sell her house to fund the film's completion. Fortunately for *Desert Hearts*, several companies that dealt with more commercial independent films were beginning to take on gay and lesbian content. These indie distributors could provide a more tailored release approach and individualized attention. The Samuel Goldwyn Company acquired *Desert Hearts* after it was completed, and their interest in this and other LGBTQ films suggests an affinity for, or at least a business-savvy open-mindedness toward, gay and lesbian films.[3] Goldwyn's stated goals included the creation of a diverse range of films, "a wide spectrum of both specialized and commercial product;" they offered a "commitment to a more demanding audience and to the kinds of diversified, quality films that will meet that demand" (Ray 26). Such comments illuminate how Goldwyn was positioning itself in the marketplace. Goldwyn made money and shaped its image by choosing projects that were considered daring, provocative, and connected to emerging trends in indie cinema. Given these priorities, Goldwyn was in a position to help films like *Desert Hearts* find greater access to theatrical markets and to lend legitimacy to boundary-pushing topics. At the same time, these films helped shape Goldwyn's image and legacy, a mutually beneficial situation for filmmakers and distributor.

After years of struggle, *Desert Hearts* was heading to theaters. It began with a successful showing on the film festival circuit, including playing at Telluride, Toronto, and Sundance, where it won the Special Grand Jury Prize.[4] When *Desert Hearts* began its New York theatrical run, Deitch brought grassroots community organizing into the realm of advertising and exhibition. She noted that the "most clever marketing device" used to promote *Desert Hearts* was when she "went to the lines of the hippest New York movies I could think of… and passed out leaflets and talked the movie up" (Learner 36). This form of specialized, local, and inexpensive marketing attracted audiences and helped the film come within a few tickets of breaking the theater's weekend record.

Audience Reactions to a Landmark Lesbian Romance

Over the years, many women have approached Deitch and the lead actresses to thank them for making *Desert Hearts*, recounting how they watched the film dozens of times and how its depiction of lesbian romance held a special place in their hearts. Filmic romances often bring together people who, initially, seem too different to belong with each other. Such is the case with Cay and Vivian, who occupy a number of dichotomies (geography, education and class status, sexual history, and even appearance).[5] These differences dissolve as the two women spend time together, and the film "presents romantic union as the solution to the problems facing these two women: Each can encourage the other to express that part of herself that she has denied" (Wartenberg 194). Presenting same-sex love in a classic romance structure caused many audience members to feel seen in a new way, to feel like their lives and relationships were somehow legitimized because they could identify with images on the screen. Screenwriter Natalie Cooper talks about making people feel valid, and not shoved to the side; "It isn't so much the content. It's a matter of identification with it and the way it's been presented... this is our movie" (qtd. in Gross).

Not all audience members, however, were as effusive. Some faulted the film's slow pace, predictability, and lack of political engagement with contemporary issues. The *LA Times* review, for example, remarked that "For all its love of risk, it's a remarkably old-fashioned, cliché-fettered work" (Benson). The mixed response is summed up in a *Gay Community News* review of the film:

> *Desert Hearts* will make you laugh, it will make you cry, and it will make you yawn. But you can't have everything... Alright, here's the real deal. It's corny. Some of it is so corny that it's downright embarrassing. It's a corny love story with very little tension. But, I know and you know that you're going to see it and something about the experience will feel exciting. Because even though *Desert Hearts* is not the greatest film ever made, it is going to be important to a lot of people. It might even make a difference in their lives. So, just get ready to enjoy yourself and giggle and groan, then get up and go see *Desert Hearts*. Later you'll want to say that you were there.
> *("Desert Hearts")*

While acknowledging some of the limitations of the film, this review points to its vital role in people's lives and, looking forward, its position as a landmark of lesbian cinema. Seeing the film in theaters meant being a part of history.

Jackie Stacey offers a compelling argument for why the film received mixed responses from lesbian audiences. The romance film focuses on a love relationship "whose fulfillment is threatened by a series of problems" (Stacey 97). A lesbian romance film offers an unappealing selection of possible problems, including competition from male characters (a return to compulsory heterosexuality) and homophobia, whether internal or external. In creating *Desert Hearts*, Deitch was faced with a challenging "double-bind," since she wanted to create positive representations, and these obstacles "reinforced definitions of lesbianism as a negative category" (98). Although the film does present some lesbian-specific impediments (e.g., Darrell vying for Cay's affection and Frances kicking Vivian off of the ranch), they are easily overcome:

> It is precisely because these characters do not present convincing problems for Cay and Vivian that there is a lack of narrative involvement and the sense of emotional flatness about which many lesbians complained... All the problems which were put in the way of their romance, including that of Vivian's homophobia, seemed to find relatively easy solution: we never

really felt on the edge of our seats, willing the relationship to succeed, fearing that without our collective desire for its fulfillment it would surely fail.
(102, 111)

While *Desert Hearts* in many ways replicates the conventions of the romance genre, the desire to capture a lesbian relationship through a positive lens, ironically, takes away some of its genre-specific thrill and emotional power.

Spurring a Gay New Wave

Desert Hearts, while fascinating to study in its own right, fits into a larger trajectory of LGBTQ cinema. In February and March of 1986, *Desert Hearts* was released alongside two other gay-themed works, *My Beautiful Laundrette* (Stephen Frears), and *Parting Glances* (Bill Sherwood). That same year, William Hurt won the best actor Academy Award for portraying an openly gay man in *Kiss of the Spider Woman* (Hector Babenco). The release of these films and the attention directed toward gay and lesbian themes caused some critics to suggest the appearance of a "Gay New Wave," the first stirrings of an LGBTQ film movement. Unfortunately, there were not enough gay and lesbian films in the late 1980s to expand discussions of a movement. Distributors also utilized marketing tactics that downplayed a film's gay content in an attempt to reach wider audiences. Jeff Lipsky, VP of Marketing for Goldwyn, said of *Desert Hearts*, the film is not a "sexual-political tract – it's a love story," and the distributor's goal was "not to characterize it as a lesbian or gay movie" (qtd. in Gold). A full movement would not happen until the 1990s, with New Queer Cinema. These 1980s films, however, played a critical role in the development of LGBTQ filmmaking.

Given the high cost of feature filmmaking, there needs to be the potential for profit to attract commercial companies to invest in films. *Desert Hearts* and other 1980s gay and lesbian films provided returns on investments, which paved the way for future films to be more explicit in their connections with LGBTQ audiences and content. *Desert Hearts* made $2.5 million in theatrical release off a $1.5 million budget.[6] While this is nothing next to a Hollywood blockbuster's theatrical revenue, it was a substantial profit for a small independent film, and it demonstrated that there was a market for films with lesbian content. In addition to theatrical releases, the rise of the home video market helped to sustain a growing gay and lesbian filmmaking niche. Vestron Video handled the home video release for *Desert Hearts*, and the company made a considerable profit and visible impact with the film. The film debuted as the fifth most popular wholesale acquisition in the UK ("Video Top 20"), and in the United States the film made it onto *American Film*'s "Best bets among this month's releases on tape," a substantial feat during a holiday buying month ("Fast Forward"). Gay and lesbian video sales facilitated significant audience growth and access to previously unserved communities. It enabled filmmakers to reach untapped markets, those gay men and lesbians who lived outside of major cities and therefore did not have access to film festivals or art house theaters. The financial success of projects like *Desert Hearts* inspired filmmakers,[7] provided a model for grassroots production techniques, and encouraged companies to invest in future films, aiding in the growth of LGBTQ cinema more broadly.

Conclusion

Creating lesbian images on film presented a number of challenges, but, as *Desert Hearts* demonstrated, independent cinema provided a space for this representation. The film did not find mainstream support before its completion, and even though audience's reactions were somewhat mixed, it holds a significant place in the history of LGBTQ cinema. *Desert Hearts* bucked the trends in lesbian representation, in part because, as Mandy Merck notes, it is "set in a fantasized Wild West (where anything goes, pardner) in an idealized retro-chic fifties, without any of the fifties' circumstances" (380). Deitch intentionally removed the film from contemporary politics to offer a never-before-seen, widely accessible romance. While we can critique this decision, I would ask, why not tell a simple love story? Hollywood is a dream factory that has been doling out fantasies of heterosexual romance for over a century. Why shouldn't lesbians have this as well? Why should lesbian films constantly rehash harsh realities? Deitch broke the cycle of tragic endings and gave people hope by reworking a classic genre. As the spirited, openly queer Cay said of Vivian, "She just reached in, put a string of lights around my heart." This film likewise reached in and put a string of lights around so many hearts, becoming a cult classic precisely because this independent production opened the world of silver screen fantasies to lesbian audiences.

Notes

1 For more on the history of LGBTQ representation, see Harry Benshoff and Sean Griffin's *Queer Images* and Vito Russo's foundational text, *The Celluloid Closet*.
2 The concept of positive representation comes with its own complexities. Some LGBTQ filmmakers, including those associated with the early 1990s New Queer Cinema, brushed off the idea of positive representation as bland and limiting. Still, we can point to the importance of representation and having self-affirming images of LGBTQ individuals.
3 Including *Longtime Companion* (1990), *Peter's Friends* (1992), *The Wedding Banquet* (1993), and *Go Fish* (1994).
4 *Desert Hearts* was not initially released on the gay and lesbian film festival circuit. This was likely a marketing decision, as showing in a gay film festival was perceived to restrict a film's commercial prospects.
5 As noted in Merck, these differences were added to the film and did not exist in the original novel. Deitch and screenwriter Natalie Cooper likely developed these distinctions in order to better fit the genre conventions of the romance, and perhaps the western.

6 *My Beautiful Laundrette* made $2.45 million on a $940,000 budget, and *Kiss of the Spider Woman* made a remarkable $17 million on a $1.8 million budget.
7 Kimberley Pierce, director of *Boys Don't Cry* (1999), for example, cited Deitch as an inspiration (Rich 86), as did *Go Fish* director Rose Troche.

Works Cited

Benshoff, Harry, and Sean Griffin. *Queer Images: A History of Gay and Lesbian Film in America*. Rowman & Littlefield Publishers, 2006.

Benson, Sheila. "2 Brisk Parts Can't Stir Pulse in 'Desert Hearts.'" *Los Angeles Times*, 25 Apr. 1986, https://www.latimes.com/archives/la-xpm-1986-04-25-ca-1592-story.html.

Carlin, Shannon. "The LGBT Film 'Desert Hearts' Is More Important Now Than Ever." *Bustle*, 17 July 2017, https://www.bustle.com/p/the-groundbreaking-lesbian-film-desert-hearts-is-more-necessary-now-than-ever-before-70504.

"Desert Hearts." *Gay Community News*, Apr. 1986. Reprinted in Sarah Schulman. *My American History: Lesbian and Gay Life during the Reagan and Bush Years*. Routledge, 1994, pp. 154–156.

"Director's Commentary." *Bonus Materials. Desert Hearts*, Criterion DVD, 2017.

Dry, Judy. "How Lily Tomlin and Gloria Steinem Helped Fund the Lesbian Film Classic 'Desert Hearts.'" *IndieWire*, 20 July 2017, https://www.indiewire.com/2017/07/-desert-hearts-donna-deitch-interview-lesbian-lgbt-lily-tomlin-1201857397/.

"Fast-Forward: Best Bets Among this Month's Releases on Tape." *American Film*, 1 Dec. 1986, p. 59.

Finch, Mark. "Home on the Range." *Gay Times*, no. 95, 1986, pp. 44–46.

Garfield, Kim. "Donna Deitch: Giving Bloom to 'Desert of the Heart.'" *The Advocate*, no. 341, 29 Apr. 1982, pp. 45+46.

———. "Desert Hearts: A Lesbian Love Story Heats Up the Silver Screen." *The Advocate* 440, 18 Feb. 1986, pp. 43–47.

Gold, Richard. "Gay-Themed Features Hot B.O. Stuff." *Variety*, 9 Apr. 1986, p. 5.

Goldstein, Richard. "The Gay New Wave." *Village Voice*, 22 Apr. 1986, p. 51.

Gross, Larry. *Up from Invisibility: Lesbians, Gay Men, and the Media in America*. Columbia University Press, 2001.

Learner, Richard. "Gay Films Stay Strong at the Box Office – Priming audiences for More to Come?" *The Advocate*, no. 449, 24 June 1986, p. 36.

Merck, Mandy. "Desert Hearts." *Queer Looks: Perspectives on Lesbian and Gay Film and Video*, edited by Martha Gever et al. Between the Lines, 1993. pp. 377–382.

Montgomery, Clifton. "Taxis, Tokens and Quick Takes at the Movies." *The Advocate*, no. 335, 21 Jan. 1982, p. 47.

Ray, Bingham. "Goldwyn and the Future of Independent Film Distribution." *Boxoffice*, vol. 123, no. 5, 1 May 1987, pp. 25–26.

Rich, B. Ruby. "Sharp Shooters." *The Advocate*, 15 Aug. 2000, pp. 85–87.

Russo, Vito. *The Celluloid Closet*. Quality Paperback Book Club, 1987.

Silverstein, Melissa. "Interview with Donna Deitch, Director of Desert Hearts." *Huffington Post*, 9 July 2008, http://www.huffingtonpost.com/melissa-silverstein/interview-with-donna-deit_b_111723.html.

———. "'Desert Hearts' Director Donna Deitch Talks Love Scenes, Gloria Steinem, and the Sequel." *Women and Hollywood*, 18 July 2017, https://womenandhollywood.

com/desert-hearts-director-donna-deitch-talks-love-scenes-gloria-steinem-and-the-sequel-897f1a6e7d0b/.

Stacey, Jackie. "'If You Don't Play, You Can't Win': *Desert Hearts* and the Lesbian Romance Film." *Immortal, Invisible: Lesbians and the Moving Image*, edited by Tamsin Wilton. Routledge, 1995, pp. 92–114.

"Video Top 20." *Screen International*, 2 May 1987, p. 398.

Wartenberg, Thomas. *Unlikely Couples*. Westview Press, 1999.

Weiss, Andrea. "From the Margins: New Images of Gays in the Cinema." *Cineaste*, vol. 15, no. 1, 1986, pp. 4–8.

26
DOWN BY LAW (1986)

Yannis Tzioumakis

When Jim Jarmusch's *Down by Law* was released in North American theaters in the autumn of 1986, some critics perceived it as a "carbon copy" (qtd. in Pierson 223) of *Stranger than Paradise* (1984), the filmmaker's previous film that had been both critically and commercially successful. More sustained analyses that came in later years seemed to agree with that view.

For Geoff Andrew, *Law* was essentially a "reworking" of *Stranger*: "its tripartite structure – basically depicting self-willed inertia, enforced inertia and a journey towards freedom (or even, perhaps Hell, Purgatory and Paradise) – again featured feckless, self-regarding, determinedly cool no-hopers vaguely revitalized by the unexpected arrival in their lives of a foreigner" (Andrew 141). Suárez, on the other hand, noted that *Law* had "a tighter plot [...] held together by sustained actions and motivations" but that it also was linked through "numerous formal and thematic continuities with Jarmusch's earlier film." When it came to form, Suárez highlighted similarities in terms of the use of black and white cinematography, deep focus, wide-angle lenses, leisurely narrative pace, a privileging of long takes, a relative absence of sequence shots, an emphasis on non-dramatic events, trivial dialogue or silence, and an insinuation of dramatic events through the use of ellipsis (Suárez 49–50).

Although such views are certainly valid, the critics' emphasis on the similarities between the two films obscured almost fully certain fundamental differences. *Stranger* was composed of 67 long takes, while *Law* consisted of a much larger number of shots edited in rhythmical patterns. The earlier film was governed by a more clearly delineated screen time, with its second part taking place a year after the first and the third immediately after the second. The narrative of *Law*, on the other hand, took place at a much more indeterminate time. *Stranger's* engagement with genre was rather understated, with the protagonists' trips to Cleveland and rural Florida linking it to the road movie (Murphy 28). *Law* was

DOI: 10.4324/9781003246930-27

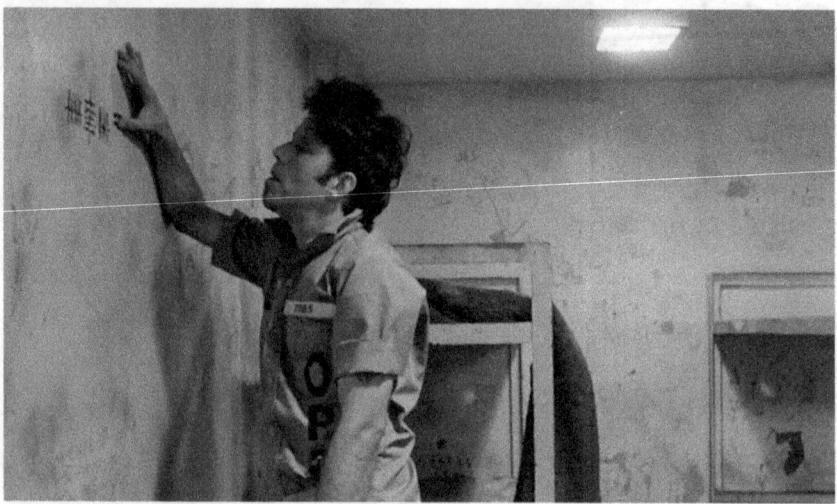

FIGURE 26.1 Has Zack been in prison for 19 days (as the markings on the wall imply) or is Jarmusch playing games with narrative time?

firmer in its use of genre with the frameworks of the prison escape film and the noir comedy providing opportunities for both adhering to and experimenting with genre conventions. Finally, *Stranger* made a point to demonstrate how narrative similarities and thematic repetition operates from one section/act of the film to the next. In *Law*, similarities and repetition become a focal point from the opening sequence and, through the help of symmetrical compositions and rhythmic editing, provide the foundation for a very different aesthetic experience compared with the earlier film. They also help viewers understand the film's main point that underneath superficial differences there are deeper structures that bind people and can help them make connections.

From Relative Failure to Slow Critical Recuperation

In a sector like American independent cinema where critics' views tend to carry a lot of weight with audiences, their emphasis on the film's similarities with *Stranger than Paradise* may have impacted *Down by Law*'s commercial performance. It grossed ~$1.5 million at the North American box office,[1] labeled by Pierson a "quiet commercial disappointment" (76). Two years prior, the domestic box office for *Stranger than Paradise* was $2.5 million, a substantial figure for an independent film that had cost just over $100,000 to produce (Levy 188). However, as the production of *Law* was estimated to have cost more than $1 million and as it was seen as a much more ambitious film than *Stranger* in terms of box office potential (Meisel 25), its $1.5 million can, indeed, be perceived as a disappointment. By 1986, the year of the film's release, certain American independent films had started to do spectacular box office business. *Kiss of the Spider Woman* (1985),

The Trip to Bountiful (1985) and *She's Gotta Have It* (1986) took $17 million, $7.5 million, and $7.1 million, respectively, in North America alone, with the first two also receiving several Academy Award nominations and even two awards.

The company behind the success of *Kiss of the Spider Woman* was Island/Alive, one of the key independent distributors of the 1980s, while, as Island (following the dissolution of its partnership with Alive in 1985), it was also responsible for releasing *The Trip to Bountiful*. With these two unexpected box office hits demonstrating the commercial potential of independent film, Island decided to expand into production. *Down by Law* was its first film as a (co-)producer-distributor, financed partly from the profits of the distribution of *Kiss of the Spider Woman* ("Fueled" 26), while a host of young executives who would become major players in the independent film scene in the years to come were involved in the film's production: Tom Rothman (who would establish Fox Searchlight in 1994), Russell Schwartz (who would be president of USA Films in 1999) and Cary Brokaw (who would found Avenue Pictures in the late 1980s). Within this context, *Down by Law*'s domestic box office must have been more than a "quiet disappointment" for the company. *Law* also failed to receive any awards at the 1986 Cannes Film Festival, when two years prior *Stranger than Paradise* had famously won the *Camera d'or*. It did not win either at the 2nd Independent Spirit Awards, with *Platoon* (1986), *Blue Velvet* (1986), *Salvador* (1986) and *She's Gotta Have It* winning the main prizes.

But even in more recent critical accounts of American independent cinema, *Down by Law* has not attracted significant interest. Where it receives some attention, it tends to be perceived, if not as a minor entry in Jarmusch's oeuvre, as a film that was a "hard sell" (Merritt 325) and that sustained Jarmusch's reputation as an important artist before his "work declined severely" (Levy 189). And when it is discussed in terms of its material contribution to American independent cinema it is primarily to showcase a "maverick filmmaker's" approach to independent film (Andrew 141–145; Levy 188–189) or to illustrate techniques that contribute to independent film aesthetics, as exemplified by its use of "narrative obliqueness" (King 72–73). Intriguingly, even in the Jarmusch literature, *Down by Law* has received little attention and even less sustained analysis compared with his other films.

However, despite this relative lack of interest, the film has carved a niche in American cinema and, 37 years since its release, it has been recuperating well from its lukewarm reception. Its 2014 theatrical re-release received rave reviews, with the *Guardian* calling it "effortlessly laidback and superbly elegant" and confirming that it has a "deserved reputation for cinematic cool" (Bradshaw). In the Internet Movie Database *Down by Law* has been enjoying more attention from cinephiles than *Stranger than Paradise* at least in terms of votes (53K against 38K).[2] Furthermore, the subsequent success, visibility, and cachet of the talent involved in the film have certainly helped it find new audiences. Italian comedian-director Roberto Benigni's Oscar-winning *Life is Beautiful* (1997) and Ellen Barkin's Hollywood stardom, together with the uncompromising quality and iconic cool of musicians-actors Tom Waits and John Lurie (who besides playing the main leads also contributed the credit songs and the score to the film, respectively), have all helped enhance the film's stature in the intervening years. This is, of course, in tandem with Jarmusch's uninterrupted association with American independent cinema as a filmmaker who never sold out to Hollywood and who has continued to work without interference more than 40 years after his debut.

In the rest of this chapter, I will demonstrate why this relatively overlooked film is an important example of American independent cinema, focusing primarily on the film's formal design. My argument is that the film may have "disappointed" because it was expected to showcase a more clear-cut evolution of Jarmusch as a filmmaker in the vanguard of independent cinema in the United States. This, significantly, would also dovetail with the evolution of an American independent cinema that in the mid-1980s had started to be more commercially ambitious than earlier in the decade and was supported institutionally by a variety of companies and organizations. This evolution would reach a tipping point at the end of the 1980s with the critical and commercial triumph of *sex, lies, and videotape* (1989), *Drugstore Cowboy* (1989), and *Do the Right Thing* (1989).

Jarmusch, however, had no interest in the increasing institutionalization of American independent cinema. Furthermore, the more popular aspects of *Down by Law* on which Island might have been depending for the commercial success of the film (faster editing, play with genre, presence of minor stars, pre-sold Tom Waits songs from the album *Rain Dogs* (1985) released by Island Records and opportunities for synergies) were swiftly subsumed into Jarmusch's overall approach to filmmaking that continued to be defined by the set of stylistic and narrative hallmarks that made *Stranger than Paradise* such a critical and commercial success. As a result, the new choices Jarmusch made (eschewing single takes in favor of symmetrical compositions and rhythmic editing, prominent experiments with narrative time versus screen time, and play with different genre(s) such as the prison film and the noir comedy) ended up receiving little or no attention.

Ironically, some of these elements would characterize the more commercial indie cinema of the 1990s, but as part of more accessible narratives and/or more overstated examples. For instance, the non-linear narrative time in Quentin Tarantino's *Reservoir Dogs* (1992) and especially *Pulp Fiction* (1994) was much easily accepted by critics and audiences within the context of the crime film, while rhythmic editing, symmetrical compositions, and montage sequences consisting of tracking shots became a trademark of Wes Anderson's colorful approach to filmmaking, starting from *Bottle Rocket* (1996). In *Down by Law*, however, such elements do not attract attention in themselves; rather they become integrated into the "Jarmusch style," with the filmmaker continuing to experiment with these elements in later films such as *Mystery Train* (1989) and *Night on Earth* (1991).

Symmetry, Rhythm, and Narrative Time

The key organizing principle of the aesthetic of *Down by Law* is a very particular type of formal symmetry that is the product of both stylistic and narrative choices. This formal design often clashes with an otherwise linear narrative and often questions the latter's linearity. Although critics assume that the narrative events in the first act of the film take place simultaneously, during the same night (see, for instance, KL 52), this is not *necessarily* the case; the events that lead the two main characters, Jack (John Lurie) and Zack (Tom Waits), to prison could have taken place days or even weeks apart. *Necessarily* is the key word here. Linear narratives in mainstream Hollywood films tend to be characterized by direction, clarity, and unity that stand up to scrutiny and contribute to the classicism that has characterized Hollywood for most of its history. In *Down by Law*, however, narrative direction and clarity can be questioned, especially as narrative time is often placed at the service of a formal symmetry that invites viewers to make non-linear connections between events and defines the film's aesthetic. This, I argue, is the key contribution of the film to the expanding aesthetics of American independent cinema in the mid-1980s. It is also a good reason to consider that contribution significant as it stands at the opposite end of a Reaganite cinema defined by narrative drive, direction and linearity and designed to "foregroun[d] the experience of cinema as an immediate and affective one" (Needham 316).

The opening tracking shots of run-down New Orleans neighborhoods, accompanied by the music and lyrics of Tom Waits's "Jockey Full of Bourbon," provide the key to understanding the carefully arranged rhythm of the film's structure. The first scene consists of nine tracking shots with the camera moving from right to left, creating a montage of a stylized but rather unappealing New Orleans. After the ninth shot, the music fades and viewers are introduced to Jack in a three-shot scene. He gets out of bed where he is lying with his lover Bobbie, goes to the terrace of his house, and checks on what looks like a sex worker sitting on a chair, before returning to bed. As he goes back to sleep, Bobbie, with her back against him, opens her eyes, revealing to the viewer that she was pretending to be asleep, which may suggest that she is not happy with him. "Jockey Full of Bourbon" comes back on, accompanying another montage of tracking shots, with the camera moving this time from left to right. At the end of the third shot, the music fades again and we have another three-shot scene during which we meet Zack coming into his house in the early hours of the day. He takes his top off and gets in bed. His lover Laurette seems to be asleep. Again with her back against him, she opens her eyes for the benefit of the viewer, showing that she was also pretending, and by the look on her face it is suggested that she is also unhappy. The opening song returns a third time as another montage of six tracking shots, with the camera moving again from right to left, continue to show desolate New Orleans landscapes before the opening credits of the film appear over a black screen.

As it is clear from this pre-credit prologue, the key objective is for the spectator to make connections between the two sets of characters. As both sets were introduced in three-shot scenes that were similar in terms of composition and mise-en-scène, and privileged omniscient narration, and as these scenes were interspersed with three montage sequences, one consisting of nine shots and two shorter ones that also add to nine shots, under the sound of the same non-diegetic song, it is clear that the focus is (or should be) on this symmetry and the ways in which it will help viewers make sense of the narrative events that are due to unfold.

Following the credits, the first "problems" with narrative structure appear immediately. Both sets of characters are presented in two successive four-shot scenes. In the first, Laurette is screaming at Zack and throws his belongings out of the window as she realizes they do not have a future together given Zack's apathy and inability to compromise and keep his job. In the second, Bobbie berates Jack for being unambitious, unorganized, and not even a good pimp, while at some point, she contemplates shooting at him with a gun. Although both scenes explain why the two women may have been unhappy in their earlier introductory scenes and move the narrative forward, what is arguably more interesting is the further connections that are established between Zack and Jack as we learn more about them as characters.

Even more interesting is the extent to which these two scenes happen simultaneously. Although in terms of screen time, they are presented successively and follow logically from the two introductory scenes before the credits, small details in the mise-en-scène suggest that they neither necessarily take place at the same time nor do they take place immediately after the opening scenes. For instance, while in the introductory scene early morning sunlight punctuated Zack's arrival at home, it is now clear that it is nighttime as Laurette throws his belongings out of the window into the darkness. An even more nuanced clue is that in the earlier scene, Zack was wearing black trousers with stripes while in the second scene, he is wearing black check trousers. It is evident that the second scene could have been taking place at any time, even though screen time and narrative direction prompt viewers to think that it is taking place immediately after Zack's opening scene.

Jack's second scene, on the other hand, provides no clues about whether it is taking place at a different time. He is wearing the same vest and his lover is still in bed, which implies that it is taking place later the same day. However, the possibility that the scene is taking place in the same room on a different day remains open. Given its structural similarity to the scene that preceded it, the question to ask is why the two storylines connect formally in such a *precise* manner. The answer is provided later in the film when it becomes apparent that its mode of storytelling is as important as the narrative itself; a narrative that is not (only) about linearity, cause-effect logic, and character goals but that is (more) about connections between people made because of circumstances that look different on the surface but are similar in reality.

As the narrative progresses, the symmetries continue. Both Jack and Zack (note also the structural similarity of their names) are framed by people they know and end up getting arrested. Both setups are executed over two sequences of nine shots each and both end with the two protagonists protesting their innocence. In the prison scenes that take up the whole of the film's second act and which feature the two main characters (and later a third one, exuberant Italian Bob [Roberto Benigni]) in the same space, similar medium close-up shots of each character on their bunker beds punctuate the narrative. However, Jarmusch uses this part of the film primarily to experiment with narrative time and screen time, often in radical ways, and therefore continue to undermine the linearity of the story. To put it differently, it is very difficult to get a sense of how long the characters were in prison before escaping in the third and final act of the film, which once again serves the film's effort to focus on the characters' budding relationship rather than on a genre determined plot that seems to emerge at the same time.

Specifically, Zack is already behind bars when this part of the film starts. In the third shot, we see him marking lines on the wall which, prison film conventions suggest, represent the number of days incarcerated. At that point, there are 19 lines on the wall, as seen in this chapter's image, but it is not clear if Zack made them all or even if they do represent days in prison as they are in groups of five and six (and not of seven which would connote a week). In the fourth shot, Jack is brought in to share the cell with Zack. If they were both arrested on the same night and Zack has been marking days behind bars, why is Jack sent to prison – seemingly – 19 days after Zack? Perhaps the idea that Zack and Jack were framed on the same night must be discarded. Three shots later the "days" on the wall seem to be close to 60 (the framing does not allow a clear view to count them precisely). And yet, the two characters argue as if they have just met, with body movements and dialogue suggesting that they may have not been in prison together for too long a time. However, after another two shots, Jack complains that Zack has not spoken in three days, while on the wall one can clearly see 65 "days," which implies that three actual days *may* have passed from their earlier argument when the lines on the wall were close to 60.

Another two shots later, the marks on the wall are 110, while following a fade out (which routinely connotes the passage of time) and the arrival of Bob, narrative time is complicated further. We do not see on which day Bob joins them in the cell but three shots after his arrival we see ~165 marks on the wall, while Jack asks Bob to get his and Zack's name "straight" "after all this time." In the next shot, Zack seems to be drawing more days on the wall, while three shots later, in the famous "I scream, you scream" sequence, the lines on the wall are 193, suggesting six and a half months of prison time (at least for Zack who was the first one to be seen in the cell). Have they really been in prison for that long? Bob's command of English seems to have improved but that is the only other clue about narrative time. But does it really matter how long they have been in prison?

And does it really matter how they escape from it, given both the film's emphasis on character relations and the overall "narrative obliqueness" that draws attention away from the plot and to the nature of such relations? The third and final act picks up the rhythmic editing (most obviously in the scene where Bob is cooking a rabbit and Jack and Zack, following yet another fight, walk off-screen and are seen successively bursting into monologues). It also continues the narrative time experiments (with their facial hair suggesting that they were wandering in the Louisiana swamps for ~a week, even though the fact that they end up near the Texas borders suggests that they have traveled for much longer than a week). On the other hand, the film's final undermining of narrative linearity and its focus on human connection based on circumstance comes in the unlikely pairing of Bob with Nicoletta (Nicoletta Braschi). Introduced just 13 minutes before the end of the film, Nicoletta is an Italian woman who, because of a number of coincidences in her own life, ended up moving from Genoa, Italy to manage her deceased uncle's roadside cafe in the Louisiana-Texas border. Within the space of hours of narrative time, the two Italians fall in love and decide to start a life together, while after a night's stop at Nicoletta's house Jack and Zack "disconnect" by taking different paths when they reach a bifurcated dirt road. By that time, however, they have made peace with each other (and themselves) and are ready to start life anew. Rather improbably, none of the three characters seems to be concerned about the Law catching up with them but, once again, this is not narratively significant.

Jarmusch stated in an interview that *Down by Law* is a more imaginative film than *Stranger than Paradise*, and that imagination is a key theme of the film (Von Bagh and Kaurismäki 73). In her examination of the use of imagination in the films of a number of contemporary filmmakers, including Jarmusch, Patrizia Lombardo noted that for the filmmaker, "unity of effect does not mean rigid narrative structures, but the coherence of attitude, and often the coherence found in a very ancient form of narration: narration that is punctuated by episodes" (121–122). While this kind of narration also characterized *Stranger than Paradise*, in that film it was based on the slow, nonchalant impact of the long take, the static camera, and the fade out that commented on the dreary existence of the main characters and the impossibility of human connection. *Down by Law*, on the other hand, embraces rhythmic editing, symmetrical compositions, and radical experimentation with narrative time that enables connections, even if they seem unlikely or unrealistic. It is perhaps this irreverent use of modernist aesthetics to support a film that combines "bleak existentialism with fairy tale brightness," as a reviewer put it (KL 52), that may not have been as palatable for American independent cinema in the mid-1980s. 37 years later it looks like *Down by Law* has been ahead of its time.

Notes

1 All box office figures cited in this chapter were obtained from individual films' Internet Movie Database pages (www.imdb.com) and refer to domestic (i.e., North American) box office gross.
2 The number of votes were taken from the films' pages on the Internet Movie Database.

Works Cited

Andrew, Geoff. *Stranger than Paradise: Maverick Film-makers in Recent American Cinema*. Prion Books, 1998.

Bradshaw, Peter. "Jim Jarmusch Masters Cinematic Cool." *Guardian*. 11 Sept. 2014, https://www.theguardian.com/film/2014/sep/11/down-by-law-review-jim-jarmusch-tom-waits.

"Fueled by 'Spider Woman' Coin, Island Steps Up Prodn, Releases." *Variety*, 26 Feb. 1986, p. 26.

King, Geoff. *American Independent Cinema*. I.B. Tauris, 2005.

KL. "Down by Law." *Film Journal*, 1 Oct. 1986, pp. 52+

Levy, Emanuel. *Cinema of Outsiders: The Rise of American Independent Film*. NYU Press, 1999.

Lombardo, Patrizia. *Memory and Imagination in Film: Scorsese, Lynch, Jarmusch, Van Sant*. Palgrave, 2014.

Meisel, Myron. "Island Thrives with Two Oscar Wins." *Film Journal*, 1 May 1986, pp. 6+.

Merritt, Greg. *Celluloid Mavericks: A History of American Independent Film*. Thunder's Mouth Press, 2000.

Murphy, J.J. *Me and You and Memento and Fargo: How Independent Screenplays Work*. Continuum, 2008.

Needham, Gary. "Reaganite Cinema: What a Feeling." *The Routledge Companion to Cinema and Politics*, edited by Yannis Tzioumakis and Claire Molloy. Routledge, 2016, pp. 312–322.

Pierson, John. *Spike, Mike, Slackers and Dykes: A Guided Tour Across a Decade of American Independent Cinema*. Hyperion, 1995.

Suárez, Juan A. *Jim Jarmusch*. University of Illinois Press, 2007.

Von Bagh, Peter, and Mika Kaurismäki. "In Between Things." *Jim Jarmusch Interviews*, edited by Ludwig Hertzberg. University Press of Mississippi, 2001, pp. 71–80.

27

SHE'S GOTTA HAVE IT (1986)

Apryl Lewis

In 1983, Spike Lee premiered his student short film *Joe's Bed-Stuy Barbershop: We Cut Heads* and won a Student Academy Award. This initial success seemed like a seamless beginning for someone whose artistic prowess is ongoing and often praised. However, Lee's debut feature film *She's Gotta Have It* (1986) was far from effortless.

The film follows protagonist Nola Darling, a young, attractive artist, and her romantic involvement with three men. Jamie Overstreet, Greer Childs, and Mars Blackmon each want Nola for themselves, but Nola is unable to choose one man. The film ends with Nola reclaiming her carefree, sexually liberated lifestyle and rejecting all three suitors. *She's Gotta Have It* was filmed in 12 days on a budget of $175,000 and involved a series of exchanges with various film distributors before finally getting picked up by Island Pictures. These humble beginnings established not only Lee's independent filmmaking status and his tenacity as a storyteller and filmmaker but also the foundation of Lee's vision for what films about, by, and for Black people can do.

Lee's resilience and visionary determination are widely recognized by scholars, critics, and industry players such as John Pierson, Roger Ebert, Todd McGowan, and Ed Guerrero. Pierson and Ebert have recognized the potential of Lee's work, including and beyond *She's Gotta Have It*, to uniquely capture African American life and experiences that would differ from mainstream Hollywood filmmaking efforts. McGowan expands on this, arguing that Lee's films compel viewers to "confront their own unconscious, whether this unconscious is associated with their own singularity as subjects, their racism, their membership in a community, or whatever else" (3). Accordingly, *She's Gotta Have It* forces viewers to reckon with their unconscious biases about seeing the African American experience on screen. Finally, Guerrero considers Lee to be one of the few directors to survive the "new black film wave" because of his ability to maintain consistent production of media content on his own creative and financial terms.

FIGURE 27.1 Nola Darling sits alone in her bed, staring at the audience.

While some of Lee's films like *Do the Right Thing* (1989), *Malcolm X* (1992), and *Crooklyn* (1994) have been distributed by major companies including Universal Pictures and Warner Bros., he is still regarded as an important American independent filmmaker. A "cultural artifact of the 1980s" that "contributed to intense contemporary debates on multiculturalism, feminism, sexuality, and many other controversies" (Foote 226), Lee's debut film aided in propelling American independent film and shaping ideas of Black cinema. Importantly, as Thelma Willis Foote and others have noted, it also contributed – particularly through its portrayal of a Black female protagonist – to debates on a range of interrelated aspects of Black life in America. I argue in this chapter that Lee's *She's Gotta Have It* provides a key reference point for considering the intersectional relationship between race, gender, and sexuality, specifically in discussing ingrained prejudice against Black women (misogynoir) and how that is presented.

Strength in Numbers

When Spike Lee emerged on the independent film circuit, he navigated personal and financial adversity. In fact, *She's Gotta Have It* was not Lee's first attempt at filmmaking. Lee failed to make his film, *The Messenger*, in the summer of 1985 (Simmonds 13). Lee described the experience as a "disaster," and he was "determined to do another film for as little money as possible" (qtd. in Simmonds 13). Moreover, from a financial standpoint, Lee had trouble procuring the finances necessary to shoot his debut feature film. According to Larry Rother, "a $20,000 grant from the American Film Institute fell through" and this reality forced Lee to improvise. In the end, his film came together with a total budget of just $175,000. The film's small budget, especially in comparison to the multi-million-dollar budgets of mainstream films at the time, reflects a prevalent attribute of American independent cinema.

Despite financial precarity, Lee's film was a "turning point in American cinema because it demonstrated once again the underestimated potential crossover between independent art cinema and African American cinema – and, crucially, crossover between their paying viewers" (Francis 16). In *Spike, Mike, Slackers & Dykes*, John Pierson recalls a sold-out screening of Lee's film at the 1986 San Francisco International Film Festival. One advantage of screening at this festival early in the film's festival run was its proximity to a large Black population (Pierson 54). The film continued to be well-received as the screenings continued, and Pierson contends that the crowds were typically 75 percent Black, which reaffirms the demand at the time for films like *She's Gotta Have It*, regardless of any Hollywood backing. Critics and scholars further noted that Lee's film "undermined the mystique of Hollywood's aesthetic of seamlessness and linearity as well as its expensive budgets" (Francis 16). His first feature then undoubtedly aligns with several critical attributes associated with American independent films, specifically the film's budget, production through Lee's own company – 40 Acres and a Mule Filmworks, its aesthetic sensibility, and its subsequent circulation via Island Pictures instead of a major distribution company.

Lee's Personal Vision on Black Representation and Black Sexuality in Film

Along with all Black casting and a sexually provocative storyline, Lee developed a "strong personal vision" for his film that ran counter to what he saw in the industry for Black actors. "It's rare enough," he noted at the time, "that black people are seen in films, but even when we are, it's always in stereotypical roles of making people laugh, or as singers and dancers" (Rother). Although Black representation in film is important, that representation has historically been reduced in American cinema to either depictions of trauma or reaffirming harmful stereotypes.

Steven Spielberg's 1985 film *The Color Purple*,[1] released the previous year, also contains a predominantly Black cast and Black female protagonist. Though the film was generally well received by audiences and received multiple Oscar nominations, many critics and viewers responded negatively to the film's portrayal of Black men as violent and abusive toward women.[2] However, "[t]he problem...is not so much the portrayal of violence itself as it is the absence of other narratives and images portraying a fuller range of Black experience" (Crenshaw 1256).[3] Even the well-known Black feminist writer bell hooks, a notable critic of Lee's films, acknowledges that *She's Gotta Have It* contains multidimensional male characters with qualities and attributes that make them appear unique (296). Though Lee's film includes what he calls "the dog scene," where a group of Black men appear on screen and deliver pick-up lines directed at women, Lee regards the principal male characters in his film – Jamie, Greer, and Mars – to be an extension of his efforts at challenging and critiquing Black male sexuality filtered through a white, mainstream gaze.

A film like *The Color Purple* reaffirms for Lee that, though there may be a predominantly Black cast, a shift from stereotypical representations of Black people is just as important. So at age 29, Lee set out "to show a slice of black city life the way he wants" by writing, directing, editing, and producing a film with an all-Black cast that showcases romance among Black people (Rother). Having an all-Black cast "releases the film from the race issues that surface in any film with a black and white cast" (Simmonds 13). Furthermore, "[t]he lack of racial tension in *SGHI*, and the [humor] of the film, give it a fresh, relaxed air, and helps us to swallow what would otherwise be bitter and painful messages about black sexual politics" (13). Simmonds's sentiment also ties back to an observation Lee makes about not seeing Black sexuality portrayed on screen, or at least in a manner that is not filtered through white supremacy or other racist tropes (13).

Those traditional depictions of Black sexuality and humanity by white storytellers create distorted Black images that run counter to how Black people see themselves. Lee attempts to provide a new narrative on Black male sexuality that does not resort to brutality or having Black men depicted as sexual predators. His "portrayals of sexual love are unabashedly male-oriented and heterosexual; for Lee, 'it is a dick thing.' The 'dick thing' returns the genitals to the Black man" (Elise and Umoja 13). Efforts to reclaim Black male sexuality may have been an underlying factor in Lee's adamance about keeping the pixilated sex scene between Nola and Greer intact, much to the chagrin of the Motion Picture Association of America (MPAA). Although Lee begrudgingly cut out some portion of the sex scene due to pressure from the MPAA, he still presented Black sexuality on his terms (Pierson 68). In Lee's film, Black male sexuality is placed at the forefront. Although filtered through a male viewpoint, *She's Gotta Have It* provides a perspective on Black men's and women's experiences that do not rely on traumatic circumstances, such as slavery, to tell a story.

She's Gotta Have... a Voice: Nola Darling and Black Feminist Critiques

Although Lee had a particular vision for the film that is inclusive of Black men's experiences, the film follows a Black female protagonist. Lee wanted to showcase a young Black woman whose approach to sexuality would cause men and women alike to reconsider societal norms toward dating and relationships. Lee recalls how during a question-and-answer session "one man remarked how unusual it was to see 'the shoe on the other foot'" (Rother). In other words, the woman is the one courting multiple men rather than the other way around. Reflecting on the cultural moment, one recent critic noted: "When written, Nola Darling was light-years ahead of most Black female characters who'd come before her in the nearly forty years prior." Nola is a sexually confident woman who has a career and, to a significant degree, takes control of her sexuality regardless of what others think. On the one hand, "the openness of her sexual desires, the intimacy of her love scenes, during the '80s was startling, especially for a narrative about a Black woman" (Daniels). On the other hand, some scholars criticize Lee's execution of Nola Darling, particularly for how underdeveloped she is as a character and for his treatment of Nola in the rape scene.

Much of the debate surrounding *She's Gotta Have It* stems from feminist readings and analyses of the film. One such notable critique comes from bell hooks. Writing shortly after the film's release, she noted: "there has been no widespread feminist response to the film, precisely because of the overwhelming public celebration of that which is new, different, and exciting in this work" (hooks 293). One line of reasoning for the lack of feminist responses includes antifeminist rhetoric in popular culture. Trepidation toward feminism and the women's movement correlates with the 1960s Black Power movement (Simmonds 14). One of the messages from the Black Power movement is that Black women do not act or carry themselves in a way that would threaten Black manhood. As such, Black women's sexual liberation was seen as a direct threat to Black masculinity and patriarchal norms. These messages are not limited to the 1960s; rather, they persisted into the 1980s and beyond (Simmonds 15). One can surmise that Lee was aware of the negative sentiments about feminism and Black women's sexuality while filming *She's Gotta Have It*. Nola Darling is "the very embodiment of a black woman's threat to black manhood" because she is "beautiful, independent, and black" (15). By characterizing Nola as a sexually free, independent Black woman, Lee's film becomes a visual representation of Black men attempting "to restrict a Black woman's ability to assert her independence" (15). Restricting Black women's ability to assert themselves physically, sexually, or otherwise, is an act of misogynoir.[4] Like Nola, many Black women do not want to reaffirm or succumb to patriarchal, sexist ideas about themselves in relation to Black men. In the film, Nola resists her suitors, friends, and family's desires for her to conform to more traditional, patriarchal sexual norms rooted in misogynoir. Hence, Nola's relationships with Jamie, Greer, and Mars provide a visual representation of the contentious dynamic between Black men and women regarding sexuality.

Lee sought to direct and produce a film that presents a more balanced view of relationships between men and women (Rother). But in his efforts to highlight Black masculinity, Lee also inadvertently criticizes Black feminism and Black female sexuality. Specifically, Lee wanted his film to be a "defense of black manhood against black feminist misrepresentation in the media" (Foote 218). Yet as Lee elevates and prioritizes the representation of Black men and manhood in *She's Gotta Have It*, he does so at the expense of more nuanced depictions of Black womanhood and women. We see this critique of Black feminism and sexuality emerge particularly in Nola's dream scene. In the scene, three Black women appear and surround Nola. The three women – Jamie, Greer, and Mars's respective girlfriends – denounce Nola as a homewrecker. The women proceed to set Nola on fire. In addition, Lee has the women lament that too many "decent" Black men are preoccupied with women like Nola.

In the film, Nola's dream demonstrates that many Black women are pitted against one another due to a seemingly scarce number of available, eligible Black men. Thus, according to the film, if a Black man is not incarcerated or gay, they must be in the clutches of promiscuous or sexually deviant Black women. Such denigration of Black women is another form of misogynoir, although the stereotypes are coming from women within the Black community. The three women in Nola's dream utilize a common stereotype used against Black women: the Jezebel, which is the "embodiment of deviant black female sexuality" (Harris 5). This stereotype positions Black women as incapable of chastity in a society that demands the innocence of women (5). One of Nola's lovers, Mars Blackmon, cosigns with the Jezebel stereotype when he says, "Men want freaks, but not for a wife." Mars's sentiment suggests that a Black woman's sexual liberation and prowess is an asset until the man is ready to marry and settle down. Then, that same sexual freedom becomes a liability or a detriment for a Black woman who desires a husband. Unfortunately, Nola is subjected to the Jezebel stereotype in the film not only by her lovers but also by her female friends.

Nola's friend and ex-roommate Clorinda Bedford disapproves of the numerous male lovers Nola entertains. Clorinda's sentiment about Nola's sexual independence coincides with the Jezebel stereotype. Moreover, "Clorinda and the male lovers reiterate the dominant culture's demand that Nola conform to the communal ideal of normative female sexuality by entering a monogamous relationship with a male partner" (Foote 222). Nola's friend Opal Gilstrap – a lesbian who has unrequited, romantic feelings for Nola – provides another example. Like the male lovers, Opal objectifies Nola by "insisting that Nola epitomizes subjugated female sexuality waiting to be liberated from male domination" (221). Unlike the male lovers, Nola offers Opal platonic friendship instead of sensual or sexual pleasure through her body and hooks connects her response to Opal to her overall sexual behavior, arguing: "Nola does not find it difficult to reject unwanted sexual advances from another woman, [or] to assert her body rights [and] her preferences" (300). Just as she does with Clorinda, Nola prioritizes her relationships with the men in her life and pushes her friend Opal away. Even when Dr. Jamison, a Black female therapist, tries to convince Nola that she has more to offer people than sex, Nola rejects this notion and further isolates herself from the Black women in her life.

Not only does Nola experience isolation from the Black women in her life, but she also becomes isolated from her lovers in the aftermath of the film's highly debated rape scene. After Jamie breaks up with Nola due to her refusal to end her relationships with Mars and Greer, Nola begs Jamie to come over. He agrees and listens as Nola promises to commit to only him and asks him to make love to her. Simmonds, hooks, and Foote have analyzed this scene and discussed how the film equates rape as a form of punishment for Nola's desire to be a sexually liberated woman and define her own sexuality. In the film, Nola blames herself for driving Jamie to what she calls a "near rape." She inadvertently denies her own vulnerability to sexual victimization by downplaying the traumatic magnitude of the rape. Even if Lee did not intend for the "rape as punishment" narrative to come across in his film, Simmonds explains that "Spike Lee, as a black director, is treading dangerous ground by using his first film to be the teller of this 'truth' about black women's sexuality" (18). The "truth" in this case is referring to the misogynistic idea that women want to be sexually dominated by men and that sexual violence is desired. Furthermore, the rape scene runs counter to Lee's declaration that the film is a defense of "black manhood against black feminist misrepresentation." Although he created male characters that are not "one-dimensional animals," one of his multifaceted male characters still commits sexual violence against a Black woman (Foote 218). Ultimately, Lee does not encapsulate Black women's complexity and nuance as thoroughly as he does with his Black male characters.

Conclusion

Though this chapter is critical of Lee's depiction of women in his film and includes scholarship that highlights the magnitude of the film's climatic rape scene, Lee has, more recently, also critiqued his own decision-making with this polarizing film scene. In 2014, while promoting his remake of *She's Gotta Have It* (2017), a Netflix original series, Lee stated that his biggest regret as a filmmaker was the rape scene. In the interview, he goes on to say:

> If I was able to have any do-overs, that would be it. It was just totally... stupid. I was immature. It made light of rape, and that's the one thing I would take back. I was immature and I hate that I did not view rape as the vile act that it is. I can promise you, there will be nothing like that in *She's Gotta Have It*, the TV show, that's for sure.
>
> *(Fleming)*

Also, when interviewed by activist and leader of the MeToo movement Tarana Burke in 2019, he once again expressed regret about including the rape scene in the film, explaining how his works changed direction after he married his wife Tonya Lewis Lee in 1993. During that 2019 interview, Lee notes how his films such as *Malcolm X*, *Girl 6* (1996), and *BlacKkKlansman* (2018), provide more positive, multifaceted portrayals of Black women (Silver). Lee's remarks do not negate the scholarly response to the rape scene in *She's Gotta Have It* but rather showcases the evolution of his views on gender and sexuality, along with his development as a Black man and filmmaker.

Certainly, Lee's debut film brought in a new era of Black independent film, which was critical after the dissolution of Blaxploitation films in the 1970s. Lee contends that many Black Americans were waiting for a film like his to challenge what was becoming the status quo of the Hollywood system: having Black experience filtered through the lens of white directors. Lee's success shows that Black filmmakers are just as, if not more, capable of conveying stories about

Black people and for Black people. His contributions to American independent cinema and especially Black cinema are indisputable and his work, including *She's Gotta Have It*, has been heralded by scholars, critics, and audiences, even as each of these groups continues to confront, challenge, and question the ideas Lee puts forth in his films. This chapter has highlighted the significance that Black Feminist analysis can play in advancing such work and especially in intersectional discussions of *She's Gotta Have It*, Spike Lee's films, and American independent cinema.

Notes

1 Spielberg's film is an adaptation of Alice Walker's 1982 novel of the same name.
2 Lee stated at the time that he considered his film to be "an antidote to how the black male is perceived in *The Color Purple*" (Fuchs 9). In a separate interview, he elaborated further:

> The difference between [*She's Gotta Have It*] and 'The Color Purple' is that even though there are some dog black men in [my] film, you can tell there is a difference…none of the men here are one-note animals, like Mister was in 'The Color Purple'
>
> (Rother)

3 Crenshaw considers the criticism of Alice Walker's *The Color Purple*, which I extend here to the film adaptation.
4 Coined by Moya Bailey in 2010, misogynoir is described as a particular form of hatred rooted in misogyny and racism directed at Black women, especially in American visual and popular culture. For more on misogynoir, see Bailey and Boom.

Works Cited

Bailey, Moya. *Misogynoir Transformed: Black Women's Digital Resistance*. NYU Press, 2021.
Boom, Kesiena. "4 Tired Tropes That Perfectly Explain What Misogynoir Is – And How You Can Stop It." *EverydayFeminism.com*, 3 Aug. 2015, https://everydayfeminism.com/2015/08/4-tired-tropes-misogynoir/.
Crenshaw, Kimberlé. "Mapping the Margins: Intersectionality, Identity Politics, and Violence against Women of Color." *Stanford Law Review*, vol. 43, no. 6, 1991, pp. 1241–1299.
Daniels, Robert. "The Racial and Sexual Revolution of 'She's Gotta Have It.'" *The Spool*, 7 Mar. 2020, https://thespool.net/reviews/movies/shes-gotta-have-it-spike-lee-retro-review/.
Ebert, Roger. "It's High Tide for Black New Wave." *RogerEbert.com*, 26 May 1991, https://www.rogerebert.com/roger-ebert/its-high-tide-for-black-new-wave.
Elise, Sharon, and Adewole Umoja. "Spike Lee Constructs the New Black Man: Mo' Better." *The Western Journal of Black Studies*, vol. 16, no. 2, 1992, pp. 1–18, https://faculty.csusm.edu/selise/documents/elise_umoja_spike_lee_constructs.pdf.
Fleming, Mike, Jr. "No Cannes Do: Why Spike Lee Nixed 'Do The Right Thing' Silver Anniversary for Black Fest Fete." *Deadline*, 13 May 2014, https://deadline.com/2014/05/no-cannes-do-why-spike-lee-nixed-do-the-right-thing-silver-anni-for-black-fest-fete-729355/.

Foote, Thelma Willis. "Happy Birthday, Nola Darling! An Essay Commemorating the Twentieth Anniversary of Spike Lee's 'She's Gotta Have It.'" *Women's Studies Quarterly*, vol. 35, no. 1/2, 2007, pp. 212–233.

Francis, Terri Simone. "Flickers of the Spirit: Black Independent Film, Reflexive Reception, and a Blues Cinema Sublime." *Black Camera*, vol. 1, no. 2, 2010, pp. 7–24.

Fuchs, Cynthia, editor. *Spike Lee: Interviews*. University Press of Mississippi, 2002.

Guerrero, Ed. "Spike Lee: A New Black Wave of Cinema." *ACMI*, 28 Dec. 2016, https://www.acmi.net.au/stories-and-ideas/spike-lee/.

Harris, Tamara Winfrey. *The Sisters are Alright: Changing the Broken Narrative of Black Women in America*. Berrett-Koehler Publishers, 2015.

hooks, bell. "'Whose Pussy Is This?' A Feminist Comment." *Reel to Real: Race, Class and Sex at the Movies*. Routledge, 1996, pp. 291–302.

McGowan, Todd. *Spike Lee*. University of Illinois Press, 2014.

Pierson, John. *Spike, Mike, Slackers & Dykes: A Guided Tour Across a Decade of American Independent Cinema*. University of Texas Press, 2014.

Rother, Larry. "Spike Lee Makes His Movie." *New York Times*, 10 Aug. 1986, https://archive.nytimes.com/www.nytimes.com/library/film/081086lee-filmmaking.html.

Silver, Stephen. "Spike Lee and MeToo Founder Debate His Portrayal of Women." *Philly Voice*, 3 Aug. 2019, https://www.phillyvoice.com/black-star-film-festival-spike-lee-and-metoo-founder-tarana-burke-talk-do-right-thing-and-his-portrayals-women/.

Simmonds, Felly Nkweto. "'She's Gotta Have It': The Representation of Black Female Sexuality on Film." *Feminist Review*, no. 29, 1988, pp. 10–22.

28
EIGHT MEN OUT (1988)

Aaron Baker

American independent film often does not conform to what most mainstream Hollywood movies do, namely telling utopian stories in which everything works out: protagonists whom we are asked to like get their questions answered, fix their problems, achieve success, find love, and have justice restored.

Consider Lulu Wang's 2019 independent film *The Farewell* as an example. Its Chinese American and Chinese ensemble of characters have a problem: the matriarch of the family, Nai Nai (Zhao Shu-zhen), is dying of cancer and her children and grandchildren do not agree about whether to tell her. This problem of Nai Nai's terminal illness and its impact on the family cannot be "fixed." At best an uneasy consensus is reached that it is better not to tell her so she can enjoy her remaining time. Nai Nai's granddaughter Billi (Awkwafina) and the other main characters are sympathetic enough but hardly empowered or in control of the narrative as we are used to with Hollywood movies. Like most independent films, *The Farewell* is mostly about the challenges and frustrations of the real world. Its main appeal to viewers is not to offer happiness in stories about characters who demonstrate that success can be realized if we just have the courage to go find it. Rather, many independent films reassure us that we are not alone in facing a difficult world.

Besides such real-world narratives, some independent films also diverge from Hollywood movie-making by taking chances stylistically, breaking from the standard continuity aesthetic to foreground how they tell their stories and therefore challenging viewers to think about form. One example is *Stranger than Paradise* (1984), the Jim Jarmusch film full of long takes that transition to the next shot by going to black. The film does not have the kind of invisible editing seen in most Hollywood films. As such, it works explicitly as an independent film promoting viewer reflection rather than absorption in the central narrative.

FIGURE 28.1 Joe Jackson (D.B. Sweeney), banned from baseball for his role in the 1919 World Series scandal, continues to play under a different name at the end of *Eight Men Out*.

Since he began his filmmaking career in the late 1970s, writer and director John Sayles has become known as one of the most prominent representatives of American independent cinema. David Shumway calls Sayles "America's leading independent filmmaker" (1) and Diane Carson, writing in 2004, adds, "John Sayles did not invent independent filmmaking, but he has championed it longer and practiced it better than anyone else" (125). A big part of Sayles's independence as a filmmaker comes from how he has made movies outside of the Hollywood industry, financing them with his own money earned working as a screenwriter on other people's projects. Such economic independence has allowed Sayles to make films about issues of social injustice not typically shown in mainstream movies including racism, sexism, the denial of workers' rights, homophobia, and American imperialism. In Sayles's own words, independent film is "when filmmakers started with a story they wanted to tell and found a way to make that story" (Carson 129).

Of his 18 feature films, only one, *Baby It's You* (1983), was a studio movie (Paramount Pictures) for which Sayles did not have the final cut. Because he has usually self-funded his films, Sayles has adopted a pared-down formal style that allows him to work quickly and cheaply. While directors like Jarmusch show the influence of international art film in their aesthetic composition and storytelling, Sayles does not diverge from a Hollywood continuity style. He avoids overt stylization to make his films accessible to the biggest audience possible despite the limitations of his small budgets. Where Sayles challenges viewers is not at the formal level but with the narrative complexity of his movies: their multiple perspectives and avoidance of easy resolutions to difficult problems. That move away from the utopian simplicity of Hollywood matters most for Sayles as an assertion of independence. The positive feeling he offers in his films is not that the world is fair, assuring us of opportunities, but rather coming instead from a better understanding of how things work.

Sayles played a prominent role in the growth of American independent film in the 1980s. Using money earned from writing genre films for Roger Corman's New World Pictures, in 1979 Sayles directed *The Return of the Secaucus 7*. Its story of a group of 1960s activists spending a weekend together as they approach age 30 was a response to the conservative turn in American society that was underway and would continue during the Reagan administration in the 1980s. His next film, *Lianna* (1983), about a woman's realization of her lesbian sexuality, was one of several independent coming-out films such as *Personal Best* (1982) and *Desert Hearts* (1985). With his next two movies, *Baby It's You*, a love story about class and ethnicity, and *The Brother from Another Planet* (1984), set in Harlem and made with an African American lead (Joe Morton), Sayles cemented his commitment to films about politics and social identity.

From 1987 to 1996, Sayles reached the highest point of his career with four films that were well-reviewed and drew his biggest audiences: *Matewan* (1987), *Eight Men Out* (1988), *City of Hope* (1991), and *Lone Star* (1996). *Matewan* tells the story of a coal miners' strike in West Virginia in the early 1920s, with Chris Cooper giving a strong performance as union organizer Joe Kenehan that launched his career and Haskell Wexler earning an Academy Award nomination for his cinematography. In *Eight Men Out* Sayles tells another story of the conflict between owners and workers, and *City of Hope* again demonstrates his ability to offer complex, ensemble stories offering multiple perspectives, transcending Hollywood's tendency for simplistic narratives. The other big success for Sayles from this period was *Lone Star*, a revisionist western about class, race, and immigration on the border with his signature ensemble cast. One of the few of his movies that made it into the multiplexes, *Lone Star* earned $25 million, the biggest box office of the filmmaker's career, and won an Oscar nomination for Sayles's original screenplay.

Sayles's insistence on the story he wants to tell is exemplified by his interest in putting social history on the screen. Three of his films, *Matewan*, *Eight Men Out* and *Amigo* (2010) are explicitly historical, and several others, including *Lone Star*, *Men with Guns* (1997) and *Sunshine State* (2002) invoke historical events. In an interview with historian Eric Foner, Sayles explained that his attraction to history comes from how it offers "good stories" that help "in getting something new into the conversation that may have been overlooked" (11–12). Foner ties such exclusion to Hollywood's tendency to present "celebratory" history that makes audiences "feel good" by focusing on the accomplishments of individuals (12). Sayles agrees about this distortion of history in most commercial films and states that he instead seeks to present complexity in his historical stories told not by overemphasizing the achievements of individuals but rather by showing "ensemble situations" (11). Such ensemble situations involve stories built around a group of characters who offer multiple perspectives and interests. Although most of Sayles's films comment on social issues that are grounded in the present, he has also looked back to offer an understanding of the past that can better inform how we see our contemporary world. This essay looks at one of Sayles's historical films, *Eight Men Out*, to trace how it presents his typical divergence from the utopian simplicity of Hollywood to show how social inequality, specifically the power of money and class difference, impacted professional baseball in particular and American society more generally, the former just after World War I and the latter at the time when the film was made.

Critical Analyses of *Eight Men Out*

Despite his realization that most viewers are not used to stories with more than a few principal characters, Sayles insisted on an ensemble approach for *Eight Men Out* based on Eliot Asinof's book about the fix of the 1919 World Series. He explains that "I wanted to tell that story, *Eight Men Out*. Not *One Man Out*" (Foner 14). The film, therefore, recounts the history of eight Chicago White Sox players caught up in a deal with gamblers to intentionally lose the 1919 World Series. Sayles foregrounds the greed of owner Charles Comiskey (Clifton James), and his failure to pay his outstanding team fairly, as a major cause of the scandal. While the White Sox, as the best team in baseball, were an extreme example of such economic injustice, in fact, standard contracts at the time prevented all players from negotiating with other teams, resulting in most major leaguers being severely underpaid.

Within Sayles's use of an ensemble of characters, including the players, gamblers, journalists, fans, Comiskey, and baseball officials, Chicago third baseman Buck Weaver (John Cusack) is the closest the film has to a protagonist. Even though he knows about the gamblers paying his teammates, Shumway notes that Weaver is "the most sympathetic of the players" because he shows compassion in his conversations with young fans, appreciating how important the team is to the boys, and moreover because he plays well and does not participate in the fix (61).

Yet, while Weaver may get the most attention, true to his ensemble form Sayles attempts to show the motives and actions of a large group of characters on various sides. For Shumway, this concern with historical accuracy makes the story hard to follow. As he puts it, "the viewer who does not have the benefit of a recent reading of Asinof's book may not have enough information to understand the plot points presented" (66). Shumway views *Eight Men Out* as keeping the authorial commentary that most US independent films in the 1980s borrowed from the international art cinema, yet embedded within an ambiguous narrative that reduced its audience appeal. He concludes that *Eight Men Out* "in not simplifying...fails to engage us narratively and therefore it does not help viewers develop a strong emotional investment in the story or the characters" (66). Michael Z. Newman notes that as American independent film became more popular in the 1980s, it effectively "came to replace foreign imports as the bread and butter of art house programming" by offering viewers a more easily digestible kind of narrative movie with well-defined characters, clearer connection between plot events and less open-ended conclusions (27). Such independent films in Newman's view gave audiences the sophistication and cultural distinction of art films but without as much narrative ambiguity (27). For Shumway, the problem in *Eight Men Out* is that it does not stick to such narrative clarity, and therefore "the film's refusal to offer the viewer an easy, consistent point of identification" (68). Sayles tells Foner that he saw such complexity and ambiguity as essential parts of the history he was representing and that "one thing I definitely do in my movies is allow people to draw their own conclusions" (28). For Sayles, the complexity of history required that an independent film like *Eight Men Out* moved closer to art cinema, making viewers interpret the social implications of the narrative.

Sayles understood the complexity of his ensemble story as not only necessary for accurate history but also to represent the issues of social injustice central to his version of independent filmmaking. Such a need for multiple viewpoints had also informed his previous film *Matewan*. Like *Eight Men Out*, *Matewan* draws from history to tell a story about the conflict between owners and workers. Both movies offer examples of the need for, but the ultimate failure of, worker unity to advance their rights and opportunities. Although the miners in *Matewan* at least temporarily find strength in a collective response to the low pay and unsafe working conditions that their employers impose on them, in *Eight Men Out* the players fail to achieve such selfless unity at all. Warily they band together to fix the Series, but the gamblers who are their co-conspirators betray them and the ballplayers arrive at a disastrous end when they are banned for life. Besides their shared focus on labor conflict, *Matewan*, like *Eight Men Out*, alludes to the idea of baseball as a symbol for the unrealized promise of opportunity in American society. There is a brief scene in the earlier film of White, Black, and Italian miners playing baseball together. While such unity is short-lived, Sayles uses the game in this scene to illustrate how the miners by banding together are able to find some belief in the promise of opportunity that the national pastime offers.

Daniel Nathan emphasizes how Sayles in *Eight Men Out* portrays the White Sox players critically for their lack of class consciousness and collusion with gamblers. He writes that the "underpaid" players become "victims of their own financial insecurity, unscrupulous gamblers and a baseball establishment" represented by Comiskey (178). However, Nathan seems to understand Sayles's preference for historical accuracy rather than an ideological statement and he defends the complexity of the film's ensemble storytelling (181). He compliments Sayles for having the courage to present the 1919 World Series scandal as a "fragmented story in a fragmented manner and to destabilize audience expectations…because [it] was…often difficult to follow" (181).

Eight Men Out and Class in 1980s America

Just as *Eight Men Out* reveals unpleasant truths about America's past, it also resonated with similar problems of economic inequality in the 1980s when the film came out. Robert Elias reads nostalgic Hollywood baseball films of the 1980s like *The Natural* (1984) and *Field of Dreams* (1989) as using a utopian narrative to avoid recognizing how greed and the power of big money – supported by the conservative policies of the Reagan Administration – were making life increasingly difficult for working people (21). *Eight Men Out* by contrast looks back on the 1919 Series to present an earlier historical example of ongoing class division in American society typical of Sayles's independent aesthetic. Sayles, therefore, makes his movie an allegory of the financial forces of the 1980s, showing the underpaid White Sox players caught between their owner and the gamblers – both of whom exploited them, as like working Americans in the 1980s caught between corporate greed and a complicit federal government.

Working during this time when wealth in American society was flowing to the top, Sayles tells the story of the 1919 fix as driven by the desire of the players to get a fairer share of the money that their talent on the field generated. As the film's exposition introduces those involved and sets the scene for the deal, Sayles presents several statements about the players' excellence and lack of fair pay. Discussing who might take a bribe, former player and now gambler Bill Burns (Christopher Lloyd) describes Sox second baseman Eddie Collins (Bill Irwin) – whose 15,000-dollar salary was second highest in the American League and almost double that of any of his teammates – as "the only one getting paid what's he's worth." When another gambler, Sport Sullivan (Kevin Tighe), talks in a bar with first baseman Chick Gandil (Michael Rooker) he asks incredulously, "Seven men on the best ball club that ever took the field willing to throw the World Series?" To which Gandil responds. "You never played for Charlie Comiskey." Major League players making deals with gamblers to supplement their salaries kept low by restrictive contracts were not uncommon around the time of the 1919 fix. Bill James has documented how, in the period from 1917 to 1927, "thirty-eight players were either banished from baseball or at the least had serious charges brought against them for game-throwing" (Rader 118). In reaction, Benjamin Rader explains that "terrified that disclosure might undermine public confidence in the game and result in the loss of valuable property (in the form of players), the owners had tried to maintain a cloak of absolute secrecy while suppressing all evidence of game-fixing" (118).

Although Comiskey was reluctant to lose his star players, American League President Ban Johnson and the other club owners were anxious to limit the damage brought by the 1919 fix to the veracity of their product, so they hired federal Judge Kenesaw Mountain Landis and gave him unlimited power as commissioner of baseball to clean up the reputation of the game. Even after the eight White Sox players were exonerated on conspiracy charges by a Cook County grand jury in August 1921, the new commissioner banned them from organized baseball for life (Rader 117).

Although Sayles shows how Landis banished the players to protect the authority of the owners, the storytelling in *Eight Men Out,* focusing on the punished players, other team members, as well as the gamblers, journalists, fans, Comiskey, and league officials allows Sayles to make clear the unfairness of the new commissioner's harsh blanket judgment. Regardless of the challenge in presenting multiple points of view in a story, Sayles pursues the historical complexity needed to explain the complicated events of the 1919 World Series fix with as many perspectives as there were banned ballplayers. On the White Sox, there are two players, Buck Weaver and Joe Jackson (D. B. Sweeney), who knew of the deal with gamblers but still played very well. Weaver hit .324 in the Series and Jackson, although he took money from the gamblers, led both teams with a .375 average. A second point of view is that of the six players on the White Sox who accepted money to lose. Nathan correctly observes that Sayles criticizes these conspirators "for 'selling out' their own teammates" who wanted to win and for making a deal that turned out to be disastrous in that it led to a lifetime ban for them as well as for Weaver and Jackson (180).

Sayles also represents competing interests among the gamblers in terms of those who do not and those who do have the money to control the deal, a division reflective of the larger class politics of the story. Billy Maharg (Richard Edson) and Bill Burns come up with a plan to fix the series but are pushed aside by the money and muscle of gambling kingpin Arnold Rothstein (Michael Lerner). A fifth perspective in the film is that of the two journalists Ring Lardner (Sayles) and Hugh Fullerton (Studs Terkel) who try to untangle what happened. Rader explains that Maharg, whom he describes as "a small time Philadelphia gambler," was "embittered because he had not received his promised cut of the take" and therefore was a key source in revealing to the press that to lose the series "eight Chicago players had been promised $100,000, most of which they never received" (116). *Eight Men Out* shows that, even in their fix with gamblers, the White Sox players again were underpaid.

In addition to the players, gamblers, and journalists, we also see the perspective of Chicago owner Comiskey, at first trying to promote his first-place team to the sports writers he wines and dines to help him drum up excitement and ticket sales for the Series, and then increasingly outraged as the Sox lose and the fix becomes apparent. A seventh point of view in the film is that of the new commissioner brought in to address the problem. Judge Landis (John Anderson) seems at first eccentric and self-interested but acts decisively to ban the eight White Sox players to protect the interests of the owners – except for Comiskey – who need to defend the integrity of their sport. Last and least empowered, we see the scandal from the vantage point of the fans, represented poignantly by two young boys, Bucky (Tay Strathairn) and Scooter (Jesse Vincent). They embody the interest of loyal Sox fans whose belief in heroism is betrayed by the fix.

Independent from the Baseball Film

Understanding how *Eight Men Out* is independent of Hollywood involves analyzing it as typical of John Sayles's interest in telling stories that represent history with all its ambiguity and complexity, even if that puts his movies at odds with the more accessible stories in American independent film that became popular in the 1980s. Analysis of his portrayal of history in *Eight Men Out* also brings up the authorial commentary that the writer and director has often presented in his films, what Shumway calls "Sayles's critical stance toward American society and its politics [that] is the defining characteristic of his cinema" (5). In this case, that critical commentary focuses on the class conflict central to the 1919 World Series that had resonance for American society in the 1980s increasingly being divided between the haves and have-nots (Levy).

However, another aspect of how *Eight Men Out* defines an independent position comes from its difference relative to most films about baseball. Combining the conventions of newspaper, radio, and TV representation of the sports world with its talent for affirmative stories and happy endings, Hollywood has made hundreds of films about athletes who dream big and are determined to win. Baseball has been the subject of many of those films, and such movies have often endorsed the idea that success in American society comes from the same hard work, self-discipline, and team collaboration needed to prevail on the field.

Yet even the most utopian Hollywood baseball movie must appeal to baseball fans with a degree of plausibility based on its resemblance to the real business of professional sports. The presence of such realism often shows the lack of promised opportunity and reveals the conflicting interests in big league baseball in ways that complicate its stories. John Sayles's interest in representing the history of the 1919 World Series in all its social complexity exemplifies this realism, and to the degree that *Eight Men Out*, therefore, shows players who followed the rules and achieved excellence but were denied the promised rewards, it becomes a movie independent of typical Hollywood ideological messaging.

Works Cited

Carson, Diane. "John Sayles, Independent Filmmaker: 'Bet on Yourself'." *Contemporary American Independent Film: From the Margins to the Mainstream*, edited by Chris Holmlund and Justin Wyatt. Routledge, 2004, pp. 125–139.
"A Conversation Between Eric Foner and John Sayles." *Past Imperfect: History According to the Movies*, edited by Mark C. Carnes. Henry Holt, 1995, pp. 11–28.
Elias, Robert. *Baseball and the American Dream*. M.E. Sharpe, 2001.
Hemphill, Jim. "'We Got Over 90 Setups One Day': John Sayles on *Eight Men Out*." *Filmmaker Magazine*, 15 Nov. 2015, pp. 1–12.
Levy, Frank. *Dollars and Dreams: The Changing American Income Distribution*. Norton, 1988.
Newman, Michael. Z. *Indie: An American Film Culture*. Columbia University Press, 2011.
Rader, Benjamin. *Baseball: A History of America's Game*. University of Illinois Press, 2002.
Shumway, David. *John Sayles*. University of Illinois Press, 2012.

29
SEX, LIES, AND VIDEOTAPE (1989)

Michael Z. Newman

Much discussion about *sex, lies, and videotape* (1989) has focused on its place in the American indie movement that developed in the 1980s around films linked to the Sundance Film Festival and distributors like Miramax regarded as alternatives to the mainstream Hollywood studios. The year of its release was almost instantly felt to be a watershed, "the year it all changed" according to film producer John Pierson's popular chronicle of the period, *Spike, Mike, Slackers & Dykes*. *sex, lies, and videotape* was critical to this moment. It arrived with a wave of new American films, including *Do the Right Thing* (1989), *Roger & Me* (1989), and *Slacker* (1990), that excited critics and audiences by being offbeat and quirky, different enough from major multiplex releases to appeal to a vanguard sensibility.

An intimate adult drama shot on a modest budget by a filmmaker in his twenties, the film was a Palme d'Or winner at the Cannes Film Festival. With the aid of a tantalizing marketing campaign, it became a crossover hit. It marked the auspicious debut of a writer-director, Steven Soderbergh, who would go on to establish a reputation as one of the most intriguing American filmmakers of his generation, adept at toggling between the fringes of popular cinema and its more commercial and crowd-pleasing center. It also helped Miramax, the upstart New York outfit run by brothers Harvey and Bob Weinstein, establish its business model of releasing edgy, adult-oriented fare produced and released without the lavish resources of major studios to find audiences via the cachet of critical acclaim and awards buzz (Perren) and engaging with topical issues such as "safe sex" and gay rights (Wyatt 79–81). It was the epitome of a kind of film positioned within the commercial film business as not very Hollywood while also not so divergent from commercial cinema that it would alienate audiences. In other words, it was a classic *indie*.

All of these details make for an ideal case study of the emergence of this mode of cinema as a popular alternative to Hollywood blockbusters that made a strong

FIGURE 29.1 The video image in *sex, lies, and videotape* – with visible scan lines and flicker, lack of sharpness, along with tight close-up framings – indicates the authenticity and intimacy of Graham's homemade recordings.

cultural and industrial impact in the 1980s, 1990s, and early 2000s in parallel with the rise of alternative music and other cultural forms under the banner of indie style.[1] But *sex, lies, and videotape* is also a film that tells a particular kind of story about a group of four central characters in a specific setting, against the background of a cultural context and moment in time, the late 1980s. This chapter focuses on the film as a narrative of human relationships mediated by the then-emerging technology of amateur video. The film tells a kind of story that marks it in subtle ways in relation to dominant forms of media. Video in this text is positioned as novel and sexy, but also as alternative and personal. These are values that fit the cultural moment both in terms of media technology and styles of commercial cinema.

The image in *sex, lies, and videotape* regularly shifts between one format and another, integrating amateur video into its cinematic text. In critical moments, it cuts from a 35mm film image typical of professional motion pictures to an 8mm video image produced within the narrative world by Graham (James Spader). We see him record video with a Sony Handycam, a compact consumer-electronics product popular in the later 1980s. We also see him watch his videos, all of which are recordings of interviews he has conducted with women about their sexual experiences, using the Handycam as a source input to the television. The distinction between video and film – the alternating image formats, homemade camcorder images interpolated into a cinematic text – runs in parallel to independent cinema's distinction from mainstream film. Indie and Hollywood, film and video: both have elements in common, but both are also marked by contrasting values and relational status. By integrating video as the medium of the character's own moving-image practice, *sex, lies, and videotape* foregrounds authentic and personal storytelling and representation.

sex, lies, and videotape represents media production on an individual rather than a professional scale. The film portrays a process of media production and consumption that contrasts the look of homemade tapes against the film's typical scenes of realist drama. It uses videotape as a medium rich in connotations and dramatic potential. Video becomes its own cinematic device as an audiovisual format distinct in quality from the rest of the text. It lacks the sharpness and color of 35mm film, flaunting evidence of being mediated imagery. It represents characters and settings indirectly, showing traces like scan lines and flicker. The unsteady framing of the video image captures the character's own bodily movements as they manipulate the camera, a technology designed to be handheld. Video is marked as the rough and real format of an individual in contrast to a polished commercial product like a feature film, even one made on a small budget like *sex, lies, and videotape*.

While the video image is marked as different and degraded, it also promises privileged access to powerful effects of recording and playback in the way it is used by the film's central character. Unlike professional media, the movies made by the protagonist of *sex, lies, and videotape* have primarily private use and value, but the film suggests that they match or exceed professional media in their ability to conjure powerful effects. Videotape is figured as a medium used to capture and reproduce reality to satisfy individual desires. This picks up on a discourse of new media that circulated within popular culture in the later 1980s, ideas about the liberatory potential of video as a medium that would transform the everyday lives of ordinary people (Newman).

Videotape had been a technology widely used in professional media production and within the television industry beginning in the 1950s, but as a consumer-grade technology, its use developed more slowly, first as a device for recording television programs or viewing movies at home. Sales of consumer-grade video cameras like the one in *sex, lies, and videotape* took off in the 1980s as a form of home electronics with a strong "democratizing" potential. While home movies shot on 8mm or Super 8 film had been a feature of American life for many decades before camcorders, the new technology allowed for much cheaper and easier recording of everyday life that required no lab processing or separate projection apparatus, working as part of the ensemble of home video components that included a TV set and its peripherals like cable boxes and videotape decks (VCRs).

At the same time as camcorders were becoming a popular consumer-electronics technology in the US, pornographic movies were exploding as a videotape rather than a film genre, and the previous generation of X-rated films screened in urban movie houses gave way to a new format and setting for pornographic consumption in the home on videocassette (Alilunas). The salaciousness of a title linking sex and video would have drawn on the suggestiveness of pornographic media, and on video's possible use in recording sex. In this way, the film's contents and its marketing were mismatched. While the lies of the title are a central theme of the film and instances of honesty and dishonesty are key plot devices and character-defining moments, the sex is treated tastefully and with deft editing to signal passion without showing too much. We see a modicum of skin and nothing explicit or graphically sexual. Videotape is a central motif and device, but the contents of Graham's tapes are different from what the title offers in the context of sexualized video in the 1980s. He turns out to be more of a documentarian than a pornographer, even as his tapes are a visual aid to solo pleasure.

When Graham is introduced during expository opening shots, he is driving a convertible and changing and washing up in a men's room off a bait shop. This establishes the setting and shows Graham as an itinerant character on his way someplace. Evoking a mythical figure in American cinema, a man on the open road, Graham turns out to be, among other things, a videographer who records his encounters with women in the different places where he stops. When we see inside his trunk, the open box containing his camcorder is one of the small number of possessions that sketch him as a mysterious light traveler carrying around the secrets of his past. This early image establishes the video camera as one of the motifs that defines Graham. He has so few other possessions, just a car and a duffel bag, and he says he is reluctant to rent an apartment as he likes having just the one key.

Graham is the classic wanderer reluctant to put down roots. By recording videos, he keeps the company of his interview subjects while having little in the way of community aside from the three other characters who enter his life as the film's narrative begins. They are John (Peter Gallagher), the college friend Graham has not seen in nine years who has become a successful lawyer (to judge by his spacious office and nice suits) and has married Ann (Andie MacDowell), his beautiful wife who does not work outside of the home and goes to therapy. Ann's sister Cynthia (Laura San Giacomo) is the fourth main character, a sexually adventurous artist earning a living as a bartender and having a secret affair with John.

The enigma of Graham begins to get revealed in an early scene with Ann as they are out apartment hunting and stop at a restaurant. He tells her that he is impotent and unable to have sexual relations with a partner. This establishes not only his sexual identity but also his commitment to telling the truth and being comfortable with self-revelation, a confessional mode of honest conversation (Templeton). He has a past in which lying was a problem for him and has tried to go right by being truthful. This past involves an ex-girlfriend, Elizabeth, from the time when he and John were friends and they were all in college. While she is never seen in the film and the details of their relationship are barely filled in, Elizabeth is someone John asks Graham about early on when the characters first reunite, and someone Graham mentions when he talks about having been a pathological liar.

The characterization of Graham as impotent, a bold and intriguing revelation about a main character, is challenged early in the film during the first scene in which he watches one of his videotapes. Video and sexuality are closely connected in this narrative, and we are shown video as a medium of pleasurable spectatorship before we are introduced to Graham as the man holding the camera. In the first scene with a video, Graham sits shirtless opposite the television when his viewing is disturbed by a knock on the door. He has been watching a tape that contains a tightly framed close-up of a woman in profile, abstracted from any surroundings. She describes a sexual experience while flying on an airplane. The video image is marked by differences from the film image: scan lines and flicker are noticeable, and any color is pale and faded. The film cuts from the image on screen to the camera (functioning as a tape deck) and the collection of cassettes in their plastic cases labeled with women's names along with the dates they were recorded: Donna, Rose, Betty, Gladys, Linda, Jennifer, Diane, Barbara, Tara. Then we see Graham, undressed, touching his chest. This first appearance of video as a medium for intimate personal viewing shows it to be a way of capturing something authentic and powerful, a form of media with erotic force but also a product of the character's own practice of recording rather than a form of commercial media, like pornography.

Upon hearing the knock, Graham hurries to wrap his body in a sheet and turns off the camcorder, calling out to his visitor to come in as he withdraws into another room of the home. Graham's sexual dysfunction is not exactly impotence in the sense of inability to have an erection but is a kind of substitution of autoerotic sexuality for relationships with a partner. He has told Ann that he is unable to have an erection in the presence of another person, yet the scenes of his videotape spectatorship indicate masturbation.

Ann's reaction to Graham having this collection of homemade tapes sets in motion a series of consequences that form the film's main plot. Ann finds this somewhat shocking, which makes sense given that we already know she is not very comfortable with sex. Her relationship with her husband is lacking intimacy as she is not all that interested in being touched by him, while her husband is satisfying his sexual needs with her sister. She also seems shocked when her therapist brings up masturbation, which she admits only to having tried once. She calls Cynthia to warn her that Graham is "strange," and that Cynthia does not want to get involved with him, which intrigues Cynthia and leads her to visit Graham herself to find out what made Ann so "spooked." Graham (honest as he is) shows Cynthia the videotapes beside his TV as the cause of Ann's agitation.

This leads to the first scene in *sex, lies, and videotape* in which Graham shoots a video recording of an interview with a woman: a recorded conversation between Graham and Cynthia. He proposes that they make a video, and we see him take the camcorder in his hand in preparation. As the tape rolls, he asks questions about her sexual experiences and she narrates her stories. It is a scene of dramatic intimacy and self-revelation as Graham sits on a chair cradling the camera and she sits opposite him on the couch. After a few turns of the conversation, Graham descends from his chair to lay on the floor by her feet, and by drawing closer to her, he increases the sense of an intimate encounter. We are not shown the camera in this shot of Graham on the floor, only his medium close-up staring intently at Cynthia. The presence of visible mediation in this conversation is saved for another scene, but the use of video as a recording device instigates an episode of confessional truth-telling. She leans over the edge of the couch to speak more directly to him as the scene intensifies, with Cynthia describing a formative sexual encounter, and he returns her gaze. The setup of this exchange is a strong contrast with the earlier scene in which Ann interrupts Graham's viewing and interrogates him about the tapes, which has more friction and frustration. While we do see Cynthia speaking as she will appear on videotape, seeing the setup of the camera and subject, we do not see video images of Cynthia until a bit later.

After a gap in storytime, Cynthia departs feeling aroused, and she calls John to meet for sex in the middle of the day. But immediately after John speaks with her, the film cuts back to Graham and his videotapes. The first image back at his apartment is of Cynthia mediated by video, with the same scan lines, flicker, faded color, and tight framing as in the earlier scene of video spectatorship. In the video, Cynthia undresses (and, we later learn, masturbates), though we do not see her naked body and only hear her voice as the film holds on Graham. This reverse shot of Graham as the viewer has him naked again, this time occupying the same couch where Cynthia was positioned for the recording. Cynthia speaks about Ann and John's lack of a sexual relationship. The scene cross-cuts abruptly from this image to a dolly-zoom on Cynthia at her tryst with John representing her sexual satisfaction. Video has given her this overwhelming desire; it is a medium with the power to arouse and stimulate. It gets at the core of something deeply personal and sexual.

After Cynthia's video, the next and last character to appear on one of Graham's tapes is Ann, and it is this episode that brings the film to its dramatic climax. After discovering John and Cynthia's affair, Ann returns to Graham's apartment, upset, and says "John and Cynthia have been fucking." Her language marks a reversal from an earlier prudishness, and after a brief exchange in which Graham acknowledges that he knew about John and Cynthia from her confession on camera, Ann proposes that she and Graham make a videotape, a bold turn. He initially declines her proposal, but she persists, and he loads a tape in the camera and the recording begins. This instantly becomes a moment of intimacy between the characters who speak softly to one another. The scene cuts to black, then an exterior of Graham's house. When we return to the interior, assuming a passage of time, Graham is perched above Ann on the couch and they wordlessly look into each other's eyes. The camera is positioned on an end table across the room, out of focus in the foreground recording their encounter. We will see some of the contents of this recording in an upcoming scene, but for now, we observe a personal, romantic moment instigated by camcorder recording. And the next time Ann appears, she tells John that she wants a divorce and goes on the offensive, saying "fuck you" and informing him that she has been to see Graham. John becomes enraged when she admits to having made a videotape and this sends him, furious, to Graham's place. John assaults Graham and throws him out onto his porch.

Inside, John finds Ann's tape and begins to play the familiar wobbly video image. Low-fidelity sound comes from off-screen: Graham speaks, "I'm recording." Ann begins her confessional, with her husband as the spectator. She reveals the lack of sexual activity in her marriage and her lack of sexual satisfaction. In the recording, Ann hesitates before answering a question about whether she has thought of having sex with someone other than her husband, and the film cuts from the video image to a flashback of the recording of that interview a few scenes earlier. The flickering video gives way to the cinematic aesthetic: professional lighting, sharp facial features, and smooth camera movements. The characters speak about their interest in each other, and Graham becomes pained, unused to being the subject of an interview. He speaks about his past, his lying. These moments are intercut with shots of the camcorder: the turning tape spool and the lens.

After a few minutes of interrogating Graham, Ann picks up the camera, pressing her eye to the viewfinder, and pesters him to answer her questions. Then she cradles it against her chest, continuing the recording but giving him a reprieve from being visible in the image. After more moments of tense dialogue, Ann tells Graham she is leaving John, and he is partly responsible for it. And she sets the camera down on the table. Then she goes to Graham and touches him on the shoulder and the head, lays him down on the couch, takes his hand in hers, and touches it to her face and neck. They kiss. Only then does Graham stop the camera recording. Videotape has been the catalyst and the witness.

The TV screen turns to noise, and we are back with John at night, having viewed this scene as a spectator in Graham's apartment. John tells Graham, who has endured the duration of John's viewing on the front porch, that he and Elizabeth had sex before she and Graham broke up, and he walks away. Graham returns inside and destroys his videocassettes, breaking up the plastic and throwing it on the floor, then smashes the Handycam against the table. This is an act of cathartic violence as he puts his recording project in the past and rejects the forms of intimacy and sexuality that had been central to his identity. This dramatic moment signals that he will now have "real," unmediated human connections.

Graham and Ann have one last scene together. John and Ann have split up, and she and Graham sit together on the porch steps holding hands, now a couple, obviously happy with one another. This brief scene is the film's happy ending for the two characters least able to sustain meaningful connections to others at the film's beginning.

Amateur home video has mediated this relationship over the course of the film's narrative, only to be left out at the end, removed as a substitution of a technological process for authentic human contact. In *sex, lies, and videotape*, the medium of video is shown as a potent force, a technology capable of powerful effects of bringing people together, aiding sexual pleasure, capturing personal and intimate moments and feelings, but also provoking fear and violence. The film needs it to be left behind for its character arcs to be resolved. Ultimately this representation leaves us with an image of videotape and video recording as a way for individuals to capture their reality and fulfill individual desires, though imperfectly and problematically. This theme fits with the spirit of indie cinema as a mode of telling personal stories that run against the grain of mainstream culture, just as the outsider Graham rejects the square, white-collar ethos of his old friend John and as Ann escapes the constraints of her traditional marriage for a different kind of intimacy. The centrality of amateur video recording as an instigator of these changes in the central characters matches the positioning of independent film as an alternative mode of storytelling and culture that speaks more to authentic human experiences. The sex and lies were crucial to marketing the film and to telling a compelling story about human relationships, but the videotape would be no less central to the film's appeal as a work that speaks to its cultural moment, and as a key text in American independent cinema.

Note

1 For more on the significance of *sex, lies, and videotape* as a key indie release of its era, see Gallagher (19–44) and Perren (16–53).

Works Cited

Alilunas, Peter. *Smutty Little Movies: The Creation and Regulation of Adult Video*. University of California Press, 2016.

Gallagher, Mark. *Another Steven Soderbergh Experience: Authorship and Contemporary Hollywood*. University of Texas Press, 2013.

Newman, Michael Z. *Video Revolutions: On the History of a Medium*. Columbia University Press, 2014.

Perren, Alisa. *Indie, Inc.: Miramax and the Transformation of Hollywood in the 1990s*. University of Texas Press, 2012.

Pierson, John. *Spike, Mike, Slackers & Dykes: A Guided Tour Across a Decade of American Independent Cinema*. Hyperion, 1995.

Templeton, Alice. "The Confessing Animal in *sex, lies, and videotape*." *Journal of Film and Video*, vol. 50, no. 2, 1998, pp. 15–25.

Wyatt, Justin. "The Formation of the 'Major Independent': Miramax, New Line and the New Hollywood." *Contemporary Hollywood Cinema*, edited by Murray Smith and Steve Neale. Routledge, 1998, pp. 74–90.

30
PARIS IS BURNING (1990)

Michele Meek

Few independent documentaries by a first-time director have been the focus of as much academic inquiry as *Paris Is Burning*. Over the past several decades, high-profile scholars including bell hooks, Judith Butler, and Jack Halberstam have used the film to discuss issues around race, class, sexuality, and gender identity. Directed by Jennie Livingston, *Paris Is Burning* depicts Black and Latinx drag balls in Harlem, New York City in the 1980s featuring interviews with several of the house "mothers" – Dorian Corey (House of Corey), Angie Xtravaganza (House of Xtravaganza), Willi Ninja (House of Ninja), Pepper LaBeija (House of Labeija), and Paris Dupree (House of Dupree) – as well as numerous house "children" who adopt the name of their house as a surname. The documentary showcases the participants as they walk the "runway" of the balls in street clothes, evening gowns, and military wear or compete in voguing dance contests.

The film has been credited with drawing attention to drag as well as concepts like voguing, reading, mopping, and throwing shade, many of which became later coopted and further mainstreamed by the series *RuPaul's Drag Race* (2009–2023) and *Pose* (2018–2021), for which Livingston directed one episode. *Paris Is Burning*, which is often cited as an example of New Queer Cinema, was acquired by Miramax, and on its $500,000 budget, it grossed nearly 4 million dollars in the United States.[1] It won the Grand Jury Prize at Sundance Film Festival in 1991; prestigious awards from critics' associations in Boston, New York, and Los Angeles; Outstanding Documentary from the GLAAD Media Awards; and a Teddy Award from Berlinale. In 2016, *Paris Is Burning* earned another rare distinction for an independent film – inclusion in the National Film Registry at the Library of Congress. In 2020, the Criterion Collection acquired and restored the film for redistribution, presenting an additional hour of previously unreleased footage. In its era, *Paris Is Burning* resonated for shedding light on a world unfamiliar to mainstream America – today it appears prescient for its groundbreaking

DOI: 10.4324/9781003246930-31

FIGURE 30.1 The film's representation of Venus Xtravaganza, a Latinx trans woman, has evoked both scholarly praise and critique.

portrayal of the deconstruction of gender and intersectional identities at a moment when scholars had begun to theorize the concepts.

"Realness" and Representation in *Paris Is Burning*

Paris Is Burning emerged in tandem with academic discourse on the pliability of gender and sexuality. In the influential 1990 book *Gender Trouble*, Judith Butler used drag to demonstrate the "performativity" of gender, or the way gender is enacted by, through, and on us. In the book, Butler counters the concept of any "primary gender" noting that "*In imitating gender, drag implicitly reveals the imitative structure of gender itself – as well as its contingency*" (Butler, *Gender Trouble* 187, emphasis in original). According to Butler, there is no "original" gender or sexuality, but rather only a copy of a copy of a copy. Such a framework exposes the inherent instability of gender and sexuality. In other words, if everyone were to stop reiterating certain heteronormative norms, such paradigms would cease to exist.

The film *Paris Is Burning* became an apt example in Butler's subsequent book *Bodies That Matter: On the Discursive Limits of Sex* (1993). In the chapter "Gender is Burning," Butler points to how the film's drag performances show evidence of this "denaturalization of gender" (Butler, *Bodies That Matter* 82). However, Butler clarifies how the film exposes that drag itself is not always a subversive act that breaks down gender/sex norms. Sometimes an aspiration to "realness" can be another way of upholding, enforcing, and rewarding existing binaries. Butler makes it clear that it is not a case of either/or but both, concluding, "*Paris Is Burning* documents neither an efficacious insurrection nor a painful resubordination, but an unstable coexistence of both" (Butler, *Bodies That Matter* 89).

The instability of gender alongside the persistence of gender norms comes through in the film's footage from the balls where individuals are judged on their "realness" in categories like "Going to School," "Military," "Town and Country," and "Executive." On the one hand, the balls enable contestants to simulate fitting into segments of society from which they felt excluded. Corey states in the film, "Black people have a hard time getting anywhere. And those that do are usually straight." The balls provide the space to counter this reality. Corey explains,

> In a ballroom, you can be anything you want. You're not really an executive, but you're looking like an executive. And therefore, you're showing the straight world that 'I can be an executive. If I had the opportunity, I could be one because I can look like one.' And that is like a fulfillment. Your peers, your friends are telling you, 'Oh you'd make a wonderful executive.'

Corey clarifies that it is "not a take-off or a satire" – rather aspiring to "realness" enables one to "give the society that they live in what they want to see so they won't be questioned." The goal of realness is "to be able to blend" and "to look as much as possible like your straight counterpart." On the other hand, as Corey bluntly adds at one point, "It's really a case of going back into the closet." Interviewees in the film clarify how not adhering to "realness" is disciplined. If one finds a "flaw," they are subject to "reading" or "the real art form of insult." As Corey explains, while being called a "drag queen" would be a slur coming from a straight person, two queer people cannot use terms like this to insult each other. Corey describes, "If I'm a Black queen and you're a Black queen, we can't call each other 'Black queens'…. That's not a read; that's just a fact. So, then we talk about your ridiculous shape, your saggy face, your tacky clothes." A more "developed form" of reading, Corey describes, is "shade." Corey explains the subtleties of "shade" by stating, "I don't tell you you're ugly, but I don't have to tell you because you *know* you're ugly."

Performers in the film often emulate affluent white heteronormative culture and draw from racist stereotypes for the categories of the ball. For example, the "Banjee" category means, "looking like the boy who probably robbed you a few minutes before you came to Paris's ball" or "impersonat[ing]…the gum-chewing round-the-way girl on welfare or the crackhead gangbanger on the block" (Parkerson). Reviewers and scholars often note how the film lays bare how racist, sexist, and cisist ideals infiltrate both the ball culture and the individuals' personal aspirations. Numerous interviewees express their desires to be rich and famous – Octavia St Laurent says, "I want to be somebody. I mean I am somebody. I just want to be a rich somebody"; Willi Ninja says, "I want [voguing] to be known worldwide, and I want to be on top of it when it hits"; and Venus Xtravaganza says, "I would like to be a spoiled rich white girl." Many of these aspirations when further examined represent a yearning for conventional suburban life, for example when Venus, a Latinx trans female performer, expresses, "I want to be with the man I love. I want a nice home, away from New York – up the Peekskills or maybe in Florida, somewhere far where no one knows me. I want my sex changed. I want to get married in church in white. I want to be a complete woman." Soon after Venus expresses these longings, we learn in an interview with her house mother Angie that Venus was discovered strangled in a "sleazy" hotel.[2] Although the case was never solved, the presumption remains that she was murdered by a male client who discovered that she was trans. As a result, Venus's inclusion in the film has come to epitomize larger issues of the oppression of and violence against trans individuals of color. The tenuousness of Venus's unrealized dreams is further compounded by the fact that within three years of the film's release, five of the nine performers featured in the film had died, several from AIDS.

Can the Queens Speak?[3]

The same year as *Paris Is Burning*, Madonna released the song and music video *Vogue,* featuring the style of dance performed in the film by Willi Ninja, "the godfather of voguing." However, Ninja played no role in the video; instead, Madonna's video was choreographed by and stars José Gutierez Xtravaganza and Luis Camacho Xtravaganza. Still, Madonna's appropriation of voguing without apparent credit to its Black and Latinx roots has been often criticized. As Essex Hemphill wrote in a 1991 review of the film, the "litany of names [Madonna] calls in the song as representative of style and attitude" omit people of color, allowing the conclusion that Madonna believes they "have contributed nothing to the theater of style and attitude originating in this country" (27). While Ninja did achieve unprecedented fame as a dancer due to the popularity of voguing, this cultural appropriation of voguing into white culture has continued to be critiqued.

In a similar vein, *Paris Is Burning* has been a flashpoint for criticism at times, specifically because Livingston, a Jewish Ivy League-educated queer/genderqueer person, crafts the story from outside, not within, the community. After the success of the film, several of the main subjects, not including Willi Ninja and Dorian Corey, sued for additional payment after seeing the film's popularity. Since Livingston had obtained signed releases from interviewees, however, the cases were dropped. Nevertheless, after Miramax bought the film, Livingston voluntarily took $50,000 from an initial guarantee of $250,000 to pay the performers in the film. In a *New York Times* article, Pepper LaBeija reported being given $5,000 of "hush money" adding "at least it brought me international fame," while Dorian Corey stated, "a lot of the girls hate Miss Jennie, but that's just greed," adding, "I didn't do it for money anyway. I did it for fun. Always have" (Green). Livingston has expressed how they "didn't get rich" from the film and that their status as queer and gender-nonconforming are what enabled them to be welcomed into the ball culture (Green). Livingston recalls being drawn to the balls because it gave them a "visceral feeling of the construction of gender," which resonated because of Livingston's own experience with gender, as Livingston explains,

> I never felt comfortable with the gender system. I wanted to be a little boy when I little. Then I was queer, and there was more room, but I just didn't get it. I just never felt like a woman, and I didn't really want to be a man
> *(Livingston)*[4]

The critique of the film points to an underlying concern within any documentary about minoritized subjects. In a 1993 interview, Livingston stated, "If they wanted to make a film about themselves, they would not be able....I wish that weren't so, but that's the way society is structured" (Green). More recently, Livingston has clarified, "They weren't making films because there wasn't enough resources, enough entitlement, and enough sense that you *should* be able to make a film about your own community, your own experience" (Livingston). While noting how "that's completely changed" today, Livingston also states that still "systemically there is not an all-pervasive inclusiveness and equity happening in the film and TV world" (Livingston). Such a premise – that a minoritized population cannot speak for themselves and thus can only be represented by a more privileged person – evokes the groundbreaking question raised by Gayatri Chakravorty Spivak in the 1988 essay, "Can the Subaltern Speak?" Thus, some analyses of the film point to a concern common to all documentary films – whose story is this? In an essay on the film in the book *A Companion to Contemporary Documentary Film*, Eve Oishi argues that the film presents its own attempt at "realness" as it "grapple[s] with the challenge" of "bridging the gap between the dynamic political and cultural worlds that are the subject of the films and the forms available for representing them" (266). Ultimately, Oishi suggests that the "documentary gaze" always falls short in its effort to represent its subjects' reality – a "testimony to the impure tools of film" (267). Documentary, in other words, is never the same as reality.

Livingston's connection to the film's subjects has been a recurring theme in the analysis of the film. Soon after the film's release, bell hooks lambasted *Paris Is Burning* as an example of the exploitation of queer individuals of color in her chapter "Is Paris Burning?" in *Black Looks: Race and Representation* (1992). hooks argues that reviewers and audiences were drawn in by the "pageantry of the drag balls," but that the film fails to problematize the race and class issues that underpin the lives of the real individuals featured. In particular, hooks takes aim at Livingston's portrayal of queer individuals of color who aspire to be white, while "the film in no way interrogates 'whiteness'" (149). As a result, hooks argues that the film presents a "reassuring" portrayal in which people of color are "all too willing to be complicit in perpetuating the fantasy that ruling-class white culture is the quintessential site of unrestricted joy, freedom, power, and pleasure" (149). hooks suggests that Livingston exploits her characters of color in service to an agenda that ultimately upholds white hegemony. In the essay, hooks points specifically to the example of Venus Xtravaganza – a "tragedy" in the story that offers no "mourning," so hooks criticizes that, "her dying is upstaged by spectacle. Death is not entertaining." Such an emphasis on "spectacle," hooks suggests, conceals any "pain and sadness" alluded to in *Paris Is Burning* (149). Other scholars have built upon hooks's argument. For example, Kimberly Chabot Davis compares *Paris Is Burning* with the 1994 film *Hoop Dreams* – a film directed by two white male filmmakers chronicling several years in the lives of two Black boys who aspire to be in the NBA. Davis argues that although the use of irony in these films has "subversive potential," ultimately both "underscore[] the marginality and exclusion of a few black, Latino, and transsexual subjects, while reasserting the superiority of primarily white, privileged viewers who see through the same cultural lens as the filmmakers" (44).

Still, not all scholars and critics of colors have found the film problematic. For instance, Jackie Goldsby in the 1993 essay "Queens of Language," argues that Livingston "can tell this story because her identity is not implicated in it" (115). Of course, Goldsby recognizes the implications "for Livingston, a white woman, to give the members of the ball world a public voice," which ensures "that the cultural and social privilege of the filmmaker is inscribed into the film, however unobtrusive she strives to be" (115). However, Goldsby's conclusion is not that Livingston should not have made the film or that a version of the film directed by a person of color would have been different. Rather Goldsby expresses being "thankful" that Livingston made a film "as performance and oral text" that is "so irresistible to my eyes and ears" even as the film ultimately "signal[s] that we can't know this world fully" (115). Essex Hemphill, a Black and openly gay poet and activist, in a 1991 *Guardian* review republished in a booklet accompanying the re-released DVD, also argued although the film ran the "risk" that Livingston "could have mistakenly imposed her personal cultural presumptions and interpretations upon the material," the film avoids such a "travesty." Instead, Hemphill suggests that "We are not exposed to any of Livingston's judgements, if she has any, of the subjects. The authentic voice of this community emerges unfettered." Like hooks, Hemphill points to numerous interviewees in the film who aspire to be rich, white, and heterosexual. But the conclusions he draws are different from hooks's. Instead, he notes the irony embedded in the articulated dreams of performers who want to be "white and female, clearly an escapist longing, a longing that if realized would then place them in collusion with white supremacy – the primary source of their disempowerment." Certainly, what continues to resonate in Livingston's film is how unsettling it is to see queer people of color aspiring to ideals that have kept them oppressed, or as Hemphill puts it, "They want to be stars in a world that barely wants to see them alive." In the DVD commentary for the film, Willi Ninja tries to clarify these scenes expressing, "It's not that we wanted to be white. We just wanted to have the same things that most of white America have." Although the film does not "interrogate" whiteness, as hooks argues, it does render visible the power dynamics of a white cis heteronormative society that has convinced many of its outcasts that their only hope is to join the ranks of the oppressors themselves.

Trans Lives and Intersectionality in *Paris Is Burning*

Of course, race and class are not the only sites of oppression for the performers in *Paris Is Burning*. Livingston's film was released only one year after Kimberlé Crenshaw coined the term "intersectionality" to describe how individuals' identities are comprised of a complex array of privileges and oppressions, but the film remains to this day an apt example of the term. The performers in the film are oppressed on many levels – through race, class, sexuality, gender expression, and gender identity. Thus, the film resists a reading on only one aspect of the performers' identities – or the filmmaker's for that matter. Butler points to this irony – while agreeing that

> hooks is right to argue that within this culture the ethnographic conceit of a neutral gaze will always be a white gaze, an unmarked white gaze, one which passes its own perspective off as the omniscient, one which presumes upon and enacts its own perspective as if it were no perspective at all

Butler follows with the question, "But what does it mean to think about this camera as an instrument and effect of lesbian desire?" (Butler, *Bodies That Matter* 89). In interviews, Livingston also has articulated how hooks's critique comes from the standpoint of a Black cis straight woman who might not recognize how much the film resonated with queer and trans audiences of color, many of whom saw themselves empathetically and positively represented in the film for the very first time. Others have taken issue specifically with how hooks compares the gender-bending performances of *Paris Is Burning* to Black comedians' crossdressing, which hooks suggests "give public expression to a general misogyny, as well as to a more specific hatred and contempt toward black woman" (146). Since many of the performers in the documentary identify as trans, such a comparison overlooks how many ball performers were not motivated by misogyny or levity, but simply the fact of their own gender identity and expression. For this reason, trans scholar Jack Halberstam lauds the film for providing a "fairly extensive visual account of trans* life in the 1980s, well before transgender identities were part of the national conversation" (65). Scholars also have often noted the kinship system represented through the "houses" depicted in the film, particularly how they enabled queer and trans people of color – often ostracized from society and their own families – to form intergenerational bonds.

While the issue of representation embedded in *Paris Is Burning* initially focused on people of color, more recently, scholars have highlighted a similar urgency regarding trans and nonbinary individuals. Numerous trans scholars have taken issue with how drag has been seen as "the exceptional locus of gender trouble" (Benavente and Gill-Peterson 25). In the book *Invisible Lives*, Viviane K. Namaste critiques how gender theorists like Butler have "contained" drag "as a performance in itself" – while sexuality is often seen as something "prior to performance" (Namaste 13). While Butler articulates all gender and sexuality iterations are performative, Namaste argues that Butler does not properly prioritize trans identity, stating, "Butler elides both Xtravaganza's transsexual status and her work as a prostitute. Here is the point: Venus was killed because she was a transsexual prostitute" (Namaste 13). In other words, Namaste argues that it is not merely Venus's status as a person of color or as a woman that leads to her murder, but it is her status as a trans sex worker which puts her at risk. Interviewed in the documentary about Venus's death, Angie mourns losing "her right hand" and "the main daughter of my house," adding, "But that's part of life, that's part of being a transsexual in New York City and surviving."

While both the film and drag itself have been "read" countless times since 1990, more recent critiques have started to problematize concepts like "passing" for trans and nonbinary individuals. Although categories have existed in the balls – then and now – where "passing" is not the main criteria, the emphasis on "realness" in the film offers another aspect to problematize as trans scholars and activists seek not only to render visible trans lives but also to make space for more varied and disparate gender identifications and manifestations.

Although drag has been adopted in countless ways into mainstream culture, *Paris Is Burning* remains unique in its direct interviews with the ball participants about their aspirations, fears, and beliefs. As Halberstam notes, although the film "has been critiqued over the years…it remains an important record of a subcultural world at a particular point in time" (65). While the film is not merely a fact-based historical document nor necessarily an embodiment of contemporary ideals, it has cemented its place as a groundbreaking and important work in the US independent film canon, and it continues to be an extraordinarily generative text in the study of intersectionality, kinship, gender performativity, cultural appropriation, and trans studies.

Notes

1 According to Livingston, the production budget was $250,000 and music licenses cost $250,000. It grossed $3.8 million in the US.
2 In an interview in *Paris Is Burning*, Angie Xtravaganza uses the word "sleazy" to describe the hotel
3 Several performers in the film refer to themselves as "queens." However, according to Livingston performers like Willi, Freddie, Kim, Junior, Sol called themselves "butch queens."
4 Livingston has expressed being comfortable with either they or she pronouns. While I use them, other quotes here refer to Livingston by female pronouns.

Works Cited

Benavente, Gabby, and Julian Gill-Peterson. "The Promise of Trans Critique." *GLQ: A Journal of Lesbian and Gay Studies*, vol. 25, no. 1, 2019, pp. 23–28, https://doi.org/10.1215/10642684-7275222.

Brathwaite, Les Fabian. "The Ultimate *Paris Is Burning* Viewing Guide." Out.com, 1 Feb. 2017, https://www.out.com/movies/2017/2/01/ulimate-paris-burning-viewing-guide.

Butler, Judith. *Gender Trouble*. Routledge, 1990.

———. *Bodies That Matter: On the Discursive Limits of "Sex."* Routledge, 1993.

———. "Gender Is Burning: Questions of Appropriation and Subversion." *Feminist Film Theory A Reader*, edited by Sue Thornham. Edinburgh University Press, 1999, pp. 336–352.

Crenshaw, Kimberlé. "Demarginalizing the Intersection of Race and Sex: A Black Feminist Critique of Antidiscrimination Doctrine, Feminist Theory and Anti-racist Politics." *University of Chicago Legal Forum*, vol. 1989, no. 1, article 8, http://chicagounbound.uchicago.edu/uclf/vol1989/iss1/8.

Davis, Kimberly Chabot. "White Filmmakers and Minority Subjects: Cinema Vérité and the Politics of Irony in *Hoop Dreams* and *Paris Is Burning*." *South Atlantic Review*, vol. 64, no. 1, 1999, pp. 26–47, https://doi.org/10.2307/3201743.

Goldsby, Jackie. "Queens of Language: *Paris is Burning*." *Queer Looks: Perspectives on Lesbian and Gay Film and Video*, edited by Martha Gever et al. Routledge, 1993, pp. 108–115.

Green, Jesse. "Paris Has Burned." *New York Times*, 18 Apr. 1993, https://www.nytimes.com/1993/04/18/style/paris-has-burned.html. Accessed 9 Nov. 2021.

Halberstam, Jack. "Trans* Generations." *Trans*: A Quick and Quirky Account of Gender Variability*. University of California Press, 2018, pp. 63–83.

Hemphill, Essex. "To Be Real." *Guardian*, 3 July 1991. Republished in *Paris Is Burning* DVD Booklet.

hooks, bell. "Paris Is Burning." *Black Looks: Race and Representation*. Routledge, 2014, pp. 145–156. Juzwiak, Rich. "*Paris Is Burning* Director Jennie Livingston on Legacy, Controversy, and Harvey Weinstein." *Jezebel*, 28 Feb. 2020, https://jezebel.com/paris-is-burning-director-jennie-livingston-on-legacy-1841954416.

Livingston, Jennie. Personal interview. 14 Nov. 2021.

Namaste, Viviane K. *Invisible Lives: The Erasure of Transsexual and Transgendered People*. University of Chicago Press, 2000.

Ninja, Willi, et al. Audio Commentary. *Paris Is Burning*. Directed by Jennie Livingston, Criterion Collection, 1990. DVD.

Oishi, Eve. "Reading Realness: Paris Is Burning, Wildness, and Queer and Transgender Documentary Practice." *A Companion to Contemporary Documentary Film*, edited by Alexandra Juhasz and Lebow Alisa. Wiley Blackwell, 2015, pp. 252–270.

Parkerson, Michelle. Review of *Paris Is Burning*. https://www.criterion.com/current/posts/6832-paris-is-burning-the-fire-this-time. Accessed 9 Nov. 2021.

31

TEENAGE MUTANT NINJA TURTLES (1990)

Cortland Rankin

The inclusion of *Teenage Mutant Ninja Turtles* in this collection likely strikes the reader as odd. As part of a massively popular franchise, the first *Teenage Mutant Ninja Turtles* movie (*TMNT*)[1] seems antithetical to everything "independence" was once commonly thought to stand for, a position best summarized in Emanuel Levy's essentialized definition of an independent film as "a fresh, low-budget movie with a gritty style and offbeat subject matter that expresses the filmmaker's personal vision" (2). And yet this live-action adaptation of a comic book, television series, and toy line is one of the highest-grossing independent films of all time.

But how can a high-concept franchise film about four pizza-loving, crime-fighting turtles and their wise rat sensei be thought of as "independent" and what does its inclusion in that category tell us about American independent cinema at the dawn of the 1990s? The story of Leonardo, Donatello, Raphael, and Michelangelo's journey to the big screen sheds light on several interrelated facets of independent cinema, including the fluid dynamic between independent and mainstream cultural products, the place of exploitation and commercial filmmaking in the independent sector, and the realignment of the independent film industry itself that came about partly as a result of the success of *TMNT*.

To understand how *TMNT* qualifies as an independent film, it is first necessary to articulate exactly what is meant by "independent," a task on which film scholars have spilt much ink over the years. For Geoff King, independence is a "relative rather than an absolute category" best defined through three points of orientation: a film's industrial location, its formal and aesthetic strategies, and its sociocultural, political, and ideological disposition (9, 2). Yannis Tzioumakis clarifies King's "relativity" in asserting that independence should be thought of as a historically contingent "discourse that expands and contracts when socially authorised institutions (filmmakers, industry practitioners, trade publications,

FIGURE 31.1 Teenage Mutant Ninja Turtle Raphael at home in the sewers of New York City.

academics, film critics, and so on) contribute towards its definition" (*American Independent Cinema* 10). Many critics and scholars (Biskind 40; Levy 94; King 261) have pointed to the 1989 release of Steven Soderbergh's *sex, lies, and videotape* as the watershed moment that inaugurated a new era in which a film's formal, aesthetic, sociocultural, political, and ideological characteristics became equally valid credentials for defining an "indie" film rather than just a marginalized industrial location (Staiger 22). While tough to categorize as an "indie" film, the phenomenal success of *TMNT*, released by New Line just a year after Soderbergh's film, nonetheless had significant implications for both the rhetorical project of defining independent film and the industrial landscape of independent cinema.

The most obvious aspect of *TMNT* that complicates any traditional reading of it as an independent film is its status as part of a larger pre-existing transmedia franchise. Instead of bracketing off this broader lineage as a tangent, however, attending to the relationship between independent and mainstream iterations of the Turtles across this franchise actually enriches our appreciation of the film's unique independent credentials. Before the film, TV show, and toys, the Teenage Mutant Ninja Turtles were characters in an independent comic book. As comic books became increasingly niche cultural products sold primarily at specialty shops, an independent comic scene developed in the 1970s to appeal to a demographic of largely educated adult men (Kidman 147). Like their cinematic counterparts, independent comics tended to be "more flexible in terms of available genres, artistic styles, content, and expression" than mainstream comics and not bound by the same self-censorship guidelines stipulated by the Comics Code Authority (Kim ix). The original *TMNT* comic was not only classically independent in terms of its production but also a prime example of the critical disposition toward genre that often develops at the margins of mainstream cultural industries. The Turtles started as an in-joke between Kevin Eastman and Peter Laird, two comic book artists/writers who had recently founded Mirage Studios in the living room of their house in Dover, New Hampshire (the mirage being the illusion of an actual studio). The comic would be a work of pastiche, combining story elements from Frank Miller's *Daredevil* comics (Marvel, 1979–1983) and his limited series *Ronin* (DC, 1983–1984) with Chris Claremont's *X-Men* spin-off *The New Mutants* (Marvel), which debuted in 1982. Although still associated with the superhero genre, the original *TMNT* comic, unlike most subsequent franchise installments, was darker and more violent than anything coming out of Marvel and DC and appealed primarily to adult readers. Inspired by the success of Dave Sim's self-published comic *Cerebus* (1977–2004), which was itself a parody of Marvel's *Conan the Barbarian*, Eastman and Laird self-published 3,275 copies of *Teenage Mutant Ninja Turtles* #1 in May 1984. Printed in black and white in an oversized magazine-style format, the stand-alone issue unexpectedly found a readership and demand for subsequent issues rose quickly. But the original comics appeared at a moment of great change in the comic book industry when the licensing of comic book characters as intellectual properties rather than the sale of comic books themselves had become the primary source of profit, a shift that would have profound implications for both the Turtles and their creators (Kidman 36).

The Turtles moved out of the shadows and into the limelight of popular culture with the phenomenal success of the TMNT toy line and animated TV series. Eastman and Laird had licensed a tabletop role-playing game in 1985 and collectible lead figurines in 1986, but it was only after the Turtles caught the attention of licensing agent Mark Freedman, who was hunting for emerging intellectual properties to sell to toy manufacturers, that the Turtles' rise to fame began in earnest. Turned down by the major toy companies, Freedman nonetheless managed to interest the Hong Kong-based Playmates Toys, which was looking to launch its own action figure line to compete with Mattel's Masters of the Universe and Hasbro's G.I. Joe and Transformers properties. To help market the action figures, Playmates took inspiration from Hasbro and Mattel and commissioned its own animated television series from the Ireland-based animation studio Murakami-Wolf-Swenson. This TV series is the source of some of the franchise's most iconic elements, including the unique personalities and color-coded masks of each Turtle, their love of pizza, and their surfer lingo (i.e., "cowabunga!"), all of which would eventually find their way into the first feature film. Debuting as a five-part miniseries in December 1987, the *TMNT* TV series eventually ran for ten seasons (most premiering on CBS) until 1996, indelibly imprinting the Turtles in the imagination of a generation. By 1989, just a year after Playmates rolled out its line of action figures and vehicles at Toys "R" Us retailers, TMNT was the top-selling toy in America ("Teenage Mutant Ninja Turtles"). At the height of "Turtlemania" between 1988 and 1992, over a billion dollars in Turtle merchandise was sold and the "heroes in a half-shell" could be found on everything from school supplies and breakfast cereals to pinball machines and arcade games (Wood). In just five years, TMNT had evolved from a self-published independent comic to a record-breaking franchise generating hundreds of millions of dollars in revenue annually. While it would seem that a live-action film adaptation of TMNT would be the next logical step, it was actually the uncertainty surrounding that prospect that provides the prologue for the film's pathway to independent cinema.

It is strange to think from the superhero-saturated perspective of the early 21st century that comic book properties were ever anything but cash cows, but a live-action *TMNT* was initially thought of as a risky endeavor. In the 40 years between 1950 and 1990, only 20 comic book-based films appeared in theaters. Although *Superman* grossed over $300 million worldwide in 1978, it was largely seen as an aberration given the iconicity of its protagonist; Tim Burton's 1989 *Batman* had yet to be released when *TMNT* went into production (Kidman 183).[2] Proving the received wisdom that live-action comic book adaptations were too expensive to make and had limited audience appeal was the commercial failure of two films with much in common with *TMNT*: 1986's *Howard the Duck* (budget: $37 million, domestic gross: $16.3 million), which was adapted from a niche comic and built around an anthropomorphized protagonist that required the use of animatronics, and – more consequentially here – 1987's *Masters of the Universe* (budget: $22 million, domestic gross: $17.3 million), which was based on characters from a top-selling toy line with its own popular animated TV series.

The studio that ultimately greenlit *TMNT* would not be Warner Bros., Fox, or Disney, but rather the Hong Kong-based Golden Harvest best known in the United States for co-producing and distributing martial arts films like Bruce Lee's *Enter the Dragon* (1973) and Jackie Chan's *The Big Brawl* (1980). Irish-British filmmaker Steve Barron, who made his name helming visually innovative music videos including Michael Jackson's "Billie Jean" (1983), Dire Straits's "Money For Nothing" (1985), and a-ha's "Take On Me" (1985), was brought on to direct. Barron wanted to synthesize elements from the TV series that younger audiences would expect with storylines and the darker tone of the original comics to entice older viewers, a decision that pleased Eastman and Laird. Having directed several episodes of Jim Henson's puppet-based TV series *The StoryTeller* (1987), Barron was able to convince Henson to lend the talent and resources of his London-based Creature Shop to the task of developing the foam rubber latex suits and animatronic heads the actors playing the Turtles would wear. Shot at Wilmington's North Carolina Film Studios over the summer of 1989 with limited location shooting in New York, *TMNT* ultimately came in at a cost of $13.5 million. While Golden Harvest footed most of that bill, they also secured financing from independent distributor New Line Cinema in exchange for the rights to distribute the film theatrically in North America, a process that involved not only the physical distribution of film prints but also marketing (Schatz 130). It is precisely the distribution of *TMNT* by New Line rather than a major studio that technically qualifies it as an independent film. However, the success of *TMNT* was also crucial to New Line's project of reinventing itself.

Founded by Bob Shaye in 1967, New Line Cinema started as a non-theatrical distributor catering to college campuses before moving into theatrical distribution in 1973. As with other independent distributors like New Yorker Films and Cinecom, New Line covered markets that the Hollywood majors ignored, including foreign art cinema, but it specialized in distributing exploitation films like the re-released stoner classic *Reefer Madness* (1936), John Waters's *Pink Flamingos* (1972), and the proto-slasher flick *The Texas Chain Saw Massacre* (1974) (Schatz 128). New Line started producing a modest number of primarily low-budget horror films in 1978 and finally found significant commercial success with Wes Craven's *A Nightmare on Elm Street* in 1984. Made for only $1.8 million, *Nightmare* grossed over $25 million domestically and launched a lucrative franchise that New Line used to expand its production and distribution operations, a business model that Justin Wyatt likens to Paramount's "tent-pole" approach of the 1980s that compensated for less profitable mid-level releases with blockbusters (78). Alongside its rival Miramax, New Line entered the 1990s as a major force in American independent cinema. In contrast to Miramax's strategy of bringing controversy-courting and/or award-baiting independent art-house films to mainstream audiences, New Line continued to concentrate on the distribution of independently produced genre and exploitation films. *TMNT* then represented to New Line's executives another potentially franchise-worthy property in the *Nightmare* vein. On top of $3 million in financing, New Line invested $12 million in marketing the film and when *TMNT* hit cinemas on 30 March 1990, the payoff was immediate (Schatz 130). The film took in more than $25 million on its opening weekend alone and went on to gross $135.4 million domestically and over $200 million worldwide, notably outperforming several of that summer's studio-backed blockbusters like the Tom Cruise starrer *Days of Thunder* (Paramount), the Arnold Schwarzenegger sci-fi film *Total Recall* (Sony), and the year's other major live-action comic book adaptation, Disney's *Dick Tracy* (Schatz 130). Not only was *TMNT* one of the top ten highest-grossing films of 1990, but it was also the highest-grossing independent film of all time until the 1999 release of *The Blair Witch Project*. *TMNT*'s blockbuster-level performance landed New Line firmly in the black for 1990 and paved the way for two prompt sequels: *Teenage Mutant Ninja Turtles II: The Secret of the Ooze* (1991) and *Teenage Mutant Ninja Turtles III* (1993), both of which were also produced by Golden Harvest and distributed by New Line (Wyatt 77).

Together with the profitable *Nightmare on Elm Street* (1984–1994) and *House Party* (1990–1994) franchises, the *TMNT* films enabled New Line to grow and diversify its operations. This included opening Fine Line Features, a specialty division that would bite into Miramax's market share of independent art cinema by distributing films with more traditional "indie" credentials like Gus Van Sant's *My Own Private Idaho* (1991) and Tom Kalin's *Swoon* (1992), both identified with the New Queer Cinema (Wyatt 76–78; Tzioumakis, *Hollywood's Indies* 7–8). Tzioumakis argues that the establishment of Fine Line in 1991, the first new such specialty division in seven years, was "[l]ess 'epic' but arguably equally important" as Miramax's vaunted release of *sex, lies, and videotape* ("'Independent', 'Indie'" 33). Indeed, Fine Line would presage a new wave of studio-owned specialty divisions that would characterize the increasing interdependence of mainstream and independent filmmaking in the late 1990s and 2000s (Schatz 132).

The success of the *TMNT* film franchise had an additional consequence for New Line – it helped make the company ripe for acquisition. 1993 was another watershed year in the history of American independent cinema as both New Line and Miramax were absorbed into major media conglomerates, with Disney acquiring Miramax and Turner Broadcasting System buying New Line for over $500 million (Biskind 200). Writing on the eve of the Turner buyout, Jim Hillier singled out New Line as an emerging "mini-major" that, like Orion Pictures, emulated the operations of a major studio (19). But unlike Orion, which declared bankruptcy in 1992 despite winning back-to-back Oscars in 1990 and 1991 with *Dances with Wolves* and *The Silence of the Lambs*, New Line was able to parlay its success as a standalone independent into its role as a Turner subsidiary. The acquisition was a game changer in many ways for New Line, enabling it to broaden its distribution slate, plan wider releases and more extensive (and expensive) marketing campaigns, and expand its production operations (Schatz 133, 137). But it also posed serious questions for the studio's "independence," an ambivalence reflected in Wyatt's use of the term "major independent" to characterize the liminal post-acquisition status of both New Line and Miramax (87). Tzioumakis takes issue with both "mini-major" and "major independent" since the first "presents the companies simply as smaller majors and does not allow space for qualitative differences" while the second "uses the term 'independent' when a company is a subsidiary of a conglomerate" (*American Independent Cinema* 205). But both terms capture the gray area between the independent and mainstream realms in which New Line operated to an extent before, but certainly after the buyout. The mergers and acquisitions did not stop there. Turner Broadcasting System eventually merged with Time Warner in 1996 and, as a subsidiary of Time Warner, New Line continued to produce and distribute mid-level indie films like *Boogie Nights* and *Wag the Dog* (both 1997) and again found major commercial success with the *Rush Hour* (1998–2007), *Austin Powers* (1997–2002), and *Lord of the Rings* (2001–2003) franchises. In 2008, New Line was folded into Warner Bros., a name-brand Hollywood major. What started as an independent distributor of exploitation films in the 1960s and 1970s eventually became part of a constellation of companies under the banner of a massive multinational media and entertainment conglomerate known as WarnerMedia following its acquisition by AT&T in 2018 and as Warner Bros. Discovery after AT&T sold its WarnerMedia assets to Discovery in 2022. Though by no means the sole cause, New Line's trajectory from the margins to the mainstream was nonetheless notably accelerated by the success of *TMNT* and its sequels in the early 1990s.

While *TMNT*'s production and distribution circumstances are primarily responsible for its independent status, there are also select narrative and aesthetic elements that align it with independent cinema. One is the consummate outsider status of the film's protagonists. In contrast to most other superheroes with white male (not to mention human) alter egos, the Turtles have "no social status whatsoever" to the extent that Richard Rosenbaum calls them "the ultimate superheroes of the subaltern" (16). On one level a manifestation of postmodern hybridity, each component of the Turtles' identity also connotes social marginalization (22). Suspended in limbo between childhood and adulthood, the Turtles are perennial teenagers and each one personifies some aspect of adolescent non-conformism, from Raphael's tempestuousness to Michelangelo's tomfoolery. As mutants they likewise exist in a liminal state of ontological uncertainty – "no longer one thing but not yet quite another" (37). Trained in the Japanese martial art of ninjutsu by their surrogate father and sensei Splinter, but steeped in contemporary American popular culture, the Turtles can be read as "symbolic Nisei" (Cobb 96), although the film treads a fine line between honoring and exploiting Japanese culture. This ambivalence seems mild and even moderately progressive when compared to the resurgent anti-Japanese rhetoric present in many American cultural and political discourses of the 1980s, a decade that witnessed Japan's growth as a major economic competitor. Finally, the Teenage Mutant Ninja Turtles are, at the end of the day, turtles. Despite being significantly anthropomorphized, *TMNT*'s instrumentalization of non-human agents as a force for social good inverts the stereotypical and frequently racialized equation of animality with criminality. While these sewer dwellers' status as part of a literal "sub" culture aligns them with many outcast indie characters, the film's aesthetics also gesture toward an oft-overlooked component of independent cinema – exploitation films.

In addition to its franchise lineage, for Thomas Schatz the other factor that complicates *TMNT*'s status as an independent is its reliance on the aesthetic conventions of genre and exploitation films, which places it "categorically (and aesthetically) at odds with the implicit equation between the indie movement and art cinema" (130). However, exploitation filmmaking has long been an important part of American independent cinema and several scenes in *TMNT* seem to explicitly acknowledge this history. Fittingly, two of them concern origin stories narrated in flashback by Splinter (voiced by Kevin Clash). The first, spoken to reporter April O'Neil (Judith Hoag), details how he came upon four baby turtles wallowing in radioactive ooze in the New York sewers and trained them as they grew (and mutated) in their ninja ways. The second flashback, told to wayward youth Danny (Michael Turney), relays the story of how Splinter learned ninjutsu by mimicking his master Hamato Yoshi and Yoshi's murder at the hands of his rival Oroku Saki (aka the villainous Shredder). Using minimalistic sets and shot on small gauge film stock, both scenes look as if they were lifted from earlier B movies. Shots of Yoshi and Saki shadowboxing in front of stark black backgrounds echo the kung fu films for which Golden Harvest was famous. Likewise, the simple animatronics used for Splinter as an "ordinary" rat and the fledgling Turtles recalls not only low-budget sci-fi and monster movies, but in particular the campy stylings of *Tales from the Crypt*, which had also made the jump from indie comic to big and small screens in 1972 and 1989, respectively. One can also see echoes of a previous era's cautionary tale films about juvenile delinquency in a scene set in Shredder's warehouse in which the camera surveys the litany of "vices" used to attract "lost" kids like Danny to the Foot Clan, including video games, graffiti, gambling, skateboarding, punk rock, rap, cigarettes, and junk food. These aesthetic homages not only acknowledge the exploitation heritage of *TMNT* but also implicitly point out the kinds of films on which New Line itself was built.

The transmedia franchise of which *TMNT* was but a part provided an important precedent for the type of synergy built around comic book properties that would thrive in the conglomerate-dominated media and entertainment landscape of the 21st century. And that franchise continues to evolve to this day. For Rosenbaum, mutation and hybridity not only inform the Turtles' diegetic mythos but also capture the ways in which the TMNT intellectual property has been adapted across different media, from comics, toys, and TV shows to films and video games (22). Kevin Eastman sold his TMNT rights to Peter Laird in the early 2000s and Laird ultimately sold his rights to Nickelodeon in 2009 for $60 million, although both remain involved with the TMNT comics. Rosenbaum laments this turn in the Turtles saga, writing:

> The sale to Nickelodeon shocked fans and caused not a little outrage. One of the things we appreciated about TMNT was that, since its very beginning, it had been *independent*. It was created by these two guys, not by some corporate culture factory. And that independent spirit was part of its very ethos.
>
> *(101–102)*

It seems strange, however, to pick this moment as the definitive time of death for TMNT's "independence" given how much the meaning of the term itself has changed. A more interesting conversation concerns what TMNT's evolution can teach us about the mercurial relationship between independent and mainstream cultural products and the historically specific ways in which independent films have been defined. By examining the industrial context of *Teenage Mutant Ninja Turtles*'s production and distribution and, to a lesser degree, its narrative and aesthetic dimensions, we can clearly see that not only is the notion of independence highly contingent but, much like the franchise's principal characters, also susceptible to mutation.

Notes

1 Hereafter I use the italicized "*TMNT*" to refer to the film and other media objects that share the title *Teenage Mutant Ninja Turtles* while the non-italicized "TMNT" refers to the characters or to the franchise more generally.
2 All budget and box office figures come from Box Office Mojo.

Works Cited

Biskind, Peter. *Down and Dirty Pictures: Miramax, Sundance, and the Rise of Independent Film.* Simon & Schuster, 2004.

Cobb, Nora Okja. "Behind the Inscrutable Half-Shell: Images of Mutant Japanese and Ninja Turtles." *MELUS,* vol. 16, no. 4, 1989, pp. 87–98.

Hillier, Jim. *The New Hollywood.* Continuum, 1994.

Kidman, Shawna. *Comic Books Incorporated: How the Business of Comics Became the Business of Hollywood.* University of California Press, 2019.

Kim, Minjung. *Teenage Mutant Ninja Turtles: Evolution of an Independent Comic to a Multimedia Icon.* 2015. Fashion Institute of Technology, MFA Thesis. *ProQuest Dissertations and Theses.*

King, Geoff. *American Independent Cinema.* Indiana University Press, 2005.

King, Geoff, Claire Molloy, and Yannis Tzioumakis, editors. *American Independent Cinema: Indie, Indiewood and Beyond.* Routledge, 2012.

Levy, Emanuel. *Cinema of Outsiders: The Rise of American Independent Cinema.* NYU Press, 1999.

Rosenbaum, Richard. *Raise Some Shell: Teenage Mutant Ninja Turtles.* ECW Press, 2014.

Schatz, Thomas. "Conglomerate Hollywood and American Independent Film." King et al., pp. 127–39.

Staiger, Janet. "Independent of What?: Sorting Out Differences from Hollywood." King et al., pp. 15–27.

"Teenage Mutant Ninja Turtles." *The Toys That Made Us,* season 3, episode 1, Netflix, 15 Nov. 2019. *Netflix,* https://www.netflix.com/watch/80994013.

Tzioumakis, Yannis. *American Independent Cinema: An Introduction.* 2nd ed., Edinburgh University Press, 2017.

———. *Hollywood's Indies: Classics Divisions, Specialty Labels and the American Film Market.* Edinburgh University Press, 2012.

———. "'Independent', 'Indie' and 'Indiewood': Towards a Periodisation of Contemporary (Post-1980) American Independent Cinema." King et al., pp. 28–40.

Wood, Robert W. "'Teenage Mutant Ninja Turtles' Is Surprisingly All About Taxes." *Forbes,* 11 Aug. 2014, www.forbes.com/sites/robertwood/2014/08/11/teenage-mutant-ninja-turtles-is-surprisingly-all-about-taxes/?sh=2942473529cb. Accessed 18 Sept. 2021.

Wyatt, Justin. "The Formation of the 'Major Independent': Miramax, New Line and the New Hollywood." *Contemporary Hollywood Cinema,* edited by Steve Neale and Murray Smith. Routledge, 1998, pp. 74–90.

32
MY OWN PRIVATE IDAHO (1991)

Daniel Herbert

Directed by Gus Van Sant and featuring rising teen stars River Phoenix and Keanu Reeves, *My Own Private Idaho* bears many characteristics associated with indie cinema. The film tells the story of two prostitutes, one from a wealthy background, played by Reeves, and the other of whom, played by Phoenix, is destitute, suffers from narcolepsy, and is in search of his mother. Its picaresque structure follows the characters as they engage with clients around Portland and later travel to Idaho and Italy in search of the mother. Similar to Van Sant's *Drugstore Cowboy* (1989), much of *My Own Private Idaho* is slow-paced and meditative.

But this contemplativeness is interspersed with energetic, often humorous scenes with different clients; it also features several rambunctious sequences with a gaggle of fellow hustlers and their leader, Bob, who is modeled on the Falstaff character from several Shakespeare plays and Orson Welles's adaptation *Chimes at Midnight* (1965). Stylistically, *My Own Private Idaho* is further distinguished by featuring a number of impressionistic, surreal vignettes as Phoenix's character experiences visions during narcoleptic episodes. Thus, with its narrative focus on social outsiders, its mix of disparate cultural references, and its stylistic mélange of realism and oneiricism, *My Own Private Idaho* stands out as artistically unusual and deviates from Hollywood conventions of the time.

The film's engagement with queer sexuality also aligns it with a cycle of related films from the early 1990s. B. Ruby Rich coined the term "new queer cinema" in 1992 to describe this recent wave of movies made by queer-identified filmmakers that represented queer sexuality in new and complex ways. Along with *Poison* (1991) and *Swoon* (1992), among other films, Rich mentions *My Own Private Idaho* as a key example of this cycle and sensibility. The film has continued to attract the attention of critics and scholars, many of whom examine its representation of queerness (Arthur and Liebler; Lang; Levy; Román; Tinkcom), although others attend more to the film's connections to Shakespeare (Barnaby,

FIGURE 32.1 Alone on a highway in Idaho, Mike (River Phoenix) searches for human connection.

Davis, and Protic), while others include it within discussions of Van Sant as an auteur (Staiger). If we consider that auteurial vision and cultural pedigree are common elements of American "indie" cinema, then *My Own Private Idaho* clearly conforms to this label. Yet calling this film "indie" does not fully account for the film's engagement with queerness; rather, doing so raises the very issue of how queerness relates to independent cinema.

Although scholars have examined multiple aspects of *My Own Private Idaho*, they have not looked at it from discursive and industrial perspectives in a dedicated way. One can define "independent film" industrially, and *My Own Private Idaho*'s development, distribution, marketing, and publicity all illuminate key tendencies of the independent cinema industrial sector. The film's identity, as associated with queer sexuality, auteurial vision, and cultural distinction, is not only to be found within its formal features and narrative but also through the way in which it was distributed, marketed, and discussed in the press. This film was defined as both "indie" and "queer," and this essay will show how these meanings and associations came about through industrial practices and the film's circulation through culture.

Van Sant developed *My Own Private Idaho* over many years as he established his career. His first feature was *Mala Noche*, which featured a queer romance and gained considerable press as it played in prestigious festivals in 1986. This success allowed him to make *Drugstore Cowboy* with a multi-million-dollar budget and a cast that included star Matt Dillon. *Drugstore Cowboy* was released in 1989 and also earned widespread praise and awards. Although these achievements brought Van Sant to Hollywood's attention, he pursued *My Own Private Idaho* despite the lack of studio interest in the project (Andrews; McKenna, "Will

Hollywood"). The director made multiple statements that articulated a desire to make *My Own Private Idaho* an independent picture (Andrews; Taggart). The director stated,

> Sure there are people chomping at the bit to give me big bucks, but they won't give me money to make *my* next movie.... *My Own Private Idaho* is of a nature that doesn't suggest wide audience appeal, so it will be an independently financed low-budget film.
>
> *(McKenna, "Will Hollywood")*

Here he provides a serviceable definition of indie cinema: low budget, outside Hollywood, personal, and artistically distinct.

Van Sant's statement also suggests the way in which *My Own Private Idaho*'s queer subject matter was embedded within his artistic vision and the film's industrial independence. Even the earliest press about the project indicated that it featured queer characters (Andrews; McKenna, "Will Hollywood"), and the press continued to discuss the film's sexual themes and content throughout its circulation in festivals, theaters, and on video. Further, Van Sant was known to be gay himself, and articles about the director regularly identified him as "openly gay." Through its content and its director, *My Own Private Idaho* was identified as queer from the very start, and this quality was entirely tied up with its industrial independence.

The film attained production funds and a distribution deal from the independent company New Line Cinema. After eking out a small business at the margins of the film industry in the 1960s and 1970s, New Line grew enormously during the 1980s with the *A Nightmare on Elm Street* franchise and, in 1990, with the *Teenage Mutant Ninja Turtles* film. New Line was in a transition when it picked up *My Own Private Idaho*, aiming to produce higher-profile movies with recognizable stars while also continuing to exploit the niche markets and genres that it had a history with, including "specialty" films.

My Own Private Idaho reflects both New Line's interest in producing star-driven films as well as its interest in specialty cinema. The film was important enough to the company that it placed *My Own Private Idaho* at the top of advertisements for its upcoming slate of films, and the ads highlighted that River Phoenix and Keanu Reeves would star in the film. In truth, New Line only committed to producing *My Own Private Idaho*, budgeted at $2.5 million, after Phoenix and Reeves joined the project (Mahar). New Line's interest in the art-house film market grew considerably following the success of *sex, lies, and videotape* in 1989. As Alisa Perren has written, "*sex, lies, and videotape* served as both an example and model for the future of low-budget film" because it demonstrated the commercial potential for "quality" cinema as an alternative to Hollywood blockbusters (39). Spurred by this film's success, every Hollywood studio either launched a specialty division or purchased an existing specialty distributor over the course of the 1990s (4).

New Line spearheaded this trend with the creation of Fine Line Features in 1990, a division devoted to smaller, artistically sophisticated works. *My Own Private Idaho* became the division's first hit and, ultimately, helped establish Fine Line's status and identity within the film industry. Like the company's subsequent breakout hit *The Player* (1992), *My Own Private Idaho* was an English-language film made by a distinguished auteur and featured a cast of marketable stars. These traits helped distinguish Fine Line within the field of independent distributors at the time, which commonly also distributed foreign-language art films.

The film's queer subject matter was not unusual for the fledgling division. Prior to Fine Line's creation, New Line had handled some queer cinema in the 1970s, including *A Very Natural Thing* (1974) and, in a very different style, the films of John Waters. The company also released *Torch Song Trilogy* in 1988, a queer romance adapted from the Harvey Fierstein stage plays. Further, Fine Line President Ira Deutchman handled some important queer films when he worked at Cinecom Pictures during the 1980s, including *Parting Glances* (1986).

Despite such previous work with queer film subjects, however, Fine Line's handling *My Own Private Idaho*, from publicity, through marketing and advertising, through its circulation at film festivals and commercial theaters, as well as the public discourse these activities generated, reveals a complex negotiation with multiple qualities associated with "indie film" and queerness. An internal memo indicates that, prior to its release, Fine Line considered that the film's director and stars offered "a great package," but that "the subject matter makes it a very tough sell" ("Fine Line Features: Business Plan 1992"). Thus the company appears to have conceived of the film primarily as an indie picture with a solid artistic pedigree and considered the film's queerness as a possible hindrance that needed to be overcome.

As is common with specialty cinema, Fine Line first sought publicity for the film by entering it into film festivals. Although *My Own Private Idaho* did not get into Cannes, the film gained praise and awards when it played at the Venice, Toronto, Chicago, and Deauville festivals in 1991 (Hartl; Kehr). Fine Line caused a bit of a stir, however, by *not* entering *My Own Private Idaho* into festivals specifically dedicated to gay and lesbian cinema. The film gained negative attention as "the highest profile" film to have been "blocked" from the Los Angeles Gay & Lesbian Film/Video Festival (Fox, "Gay Film Fest"). The festival's director expressed disappointment and even a sense of betrayal about director Gus Van Sant. "Private Idaho is a gay film and they're not looking at the audience that first embraced Gus," the festival director said, since *Mala Noche* had played at that festival previously (Fox, "Gay Film Fest"). The film's publicist, Mickey Cottrell complicated the issue by stating that, "The distributor doesn't want the film positioned as a gay film... Then many people would be frightened away. It's better to have the critics say how wonderful it is in dealing with gay characters" (Fox, "Gay Film Fest"). Thus, in its festival run, which is precisely where it gained the attention of B. Ruby Rich, *My Own Private Idaho* was identified as queer *and* as indie, with indie being positioned as the dominant quality and its queerness as a secondary aspect of the film.

Fine Line gave *My Own Private Idaho* a "platform release" typical of specialty films. It initially played in two theaters in New York City in late September, where it did considerable business ("Film: Weekly Box Office Report"), and then expanded to over 70 screens around the country in mid-October (Fox, "DeVito Comedy Dethrones 'King'"). Fine Line engaged in a publicity campaign coordinated with the film's theatrical expansion, spending roughly $1.5 million on direct advertising costs in newspapers, magazines, and on television, and an additional $350,000 on other publicity and marketing activities ("Film P&L Estimate: My Own Private Idaho"). Reeves and Phoenix supported the film with publicity events, including appearing on an episode of the *Today* show ("Other 22 – No Title"), while Van Sant was interviewed on NPR's *Morning Edition* ("My Own Private Idaho: Film About Gay Hustler"). Fine Line also partnered with *Detour* magazine to throw a premiere screening and after-party in Los Angeles and Drew Barrymore, Winona Ryder, and Christian Slater were among the many young stars who attended (Allman).

Fine Line's print advertising largely deflected away from the film's sexual content and instead focused on its stars and auteur. A one-sheet for the film played up the characters' class differences, featuring an image of Phoenix lying on a sidewalk and an image of Reeves riding in a limousine ("'My Own Private Idaho,' Publicity Photo"). Newspaper advertisements for the film likewise made no reference to the characters' sexuality but rather featured close-ups of the two stars arranged as a series of fragmented pictures, as well as pull quotes from the film's many positive reviews ("Display Ad 34 – No Title"). Print ads for the film also featured the slogan, "Wherever, Whatever, Have a nice day" ("Display Ad 343 – No Title"), which implied a generalized Gen-X, slacker sensibility that aligned with the star personae of the film's lead actors.

Alternatively, the film's theatrical trailer indicates that Phoenix and Reeves play hustlers and features a number of moments of the characters engaging romantically with both male and female characters. Additionally, the trailer includes many of the surreal interludes from the film, including a barn falling from the sky into a highway. The trailer showcases the stars throughout, and also plays upon auteurism by noting that the film is "from the director of *Drugstore Cowboy*." The trailer concertedly highlights moments that suggest that family, and a search for belonging within a family, is the film's central theme. This includes interactions between Reeves's character and his father, Phoenix's dreams of his mother, and dialogue in which Phoenix directly states that he wishes he had a normal family. On the one hand, the trailer threatens to subsume its markers of queerness and indie-ness with a conventional notion of "family" as a normative social formation. On the other hand, this invocation of "family" resonates with ideas about "family of choice" that circulated at the time, especially about and within the LGBTQ community.

Promotional interviews and press coverage about the film were more direct in addressing its queerness, and this discourse regularly related this topic to the film business. One reviewer asserted, "the biggest commercial gamble

[Van Sant] takes is making his lead character gay...For all the advances gay culture is making toward integrating with mainstream society, gay themes still aren't exactly box-office magic" (McKenna, "Another Risky Road"). One interviewer asked Van Sant whether he thought the queer material in the film would affect its box office performance, but he was characteristically circumspect and replied, "I don't know. Maybe. We'll see" (Terry). Another article noted that "Hollywood actors are notoriously paranoid about playing gay roles" (Ansen). The press universally felt compelled to identify the actors as straight, and one writer even referred to them as "macho" (Terry). The actors were often lauded for taking the roles, as though doing so was a sign of bravery on their part (e.g., Farley; Schwager). One reviewer wrote, "River Phoenix and Keanu Reeves take major gambles with their teen-idol images to play street hustlers" (Orme).

Interviewers also commonly asked Van Sant to comment on the film's sexuality. But the director's statements aimed to be slippery and un-proscriptive, such as when he told the *Advocate*, "I think it would be odd to pigeonhole it as a gay film," and further that, "I don't see [the characters] as gay or straight" (Block). Van Sant was similarly inexact about how his own sexuality might affect *My Own Private Idaho*. One interview stated that Van Sant "doesn't particularly address himself to a gay audience," and quoted the director saying "I try and speak to everyone, not just a select group" (Howe). Van Sant occasionally gestured toward the film's social relevance, stating, "That's a good thing about filmmaking – you can comment on social issues and bring things up for discussion that people tend to shy away from." But he quickly tried to universalize this statement by adding that, "Everyone can listen to a good story" (Farley).

Reviews for the film were largely positive and focused on elements that endowed it with artistic distinction, and thus helped to define *My Own Private Idaho* as "indie." Critics often held up Van Sant as a visionary and idiosyncratic auteur (e.g., Schwager). One piece compared the director to David Lynch and John Waters as "the latest celluloid original" (Loud), and another asserted that, "Gus Van Sant Jr. makes a big bold leap to join Jim Jarmusch and the Coen brothers in the front ranks of America's most innovative independent filmmakers" (Canby). Reviewers regularly praised the film's acting and especially commended Phoenix's performance (Upchurch). Many reviews gestured toward its prestige by discussing its use of Shakespearean elements (e.g., Loud, Mathews, Mondello, and Upchurch), while others compared it with Dickens (Ansen).

But reviewers commonly discussed these qualities of artistic "quality" alongside a devoted if irregular concern with the film's queerness. One reviewer wrote that Phoenix's character, "lives a sordid life, sleeping on the street when he isn't having sex (with men and women) for money" (Salamon), while another asserted:

> For a story about two gay hustlers, film deals very little with sex. While the milieu may be enough to put off many viewers, other may complain that

the two leads' predilections are not adequately clarified. Still others may be offended at the lack of mention of AIDS.

(McCarthy)

Along a similar line, Vincent Canby noted that the lack of any reference to AIDS in *My Own Private Idaho* was so conspicuous that it made the film seem fantastical. Reviews such as these held *My Own Private Idaho* up as a representative text for understanding queer identity, the real-life queer community, and the politics of queer representation. In their cumulative effect, however, the reviews did not pin down the sexuality of *My Own Private Idaho* in a clearly defined manner. The film's fluid identity was especially noted by the reviewer for *Gay Community News*, who wrote, "Part of the trouble in looking at My Own Private Idaho as a 'gay film' is that it isn't a gay film, at least not in the usual sense of that overused and under-explicated term" (Bronski). *My Own Private Idaho* confounded expectations about sex and sexuality on multiple fronts, and its representation of *fluid* rather than fixed sexual identities makes the film all the more radical within its historical context.

In addition to garnering positive reviews, *My Own Private Idaho* won three Independent Spirit Awards (Fox, "'Rose' Named Best at the Alternative Oscars"), and Phoenix won the best actor award from the National Society of Film Critics ("'Life is Sweet' Tops Film Awards"). Further, the film was also financial success. By the time it was reaching the end of its theatrical run in 1992, it had earned $6 million at the box office (Deutchman; "US Box Office") and nearly $1 million in pay TV licenses ("'My Own Private Idaho,' Domestic Profit/Loss Statement"). Based on this revenue, Fine Line expected to make over $2.5 million in profit on the film ("'My Own Private Idaho,' Domestic Profit/Loss Statement").

My Own Private Idaho was thus a remarkable film – as indie, as queer, and as a film that melded these qualities in complex ways. Not only did it help crystalize the "new queer cinema," but it also contributed greatly to the indie cinema boom of that moment. Indeed, *My Own Private Idaho* was held up in the press as a key example of how small, specialty films could generate impressive business (Natale). The film cemented Gus Van Sant's status as a distinctive auteur. Further, *My Own Private Idaho* was a defining film for Fine Line, with President Ira Deutchman writing in a memo, "This is...a perfect example of everything a Fine Line film should be – a true art film that has promotable elements" ("Fine Line Features: Business Plan 1992").

This was precisely the formula that the company found in the next major hit, *The Player* by Robert Altman. And despite Fine Line's ambivalent treatment of *My Own Private Idaho*'s queerness, the film's success prompted the company to treat "queer" as a clear element of "indie," an associative linkage that the company would draw upon in subsequent releases. The company became even more strongly linked with the "new queer cinema" when it released *Edward II* in 1992, which also gained much press for its portrayal of queerness. When Fine Line released *Swoon* later that year, it promoted the film's queerness directly, as a salable quality. Thus, much in the way that the characters in *My Own Private Idaho* wander street corners and lonely rural highways, the film itself paved an unusual and twisting path for indie and queer cinema in the 1990s.

Works Cited

Allman, Kevin. "A Private Premiere and Party." *Los Angeles Times*, 16 Oct. 1991.
Andrews, Paul. "Private Screening – Director Gus Van Sant Gives Movies That Feel Like a Reality Check." *Seattle Times*, 9 Sept. 1990.
Ansen, David. "Prince Hal in Portland." *Newsweek*, 15 Apr. 1991, p. 69.
Arthur, Paul, and Naomi Liebler. "Kings of the Road: *My Own Private Idaho* and the Traversal of Welles, Shakespeare, and Liminality." *Postscript*, vol. 17, no. 2, Winter/Spring 1998, pp. 26–38.
Barnaby, Andrew. "Imitation as Originality in Gus Van Sant's My Own Private Idaho." *Almost Shakespeare: Reinventing His Works for Cinema and Television*, edited by James R. Keller and Leslie Stratyner. McFarland & Company, 2004, pp. 22–41.
Block, Adam. "Inside Outsider Gus Van Sant: The Director of *My Own Private Idaho* Is Casual About Hi Sexuality, Compulsive About His Filmmaking." *Advocate*, 24 Sept. 1991, pp. 80–84.
Bronski, Michael. "Underground Like a Wild Potato." *Gay Community News*, 2 Nov. 1991, p. 16.
Canby, Vincent. "A Road Movie about Male Hustlers." *New York Times*, 27 Sept. 1991.
Davis, Hugh H. "'Shakespeare, He's in the Alley': *My Own Private Idaho* and Shakespeare in the Streets." *Literature/Film Quarterly*, vol. 29, no. 2, 2001, pp. 116–21.
"Display Ad 34 – No Title." *New York Times*, 27 Sept. 1991.
"Display Ad 343 – No Title." *Chicago Tribune*, 13 Oct. 1991.
Farley, Christopher John. "Van Sant Stays True to His Own Private Vision." *USA Today*, 29 Oct. 1991.
"Film P&L Estimate: My Own Private Idaho." University of Michigan Special Collections Library. Ira Deutchman Papers. Box 18 – Prod. Companies – Fine Line – Business Plans, 1992.
"Film: Weekly Box Office Report." *Variety*, 7 Oct. 1991, p. 14.
"Fine Line Features: Business Plan 1992." University of Michigan Special Collections Library. Ira Deutchman Papers. Box 18 – Fine Line – Business Plans, 1992.
Fox, David J. "Gay Film Fest Loses Out on Four Films." *Los Angeles Times*, 9 July 1991.
———. "DeVito Comedy Dethrones 'King'." *Los Angeles Times*, 22 Oct. 1991.
———. "'Rose' Named Best at the Alternative Oscars." *Seattle Times*, 31 Mar. 1992, p. F2.
Hartl, John. "His 'Private' Triumph – 'Saint Gus' Has Become a Quirky, Moody Poet of Urban Alienation." *Seattle Times*, 13 Oct. 1991, p. J1.
Howe, Desson. "Van Sant's 'Private' Eye." *Washington Post*, 18 Oct. 1991, p. 52.
Kehr, Dave. "Van Sant Outdoes Himself." *Chicago Tribune*, 15 Oct. 1991.
Lang, Robert. *Masculine Interests: Homoerotics in Hollywood Film*. Columbia University Press, 2002.
Levy, Emanuel. *Gay Directors, Gay Films?: Pedro Almodóvar, Terence Davies, Todd Haynes, Gus Van Sant, John Waters*. Columbia University Press, 2015.
"'Life is Sweet' Tops Film Awards." *Seattle Times*, 6 Jan. 1992, p. B2.
Loud, Lance. "Shakespeare in Black Leather." *American Film*, vol. 16, no. 9, Sept. 1991, pp. 32–37.
Mahar, Ted. "Van Sant's Next Move a Bold One." *Oregonian*, 9 Dec. 1990, p. D01.

Mathews, Jack. "New York Film Festival: Desperately in Search of their Own Private Love." *Newsday*, 27 Sept. 1991.
McCarthy, Todd. "Telluride Fest – My Own Private Idaho." *Variety*, 9 Sept. 1991, p. 64–65.
McKenna, Kristine. "Will Hollywood Rope the Director of 'Drugstore Cowboy'." *Los Angeles Times*, 26 Dec. 1989.
———. "Another Risky Road After 'Drugstore Cowboy'." *Los Angeles Times*, 13 Oct. 1991.
Mondello, Bob. "*My Own Private Idaho*: Profane & Awesome." NPR, Washington, D.C., 5 Oct. 1991.
"'My Own Private Idaho,' Domestic Profit/Loss Statement." University of Michigan Special Collections Library. Ira Deutchman Papers. Box 18 – Fine Line – Management Reports – 1991–1994, Folder 1 of 4.
"My Own Private Idaho: Film About Gay Hustler." NPR, Washington, D.C., 30 Sept. 1991.
"'My Own Private Idaho,' Publicity Photo." Ira Deutchman Papers. Box 10 – Personal – Press – Fine Line, 1993–2004 – Folder 1 of 3.
Natale, Richard. "Indies Snare their Share of Xmas Screens." *Variety*, 2 Dec. 1991.
Orme, Terry. "At the Movies." *Salt Lake Tribune*, 7 Feb. 1992.
"Other 22 – no Title." *Los Angeles Times*, 25 Sept. 1991.
Perren, Alisa. *Indie Inc.: Miramax and the Transformation of Hollywood in the 1990s*. University of Texas Press, 2012.
Protic, Nemanja. "Where is the Bawdy? Falstaffian Politics in Gus Van Sant's *My Own Private Idaho*." *Literature/Film Quarterly*, vol. 41, no. 3, 2013, pp. 184–196.
Rich, B. Ruby. "New Queer Cinema." *Sight & Sound*, Sept. 1992, pp. 30–35.
Román, David. "Shakespeare Out in Portland: Gus Van Sant's *My Own Private Idaho*, Homoerotics, and Boy Actors." *Genders*, no. 19, 1994, pp. 311–333.
Salamon, Julie. "Mamet's Cop in Search of Himself." *Wall Street Journal*, 3 Oct. 1991.
Schwager, Jeff. "Reviews: *My Own Private Idaho*." *Boxoffice*, 1 Oct. 1991, pp. 109–110.
Staiger, Janet. "Authorship Studies and Gus Van Sant." *Film Criticism*, vol. 29, no. 1, 2004, pp. 1–22
Taggart, Patrick. "Many Talents, Few Words – 'Drugstore' Gives Reticent Director an Arthouse Hit." *Austin American-Statesman*, 19 Nov. 1989.
Terry, Clifford. "Beyond the Fringe: 'Idaho' Writer-Director Takes the Alternate View." *Chicago Tribune*, 13 Oct. 1991.
Tinkcom, Matthew. "Out West: Gus Van Sant's *My Own Private Idaho* and the Lost Mother." *Where the Boys Are: Cinemas of Masculinity and Youth*, edited by Murray Pomerance and Frances Gateward. Wayne State University Press, 2005, pp. 233–245.
Upchurch, Michael. "Roads Less Traveled – Looking for Love, Home and Family in Van Sant's Chaotic 'Idaho'." *Seattle Times*, 18 Oct. 1991, p. 3.
"US Box Office." *Screen International*, 14 Feb. 1992, p. 24.

33

TWIN PEAKS: FIRE WALK WITH ME (1992)

Rick Warner

For more than a decade after it flustered audience members at the Cannes Film Festival, received mostly negative reviews, and had an unprofitable theatrical run, David Lynch's *Twin Peaks: Fire Walk with Me* was widely regarded as an abstruse mess of a film, rivaling *Dune* (1984) as its director's worst misstep. Billed as a prequel to the 1990–1991 television series Lynch had co-created with Mark Frost for ABC, the film revisits the small, enchantingly weird Pacific Northwest town of Twin Peaks to detail the traumatic last days of Laura Palmer (Sheryl Lee), the homecoming queen whose murder attracts a convoluted FBI investigation. But the film is more aggressively experimental in its style, as well as more relentlessly disturbing in its tone and content.

Now backed by a French independent production company, Ciby 2000, that allowed much freer rein to explore dark material, Lynch could reinvent *Twin Peaks* without yielding to network television protocols of making palatable the horror of Laura's experience, which involved incest and rape. These changes go some way to explain why the film upset viewers who expected more of the cozy, pie-and-coffee charms of the original show.

The film's antagonistic reception had just as much to do with the equivocal nature of the *Twin Peaks* universe, its mutability between mainstream and avant-garde impulses. Lynch, on the strength of *Eraserhead* (1977) and *Blue Velvet* (1986), had already established himself as American independent cinema's leading surrealist. Network television seemed an unlikely and unsuitable home for his work, but *Twin Peaks* launched him to unforeseen heights of popularity and affirmed Pauline Kael's hypothesis, in a review of *Blue Velvet*, that he "might turn out to be the first populist surrealist – a Frank Capra of dream logic" (1114). The surrealism afoot in the ABC series is partly tamed for accessibility. Bursts of radical experimentation with form and mood punctuate the episodes Lynch directed – most memorably the surreal scenes inside the Black Lodge, an extradimensional maze of hallways and

FIGURE 33.1 Laura Palmer (Sheryl Lee), or a version of herself, finds a postmortem refuge in the Black Lodge.

waiting rooms – but these moments are, for the most part, contained by familiar narrative devices in a serviceable mix of murder mystery, police procedural, film noir, melodrama, and teen romance genres. *Fire Walk with Me* resumes this combination but invests more amply in psychological horror that veers into abstractions. The film tilts the balance toward the avant-garde, leaving a mainstream audience in the lurch and looking ahead to Lynch's elaborate identity switches and parallel universes in *Lost Highway* (1997), *Mulholland Drive* (2001), and *Inland Empire* (2006). As became his custom after the Hollywood setback of *Dune*, Lynch, in exchange for a reduced budget, retained final cut with Ciby 2000, a company that catered to international arthouse auteurs such as Pedro Almodóvar, Bernardo Bertolucci, Jane Campion, Wim Wenders, Mike Leigh, and Emir Kusturica. Brashly independent in the industrial, formal, authorial, and experiential senses of the term, *Fire Walk with Me* revives *Twin Peaks* not as a franchise so much as a sorcerer's workshop. The film tests out new ideas and multisensory forms while sustaining a hypnotic, unresolved feeling of mystery that exceeds genre conventions.

Fire Walk with Me has been reevaluated in recent years, with commentators building on insights of early defenders such as Michel Chion and Martha P. Nochimson. My essay adds to this rehabilitation effort by explaining the film's narrative complications, its eerie atmospheric disturbances, and its harrowing portrayal of an ultimately opaque protagonist. These traits – all of which seem unmotivated according to the dictates of "proper" storytelling – follow directly from the film's independent status. Giving them their due will illustrate how *Fire Walk with Me* embodies independence not just as a production mode but as a sensibility that craftily negotiates between popular and experimental aesthetics.

Twin Peaks Redoubled and Rewired

The opening title sequence of *Fire Walk with Me* immediately signals its departure from the feel of the ABC series. Angelo Badalamenti's musical combo of synth strings and a muted trumpet differs from the score he composed for the show.

Still slower, more sorrowful "*doom* jazz" instead of "cool jazz" (Norelli 118), it accompanies the credits on an abstract field of blue (a color Lynch strictly limited in the TV series' décor).¹ The camera gently withdraws, revealing this volatile blue texture to be electronic static on a TV set that is soon destroyed by a shadowy figure wielding an ax. Out of frame, as if behind the audience, a woman screams. With a cut to black, triggered by the dark figure engulfing the entire shot, we hear a dull thud and then silence, or rather an ominous room tone.

In addition to establishing a more somber and frightening mood, this obscure event (who are these people? where is the scene located?) stages a contrast between the square television set and the wider dimensions of Lynch's 1.85:1 film frame. Many have taken the destruction of the TV to indicate Lynch's animosity toward the televisual medium and what the ABC series had become in its second season, when it fell into hackneyed script ideas. More crucially, this self-reflexive opening works as spectator address by playing on our interface with the film screen. The frame-within-the-frame display of the monitor and its blue conduction of energy make us mindful of technological mediation – a motif that soon becomes associated with supernatural forces and passageways. This entrancing blue static, our first important clue, seems to bear on the assault we do not quite witness. In time we will learn that this opening implies the murder of Teresa Banks (Pamela Gidley) – a double for Laura – at the hands of Laura's demon-inhabited father, Leland Palmer (Ray Wise). For now, this opening, with its portal-like screen and bleak atmosphere, indicates this version of *Twin Peaks* will need to be perceived and puzzled over in different ways.

Although it uncannily echoes the network series' pilot episode, the film's first half-hour continues to foil expectations as we follow the FBI inquiry into Teresa's disappearance. We are introduced to a new locale, the town of Deer Meadow, an inverse replica of Twin Peaks with a lifeless diner and police station. Sluggish in its narrative pace, the film dawdles in this setting and introduces characters who are bland substitutes for their Twin Peaks counterparts. Instead of the beaming-with-charisma-and-intellect FBI Special Agent Dale Cooper (Kyle MacLachlan), whose role has been abridged, we tag along with the depthless Agent Chester Desmond (Chris Isaak) and his forensic examiner companion as they less capably weigh the evidence that suggests a paranormal weave of factors.

Along with these deglamorizing shifts in setting and character, modifications surface at the level of narrative style. Geoff King, in his study of American independent cinema, engages Lynch's work in general as an example of alternative narrative strategies that openly flout the clear, linear, efficient, rational, and action-focused plotting of the Hollywood mainstream (101). Lynch's deviations assert his authorial presence (148) and draw attention to unsettling formal operations that ambiguously drift, in their expressive register, between character subjectivity and the overall texture of the film's world (132–134). We contend with resonances of form and feeling that make cause-and-effect relations elusive. For King, Lynch's independent approach, from *Eraserhead* onward, incorporates traditional forms only up to a point, injecting them with strangeness through slow pacing, deadpan acting, and uneventfulness (133). In line with these tendencies, the Deer Meadow segment renders the action banal while using low sonic drones, lap dissolves, and sinuous camera movements to alert us to mysterious forces that outstrip the detectives. Such atmospheric devices underscore details at the Fat Trout Trailer Park where Teresa resided: her blonde hair and blue eyes in a photograph; a green signet ring; a grime-covered vagabond; humming electrical wires; and a note, "Let's Rock," in fuchsia lipstick on Agent Desmond's windshield. These clues point to the Black Lodge, but it takes time, effort, and likely more than one viewing to infer this.

Absurdist comedy, not to be confused with cynicism, informs the film's self-conscious handling of clues and coded information. In a droll scene, FBI Regional Bureau Chief Gordon Cole (David Lynch) shares highly classified details with Desmond through a clownlike figure, Lil (Kimberly Ann Cole), whose encrypted pantomime reveals this is a "Blue Rose" case. The scene parodies the activity of interpretation itself. Although Desmond deciphers Lil's routine, this same symbolic language, used to safeguard FBI clearance levels, is futile in the face of the infinitely more profound, metaphysical mystery it implicates. For the viewer, the scene mocks the notion that the film itself is a code to be broken with neat finality. That said, this *blue* rose resonates with salient clues: it recalls the TV static from the opening and primes us to notice blue accents in the visual field that imply crossings between alternate worlds (e.g., the retro automobiles of Leland and Desmond, the eyes of both Teresa and Laura, the spotlight on Julee Cruise as she sings "Questions in a World of Blue," and the strobing light that enfolds Laura in the final scene). Blue, the color of flames at peak intensity, relates to the "fire" in the film's title, whose meaning I will explain shortly.

Lynch's humorously drab recasting of the procedural genre also sets the stage for Laura's arrival as the protagonist. As Nochimson has argued, the flatly portrayed FBI officials – hamstrung as they are by their incapacity to see beyond concrete parameters of time and space – open up the narrative possibility for Laura to become, in effect, the authority in her own life as she navigates a matrix of intersecting realms (177–191). Together with the sidelining of Agent Cooper, who had been a steady guide in the series, the FBI's inefficacy disrupts the mainstream genre convention whereby patriarchal authorities preside over the fates of victimized women and serve as the locus of audience identification. As the prequel "plunges us into the life of Laura Palmer, surprisingly we are liberated from the limitations of the would-be rescuers" (174). Nochimson writes that it is *Laura's* knowledge – her abiding "ownership of her own story, which no one else can tell" – that calls for a prequel in the first place (175).

Laura's Voyage

Independence from mainstream decorum allows *Fire Walk with Me* to lay bare the fact that the quaint veneer of Twin Peaks is everywhere predicated on Laura's brutal suffering. The narrative's focalization around her point of view, after the

Deer Meadow segment, is Lynch's starkest change from the ABC series in which Laura, already dead from the start, serves as the blonde, beautiful object of everyone else's fascination. The prequel transforms Laura from the one who haunts to the one who is haunted. It assigns a much more demanding role to Lee, an untried actress before being cast for the series, yet her performance is one of 1990s independent cinema's most poignant.

Laura's first appearance is scored to the strategically delayed main theme from the series. As she saunters to school with her best friend Donna Hayward (Moira Kelly), this familiar, lulling music is countered by intimations of dread. Dennis Lim observes how "the camera hovers along and behind the girls as they walk along tree-lined streets in an echo of the stalking perspectives of John Carpenter's *Halloween* [1978]," driving home the film's "disconcerting atmosphere of sunlit terror" (118). A sinister presence seems to lurk obscurely amid the rows of middle-class facades with manicured lawns. In its interrogation of the bourgeois domestic sphere, the film intertwines family melodrama (Nieland 79–94) with a female gothic variety of psychological horror. Much has been remarked about Lynch's evocations of 1950s Hollywood melodramas such as Mark Robson's *Peyton Place* (1957), but *Fire Walk with Me* also has strong affinities with contemporaneous, independent riffs on the genre such as Todd Haynes's *Safe* (1995) and Sofia Coppola's *The Virgin Suicides* (1999), with their lush yet stifling suburban environments that become horrific for their female protagonists.

Laura's story hinges on her discovery that her father is uncannily fused with Bob (Frank Silva), the feral rapist who has been visiting her bedroom at night since she was 12, and who has been tampering with her diary.[2] In-the-know viewers foresee this plot point, which the series had already offered, but the film still generates *atmospheric* suspense as it filters this revelation through Laura's subjectivity. Take the eerie scene in which she inspects the rosy interior of her seemingly unoccupied house. A quiet ambience – marked by a whooshing ceiling fan above the stairs, a key motif in *Twin Peaks* linked to Laura's abuse – leads to a convulsive reveal of Bob in her bedroom. This jump scare flings us into the middle of Bob's and Laura's superimposed screams: the image dissolves into an abstract close-up of a fleshy, blue-tinged throat, and then dissolves again into an exterior long shot of the house as Laura flees and takes refuge beneath a hedgerow – only to be jolted anew when her father, who ought to be at work, exits the front door and drives away in his blue retro convertible.

The overlapping imagery defines the Palmer household as a mouth ready to devour. Part of what makes the film a grueling watch is that it overtly spotlights domestic abuse. Leland's possession by Bob is only once, and briefly, treated as a cause of sympathy toward him. The ABC series tempers his crimes of incest and filicide with ironic humor and tragic compassion, but the prequel moves him closer to Jack Torrance (Jack Nicholson) in *The Shining* (1980) and Ed Avery (James Mason) in *Bigger Than Life* (1956). As a grotesque patriarch, he now exudes deranged qualities *in excess of* his demonic possession, a malicious and controlling demeanor from which neither Laura nor the viewer has relief. His presence interrupts the mundane rituals of family life in the form of menacing awkwardness. Portrayed from a low angle while insisting that Laura wash her hands before dinner ("Look, there is dirt way under this fingernail"), Leland is no less monstrous than Bob. The extent to which Bob inhabits Leland is unclear, but if he everywhere controls Leland's actions, he does so, it seems, by ratcheting up malign tendencies Leland already has.

Some have claimed Lynch relishes the cruelty Laura endures until her death, a charge of misogyny that the *Twin Peaks* series and other Lynch works have drawn in debates about their gender politics (Lafky). The film's depiction of Laura's anguish has, with time, received more sympathetic discussion (McGowan; Rennebohm and Howell). Ahead of the reappraisal curve, Nochimson argues that the film is keyed to Laura's "passage toward choice and freedom," her escape from Leland/Bob's abuse, as well as from ordinary reality itself and its "flawed social systems." Laura attains "new powers" of perception that allow her to pass through treacherous spaces where dreams and reality converge (183–189). With the vague assistance of otherworldly intercessors – such as an elderly woman and her grandson who give Laura a picture of a door to hang on her bedroom wall – Laura discovers how to navigate the very interdimensional pathway that stumps the FBI agents at Fat Trout Trailer Park.

As in a female gothic framework, the film aligns us with our investigative heroine as she grapples with supernatural impressions and enticements. In a dream sequence, the picture on her bedroom wall becomes a portal through which she enters the Black Lodge, where a man in a red suit (Michael J. Anderson) offers her a green signet ring (the same ring we saw on Teresa Banks's finger). Agent Cooper, whom Laura has never met, urges her to refuse. These rival emissaries address her while directly facing the camera, as we share her first-person perspective. Her negotiation of obscure signs, events, and personages thus overlays with our struggle to decode not just the film's plot but its increasingly abstract expressive system, which burdens us with the task of sorting out an associative tangle of clues, from objects and colors to textures and sounds.

Laura awakes to find the ring in her hand. And yet, whether this transaction with the man in red dooms or liberates her is uncertain, even by the finale, in which she weeps (tears of joy?) in the Black Lodge, overseen by a female angel. For Nochimson, the ring grants Laura future transit between worlds and *opens an escape route* (183–197). The film thus invites us to see her fate as an evasion of being preyed upon, of being possessed – a *victory* at ruinous cost only to a tortured existence that she transcends (190–191). She ultimately escapes Leland and Bob, who feed on what Black Lodge dwellers call "garmonbozia," the pain and sorrow of humanity. But doesn't she also elude the spectator? Despite our closeness to her point of view, Laura remains in large measure unknowable beneath the clichéd identities that others project onto her (McGowan 130–136). This elusiveness wards off the spectator who – desiring what character-driven narrative usually offers – seeks a gratifying experience of psychological identification. Such a spectator, it must be said, feeds on "garmonbozia" too.

Lynch conducts Laura's journey in a formally daring manner that tests the literacy even of viewers primed for independent cinema's idiosyncrasies. The film's surrealism, some have argued, is better understood in the context of the avant-garde. Identifying parallels with Maya Deren's experimental dream film *Meshes of the Afternoon* (1943), Nicholas Rombes observes that Laura – like Deren herself in both *Meshes* and her later film *At Land* (1944) – undergoes a bodily schism and duplication as she "crosses and exists in multiple spaces simultaneously, and gazes upon herself as she does so" (72).

The Primacy of Atmosphere

The complexity of *Fire Walk with Me* comes down to questions of atmosphere. Lynch's style requires leeway to revel in atmospheric experimentation that is too obscure, autonomous, and slow-moving for Hollywoodian narrative. A film's atmosphere is produced and controlled through stylistic operations that palpably spatialize feeling. If popular cinema tends to reduce atmosphere to a mere backdrop, many devices in Lynch's work (aural murmurs, music, color, lighting, camerawork, superimpositions, and mise-en-scène) raise it to a primary role. Critics often use "atmosphere" as a synonym for "tone" and "mood," yet it should be carefully defined in a way that includes an embodied viewer's immersion in a *world*. According to its etymology, atmosphere consists of a "vaporous globe," diffuse in space and emanative. In terms well suited to Lynch's ambient style, Robert Spadoni theorizes film atmosphere as a kind of aesthetic weather system that reaches beyond the setting and radiates outward to envelop us (59). Modulating emotions and shaping attention, it "forms a seam of contact," as Spadoni puts it, "between the film's world and its viewers" (58).

The atmospherics of *Fire Walk with Me* might seem gratuitous when in fact they steer the drama, build suspense, and not only confound but also *differently attune* our perception, making analysis possible amid narrative opacity. The phrase "fire walk with me," which comes from a shamanic poem in the ABC series and evokes fire as primal technology, is a passkey that opens gateways between the Black Lodge and Twin Peaks. In the film's vocabulary of motifs, "fire" assumes the form not just of flames but electrical power and mediation, from the blue TV static to the utility wires that emit an undulant zap. A circuit of "fire" connects Laura's voyage to the Deer Meadow segment and mingles with thunder, wind, and flowing rivers. Largely through Lynch's experiments with layered sound (Chion 142), we feel exposed to cryptic forces at play in the diegesis. Across multiple set pieces, a pyrotechnics of atmosphere disturbs the narrative and teases us with sensory hints. For instance, when the missing Agent Jeffries (David Bowie) resurfaces at the blue-carpeted FBI headquarters, a flurry of superimpositions erupts on screen and reveals, via blue static and a video surveillance system, a liminal room above a convenience store: a portal to the Black Lodge. These moments make the film intuitively graspable yet deepen its mysteries, ignoring the orthodox rhetoric of closure (King 61).

Lineages, Missing Pieces, and Returns

While the ABC series has inspired endless imitations, the legacy of *Fire Walk with Me* is less prevalent. Granted, several North American independent directors bear affinities to Lynch's work in general: Charlie Kaufman, David Cronenberg, Richard Kelly, Ana Lily Amirpour, Denis Villeneuve, Atom Egoyan, and David Robert Mitchell, to name a few. Further afield, Jonathan Glazer (UK), Philippe Grandrieux (France), Gaspar Noé (France), and Joachim Trier (Norway) each display Lynchian traits crucial to their independent projects. *Fire Walk with Me* has been championed by John Waters (US), Bong Joon Ho (South Korea), Céline Sciamma (France), and Bertrand Bonello (France) – with Bonello directly taking cues from its soundscape, but the film is too singular to be repeated outright.

Fire Walk with Me has assumed a vibrant afterlife within Lynch's evolving corpus. The DVD release of *Twin Peaks: The Missing Pieces* (2014), a Lynch-edited compilation of deleted material from *Fire Walk with Me*, reawakened interest in the film and dropped new clues. With *Twin Peaks: The Return* (2017), a third season he directed in toto at the age of 70 (now for Showtime instead of ABC), Lynch retooled *Twin Peaks* yet again for the digital streaming era. *The Return* reignites the fiery, mediational play of energy and, in Part Eight, extends it to include nuclear power: the US military's atmospheric testing of the atom bomb in 1945 figures as the source from which Bob and the world of *Twin Peaks* derive. Laura's tragedy becomes tied (or rather, wired) to a catastrophic history of war, resource capitalism, and American triumphalist values. The ABC series, for all its ironies, almost enshrines its conservative, eternally 1950s milieu, but *Fire Walk with Me* and *The Return* sneeringly deflate the American Dream and its anachronisms, locating horror, exploitation, and banality at its roots. Lynch's surreal atmospheric style, far from being a private affectation, is a vehicle of social commentary.

Since the confrontational slashing of the eyeball at the start of Luis Buñuel and Salvador Dalí's *Un chien andalou* (1929), surrealist cinema has sought to transform its spectators' habits of making sense. *Fire Walk with Me* channels this aim through the experiential dimensions that are part of the film's independent status. We are lured into an atmospheric way of connecting motifs and resonances, yet we must acquire this perceptual skill as we go, without having our intuitions confirmed. Because the film's world is infinitely steeped in mystery, this process may well involve independent cinema's "economy of multiple viewing" (King 100). Neither story resolution nor characterological depth is on offer, nor a pretentious exercise in confusion, but, rather, a hypnotic call of the weird inviting us to embrace cinema as a medium primarily of affective sensations.

Notes

1 Directors hired for 1990–1991 *Twin Peaks* episodes could not introduce blue mise-en-scène unless Lynch approved (Dukes 280). Blue defines zones of liminality between worlds, much as it does in *Mulholland Drive*.

2   In both criticism and fan discussions, it has become customary to refer to this character as "BOB" (in all caps), an acronym that evokes "Beware of Bob" and accords with Laura's diary. But *Fire Walk with Me*'s end credits list him as "Bob," as do the credits for both the ABC show and *Twin Peaks: The Return*. More pivotal than the issue of capitalization is the name's palindromic aspect as it relates to language games and mirror motifs associated with the Black Lodge.

Works Cited

Chion, Michel. *David Lynch*. Translated by Robert Julian, 2nd ed., BFI, 2006.
Dukes, Brad, editor. *Reflections: An Oral History of Twin Peaks*. Short/Tall Press, 2014.
Kael, Pauline. "*Blue Velvet*: Out There and In Here." 1986. *For Keeps*, Plume, 1996, pp. 1109–1115.
King, Geoff. *American Independent Cinema*. I.B. Tauris, 2005.
Lafky, Sue. "Gender, Power, and Culture in the Televisual World of *Twin Peaks*: A Feminist Critique." *Journal of Film and Video*, vol. 51, no. 3/4, 1999/2000, pp. 5–19.
Lim, Dennis. *David Lynch: The Man from Another Place*. New Harvest, 2015.
McGowan, Todd. *The Impossible David Lynch*. Columbia University Press, 2009.
Nieland, Justus. *David Lynch*. University of Illinois Press, 2012.
Nochimson, Martha P. *The Passion of David Lynch: Wild at Heart in Hollywood*. University of Texas Press, 1997.
Norelli, Clare Nina. *Soundtrack from Twin Peaks*. Bloomsbury, 2017.
Rennebohm, Kate, and Simon Howell. "Fire Walk with Me (ft. Adam Nayman)." *The Lodgers: A Twin Peaks Podcast*, 31 Jan. 2019, https://twinpeakspodcast.fireside.fm/episode-fourteen-fire-walk-with-me.
Rombes, Nicholas. "Blue Velvet Underground: David Lynch's Post-Punk Poetics." *The Cinema of David Lynch: American Dreams, Nightmare Visions*, edited by Erica Sheen and Annette Davidson. Wallflower, 2004, pp. 61–75.
Spadoni, Robert. "What Is Film Atmosphere?" *Quarterly Review of Film and Video*, vol. 37, no. 1, 2020, pp. 48–75.

34

PULP FICTION (1994)

Scott L. Baugh

Retrospection

When Vincent arrives for his not-a-date "date" with Mia, an old-fashion handwritten note, read in voiceover by her, greets him. Inside the Beverly Hills mansion, like a multimedia museum, High-Modern and eclectic artwork intermingle with 1969 pop music by Dusty Springfield playing on vinyl, a reel-to-reel that will feature 1992 alt-rock Urge Overkill (covering 1967 Neil Diamond), and stacks of CDs. Mia operates a surveillance camera, twice revealing Vincent in ceiling-high grainy black-and-white footage, and directs him to an intercom. An extreme close-up emphasizes the microphone Mia uses as much as her speaking lips. Like fragmented clues here, *Pulp Fiction*'s reflections on media and its discursive-powerful dynamics – broadly and the film's own – both look backward and situate the film in its present media moment.

To look back, retrospection equally engages contemplation of select past events as well as reconciliation and affirmation of some present moment. Across instances of this idea, this chapter itself serves as a brief retrospective on the significance of *Pulp Fiction* to the contemporary institution of US independent-commercial cinema at the inauguration of Indiewood. Students of the film can benefit from appreciating its impact at the time of its release in the mid-1990s and recognize now its canonical placement in cinema, the second feature film written and directed by Quentin Tarantino. The film itself, too, enacts retrospection in its address to viewers and its treatment of stories and themes, embodying and relaying its own version of an indie film history that looks to the past to establish and comment upon its vaguely near-present-1994 story and milieu.

A cue to retrospective readings lies in *Pulp Fiction*'s metafictional qualities – its story about stories and storytelling; its notion of authorship about authorship; and

DOI: 10.4324/9781003246930-35

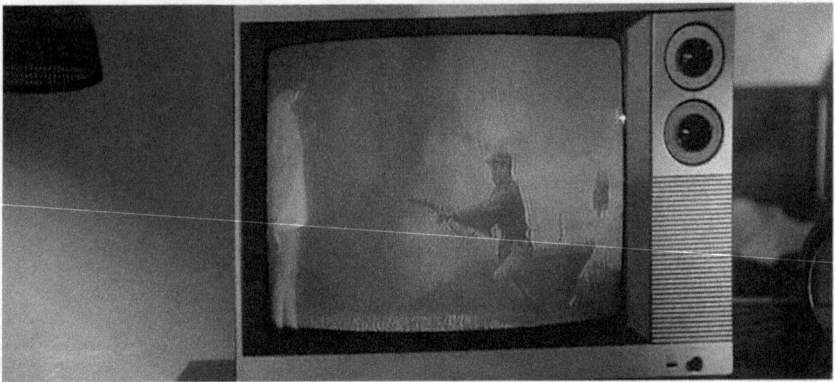

FIGURE 34.1 Form playfully exemplifies retrospective metafiction, enacts story-in-story mise en abyme, mocks cinematic techniques, and casts (a reflection of) Fabienne now starring in genre-fusing multimedia.

its filmmaking model about filmmaking models with comparative exploitations of exploitation.

About Story

The film's title references the literary genre, "pulp fiction," noted for exploiting sensationalism and following generic formulas for popularity and sales, advancing from the 1880s through literate but common rather than elite readers with opportunity for leisure reading, and being frugally produced, affordable for mass markets. The film's opening inserts definitions for "pulp": "/pəlp/ *n*. (1) A soft, moist, shapeless mass of matter. (2) A magazine or book containing lurid subject matter and being characteristically printed on rough, unfinished paper." In the context of this chapter, the "shapeless mass" may refer to *Pulp Fiction*'s shape-shifting narrative, authorship, and production scheme as much as to the 1990s audiences and markets indie-cinema businesses are trying to formulate; "lurid" aspects reference exploiting commercial-entertainment boundaries; and innovative approaches can be found in the seemingly "rough, unfinished" quality of the finished and marketed product. From the epigraph forward, metafictional aspects of *Pulp Fiction* multiply.

The subtitle on *Pulp Fiction*'s screenplay cover page, also, usefully references, triples, and then reunifies itself: "three stories… about one story" (Tarantino). But what is this "one story" really about?

Pulp Fiction marks the beginning of a sea-change moment in contemporary US independent-commercial cinema, signaling the mid-1990s "imminent arrival" of Indiewood (Tzioumakis 263). Pinning down profound meanings to symbols and themes, analyzing characters, their dialogue, and actions, or reading for ideologies and issues in this film can be as entertaining as they are critically engaging. Highlighting metafictional qualities resolves some of the riddles.[1] *Pulp Fiction* proves, through this reading, to be mostly *about* itself as a film and specifically, this chapter offers, about being an independent American film in the 1990s, pasting together mainstream, art, and exploitation cinemas and entertainment cultures. Perhaps its "one story" is about being indie.

Three titled stories aggregate in fascinating ways to look at a fictionalized (nay, meta-fictionalized), vaguely 1990s Southern California crime environment. "Vincent Vega and Marsellus Wallace's Wife" relates John Travolta's henchman Vincent buying heroin from Lance (Eric Stoltz) and entertaining Uma Thurman's Mia that evening at the request of his LA crime-leader boss and her husband Marsellus Wallace (Ving Rhames) while he is out of town – screwball rom-com injected with illicit drugs meets crime-story violence. "The Gold Watch" invokes the boxer-film genre, as Bruce Willis's Butch, an aging "palooka," decides not to throw a fight (for Mr. Wallace), must retrieve an enigmatic but prized wristwatch, gets entangled in a pawnshop/dungeon misadventure circumscribing the *chanbara*-samurai actioner but ultimately rides off into the proverbial sunset (the Western but on a chopper ala biker film) perhaps happily ever after with his love interest Fabienne (Maria de Medeiros). "The Bonnie Situation" takes Vincent and fellow hitman, Samuel L. Jackson's Jules Winnfield, through a series of *noir*-mystery and gangster adventures, including the retrieval and delivery of Mr. Wallace's enigmatic but prized suitcase, a "hit" on his "business partners," the clean up afterward at Jimmie's (Tarantino) with "The Wolf"/Winston Wolf (Harvey Keitel), Jules's contemplation to quit "the life" of crime, and a partly failed diner heist by Yolanda/Honey Bunny (Amanda Plummer) and Pumpkin/Ringo (Tim Roth).

Intertitles announce each of the three stories, but these markers cannot be taken literally or discretely, as the plot intertwines episodes across shifts in diegetic time. For example, two story moments (the hit around retrieval of the suitcase and the diner heist) replay in revised, retrospective forms, interconnecting the short stories. The first thing the plot reveals in the named "Vincent" story focuses instead on Butch and some suggestion of principles ("Gold Watch" storyline) and then delivery of the suitcase ("Bonnie" storyline); not until the drug-deal scene do viewers begin receiving the mainline of the "Vincent" story. The film begins *in medias res* (here and throughout, literally "in the middle" of conversations) at the diner after the hit – later in the story but earlier in the plot. Viewers may be puzzled by how pieces fit together as well as where several pieces begin and end – and furthermore, what picture they reveal when assembled.

While not world-shattering (nor storyworld-shattering) for viewers, as slippages in time may even be somewhat expected in novels, literary short-story cycles, and episodic television, in *Pulp Fiction* they nevertheless disrupt mainstream viewing expectations and classical style. That is, as the "classical paradigm" primarily regulates the plot/*syuzhet* toward an efficient delivery of the story/*fabula*, it advantages linear causality, particularly through character motivation, stresses seamlessness in the storytelling, and prohibits stylistic "excesses" (Bordwell, *Narration* 50–51). And in 1994, there was a buzz of excitement about the originality of *Pulp Fiction*. It leads a wave of contemporary "puzzle films" whereby complex storytelling invites viewers to sort its riddled pieces and play along to help arrange its stories (Buckland 1–4). While innovations rely upon traditional storytelling, this 1990s trend particularly engages "off-Hollywood" cinemas and reconstructs familiar devices for audiences "drenched in modern media" (Bordwell, *The Way* 72–82). *Pulp Fiction*'s critical attention, popularity, and blockbuster-level profitability prove the "tricky storytelling" concept, particularly through a "fresh take" on genres and exploitation (72–74).

"Example?," as Jules demands. In the hit on Brett and Flock of Seagulls, the impact of the gunfire occurs off screen. Slight red tinting hints at the violence, distracts from the graphic gangster content, and redirects to a transitional point in the narrative – only to be returned to later in replayed retrospection. After their elevator exit, a moving camera follows their left-right-right then proceed-pause-and-return circumvention through the apartment building. Their dialogue seems equally guided by distraction and misdirection. The hitmen are not lost but certainly forsake a conventional or efficient route, actions that mirror the film's tricky narrative. Further, the conversation detours to how "pilots" operate within, sarcastically, this "invention called television," and Jules initiates the hit with "let's get into character," shifting tone and bridging metafictional entertainment-media references.

Jules's delivery of the Ezekiel passage is fully rehearsed, a contract-killer performance; it is also less Biblical allusion than media retrospection. The Ezekiel passage, delivered, replayed in revision, and even explicated for reinterpretation by Jules, across several instances, cites the martial-arts film *The Bodyguard* (1976) – and then retrospectively enriches the exploitative qualities. Hitchcock gets cited too – Marsellus halting Butch at the stoplight echoes *Psycho* (1960), while Butch changing in the cab after the fight echoes *Strangers on a Train* (1951). *Pulp Fiction* is riddled with various entertainment-media citations, complicating the puzzle's realization.

A decision to situate the diner heist as more a part of the "Bonnie" story than as a separate prologue, which many viewers do because it bookends the film and envelopes the minor Honey Bunny-Pumpkin portion of the narrative, is interpretive: to be sure, the puzzle-plot engages the viewer subversively through how the story is being told as much as or more than what information is conveyed.

Among other things, the metanarrative story moments highlight the major-minor differences across a network of characters and storylines and reveal how major-minor power dynamics operate for this indie film, fusing past and present mainstream, independent, and exploitation entertainment media. As Tzioumakis argues, a "power struggle" involves "the usage of 'independence' and in effect justifies an approach" to conceptualizing early-1990s Indiewood not just as an industrial space for filmmaking but also as a "discourse" in itself (12, 224–225). While "independence" has traditionally implied increased autonomy (creatively if not also financially), the issue remains the degree of that autonomy discursively balanced with Indiewood's inherent dependence. And while I argue that this fundamental issue operates across the history of commercial- and non-commercial-independent cinemas, in *Pulp Fiction*, story-level moments metafictionally highlight the balancing act for 1990s indie cinema.

Consider when Mia and Vincent arrive at Jackrabbit Slim's, an excessive parody of the 1950s-era diner, Tarantino's screenplay invites value judgment, "[e]ither the best or the worst, depending on your point of view" (38A). An anticipatory shot reveals Vincent's classic Chevy Malibu convertible pulling into the bustling parking lot – bumper and California plates to the grill to the hood to the windshield, each rectangular shape resonating with *Pulp Fiction*'s own widescreen 2.39:1 frame itself. As the car pulls to a stop, a 24-second two-shot holds on Mia and Vincent's conversation about this restaurant, a miniature retrospection on classic mid-century entertainment reformulating 1990s indie entertainment, a "wax museum with a [cinematic] pulse."

Lacking a reverse-shot or true establishing shot, the restaurant front and neon signage appear mirror-reversed as a reflection on the windshield. "What the fuck is this place?," provides part of Vincent's value judgment, to which Mia answers: "Jack-rabbit-Slim's." Mia enunciates each word instructionally and, with a lit cigarette between her fingertips, indicates the sign/reflection in the car windshield. Mia invites Vincent to time travel through the popular cultures with her, calling him an "Elvis man" and "daddy-o," to which he warms with "kitty cat." Mia seals the deal by cajoling him, "don't be a—," and the fill-in-the-blank leaves the viewer to answer "—square." Mia, however, traces with fingertips not a "square" but a rectangle that extradiegetically appears on screen in white perforated lines. This shape emblematizes the film's own industrial-standard form, mise en abyme with the windshield-as-frame and film frame, each in widescreen aspect ratio.

From Mia's cue, *Pulp Fiction*'s metafiction redraws storytelling devices across entertainment and cultural traditions, depicting Indiewood's balancing institutional reliance with innovation. The metafictional examples multiply almost beyond count once inside Slim's – remediated Marilyn Monroe, Mamie Van Doren, James Dean, Ricky Nelson, and even Speed Racer, all hosted by Ed Sullivan, curated by Vincent, and updated for and as 1990s Indiewood. Worth noting, 1990s viewers see Uma Thurman performing Mia, who was a failed TV actor, being served by Steve Buscemi (Mr. Pink in *Reservoir Dogs* [1992]) performing a waiter, who is performing a simulacrum of Buddy Holly, who is not "much of a waiter" after all. The tone verges on artful absurdity in this game of "trivial pursuit." The meta-formality perforates commercial-cinematic tradition and enacts the metafictional aspects of the story to follow, melting mid-century entertainment culture with the vague present of the storyworld. Older media continue multiplying into newer media for formative audiences and markets for Indiewood.

About Auteur

The iconicity of Tarantino as "video-store clerk-turned-artist" precedes himself, and his career is riddled with controversy almost as much as it is celebrated.[2]

Metafictional aspects of *Pulp Fiction* promote Tarantino's auteur status as much as his auteur status helps promote the film and a "cool" 1990s generation on the rise.

Tarantino helps formulate what has been called a "cinema of cool" (Perren 95–100; Polan 65). Alongside Kevin Smith and Robert Rodriguez, also working with indie-major Miramax in this formative early-1990s period, Tarantino's auteurism exemplifies several definitive aspects of "cool." Most importantly, Tarantino represents a video-store generation. According to his auteur lore, Tarantino trained for filmmaking through repeated viewings, play-pause-replay inquisitions, of an eclectic body of films themselves, available in unprecedented ways for the VHS-era generation of viewers. As a result, his cinema of cool reflects resourcefulness particularly in terms of economics (character- and dialogue-driven narratives over costly effects-driven spectacles, notably early in his career) and recycling previous films and entertainment media (most visible in his fusion of genres and repurposing pop-culture iconography). Comparably, cool aesthetics and narration subtly revise Hollywood's classicism. Cool style typically fulfills but reinvents classical-paradigm demands. It pushes the boundaries toward stylistic excess in one direction for art and another direction for vulgarity in its unique vernacular. The cinema of cool often finds balance across three fields – mainstream, art, and exploitation – which results in exploiting markets traditionally siloed from one another. By the diner heist *denouement*, "cool" invokes *Happy Days*-to-*American Graffiti* (1974–1984; 1973) – film-to-television-back-to-film references: New Hollywood, broadcast television, Indiewood retrospection – as a means to diffuse the standoff.

About Production

"Once upon a time" (in… Hollywood), Umberto Eco narrates, "there were the mass media, and they were wicked (of course), and there was a guilty party. Then there were the virtuous voices that accused the criminals. And Art (ah, what luck!) offered alternatives, for those who were not prisoners of the mass media" (150). The conclusion to Eco's fable is both that "it's all over" and also that we have new pathways: independent-commercial cinema must "start again from the beginning," retrospectively reaffirming "what's going on" (150). As chronicled by Yannis Tzioumakis, the mass media "age of conglomerates" (1966–present) takes a revolutionary turn by the 1990s toward concentrations in entertainment-and-leisure fields (175–200, 203–204). And Hollywood begets Indiewood.

Miramax uniquely reflects the creation of Indiewood (King, *Indiewood* 93). Alisa Perren, foremost authority on Miramax, ascribes to Disney's 1993 purchase of Miramax nothing short of "the beginning of a transformation of the economics and culture of the entertainment world," and a "new era" in Hollywood (Perren 58–70, 73). And Miramax, according to its executive statements, stands as "the house Quentin Tarantino built" (Holson). With its blockbuster-level commercial success as one of the first independent films to make over $100M dollars domestically, *Pulp Fiction* initiates Miramax's ascension as a definitive indie-major company during this age of entertainment conglomerates (1994–2004).

Miramax forms in 1979 primarily as an independent distributor. Its house style and business philosophy engage controversial, risqué and risky, material in both film subjects and their marketing campaigns (King, *American* 32). With Miramax as primary distributor, Tarantino's debut feature, *Reservoir Dogs*, modestly turns a reported $1.2M budget into $2.8M domestic gross, but finances suffer overall from ineffective promotion and slow traction with audiences. Bad for Miramax, co-producer LIVE Entertainment holds rights to the home video market, which Miramax had been unable to purchase and so saw little direct profit from the cult following the film gains. Worse for Miramax, there is competition for Tarantino's next project, which would become *Pulp Fiction*. Through co-producers at Jersey Films, Tarantino secures a development deal in 1991 for a reported $900,000 with TriStar-Columbia.

The dialogue in between Tarantino's first two films highlights three main initiatives for Miramax entering the 1990s: retain their talent, promote material with crossover potential, and acquire projects earlier or bring them in-house in order to manage as many rights as affordable. The answer will be financial leverage.[3] The TriStar deal with Tarantino falls through by 1993. ("That's one way to say it," as Vincent says.) Another way is that the deal falls through because TriStar chief Mike Medavoy and an executive committee found the in-development screenplay, delivered late and overly long, filled with material too controversial for their strategic vision and definition of audience, namely the tone-shifting violence and the heroin set piece, and so they put it in "turnaround" (Clarkson 201). And even another is that Miramax wooed Tarantino through an aggressive acquisition deal, matching the larger studio's $900,000, promising creative autonomy, and configuring those controversial elements within their strategic vision (King, *American* 47). Across these versions of the dealings, Tarantino never compromises creative ideas under development for *Pulp Fiction*.

In relation to traditional independent cinema, the 1990s arrival of "indies" entails, optimistically: greater financial security, the diversified corporation buffering risks around the single project; relative increases in financing, often medium-size budgets in between the lower-budget constraints of traditional independent cinema and the big-budget demands of blockbusters; increased promotion and distribution for independently funded and co-financed production; provisions for select star casting; increased demand for product; and allowance for alternative-to-mainstream material to gain wider audiences. On the downside, the indie gets held to new standards of commercial success across platforms, the acquisitions market sees inflation, and the gulf between "haves" and "have-nots" widens (Schatz 20–22; King, *American* 32–34; Perren 73, 102).

Very few film companies post-1980s thrive or even survive economically without financial support from and ties to entertainment conglomerates, infusing the formative institution of independent-commercial cinema with varying degrees of inter-dependence and co-dependence across these entities, reshaping the very discourse of independence (Tzioumakis 203–204, 224–229; Perren 17–18). Again, Eco offers our retrospection some direction, that as "expectation horizons" shift, "value judgments" demand "different parameters" (147). For better or for worse, this independent-institutional process initiates in many respects with *Pulp Fiction* – Tarantino and producer Lawrence Bender's shingle A Band Apart (its name honoring Godard's French New Wave film, *Bande à part* [1964]) co-producing with Jersey Films at indie-major Miramax.[4]

Alongside New Line, Miramax exemplifies what Justin Wyatt identifies as the "major independent," a "curious hybrid" production/distribution company that maintains brand identity and creative autonomy after being taken over by a major corporation – Disney purchasing Miramax in 1993, only months before *Pulp Fiction*'s release, and Turner purchasing New Line in 1994 (74–75). One organizational scheme for New Line generally segments its character- and story-driven projects in its specialty division Fine Line, while keeping mainstream-ready projects for the New Line brand (King, *American* 32–33). *Pulp Fiction* at Miramax touches all these audience bases at once: its Palme d'Or win at Cannes reflects a "prestige" appeal, fully appreciated by art-house "elite" audiences (Wyatt 81). Its edgy treatments of violence and illicit drug use advance the boundaries of exploitation; its revision of Hollywood genres (boxer film, romantic comedy, gangster) as well as its invocation of exploitative genres (martial arts, biker film, teenpic) bridge niche and mainstream viewers. Its allusions to entertainment culture and technology marry cinephiles, movie-nerds, and 1990s media-drenched consumers. Critical appreciation – at Cannes as well as a Best Screenplay Oscar and seven other Academy Award nominations including Best Picture and Best Director – and commercial success – especially reaching the blockbuster benchmark with a reported $108M domestic box office (and another $50M in VHS sales alone) on its reported $8M budget – justified *Pulp Fiction*'s approach for Miramax. Disney money afforded wide release and promotion. Miramax lost some gambles, but with *Pulp Fiction* arrives a new era for the indie.

About Entertainment

If *Pulp Fiction*'s "one story" is about being indie, then the moral of that story is: entertainment pays. (Another way is to say *Pulp Fiction* is about "entertaining" itself, pun intended, recognizing Tarantino's indulgences.) Recall the 69-second heroin set piece: a deal-breaker for TriStar becomes selling feature for Miramax. Ultra-stylized imagery (hand-crank effect, expressionistic angles, chiaroscuro shadow-play, upcycled process shot) metafictionally translates exploitative subjects to reconceive mainstream audiences for Indiewood.

The oldest part of *Pulp Fiction*'s story revolves around young Butch receiving his gold watch – technically, the film's only flashback. Viewed from center, young Butch sits legs-crossed on the floor near a console television. From opposite, Captain Koons approaches "little man" Butch. A stageline cuts the room lengthwise, but this is never fulfilled with an establishing shot. The reconditioned shot-countershot convention paradoxically both aligns and detaches perspective. Historical references throughout this one-sided conversation – to wars, to wristwatch technology – seem like disconnections too. Delivered in Christopher Walken's intense, deliberately paced performance, held by several long takes, Koons loosely reincarnates Walken's Nicky from *The Deer Hunter* (1978).

The "one story" in this sequence initially may seem like throw-away images and get overlooked. From fade-in, three images remediate material from the cartoon young Butch is watching on the console television, *Clutch Cargo* (1959–1960). First, the aesthetic of this cartoon was unique and recognized for its inventive yet minimalist animation methods. The technique utilizes Syncro-Vox, an optical system that superimposes live-action human mouths talking over limited animation. Further, these three shots, divorced from Butch's perspective, successively imitate the pan-and-scan technique that VHS-era distributors use to reformat widescreen imagery for home television's 4:3 aspect ratio.

The morning after the fight, Butch awakens, startled by "explosions and war" – which look backward to Koons, prophesize escapades to come, and re-situate in the present motel room. A tabletop television plays a biker-war film, *The Losers* (1970), directed by noted exploitation filmmaker Jack Starrett. A series of shots demonstrate the act of transposing the film-within-a-film on a TV screen – this time a 1.85:1 widescreen view collapses through pan-and-scan for the video-television release's 4:3 aspect ratio, a selection retrofitted into *Pulp Fiction*'s 2.39:1 frame. If that's not enough, Fabienne's reflection appears across the TV screen, again, mimicking a process shot but ludicrously re-setting her in a pajama top in the middle of the bikers' battle. *Pulp Fiction* artfully replays exploitation for a 1990s new-era mainstream.

Through multimedia museums, screen reflections, windshield tropes, cinematic effects dismantled and reconstructed, one metafictional example after another, the entertainment seems to serve itself, suspending some critical assessment in its place. *Pulp Fiction*'s "one story" coalesces metafictional elements for formative 1990s audiences and highlights its own significance to the emergence of Indiewood, retrospectively, in and of itself.

Notes

1 Roche focuses on cinematic metafiction across Tarantino's films.
2 Several controversies surround Tarantino's career. Nama smartly clarifies issues around race, representations, and language in Tarantino's films. Diapolo discusses Tarantino's recent associations with #MeToo and related issues. Roche surveys "identity politics" throughout Tarantino's career. This chapter cannot resolve these controversial aspects of Tarantino's career or films, which are largely outside its scope, and yet it hopes to inform thoughtful discussion that these timely and crucial issues demand.
3 For fuller discussion, see Perren (90).
4 For fuller discussions, see King (*American* 26) and Wyatt (75, 79–81).

Works Cited

Bordwell, David. *Narration in the Fiction Film*. University of Wisconsin Press, 1985.

———. *The Way Hollywood Tells It: Story and Style in Modern Movies*. University of California Press, 2006.

Buckland, Warren, editor. *Hollywood Puzzle Films*. Routledge, 2014.

Clarkson, Wensley. *Quentin Tarantino: Shooting from the Hip*. Piatkus, 1995.

Diapolo, Marc. "#MeToo and the Filmmaker as Monster." *Next Generation Adaptation: Spectatorship and Process*, edited by Allen H. Redmon. University of Mississippi Press, 2021, pp. 185–208.

Eco, Umberto. "The Multiplication of the Media." 1973. *Travels in Hyperreality*. Translated by William Weaver, Harcourt, 1986.

Holson, Laura M. "New Tarantino Film to Be Released in 2 Parts." *New York Times*, 16 July 2003, p. E1, https://www.nytimes.com/2003/07/16/movies/new-tarantino-film-to-be-released-in-2-parts.html?.

King, Geoff. *American Independent Cinema*. Indiana University Press, 2005.

———. *Indiewood, USA: Where Hollywood Meets Independent Cinema*. I.B. Tauris, 2009.

Nama, Adilifu. *Race on the QT*. University of Texas Press, 2015.

Perren, Alisa. *Indie, Inc.: Miramax and the Transformation of Hollywood in the 1990s*. University of Texas Press, 2012.

Polan, Dana. *Pulp Fiction*. BFI, 2000.

Roche, David. *Quentin Tarantino: Poetics and Politics of Cinematic Metafiction*. University of Mississippi, 2018.

Schatz, Thomas. "New Hollywood, New Millennium." *Film Theory and Contemporary Hollywood Movies*. Routledge, 2009, pp. 19–46.

Tarantino, Quentin. *Pulp Fiction: A Screenplay*. Hyperion, 1994.

Tzioumakis, Yannis. *American Independent Cinema: An Introduction*. 2nd ed., Edinburgh University Press, 2017.

Wyatt, Justin. "The Formation of the 'Major Independent': Miramax, New Line and the New Hollywood." *Contemporary Hollywood Cinema*, edited by Steve Neale and Murray Smith. Routledge, 1998, pp. 74–90.

35

EVE'S BAYOU (1997)

Kristi McKim

An exemplar of independent film in its precise rendering of first-time writer-director Kasi Lemmons's pioneering vision, *Eve's Bayou* opened worlds for stories and characters beyond mainstream white, male-centered films. Despite success as an actress in major Hollywood features (such as *The Silence of the Lambs* (1991) and *Candyman* (1992)), Lemmons experienced professional disappointment: "I couldn't empty my soul because the parts I was playing would not allow that sort of artistic relief: Black Girl Best Friend, Black Girl Next Door, Black Girl Cop. I was frustrated and I had this story inside me" (Muhammad).

Lemmons took a season off from auditioning to write "an experiment in creating a form...a hybrid of a novel and a screenplay," featuring voices truer to her experience (Nocenti). This experiment would become *Eve's Bayou:* the highest grossing independent film of 1997, the Independent Spirit Awards Best First Feature, the National Board of Review's Outstanding Directorial Debut, and an addition to the Library of Congress National Film Registry in 2018.

Lemmons's page-to-screen process took over four years, a period during which independent films made by Black artists about Black communities were experiencing greater theatrical success. In 1991, Julie Dash wrote, produced, and directed *Daughters of the Dust*, a poetic matriarchal history of generational trauma and healing, which was the first feature by a Black female director to receive a theatrical release in the United States. Also in 1991, John Singleton's *Boyz 'n the Hood* – a compassionate rendering of human yearning eclipsed by street crime – enjoyed critical and commercial success (which earned $57.5 million on a $6.5 million budget); Singleton became the youngest person and first Black filmmaker whose film was nominated for Best Picture at the Academy Awards. Cheryl Dunye's mockumentary *The Watermelon Woman* (1996) – featuring Dunye as a Black lesbian filmmaker, searching film archives for

FIGURE 35.1 Framed together in a sibling portrait, Eve, Cisely, and Poe Batiste share a secret champagne toast at their family's house party.

traces of a (fictionalized) marginalized Black actress – made history as the first American feature directed by an out Black lesbian. More accessible to mainstream audiences than the (comparatively) experimental *Daughters of the Dust* or self-reflexive *Watermelon Woman* and more feminist than *Boyz 'n the Hood*, Lemmons's *Eve's Bayou* situates Black female interiority as the locus of power and feeling. In framing a newly-centered film subject (Black women's experience) within an accessible genre (melodrama) via an inventive form, *Eve's Bayou* makes history.

Production and Power

Eve's Bayou's historical success with audiences and critics – and its legacy, which has only grown since its release – results from Lemmons's uncompromised vision and tenacity. Having received positive feedback from early readers of her screenplay, Lemmons then earned the support of producer Caldecot Chubb and decided – awaking with inspired clarity on her birthday – that she should also direct the film. With Chubb's investment, Lemmons directed a short film based on her script, *Dr. Hugo* (1996), starring Vondie Curtis-Hall (Lemmons's husband) as the titular character. *Dr. Hugo* caught the attention of Samuel L. Jackson, keen to play the complex lead in the feature. With Jackson and Chubb on board, and with the ultimate greenlight happening in her ninth month of pregnancy, Lemmons brought together a remarkable crew and cast. Lemmons describes the unlikeness of this outcome, as she recalls preparing to pitch the film in a meeting that ultimately proved successful: "[Friends] told me I was out of my mind. You're not only a woman, you're a black woman. And you're not just a black woman, you're a pregnant black woman" (Thompson). Yet the uniqueness of

Lemmons's authorship gives rise to "one of the greatest writer-director debuts in American cinematic history," according to critic Angelica Jade Bastién.

After three months of leave with her newborn son, Lemmons began to bring her feature to life. *Eve's Bayou* literally emerges through the perspective of a new mother, lending visible form to her dreamed world, itself foregrounding children's perception. *Eve's Bayou* privileges the ten-year-old Eve (Jurnee Smollett, in her first film role) as its protagonist, her interiority structuring the film. Writes Frances Gateward in *Black Camera*, "so rarely in the cinema are we given narratives which focus on adolescent girls, and perhaps even more scarce are those about African Americans."

Set in 1962 rural Louisiana, *Eve's Bayou* pictures an affluent Black community in a picturesque landscape. Despite pressure from producers to include white characters, Lemmons "wanted to make a movie with all Black people. ... about a place that had kind of merged into one race." Lemmons continues: "To me it's a fable; *Eve's Bayou* was full of Black people that had sprung from masters marrying slaves. What became important was that they were *any* family. And that they didn't sit around obsessing about race. They never really mention it." (Holmes). In picturing Black communities framed by but not contingent to white supremacy, *Eve's Bayou* offers much-needed mirrors for Black female spectators and a corrective for white audiences' limited imagination, given how media conceptions of "family" – and, often, political categories of "American" – have excluded Black experience. Spencer celebrates *Eve's Bayou* as "a film directed by a Black woman which not only achieved critical and financial success but did so without compromising its cultural integrity."

Black feminist scholar bell hooks traces her experience of films as originating in her dawning awareness that "[t]here is power in looking," a way that slaveholders would exercise power or that children would challenge parental authority; hooks explains that Black female spectators develop an "oppositional gaze" that questions instead of escapes into the white patriarchal fictions that exclude or malign Black female experiences (hooks). *Eve's Bayou*'s titular young Black female character learns to appreciate her own "power in looking," a power with the capacity both to rupture and heal. Foregrounding how an ecologically diverse bayou setting and life-filled Southern family quietly carry slavery's trauma, *Eve's Bayou* illustrates how bearing witness involves a layered history of perception.

Opening the Film: First Two Sequences

This film makes us aware of the power and responsibility of looking. "Memory is the selection of images, some elusive, others printed indelibly on the brain. The summer I killed my father, I was 10 years old." So begins *Eve's Bayou*, these sentences offered in voiceover by an older Eve Batiste (Tamara Tunie), over black-and-white images of an eye in extreme close-up (aligning the object of the audience's sight with the character's own senses and eventual "second sight") and untethered landscape shots of breeze-blown grasses. The first sentence's abstract and dreamy qualities (memory as imagistic, precise yet vague) contrast with the second sentence's blunt precision (describing a particular season, age, and violent act). Driven by the suspense of how or why Eve kills her father, *Eve's Bayou* opens into a movie both accessible (a period melodrama) and itself "elusive", about far more than this immediacy, invoking the history of slavery, power, perception, medicine, healing, spirituality, and epistemology.

Within the first minutes, the retrospective Eve announces her family as the descendants of the former enslaved woman Eve and her slave owner, General Jean-Paul Batiste: Eve saved his life; in return, he granted her freedom and gave her the bayou; "perhaps in gratitude" she bore him 16 children. Though this historical tracing appears as mere mention and ghostly figures fade within the image, the film establishes from the outset that not only the titular land but also the family itself has arisen through inequitable power, that the aliveness of its present is situated within slavery's dehumanizing history,

Eve thus reaches back to incorporate her namesake's traumatic history: a beginning – hardly a "once upon a time" origin story – that situates Eve's identity within a radically imbalanced power dynamic. At once, Eve's opening voiceover provides helpful exposition: the bayou has a history, after all, and so does this family; furthermore, this voiceover tightens the narrative strings and anticipates the unfolding plot; invoking *Citizen Kane* (1941) and *Sunset Blvd* (1950), *Eve's Bayou* begins by announcing Eve's father's death, which charges the subsequent film with suspense. But in ways that move beyond the aforementioned Hollywood films, *Eve's Bayou* historicizes its very setting and traces back the family narrative that has birthed our present-day Eve Batiste. This historical weight and suspense narrative invoke both individual guilt (Eve killed her father!) and intergenerational trauma ("we are the descendants…"), a lineage of caretaking and sacrifice, rendered via images that complicate more than rationalize the voiceover.

This experimental black-and-white exposition quickly gives way (via an editing wipe of the bayou itself) to the full-color sprawling Batiste home, nestled amidst old trees and overhanging Spanish moss, where cars arrive and zydeco music registers the festive atmosphere. Inside, a full-on multi-generational glamorous house party is joyously enlivened by a film camera that appreciates bodies of all ages and movement of every sort: the wise-cracking older women raise eyebrows about the sensual dancing; Uncle Harry (Branford Marsalis) performs magic tricks and takes photographs; ten-year-old Eve takes in the splendor with her wide eyes; Eve's younger brother Poe (Jake Smollett) tries to keep up with his older siblings, while eldest sister (Meagan Good) moves about the space with the dawning grace of a young woman learning how to be inside of her changing body.

With a film camera aligned with Eve's curiosity, Amy Vincent's cinematography drinks in the celebration with ease, establishing a genre altogether different from the prior gothic and suspense frames. The film's promise shines clear in just these opening minutes: musical and community joy; vibrant color and texture; magic, tricks, and abundance, in the shadow of a traumatic past. Yet these scenes can hardly convey the moody spell of the film's duration, the long takes that sweep from overhanging trees to the ground, the light that moves through the thick foliage and dappled paths to lend everything a glittering magic, and the heavy atmosphere of both weather and plot.

The three Batiste children raise their glasses for a champagne toast, behind the production credits that read "written and directed by Kasi Lemmons," almost as if the characters *within* the film toast the writer-director *of* this film. A combination of slow-motion and tiny jump cuts elongates the children's gestures of raising their drinks, clinking in glassy accompaniment, as the diegetic party music rises in volume and the lyrics ("a little bit higher") both caption and compel the action. This scene, its audiovisual layering of production credits and character movement, introduces a broader way to read the film: as a question of causality and subtlety, of children's gestures shaped by adult influence, of finding community and intimacy through emulating and making new.

In contrast with the rupture that soon follows, this moment establishes an equilibrium among the Batiste siblings, synching their motions toward a central point, bridging the film world and existential world, plot and production aligned. Furthermore, Lemmons's film honors her own childhood memory,

> I was trying to re-create what my parents and their friends looked like to me as a child. They looked like gods. ...Their hair was fabulous, they were really dressed, their friends were gorgeous, their parties were fabulous... they looked like movie stars. I thought, why don't I see this in films?
>
> *(Nocenti)*

This glossy film moment perhaps appears further idealized via the older Eve's retrospective nostalgia for her childhood, the innocence by which she experienced the party before a critical sight and new knowledge upended her comfortable world.

Ways of Seeing

Originating in the double beginnings of the black-and-white exposition and the house party, the film's complex plot accelerates. After joking with her beloved Uncle Harry and distributing chocolates and champagne to guests, Eve jealously leaves the party, when their suave doctor father, Louis Batiste (Jackson), asks Eve's older sister Cisely to dance. Eve finds refuge in the carriage house, where she falls asleep only to awaken, startled by the nearby sounds of her father's affair with neighbor Matty Mereaux (Lisa Nicole Carson). Shocked, Eve processes what she's witnessed relative to what she feels. This tension continues, as she accompanies her father on house calls and begins to ask questions about the sultry bed-ridden women in need of "something for the pain," as they privately consult with the doctor. Beset with skepticism alongside visions (black-and-white flashes in the experimental film style of the film's opening sequence) that seem confoundingly portentous, Eve connects with her Aunt Mozelle (Debbi Morgan), who works as a "seer," helping neighbors answer questions and heal, through her second sight.

Having received a fortune from the local marketplace conjure woman Elzora (Diahann Carroll) that she ought "look to her children," and after Mozelle has a premonition of a young child's death, Roz Batiste (Lynn Whitfield) determines to keep her children indoors all summer, to protect them from succumbing to this foreseen fate. The film's second act takes place within this domestic interior, as the children perform scenes from *Romeo & Juliet*, play with costumes and dolls, read books, fight over the bathroom, and explore their limits. Yet these boundaries prove permeable: Cisely disappears and returns with a new mature hairstyle and made-up face, resembling her mother; Louis Batiste often comes home drunk at night, and Cisely waits up for him, and – in the ambiguity at the film's heart – crosses lines of propriety with his eldest daughter. Cisely tells Eve of her father's transgression, and the sisters find renewed solidarity in opposing him, Eve taking on a vengeful spirit in seeking help from Elzora to kill her father with a spell. Whether a consequence of Eve's actions or his own, Louis Batiste soon after is murdered by Matty Mereaux's jealous husband. A letter, which Eve finds posthumously in Louis's doctor bag, addressed to his sister Mozelle, writes a version of history that counters Cisely's account (according to Louis's version, Cisely lied or falsely imagined who was the instigator). Yet Eve's own powers of second sight, as she takes Cisely's hands to learn more, reveal an ambiguity that clouds clear cause and effect.[1] Comparable to yet more intimate than *Citizen Kane*'s closing revelation of "rosebud," *Eve's Bayou* ends with the sisters working together to submerge Louis's letter into the bayou, the handwriting washing away, its secret theirs to keep.

What this summary hardly glimpses, however, is the film's feel and look, its textures and nuance: the soft rose-coral and blue-green color palette that suffuses domestic interiors and natural landscapes; the patterns of floral sundresses and twinsets, denim overalls and satin partywear, curtains and doll clothing, pajamas and bed linens, that map the film's changing emotional tonality; the range of young Jurnee Smollett's expressive looks that convey emotional extremes; the light that glimmers through leafy trees and reflects on the bayou water, suffusing each scene with combined luminosity and shadow.

For all the pain and difficult learning, *Eve's Bayou* nonetheless shines with a vibrance that does not gloss over complexities. When Roz demands that her children stay indoors, for example, her pale orange shirtdress distracts from her shrillness and affords a softness that complements her relief in drawing the line and choosing safety above all else. Given our alliance with Eve's subjectivity, Roz's excessive measures seem unwelcome; yet the film visually *flatters* Roz in this moment of excess, a generosity that intimates the validity of this potentially life-saving measure. The film frames Roz's protective looks at her children in a lush style that offers compassion for Roz's desperation to find control somewhere in her otherwise unspooling family. Further, despite the plot that chronicles

Eve's coming of age, cinematographer Amy Vincent contrasts this dawning maturity with the dynamic movement of energetic children at play. Earlier in the film, Po and Eve run (and the camera moves, with wildness and dynamism akin to their youthful energy) on a grassy patch alongside the shimmering bayou. At the film's end, on this very same land, Eve and Cisely stand together, hand-in-hand, in perfect horizontal and vertical symmetry and color equilibrium among sky and water, clothing, and nature. This change from a lively, moving camera to a stable, balanced, static frame – this movement from free, youthful scampering to still steadiness – inscribes Eve's maturation in the style itself.

At the opening party scene, when Harry snaps his photos, the color cinematic image pauses in a black-and-white still, elongating the screen duration and transforming into a photographic form the party's colorful events. Despite Mozelle's insistence that Harry "put down the damn camera," Harry photographs a stunning and glamorous Mozelle and Roz – our first glimpse of them, too – putting them on display and evoking their "to-be-looked-at-ness," Laura Mulvey's phrase to describe how women conventionally appear in Hollywood narratives. Harry's black-and-white photographs echo the black-and-white prologue, yet Harry's photographic reality is *verifiable*: we have just seen the *in-color* pose and image that Harry then records. After his death, Harry's black-and-white photographic moments are then supplanted with Eve's and Mozelle's black-and-white "second sight" sequences, though their projections have hardly the reliability of the photographic index. Instead, Eve's and Mozelle's black-and-white visions create a site of uncertainty, images blurred and slowed, angles canted, faces obscured, cause-and-effect imprecise.

In terms of film style, Eve's and Mozelle's mental subjectivity looks like an experimental film situated within an otherwise exceedingly legible melodrama. Eve and Mozelle grasp at the meaning of their second sight, haunted by the pressure to interpret their visions, and the film positions us accordingly, as we try to understand what we're seeing, right alongside these characters. This film that foregrounds the "power in looking" thus dramatizes the necessity and responsibility of interpretation. More complex than Harry's photography (he neatly smiles after snapping a beautiful sight), Mozelle's and Eve's visions both heal and confuse, therein requiring an additional phase of discernment. *Eve's Bayou* features a young Black girl who learns how to understand the power of her look, and – in so doing – the film teaches the audience to open and revise the limiting structures by which films have heretofore made *sense*.

Reception and Legacy

A favorite of audiences and critics alike, *Eve's Bayou* received standing ovations at Telluride and Toronto Film Festivals. Roger Ebert's review lent crucial early support to the film:

> Lemmons emerged at this year's Toronto Film Festival as one of today's most gifted young American writer-directors... The film is one of the big

successes here, one everyone mentions when talking about the festival's discoveries.... Unlike a lot of first films, which are overeager to impress, 'Eve's Bayou' is serenely confident.

(Ebert, "Remarkable Directing Debut")

Likening Lemmons to Tennessee Williams and Ingmar Bergman, Ebert's formal review expanded this praise:

"That Lemmons can make a film this good on the first try is like a rebuke to established filmmakers.... If it is not nominated for Academy Awards, then the academy is not paying attention.[2] For the viewer, it is a reminder that sometimes films can venture into the realms of poetry and dreams.

(Ebert)

Lemmons keeps a framed print of his review in her house, so valuable his support is at a crucial time.

While all critics appreciated the film's value, debate arose as to whether the film was a "black" film or a "universal" film. Earning nearly $15 million gross on a roughly $4 million investment in an independent film by a Black female debut writer-director led studios to research audience demographics and discover that

over half of *Bayou*'s moviegoers were white. Not only was it a major crossover vehicle – playing in art houses and mainstream theaters alike – it also dominated the NAACP's Image Awards nominations...What's at issue...is whether *Eve's Bayou* is too well made, too universal in its appeal, and too sophisticated in subject matter to be considered a 'black' film,

writes film scholar Mia Mask. Mask points to critic Andrew Sarris – renowned for his pantheon of (white, male) auteurs – as a case in point. Sarris offers backhanded praise: "To hail *Eve's Bayou* as the best African American film ever would be to understate its universal accessibility to anyone on this planet" (27). Yet Mask concludes that "the statement reinscribes the hegemony of whiteness as the locus of universal humanism" (27). Mask appreciates "Lemmons's portrait of a rural, affluent, French-speaking black family [as] threaten[ing] essentialist notions...of black experience as definitely urban, ghetto-centered, and youth-culture dominated" and argues for an expansion of Black experience on screen.

Film scholar Kara Keeling critiques the logic that attributes *Eve's Bayou*'s financial success to the fact that "it wasn't 'black,' but 'human'" (156). Keeling celebrates the film's "irrational" images, "nonchronological time," in tandem with its "valorizing living images that are capable of making those irrational images common." Instead of *adding* the experience of Black women to the category of "the human," Keeling claims that the formal inventiveness of *Eve's Bayou* "explode[s] the human by excavating an outside within cinematic reality and laboring to make that outside common" (157). In other words, *Eve's Bayou* does not reductively press Black experience into white forms of expression; rather, this film argues for Black *female* experience as a complex subject that can transform film art.

Writes bell hooks, "[l]ooking and looking back, black women…see our history as counter-memory…a way to know the present and invent the future" (131). Including and beyond Lemmons's success, and especially possible for an independent feature (without pressure – or budget – to hire established crew), *Eve's Bayou* has shaped the future for many new artists, as the first feature film for cinematographer Amy Vincent, editor Terilyn A. Shropshire, and costume designer Karyn Wagner. As an example of just one branch of this continuing influence, Shropshire – a Black female editor, successful in her own right – went on to mentor Joi McMillon as an apprentice editor on Lemmons's *Talk to Me*. For *Moonlight* (2017), McMillon became the first Black female editor – and only the second Black editor – nominated for an Academy Award (with co-editor Nat Sanders). Lemmons has gone on to direct and co-write (with Gregory Allen Howard) the award-winning *Harriet* (2019); Lemmons has most recently collaborated with Julie Dash, Gina Prince-Blythewood, and Tina Mabry on *Women of the Movement* (2022), a series about Mamie Till-Mobley, Emmett Till's mother. Itself mindful of history and memory, *Eve's Bayou* gives rise to a legacy of cinematic counter-memories that open the future by centering Black female experience on screen.

Notes

1 In Lemmons's director's cut, a character Uncle Tommy – wheelchair-bound and residing in the house, though he cannot himself speak – witnesses the night in question. For the theatrical release, a financier insisted that his presence be scrubbed from the film. Lemmons explains this difference as technically slight but with major implications: the director's cut places knowledge *in* a character who can see but not tell his truth; the theatrical release makes slippery the existence of any such truth.
2 Almost 20 years before #Oscarssowhite, the Academy did not recognize *Eve's Bayou* with any nominations. In 2020, Kasi Lemmons's extraordinary *Harriet* received two Oscar nominations: for Best Performance by an Actress in a Leading Role (Cynthia Erivo) and Best Achievement in Music (Erivo and Joshuah Brian Campbell).

Works Cited

Bastién, Angelica Jade. "20 Years Later, Eve's Bayou Is Still a Stunning Portrait of Black American Life." *Vulture*, 16 Nov. 2017, https://www.vulture.com/2017/11/eves-bayou-is-a-beautiful-portrait-of-black-identity.html.

Ebert, Roger. "'Eve's Bayou' a Remarkable Directing Debut." 11 Sept. 1997, https://www.rogerebert.com/festivals/eves-bayou-a-remarkable-directing-debut.

———. "Eve'sBayou." 7 Nov. 1997, https://www.rogerebert.com/reviews/eves-bayou-1997.

Gateward, Frances. "Eve's Bayou." *Black Camera*, vol. 13, no. 1, 1998, p. 7.

Holmes, Maori Karmael. "An Interview with Kasi Lemmons." *The Believer,* 2 Dec. 2019, https://believermag.com/an-interview-with-kasi-lemmons/.

hooks, bell. *Black Looks: Race and Representation*. South End Press, 1992.

Keeling, Kara. "Reflections on the Black Femme's Role in the (Re)production of Cinematic Reality: The Case of *Eve's Bayou*." *The Witch's Flight: The Cinematic, the Black Femme, and the Image of Common Sense*. Duke University Press, 2007, pp. 138–158.

Mask, Mia L. "Eve's Bayou: Too Good to Be a 'Black' Film?" *Cinéaste*, vol. 23, no. 4, 1998, pp. 26–27.

Muhammad, Erika. "Kasi Lemmons: The Woman Behind *Eve's Bayou*." *Ms.*, vol. 8, no. 5, Mar./Apr. 1998, pp. 74–75.

Nocenti, Annie. "Writing and Directing *Eve's Bayou*: A Talk with Kasi Lemmons." *Scenario*, vol. 4, no. 2, Summer 1998, pp. 192–199.

Thompson, Gary. "Giving Birth." *Chicago Tribune*, 20 Nov. 1997, https://www.chicagotribune.com/news/ct-xpm-1997-11-20-9711200344-story.html.

36

DONNIE DARKO (2001)

Claire Parkinson

Richard Kelly's debut feature, *Donnie Darko*, premiered at the Sundance Film Festival in January 2001 and had its theatrical release in October of the same year. At early festival screenings, writer-director Kelly was heralded as one of a new group of "indie *auteurs*," directors who could balance their distinctive style with commercial sensibilities (Kilday).

There were high expectations for the film, which was distributed by a newcomer to the independent sector, Newmarket. The company achieved success with the indie "hit of the year," Christopher Nolan's breakout film *Memento* (2000). Following advice from Nolan and *Memento* producer Emma Thomas, Newmarket executives decided that *Donnie Darko* would be the company's next release. Unexpectedly, the film fared badly at the box office but despite these initial problems, *Donnie Darko* eventually went on to acquire cult status (Mathijs and Mendik 67). Many cult films come from the independent sector and the pleasures derived from movies such as *Donnie Darko* are due, at least in part, to the audience's perception of opposition to what is thought of as "mainstream." In the case of *Donnie Darko*, the film's box office failure added to its cult appeal with fans valuing it as a film that was unappreciated by the mainstream. Oppositionality can give films cultural value and the appeal of *Donnie Darko* to cult audiences is due to the same qualities that are associated with its "indieness": its low-budget origins, the backstory of the struggling indie *auteur*, the film's countercultural value that sits in opposition to mainstream tastes, and experimentation that invites multiple viewings (Newman 213–215). Interestingly, many of these same characteristics place *Donnie Darko* in the company of other films which have been labeled "smart cinema." As such, the film's box office failure, low budget, independent financing and distribution, blend of generic conventions, and complex narrative mark *Donnie Darko* out as a cult indie feature with a smart film sensibility.

FIGURE 36.1 The dysfunctional suburban family at the evening dinner table.

Indie *Auteur*

2001 was declared by *Variety* "the year of the *auteur*" (Kilday) with Richard Kelly featuring as one of a new group of indie directors that included Henry Bean (*The Believer*), Todd Field (*In the Bedroom*), and John Cameron Mitchell (*Hedwig and the Angry Inch*). The article argued that this group deserved the title of *auteur* due to their "uncompromising vision" and refusal to "buckle under to overly commercial considerations, nor create statements so underground that they're precluded from normal distribution routes" (Chagollan). Used by postwar French film critics to discuss Hollywood studio directors' authorship, the term *auteur* was widely appropriated in the early 2000s by the trade press and film industry in relation to independent filmmaking. The concept of the indie *auteur* was a way to differentiate certain directors; it signified autonomy and the value of their creative work in a wider market where it could be understood in opposition to formulaic studio filmmaking. However, although the indie *auteur* is defined here as a director who has creative freedom and manages to make films on their own terms, the context in which their films are made is still reliant on support from executives and independent producers and having a project that will achieve the right balance between art and commerce to satisfy the discerning audiences for independent films (Schatz 28).[1] Genre-defying with a complex narrative, *Donnie Darko* was initially considered by the trade press and independent distributor Newmarket to hit the right balance of indie with crossover appeal that would attract audiences with a taste for films that sat outside the mainstream. The narrative of Kelly's struggle to make *Donnie Darko* only increased its attractiveness to the trade press and secured the filmmaker's identity as an indie *auteur*.

The route by which *Donnie Darko* was eventually made fits well with the circulating indie *auteur* narratives of the time.[2] These were stories about new emerging directors that had become commonplace in film marketing in the 1990s and early 2000s. Used to market both the films and their directors, the narratives of indie filmmakers usually included an acknowledgment of their passion for the art of filmmaking, the struggles they faced to make their first feature, followed by eventual wider critical recognition of their talent, vision, and originality at film festivals: "Such stories contributed to a myth of independent film in which talent and artistic endeavour, working outside the mainstream system and driven by a love for film, were eventually recognised and rewarded" (Molloy, *Memento* 34). Filmmakers' "origin stories" are important; they are the foundation of their biographies and the narratives of the difficulties they faced in making their films outside the established production system are especially valued by audiences for independent films (Newman 214).

In accounts of the struggle to get *Donnie Darko* made, Richard Kelly is positioned as an artist who maintains autonomy and brings his vision to the screen. This ability to realize a creative concept is intrinsically bound up with notions of the indie *auteur*'s autonomy which is imagined to only exist outside of the constraints of commercial filmmaking. In other words, indie filmmaking opposes a conflation of the commercial, mainstream, and formulaic that might be used to describe Hollywood more generally. In the case of *Donnie Darko*, the film's genre-blending and complex narrative were attributed to Kelly's ability to realize a creative vision unconstrained by the shackles of studio filmmaking.

Genre

Set in October 1988, against the backdrop of the approaching presidential election, the film uses nostalgic pop culture references of the time and explores themes of morality, reality, and time travel. While sleepwalking, Donnie (Jake Gyllenhaal) experiences visions of Frank (James Duval), a man from the future who wears a demonic rabbit suit. Two parallel universes exist in the film and only Donnie's eventual death can avert their catastrophic collision which will result in the end of everything. It is Frank who delivers the apocalyptic message to Donnie that the world will end in 28 days, 6 hours, 42 minutes, and 12 seconds. Donnie, guided by Frank, then undertakes a series of violent acts to restore the space-time continuum, the resolution of which is only realized when the protagonist's life is sacrificed.

Donnie Darko straddles genres, borrowing from comic book, horror, and science fiction aesthetics and, as such, defies easy categorization. This ability to cross genres clearly marks the film's departure from the norms of Hollywood filmmaking (King 52). However, genre is also central to how the narrative is understood. For example, the meaning of Donnie's death is tied to how the film is read in terms of genre. If read as a science fiction film, Donnie is a hero at the end of the film and saves the world, but an alternative reading sees Donnie as a psychotic teen unable to cope with the world (Blazer 209).[3] As a science fiction film, the focus is on the mysterious character of Frank, the jet engine event, and the impending end of the universe. In this context, Frank is the wise advisor to a savior who chooses his own fate (209–211).[4] Alternatively, if the film is read as the dream of a psychotic teenager, Frank and the jet engine are part of a delusion that leads Donnie to undertake increasingly violent actions (212).[5]

Donnie Darko can also be categorized as a teen film that explores experiences of being young that are commonly neglected in mainstream teen films (Driscoll 104). Kelly always intended Donnie Darko to be an intervention in the teen film genre and mixed the teen high school drama with teen gothic and teen sci-fi by refusing to resolve Donnie's identity via one single linear story (104–105). If read primarily as teen science fiction, Donnie Darko is comparable with Back to the Future (1985) which presented a positive nostalgic vision of the 1980s; on the other hand, Donnie Darko offers a significantly more cynical and altogether darker envisioning of the decade (Lee 124). Donnie's teenage development and angst-ridden search for agency and empowerment act as a counterpoint to Jim Cunningham's (Patrick Swayze) self-help simplification of life. Cunningham appears to have all the trappings of masculine success, but it transpires that he is involved in a child pornography ring, is morally bankrupt, and his wealth is built on empty slogans and useless rhetoric. Professor Monnitoff (Noah Wyle), while supporting Donnie's theories of time travel in private, is unable to do so in public without risking his job and Eddie Darko is shown in the dinner table scene to be a relic of outdated masculinity when he presumes that his daughter – who we find out is going to Harvard – will, in the future, rely financially on a husband. Understood as a teen movie, the story is about adolescence and the struggle for identity, agency, and empowerment, and remains consistent whether the film is read as science fiction or a supernatural or delusional experience (Driscoll 106).

Donnie Darko's genre-crossing impacted its box office performance. Indeed, the film's genre-blending made it difficult to market, and the decision to release it as a horror film left some critics and audiences confused. Significantly, a second reason for poor box office performance was the events of 11 September 2001. The film had a Halloween release and included scenes of a plane engine falling from the sky. Only six weeks after news broadcasts around the world had shown images of the 9/11 terrorist attacks during which planes crashed into the Twin Towers of the World Trade Center, the mood of the time dulled audiences' appetite for the film's imagery and apocalyptic storyline and the film grossed only $110,494 on its domestic opening weekend.[6] However, failure at the box office proved to be part of Donnie Darko's countercultural appeal for some audiences. Cult audiences were attracted to the film, in part because its initial failure categorized it as a misunderstood film that was beyond the tastes of a mainstream audience. Combined with the film's low budget, the cult value of Donnie Darko lay in its oppositional status, a quality that was equally associated with the film's "indieness." While opposition to mainstream tastes confers value on a cult film, in the case of Donnie Darko box office failure only served to further magnify this oppositional value.

Released in the United Kingdom in theaters and on video the following year with a clever marketing campaign that involved graffiti artists making work inspired by the film against a deadline of 6 hours, 42 minutes, and 12 seconds – a temporal duration that was central to the film's plot – Donnie Darko quickly found a cult following. The film played at European fantasy-film festivals, and such was its impact in Britain that the bleak title track, a cover of the Tears for Fears song "Mad World," recorded for the film by Michael Andrews and Gary Jules, became an unexpected UK Christmas hit in 2003, reaching the number one spot and remaining there for three weeks.

Donnie Darko's route to cult appreciation in the US was helped considerably by midnight screenings at the Pioneer Theater in Manhattan's East Village.[7] New audiences were attracted to the film's 1980s nostalgia while references to drugs and film classics such as *E.T.* (1982), *Back to the Future,* and *The Evil Dead* (1981) – combined with its complex narrative, camp sensibility, and philosophy of time travel – gave it a newfound oppositional appeal. The fact that *Donnie Darko* did not conform to mainstream tastes granted it cultural capital, a cult value that esteemed and even required oppositionality to the commercial norms of studio films.

Smart Film

This oppositionality also gave *Donnie Darko* a "smart film" sensibility. Smart cinema is a term coined to describe a group of films that, like independent films more generally, "are almost invariably placed by marketers, critics and audiences in symbolic opposition to the imaginary mass-cult monster of mainstream, commercial Hollywood cinema" (Sconce, "Irony" 351) but which has been further understood as having a shared set of elements that include some but not necessarily all the following: blank style; synchronicity; random fate; a fascination with the dysfunctional white middle-class family; and contemporary taste cultures (Sconce, "Smart Cinema" 434). The concept of blank style refers to a stylistic strategy that is dispassionate or disengaged no matter how strange or disturbing the story, and which leads to "a sense of dampened affect" (432). The stylistic choices that create blank style often include long takes, stationary characters, and straight-on level framing, all of which are apparent in *Donnie Darko,* particularly in the framing and editing of scenes that involve Frank, the bizarre rabbit character.

Synchronicity – unrealistic coincidences that make up a random yet meaningful structure of reality – is an organizing narrative principle and central to the time-loop strategy of *Donnie Darko* (Brereton 48). Synchronicity and random fate drive the narrative while Donnie and the audience try to make sense of the storyline (Perkins 41; Brereton 71). The key and apparently random event that propels the narrative forward and signals the existence of two parallel universes occurs early in the film when a jet engine crashes through the roof of the Darko home and into Donnie's bedroom. Donnie is not in his bed when the mysterious event occurs, instead waking up outside on a golf course after a sleepwalking episode during which he has been told by Frank of the impending end of everything. Writer/director Richard Kelly explains that "For me the jet engine was the conceit and then the quest was for me to solve the mystery of the jet engine. Then I just tried to find the most interesting voyage to solve that mystery" (Kelly xxii). *Donnie*

Darko centralizes and muses over questions of fate and coincidence through its exploration of the philosophy of time travel which can provide answers to the larger puzzle of the jet engine (King 67). Donnie must travel back through time to the point at which the jet engine falls through his bedroom ceiling and sacrifice his life to replace the reality in which he survives with another reality in which he dies. In doing so, Donnie saves the lives of Rose Darko (Mary McDonnell) – his mother – and Gretchen Ross (Jena Malone), his girlfriend. At the end of the film, Rose and Gretchen see each other from across the street and wave, their expressions a mix of recognition and uncertainty. In the new reality, they have never met but are connected in the other reality through Donnie. The encounter between two characters who, in this parallel world, are now strangers is made meaningful for audiences but the film intentionally leaves it open to interpretation. By the end of the film, the connection between the two characters can be read as both ambiguous and meaningful.

A coming-of-age story about a troubled middle-class teenager, *Donnie Darko* focuses as well on issues of alienation and familial dysfunction, a recurring theme in smart cinema. This focus lends itself to suburban settings where the ubiquitous trappings of everyday life and domesticity exist alongside the extraordinary and menacing. This is realized in recurring motifs of gates, doors, and fences and through family routines such as mealtimes (Perkins 135). At the beginning of the film, Donnie wakes up in the middle of the road on Carpathian Ridge, a cliff overlooking distant mountains. He jumps on his pushbike and cycles down the road leaving nature behind and pedaling into the suburbs. Riding past two middle-aged women powerwalking, Donnie turns the corner to approach his house and cycles out of shot as the camera pans and tracks across the front yard to Eddie Darko (Holmes Osborne) using a leaf blower. A hard cut to a slow motion sequence is used as, one by one, Donnie's family members are introduced, each involved in the mundane activities of suburban life: Eddie Darko blasts Elizabeth Darko (Maggie Gyllenhaal), Donnie's elder sister, with the air from the leaf blower as she leaves the house; Samantha Darko, the younger sister, jumps on a trampoline; and Rose Darko (Daveigh Chase), her back to Samantha, is curled up on a chair in the back garden reading Stephen King's horror novel, *It*. The camera picks up Donnie again as he walks past his mother, into the kitchen, and opens the refrigerator door which has a small whiteboard stuck to it and the note "Where is Donnie?" The choices made by Kelly and cinematographer Steven Poster to use slow motion for shots of Donnie's family create a sense of nostalgia for the utopian suburban experience. Once Donnie is again in frame, the shot returns to normal speed, a shift that is subtle but which creates a sense of disquiet and connotes the difference between Donnie and the rest of his family.

The focus on interpersonal alienation within the white, middle-class family has led to certain stock shots within smart cinema that include the "awkward dining shot," a familiar social routine that is often represented as "long shots of maladjusted families trapped in their dining rooms" (Sconce, "Smart Cinema" 436). Such scenes are common in American cinema generally, for example,

Edward Scissorhands (1990), *American Beauty* (1999), and *Pleasantville* (1998) each make use of the awkward dining scene to express underlying tensions in the suburban family dynamic. In *Donnie Darko*, the routine mealtime at the dining room table is used to emphasize generational differences as well as Donnie's growing alienation from the rest of his family. Donnie's father and mother sit at opposite ends of the table, his sisters sit together on one side of the table and across from Donnie, who sits alone. The discussion about the upcoming presidential election focuses on the political and generational differences between Elizabeth and her father. This theme of the progressive left in opposition to the traditionalist right is continued in the film, most notably through the different views on the teaching methods of the liberal English teacher, Karen Pomeroy (Drew Barrymore), who ends up losing her job for exposing students to the Graham Greene story "The Destructors." In this film, suburban living is represented as numbing and confining where education does not lead to empowerment but to violence and unhappiness (Perkins 141). The mealtime scene is also the first time the issue of Donnie's mental health is raised, as Samantha reveals that Donnie has stopped taking his medication and Donnie expresses his resentment about having to see a psychiatrist. The focus on therapy in the film aligns well with the observation that smart cinema can be historically contextualized alongside the rise of therapy culture: "The smart film's focus on the psychological state of middle-class America resonates closely with the tendency in contemporary culture to make sense of the world through the prism of emotion" (10). Moreover, a tendency in the 1990s and early 2000s cinema toward the depiction of characters with altered mental states such as *Memento* and *Fight Club* (1999) has privileged the point of view of protagonists with schizophrenia, paranoia, or amnesia in ways that cause viewers to discount the usual categories of sanity/insanity (Elsaesser 67). This, in turn, can be leveraged in a complex narrative to create ambiguity, a particular appeal of *Donnie Darko*.

Conclusion

Donnie Darko sits comfortably within the critical frames of smart cinema and cult cinema, both of which are often associated with films from the independent sector. From industrial and formal perspectives, the film's indie credentials are robust. And yet, *Donnie Darko* is marked out by some important differences from similar films of the time. Unusual for an indie film in the early 2000s, *Donnie Darko* includes special effects sequences, a choice that is reflected in the film's budget, which was increased from an initial $2.5 million to $4.5 million (Kelly xxxv). And, while there is no doubt that the film blends genres, there remains an overriding pull toward understanding *Donnie Darko* as science fiction/fantasy – atypical genres for indie filmmaking. As this chapter has shown, genre is important to the reading of the film, conferring quite different meanings on the characters of Donnie and Frank depending upon which generic lens is applied. The genre-blending also made the film difficult to promote and the decision to market *Donnie Darko* as horror to align with a Halloween release compounded the problems faced by the film in the light of the events of 9/11. It was, however, the fact of the film's box office failure that conferred a degree of subcultural value which was so important to its rediscovery as a cult film. When it comes to cult and indie film, value lies in oppositionality, and in the case of *Donnie Darko*, success was born out of failure.

Notes

1. For a discussion of the autonomy of indie *auteurs*, see my previous work: Molloy ("Indie Cinema" 375–378).
2. For more about the struggle, see: Kelly 2003.
3. The themes of sacrifice and dual realities have led scholars and critics to draw comparisons between *Donnie Darko* and the 1946 film *It's a Wonderful Life* (see for example: Lee 124; Walters 112–114). Steven Shaviro proposes that "Donnie's sacrifice offers us what Gilles Deleuze describes as the cinema's greatest gift: the restoration of our 'belief in this world'" (64).
4. The savior theme has also been explored by scholars in relation to the "Messianic Motif" (Dodd) and by comparison with *The Last Temptation of Christ* (1988) which is directly referenced in *Donnie Darko* (Walters 110–112).
5. For a Lacanian analysis of psychosis in *Donnie Darko*, see: Radley.
6. Box office figures from boxofficemojo.com
7. The "midnight movie" phenomenon is closely associated with cult movie fandom (Jancovich et al.).

Works cited

Blazer, Alex E. "A Phenomenological Approach to *Donnie Darko*." *Film-Philosophy*, no. 19, 2015, pp. 208–220.
Brereton, Pat. *Smart Cinema, DVD Add-Ons and New Audience Pleasures*. Palgrave Macmillan, 2012.
Chagollan, Steve. "Sundance Produces a New Crop of Auteurs." *Variety.com*. 8 Mar. 2001. Accessed 5 Sept. 2021.
Dodd, Kevin V. "*Donnie Darko* and the Messianic Motif." *Journal of Religion and Film*, vol. 3, no. 2, 2009, article 3. https://digitalcommons.unomaha.edu/jrf/vol13/iss2/3.
Driscoll, Catherine. *Teen Film: A Critical Introduction*. Berg, 2011.
Elsaesser, Thomas. "The Mind-Game Film." *Puzzle Films: Complex Storytelling in Contemporary Cinema*, edited by Warren Buckland. Wiley Blackwell, 2009, pp. 13–41.
Jancovich, Mark, et al. "Introduction." *Defining Cult Movies: The Cultural Politics of Oppositional Taste*, edited by Jancovich et al. Manchester University Press, 2003, pp. 1–14.
Kelly, Richard. *The Donnie Darko Book*. Faber & Faber, 2003.
King, Geoff. *Donnie Darko*. Wallflower, 2007.
Kilday, Gregg. "Year of the Auteur." *Variety.com*. 15 Jan. 2011. Accessed 5 Sept. 2021.
Lee, Christina. *Screening Generation X: The Politics and Popular Memory of Youth in Contemporary Cinema*. Routledge, 2010.
Mathijs, Ernest, and Xavier Mendik. *100 Cult Films*. BFI, 2011.
Molloy, Claire. *Memento*. Edinburgh University Press, 2010.
———. "Indie Cinema and the Neoliberal Commodification of Creative Labour: Rethinking the Indie Sensibility of Christopher Nolan." *A Companion to American Indie Film*, edited by Geoff King. Wiley Blackwell, 2017, pp. 368–388.

Newman, Michael Z. *Indie: An American Film Culture*. Columbia University Press, 2011.
Perkins, Claire. *American Smart Cinema*. Edinburgh University Press, 2012.
Radley, Emma. "Where Is Donnie? Psychosis and agency in Richard Kelly's *Donnie Darko*." *Psychoanalysis, Culture & Society*, no. 17, 2012, pp. 392–409.
Schatz, Thomas. "New Hollywood, New Millennium." *Film Theory and Contemporary Hollywood Movies*, edited by Warren Buckland. Routledge, 2009, pp. 19–46.
Sconce, Jeffrey. "Irony, Nihilism and the New American 'Smart' Film." *Screen*, vol. 43, no. 4, 2002, pp. 349–369.
———. "Smart Cinema." *Contemporary American Cinema*, edited by Linda Ruth Williams and Michael Hammond. McGraw Hill, 2006, pp. 429–439.
Shaviro, Steven. *Post-Cinematic Affect*. 0 Books, 2010.
Walters, James. *Alternative Worlds in Hollywood Cinema: Resonance Between Realms*. Intellect Books, 2008.

37

THE ROYAL TENENBAUMS (2001)

Warren Buckland

Wes Anderson's film style in *The Royal Tenenbaums* consolidated his reputation as an indie auteur. His use of reflexive techniques confronts the viewer, including the film's opening credit sequence: a series of shots of each character filmed head-on, occupying the center of a static frame, facing the camera looking directly at it, as we see in this chapter's image. At first, this appears to be a reflexive moment in the sense that the characters seem to address the film's audience. But, in fact, the characters are *not* breaking the fourth wall, for their actions reveal that each one is looking at themselves in a mirror and the camera is taking the place of that mirror. In other words, this look at the camera remains within the storyworld, and the film's audience sees what the characters see in the mirror – the characters looking at themselves. Each mirror shot in the credit sequence is therefore an optical point-of-view shot. Nonetheless, these shots are still reflexive, for the camera's image and the mirror image merge, an atypical reflexive use of style that draws attention to itself.[1] In this instance, style is used to draw attention to the film's frame (which is equated with the mirror's frame) and to the flatness of the filmic image and the screen (which are equated with the flatness of the mirror's surface).

The following chapter makes the case for Anderson's status as an indie auteur by arguing that his reputation was secured with *The Royal Tenenbaums*, not only because the screenplay he co-wrote (with Owen Wilson) was nominated for an Academy Award but also because with this film (only his third feature), he created a distinctively reflexive filmmaking style. Christian Metz identified two types of reflexivity in the cinema. In the form of reflexivity Metz calls "reflection... the film mimes itself (screens within the screens, films within the film, showing the device, etc.)"; in the version he identifies as "commentary," "the film speaks about itself, as is the case with certain 'pedagogical' voiceovers about the image... or in non-dialogue intertitles, explicatory camera movements, etc."

FIGURE 37.1 Gene Hackman as Royal Tenenbaum looks into a mirror during his introduction, though the camera presents him as gazing out at the audience.

(qtd. in Marie and Vernet 270). In *The Royal Tenenbaums*, Anderson's reflexive use of filmic techniques – both reflection and commentary – coalesced for the first time into a coherent stylistic system.

Indie Auteur

Filmmaker Karel Reisz makes a good case for privileging directors when analyzing and evaluating films. "The director should normally be in charge," Reisz argues, because the director is "responsible for planning the visual continuity during shooting" and is, therefore, the member of the production team who is "in the best position to exercise a unifying control over the whole production" (Reisz 58). Identifying the director as the central figure in a film's production is, therefore, an endeavor grounded in film practice.

From the opposite perspective – that of the auteur film critic – one finds agreement with Reisz. Auteur critics identify two types of directors – the auteur (who succeeds in exercising a unifying control over all of their films) and the metteur-en-scène (who does not). To determine if a director such as Anderson can be elevated to the status of an auteur, we can review ideas of authorship developed by Andrew Sarris, Henry Jenkins, and Michael Z. Newman. Andrew Sarris proposed three criteria to define an auteur – "technical competency" (a director's mastery of and control over their medium), a "consistent style" (evidence that a director has successfully expressed their "personality"), and "interior meaning" (which emerges from the tension between a director's personality – expressed in style – and their material – including their themes, a tension that somehow conveys their unique "inner essence"). However, Sarris applied the term "auteur" to directors working in the classical Hollywood studio system's inflexible, assembly-line mode of production, which reduced the director's position to that of an employee. For Sarris, an auteur is a director who managed to restore individuality and creativity to their position. However, contemporary Hollywood directors are not mere employees of studios but instead are freelancers, independent contractors who create film projects and sell them to the studios.[2] As a freelance worker, a director does not need to transcend an assembly-line mode of production but instead must invent a distinctive or individual style to increase their chance of being rehired. "By treating filmmakers as independent contractors," Henry Jenkins writes, "the new production system places particular emphasis on the development of an idiosyncratic style which helps to increase the market value of individual directors" (115). Jenkins implies that the freelance film market encourages the auteurist approach to filmmaking, for it impels directors to develop an individual style and personal themes. Nonetheless, despite working in different industrial contexts, the classical and contemporary auteurs share the same aim: to create added value, a differential style that is distinct from its immediate context (mainstream filmmaking, the background norm of film style).

For Michael Z. Newman, "indie" (and, by extension, an indie auteur) refers to middlebrow American films/filmmakers that offer an alternative to the popular tastes of mainstream cinema (2). Newman identifies "quirky" as a distinctive quality of indie films:

> Quirk is a kind of tone or sensibility that depends for its effect on a perception of its unusual, eccentric qualities, and this fits perfectly with the mission of indie cinema to distinguish itself against mainstream tone or sensibility or conventions of representation of characters and settings.
>
> *(44; see also MacDowell)*

It is Anderson's "quirky" storyworld, formed from his themes and reflexive use of style, that defines him as an indie auteur.

Wes Anderson: Familial Themes and Reflexive Use of Style

Thematically, Anderson's films are populated with orphans, outsiders, and alienated individuals, with strong women and insecure dysfunctional men. The traditional nuclear family is fragmented, replaced by diverse types of new "families" consisting of a group of likeminded oddball characters – such as Dignan's gang in *Bottle Rocket* (1996), Steve Zissou's crew in *The Life Aquatic* (2004), and the band of eccentric characters working at *The Grand Budapest Hotel* (2014) who act as a substitute family for the new lobby boy, the orphan Zero.

The Tenenbaum family is another dysfunctional group. It resembles a matrilineal family system, with separated parents (Etheline and Royal Tenenbaum) and three Tenenbaum children (Chas, Richie, and their adopted sister Margot) raised by their mother, who held the family together while the father remained on the periphery. The underlying themes and narrative conflicts in the film revolve around multiple rivalries within this family: Henry Sherman is a suitor for Etheline and is in conflict with Royal (who fakes an illness to return to the family home); Chas is also in conflict with Royal (who stole money from the young Chas) and is traumatized by the recent death of his wife; and Richie is in love with his adopted sister Margot, a secret desire that gradually unfurls as the film progresses. Following through on these narrative set-ups, Henry succeeds in eliminating his rival from the family home by exposing his fake illness, Chas reconciles with his father, while Margot and Richie end up acknowledging their love for each other.

Style is pushed into the foreground – becomes reflexive by drawing attention to itself – in both art cinema and indie cinema, whereas in mainstream cinema, style is subordinated to narrative. *The Royal Tenenbaums* deviates from mainstream filmmaking by foregrounding style. Furthermore, in relation to other indie auteurs whose style is similarly foregrounded, it is the *specific combination* and *variety* of foregrounded properties that define Anderson's style as distinctive, for it is rather unlikely that different auteurs would foreground an identical combination of stylistic properties.

For Sarris, what makes an auteur distinctive is their "personality," the way they impose their thinking on each film. In place of this amorphous notion, I suggest we define an auteur in terms of the distinct combination of foregrounded properties that constitute their style. Central to Anderson's style is *perpendicular vision*, an expression that suggests his films view the world from a straight or head-on angle, in which his camera is pointed directly at the world, creating a flat image that preserves the distances and angles of the filmed objects. The image is typically flat because those objects are seen from one side only, which maps directly onto the two-dimensional surface of the image. The head-on angle, therefore, makes the perpendicular vision reflexive, in the sense of Metz's first category of reflexivity – an imitative form of reflection that foregrounds the image's flatness.

Rarely do all the formal properties participate equally in the formation of a distinctive film style. Instead, a single property dominates, while subordinate properties harmonize with it. It is in *The Royal Tenenbaums* that Anderson's perpendicular vision first becomes the dominant organizing principle of his style. The film is systematically and consistently planned around tableau shots, beginning with the characters in the opening credit sequence looking into the camera/the mirror.[3] The perpendicular vision expressed in tableau shots is supported by top (birds-eye) views where the camera points straight down – including the film's very first shot, of a library book called *The Royal Tenenbaums*, but also a shot of Margot's glove with a finger cut off, a shot of Royal lying on the bedroom floor pretending to be ill, and Royal in an ambulance after genuinely falling ill. Francesco Casetti calls this birds-eye camera angle an "unreal objective shot," for it represents a look that emphasizes the "pure faculty of seeing" – that is, "a look without a determinate place" (130). This type of shot is characterized by the inability to attribute it to a character, for only the camera's look is present.

Anderson's perpendicular vision is further strengthened by and harmonizes with several additional formal properties of the film: spatially, the tableau and top-view shots are complemented by centered framing and a static camera, which add symmetry and stillness to those shots, momentarily pausing their temporal flow, while 90-degree whip pans quickly move the camera from one head-on position to another, evident in the shot of Richie leaving his cabin on the Côte d'Ivoire ship, of Etheline hailing a taxi when Margot separates from Raleigh, and of Royal and his grandchildren stealing from a corner shop. Temporally, slow motion shots artificially lengthen the filmed actions, which are employed in the centered head-on shot of Margot exiting the Green Line bus to meet Richie and in the shot of the characters leaving the cemetery at the end of the film. Montage sequences accompanied by a rock music soundtrack creatively contrast the aural continuity of the song with the visual discontinuity of the shots (forward leaps in time and sudden changes in location that take place with each cut), such as the series of shots covering several years of Margot's secretive activities and love affairs set to "Judy Is a Punk" by The Ramones. In addition, the deadpan faces of the inexpressive characters who inhabit the story world (such as Richie, Raleigh, and Margot) are foregrounded when they are symmetrically framed and filmed head-on with a static camera. When employed consistently throughout the film, these mutually reinforcing reflexive properties add up to create a unified style, a type of filming where the pure faculty of seeing becomes a form of clinical observation of the storyworld and the characters who inhabit it.

A perpendicular vision is opposed to an *oblique vision*, the view of an object from an angle, which reveals the three dimensions of that object. The resulting image attempts to render those three dimensions onto the image's two-dimensional flat surface, which may lead to images that compress or extend the perception of depth, or that distort parallel lines by translating them into converging lines. Anderson's perpendicular vision attempts to avoid these visual deformations and distortions, which downplays the three-dimensional impression of filmed space.

Reflexive Use of Storytelling

A director's reflexive use of techniques may also encompass storytelling, in which the process of telling a story is pushed into the foreground to become part of the story. The opening of *The Royal Tenenbaums* is reflexive not only via the shots of each character looking into a mirror; additionally, the opening also employs a voiceover, which comes from an unseen narrator located outside the storyworld. The presence of this disembodied voice on the soundtrack addressing the audience via commentary (Metz's second category of reflexivity) foregrounds the process of storytelling.

Anderson also employs title cards consistently throughout the film, a written mode of address that, similar to the voiceover, functions reflexively by addressing the audience. Anderson divides up *The Royal Tenenbaums* into eight chapters plus a prologue and an epilogue, with each chapter announced with a title card. (There are two additional title cards in the film: one announcing the cast of characters and the other naming the Maddox Hill Cemetery.) Similar to the voiceover, the title card foregrounds the storytelling process by addressing the audience but, unlike the voiceover, the title pauses the story when it appears on screen, momentarily taking the audience out of the storyworld.

Of course, title cards are a common feature of mainstream films, where they are traditionally limited to displaying the film's title and credits in the film's opening or closing moments. These title cards and credit sequences usually exist outside the storyworld – either on a neutral background or imposed over the image. However, Anderson does occasionally place the film's title *within* the storyworld. The title of *The Royal Tenenbaums* is not imposed *over* the image, as is traditional, but appears on the cover of a library book *in* the image (a technique Anderson used again in *The Grand Budapest Hotel*). The film's title becomes part of the storyworld and because it appears on the cover of a novel, the "source" of the story is embedded in the story itself (with the voiceover representing the novel's narrator). Furthermore, because the title cards that punctuate the rest of the film are part of this novel, they are not, strictly speaking, outside the storyworld but form part of the storyworld as well. (That is, the title cards are close-ups of the chapters of the book seen in the film's opening shot.) Nonetheless, they still address the audience and momentarily pause the storyworld.

The film's narration organizes the opening scenes into a paradigmatic structure, which is the opposite of a syntagmatic structure. A syntagmatic structure comprises the linear continuity of characters, actions, and events from scene to scene, where the story develops from one scene to the next. In a paradigmatic structure, on the other hand, each new scene presents a new storyline, a new location, and a new character (or characters). This means no continuity exists from one scene to the next, because each storyline interrupts the development of the others. In paradigmatic narration, the narrator's control and manipulation of the storytelling become reflexive (in the sense of Metz's second category of reflexivity) because their decision to stop narrating one story and to shift focus to another is foregrounded.

The Royal Tenenbaums initially follows the lives of the Tenenbaum family members individually, jumping from one character to the next rather than developing the same storyline. After the narration of the Tenenbaum children's early upbringing and the introduction of the main cast of characters in "the present" (22 years later), a title card announces, "Chapter One." This section of the film uses paradigmatic narration to present seven separate storylines within a matter of seven minutes: it jumps from Royal Tenenbaum in the Lindbergh hotel, to Richie on the Côte d'Ivoire ship, to his friend Eli Cash reading from his new novel, to Margot in the bathroom talking on the phone, to her husband Raleigh carrying out a test on his patient Dudley, to Chas carrying out a fire drill with his two sons (inadvertently leaving behind their dog Buckley), and finally to Etheline and Henry Sherman, in which Henry proposes to Etheline. In addition, each scene is punctuated with a flashback or an insert of a document: a letter to Royal asking him to vacate the hotel; the cover of *Sporting Press Magazine* reporting the end of Richie's tennis career; the cover of Eli's novel *Old Custer*; a record cover (*Desmond Winston Manchester XI*) featuring Margot (plus a flashback to her writing studio, the walls covered with posters of her previous plays); the cover of Raleigh's book *The Peculiar Neurodegenerative Inhabitants of the Kazawa Atoll*; a flashback to a plane crash that killed Chas's wife; the cover of Henry's book *Accounting for Everything*, and a montage sequence of Etheline's previous suitors. These flat documents, book covers, and flashbacks interrupt the unfolding narrative, again making the storytelling reflexive (in both of Metz's senses – miming the flat image and narrational commentary), although all are partially motivated by the voiceover, which introduces and explains these features. The narration then returns to the first storyline, Royal Tenenbaum, as he learns about Henry's proposal of marriage to Etheline. Up to this moment the narration in "Chapter One" was entirely paradigmatic, but with the reintroduction of Royal, the narration becomes syntagmatic, for it develops a previous storyline.

A new title card appears, announcing "Chapter Two." Chas's storyline is developed as he returns to the family home, before the narration shifts by focusing again on Royal. In the next scene, several storylines merge: Raleigh, Margot, and Etheline come together, and Margot decides to return to the family home (and meets up with Eli). As the film progresses, the narration gradually switches from paradigmatic to syntagmatic, as all the Tenenbaum family begin to occupy the same space and interact. However, the paradigmatic is never eliminated: the narration continues to switch between two or three storylines at any one time, with different groups of characters meeting up in each story. Overall, however, it is Royal's story that is privileged over the other characters, for the narration closely follows his attempts to disrupt the marriage of Etheline and Henry by pretending that he is dying before he experiences a moment of *anagnorisis* – a sudden recognition of his true situation. This happens when Royal's fake illness is exposed. He gets dressed and makes a short speech before leaving the Tenenbaum home. The voiceover returns – represented in the screenplay as the Narrator, who delivers his words in voiceover (VO) – to narrate his inner thoughts:

> Royal swallows one of his pills. He turns and stands in front of everyone.
>
> ROYAL (CONT'D)
> Look. I know I'm the bad guy on this one, but I just want to say that the last six days have been the best six days of, probably, my whole life.
>
> A strange, sad expression crosses Royal's face.
>
> NARRATOR (V.O.)
> Immediately after making this statement, Royal realized that it was true.

The external narrator's sudden intervention at this point in the story is once again a reflexive use of filmic technique because it foregrounds the voiceover which had remained silent for so long. But this interruption is necessary because Royal's actions had been duplicitous up to this point, and the narrator intervenes to signal Royal's moment of *anagnorisis* by proclaiming the truthfulness and sincerity of his speech. The external narrator falls silent again, and only makes a comeback in the film's final moments.

The film's final chapter, "Chapter 8," begins with Henry and Etheline's marriage ceremony. The narration shows the preparations for the ceremony, which is disrupted by Eli Cash crashing his car into the front of the Tenenbaum house, killing the dog Buckley. A long lateral tracking shot then brings all the characters together (except Margot) in the aftermath of the disrupted service. It is at this point that the external narrator's voiceover returns to narrate the fate of the main characters, in a series of brief episodes strung together using a mix of syntagmatic and paradigmatic narration: the dog Buckley is buried; Henry and Etheline are married in the Judge's chambers; Margot's new play opens ("The Levinsons in the Trees") with limited success; Raleigh and Dudley go on a lecture tour; Eli checks himself into a drug rehabilitation center; Richie teaches tennis to children; and Royal, reconciled with Chas, enjoys time with his grandchildren until he suddenly dies from a heart attack.

The reflexive use of storytelling techniques in "Chapter 8" (the voiceover and the paradigmatic presentation of events) rhymes with the voiceover and paradigmatic presentation of events in "Chapter 1." Furthermore, the rhyme itself is also reflexive: one reflexive fragment of the film ("Chapter 8") stylistically repeats – imitates or mimes – how another reflexive fragment of the film ("Chapter 1") presented the lives of the characters. However, the repetition is not purely stylistic and reflexive, for it also serves the storytelling by foregrounding character development. In other words, by repeating the reflexive storytelling techniques of "Chapter 1," "Chapter 8" narrates the transformation of the Tenenbaum family members, in the form of marriage, artistic creativity, sport, play, and death.

In sum, *The Royal Tenenbaums* consolidated Wes Anderson's reputation as an indie auteur, for the film deviates from mainstream norms in favor of a specific combination and variety of techniques used reflexively – including centrally framed static tableau shots, top views/unreal objective shots, 90-degree whip pans, deadpan acting, slow motion shots, and reflexive use of storytelling techniques such as voiceover, title cards, and paradigmatic narration – which Anderson has employed consistently and systematically across the whole film.

Notes

1 In his analysis of an identical camera set up in *Marnie* (1963), of Marnie looking at herself in a mirror/the camera, Raymond Bellour writes that such a moment "collapses the mirror into the screen" (231).
2 After co-writing the screenplay, Wes Anderson and Owen Wilson sold it to The Walt Disney Company, which produced it for $21 million under the Touchstone Pictures label and distributed it via Buena Vista Pictures, accumulating a worldwide gross of $71.4 million (figures from boxofficemojo.com). Anderson therefore developed his own distinctive film style by directing his own screenplay rather than by working against a screenplay imposed upon him within an inflexible studio system.

3 In later films such as *Moonrise Kingdom* (2012), Anderson combined the frontal shot with extensive camera movement – specifically, lateral tracking and crane shots that rigorously maintain the camera's straight on angle to the filmed objects. The camera is placed on a track and moves sideways in a straight line; objects appear from the left or right side of the screen, move across it, and disappear on the other side of the screen. Similarly, his crane shots move the camera laterally up and down the filmed objects while maintaining the straight head-on angle.

Works Cited

Bellour, Raymond. *The Analysis of Film*, edited by Constance Penley. Indiana University Press, 2000.

Casetti Francesco. "Face to Face." *The Film Spectator: From Sign to Mind*, edited by Warren Buckland. Amsterdam University Press, 1995, pp. 118–139.

Jenkins, Henry. "Historical Poetics." *Approaches to Popular Film*, edited by Joanne Hollows and Mark Jancovich. Manchester University Press, 1995, pp. 99–125.

MacDowell, James. "Wes Anderson, Tone and the Quirky Sensibility." *New Review of Film and Television Studies*, vol. 10, no. 1, 2012, pp. 6–27.

Marie, Michel, and Marc Vernet. "Interview with Christian Metz." 1990. *Conversations With Christian Metz: Selected Interviews on Film Theory (1970–1991)*, edited by Warren Buckland and Daniel Fairfax. Amsterdam University Press, 2017, pp. 243–273.

Newman, Michael Z. *Indie: An American Film Culture*. Columbia University Press, 2011.

Reisz, Karel, with Gavin Millar. *The Technique of Film Editing*. 2nd ed., Focal Press, 1968.

Sarris, Andrew. "Notes on the Auteur Theory in 1962." *Film Culture*, no. 27, 1962–1963, pp. 1–8.

38
STRANGER INSIDE (2001)

Kathleen McHugh

Stranger Inside (*SI*) tells the story of Treasure Lee (Yolonda Ross), a young Black lesbian, who intentionally commits a crime in juvenile detention so she will be transferred to a women's prison. She has heard that her mother, Brownie (Davenia McFadden), is incarcerated there. Once "inside," Treasure finds and then tries to get close to her mother, a butch lesbian lifer, who runs a prison gang. The film engages a known exploitation genre, the women-in-prison (WIP) film, to depict an underrepresented community, incarcerated lesbians of color. *SI*'s significance to American Independent film derives from director Cheryl Dunye's indie auteurist voice and practice, the film's subject and treatment, and the industrial context in which it emerged.

Dunye achieved distinction as a Black American independent filmmaker with 1996's *The Watermelon Woman* (*TWW*), her first feature and also the first theatrically released feature film directed by an out Black lesbian. The film demonstrates Dunye's innovative aesthetics-in-action, cultivated through six early short films which she called "Dunyementaries." Her aesthetics ignores or blurs distinctions between genres, media (film/TV), modes (documentary/fiction), film text and context, and filmmaker and subject. Though politically and theoretically informed and committed, Dunye's films do not overtly seek to educate, persuade or moralize but rather familiarize audiences with underrepresented perspectives through popular media modes.

Centering a Black lesbian point of view through the blurring of aesthetic and referential binaries, Dunye's practice and subject matter ultimately question the (white, male) privilege underlying distinctions between fiction and fact, history and imagination, inside the text and out. Possessing the "outsider" perspective and "social engagement" often informing American independent film (Holmlund 1–2), her films worked, in an albeit limited way, to progressively familiarize industry and audiences with her name, sensibility, and community.

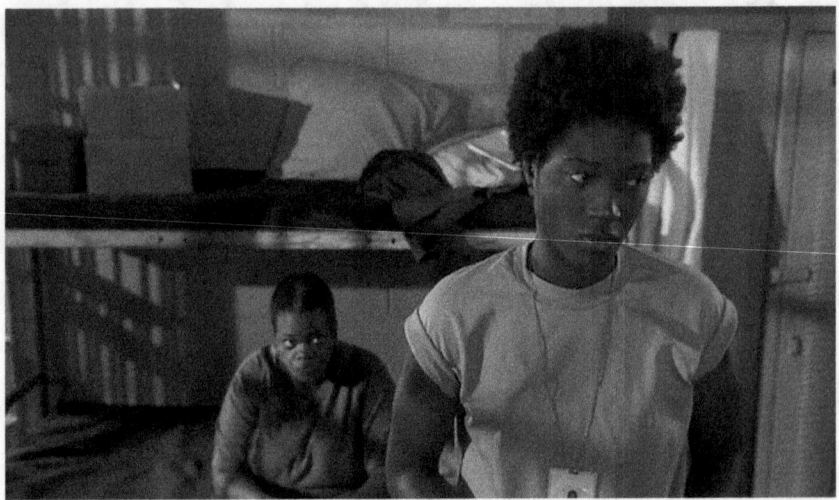

FIGURE 38.1 Treasure (foreground) grows disillusioned as Brownie (seated, glaring) extracts a greater and greater price to be her "daughter."

Though a made-for-TV movie funded by HBO, *SI* had a brief theatrical release. HBO's oft-cited industrial, financial and philosophical blurring of film and TV and its aim to produce "small-budget independent films" that were "edgier and more diverse" enabled *SI*'s financing and release (Heller 43–44). Partaking of both marginalized Black independent film *and* the transformative industrial force of HBO, *SI* embodies the paradoxes of American independent filmmaking of the last several decades. It moves from the "margins to the mainstream" (Holmlund/Wyatt). Along with HBO, Netflix, and Amazon's colonization of "diverse" and "edgy" as niche products, the very idea of American independent film becomes a point on an industrial production continuum rather than a genuine alternative. And yet, we see and hear different stories and voices.

From Doc to Dunyementary

Cheryl Dunye decided to be a filmmaker when she heard Spike Lee say that if people did not like his representation of Black women, they should go make their own films (Francis 46). She began from the autobiographical premise that she was her own text. Younger than, but like other emergent 1990s filmmakers-of-color (Lourdes Portillo, Marlon Riggs, Rea Tajiri), she blended documentary and autobiography but also added popular generic approaches. She counted 1970s TV sitcoms among her creative influences as well as Black/feminist/LGBTQ theory, documentary, and experimental film (McHugh 339). The Dunyementaries activate an imaginative, lived version of Patricia Hill Collins's Black feminist standpoint theory within the format of a TV sitcom. Collins identified Black feminism as a situated knowledge arising from intersectional oppressions and histories and the coping mechanisms those entailed (24, 270–271). In their composition and address, the Dunyementaries mobilize pleasure, situated knowledge, and wit to fulfill Dunye's goal to make "her life and her community accessible and familiar in an ongoing experimental sitcom of black lesbian life" (Dunye, qtd in McHugh 340).

This goal was aesthetic as much as political. Dunye wanted her films to evince an active, creative Black feminism doing things with form – an aesthetics-in-action. With Barbara Christian, she believed that, for African Americans, theory was a verb, not a noun (52) and, along lines contemporaneously outlined by Valerie Smith, Dunye mined a distinctly African American documentary impulse that employed "the fictional or artificial in an attempt to enter suppressed narratives into public discourse" (57). Exemplified in her final Dunyementary, *TWW* documents aspiring filmmaker "Cheryl's" search for a creative predecessor, an uncredited African American actress who played mammies in 1930s plantation films. At the end of the film, Dunye narrates "Faith Richardson's" biography in voiceover as we see the visual evidence of Richardson's life that Cheryl (as a character) has unearthed and that Dunye (as director) documents. A final text transforms the film's meaning and its mode: "Sometimes you have to create your own history. The Watermelon Woman is a fiction."

TWW familiarizes its spectators with Cheryl's painstaking (re)search, implicating them in her (historiographic) longing and frustrated desire "to inhabit grand narratives of American history and American cinematic history" (Francis 47). At the same time, the film, through Dunye's creative ruse, gives us to understand precisely and affectively what is false and lacking in those very histories (Sexton 162). Recalling Barbara Christian's idea that Black women theorize through a riddle, hieroglyph, and "the stories we create" (52), Dunye's aesthetic practice also anticipates, in "fake documentary" form (Juhasz 7), the contemporary speculative historiography practiced by Black cultural theorist Saidiya Hartman. Hartman imagines and documents "intimate" and "alternative modes of life" lived by "anonymous" Black women and children whose images she finds in early 20th C archival photographs (*Wayward Lives* 19).[1] Dunye invents and Hartman imagines the undocumented lives of Black creatives, women, and girls from and in defiance of sparse or nonexistent archives. Each thereby advisedly ignores "knowledge-based" distinctions materially, institutionally, and discursively maintained between theory and creative practice, documentary and fiction, history, and imagination – epistemological binaries that underwrite and validate "objective" histories that are nevertheless "fake" or false for many (Juhasz 17–18; Sexton 162–163). These binaries, vested in the privilege of abstract, "objective" perspective and material documentation, render Black women and lesbians, among others, historically and legally illegible, unable to be seen or heard.

Dunye, in a generative and witty act of auto-branding, labeled her films up through *TWW* "Dunyementaries," capturing their paradoxical critical blend of the popular, funny, and profound. She replaced the "docu" of nonfiction filmmaking (evidence and proof that certifies its facticity and truth) with "Dunye," putting her name to what referent-based nonfiction filmmaking obscures, cannot see, could not document. "Dunye" references text, standpoint, and historical lacunae, a Black lesbian creative perspective made genre. However playful, the Dunyementaries successively challenge documentary's epistemic procedures for validating so-called objective or historical knowledge (Collins 271); accordingly, they culminate in *TWW*'s witty but incisive indictment of American (film) history and representation.

Along these lines, Dunye notably distinguishes her aesthetics-in-action from (white) modernist experimental film's formalist efforts to *defamiliarize* or make representation difficult; rather, she commits to *familiarize* audiences with her community, knowledge, and yearning through an accessible, comedic popular genre (the sitcom). Her intermedial designation of the Dunyementaries as "an ongoing experimental sitcom" also provocatively (and proleptically) renders her independent films' accessibility in the idiom of TV; the sitcom is domestic, serial, and a part of everyday life. Writing that "Cheryl Dunye's transformational lesbian films of the 1990s fit almost seamlessly with HBO's current slate of first-person stories, such as Issa Rae's *Insecure* (2016–2021) and Terence Nance's *Random Acts of Flyness* (2018–2022)," Terri Francis underscores the Dunyementaries' intermedial significance and legacy (45). They register the different experience, status and history of Black lesbian subjectivity as a "part of everyday life," delivered through an emergent critical genre shaped by familiarization, imagination, and pleasure. They thereby innovate independent experimental and autobiographical filmmaking through their engagement with Black feminist theory, political thought, pleasure, and humor.

In her second feature film, *SI*, Dunye builds upon these critical storytelling aesthetics and production strategies she had developed to innovate the WIP film, merging it with maternal melodrama and re-shaping both through her aesthetics-in-action.

Getting "Inside" Outside the Text

Two intentions, one familial and autobiographical, the other political, motivated Cheryl Dunye to make *SI*. Recently a mother herself, she wanted to explore Black lesbian maternity and to continue to fulfill her careerlong commitment to represent marginalized women (St. John 329). Albeit inspired by her personal experience, *SI* is a fiction film, the first in which Dunye did not star. Focusing on incarcerated lesbians of color, among the most marginalized of women, she determined to explore imprisoned maternity. Her title, *Stranger Inside*, evokes many dimensions of her subject, the film, and its production, as well as of her *oeuvre*, in her ongoing efforts to familiarize the marginalized or strange to her audiences.

Motherhood begins from pregnancy, a state not unlike having a stranger, both intimate and unknown, inside, who becomes family/familiar upon parturition.

SI's backstory, a daughter taken from her mother at birth, separates biological and familial maternity and enables a number of Dunye's aesthetic innovations. It embeds a generic stranger, maternal melodrama, within a WIP film, the prison context throwing into relief the whiteness, heteronormalcy, and material privilege assumed both by maternal melodrama and commodified, sentimentalized cultural mores concerning maternity.[2] In *SI*, the maternal melo plot involves adult daughter Treasure seeking a mother she has only seen in pictures and never met. She regards her transfer from juvenile detention to the State Women's Facility as "goin' home."

Maria St. John indicates how Dunye's generic hybrid maps domestic onto carceral space:

> [T]he 'inside' of prison is generally constructed as being the farthest place possible from the domestic interior of the U.S. living room...But Dunye's production calls into question such cultural geographies and emphatically portrays prison as a home space, a place of family, and a domestic space, at the same time that it documents the deracination, the attacks on kinship, and the institutional colonization of the psyche perpetuated by the prison system.
>
> *(325–326)*

The WIP genre provides Dunye an apt exploratory vehicle by merit of its subject, location, narratives, and primary characters. As Suzanna Walters has written, WIP films "elaborate fully the creation of the marginal subject," where differences of race, sexuality, poverty and exploitation "literally explode and proliferate" (106). Generically marginalized as B melodrama, exploitation, earnest social problem film, or some combination thereof, WIP films, unlike most industry genres, pass the Bechdel test with flying colors.[3] Feminist and queer scholars have noted that, despite its often-exploitive focus on torture and sadism, WIP films, by subject and necessity, feature otherwise un-or underrepresented subjects: women's relationships with each other; their communities "inside"; and the female gaze, as women and their gazes at each other predominate (Mayne 117–118; Walters 106–107).

Nevertheless, *SI* pointedly alters other WIP film conventions concerning characterization, embodiment, and gender. They typically feature a naïve protagonist, wrongly charged or unwitting accomplice, coming into the prison's alien, hostile community of women who are nothing like her except one or two highly vulnerable, often mentally ill, who are. She must choose to "get tough or get killed" as Kitty (Betty Garde) tells Marie Allen (Eleanor Powell) in *Caged* (1950). Entering an innocent, the protagonist leaves prison hardened, "masculinized," and destined for a life of crime. By contrast, Treasure's innocence or criminality is incidental to *Stranger*'s plot. Indeed, whereas WIP films generally tell inmates' criminal backstories, *SI*, familiarizing incarcerated Black lesbians to audiences, narrates their family stories before and after they arrive in prison.

The film uses another trope of WIP film – lesbian desire and embodiment – to recast the mother/daughter dyad and indeed, the gender binary, in its centering of incarcerated Black lesbian butches on a continuum of female masculinity. Jack Halberstam writes:

> The women's prison film as genre – from John Cromwell's *Caged* (1950) to Jonathan Demme's *Caged Heat* (1974) – has circled obsessively around the idea of lesbianism while depicting relations between women as coercive: part of a general mood of perversion and pathology. Paying homage to the genre, *Stranger* makes butch-femme culture both central to prison life and crucial to survival.
>
> (qtd. in St. John 327)

Ambiguating biological (gender/sex/maternity) and moral/legal (good/innocent) binaries with the realities of choice, desire, coercion, and necessity, the film also thwarts, as did *TWW*, other binaries and distinctions upon which white privilege depends. In TWW, these had to do with history, representation, documentary, genealogy, and the archive. *Stranger* maintains the focus on genealogy and explores genre, incarcerated Black lesbian maternity, and their structural, representational relationship to racialized social status and citizenship. St John writes: "Binary oppositions such as guilt versus innocence, sociality versus criminality, naivete versus cynicism, and black versus white, which have organized traditional prison films, refuse in this one to stand apart; instead they mingle, merge, and mutate before Dunye's lens" (327). The most crucial binary that Dunye refuses in *SI* is inside and outside – the text, prison, art, and social impact.

If the Dunyementaries' aesthetics-in-action reflexively created a genre from Dunye's "I/eye" within her community, *SI*'s innovation derives from that aesthetic reflexivity directed to social impact. Her aesthetical ethos compelled Dunye to "get inside" so as to write her protagonists, characters, and script from incarcerated women's perspectives. In St. John's interview, Dunye recounted extensive preproduction research tracking down myriad newspaper articles on incarcerated women and interviewing lawyers, inmates, and social workers (329). While such research might characterize any fictional director's efforts for "realistic" representation, Dunye went much further. She consulted scholar and prison abolitionist Angela Davis and Rhodessa Jones, director of *The Medea Project: Theater for Incarcerated Women* (328). Most importantly, she herself "got inside," running an intensive screenwriting workshop for 12 inmates at the Minnesota Shakopee Correctional Facility for Women in exchange for their input on *SI*'s screenplay. She did readings of the script for the prison population and then extended preproduction so that *SI*'s cast members and crew could get inside and tour prisons before filming. And she cast inmates, who had completed their time, in her film (329–330).

Dunye's commitment to inmates' voices, experiences, and relationships shapes *SI*'s borrowings and innovations of maternal melodrama and its form. From the outset, she emphasizes confinement, metaphorical in classical maternal melodrama, and actual in prison. Save for the opening shot, she limits our visual and experiential perspective "inside," confined with the inmates. We look, with Treasure, out of the prison van's steel-meshed windows at highly obstructed views of streets, buildings, and people "outside." We watch her and three other inmates go through intake, naked and under the surveillance of male supervisor Nelson: fingerprints; rules and regulations; shower and cavity search; uniform issue. There is one speculum for the four cavity searches. When the one white woman objects – "you can't do that – it is unsanitary" – she is put in the hole for the night. Similarly, when Treasure meets her mates in Cell 2, the fact that there are only four beds for five inmates motivates her to ingeniously and successfully negotiate for one of the bunks.

While the intake sequences depict systemic violations of gendered privacy, basic hygiene, sufficient space, and the inmates' utter lack of recourse against ill or sadistic treatment, they do so from the inmates' "insider" point of view, as matter-of-fact challenges that must be navigated and mastered. In this regard, the film notably avoids the melodramatic pathos and moral outrage the maternal melo conventionally generates, usually by the audience knowing more than some or all of the characters or by the protagonist/mother's affectively motivated muteness to protect her child (*Stella Dallas*; *Madame X*). Instead, these sequences document the varied approaches and outcomes (protest and punishment; ingenuity and negotiation; resilience and accommodation) available to inmates. The characters know more than the audience about how to survive. Significantly, the muteness cultivated in prison is pragmatic (do not protest or you will be punished), survival-oriented rather than moral or pathetic.

The body of the film interweaves routine events (work, exercise, therapy, sex, sleep) and locations (laundry, prison yard, library, chapel, and cells) of inmates' daily lives with the film's maternal melodrama plot – Treasure's quest to make a family with Brownie. But the prison context in which this plot unfolds reconstrues the familial bonds, motivations, and temporality conventional to the maternal melo. *Stranger*'s plot contrasts family by nature or blood, the melodramatic (and social) standard from which Treasure has been excluded and for which she deeply yearns, with family made "inside" by necessity, choice, coercion, or "audition." As a biological daughter, Treasure does not have a claim to Brownie's maternal bond, but must compete, initially unsuccessfully, with the daughters Brownie has "made" in prison – Kit (Rain Phoenix) and Scar (Alma Yvonne Dixon). They are bound to her in instrumental relations of protection and loyalty, fiercely held and at fatal cost, if betrayed.

Brownie first rebuffs Treasure's claim to be her "blood," but later apologizes as she embraces and comforts Treasure, who weeps in her arms. It is a powerful moment. The two become inseparable, and we see, over a number of scenes, that Brownie's maternal affections and actions (she arranges for Treasure to get a Walkman) are tied to instrumental motivations and increasingly more extreme expectations: that Treasure deal drugs; beat up the "Spanish girls" who stole

Brownie's money; and finally, that she "take down" her rival and putative sister, Kit. Survival dictates that familial and criminal bonds be interchangeable, instrumental, powerful, and yet mercurial. Brownie exhibits sudden and violent rages – she stabs Kit in the thigh when her take is "short" and tries to push Treasure's face into a broken glass when she thinks Treasure has betrayed her. We learn that Brownie spent a year "in the hole" that "messed with her head" and that, similar to Treasure, Brownie "never had no mother, no family."

In the Treasure/Brownie relationship, *SI* mobilizes a melodramatic temporality, of "ceaselessly returning to a prior state" rather than the cinematic narrative's "progressive movement to an end that is significantly different from the beginning" (Modleski 330). In an immediate sense, Brownie represents one very probable future for Treasure, a regressive return. But situated within that personal regression is a systemic and institutional one. Many scholars of Dunye's first two features have noted they engage Black kinship, genealogy, and maternity linked to their precarious status in US history and culture (Michel, Sexton, and Winokur). If explicit in *TWW*, *SI* implicitly positions prison as a material legacy of US slavery, a ceaseless return "to a prior state." Like slavery, the prison industrial complex has devastated Black maternity and family through systemic resource deprivation (housing, education, job opportunities, and health care) and the overt coercion of the prison system while dominant cultural narratives and their affective attentions and imperatives have largely ignored the Black femininity, maternity, and queer sexualities upon which Dunye's films focus.

Conclusion: Ins and Outs

In the interlocutions her aesthetics in action create between fiction and fact, imagination and history, melodrama and the WIP film, Cheryl Dunye projects the anecdotal, particular, and seemingly individual maternal melo of Treasure and Brownie into trenchant critical and historical dimension. Scholars speak to her singular accomplishments in this regard, with Frann Michel citing the amalgam of Dunye's concerns: "African-American women's history, the search for mother figures and the *nature of representation*" (italics mine) (1). Mark Winokur credits Dunye with inaugurating "a genuinely new field of critical archaeology: black lesbian filmmaking" in which she is both inventor/creator by necessity as well as "heir" to her self-creation (231–232). Finally, Jared Sexton argues that her aesthetic practice unsettles normative binaries, activating them in an unstable, intersectional mobility: "*Stranger Inside* is a complex meditation on the psychopolitics of black kinship, and of black maternity specifically, as the disinherited matrix of gendering and ungendering as well as the orientation and disorientation of sexuality" (165).

Notably, each scholar aligns Dunye's insights and contributions, which extend far beyond the "inside" of her film, to her narrative attention to marginalized populations within them. From the margins, *SI* reorients the normative, sentimental, moral and generic, making them seem strange "inside." For Dunye, one of the most eloquent and insightful commentators on her own work, *SI* "was less about right and wrong and more about who is in and who is not" (St. John 336).

Dunye's sustained commitment to familiarization as an aesthetic-in-action leads her to refuse, finally, the distinctions of "inside" and "outside" the text upon which most narrative filmmaking depends. Her creative ambition to make marginalized women familiar in her films determined her filmmaking ethics in this regard: to involve her film subjects, whether her Black lesbian community or incarcerated women, in the process of their own representation. She does not speak "as" or "for" these subjects but rather "with" and "alongside" them, just as she does not speak as or for herself, but similarly with and alongside. She thereby finally evades generic and auteurist categorization (autobiography/ethnography, sitcom, or fiction film) determined by the text's relation to an "outside" referent or creator. Correlatively, the social justice impact of her practice is embedded in the singular respect she accords to what and whom she films and represents – that they are neither subject nor object, neither inside or outside of her filmmaking and film text. From this representational ethic, they make history speak differently, with and against itself, in their own words.

Notes

1 In a 2008 article, "Venus in Two Acts," Hartman's professed research method captures Dunye's creative practice: "History pledges to be faithful to the limits of facts, evidence and the archive. I wanted to write a romance that exceeded the fictions of history...that determine what can be said about the past" (9).
2 WIP films often feature pregnant inmates, miserable when their infant is taken and given to family or strangers outside. Dunye encountered two mother/daughter inmate pairs in her work with the prison population (Willis, cited in Michel 5).
3 The (Alison) Bechdel text for feature films has three measures: are there at least two named women; do they talk to each other; about something besides a man?

Works Cited

Christian, Barbara. "The Race for Theory." *Cultural Critique*, no. 6, Spring 1987, pp. 51–63.
Collins, Patricia Hill. *Black Feminist Thought: Knowledge, Consciousness and the Politics of Empowerment*. 2nd ed., Routledge, 2000.
Frances, Terri. "Structural Laughter and Constructed Intimacies: The Self-Reflexivity of Cheryl Dunye." *Film Quarterly*, vol. 72, no. 2, pp. 45–54.
Halberstam, Jack. "Doing Time: Cheryl Dunye Makes a Black Lesbian Version of the Women's Prison Film." *Girlfriends*, Aug. 2001, p. 28.
Hartman, Saidiya. "Venus in Two Acts." *Small Axe*, vol. 12, no. 2, June 2008, pp. 1–14.
———. *Wayward Lives, Beautiful Experiments*. W.W. Norton, 2019.
Heller, Dana. "Films." *The Essential HBO Reader*, edited by Gary Edgerton and Jeffrey Jones. University Press of Kentucky, 2008, pp. 42–51.
Holmlund, Chris. "Introduction." *Contemporary American Independent Film*, edited by Chris Holmlund and Justin Wyatt. Routledge, 2005, pp. 1–19.
Juhasz, Alexandra. "Introduction." *F is For Phony: Fake Documentary and Truth's Undoing*, edited by Alexandra Juhasz and Jesse Lerner. University of Minnesota Press, 2006, pp. 1–18.

Mayne, Judith. *Framed: Lesbians, Feminists, and Media Culture*. University of Minnesota Press, 2000.

McHugh, Kathleen. "The Experimental 'Dunyementary': A Cinematic Signature Effect." *Women's Experimental Cinema: Critical Frameworks*, edited by Robin Blaetz. Duke University Press, 2007, pp. 339–359.

Michel, Frann. "Eating the (M)Other: Cheryl Dunye's Feature Films and Black Matrilineage." *Rhizomes*, no. 14, Summer 2007, http://www.rhizomes.net/issue14/michel/michel.html.

Modleski, Tania. "Time and Desire in the Woman's Film." *Home Is Where the Heart Is*, edited by Christine Gledhill. BFI, 1987, pp. 326–338.

Sexton, Jared. *Black Masculinity and the Cinema of Policing*. Palgrave Macmillan, 2017.

Smith, Valerie. "The Documentary Impulse in Contemporary African American Film." *Black Popular Culture: A Project by Michele Wallace*, edited by Gina Dent. Bay Press, 1992, pp. 56–64.

St. John, Maria. "Making Home/Making "Stranger": An Interview with Cheryl Dunye." *Feminist Studies*, vol. 30, no. 2, Summer 2004 (The Prison Issue), pp. 325–338.

Walters, Suzanna Danuta. "The (R)evolution of Women-in-Prison Films." *Reel Knockouts: Violent Women in the Movies*, edited by Martha McCaughey and Neal King. University of Texas Press, 2001, pp. 106–123.

Willis, Holly. "Breaking Out: Cheryl Nabs Big Audiences on the Small Screen with Her HBO Prison Feature *Stranger Inside*." *The Independent Film and Video Monthly*, vol. 24, no. 3, June 2001, pp. 32–35.

39

FAR FROM HEAVEN (2002)

Ken Feil

When *Far from Heaven* opened to critical fanfare in 2002, one indisputable attraction remained auteur director Todd Haynes's queering of Douglas Sirk's classical Hollywood melodramas. The 1970s critical discourse had exalted Sirk, once presumed a genre hack, as an auteur; the founding argument was that the director cued Brechtian irony and ideological critique for one set of spectators cognizant of Sirk's modernist intentions, and to the unknowing, presumably female fans of melodrama, cued the suspension of disbelief (Selig 14). In addition, the 1970s Sirk critical discourse quieted queer pleasures, despite the camp readings of Sirk films offered by Rainer Werner Fassbinder, the celebrated, openly gay New German Cinema filmmaker who also remade Sirk's *All That Heaven Allows* (1955) as *Ali: Fear Eats the Soul* (1974) (Fassbinder 22–24; Dyer 183–184; Feil 39–41).[1]

Amid the flourishing of feminist cultural studies in the 1990s and the advent of queer theory, critical reassessments of Sirk coincided with the revisionary work of the New Queer Cinema.[2] One obvious example, Mark Rappaport's 1992 found-footage video *Rock Hudson's Home Movies*, reviews the actor's oeuvre to exhume traces of the movie star's gayness as well as the machinery of the Hollywood closet; Sirk's relationship with Hudson and clips from his nine Hudson films figure centrally in Rappaport's video essay.

Buoyed by the commercialization of queer filmmaking in the aftermath of the New Queer Cinema, *Far from Heaven* engages the feminist and queer interventions into Sirk and Hollywood melodrama. The film, however, fails to explore issues of race in a similar fashion (Willis 119–120). While Haynes, channeling Sirk through Fassbinder, creates a cinematic world infused with a beautifully detailed mise-en-scène disturbed by queer desire, the racial politics of the film are played out in much safer territory. To a large extent, the aesthetic perfection of Edward Lachman's cinematography, veteran composer Elmer Bernstein's score, and the carefully patterned use of color create a film that seems to fetishize the

FIGURE 39.1 Adapting Fassbinder's theatricalized, camp revision of Sirk, Haynes both curates the gay cinematic archive and emphasizes the constructed, artificial social barriers between Raymond and Cathy that ultimately render their utopian romance impossible.

aesthetics over and above the narrative and ideological strands created by Haynes and his creative team.

Set in 1957, the film focuses on upper-middle-class housewife and mother Cathy Whitaker (Julianne Moore), whose mechanical existence in suburban Hartford, Connecticut, suddenly starts to malfunction. Husband Frank (Dennis Quaid) reveals his homosexuality, and Cathy's burgeoning relationship with Raymond Deagan (Dennis Haysbert), the Whitaker's widower gardener, results in Cathy's alienation from the white, bourgeois elite of Hartford, the racist harassment of Raymond's daughter Sarah (Jordan Puryear), Raymond's estrangement from Hartford's Black community, and Raymond's decision to relocate to Baltimore.

Reviewers and scholarly critics alike confirm the film's simulation of several Sirk films: *All That Heaven Allows*, its love affair between a wealthy widow (Jane Wyman) and her younger gardener (Hudson); *Imitation of Life* (1959), its subplot about racism, passing, and interracial desire; and *Written on the Wind* (1956), its hyperbolic drama of sexual frustration and failed masculinity.[3] Along with Sirk's films, Fassbinder's *Ali: Fear Eats the Soul* is also frequently cited for inclusion in the "archive," Glyn Davis's expression for the intertextual network of films (and other texts) that Haynes "plundered and appropriated" to create *Far from Heaven* (Davis 60).[4] "Archival" filmmaking – continuing and expanding on Davis's concept – flourished among independent filmmakers of the 1990s and 2000s such as Steven Soderbergh and Quentin Tarantino who demonstrated both their knowledge of film history as well as their artistic virtuosity by referencing classic and cult movies as well as mimicking their tropes and styles.[5]

Haynes's archival project in *Far from Heaven* more closely resonates with Ann Cvetkovich's perception of independent lesbian films and videos of the 1990s that "demonstrate the profoundly affective power of [...] an archive of sexuality and gay and lesbian life, which must preserve and produce not just knowledge but feeling" (109–110). A queer film's archive also serves a related function pertaining to authorship: the formation of an intertextual "canon" of texts, which reflects both the queer artist's "readerly act of consumption as production" and a broader history of LGBTQIA+ fan culture (Gerstner 15, 18–20; Cvetkovich 116). Haynes's archive nevertheless represents a specific queer fan formation: post-Stonewall gay culture and identity politics, in which the specificity of sexuality overshadowed the sense of intersectionality and preempted the critique of white male hegemony within gay identity politics. These limits of *Far from Heaven* remain largely unexamined, along with their impact on perceptions of the film's critical and affective contours.

I am arguing for a tour through *Far from Heaven*'s queer archive both unfettered by auteurism and situated squarely in the context of queer independent film and video history. Considering *Far from Heaven* together with two "archive films" produced during the New Queer Cinema of the 1990s – Rappaport's *Rock Hudson's Home Movies* and Cheryl Dunye's *The Watermelon Woman* (1996) – this discussion both draws forward approaches to cinematic appropriation found in several contemporaneous independent films and challenges the normative limits of auteurist approaches that have more commonly curated the queer media archive, established authorial pantheons (including Haynes's), and defined media canons.

From Hudson to Heaven

At first glance, *Far from Heaven* appears an inheritor of the camp interventions of *Rock Hudson's Home Movies*, which, according to Mary Desjardins, "suggests that it is possible to read, or perhaps reread, what were once thought to be signs of heterosexual masculinity as Hudson's signature of a gay authorial position" (210). Davis reasons similarly that *Far from Heaven* employs homosexuality as "a strategy of fantastic re-imagining" involving "audience knowledge about Hudson's real identity, and the camp appreciation of Sirk's films" (37).

A kind of replay of codes of the closet – the performance of passing, older/younger male pairings, secretive glances, and encrypted communication – occurs in *Far from Heaven*. Frank, vacationing with Cathy in Miami after enduring psychotherapy to "cure" him of homosexuality, furtively admires a young blond man in a large family staying at the same hotel. At the hotel's New Year's Eve fete, the family proceeds by Frank and Cathy, and after Frank notices the "prettiest" of the sons (in Haynes's description in the screenplay), eyeing him with interest, he proclaims to the father, "You have a lovely family." (Haynes).[6] Sharon Willis's argument that *Far from Heaven*'s teasing out of the "ironic potential" (153) underpinning Sirk's melodramas applies just as much to *Rock Hudson's Home Movies*, insofar as both films unearth the irony of heteronormative gravity set against insight into closeted queer desire.

Far from Heaven nevertheless distinguishes itself by meticulously remaking the sights and sounds of a Sirk melodrama and by extending its identity politics. Replacing Hudson with Dennis Haysbert as the gardener and moral center of the story, Lynne Joyrich explains, the film connects the taboo element of homosexual desire repressed in Sirk's Hudson vehicles to the plotline about interracial desire (189). Acknowledging "the richness of this layered archive," Willis nevertheless points to one of the pitfalls of this strategy: "*Far from Heaven* seems to confine itself to examining the terms of Sirk's model rather than those of interracial melodrama"; as a result, the storyline involving Raymond "faithfully reproduces the racial imaginary of its diegetic period," "the Poitier effect," which renders Raymond "innocent," isolated, and "a screen for white projections" (123, 155). Raymond bears "the burden of a certain unironic authenticity," furthermore, "largely lacking the critical mediation that shapes *Far from Heaven*'s rewriting of Sirk" because "the familiar tropes of Poitier's films largely escape [*Far from Heaven*'s] ironies" (121–122). A similar polarity emerges briefly in *Rock Hudson's Home Movies* during a clip featuring Hudson and Sidney Poitier from *Something of Value* (1957), a drama about the Mau Mau Uprising in Kenya. Without referring to the colonialist racial politics of the film, the clip hones in on Hudson and Poitier evoking two star-crossed lovers: Hudson implores, "We'll start over again. This time it'll be different." "No," states Poitier, "It is too late for you and me." Hudson's imagined critical commentary follows, which reinstates the video's colorblindness simultaneous to revealing Hudson's camp insight and his costar Poitier's unawareness: "Boy! It was never this deep or steamy with Doris" quips Rock, referring to the Hudson/Doris Day romantic comedies.

A disparity of knowledge and performative agency indeed emerges in *Far from Heaven* correlating with Black heterosexual authenticity and white gay performativity, within the diegesis as well as in terms of Haynes's archival filmmaking. Although Raymond reveals a mischievous recognition of social barriers in the scene at Ernie's Bar and Grill, a Black establishment where he takes Cathy, Raymond's transparent sincerity soon returns concurrent with the spiraling strains of heterosexual romance, stylized social commentary, and movie references reflective of Haynes's gay film archive. Amid a chilly reception from the regulars and Ernie's and Cathy's ensuing embarrassment, Raymond employs playful irony to cultivate an alternative social space. "Well I hope you find this very amusing," mutters a mortified Cathy, to which Raymond replies grinning, "What do you mean? It's a very welcoming place!" After getting their drinks, Raymond's toast cheerfully acknowledges their now mutual positioning as social deviants: "Here's to being the only one." Raymond's humor finally encourages Cathy to lose her patronizing formality, but ironic awareness rapidly dissolves when Cathy invokes romantic melodrama: "Would you [...] Ask me to dance?" When the couple dance, bathed in blue light and splashes of white reflected off a glitterball, numerous critics have observed that the stylized shot quotes a similar moment in Fassbinder's *Ali: Fear Eats the Soul*, which also reinterprets the relationship from the Sirk original as doomed due to racist and classist social structure (Gill 91–93; Davis 60; Joyrich 212). Adapting Fassbinder's theatricalized, camp revision of Sirk, Haynes both curates the gay cinematic archive and emphasizes the constructed, artificial social barriers between Raymond and Cathy that render sustaining this utopian moment of togetherness impossible.

This differs from the complexly campy, misogynistic outburst that Frank performs at the Whitaker's seasonal party earlier in the film, where he sits cross-legged and bitchily, drunkenly derides Cathy after their guests compliment her beauty: "Smoke and mirrors, fellas! That's all it is. You should see her without her face on!" Frank's irony bursts out as, not the peacebuilding yet provocative humor Raymond mobilizes, nor the liberatory "new" camp of the queer, AIDS-activist era characteristic of *Rock Hudson's Home Movies,* but a pre-Stonewall variety of gay camp wit, fueled by resentment toward enforced secrecy and hegemonic gender roles, yet targeted at women (Doty 86–87; Musto). Inasmuch as the film renders Frank unsympathetic, especially when he smacks Cathy after the guests leave, such acting out unearths the tyranny of the closet, the self-hatred it imposes, and the misogyny with which it works in concert. Raymond's brief moment of humor, by contrast, hits out at no one and disavows the appearance of a threat, making light of it. Where Raymond's humor enables a romantic fantasy momentarily to unfold, his agency is for naught since their romance is doomed to failure. Also trapped, Frank nevertheless signals Sirkian trouble in bourgeois paradise and resonates with Haynes's role as social critic and curator of an archive of gay culture.[7]

Queering Hollywood's Racialized Gazes

Far from Heaven inspired what John Gill calls "intertextual ping-pong matches" among critics (103), a testament to the archival dimension of the film and its writer-director's role as a gay film fan. Implementing "elements and tactics from [...] gay/queer alternative and art-house films" familiar to "subcultural denizens and the art-house elite" (Davis 107), Haynes's film remained in keeping with archival queer films and videos of the 1990s. Beyond *Rock Hudson's Home Movies,* which has been significantly addressed above, this also encompasses the lesbian documentaries on which Cvetkovich concentrates as well as numerous other works, including Isaac Julien's signature documentary *Looking for Langston* (1989), which combines found footage and stylized tableaus to register historical and contemporary expressions of Black gay culture and identity; Leslie Singer's *Taking Back the Dolls* (1994), a queercore parody of *Valley of the Dolls* (1967) that inventories and quotes from a range of popular culture; and a film explored further below, Dunye's *The Watermelon Woman*, which searches for Black lesbian cultural history through a narrative combining satire, romantic comedy, documentary, and the parodic imitation of classical Hollywood melodrama.

The problem presented by *Far from Heaven* pertains, paraphrasing Jack Halberstam, to "the excessively small archive" sampled in the film, a "canonical archive" of post-WWII white, male, gay culture that narrows both the archaeological revelations and the "archive of feelings" the film's intervention represents (109). This lacuna not only reinstates the canonical archive (Sirk, Fassbinder) but, by disclaiming newer participants from the New Queer Cinema (NQC), also undercuts the innovations of film form and address that these fresh works incited. *Tongues Untied* (1989) and *Looking for Langston*, for instance, rethought the patterns and power relationships governing the representation of interracial desire and, as Kobena Mercer argued regarding these incipient NQC films,

> as black lesbians and gay men we cannot separate the different aspects of our identities precisely because we value both our blackness and our homosexuality. It is this contrast between both/and against either/or that is at stake in the problem of 'identity politics' – in the pejorative sense of the term.
>
> *(239)*

Far from Heaven replicates the either/or by relocating gay desire and camp irony from Hudson's gardener in the Sirk film to Frank, a gesture that renders the character Raymond solidly heterosexual and unambiguous. These maneuvers preserve the constructed equations of "queer" with "white" and "Black" with "heterosexual," a dichotomy that writer-director Dunye scrutinizes in *Watermelon Woman* through the replication and dismantling of Hollywood norms. Dunye avoids, furthermore, the "left-wing melancholy" that Richard Dyer locates in Fassbinder's films (176) and Haynes reproduces in *Far from Heaven* through Raymond and Cathy's doomed interracial relationship.

Dunye's *The Watermelon Woman* presents a forerunner of sorts to *Far from Heaven*, most evidently by simulating classical Hollywood film styles in addition to independently produced "race movies" made for Black audiences prior to integration. In Dunye's film, the protagonist Cheryl (played by Dunye), a documentary filmmaker, conducts archival research on fictional Black actress Fae Richards (Lisa Marie Bronson), nicknamed "the Watermelon Woman" and rumored to be the lover of a fictional white director, Martha Page (Alexandra Juhasz).[8] As Cvetkovich opines, Dunye "weaves a visual archive of old photographs, film clips, and newsreels into its drama, simulating the look of these genres so well that it is hard to believe that Fae Richards is Dunye's creation and not an actual historical figure" (108).[9] More directly than Haynes's reflection and refraction of Sirk, Dunye enlists Fae's relationship to Page to scrutinize an emergent queer canon figure in 1990s cinema studies, director Dorothy Arzner. The sole woman among Hollywood directors during the first two decades of the sound era, Arzner's films engaged in "lesbian irony," according to Judith Mayne, which unsettled Hollywood's heteronormative male gaze through subcultural coding and narratives that emphasized nurturing, homoerotic women's friendships (Mayne 118–122).

The sense of irony regarding the history of racist imagery that both Dunye's protagonist and film exude also helps waylay melancholy, self-righteous piety, or sentimentality. A few scenes after announcing plans to make a film about Fae, Cheryl interviews Lee (Brian Freeman), a Black gay collector of "race memorabilia" with a vast home archive. Lee's tour concludes with snippets of actual archival footage from race movies, then the scene cuts to Cheryl with a bandanna wrapped around her head, perched next to the TV as the scene from *Plantation Dreams* replays, jokingly mouthing Fae's dialogue. In contrast to the overall earnest tone of *Far from Heaven*,[10] *The Watermelon Woman*'s subplots also ring with irony, about Cheryl's friendship with filmmaking partner Tamara (Valarie Walker) and her romance with a white woman, Diana (Guinevere Turner). Where Tamara cannot grasp Cheryl's interest in "mammy shit from the '30s" despite Fae's lesbian liaison with Martha, Diana replicates the racialized power dynamic between Fae and Martha by objectifying Cheryl and trying to take over her film project. The film concludes with Cheryl's short "documentary" about Fae Richards, and a final title card informing, "Sometimes you have to create your own history. The Watermelon Woman is fiction."

Both *Rock Hudson's Home Movies* and *The Watermelon Woman* exemplify New Queer Cinema "archive films" that, beyond the familiar examples of cinematic intertextuality in 1990s independent cinema, set the scene for *Far from Heaven*: flaunting cinematic influences as well as scrutinizing them and devising critical interventions into classical cinema's racism and heteronormativity through stylized imitations of genre norms, both revising and updating them. Dunye in particular anticipated some of the representational issues that *Far from Heaven* overlooks, related to representing Black subjectivity, Black queer desire, interracial desire, and the queer Hollywood archive: first by fabricating an old Hollywood melodrama indicative of racist, heteronormative social barriers, then enabling her protagonist to critique it, and finally, to transcend it. Haynes's film, on the other hand, is fine with ignoring the underlying racial tensions and fissures, choosing instead to create a fetishized cinematic world through the prism of queer identity politics. Locating *The Watermelon Woman* and *Rock Hudson's Home Movies* within *Far from Heaven*'s archive acknowledges the curatorial power that critics as well as creators have on audiences' perceptions of film history, authorial pantheons, and the contents of media canons.

Notes

1 I remain grateful to the editors Justin Wyatt and Wyatt Phillips for their vital and generous contributions to this chapter.
2 For additional examples of such critical reevaluation, see: Klinger, Henke, and Metz.
3 Frank's alienation at work also recalls the protagonist of Sirk's *There's Always Tomorrow* (1956).
4 Haynes and numerous critics also include here Max Ophüls's Hollywood melodrama, *The Reckless Moment* (1949).

5 For more on this, see Gallagher. New Hollywood directors such as Brian De Palma were also well known for such acts of appropriation, particularly from classical Hollywood cinema.
6 Another gay auteur film materializes in this scene, Luchino Visconti's *Death in Venice* (1971). My thanks to the editors for making this observation.
7 Frank's flare-up is similar to *Imitation of Life,* in which Sarah Jane's outburst at Laura's party strikes as a critique of racist stereotypes and performance as well as Sarah Jane's disrespectfulness (Gates 125; Willis 139).
8 Juhasz was also a producer on the film and is also a film scholar. Her chapter on Stephen Winter's *Jason and Shirley* (2015), which takes up other questions of archives and canons related to independent cinema, can be found in this collection as well.
9 See Kumbier on Dunye's "archive activism" and Francis on Dunye's historical work and genre play. Though a very different film, Dunye's *Stranger Inside* (2001) is addressed by Kathleen McHugh in this collection.
10 Haynes's films are of course ironic, but the critical distance he employs is such that the recognition of irony requires the viewer to be aware of the intertexts he is citing.

Works Cited

Cvetkovich, Ann. "In the Archives of Lesbian Feelings: Documentary and Popular Culture." *Camera Obscura* vol. 17, no. 1, 2002, pp. 107–147.

Davis, Glyn. *Far from Heaven*. Edinburgh University Press, 2011.

Desjardins, Mary R. *Recycled Stars: Female Film Stardom in the Age of Television and Video*. Duke University Press, 2015.

Doty, Alexander. *Making Things Perfectly Queer: Interpreting Mass Culture*. University of Minnesota Press, 1993.

Dyer, Richard. *The Culture of Queers*. Routledge, 2002.

Fassbinder, Rainer Werner. "Fassbinder on Sirk." Translated by Thomas Elsaesser. *Film Comment*, vol. 11, no. 6, 1975, pp. 22–24.

Feil, Ken. "Ambiguous Sirk-Camp-Stances: Gay Camp and the 1950s Melodramas of Douglas Sirk." *The Spectator*, vol. 15, no. 1, 1994, pp. 31–49.

Francis, Terri. "Structural Laughter and Constructed Intimacies: The Self-Reflexivity of Cheryl Dunye." *Film Quarterly*, vol. 72, no. 2, 2018, pp. 45–54.

Gallagher, Mark. "Discerning Independents: Steven Soderbergh and Transhistorical Taste Cultures." *American Independent Cinema: Indie, Indiewood and Beyond*, edited by Geoff King et al. Routledge, 2013, pp. 83–95.

Gates, Racquel J. *Double Negative: The Black Image and Popular Culture*. Duke University Press, 2018.

Gerstner, David A. "The Practices of Authorship." *Authorship and Film*, edited by David A. Gerstner and Janet Staiger, 1st ed., Routledge, 2003, pp. 3–25.

Gill, John. *Far from Heaven*. BFI, 2011.

Halberstam, Jack. *The Queer Art of Failure*. Duke University Press, 2011.

Haynes, Todd. *Far from Heaven, Safe, and Superstar: Three Screenplays*. Grove/Atlantic, Inc., 2003. ProQuest Ebook Central, http://ebookcentral.proquest.com/lib/emerson/detail.action?docID=5755213.

Henke, Richard. "Imitation of Life." *Jump Cut*, no. 39, 1994. http://www.ejumpcut.org/archive/onlinessays/JC39folder/imitationLife.html.

Joyrich, Lynne. "Written on the Screen: Mediation and Immersion in *Far from Heaven*." *Camera Obscura*, vol. 19, no. 3, 2004, pp. 186–219.

Klinger, Barbara. *Melodrama and Meaning: History, Culture, and the Films of Douglas Sirk*. Indiana University Press, 1994.

Kumbier, Alana. "Inventing History: *The Watermelon Woman* and Archive Activism." *Ephemeral Material: Queering the Archive*. Litwin Books, 2009. ProQuest Ebook Central, http://ebookcentral.proquest.com/lib/emerson/detail.action?docID=3328242.

Mayne, Judith. "Lesbian Looks: Dorothy Arzner and Female Authorship." *How Do I Look?: Queer Film and Video*, edited by Bad Object Choices. Bay Press, 1991, pp. 103–135.

Mercer, Kobena. "Dark and Lovely Too: Black Gay Men in Independent Film." *Queer Looks: Perspectives on Lesbian and Gay Film*, edited by Martha Gever et al. Routledge, 1993, pp. 238–256.

Metz, Walter. "Pomp(ous) Sirk-umstance: Intertextuality, Adaptation, and *All That Heaven Allows*." *Journal of Film and Video*, vol. 45, no. 4, 1993, pp. 3–20.

Musto, Michael. "Old Camp New Camp." *Out*, April/May 1993, pp. 32–39.

Selig, Michael E. "Contradictions and Reading: Social Class and Sex Class in *Imitation of Life*." *Wide Angle*, vol. 10, no. 4, 1988, pp. 14–22.

Willis, Sharon. *The Poitier Effect: Racial Melodrama and Fantasies of Reconciliation*. University of Minnesota Press, 2015.

40
REAL WOMEN HAVE CURVES (2002)

Mirasol Enríquez

Tired of the lack of stories about Chicanas who look like her and share her experiences, Josefina López began writing the play *Real Women Have Curves* at 18 years of age ("Necessary Theatre"). Produced for the stage in 1990, it immediately gained the attention of Hollywood film executives interested in adapting the play for the big screen. Nothing materialized, however, until after López hired co-writer and producer George LaVoo to assist with the adaptation. LaVoo was able to connect to the art house division of HBO and the film *Real Women Have Curves* (2002) was made under the HBO Films banner, though originally intended solely for cable television. According to López, after 11 years of trying to get the film made, it was finally "made by an independent producer outside of the Hollywood system…. So that movie got made no thanks to Hollywood" (Gelt).

The critical and commercial success that *Real Women Have Curves* (henceforth *RWHC*) enjoyed seemed to signal what many hoped was a change in tides for Latinas in mainstream film. Jillian Báez has noted there were "shifts in Latina representation in mainstream popular culture before and after the 'Latin explosion'" of the 1990s (Báez 112), and she discusses *RWHC* alongside *Selena* (1997) and *Girlfight* (2000) as films in which "moments of female agency among and between Latinas" emerged. Latina filmmakers had, in fact, been making inroads in the world of independent filmmaking since the 1990s, and while not the subject of her study, it is notable that the majority of the other films Báez mentions were examples of this trend and most were directed and/or written by Latinas.[1] Part of what was so exciting about *RWHC* was that independent Latina filmmakers were telling a distinctly Latina story and making their way into the mainstream. Unfortunately, more than 20 years after the film was made, opportunities for Latinas in the film industry have not improved. *RWHC* remains what actor America Ferrera (who played Ana, the film's protagonist) calls "an anomaly" ("PST LA/LA").

DOI: 10.4324/9781003246930-41

FIGURE 40.1 Ana looks longingly at Jimmy as she awaits confirmation that he agrees about their relationship coming to an end.

RWHC is unique in that it both provides a Chicana feminist perspective on a coming-of-age narrative (usually reserved for white girls and, more often, boys) and it was one of HBO's first forays into theatrical distribution. While scholars have explored Hollywood studios' Indiewood shingles as a sort of middle ground that blurs the lines between Hollywood and independent film, *RWHC* was produced in yet another "in-between" context in that period that has generally been under-explored: between film and premium cable television. This chapter highlights the significance of *RWHC*'s position both between Hollywood and independent film and between the Hollywood film and television industries – particularly the "quality" branded channels like HBO, which both helps to explain the unique moment that gave rise to the film and the reasons why similar opportunities have not continued to be available to Latina filmmakers in the years since.

Although López's previous comments regarding the initiative independent producer George LaVoo took with *RWHC* are certainly worth noting, his status as an "independent" should not be overstated. LaVoo had previously worked in acquisitions at Fine Line, the specialty division of New Line Cinema (Chagollan), which was an independent production and distribution company bought by Turner Broadcasting in 1994 and then acquired by the media conglomerate Time Warner in 1996.[2] Although an independent producer at the time he met López, LaVoo would have had an understanding of what studios' specialty divisions were looking for when considering a film for acquisition. This insight was surely invaluable as he and López made adjustments to the screenplay, which they hoped would attract potential investors.

Media industry scholars like Alisa Perren similarly warn against making such clear distinctions between both Hollywood and independent film, and between the film and television industries. In her essay, "A Big Fat Indie Success Story? Press Discourses Surrounding the Making and Marketing of a 'Hollywood' Movie," Perren analyzes the production and distribution of *My Big Fat Greek Wedding* (2002), another film with an ethnic female lead, released just months before *RWHC*. She notes that HBO, "one of the most lucrative subsidiaries of the AOL Time Warner empire" (20), provided half of *My Big Fat Greek Wedding*'s funding. She explains, "from the outset, there was involvement by a Hollywood major – by way of a subsidiary company – in a so-called independent production." *RWHC*, which followed closely on the success of that film, should similarly be considered in terms of its proximity and relation to the mainstream Hollywood industry – neither wholly inside nor wholly outside its structures. This chapter considers *RWHC*'s industrial position and the unique opportunity it represented for Latina filmmakers to reach mainstream audiences from a Chicana/Latina feminist perspective. The film's "in-between" status helps to explain the tension between the strong feminist message in the film and the way it forwards dominant ideological positions that have marginalized Latina/os in Hollywood for so long.

Changing the Story: Perhaps Not Hollywood, but of it

The film *RWHC* is about Ana, a young, overweight, Mexican American woman from the working-class neighborhood of Boyle Heights in Los Angeles. At the end of her senior year, Ana secures a scholarship to Columbia University but struggles against the expectation that she turn down the scholarship to continue helping her sister Estela in her sewing factory. Ana's mother Carmen is particularly invested in making sure Ana fulfills what she sees as her familial obligations in Los Angeles and the two women are at odds throughout the film. Carmen berates Ana incessantly, calling her fat, promiscuous, and selfish. She imposes her patriarchal values on Ana, who questions the expectations placed upon her and women, more generally speaking. Viewers witness Ana transform into a confident young woman who finally moves to New York, against her mother's wishes, to attend college and secure a better future.

The play, by contrast, is a dual-protagonist ensemble piece that explores the lives of five undocumented Latinas who work in a Los Angeles sewing factory. The immigration plot that revolves around Estela, who owns the factory, is not present in the film, and López says they made Ana the protagonist of the film because she was the one who would be most accessible for a "non-Latino audience to go into this world of a sewing factory" ("Necessary Theatre"). She explains it was the film's co-writer LaVoo who "brought a new point of view and helped open [*RWHC*] up more to be accessible to so many people" (Fischer). LaVoo's experience at Fine Line surely equipped him with insight as to how the specifics of Ana's Chicana experience might translate into a more universal story that would resonate with a broader audience. It is notable that the positive response he received to the new screenplay was from HBO Films, another subsidiary of

AOL Time Warner, the same conglomerate under which New Line Cinema (the parent company of LaVoo's previous employer, Fine Line) operated. It is likely then that the film was ultimately produced at least in part as a result of LaVoo's connections to "Indiewood," which Geoff King has defined as the "area in which Hollywood and the independent sector merge or overlap…offer[ing] an attractive blend of creativity and commerce…[where] some of the more innovative and interesting work [is] produced in close proximity to the commercial mainstream" (1).[3]

Colin Callender, then president of HBO Films, aligned the Hollywood-adjacent production company with the kind of artistic freedom previously associated with independent filmmaking. In an interview with the *Village Voice* in 2002 he was paraphrased as claiming: "HBO can provide respite from the dog-eat-dog worlds of creatively conservative Hollywood and financially strapped Indiewood" (Kaufman). Continuing, in his own words, Callender added, "Because we're freed up from the traditional pressures of the box office and the ratings [...] we're making smaller films that are having an increasingly difficult time being made elsewhere" (qtd. in Kaufman). Hispanic Hollywood had grown during the 1980s and 1990s, proving there was an audience for Latina/o-themed films, and Latina celebrities such as Jennifer Lopez and Salma Hayek were being celebrated for their curves in the mainstream media. Callender explains why HBO Films decided to move forward with *RWHC* specifically: "We made [the film] because it was about two things: curvy girls… and a Mexican American world" (Toushin).

With regard to on-screen talent, Patricia Cardoso, the film's director, says it was important to HBO that the cast be Latino. They also made sure that a Latina directed the film, despite the fact that LaVoo expressed interest in doing so. Cardoso was selected to direct the film after a series of interviews with HBO executives, and López is quick to credit her for many details of the story. Similarly, Cardoso is clear that she is not a writer, but explains that López and LaVoo incorporated many of her ideas into the story. Although not Mexican American herself, Cardoso's husband is Mexican and she says she is familiar with the culture. Her background as an anthropologist also compelled her to spend a lot of time doing research, talking with people in Boyle Heights, scouting locations, and walking the streets of the neighborhood. Cardoso added certain cultural details such as Carmen having a pet bird in the film, explaining that every Mexican woman she knows, including her mother-in-law, has a bird. She felt it made Carmen's character more sympathetic, which is important considering that Cardoso was also partially responsible for heightening the animosity between Carmen and Ana in the film. In addition, Cardoso was the one responsible for convincing HBO to include Spanish language dialogue in the film ("Patricia Cardoso: Director"). For example, one of the more tender moments between Ana and her mother takes place in the sewing factory when, after Ana burns herself with the steam iron, Carmen says, "*sana, sana, colita de rana*," which literally translates to "heal, heal, little frog's tail." Spanish-speaking Latina/o viewers recognize this culturally specific detail as something mothers tell their children as they encourage their wounds to heal.

Other script changes, however, including the increased focus on the strained mother/daughter relationship and the introduction of male characters, created contradictions not present in the play. Carmen, in fact, ends up being the one who represents the rule of patriarchy, which undercuts the feminist message of the play in that it reinforces problematic post-feminist patterns in which men are portrayed as being more feminist than women (Báez 123). Also notable in the film adaptation is the absence of a scene in which Carmen discusses her pregnancy with the other women in the sewing factory. In her essay on the play, Lizeth Gutierrez explains,

> While Carmen does not explicitly say that her husband rapes her to get her pregnant, she makes known that she fears her husband in relation to sex and her body. In fact, she gains weight to protect herself from sexual advances by discouraging her husband from touching her again.
>
> *(112)*

The absence of this scene changes the way viewers understand Carmen's relationship to her body and the way that she understands gender roles. In the play, Carmen does not see her body as something for the pleasure of men but, in fact, she attempts to control her own body to avoid abuse. While shifting the focus of the film to a body-positive message that has the potential to resonate across numerous identity markers makes it more accessible to general audiences, removing Carmen's complicated relationship with her body erases the Chicana feminist critique related to domestic and sexual abuse while downplaying "women's homosocial networks," which Gutierrez notes are highlighted in the play (113).

There are, in fact, several ways in which the Chicana feminist critique present in the play was softened in the film adaptation so that the film itself portrays moments that both emphasize and undercut its feminist ideals. Take, for example, what is undoubtedly the most famous scene in the film: While working in the sewing factory on a very hot day, Ana convinces all the women except her mother to strip down to their underwear to cool down. She simultaneously encourages them to recognize "how beautiful [they] are." Cardoso says it was important that the women feel comfortable, so she insisted they choose their own underwear and she took particular care to assure that the women looked beautiful in this scene ("PST LA/LA"). Witnessing the women embrace what society has told them are flaws creates, for the viewers, a powerful sequence. It is empowering, for example, to watch Ana confidently tell her mother, "This is who we are, mama: real women." Yet, it is also disheartening to hear Ana's final words in the scene: "Who cares what we look like *when nobody's watching?*" (author's emphasis) – raising the specter of what it would mean if someone (male, Anglo, etc.) were watching.

The scene which brings Ana's relationship with her Anglo boyfriend to an end is similarly wrought with conflicting messages. On the one hand, it is through Ana's sexual relationship with Jimmy that she gains "her sexuality and her own power" (McClain 748). Ana claims agency when she responds to Jimmy's interest in her, despite what audiences can assume would be her mother's disapproval. She is the one who initiates sex with Jimmy, and her self-acceptance and self-love are clearly exhibited when she insists that they keep the lights on when they sleep together for the first time. She does not allow her mother, boyfriend, or culture to dictate with whom she can and cannot have sex. However, Ana is shown to understand the limits of her control as an overweight, working-class, Mexican American woman when Jimmy says he will write her after he moves away for college and she protests, "Once you get to college, we won't have anything to talk about anyway and, I don't know, you'll probably end up meeting some skinny girl, right?" Jimmy responds, "I'm really gonna miss you." However different the story leading up to this moment may be, Ana cannot – in the end – be partnered with the affluent, Anglo love interest. The conclusion is similar to what many mainstream films have communicated to Latina/os for so long: romantic and social coupling is restricted based on ethnicity and socio-economic class.

The film ends without a happy Hollywood ending, which might have included Ana and Jimmy remaining together or Ana and her mother resolving their issues so that Ana can move to New York City and live happily ever after. Cardoso says that in fact, they "shot a happy ending" but it did not feel right to her so she opted for something "more real" (Calder). Peter Calder quotes Cardoso in relation to the ending: "It's real life: you don't know what's going to happen. I was surprised the producers allowed me to have that ending, but they agreed, so it was a happy ending for me." With regard to the end of the film, media scholar Scott L. Baugh also observes that

> New York has taken Ana from her origins. And yet, perhaps that exactly is the social and political statement behind the story, and one that sets Ana, the story, and the film apart from a longer tradition of Latina cinema.
>
> *(224)*

In this view, what has ended up being one of the most enduring and celebrated Latina films is also one that is out of step with other Latina films and, drawing again on its production history, in line with Hollywood, seen here specifically in the longstanding themes of individualism over family ties and cultural assimilation in pursuit of the American dream.

Conclusion: Recognizing *Real Women*

At the time that LaVoo approached HBO with *RWHC*, the play had proven to be successful and the Latina/o market was of great interest to the film industry. HBO took a chance and planned to do what they do well: address a niche audience via cable. The film was made for the Latina/o audience for under $4M and they planned to cablecast the movie during Hispanic Heritage month ("Patricia Cardoso: Director"). In that sense, there was little risk involved in the production. In his book-length study, *The Promotion and Distribution of U.S. Latino Films* (published in 2011), Henry Puente notes that US Latino films have

> had a difficult time securing distribution deals because these films were unproven commodities. Over time, more studio and studio specialty divisions acquired and circulated more U.S. Latino films ... However, many film distributors do not understand the nuances of the U.S. Latino market and how to promote these films.
>
> *(3)*

Hollywood players such as Miramax and Artisan expressed their interest in distributing *RWHC* but were dissuaded by HBO's insistence that the film premiere on their cable channel (Kaufman). Callender explains, "there had never been a compelling business reason" for HBO to expand into theatrical distribution (Mohr).

RWHC's success at Sundance in January and Cannes in May 2002 proved to Callender that there was an "appetite in the marketplace" for films like it (Mohr). That summer, *My Big Fat Greek Wedding* proved to be a box office success and *RWHC*'s festival success "compelled HBO to develop a distribution partnership with Newmarket," whose Bob Berney had previously spearheaded the marketing campaigns for *My Big Fat Greek Wedding* as well as *Y Tu Mama También* (2001) (Puente 145). HBO Films took a risk on theatrical distribution and Callender said *RWHC* would "likely be a one-off as HBO uses [it] as a 'learning experience'" (Mohr). Berney led the *RWHC* marketing campaign and would go on, three years later, to lead Picturehouse, the "independent" film production and distribution company resulting from the joint venture (under the AOL/Time Warner conglomerate umbrella) between HBO Films and New Line Cinema. To Perren's point, in the early 2000s, just as the boundaries between Hollywood, independence, and Indiewood were difficult at times to draw, so too were the boundaries between film and television.

Though it took a long time to get *RWHC* made and distributed, it took even longer for it to achieve a broader cultural and critical recognition. In 2019, the film was added to the National Film Registry, a list of "culturally, historically or aesthetically significant" American films selected by the Library of Congress. Of additional significance, its selection also made Patricia Cardoso the first Latina director included in the National Film Registry. It is worth noting that the increased recognition came on the heels of controversy surrounding the striking similarities between *RWHC* and the 2017 independent film *Lady Bird* (Greta Gerwig), which was nominated for and won a number of high-profile awards. Like *RWHC*, *Lady Bird* is a coming-of-age story about a young woman who has a troubled relationship with her mother, who is opposed to her going away to college. Both films have been noted for their combination of comedy and drama, and each looks at the struggles their protagonists deal with as a result of their working-class backgrounds. Journalists have written about the similarities between the two films, noting that the main difference is that *Lady Bird* is a film about and directed by white women (Machado). *Lady Bird* also flaunts a "quirky" sensibility that has long been attached to independent film (MacDowell). What marks Ana as being different, however, is not that she is quirky, but that she is Latina, which is also what drew the attention of film production companies looking to reach a niche market.

As this chapter has shown, the filmmakers behind *RWHC* were allowed substantial creative freedom to communicate a message that challenged the status quo on a number of different levels. The film is widely celebrated for its uniquely Latina perspective, but the filmmakers also worked with an eye toward wide distribution, which resulted in some significant changes in the story. As award-winning filmmaker Lourdes Portillo has said about *RWHC*, it "marked and gave us a taste of what the beginning of a feature Latina film industry would be like in the U.S." ("PST LA/LA"). The specific conditions that gave rise to the film in the early 2000s have not been replicated as of yet, and Latinas have remained without a foothold in the US film industry (Enríquez). They do, however, continue to take advantage of opportunities wherever they can be found, whether independent, mainstream, or – as with *Real Women Have Curves* – somewhere in between.

Notes

1 Independent films *Mi Vida Loca* (Alison Anders, 1993) and *Girlfight* (Karyn Kusama), while not directed by Latinas, were directed by women; *Selena* was directed by Latino filmmaker Gregory Nava. Additional films to which Báez refers include *The 24 Hour Woman* (Nancy Savoca, 1995), *Luminarias* (Jose Luis Valenzuela, 1999), written by Evelina Fernández; *Tortilla Soup* (2001), directed by Spanish filmmaker María Ripoll; and the Hollywood film, *Chasing Papi* (Linda Mendoza, 2003). Other independently produced Latina-themed films of note include *Rum and Coke* (María Escobedo, 1999) and *The Blue Diner* (Jan Egleson, 2001), co-written and produced by Natacha Estébanez.
2 By the time *RWHC* was produced, Time Warner had gone through another merger (in 2001) to form AOL Time Warner.
3 For more on Indiewood, see Tzioumakis (261–271) and Perren (*Indie, Inc.*, 217–223).

Works Cited

Báez, Jillian. "Towards a *Latinidad Feminista*: The Multiplicities of Latinidad and Feminism in Contemporary Cinema." *Popular Communication*, vol. 5, no. 2, 2007, pp. 109–128.

Baugh, Scott L. "*Real Women Have Curves* (2002)." *Latino American Cinema: An Encyclopedia of Movies, Stars, Concepts, and Trends*. Greenwood, 2012, pp. 224–225.

Calder, Peter. "Fat Is a Familiar Theme for Movie's Director." *New Zealand Herald*. 5 Mar. 2003.

Chagollan, Steve. "10 Producers to Watch: George LaVoo." *Variety* Special Issue: Cannes Film Festival, vol. 386, no. 13, 13–19 May 2002, p. 50.

Enríquez, Mirasol, "Trying to Sell Ketchup in a Salsa Bottle: *Chasing Papi* and the Hispanic Audience." Latina Media Histories [Special Issue], *Feminist Media Histories*, vol. 7, no. 4, 2021, pp. 55–79.

Fischer, Karen. "Enduring Legacy: Playwright Josefina Lopez [sic] Reflects on 'Real Women Have Curves.'" *Bitch Media*, 14 Dec. 2020, https://www.bitchmedia.org/article/josefina-lopez-real-women-have-curves-interview. Accessed 25 Sept. 2021.

Gelt, Jessica. "Patricia Cardoso's 'Real Women Have Curves' Was Landmark Latina Cinema, But Hollywood Shut Her Out. Until Now." *Los Angeles Times*, 7 Sept. 2021, https://www.latimes.com/entertainment-arts/story/2021-09-12/patricia-cardoso-real-women-have-curves-academy-museum. Accessed 18 Sept. 2021.

Gutierrez, Lizeth. "Queer Chisme: Redefining Emotional Security in Josefina López's *Real Women Have Curves*." *Aztlán: A Journal of Chicano Studies*, vol. 42, no. 2, 2017, pp. 111–138.

Kaufman, Anthony. "Thinking Inside the Box." *Village Voice*, 12 Mar. 2002, p. 124.

King, Geoff. *Indiewood, USA: Where Hollywood Meets Independent Cinema*. I.B. Tauris, 2009.

MacDowell, James. "Quirky: Buzzword or Sensibility?" *American Independent Cinema: Indie, Indiewood and Beyond*, edited by Geoff King et al. Routledge, 2013, pp. 53–64.

Machado, Yolanda. "'Lady Bird' Was Influenced by 'Real Women Have Curves' and No One Outside the Latinx Community Is Acknowledging It." *Marie Claire*, 1 Feb. 2018, https://www.marieclaire.com/culture/a15931477/lady-bird-real-women-have-curves/.

McClain, Linda C. "*Bend it Like Beckham* and *Real Women Have Curves*: Constructing Identity in Multicultural Coming-of-Age Stories." *DePaul Law Review*, vol. 54, no. 3, 2005, pp. 701–754.

Mohr, Ian. "'Curves' a New Turn for HBO Films, Newmarket." *Hollywood Reporter*, vol. 374, no. 27, 31 July 2002, p. 1.

"Necessary Theatre: Josefina Lopez II." University of California Television, 1 July 2003, https://www.uctv.tv/shows/Necessary-Theatre-Josefina-Lopez-II-7362

"Patricia Cardoso: Director (Colombia)." *Pacific Standard Time: LA/LA at the Academy*, 15 Apr. 2015, https://pstlala.oscars.org/interview/patricia-cardoso/.

Perren, Alisa. "A Big Fat Indie Success Story? Press Discourses Surrounding the Making and Marketing of a 'Hollywood' Movie." *Journal of Film and Video*, vol. 56, no. 2, 2004, pp. 18–31.

———. *Indie, Inc.: Miramax and the Transformation of Hollywood in the 1990s*. University of Texas Press, 2012.

"PST LA/LA at the Academy: 'Real Women Have Curves.'" *YouTube*, 16 Oct. 2017. https://www.youtube.com/watch?v=GWC01UOueRo&t=199s. Accessed 15 Sept. 2021.

Puente, Henry. *The Promotion and Distribution of U.S. Latino Films*. Peter Lang, 2011.

Toushin, Abbi. "'Women' on the Verge." *Variety*, vol. 388, no. 10, 21 Oct. 2002.

Tzioumakis, Yannis. *American Independent Cinema*. 2nd ed., Edinburgh University Press, 2017.

41

AMERICAN SPLENDOR (2003)

Alberto Zambenedetti

In memory of Brian Doan (1973–2017)

"I'm no showbiz phoney, I'm telling the truth!" proclaimed Harvey Pekar (1939–2010) on his first appearance on *Late Night with David Letterman* on 15 October 1986 ("Harvey Pekar Collection" 02:35–02:39). Wearing a crumpled denim shirt under a pin-striped jacket, blue jeans, and sneakers, the late Cleveland comic book author did not appear to be ready for his close-up. By positioning himself as an outspoken outsider of the entertainment business, which he manifestly held in contempt, he defined the terms of his on-camera relationship with the famed talk-show host through such adversarial tactics.

Often interrupting Letterman, remarking on his looks, calling him out on his TV mannerisms, or outright insulting him, Pekar simply refused to play along, forcing his Indiana-born interlocutor to abandon his script and counterbalance the guest's harshness by inflating his own Midwestern politeness to a paradoxical degree. The unusual repartee was so electrifying that the show booked Pekar for a string of appearances throughout the following year, during which the guest's behavior became increasingly disruptive, constantly pushing against the norms of conventional conversation, ignoring the cameras, and even jeering at the studio audience.

Directors Shari Springer Berman and Robert Pulcini embed the footage of Pekar's debut on national television in their HBO Films-produced *American Splendor* (2003), a hybrid documentary and biographical picture chronicling the trials and tribulations of this idiosyncratic hero of American counterculture. During Pekar's infamous segment, the filmmakers shift their focus on Joyce Brabner (Hope Davis), his third wife and frequent collaborator, who in the *Late Night* green room grows increasingly frustrated while watching the live feed on a small

FIGURE 41.1 What's in a name? A cinematic remediation of "The Harvey Pekar Name Story."

monitor. Mise en abyme, the representation of one artwork *within* another artwork, is but one of the many non-naturalistic techniques employed by the filmmakers in their compelling tightrope act of mixed media. *American Splendor* brims with originality, much like its source material, the eponymous autobiographical comic Pekar published from 1976 to 2008. According to the periodization of American independent cinema outlined by Yannis Tzioumakis, the innovative biopic sits at the cusp between "the indie years" and "Indiewood" (33–38). Tzioumakis argues that in the late 1990s and early 2000s, independent cinema moved closer to Hollywood in both content and target audience, relinquishing the formal experimentation of the late 1980s and early 1990s for more box-office-friendly products. In this context, the great achievement of Bergman and Pulcini's low-budget *American Splendor* is its ability to be innovative in form while remaining palatable in content. In what follows, I will discuss the award-winning feature in relation to American independent cinema, Pekar's own body of work (focusing on their shared setting of Cleveland, Ohio), their formal hybridity (auto/biography and documentary), and their cultural significance.

In one of his last on-screen bouts with Pekar (31 August 1988), Letterman finally submitted to anger, calling his guest's latest collection of *American Splendor* comics a "Mickey-mouse magazine," a "little newsletter," a "clubhouse fun and games," a "little rainy-day fund for boys and girls," and a "little weekly reader deal" ("Harvey Pekar Collection" 1:18:18–1:18:40). Never was Letterman so mistaken about an artwork promoted on his late-night talk shows, as Pekar's creation is one of the most original autobiographies in American literary history. The *American Splendor* comics emerged from the underground comix movement of the late 1960s, which operated in blatant disregard of the Comics

Code Authority (CAA), a self-censoring agreement entered into by mainstream publications such as Marvel and DC Comics. Depicting drug use, sexuality, and violence, these independently produced comics were aimed at a mature audience. Pekar's principal contribution to the movement, of which he rejected the iconoclast and bohemian extremes, was his turn to experimental autobiography; his work is a motley assortment of existential musings, observations, and vignettes that render an image of the author not by means of linear narration or structured recall but by a process of unorganized, non-hierarchical accumulation of memories and experiences. The narrativization of Pekar's quotidian working-class life is fragmentary, impressionistic, and refracted through the prism of the many artists who illustrated his stories, among whom are distinguished cartoonists Robert Crumb, Don Simpson, Alison Bechdel, and Alan Moore. The only formal device tying these accounts together, except for the ones structured as epigrammatic dialogues, is Pekar's first-person narration, a blend of diegetic and non-diegetic voiceover that in some instances is translated into frontal drawings of his character addressing the reader directly. As a result, Pekar's comics are confessional, intimate, and authentic, but there is no romanticism to their outlook. Relationships, settings, or motivations are never idealized. The author did not employ any of the reflexive, ironic, or distancing techniques proper to postmodernism since he was not interested in deconstructing the medium, but instead harbored a blind faith in the poetic potential of the powerful coupling of word and image in his autobiographical enterprise (Bredehoft 105–107). Pekar instinctively mixed modernist devices such as stream-of-consciousness with stark realism: the characters in his stories speak a natural, almost anti-literary language full of contractions and swear words, and the depiction of Cleveland, where the vast majority of the stories take place, is razor sharp. The cityscape emerging from the page is unmistakable: cultural institutions, neighborhood shops, monuments, infrastructure, amusement facilities, climate (summer, winter, and then more winter), and vernacular architecture are not just background, but a constitutive element of Pekar's oeuvre. The *American Splendor* comics are about Cleveland just as much as they are about Pekar who, throughout his entire career as a pioneering author and respected jazz critic, maintained a day job as a file clerk at the local Veterans Administration (VA) Hospital.

In their film, Springer Berman and Pulcini build on the comics' formal subtleties, blending animated panels, live-action re-enactments of stories from the books, episodes from Pekar's personal life, footage from his appearances on *Late Night*, and a voiceover narration by the late author himself. Undoubtedly, this ambitious mix of techniques and stylistic flourishes reflects the film's distance from mainstream cinema, where narrative clarity, continuity editing, and character focus are imperative. *American Splendor* establishes Pekar's hoarse voice (in both literal and figurative sense) early on, which opens by fictionalizing the answer to a question Letterman asked Pekar on his 24 March 1987 interview: "Harvey, why don't you make yourself a superhero?" ("Harvey Pekar Collection" 38:50–38:54). Flash back to 1950, when a group of boys dressed as

Superman, Batman, Robin, and the Green Lantern are seen trick-or-treating by a single-family home for Halloween. One of them is not wearing a costume, and when questioned by a woman handing out candied apples, he rejects the need to be anything but himself: "I ain't no superhero, lady, I'm just a kid from the neighborhood!" As the film's opening scene makes salient, while obviously capable of poking and prodding Pekar for comedic effect, the legendary talk-show host failed to historicize his guest's work and ended up asking the wrong question.

Late film scholar Brian Doan poses a different question, one that better encapsulates Pekar's accomplishments and exhibits a finer understanding of his position in American comic book history:

> What would a "Cleveland super-hero" look like? Maybe he would be Harvey Pekar, whose American Splendor...was shot in Cleveland and Lakewood, and is proud to identify itself with the city. Well, "proud" is always a relative term in Pekar's work: as played by Paul Giamatti, the late comic book writer – sometimes called "the poet laureate of Cleveland" – is not Captain America, or even Peter Parker, but a grumpy and decidedly down-to-earth genius, as suspicious as he is happy about his success. Whether it's working as a VA file clerk, finding a collaborator in R. Crumb, or eating at Gene's Place To Dine on Rocky River Avenue, Pekar's triumph is in getting through the day with some sense of identity and ethics intact.
>
> (qtd. in Zambenedetti 93)

Pekar's continuous interrogation of his own identity through his work is foregrounded at least twice in the film. The first occurs right after the cold opening that dismisses any automatic association of comic books with superheroes. Disappointed by the trick-or-treating debacle, the disgruntled child (Daniel Tay) hits the pavement and is quickly replaced by means of a graphic match cut with an equally sulky Paul Giamatti. Cue *Paniots Nine* by jazz saxophonist Joe Maneri and roll the title credits, which are designed as rectangular comic book panels that spell out Pekar's multiple incarnations in the film: as animated versions of *American Splendor*'s drawings, as himself, and as played by Giamatti. Later, the directors will add even more Harvey Pekars, consonantly with their daring re-mediation of the *American Splendor* comics: "If you think reading comics about your life seems strange, try watching a play about it. God only knows how I'll feel when I see this movie," quips the author in voiceover after an excerpt of the play based on his comics is performed in the film.[1]

The second instance is when the film recreates an identity-centered story from the comics almost verbatim: after fainting from the side effects of his cancer treatment, Giamatti/Pekar drifts into a white room that soon enough is revealed to be a blank page. An invisible hand begins to fill it with drawings of the recognizable features of a room (a corner, a telephone, a wall), sketching out the world around its human character. Pacing aimlessly through this virtual space, Giamatti/Pekar tells an abridged version of his "The Harvey Pekar Name

Story" (illustrated by R. Crumb), in which he discusses his bemusement at the discovery that other Harvey Pekars are listed in the Cleveland phonebook. Concluding with the existential question "Who is Harvey Pekar?," the story points to the autobiographical nature of the comic, but also to the unstable identity of its creator (at least on the page), which was occasioned and sustained by Pekar's collaborative methods. As Andrew J. Kunka notes, "Pekar's frequently described creative process involves rough, stick-figure layouts that the artists then flesh out." He continues: "each artist's unique depiction of Harvey demonstrates the instability of the subject's identity in autobiographical comics, which is especially notable because readers of autobiography assume a consistent 'I' that is the author/subject of the work" (164). Springer Berman and Pulcini's film goes to great lengths to find cinematic correlatives to Pekar's comics to further explore how his collaborative approach can both reveal and complicate the notion of identity and authorship – a highly reflexive approach typical, at least to some extent, of independently produced cinema. One such instance is the establishment of Harvey's authorial voice alongside theirs; as mentioned, the writer delivers the film's voiceover narration, but not in a traditional sense. As soon as the opening credits finish rolling, a wipe moves us from the streets of Cleveland, where Giamatti plays Pekar, to a sketched-out recording studio (the whitened background gesturing once more to a comic book page) where the real Pekar is reading the voiceover text and laying down the audio tracks to be used in the film we are watching. Jason Sperb describes and discusses this scene:

> Harvey finishes his dubbing, and then says to the filmmakers, "Okay, so now you got four takes. You oughta be able to patch one together from there." Though, on the one hand, Pekar's remark exists as one of the film's many distinctive deconstructive asides, calling attention to the artifice at work, the imagery he establishes also serves as a framework and strategy for the entire act of autobiography in *American Splendor*. Several takes of Harvey Pekar are presented, and "you" (however defined) must "patch one" Harvey together from there.
>
> *(131)*

According to Sperb, this technique ends up negating the idea that there is such a thing as an "original" Pekar to begin with, but rather that the author "is always constituted and fragmented by a series of simulations" (132). I would argue that the collaborative filmmaking practices on display in *American Splendor* complicate and partially contradict Sperb's conclusion. In fact, the scene continues with Springer Berman (off screen) asking Pekar if he has actually read the film's script. Stuttering through the answer, an embarrassed Pekar responds "Naaaa. A little bit. Just to check the construction," as he nervously crosses his legs. Pressed by an amused Springer Berman ("Do you feel weird saying this now?"), Pekar shifts the topic to his own voice, remarking that "I don't know how long my voice is going to hold up," and he brings the questioning to a close by taking a sip of his orange soda. The establishment of Pekar's physical (his narration) and metaphorical (his poetics) voice is key to the film's aesthetics, which deliberately oscillate between fiction (applying the generic conventions of the biopic and its claims to "authenticity") and documentary (invoking the form's intrinsic negotiation with "reality"). Moreover, while the reins of *American Splendor*'s construction, as Pekar puts it, are firmly in the expert hands of Springer Berman and Pulcini, the film's content and form arise from a dialogue between the directors and their subject – understood both as the author himself as well as his literary avatar.

According to comic book scholar Nina Mickwitz, not even Pekar's own comic books are strictly his own:

> In terms of genre, *American Splendor* is commonly considered as autobiography, although Pekar's collaborative practice complicates the notion of authorship in ways not adequately reflected by such a label (Bredehoft) and its formal diversity makes it resistant to categorization based on stylistic markers.
>
> *("A profusion of signs" 294)*

In her book-length study about the relationship between a broadly-construed, intermedial documentary form and non-fiction comics, Mickwitz proposes that

> those comics that take the actual and historical real as their subject and documentary (more commonly assumed to be identified by its use of recording technologies) share an ambition to narrate and visually represent real people, events, and experiences, and consequently offer their readers and audiences comparable positions.
>
> *(Documentary Comics 9)*

The scholar thus considers Pekar's comics to be an example of such a relationship between these media as well as a challenge to it, since through its unconventional depiction of sound *American Splendor* "critically undermines the perceived conflation of the real and its representation that marks documentary realism" (9–10). It is precisely the rendering of Pekar's voice in the books that Mickwitz analyzes, describing how its fluidity and unstable status within the comics' diegesis underscore the continuous formal negotiations that make *American Splendor* a literary hybrid of autobiography *and* documentary.

Similarly, Springer Berman and Pulcini's film is a Harvey Pekar biopic *and* a documentary about the unlikely genesis and the unsteady rise to critical acclaim of the *American Splendor* comics. Tackling both film genres at once, the directors maintain the traditional narrative arc of a fictionalized biography: they establish the protagonist as a gifted and unique individual (albeit not in the traditional sense), describe the challenges he faces in getting his talent recognized, show his ability to persevere and succeed, identify an obstacle that seems insurmountable, and conclude with the conquering of said adversity. If the formulaic nature of the biopic genre is what often stands in the way of authenticity (not all "exceptional" lives can be neatly subsumed under its agenda), for Springer Berman and Pulcini it provides a familiar structure to help the viewer wade through the intricacies of their remediation of the (documentary) comic books. In an effort to sustain the biopic's traditional arc, the filmmakers conclude the film after Pekar wins his battle with testicular cancer (which would return soon after the making of the film) and retires from his day job, finally securing the pension he so adamantly pursued his whole life – as he stressed numerous times in his Letterman appearances. In the closing scene, a bevy of coworkers crowds around a small desk piled with files, sharing a yellow-colored sheet cake emblazoned with the simple send-off "Happy Retirement Harvey." Recognizable among them are Joyce Brabner, their adopted daughter Danielle Batone, and Toby Radloff, Pekar's friend and colleague at the VA hospital. In the film, the three are played by Hope Davis, Madylin Sweeten, and Judah Friedlander respectively, and in the case of Brabner and Radloff, they also make various appearances as themselves. In discussing this duplication, Jason Sperb focuses on one earlier scene in particular in which Giamatti and Friedlander

> take a break from their performance and sit down, with the real Harvey and Toby interacting in front of the two actors, [who] appear to watch their real-life counterparts in amazement – making asides to one another – as though astonished and amused that two such *characters* could really exist. [...] the shot also invites the audience to join the actors in seeing the real Harvey and Toby not as real, but as a mythic spectacle.
>
> *(137)*

Sitting on folding director chairs, the actors undeniably direct their gazes at Pekar and Radloff who, standing by the catering table, launch into an inane conversation about jellybeans. However, I do not believe that the two friends are reduced to a "mythic spectacle" for the diegetic and extradiegetic audience. Conversely, the true achievement of Springer Berman and Pulcini's film is that it never patronizes its subjects, unlike the peculiar Music Television (MTV) segments featuring Radloff who, after Pekar's appearance on Letterman, suddenly begins to shine of his friend's reflected light, and books a gig with the network. The directors embed the original MTV segments in their film, making the sincerity of Radloff's love and pride for his city and his status as a self-declared nerd clash with MTV's snarky tone. In his voiceover, Pekar notes that he is not fooled by his friend's newfangled notoriety:

> That day I had an epiphany. It seemed that real, salt-of-the-earth people like Toby and me were getting coopted by these huge corporations. We were getting held up and ridiculed as losers in the system. What can I say? It was the '80s, man!

As in many other scenes throughout the film, Springer Berman and Pulcini perform an act of mediatic prestidigitation by introducing the topic of Radloff's befuddling MTV fame with a clapboard snapping in front of Friedlander/Radloff's face as he is framed by a 4:3 TV camera (the film's aspect ratio is the traditional cinematic 1.85:1), and then cutting to Giamatti/Pekar wandering through a set on the parking lot of a White Castle restaurant, where Friedlander/Radloff is getting ready to shoot his segment. After mooching a donut from the caterer and putting his foot through a light bounce disk, Giamatti/Pekar exchanges choice words with the ridiculously coiffed director, who is set up by the film as the contrived foil to the genuine Cleveland folk. Two decades later, in other words, MTV gets a taste of its own condescension.

In a 1992 interview, Brabner expounded on the fraught rapport between the coastal media and Cleveland's artistic and intellectual community:

> I'll tell you the relationship between New York and Cleveland. We are the people that all those anorexic vampires with their little black miniskirts and their black leather jackets come to with their video cameras to document Rust Belt chic. MTV people knocking on our door, asking to get pictures of Harvey emptying the garbage, asking if they can shoot footage of us going bowling. But we don't go bowling, we go to the library, but they don't want to shoot that. So, that's it. We're just basically these little pulsating jugular veins waiting for you guys to leech off some of our nice, homey, backwards Cleveland stuff.
>
> *(qtd. in Piiparinen and Trubeck 26)*

Writer of political comics such as *Real War Stories* (1987–1991) and *Brought to Light* (1988), and co-author of *Our Cancer Year* (1994) with Pekar, Brabner referred to "Rust Belt chic" to acerbically remark that Los Angeles and New York viewed the Rust Belt, and Cleveland in particular, as a place of quaint decrepitude and backward Americana. An active cultural agent in the Midwest and beyond, Brabner was concerned about the lack of Rust Belt voices in the national conversation and underscored the dangers associated with the mapping onto the region the sociopolitical discourses originating elsewhere. But since the 2003 theatrical release of *American Splendor*, whose success prompted the creation of HBO Films Domestic Theatrical Releasing in partnership with Fine Line Pictures, the infamous expression underwent a two-pronged process of reclamation: on the one hand, the local literati began utilizing it to legitimize a grassroots cultural movement that aims at repositioning the Rust Belt as a bedrock of a new American post-industrial intellectualism. On the other hand, a bevy of small and mid-size enterprises (from restaurateurs to tour operators) commodified the idea of the Rust Belt by molding it into a brand, a two-dimensional logo adorning T-shirts, coffee mugs, and craft beer bottles.

Undoubtedly, 21st-century Cleveland has found itself occupying a place in the national discourse, primarily for numerous controversies arising from the worlds of politics and sports. Conversely, the city's gradual involvement in the structural decentralization of the American film industry via its increased connection to regional filmmaking has not garnered equal attention – with many of the films shot in Ohio continuing to be set elsewhere. However, as Mary P. Erickson notes, while

> The regional filmmaking landscape is one of small-scale industry, characterized primarily by small businesses, limited profits, close-knit partnerships, and community input [...] regional indie filmmakers participate in an industry that operates regionally, nationally, and internationally, and few filmmakers can exist without support or involvement from elsewhere.
> *(308)*

In this light, it becomes clear that the location shooting of *American Splendor* has contributed enormously to the slow-but-steady solidification of a local grassroots film industry that eventually led Marvel Studios to take full advantage of the region's capabilities in films such as *The Avengers* (2012) and *Captain America: The Winter Soldier* (2014).

The nuances of a place emerge only through a profound engagement with its local culture, and with their film, Springer Berman and Pulcini recognize that Pekar and Brabner belong to a handful of artists whose pioneering work in the 1970s and 1980s contributed to putting Greater Cleveland on the map of American indie/counterculture. It is thanks to their legacy that journalist Roldo Bartimole can quip, with a mixture of sadness and pride, that "Cleveland is a poverty-ridden city of great wealth" (qtd. in Piiparinen and Trubeck 91). As the success of *American Splendor* proved, this decentralized, off-the-beaten-path wealth can lead to artistic experimentation and stylistic innovation. Two decades later, Harvey Pekar's biopic remains one of the most daring takes on the genre.

Note

1 On stage, Pekar is played by yet another actor, Donal Logue, and Brabner by *Saturday Night Live* alumna Molly Shannon.

Works Cited

Bredehoft, Thomas A. "Style, Voice, and Authorship in Harvey Pekar's (Auto)-(Bio)Graphical Comics." *College Literature*, vol. 38, no. 3, 2011, pp. 97–110.

Erickson, Mary P. "The Pull of Place: Regional Indie Film Production." *A Companion to American Indie Film*, edited by Geoff King. Wiley-Blackwell, 2017, pp. 301–324.

"Harvey Pekar Collection on Letterman, 1986–1994." YouTube, uploaded by Don Giller, 17 Aug. 2017, www.youtube.com/watch?v=biOodnioY8c&t=2108s.

Kunka, Andrew. *Autobiographical Comics*. Bloomsbury Academic, 2017.

Mickwitz, Nina. "A Profusion of Signs: Jacques Rancière's Politics of Aesthetics and the Implications of Reading *American Splendor* Through the Lens of Documentary." *Studies in Comics*, vol. 3, no. 2, 2012, pp. 293–312.

———. *Documentary Comics: Graphic Truth-Telling in a Skeptical Age.* Palgrave Macmillan, 2016.

Piiparinen, Richey, and Anne Trubeck, editors. *The Cleveland Anthology.* 2nd ed., Belt Publishing, 2014.

Sperb, Jason. "Removing The Experience: Simulacrum as an Autobiographical Act in 'American Splendor.'" *Biography,* vol. 29, no. 1, 2006, pp. 123–139.

Tzioumakis, Yannis. "'Independent', 'Indie' and 'Indiewood': Towards a Periodisation of Contemporary (Post-1980) American Independent Cinema." *American Independent Cinema: Indie, Indiewood and Beyond,* edited by Geoff King et al. Routledge, 2012, pp. 28–40.

Zambenedetti, Alberto, editor. *World Film Locations: Cleveland.* Intellect Books, 2016.

42

PARANORMAL ACTIVITY (2007)

Aslı Ildır

One of the cornerstones of the found-footage horror genre, Oren Peli's debut feature, *Paranormal Activity*, has expanded since its 2007 debut into an eight-film series and corresponding universe. After being discovered and acquired by a major studio, Paramount, the film became a textbook example of a low-budget indie flourishing commercially. Drawing mainly on the established conventions of found-footage horror films, inaugurated to a significant degree by its most famous predecessor, *The Blair Witch Project* (1999), *Paranormal Activity* is a relatively late example of the genre.

Associated with stylistic features distinct from traditional Hollywood filmmaking such as amateur aesthetics, the use of handheld or surveillance cameras for verisimilitude, and a signature rawness (Heller-Nicholas), found-footage horror was already well-known to the studios for its commercial appeal and profit potential. In addition, the film was released at a time when the horror audience was already familiar with the genre's conventions and no longer surprised by the transmedia circulation of information about the supposed authenticity of the film.

The film tells the story of Katie and Micah, a young couple that is haunted by an invisible demon. They set up a home video camera to capture a recording of the demon, which causes the demon to attack more aggressively. As Micah insists on using the camera day and night, the demon gets increasingly hostile and increases its influence over the house and Katie, leading to tragic events in the end. The realistic and authentic look of the film is mainly achieved by its raw aesthetics and the non-scripted performance of the actors. Peli states that he aimed to break the "mental barrier when audiences see a regular film" by avoiding stars, script, and a professional crew (qtd. in Turek).

The original budget of the film was just $15,000, and it was initially screened at Screamfest Horror Film Festival in 2007. After being discovered by executives

FIGURE 42.1 Micah recording Katie with his new handheld camera.

from Miramax Films and DreamWorks – including Steven Spielberg – it was ultimately acquired and then theatrically released by Paramount Pictures in 2009, though with several changes to the film.¹ The most significant difference between the original film and the studio version was the ending of the story, as discussed in further detail below. *Paranormal Activity* became one of the most profitable films ever made, earning almost $193 million in box office revenue worldwide. Peli helped to fuel this, in part, by starting an online "demand" campaign from a website set up by the marketing team, where he called upon internet users to vote to bring the film to a movie theater near them, prompting the audience's participation in the film's internet marketing.

In my discussion on *Paranormal Activity*'s journey to the mainstream as an independent film, I mainly adopt Emanuel Levy's more limited, but here effectively so, definition of "indie" in his work on American independent cinema: "Ideally, an indie is a fresh, low-budget movie with a gritty style and off-beat subject matter that expresses the filmmaker's vision.... The independent label evokes audacious movies that require a leap of imagination on the part of viewers" (3). Levy's definition provides an idealized version of indie, as imagined by the industry, critics, or the audience. This ideal often becomes roughly equivalent to a branding strategy in promotional campaigns, especially when commercially successful low-budget films are reframed as success stories. The incorporation of this independent branding by a major studio was a crucial part of the hype around *Paranormal Activity*.

This chapter is organized around two aspects of Levy's definition, which I take as the most consequential to positioning found-footage horror as a genre of particular relevance to independent cinema. The first is an emphasis on the filmmaker's vision, which is inherently an issue for the genre due to its portrayal of a diegetic filmmaker/camera operator. The second is the participatory marketing strategies and the film's interactive aesthetics defined by huge negative spaces that invite the viewers to scan the frame from one end to the other. After briefly introducing *Paranormal Activity*'s position within the history of the genre, I will discuss how the studio reframed the film as an "indie blockbuster" (Castonguay). In the last two sections, I engage primarily in textual analysis and explore the characters' reflection of the film's (and Peli's) position within the industry and the way the film deals with the theme of interactivity. Providing a retrospective reading, I argue that *Paranormal Activity*'s journey as an "independent blockbuster" is embedded in the text through Micah's (or the filmmaker's) double position: a gritty, independent filmmaker with "a vision" and a profit-seeking, technophile day trader. Lastly, I argue that the demon can be read, in conjunction with this analytical approach, as an older, traditional form of content, one that is disturbed, disrupted, and exploited by its new rivals: Micah, and (especially) his digital camera.

Found-Footage Horror: From Amateur Filmmaker to Technophile

The lineages that found-footage horror has primarily drawn from are low-cost independent genres such as reality horror, snuff fiction, cinema-verité documentaries, or any other film at "the intersection between death, film and the real" (Heller-Nicholas 6). The textual link between "filming" and "killing" is crucial for the genre, also drawing on older cult classics exploring this relation such as *Peeping Tom* (1960). The overlapping of the diegetic camera in the story and the actual camera in the film's production adds an additional layer of meaning to the image, and the camera itself becomes a character, weapon, or any other device that has an active presence, drastically affecting the course of events. A key element of the genre is the narrative plausibility based on cinematic verisimilitude, an element that is directly related to the audience's relationship to the film. There is almost a reverse kind of suspension of disbelief at work for the found-footage horror, where the audiences generally convince themselves that what they see is not actually real. It is not only a formal or narrative device that creates this effect but also extradiegetic elements such as promotional campaigns that "spread the word" of a film's alleged authenticity. However, the event status of the films associated with this genre decreased over time, and a certain "degree of security" emerged between *The Blair Witch Project* and *Paranormal Activity*, where audiences became familiar with the genre and its strategies (Heller-Nicholas 7).

The Blair Witch Project is considered the first full-fledged example of the genre, and the ten years between it and *Paranormal Activity* is the period where the generic conventions of the genre were established. There were many independent found-footage films both domestically and globally during this time, including *909 Experiment* (2000), *Black Door* (2001), *FeardotCom* (2002), and *Suicide Club* (2002), which did not reach a wide audience but still prepared the way for the found-footage horror blockbusters in the next decade. The gradual decline in the popularity of the genre until *Paranormal Activity* was partly due to another trend of horror that emerged in the 2000s, known as the post-9/11 "torture porn" cycle, popularized with films like *Saw* (2004) and *Hostel* (2005) (Heller-Nicholas 4). Meanwhile, *Paranormal Activity* also belongs to the mid-2000s supernatural horror cycle, defined by "less gory and more subtle horrors that allegedly appeal to our fear of the unknown and the imagined" (Liu 61). Among the more imaginative readings of the film are viewing its ubiquitous demon as an ominous foreshadowing of the 2008 housing crisis (Leyda) and considering the voyeuristic use of the handheld digital camera as a sign of a new post-cinematic aesthetic (Shaviro).

As a genre that has emerged, fully shaped, within the digital era, found-footage horror is also notable in its portrayal of home-video technologies. The genre regularly features an "independent filmmaker" as a character, sometimes an amateur filmmaker or film student, as in *The Blair Witch Project*, and sometimes just a "regular" technophile, as in *Paranormal Activity*. Therefore, the camera's diegetic presence coupled with the character that operates the camera within the story/film also evokes a certain "indie spirit" in found-footage horror films, in addition to its low-budget aesthetics.

Reframing the "Independent Blockbuster"

The main distinguishing feature of contemporary found-footage horror is its amateur aesthetics based on verisimilitude with a commercial, mainstream appeal, positioning the sub-genre in the intersection of independent and mainstream cinema. While the horror genre has always existed in this gray area as one of the most profitable genres (e.g., New Line Cinema's *A Nightmare on Elm Street* series [1984–2010]), found-footage horror often takes an additional step beyond its predecessors in its low-budget production methods. These low-budget roots and raw aesthetics of found-footage horror suggest the genre is "independent" – though not anti-mainstream – by definition. On the other hand, the marketing, distribution, and exhibition practices of some of the genre's popular examples complicate the picture. The rhetoric of "independent blockbuster" plays a major role in shaping films' reception and circulation, where the marketing campaigns by big studios convert many commercial disadvantages of these movies into advantages (Heller-Nicholas 192).

James Castonguay discusses this hybrid status of "indie blockbusters" such as *The Blair Witch Project* from a political-economic perspective. In the post-*Jaws* (1975) era, the New Hollywood studio system consisted of two main types of production models: big-budget blockbusters (or blockbuster aspirants) on one end and middle-to-low-budget films on the other, with independent films generally located at the lower end of this range. The latter is mainly produced for niche audiences with low financial risk and opens a space for generic and formal experimentation (75). On the other hand, *The Blair Witch Project* illustrates a strong case of Hollywood's deployment of the talent and creative labor of independent filmmakers. The aggressive promotional discourse around the film and its emphasis on the filmmakers' success as independent creators "function to propagate a myth of independent cinema by falsely suggesting that this film disproved the rule of New Hollywood's hegemony in an age of unprecedented media conglomeration" (80).

Despite *The Blair Witch Project* and *Paranormal Activity* being framed as similar success stories, the latter had a longer and more involved relationship with Hollywood prior to its theatrical release. Initially, the film did not get enough attention in festivals to lead to a distribution deal. After it came to the notice of DreamWorks and Spielberg, the film was purchased by Paramount (Dreamworks was a subsidiary of Viacom, also Paramount's corporate parent, at the time) and Peli was offered $350,000 for a remake. However, Paramount decided to release the original version (with a new ending) on a limited theatrical basis after a test screening, and Paramount used social media to aggressively promote the film with a $2 million advertising budget – tiny for Hollywood but immense for low-budget films. Castonguay's argument regarding the significance of Hollywood marketing budgets for "indie blockbusters" is valid in the case of *Paranormal Activity*: to fit the film into the narrative of "supposed indie marvel" (Heller-Nicholas 99), the significant amount of money spent for its marketing and promotion has to be largely ignored. On the other hand, Peli's personal call to viewers to "demand" the film helped knowledge of it to virally circulate through the internet and find a broader audience of horror film fans. Therefore, in addition to the traditional promotional efforts of the studios, *Paranormal Activity* – like *Blair Witch* but to a degree unlike most other films in the genre – aggressively included fan networks and labor activated principally through the internet.

The audience's desire to participate is also significantly related to the YouTube and DIY culture that emerged and flourished between the two films and the average viewer's increasing familiarity with home video technologies and mobile cameras. The films' amateur aesthetics and signature rawness were now a more common part of the audience's daily life. In turn, fans were often also an active part of that DIY media culture which helped the film become not only a commercial success but also something of a cult success.[2] Some fans even accessed the original version of the movie via online channels, tracing back the film's independent roots and demanding the original and hence (for them) the "authentic" version.

The aggressive marketing strategies utilized by Paramount with *Paranormal Activity*, which leveraged significant amounts of fan labor, also illustrates for Alexandra Heller-Nicholas a case of Hollywood "swallowing up" independent films (100). The difference between the two endings is key to observing some of the textual reflections of the studio intervention in the film. While the original film ends with the demon possessing Katie, killing Micah, and Katie's body getting killed by the police, the Paramount version ends with Katie killing Micah *and* the camera, and escaping. The endings differ in their positioning of Katie as a possessed "final girl"[3] and their relationship with the audience. In the studio version, the demon attacks the camera and destroys it, a metaphorical assault on the audience and its voyeuristic gaze. On the other hand, the "indie version" with more authorial control is less violent toward the camera/medium and audience but more violent toward its heroine. The ending offered by the studio "eats" and absorbs the audience in a manner, leaving the spectator in a vulnerable state by leaving them in complete darkness and breaking their identification with the camera (Benson-Allott 190). This identification is also significant on a metaphorical level, with the studio version of the demon "swallowing up" the camera or apparatus of "an independent filmmaker" (Micah/Peli), mirroring the studio's acquisition of *Paranormal Activity*.

Taking the Risk: Micah as an Independent Filmmaker

Peli's debut also reflected the tensions and anxieties of the transition to a more interactive era, both in terms of audience experience and film distribution and exhibition practices. In addition to the interactive promotional campaign, the text itself deals with the issue of interactivity. There are different layers of this industrial anxiety in film, loosely embodied in the four main characters: Katie, Micah, the demon, and the camera. Micah is mainly the filmmaker/camera operator and Katie is – through most of the film – the traditional object of his male gaze. The camera, on the other hand, is the basic means of production of the film and a witness to the events. Though its presence ultimately affects the course of events as a result of the aggressive interaction between Micah and the demon, the camera – on its own – is presented as passive and immobile.

Since we, as viewers, look from the camera's perspective onto the story world, it can also be interpreted here as representative of the spectator within the diegesis, who (also) engages in a filtered act of witnessing. The camera's physical existence results in a textured and digital look (or filter) that constantly reminds the viewer of their position on the other side of the screen. While the diegetic filmmaker (Micah) actively operates the camera in his attempt to capture the demon on video, the role of the spectator is more limited as the viewer's gaze is reduced to what his camera sees. On the contrary, when the camera is fixed on the tripod at night without an operator, our gaze is more active as we scan the room to see where and how the demon will appear.

Looking back at Levy's definition of independent film, we can apply this to the diegesis of the film and consider the character of Micah as an amateur (and hence independent) filmmaker[4] that approaches an "off-beat subject" – a supernatural entity – with a "gritty style," manifest here through consumer-grade technologies and simple (handheld and static camera) techniques. That the characters turn a blind eye to the warnings and persist with their behaviors is a familiar trope in the horror genre, but here we can also read Micah's obstinance in relation to the kind of ambition attributed to independent filmmakers who assume personal and financial risk to make their films. Alternatively, Micah is also the one that attempts to monetize the demon by "catching a story" – just as we can say the studio did with *Paranormal Activity*. Micah works as a day trader, a job mainly associated with finance capitalism, and considers himself capable of turning everything into a tradable product. The demon, which is a highly intangible, formless, and invisible entity, becomes something tangible and materialized and therefore exchangeable in the hands of Micah. In this scenario, the camera corresponds to a technology that serves as a double-edged sword for the industry: it can be creatively freeing for the independent filmmaker and, as such, cause a disruption within the industry, or it can turn into a profit-making companion for the studio. Looking specifically at *Paranormal Activity*'s "success story," the camera (and, more broadly, new filmmaking and storytelling technology) has been a companion, consolidating the film's transmedia circulation and interaction with the viewers and forming it into a profitable horror film franchise.

The Demon and The Loss of Aura

The demon's intangible and formless nature also poses analytical challenges, in addition to the anxiety it creates for the characters. Like many "monsters" of the horror genre, it gets more aggressive when it is disturbed and assaulted by Micah and the camera. Since it has been following Katie since she was a child and (we find out in the later films) haunting the family for generations, we can conclude that it is older than any of the characters and technologies within the film. In this context, we might also read the demon as a metaphor for an older or traditional form of content produced initially to be experienced in a specific time and place – like a feature film in a movie theater. It is disrupted and triggered by new technology (digital camera), and a younger rival (Micah), which results in the destruction of both.

Micah, as the technophile of the household, tries to capture the demon to "watch it later," whenever he wants (shifting time) and wherever he wants (shifting space) – his computer, his TV, or the screen of the camcorder. Micah uses the recordings as he would any form of home video: he rewinds, fast-forwards, zooms in or out, and even plays with and manipulates the sound levels. The whole process of understanding and defeating the haunting is undertaken by Micah like a puzzle he can solve or a game he expects to win; as a technophile and a successful day trader, he presumes that abstract concepts (global finance and supernatural entities) can be turned into a set of composite data that can then be sufficiently understood and then manipulated to his advantage. Following the metaphor of the demon as a traditional form of content, we can say that the demon's rage results from losing what Walter Benjamin referred to, in a different historical context, as its "aura." The demon is experienced in a fragmented way through new technologies and in different times and spaces. It mainly emerges during the night, when the characters are asleep, but Micah records the demon to view and analyze it at a time that is convenient for him. The demon, applying Benjamin's ideas of "uniqueness," loses power because the digital technology and handheld camera absorb it to mechanically reproduce it, giving temporal and spatial control to someone else (the diegetic filmmaker and the audience). In this reading, the rivalry is not only between Micah and the demon, but it is also between digital technology and traditional (analog) forms of content. Pushing this reading even further, the theatrical ending provided by the studio – and Paramount as a film studio whose history extends back to the origins of Hollywood – is significant in terms of this rivalry: the demon (traditional media) assaults the digital camera (new media) to shut it off and recover its power and control.

Conclusion

Found-footage horror is a very rich genre open to experimentation due to its low-budget roots and fundamental subject matter: filmmaking. Since it features a diegetic camera and its resulting products (film, video, or a digitized image) to connect the story world with the audience, it is inherently self-reflexive. There is almost always a filmmaker/camera operator within the story that takes risks by filming the monster, horror, or terror. The footage seems more intimate, authentic, raw, and untouched within the diegesis; this is, as this chapter has argued, similar to the way in which the resulting narrative film circulates and is experienced by its audience. This intimacy and self-reflexivity occur in many different forms in *Paranormal Activity*. However, what makes it especially interesting in terms of American independent cinema of the 2000s is the way it reflects the ongoing and repeated incorporation of independence by the industry on both textual and extratextual levels.

Notes

1 This acquisition of *Paranormal Activity* by a Hollywood studio was distinct from the typical practices of Indiewood that became common starting in the mid-1990s in which independent films were produced and financed by subsidiaries of Hollywood companies. *Paranormal Activity*, as a negative pick-up, was incorporated into the mainstream industry only after it was initially completed by the filmmaker.
2 For more on cult cinema, see: Mathijs and Sexton.
3 "Final girl" is a term coined by Carol J. Clover for the slasher films from the 1970s and 1980s. The final girl is mainly the last survivor of a young group of people who all become victims of the villain.
4 Amateur and independent filmmaking are generally considered separate creative practices, though they are similar in that they both exist outside the dominant structures of the profession.

Works Cited

Benjamin, Walter. *The Work of Art in the Age of Mechanical Reproduction*. 1935. Penguin Books, 2008.

Benson-Allott, Caetlin. *Killer Tapes and Shattered Screens*. University of California Press, 2013.

Castonguay, James. "The Political Economy of the Indie Blockbuster: Fandom, Intermediality, and *The Blair Witch Project*." *Nothing that Is: Millennial Cinema and the* Blair

Witch *Controversies*, edited by Sarah L. Higley and Jeffrey Andrew Weinstock. Wayne State University Press, 2004, pp. 65–85.

Clover, Carol J. *Men, Women and Chain Saws: Gender in the Modern Horror Film*. Princeton University Press, 1992.

Heller-Nicholas, Alexandra. *Found Footage Horror Films: Fear and the Appearance of Reality*. McFarland, 2014.

Levy, Emanuel. *Cinema of Outsiders: The Rise of American Independent Film*. NYU Press, 1999.

Leyda, Julia. "Demon Debt: *Paranormal Activity* as Recessionary Post-Cinematic Allegory." *Post-cinema. Theorizing 21st-Century Film*, edited by Shane Denson and Julia Leyda. Reframe Books, 2016, pp. 398–432.

Liu, Linda. "Occult Anxieties and the Recessionary Imaginary in the *Paranormal Activity* Franchise." *Camera Obscura: Feminism, Culture, and Media Studies*, vol. 30, no. 3, 2015, pp. 61–91.

Mathijs, Ernest, and Jamie Sexton. *Cult Cinema: An Introduction*. John Wiley & Sons, 2011.

Shaviro, Steven. "The Glitch Dimension: Paranormal Activity and the Technologies of Vision." *Indefinite Visions: Cinema and the Attractions of Uncertainty*, edited by Martine Beugnet et al. Edinburgh University Press, 2017, pp. 316–333.

Turek, Ryan. "Exclusive Interview: Oren Peli." *Comingsoon*, 2008, https://www.comingsoon.net/horror/pb_article_type/709072-exclusive-interview-oren-peli.

43

THE GREAT FLOOD (2012)

Dale Hudson and Patricia R. Zimmermann

Considered the greatest "natural disaster" in the United States, the Great Mississippi River Flood of 1927 displaced nearly 630,000 humans and an undocumented number of animals in Arkansas, Louisiana, and Mississippi. As much as nine meters (29.5 feet) of water submerged farms and villages. The flood exposed structural racism and environmental devastation, yet it remains peripheral in US history. It disproportionately affected Black families, with 200,000 displaced. As part of the Great Migration, many resettled in the Midwest and North. Although Bill Morrison's collaboration with musician Bill Frisell – two White men – on *The Great Flood* does not necessarily convey Black perspectives, the documentary recognizes Black contributions to rebuilding and to music within systemic racial and environmental injustice.

The film excavates repressed histories from archival newsreels and amateur films never screened publicly. Like many independent documentaries, it intervenes in public perceptions by including marginalized perspectives on national events. It *interprets* archival footage through selection, sequencing, editing, and music. The film does more than reactivate archival footage by placing it back into circulation. It rejects facts and figures that dominate news and history. Rather than statistics of land submerged or populations displaced, the film juxtaposes images to show how structural racism and environmental devastation entwine with settler colonialism's logic where nature and Black citizens are inexhaustible resources for White people to exploit.

National exceptionalism – a belief that "America" is uniquely superior and benevolent – camouflages this logic, recasting the extent of damage in events like the Great Flood of 1927 as entirely natural. Without characters or interviews, the film exposes layers of power and disempowerment. Morrison's collaboration with Frisell allows excluded perspectives to seep into the footage. Unexplored in the archival footage, racial and environmental violence become undeniable. *The*

FIGURE 43.1 Archival footage of White man surveilling Black refugees, who await trains after being dispossessed from homes built beside rivers, severed from floodplains by levees.

Great Flood rejects human-centric and racially-blind views of so-called natural disasters. It unfolds and then entwines stories of land, ecosystems, natural and built structures, and racialized labor histories.

Understanding Compilation Films

Compilation films select and rework existing footage. Filmmakers mostly work independently from studios and corporations. They appropriate commercial media images and then transform their meaning. Compilation films often interest historians more than film scholars. Bill Nichols contends compilation allows seeing archival images and history in new ways (149–151). Compilation films offer opportunities to understand how documentary never stabilizes meaning. It appropriates images produced for one context and cuts them together with images from another context to destabilize assumed meaning and offer new meaning (149). Although undervalued, compilation films are important in film studies. Compilation films require thinking about filmmaking through different frameworks.

Working with archival footage involves choices about content and structure. Archival footage requires filmmakers to consider story construction *in relation to stories already constructed by the original filmmakers*. Through intercutting, archival footage becomes a literal citation of another film, marked by the material mode and historical moment of production. Images might be faded or scratched or play at a different speed. In contrast to commercial filmmaking which unifies footage through color correction, compilation films allow differences in image quality to register as much as differences in image content. Films might compile black-and-white and color footage shot by both amateur and professional operators. Compilation filmmakers make visible the seams between different original films. Filmmaking becomes assembling bits of films. It exposes what Hollywood production hides through its "invisible" style and what US news media conceals through pretenses of objectivity.

The Great Flood intersects with Hal Foster's ideas about "an archival impulse" in the visual arts where artists re-present or present-anew lost or misplaced historical information (4). Ernst van Alphen argues that archives are not neutral or just storage, but rather a source of knowledge and power (14). Morrison's structuring and editing of archival footage exceed the content's denotative value as evidence. Jaimie Baron considers the archive's authority beyond a physical place and linked instead to audience experience of images "coming from another, previous – and primary – context of use or intended use," which she terms "the archive effect" (7). Archival films entwine and complicate relationships between different filmmakers and different kinds of footage that would never have been exhibited in the same place. Filmmakers engage in acts of "media piracy" – not stealing but repurposing archival footage to contest its assumed meaning (Zimmermann), often official history, both as it is represented on film and as film is itself archived (Hudson).

Two vectors drive *The Great Flood's* structure: image content and the material condition of the footage. Aerial images of flooded homes dissolve into destroyed images, as though water damaged the celluloid. Phillip Gentile observes the film links the "instability of the nitrate film stock with the precariousness and vulnerability of human life" (131). Both humans and nonhumans are flood victims; dogs and cows are displaced. The film reveals the precarious vulnerability of ecosystems. Human life cannot be disentangled from more-than-human life such as amphibians, birds, insects, mammals, microbes, minerals, plants, reptiles, and trees, whose suffering the archival footage obscures. The anthropocentric representations of the flood mark a moment of human vanity more than vulnerability. As Morrison's edit makes clear, not all humans could access the privileges of legal and social recognition.

History is invariably contested in settler colonies that construct elaborate myths of divine rights such as the Manifest Destiny to legitimize genocide of Indigenous people, enslavement of Africans, and servitude of Asians. When filmmakers excavate footage from official archives and intercut it with footage excluded, political tensions become palpable. Archives contain images that might be striking today but have intentionally been made inaccessible and unshowable. The archive can be a place of censorship and erasure. Ariella Azoulay notes how the archive's power implicates us. As spectators, we participate in the event and its constituent violence, thus abandoning "our responsibility as citizens" (157).

Rejecting the archive as a shrine, she describes the potential of archives to provide access to the commons of resources available to everyone (154). *The Great Flood* reflects on archival power and representation, restoring the images to a commons, defined by responsibility.

The Great Flood draws on archival footage from the Fox Movietone Newsfilm Library and the National Archives. It emerges from long traditions of archival image recontextualization through a montage, such as work by Bruce Conner, Peter Delpeut, Péter Forgács, Yervant Gianikian and Angela Ricci Lucchi, Raphael Montanez Ortiz, and Esfir Shub. Differing from archival footage as evidence and elaboration of a point expressed in interviews, this other compilation history elevates the footage to primary rather secondary importance: it emphasizes visual qualities, ideological terrains, and materialities of representations.

Rejecting commercial independent filmmaking (Hollywood's "Indiewood") romanticized auteurism, compilation films involve collaboration with past generations who either shot footage or preserved it. While transnational corporations claim copyright or intellectual property that prohibits creativity through appropriation, compilation films represent disobedience. They reject pro-profit media's proprietorial economies for collective custodianship and co-creation sharing economies. Although they focus on the film's materiality, compilation films are the forerunners of supercuts. While digital images deteriorate with substantial compression, analog images endure over time. Artist and theorist Hito Steyerl praises "poor images" for their ability to reveal the shared history and to open new public debates outside the corporatized intellectual property. Acid damage marks the nitrate footage in *The Great Flood*. Gentile notes this offers "an aesthetic of reenactment [...] that provides the spectator with a heightened experience of another temporal frame of reference" (126). The materiality of celluloid is central to the film's political interrogation of the past, rather than auteurist individualism.

Compilation films suggest a feminist intervention into documentary histories of White men with cameras. In early filmmaking, women were relegated to the editing table. Esfir Schub's *The Fall of the Romanov Dynasty* (1927) intercut lost official and amateur footage to create a new perspective on historical events culminating in the Bolshevik Revolution. Unlike Sergei Eisenstein's tributes to the October Revolution, Schub starts history in February 1917. Rather than creating a dynamic fragmented world through editing, she worked with "authentic material" toward a "cinema of fact." She employs essayistic rather than revolutionary collision editing, providing context as a counterpart to newsreels of meetings and parades (Leslie 11).

Canonical compilation films include Joseph Cornell's *Rose Hobart* (1936) and Bruce Conner's *A Movie* (1958). Celebrating the commercial Hollywood industry, Chuck Workman's *Precious Images* (1986) is preserved in the US Library of Congress's National Film Registry (Hudson and Zimmermann). Other films interrogate the industry's racism and sexism, such as Tracey Moffatt with Gary Hillberg's *Lip* (1999) and Jacqueline Salloum's *Planet of the Arabs* (2005). In contrast, Morrison's filmmaking directs attention to what is saved and what decays. The content is often less important than the abstract beauty of decaying film. *Decasia: The State of Decay* (2002) compiles nitrate film in various states of deterioration. *The Great Flood*, however, produces a pointed political argument about the past through Morrison's sequencing of images.

Identifying Structure

Rather than constructing a linear causal story or an argument based on contrast, Morrison's chapters reverberate. Meaning accumulates like the waters at the edge of the levees, then bursts free in tragedy and triumph. The film reveals how racial and environmental injustice entwine. Chapters offer different conceptual frameworks for understanding the flood by focusing on the content, not as self-evident documentation, but as evidence of historical events demanding reinterpretation. *The Great Flood* is organized into chapters accompanied by different musical motifs in Frisell's score. The images' material condition and the score's rhythms layer emotions and raise questions about historical memory. In one scene, a heavy bass seems to weigh down deteriorated images, conveying only what has been lost and cannot be retrieved.

To render *The Great Flood* accessible to audiences unfamiliar with compilation films, the opening chapters visually reference films in the popular imagination. Images in "Share Croppers" convey US narratives of human mastery over nature. Shot from a low angle, often in silhouette, men and mules appear monumental, paralleling visual strategies in Pare Lorentz's *The River* (1937). Morrison lingers on shots of Black people picking cotton and loading heavy sacks shot at eye level. Rather than triumph, the images ground settler colonialism within structural racism and environmental devastation.

"Swollen Tributaries" evokes *The River* with its alliterative list of the Mississippi River's numerous tributaries, conveying the scale of New Deal human interventions into environments. It also conjures Joris Ivens's *Regen* (1929) in shots of rain hitting leaves and transforming soil into mud. Water accumulates in larger and larger quantities, overflowing levees and covering villages. White people carry furniture from their houses. Rowboats cross flooded streets covered. In "Evacuation," names of villages expose settler colonialism's dispossession of Indigenous peoples. English, French, German, and Spanish names convey connections to the European subcontinent. Village names do not commemorate Black people whose lineages were destroyed by slavery.

Chapters foreground how disasters expose social hierarchies of race, gender, and species. White women in high-heeled shoes prance down planks from rescue boats. Cows are chased through flooded streets, water covering their bodies. Held at gunpoint, Black men secure the levees. Villages are washed away. Tent cities are constructed for refugees. In "Politicians," old suited-and-booted White men survey any damage. Some pose with White children; others perform concern for Black women. Riding in a power boat to another shore, they watch

Black men secure land. Younger politicians chat with Black refugees. Older politicians marvel at the river. In "Aftermath," receded flood waters reveal village streets washed away. Beds of mud fill spaces between buildings. Black men shovel mud onto sheets dragged away by mules. Mechanized large shovels haul large amounts of dirt, underscoring the enormity of manual labor needed. Structural racism cannot be denied: Black men work like mules and machines.

The final chapters convey how the Great Flood drove the Great Migration. "Migration" shows Black men dancing, and long takes of Black people sitting on flatbed train cars with their belongings. The image fades over a map of the Mississippi River. The river's waters flow southward, the migrants flow northward. The next sequence shows flooded farms and villages, photographed from the perspective of someone riding a train looking at the track and ruins; others. Amateur footage of Black people leaving a church follows footage of official documented events. The final chapter "Watershed" shifts from humans escaping a natural disaster to Black people migrating northward. The film closes with images of Black musicians and bands, rather than White people on reconstructed farms and villages. A Black man's hand strokes the strings of a guitar in a close-up. The images gradually shift to bands playing and people dancing, flood survivors who escaped Southern racism.

This sequencing of long takes from different films combines with the tempo of the musical score to convey unresolved despair and suggest hope for survival. They evoke the resilience of the most marginalized and the most privileged exploitation of people and resources. Morrison inserts a chapter compiled entirely from Sears, Roebuck, and Co. mail-order catalog images. It debuted in 1892 to seduce the rural populations into practical rather than fashionable consumerist accumulation. Competing with higher-priced general stores, the company mobilized economies of scale to lower prices and destroy local businesses, like Walmart today. This chapter connects consumerism to racial and environmental injustice.

Reevaluating History

The Great Flood exposes institutional racism after slavery officially ended and comments on the devastating reckless modifications of natural ecosystems. In the early 18th century, French colonizers built a system of levees more than 1600 kilometers (995 miles) to cordon the Mississippi River's water from floodplains destroyed for agriculture, timber, and human residences. It redirected the river's natural flow. Part of the ecosystem, floodplains absorb flood waters. Levee construction continued over the next three centuries, covering more than 5,600 kilometers (3480 miles). Pare Lorentz's *The Plow That Broke the Plains* (1936) evidences long-term damage from short-term policies. The film ends with the desertification and displacement of White migrant farmers. Produced for the US government, the film codifies official history before civil-rights, environmentalist, and animal rights movements.

The Great Flood intervenes in historical depictions of the Mississippi River in pastoral moving panoramas, which rarely addressed Indigenous peoples' dispossession (Gentile 125). In 1927, water washed over the human-built levees, flooding forests and transforming farms and villages. The Mississippi River backwaters in *The River* could not absorb water collected behind the levees. The once-in-a-century flood caused by heavy rains anticipates the effects of so-called extreme weather. These 1927 storm images resonate with Hurricane Katrina (2005) or Hurricane Ida (2021).

Floods present spectacles of nature out of control. They loom large in the popular imagination as overwhelming events destroying natural and built environments. They serve as reminders of settler colonialism's racist extractive logic. The alleged triumph over nature in New Deal propaganda like *The River* conceals a vicious cruelty towards humans and indifference to nonhumans. However, scholarly research on floods deconstructs imaginaries of chaotic and remote nature. This work exposes the impact of extractive capitalism, engineering of watersheds and flood plains, displacement and dispossession for industrialized farming, and governmental intervention to reroute rivers and construct levees and ports.

Many book-length environmental history studies explore myriad aspects of the 1927 monumental flood, ranging from racialized public policies, power politics, environmental histories of the Mississippi River watershed (one of the largest watersheds in the world), engineering to change water flows and riverbanks, and massive farming that alters ecologies (Barry; Parrish). Historian Philip Horne has explained that the flood exposed racial inequalities in the segregated South, where "Blacks were pressed into forced, unpaid labour in shoring up the levees to protect white property and thus prevented from protecting their own – usually more exposed – homes" ("High Water Marks").

Independently produced documentaries also deconstruct the spectacle of floods as so-called "acts of god" by probing how race, class, extractive capitalism, and politics propel flooding. A landmark film by the Kentucky-based community media group Appalshop, *Buffalo Creek Flood: An Act of Man* (1975) delineates the connections between pervasive West Virginia extraction mining and flooding that devastated a poor working-class rural community. A Pittson Company coal-waste dam collapsed at the top of Buffalo Creek Hollow in 1972, leaving 125 dead and 4,000 homeless. The documentary juxtaposes interviews with survivors, union and citizen's groups representatives, and company officials. Pittson executives knew of the hazard in advance of the flood and that the dam's structure violated state and federal regulations. Denying any wrongdoing, Pittston maintained the disaster was an act of God.

At the other end of the documentary spectrum, Spike Lee's four-part HBO large-budget, long-form series, *When the Levees Broke: A Requiem in Four Acts* (2006) offers a similar analysis of flooding after Hurricane Katrina. It exposes how racialized public policy and engineering produced a so-called natural disaster. This film interviews over 100 residents of New Orleans, ranging from everyday people to politicians to engineers, who share their stories *and* analysis of the hurricane's devastation of their communities. The film critiques national commercial news representation of Katrina as a natural disaster with amateur footage and local news footage.

Filmmaker and Musician as Historiographers

Renowned filmmaker Morrison has pushed compilation film's form, content, and structure by blending experimental with documentary approaches. He has produced over 41 short and feature films, including *The Film of Her* (1997), *Decasia*, *The Miners Hymns* (2011), and *Dawson City: Frozen Time* (2016). His films deploy decaying archival footage to elucidate film's materialities. Morrison explains: "I came to feel that it was powerful to show that decay visible on the films was a by-product of time, the result of an organic process" (cited in MacDonald, "The Filmmaker as Miner"). Working collaboratively with archives, his filmmaking operates quite differently than found-footage or piracy practices. His films eschew synchronous sound. Instead, they feature elaborate soundtracks composed by contemporary experimental composers such as John Adams, Laurie Anderson, Michael Gordon, Bill Frisell, Vijay Iger, Johann Johansson, David Lang, and Julia Wolfe. Morrison's films are screened in theaters, museums, galleries, and concert halls with the original scores performed live.

Because Morrison's films move through different venues, both media critics and music reviewers have reviewed *The Great Flood*. Media critics remark on the film's epic scale revealing racialized class divides by avoiding dialogue and causality. They emphasize Morrison's meditative strategy using slower editing and lingering on turgid moments which jettisons environmental disasters as spectacle. Scholarly analyses describe Morrison's films as a form of alchemy fascinated with image decay and destruction. They note his films remove archival footage from the solely evidentiary to recontextualize a new unknown history. Although most scholars analyze the films as historiographic reclamations of lost and repressed histories, they also figure them as meta-cinema, where the emulsion decay comments on cinema itself (MacDonald, "Orpheus of Nitrate"; Weschler).

Music reviewers focus on Frisell's jazz score, noting that Delta Blues and jazz styles moved from South to North. The flood not only was a landmark moment in US history but also in music history. They note Frisell's eclectic score combines Americana, jazz, and contemporary music, migrating across meditative, playful, elegiac, and sad moods. The score operates as both an emotional ethical voice of tragedy and a historiographic marker. The music pushes audiences to watch more carefully.

Frissel recorded the music live with Ron Miles on trumpet, Tony Scherr on bass, and Kenny Wollesen on drums and vibes at a Seattle screening. The music reverses a traditional score where sound supports the narrative and is subordinate to images. Instead, this intermingling jazz, Americana, and quotes from "Ole Man River" unwinds as a collective voice in dialogue with the images, encouraging audiences to look beyond the spectacle of flooding to notice structures and impact. The film's key pattern emerges in its focus on movement: water, sharecroppers, boats, people, works, cars, trains, and dancing. With free-flowing riffs and layers of sound, the music intensifies this pattern.

The music also performs an act of sonic historiography. The flood propelled not only significant change in the engineering of waterways but also, as a result of Black sharecropper migration, brought the Southern blues and guitar music to Midwestern and Northern cities such as Detroit and Chicago. Philip Horne describes how the flood contributed to the Great Migration of rural Black families to urban centers, including Chicago, where their experience can now be heard in jazz music, evident in the joyful performances at the end of the film ("Flood Songs" 65). White musicians adopted Blues informed rock-n-roll music. The guitar utilized a virtuoso Southern improvisational riffs style. As it moved North, it became electrified and infused other popular music forms. Frisell's improvisational guitar evokes the movement of Southern guitar music, a living historical record of the flood's impact. However, this historiography raises issues of White appropriation of Black pain. At the same time, it recognized Black joy. The soundtrack could be interpreted either as exploitation or as a continuation of the migration of people and music infiltrating experimental jazz.

Conclusion

The Great Flood excavates environmental racism and ecological devastation from archival footage. It questions the so-called natural disaster. Black families living in lower-lying areas were more likely to be flooded. White men exercised their power to hold Black men at gunpoint to perform unpaid labor. *The Great Flood* does not dilute racialized politics and environmental complexities for mass appeal. It challenges audiences to see land, water, environment, race, gender, and species as enmeshed, entwined, and flowing. The deteriorating damaged archival footage suggests that racialized environmental history permeates US landscapes, waterways, and cultures. *The Great Flood* reframes the flood as a consequence of settler colonialism, interferences with natural systems, and racialized capitalism.

Works Cited

Azoulay, Ariella. "Photographic Archives and Archival Entities." *Image Operations: Visual Media and Political Conflict*, edited by Jens Eder and Charlotte Klonk. Manchester University Press, 2016, pp. 151–166.

Baron, Jaimie. *The Archive Effect: Found Footage and the Audiovisual Experience of History*. Routledge, 2013.

Barry, John M. *Rising Tide: The Great Mississippi Flood of 1927 and How It Changes America*. Touchstone Press, 1997.

Fennessy, Kathy. "Director Bill Morrison and Composer Bill Frisell Remember the Great Flood of 1927." *The Stranger*, 24 Mar. 2014, https://www.thestranger.com/slog/archives/2014/03/24/director-bill-morrison-and-composer-bill-frisell-remember-the-great-flood-of-1927.

Fordham, John. "Bill Frissel/The Great Flood." *Guardian*, 14 Nov. 2012, https://www.theguardian.com/music/2012/nov/14/bill-frisell-great-flood-review.
Foster, Hal. "An Archival Impulse." *October*, vol. 110, 2004, pp. 3–22.
Gentile, Phillip. "Viewing the Iconic Mississippi: Strategies of Reenactment in River Panoramas and Bill Morrison's *The Great Flood* (2013)." *Southern Quarterly*, vol. 52, no. 3, 2015, pp. 121–136.
Horne, Philip. "Flood Songs, Dylan, and the Mississippi Blues." *Raritan: A Quarterly Review*, vol. 33, no. 2, 2013, pp. 30–66.
———. "High Water Marks." DVD insert for *The Great Flood*, Icarus Home Video, 2013.
Hudson, Dale. "Untangling Fact, Fiction, Fantasy—and Outright Lies: Compilation Films as Archival Piracy." *Social Research*, vol. 89, no. 4, 2022, pp. 1055–1083.
Hudson, Dale, and Patricia R. Zimmermann. "*Precious Images.*" National Film Preservation Board of the National Film Registry. Library of Congress, 2015, http://www.loc.gov/programs/national-film-preservation-board/film-registry/complete-national-film-registry-listing/index-of-essays.
Jahn, Pam. "*The Great Flood*: Interview with Bill Morrison." *Electric Sheep*, 18 Apr. 2014, http://www.electricsheepmagazine.co.uk/2014/04/18/the-great-flood-interview-with-bill-morrison/.
Leslie, Esther. "Art, Documentary and the Essay Film." *Radical Philosophy*, vol. 192, 2015, pp. 7–14.
MacDonald, Scott. "The Filmmaker as Miner: An Interview with Bill Morrison." *Cineaste*, vol. 42, no. 1, 2016, pp. 40–43.
———. "Orpheus of Nitrate: The Emergence of Bill Morrison." *Framework: The Journal of Cinema and Media*, vol. 57, 2016, pp. 116–137.
Nichols, Bill. "Remaking History: Jay Leyda and the Compilation Film." *Film History*, vol. 26, no. 4, 2014, pp. 146–156.
Parrish, Susan Scott. *The Flood Year 1927: A Cultural History*. Princeton University Press, 2017.
Sandhu, Sukhdev. "*The Great Flood*: Water is Transparence Derived from the Presence of Everything." *Films of Bill Morrison: Aesthetics of the Archive*, edited by Bernd Herzogenrath. Amsterdam University Press, 2018, pp. 151–166.
Scheib, Ronnie. "The Great Flood." *Variety*, 8 Jan. 2014, https://variety.com/2014/film/reviews/film-review-the-great-flood-1201037797/
Solomon, Jon. "*The Great Flood* director Bill Morrison on Collaborating with Bill Frisell." *Westword*, 17 July 2014, https://www.westword.com/arts/the-great-flood-director-bill-morrison-on-collaborating-with-bill-frisell-5799475.
Steyerl, Hito. "In Defense of the Poor Image." *e-flux*, vol. 10, 2009, https://www.e-flux.com/journal/10/61362/in-defense-of-the-poor-image/.
van Alphen, Ernst. *Staging the Archive: Art and Photography in the Age of New Media*. Reaktion Books, 2015.
Weschler, Lawrence. *The Films of Bill Morrison*. Amsterdam University Press, 2017.
Zimmermann, Patricia R. *States of Emergency Documentaries, Wars, Democracies*. University of Minnesota Press, 2000.

44

BEFORE MIDNIGHT (2013)

Chuck Tryon

Richard Linklater's "Before" trilogy chronicles the ongoing relationship between Jesse and Celine, returning to them every nine years as they age and evolve, their bodies increasingly wrinkled and Jesse's voice hoarse from years of smoking cigarettes. For many critics, the film evokes Michael Apted's magisterial *Up* (1964–2019) series, a long-running documentary that revisited a group of British people every seven years beginning in the 1960s.[1] This comparison captures both the temporal structure of Linklater's project, made in close collaboration with the film's lead actors, Ethan Hawke and Julie Delpy, and the naturalistic tone of the films, specifically the use of long takes and the extensive use of dialogue and conversation as a means for conveying how romantic relationships evolve over time as couples learn more about each other.

This sense of naturalism is linked to the broader notions of authenticity associated with the indie film movement that began in the late 1980s and persisted into the early 2000s and that is foundational to a number of Linklater's films, especially his long-running project, *Boyhood* (2014), which was shot over the course of ten years. A close examination of *Before Midnight* (2013) can reveal the ways in which the concept of authenticity is crucial to both independent film and to Linklater's project of representing human experience.

The definition of independent film has been contested for decades, both within media industry discourse and beyond, as we attempt to make sense of how the film industry operates. These debates are far from frivolous. Instead, they speak to questions about the autonomy – or perceived autonomy – of individual filmmakers and their ability to make and distribute movies without significant interference from studio executives. Defining independent film has always run into considerable challenges. For one, definitions of independence are invariably wrapped up in the conventional knowledge within the media industries that shapes what kinds of industrial practices are possible. In addition,

FIGURE 44.1 *Before Midnight*'s extended opening shot deftly updates viewers on the changes in Jesse and Celine's life, using the static camera to convey the underlying tension between them.

as Michael Z. Newman has pointed out, indie as a concept reflects a specific set of values that generally align themselves in opposition to a mainstream culture a value system that draws boundaries between "authenticity and inauthenticity, autonomy and corporate control, opposition and complicity, always figured in terms of the threat posed by mainstream society and its institutions" (35). Definitions of independence are also linked to how films are financed. As Alisa Perren reminds us, the concept of indie film emerged out of "specific industrial conditions" that enabled companies such as Miramax and New Line to thrive and positioned film festivals such as Sundance and South by Southwest as key players in shaping conversations about independence (5). This era launched in the late 1980s with the release of Steven Soderbergh's *sex, lies, and videotape* (1989) and Richard Linklater's *Slacker* (1990) movies that benefitted enormously from the hype generated at film festivals and in trade publications. This notion of independence developed alongside the emerging Generation X youth culture that was defined as rebelling against the ostensibly artificial popular culture in which they had grown up. *Slacker*, in particular, with its rambling depiction of a cynical and anti-establishment youth culture, became explicitly identified with Generation X in trade articles.[2] While narratives about generations are largely fictional – they often obscure how race, gender, sexual identity, and disability shape cultural experiences – they retain enormous power, especially within popular culture representations. However, generational identities can also provide a shorthand for speaking to shared political experiences, whether that entails the Iraq War, the global climate crisis, or the emergence of social media.

Few filmmakers have been more readily identified with independent film – or Generation X – than Richard Linklater. *Slacker*, with its episodic structure, and its philosophical dialogue, evoked a youth culture that sought to embrace authentic experience over a homogeneous mass culture. Many of the characters in *Slacker* are un- or under-employed with little hope for long-term employment. However, they are also deeply linked to the do-it-yourself production cultures that gave rise to independent cinema. As Jesse Fox Mayshark observed, the young people in *Slacker* are "not making money, but they're making music, constructing art, concocting theories, writing, reading, and – especially – talking. They are engaging with life on their own terms" (22). The production narratives around *Slacker* also reinforced narratives of authenticity and autonomy. Media accounts and other promotional discourse focused on Linklater's status as a self-taught filmmaker operating outside the commercial mainstream. Linklater's status as an independent filmmaker was cemented a few years later when *Before Sunrise* (1995), the first film in the Before trilogy, was the opening night film at the 1995 Sundance Film Festival and featured iconic Generation X actor Ethan Hawke, who had recently appeared in the self-consciously generation-defining film, *Reality Bites* (1994). Thus, although many of Linklater's films were distributed by major studios, he had carefully crafted a narrative that identifies him as a resolutely independent filmmaker.

Despite Linklater's reputation, *Before Midnight* might not appear to belong to the category of independent film. It is the product of an established movie director working with recognizable stars in Ethan Hawke and Julie Delpy. It is also the third film in an ongoing series. However, given Linklater's status as a key figure within indie culture, *Before Midnight* can still be understood both within these larger debates about indie filmmaking and, largely due to Julie Delpy's contributions to the films' screenplays, as a gendered critique of the idea of the autonomous and authentic (male) artist. As Delpy has attested in an interview in the *Guardian*, the screenwriting process for all three films, particularly *Before Sunset* and *Before Midnight*, was collaborative, and Linklater and Hawke embraced Delpy's efforts to include women's experiences. In addition, the Before films depict the ongoing evolution of Generation X as it comes to terms with its relationship to culture, work, and aging. As Christina Lee observes, the Before films "trace the progression of Generation X as it happens," tracking alongside the actual social changes taking place as the films are made (145). While *Before Sunrise* was produced just as Generation X youth culture was coming of age – in the midst of an economic boom linked to Clinton-era optimism – the latter films take place against the backdrop of the existential threats posed by the Iraq War, the ongoing climate crisis, and eventually the rise of Trumpism. Ultimately, the category of independent – or indie film – is a slippery one; however, the films in the Before trilogy not only can be understood as indies, but they also function as an ongoing engagement with the very idea of what it means to identify as independent as our culture and our technologies of distribution continue to evolve.

Before Midnight, like the other films in the trilogy, serves as an ongoing engagement with the question of authenticity, of living and working authentically within a world characterized by corporate, governmental, financial, and institutional pressures to "sell out." In *Before Midnight*, this question turns into a profoundly feminist one, as Celine, especially during the couple's extended hotel room argument, pushes back against Jesse's idea of himself as an authentic and autonomous artist, a status that we come to realize is possible, in part, because Celine assumes a greater share of the responsibilities in parenting their children and in managing their household affairs. Meanwhile, Celine's career has also advanced, and at the beginning of the film, she learns that she has been offered a job working for the government in France, a position that would enable her to advocate more effectively for environmental justice. Unlike the first two films, the tension no longer involves whether Jesse and Celine will get together. Instead, the tension revolves around whether Jesse and Celine will stay together. In turn, Linklater's camerawork in *Before Midnight* shifts away from the tracking shots that depict Jesse and Celine walking (or sometimes riding) and talking and replaces them with static shots of the couple arguing in a tourist hotel. As a result, *Before Midnight*, through both narrative and formal devices, interrogates what Lesley Speed has called the "utopian" ideal of freedom of thought, their capacity for living authentically, as it is expressed through the couple's freedom of movement through picturesque European cities and tourist destinations (104).

To make sense of how *Before Midnight* engages with the idea of authenticity and autonomy, it is useful to take a brief tour through the first two films in the trilogy. In the opening sequence of *Before Sunrise*, even before Jesse persuades Celine to get off the train with him, the two young people discuss parental pressures to pursue careers that do not reflect their authentic interests, a common trope of Generation X storytelling. Reacting to a middle-aged couple on the train arguing about their finances, they begin to discuss their own personal ambitions. Celine laments that her father is pushing her into a pragmatic career that does not address her commitment to issues related to social justice, while Jesse reflects that he found himself doing the opposite of what his elders advised. Jesse and Celine's ambivalence about pursuing careers prescribed by their parents reflects a larger rejection of a mass culture that appeared poised to stifle their individuality. Similar questions about authenticity and autonomy drive the narrative of *Before Sunset* (2004), in which Jesse and Celine reunite after Celine learns that Jesse has written a novel loosely based on their encounter. Now in their early thirties, Jesse and Celine have stepped into careers, and in Jesse's case, the responsibilities of parenthood. *Before Sunset* opens with Jesse concluding a book tour that has taken him to the famous Shakespeare and Co. Bookstore in Paris – a nod to the Before series' ongoing references to James Joyce's *Ulysses* (the first film takes place on Bloomsday). Jesse has just completed a reading of his novel and is now answering questions about the degree to which the book is autobiographical, that is, whether the book is an authentic reflection of Jesse's lived experience. During that discussion, we realize that Jesse has embellished certain details of their date in ways that make Celine appear more promiscuous. Later when asked what he is planning to write next, Jesse remarks that he is planning to write about a character who "wants to fight for meaning."

After reuniting – we learn that Celine missed their planned reunion because she was at her grandmother's funeral – Celine and Jesse discuss their lives. Like Jesse, Celine has found work that she finds emotionally rewarding through her commitment to providing "small things" that will help to pull families out of poverty. As they explore the streets of Paris, Jesse talks about his decision to marry even though he never felt fully committed to his wife. He recalls that "I had this idea of my best self, even if it might have been overriding my honest self." Once again, Jesse shows an awareness of the cultural norms that shape behavior. Like the first film, *Before Sunset* is structured around a deadline, with Jesse due to fly back to the United States and to return to his unhappy marriage. But as the film closes, Jesse chooses to stay in Paris and to work to create a relationship that had previously been only a fantasy, whether expressed through Jesse's novel or through Celine's waltz. Jesse's decision is coded as a rejection of the inauthentic, and conveniently unseen, life and marriage he has in the United States.

Before Midnight takes these notions of romantic love and authenticity – and their relationship to artistic production – and interrogates them by focusing on what happens after Jesse and Celine have built a long-term relationship together. Like the first two films, *Before Midnight* takes place over the course of a few hours, in this case on the Peloponnesian region of Greece, at a writer's retreat where Jesse has been invited to spend the summer. The film has a loose deadline structure – we know that Jesse and Celine's family will be leaving Greece the following day – but unlike the first two films, there is less overt urgency attached to the story's conclusion. *Before Midnight* opens with Jesse dropping his son from his previous marriage, Hank, at the airport, before returning to join Celine and their twin daughters for a good-bye dinner with their hosts. After the dinner, the hosts announce that they have arranged to babysit Jesse and Celine's daughters while the couple spends the night together in a luxury hotel. But rather than serving as a romantic escape, they spend much of the evening bickering and expressing resentments about their relationship together. Thus, the film subverts our expectations, exposing the previous two films as fantasies. Like the other two films, *Before Midnight* ends on a somewhat ambiguous note, although it is relatively clear that they have reached a provisional agreement to stay together.

Before Midnight, like the other films in the trilogy, uses a naturalistic approach to convey the idea of Jesse and Celine's relationship unfolding in time. This naturalistic approach is reflected formally through Linklater's extensive use of long takes and subtle camera movements that make the films appear to be improvisational, when in fact, they are highly scripted. For example, after the brief opening sequence in the airport, Linklater uses a single take that lasts several minutes, following Jesse as he leaves the airport and then goes out to rejoin Celine, who waits beside their car. The camera then pans slightly to reveal their twin daughters sleeping in the backseat before settling on Jesse and Celine as they drive to the goodbye dinner set up for them at the writer's retreat where the family has been living for the summer. During this single take, we learn a significant amount of information about Jesse and Celine's life together. Jesse laments the fact that he is separated from his son, Hank, while Celine announces that she has been offered a job with the French government that would give her much greater autonomy to implement programs that would help to eradicate global poverty and to support environmental justice. However, Jesse's concerns about his son take precedence, illustrating the degree to which Celine's work, both outside and inside the home, are devalued. Although shot while the car is in motion, the framing reinforces a feeling of claustrophobia, one that matches the sense that both Jesse and Celine feel trapped by their relationship, Jesse because he is unable to see his son and Celine because she feels forced to sacrifice her career in order to perform the domestic duties associated with motherhood. In fact, the use of the long take here is consistent with Jeffrey Sconce's observation that the so-called "smart cinema" of the 1990s deployed long takes as a means of producing "tension through dividing audience and storyworld ... as a means of fostering a sense of clinical observation" (360). Through this opening scene, Linklater deftly establishes the stakes of the conflict between the couple – who have been together for nine years since the previous film ended – by showing how the real life of raising children and pursuing careers interferes with the fantasy world of philosophical conversations in romantic European cities. We quickly learn the details of their relationship, including who is most responsible for handling domestic duties. Jesse, for his part, has thrived as an artist in part because he can rely on Celine to handle the family's household duties and by exploiting his relationship with Celine in ways that are not authentic.

Before Midnight's engagement with gender dynamics alters between comedic and dramatic depictions and is introduced early in the film when Celine reports that she had talked with Hank about dating and that he had even disclosed to her that he had kissed a girl, a detail that Hank had not mentioned to his father. Notably, Hank's departure at the airport is awkward and Hank even asks Jesse not to show up at his piano recital because of the stress it would cause. Later, when Jesse and Celine stop for supplies at a grocery store, Celine takes over, playing the role of "the general" while jokingly barking commands at her young daughters who dutifully run into the store to retrieve the needed items. Meanwhile, Jesse is simply tasked with waiting by the car because he cannot be trusted to buy the right things, a typical role for the male partner whom Celine later describes – with just a hint of resentment – as a "closet macho." While the scene is played for laughs, it helps to establish that Celine takes responsibility for managing the household, even while she has a full-time job, allowing Jesse to pursue his writing career without fully focusing on his role as a parent.

Before Midnight also addresses questions about gender and authenticity in the dinner scene. As the women prepare the dinner in the kitchen, the men are given the freedom to sit outdoors and talk about Jesse's work. This is one of the few scenes in the trilogy in which Jesse and Celine are filmed separately. While Celine helps in the kitchen, Jesse chats with the older, male novelist who is hosting him. During this conversation, we learn that Jesse has published a sequel to his first novel that depicts his reunion with Celine and a third, more ambitious book that is less explicitly autobiographical (and less financially successful). During this scene, Jesse discusses the book with Patrick and Stefanos, two of their hosts in Greece, when Stefanos described the detailed accounts of the characters' sex lives, asks, "it must be a little weird for Celine, man, the way she's in a book like that?" While Jesse dismisses Stefanos's inquiry, the film clearly shows that Jesse's exaggerated (inauthentic) depiction of Celine – and their love life – has become a source of resentment for her, one that brings to the surface how Celine has become objectified through Jesse's representation of her.

During the walk from the dinner to their hotel, Jesse and Celine remark on this shared bit of unstructured time. The brief taste of freedom provokes deeper questions about the gendered nature of work and leisure time, with Celine observing that young men are constantly "comparing themselves" and that they have "signposts" that measure their relative success. Women, by comparison, she states "struggle for 30 years or they raise kids and were stranded at home" before having the opportunity to find success. Although Jesse's career as a writer is not explicitly mentioned here, it is difficult not to hear the resentment Celine has toward Jesse because of the freedom he has had to pursue his creative interests. Celine continues her reflections on time, aging, and gender by insinuating that the young Jesse who met her on the train would no longer be attracted to her as a "fat-assed, middle-aged mom."

When they check into the hotel, a concierge asks him to sign a copy of his book and recognizes Celine as the basis for a main character in the novel, again turning her into an object to be consumed by others. Afterward, Celine demands that Jesse never use their personal life for his books again. During the argument, Jesse tries to claim that they contribute equally to parenting. But we have seen otherwise, especially during the grocery store scene. She challenges him by asking if he knows the name of the girls' pediatrician, to which he responds, "stop quizzing me." Celine further implies that he is not always at home, that he often keeps writing when he is "inspired," while reminding him of her songwriting and adding that "I get inspired sometimes, too, you know that?" Ultimately, like the other Before films, *Before Midnight*'s resolution contains a hint of ambiguity. The film closes with the two of them sitting at the same seafront restaurant where they had stopped to watch the sunset earlier in the evening. Jesse revives the time travel metaphor that he had used years earlier, in *Before Sunrise*, to convince her to get off the train with him in Vienna, when he presents her with the thought experiment that in the future, she would regret not spending time with him. However, in the updated version, Jesse pretends that he is delivering a letter from Celine as an 82-year old and that the letter assures her that she would have the best sex of her life that night. Despite her skepticism, Celine eventually seems to reconcile with Jesse, remarking to him, "It must be one hell of a night we're about to have." Celine's comment seems to confirm that for at least one more night, the couple will stay committed to each other, that they have a future together, even if it is an uncertain one.

Like many of their conversations in the Before films, this final moment revolves around the question of time and its linkage to identity, to the fragile bodies we inhabit, and to the often-fragile relationships that shape our experiences. The references to time and identity are not mere philosophical exercises. They speak to larger questions about the possibility of change – personal and political. While the passage of time has changed the dynamics of Jesse and Celine's relationship, their story continues to remind us about how our commitments to independence and autonomy are shaped by gender and culture. *Before Midnight* is acutely aware of both its status as a generational touchstone and its significance within independent cinema. The Before films play a vital role in defining a generation. Jesse and Celine's tenuous, contingent agreement to stay together provides a powerful corrective to the youthful romanticism of the previous films, interrogating the ideal of the autonomous male artist in the process. Ultimately, *Before Midnight* functions as a powerful self-critique of the past Before films and, in the process, raises questions about the idea of independent cinema and its role in crafting historically specific notions of authenticity. The broader culture of independent cinema has long been promoted in terms of its ability to cultivate authentic voices. The Before films explore that idea of authenticity – in all of its many contradictions – and in doing so, provide us with a new way of thinking about what it truly means to make independent film in an age of media consolidation.

Notes

1 See, for example, Villaça.
2 See, for example, Leonard; Duncombe.

Works Cited

Duncombe, Stephen. "We're Marketed, Therefore We Are?" *Baffler*, no. 5, 1993.
Federal Communications Commission, "Penetration Rates of Consumer Technologies (1876–Present)," https://transition.fcc.gov/Bureaus/Common_Carrier/Notices/2000/fc00057a.pdf.
Hoad, Phil, "Julie Delpy and Ethan Hawke: How We Made the Before Sunrise Trilogy." *Guardian*, 4 Nov. 2019, theguardian.com/film/2019/nov/04/julie-delpy-ethan-hawke-how-we-made-before-sunrise-trilogy-sunset-midnight.
Lee, Christina. *Screening Generation X: The Politics and Popular Memory of Youth in Contemporary Cinema*. Routledge, 2010.
Leonard, Andrew. "The Boomers' Babies." *New York Times*, 23 May 1993, sec. 7, p. 9.
Mayshark, Jesse Fox. *Post-Pop Cinema: The Search for Meaning in New American Film*. Praeger, 2007.
Newman, Michael Z. "Indie Film as Indie Culture." *American Independent Cinema: Indie, Indiewood, and Beyond*, edited by Geoff King et al. Routledge, 2012, pp. 25–41.
Perren, Alisa. *Indie, Inc.: Miramax and the Transformation of Hollywood in the 1990s*. University of Texas Press, 2012.
Sconce, Jeffrey. "Irony, Nihilism, and the New American 'Smart' Film." *Screen*, vol. 43, no. 4, 2007, pp. 349–369.

Speed, Lesley. "The Possibilities of Roads Not Taken: Intellect and Utopia in the Films of Richard Linklater." *Journal of Popular Film and Television*, vol. 35, no. 3, 2007, pp. 98–106.
Villaça, Pablo. "*Before Midnight*." RogerEbert.com, 28 May 2013, https://www.rogerebert.com/reviews/before-midnight-2013.

45
DALLAS BUYERS CLUB (2013)

Mark Gallagher

Dallas Buyers Club opens with star Matthew McConaughey having semi-public sex with two women, but not the way one might expect. Though the actor had recently delivered a showy performance as a strip-club owner in *Magic Mike* (2012) and was in the midst of a critical reappraisal after a series of well-received dramatic roles, he retained associations with what he describes as his "shirtless rom-com phase" of the 2000s (Gardner).

Critics repeatedly remarked on his successful pivot to dramatic acting beginning with 2011's *The Lincoln Lawyer* and continuing with *Magic Mike, Mud* (2012), and other films in quick succession. Perhaps even more noteworthy is the figure the actor cuts at the start of *Dallas Buyers Club*. In the shadows of a rodeo corral, tight close-ups and medium shots show a radically emaciated McConaughey, his skin sallow and face blotchy from as-yet undiagnosed AIDS, furtively servicing from the rear two women in alternation. Intercut with shots of a bull-riding competition underway nearby, the scene proclaims his character's heterosexuality in startlingly unglamorous fashion.

McConaughey, as real-life activist Ron Woodroof, and co-star Jared Leto, playing a trans woman, Rayon, with whom Woodroof forms an uneasy partnership as they pursue treatment for the HIV virus in inhospitable 1980s Texas, both earned Academy Awards for their roles. McConaughey won Best Actor and Leto Best Supporting Actor, in what remains the only Oscar nomination or victory for either man. Alexandra Juhasz and Ben Kerr observe that these awards "primarily served to recognize the vivid and notable transformation of its two handsome leading men into iconographic, emaciated 'AIDS victims' of the 1980s" (Juhasz and Kerr). This chapter focuses in particular on the two actors' performances, including the negotiation of that work in reviews and interviews. This discourse defines the film as a showcase of male performance, rather than, or in addition to, an activist account of the 1980s AIDS epidemic.

FIGURE 45.1 Ron Woodroof (Matthew McConaughey) dominates the frame as Rayon (Jared Leto) lingers in the background amid Ron's supermarket confrontation with a transphobic former friend.

The double-edged sword of its mainstream recognition notwithstanding, *Dallas Buyers Club* remains remarkable for dramatizing the onset of the US AIDS crisis, intimately rendering the physiological and psychological effects of HIV, representing the experience of transgender people and people with AIDS in 1980s Texas, and melodramatically depicting not only intolerance and indifference but also coping and resilience. The film's storytelling and camerawork involve an often intense subjectivity, with McConaughey dominating the film. Rarely off-screen, McConaughey is absent only for some scenes showcasing female lead Jennifer Garner, who plays Eve Saks, the crusading doctor overseeing part of Ron and Rayon's medical treatment, and from a handful of scenes involving Leto's Rayon (scenes often including Garner too). Leto, despite the "supporting role" designation for awards contention, earns comparable screen time to Garner and more thematic heft. The film sparingly affords Leto and Garner dramatically or emotionally weighty scenes with McConaughey's Woodroof off-screen. In Rayon's confrontation with her father shortly before her death, Leto's pained expression and listless body language highlight how literally ill-suited Rayon is for traditional, conservative Texas. Similarly, Garner becomes the focus in intermittent hospital conversations with her colleague, Dr. Sevard (Denis O'Hare), as she passionately advocates for effective HIV treatments; and in hospital-boardroom scenes in which she sits mostly silent, her concerned or anguished expressions underscoring her limited agency as a woman in the male-dominated space. These scenes foregrounding Garner and Leto pit feminized expressions of compassion against intractable patriarchal figures. Otherwise, the film follows McConaughey relentlessly, with handheld camerawork, extreme close-ups, point-of-view shots, and blurred images supplementing his performance of Woodroof's debilitating dizziness and other symptoms as the untreated virus ravages him.

Critiques of the film have questioned its approach to sexuality, as a narrative of the AIDS crisis that overwhelmingly emphasizes heterosexuality, framed through a straight male character and a trans character, both played by straight, cisgender men. Like many other films, *Dallas Buyers Club* imagines white male actors' comparatively affluent characters as the tragic victims of sexual discrimination and public-health crises. Overall, the film – in storytelling, dialogue, camerawork, makeup, and costuming – and its promotional and reception discourse amplify the distance between McConaughey and Leto's screen characters and their off-screen personas and previous roles. The reliably buff, heterosexual babe magnet McConaughey, whose characters routinely embody the actor's Texas-stoner koan "just keep livin'," becomes the skeletal, homophobic, manic Woodroof. Leto, for his part, transforms from the punchable pretty boy of *Fight Club* (1999) and *American Psycho* (2000) to object of pathos and Method-acting cross-dresser. At the same time, the film draws on elements of both men's existing personas. Woodroof repeatedly deploys McConaughey's disarming smile and comic charm, particularly for interactions with Garner's Dr. Saks. For Leto, *Dallas Buyers Club*'s Rayon echoes his *Requiem for a Dream* (2000) protagonist, Harry Goldfarb, another frail boy-man ravaged by narcotics addiction. Leto brings the fragility, weird energy, and musicophilia of many other roles (including that of singer-guitarist for alt-rock band Thirty Seconds to Mars) to Rayon, who fetishizes glam rockers T. Rex's androgynous frontman Marc Bolan. Still, the accentuated distance between actor and character in *Dallas Buyers Club* and its surrounding discourse constitutes a key part of the film's public articulation, performance – and crucially too, affirmation – of allyship. The publicized spectacle of allyship broadcasts affiliation with groups that often remain excluded, and thus not present to affirm the proposed alliance themselves.

Looking anew at *Dallas Buyers Club* in light of intervening reappraisals of film-industry inclusivity and popular-cultural treatments of contested social categories, this chapter's analysis addresses questions about acting in independent cinema; its representation of gender and sexuality; and the role of extratextual discourse, star reputation, and awards recognition in positioning performers and films. *Dallas Buyers Club* also evidences US independent cinema's contribution to loosely defined post–studio era star systems. With far greater visibility than the sphere of stage acting, independent cinema offers a space to which actors have often turned for artistic credibility; for reputation management; or following aging, a decline in bankability or both. The US film industry relies on awards recognition, often for independent releases far removed from studio practices and economics, to burnish its reputation as a site of artistically rich, historically and politically aware content. The star-acting focus of *Dallas Buyers Club*'s promotional and reception discourse establishes the film as much a calling card for the American cinema and its major producers as a historical exploration, activist effort or platform for HIV and LGBTQ+ awareness.

As film text and discursive object, *Dallas Buyers Club* fundamentally engineers a narrative of allyship, with the possibilities and pitfalls that accompany efforts from members of dominant classes to grasp marginalized groups' lived experiences. The film and its principals (McConaughey and Leto particularly) treat their own acquisition of knowledge and ostensibly raised awareness as revelatory; off-screen, the actors eagerly articulate personal and collective blind spots. The film, its surrounding discourse, and its awards recognition for acting and makeup acknowledge and in effect reward the distance between its subjects and social-historical reality. Despite – or indeed, partly as a consequence of – its avowed oversights and its framing in terms of white male subjectivity, the film powerfully dramatizes ignorance while making incremental efforts on- and off-screen to bridge gaps in knowledge and perspective.

Film Style, Storytelling, Acting, and Stardom

Costuming, makeup, body language, and vocal performance help distinguish the film's male and trans principals, Ron and Rayon. Ron favors conventional western wear of jeans and cowboy hat but at various stages of the film also displays facial lesions that mark his difference from his former tradesmen friends and co-workers, while Rayon's clothing supplements an exaggerated performance of femininity, with not only a dress and earrings but also prominent eye shadow, blush, and lipstick. (In scenes preceding her death, Rayon too develops prominent skin blemishes.) Ron's accented, connotatively authentic voice contrasts too with Rayon's affected high-pitched speech and arch vocalizations. In other respects, Ron and Rayon bear physical similarities: both are tall, gaunt, and white; both speak with Texas or broadly Southern accents; and both repeatedly appear in hospital beds, their street clothes swapped for medical gowns. Despite their strongly contrasting character types, Ron and Rayon, and the actors playing them, complement each other in notable ways too. McConaughey sometimes uses silence or introspection when Leto and others speak, his periodic taciturnity providing a counterpoint to other characters' loquacity. Both also turn laconic or high-wired as narrative events dictate. Still, Leto's overall affect – conveyed through posture, facial expressions, and speech in particular – intersects with stereotypical pop-culture representations of sad, doomed queens. In contrast, McConaughey embodies the angry, relentless fighter.

Other character and story elements further Ron and Rayon's thematic interdependence. Ron is a working-class, redneck hothead with no family ties (or baggage), while Rayon is a scion of a wealthy banker forced out of her class position and estranged from family thanks to her disreputable trans status and drug-addiction backstory. Awareness of social class and sexuality largely substitutes for attention to race relations and racial imbalances. The film never hints at anti-Black or anti-Latino racism but does narrate white characters' comparative privilege, their access to resources and ease of movement. Rayon shows resourcefulness by working alongside Ron in a quasi-legal drug sales enterprise and by contributing money from a life-insurance policy to the business. More prominently, though, the film shows Ron doing library research, making contacts to acquire medication, disguising himself to navigate border security, sparring with doctors and government officials, and testifying in court proceedings. McConaughey plays Ron as often a manic figure, moving jerkily and with an off-balance posture; while Leto endows Rayon with an air of weariness and defeat, arms hanging limply by her side and with facial expressions conveying resignation and fatigue. This performance dynamic contributes to the film's physicalization and psychologization of character, offering material for viewers' emotional investment while also establishing and reiterating whose story and subjectivity matters most. These differing arcs feed a recurring critique of the film: while it traces Ron's journey from self-destructive homophobe to humanitarian entrepreneur, it puts Rayon on a comparatively fixed, downward trajectory. She oscillates between sobriety and relapses into addiction but repeatedly takes on the tasks of educating and caring for Ron, before dying early in the final third of the film.

Diverging character arcs and screen time aside, the dynamic interplay between Ron and Rayon, and McConaughey and Leto, creates productive oppositions. McConaughey's performance recalls aspects of his past portrayals of smooth-talking Texans or Southerners. For a dinner date with Garner's Eve, he turns on the charm that viewers may recognize from previous roles: he dons a suit and is upbeat, inquisitive, and an engaging conversationalist. He brings levity to the film too, with, for example, his scene impersonating a priest at the Mexican border offering an opportunity for comic masquerade. For later drug-buying forays to Europe, he also dresses as a businessman and an airline pilot. Meanwhile, when Rayon adorns herself in male drag, an oversized man's suit, to visit her disapproving father, she appears emphatically ill at ease. Leto bows his head and bears a pained expression, and Rayon attempts an insouciant air but bounces nervously even when standing still, with handheld camera punctuating her agitated state. Ron appears far more comfortable as a priest or pilot than Rayon does in any identity, particularly one compatible with a space such as her father's ornate, wood-paneled office. Ron's ability to shift fluidly among a range of conventional gender identities underscores the challenges and anguish that confront Rayon as she struggles to outfit herself in just one. And while Ron's costume changes occur off-screen, the film repeatedly shows Rayon in dressing and grooming rituals, wearing a bathrobe and scarf, or sitting at a mirror, applying makeup and more. While such rituals are often regarded as pleasurable, the film's contrasts in this regard highlight its larger project of demonstrating the agency and the array of willing interlocutors available to historically self-assured, heterosexual white men and the loss of privilege and leverage that accompany trans existence.

Dallas Buyers Club largely eschews the artifice and fantasy characteristic of studio-produced genre films. The film's approach to gender and culture instead evidences independent films' and their viewers' tolerance or celebration of naturalistic performance and textual realism. Still, the film's character-centered oppositions attest to McConaughey's and Leto's respective star personas. Ron Woodroof extends a template that critic A.O. Scott finds in McConaughey's other early-2010s roles. Reviewing *Mud*, Scott opines that "Mr. McConaughey commands attention with a variation on a certain kind of Southern character: handsome but battered, charming but also sinister, his self-confidence masking a history of bad luck and trouble" (Scott). Leto, meanwhile, had largely disappeared from multiplex screens, playing major roles in only five films in the decade preceding *Dallas Buyers Club*'s release. In 2013, then, Leto was best known as a protean independent actor who had mostly shifted to music, while McConaughey was experiencing a mid-career revival, newly recognized for independent films in particular. For both, independent cinema offers a space to enact complex gender identities less evident in studio productions. At the same time, both continued to enjoy reputations based in part on sex appeal. McConaughey as noted had only recently exited his "shirtless rom-com phase." As for Leto, David Edelstein comments that Leto's casting as the trans Rayon would "make anyone rethink his or her prejudices" (Edelstein), implying the actor's general appeal.

Edelstein also participates in the discursive celebration of Leto's acting, remarking that "[t]he transformation is so complete – physically and vocally – that it's hard to believe he could ever be anything else," just after calling Rayon "an alluring transvestite." Few characters acknowledge this allure, however. The film carves out space for an eventual romantic interest, Sunflower, or Sunny (played by indie musician Bradford Cox), who hovers in the background for many of Rayon's scenes and merits some incidental dialogue. While Sunny sometimes occupies the motel room that Rayon, like Woodroof, uses for business, *Dallas Buyers Club* does not substantively imagine a romantic or sexual relationship involving gay or trans characters. Instead, ruminations on gay and trans interests and relationships play out largely in promotional and reception discourse.

Discourse, Reception, and Awards Recognition

With a substantial star focus, *Dallas Buyers Club*'s promotion and commentary foster a view of the film as defined by McConaughey and Leto's roles and by the actors' physical transformations. Awards recognition similarly calls attention to male performance as one of the film's key attributes. The film received six Academy Awards nominations, including for Best Picture, Best Original Screenplay, and Best Editing. It did win the Oscar too for makeup and hairstyling, but the most consistent recognition accrued to McConaughey and Leto, with their acting celebrated at the Oscars, Golden Globes, Independent Spirits, Screen Actors Guild Awards, and by many more festivals and critics' groups. The film was thus judged and enshrined above all as a showcase of quality male performance.

Reviews and commentaries also emphasize male performance as *Dallas Buyers Club*'s chief asset, paralleling or supplanting the film's ostensible subject, the first decade of the AIDS epidemic and faltering US public-health responses. Reviewers remark on McConaughey's weight loss and appraise it (and often Leto's too) in terms of an updated Method acting style – a style overwhelmingly associated with white male actors such as Marlon Brando, James Dean, and Daniel Day-Lewis – and as a sign of professional commitment. In his review, Edelstein repeats the press-kit staple that the star "lost about a quarter of his body weight" for the role and comments that "McConaughey's hollows and protruding bones are scary to behold, and they serve to set off the intensity of his performance." Similarly, Tim Masters reports in a *BBC News* piece that "Much attention has focused on the huge amount of weight that both actors lost for their roles" (Masters) – attention including that in Masters' own article. He recounts McConaughey's conversations with Woodroof's family, the actor's study of Woodroof's diaries, and screenwriter Craig Borten's audio interviews with Woodroof. McConaughey asserts that the psychological effects of weight loss attuned him to Woodroof's frenzied mindset: "I became clinically aware, almost hyper. I needed three hours less sleep a night. I had an amazing amount of energy from the head up." Woodroof similarly, by McConaughey's account, "was withering away, but from the neck up he was like a starving baby eagle – and he was just savagely clinging to life" (Masters). Such anecdotes challenge any assumptions of McConaughey's performance as surface-based and purely physical. Discourse emphasizing the male stars' preparations functions not only as testaments to professionalism and dedication to craft but also as truth claims confirming the film's historical and social verisimilitude.

The actors' inexperience playing gay or trans characters merits little press attention. Instead, McConaughey's role in the film and in extratextual discourse as advocate for HIV treatment and de facto straight spokesman for the gay community reflects what Juhasz terms "the *Mississippi Burning* ([...] 1988) legacy: tales of past American activist struggles that rely on lead characters who represent the dominant culture to tell stories of minoritarian community struggle" (Juhasz and Kerr). The role also positions him eventually as a straight ally to gay men and to people with AIDS. Leto similarly pursues ally status through his characterization and off-screen commentary. In interviews, he claims interest in comprehending the reality of trans people's lives – to prepare for his role, demonstrate his social consciousness, and shape the reception of his role and of the film overall. As he recounts in one interview,

> I met with people [in the transgender community] and I listened and I learned, and those people were great teachers. [...] It started in a very simple way: sitting down and sharing. People opening up their lives and talking about what it was like to be a young person and make the decision to start living as a woman. You know, that is a very brave and terrifying thing to do. That affected me. I understood that.
>
> *(Yuan)*

Other anecdotes, though, hint that Leto approached the part in terms of ostentatious, sexually flirtatious male homosexuality in drag. In another interview, he recalls that "I did the Skype with the director, and I reached over and got some lipstick and I put it on, and I had a little pink sweater on and flirted with him a little bit." Asked in that conversation "What was the toughest thing about that role?," he responds, "The waxing. I was smooth. [...] I waxed my legs. Oh yeah, man, I was a pro. I didn't want that stubble growing back. I waxed my eyebrows, too" (Galloway and Belloni). In this regard too, at the start of filming, he tweeted that "I just waxed my legs for this new role. Ladies, I feel your pain" (Leto). With the statement, he claims affinity with women's, but not specifically trans women's, experiences. In the interview too, Leto subtly asserts his manhood when articulating his desire to work – or in effect, fight – alongside McConaughey:

> I remember hearing that Matthew was involved, and I knew he'd already started losing weight, and I thought, 'If this guy is willing to do this, there's got to be something special, and I want to get in the ring with him right now 'cause he's killing it.'
>
> *(Galloway and Belloni)*

Notably, expectations that women maintain a hard-to-achieve thinness for screen parts remain the norm, while male weight loss continues to be regarded as a bold sign of actorly dedication. Beyond the gendering of weight change for screen roles, Leto's invocation of "the ring" and of McConaughey hypothetically "killing it" (either by losing weight or on the evidence of his other parts circa 2011 and 2012) accords with conventionally masculine codes of rigor and combat, helping balance Leto's ostensible performance of femininity.

McConaughey and Leto's framing of their roles as professional challenges and opportunities for (their own) raised awareness can appear self-serving, not just in the wake of movements for industry diversity and inclusivity but even in the comparatively less enlightened era of 2013–2014. Still, their work and the indirect advocacy of their discourse deserve attention for efforts, however partial, to forge alliances between those with considerable social capital and prominent speaking platforms and groups marginalized or erased from representation and discourse. Glossing social-sciences work on allies and allyship,[1] Bree Hadley defines a social justice ally as "a member of a dominant group – for example white, straight, able, or male – who works to support non-dominant groups to address issues of systematic privilege, prejudice, and inequality" (85). Hinting at the performative, reputational dimension of articulations of allyship, Hadley invokes the figure of the "pseudo-ally": "an ally of convenience more interested in improving one's own status than that of others" (85–86). In this regard, McConaughey and Leto's stated investments in the communities they represent on screen sit uneasily alongside their press appearances' explicit commercial function.

Owing to its representational priorities, *Dallas Buyers Club*'s formation of alliances and pseudo-alliances occurs mostly through extrafilmic discourse. The filmmakers render 1980s Texas as a conspicuously white, heterosexual milieu. And while narratively invested in Rayon's plight, *Dallas Buyers Club* overall uses its trans character instrumentally, to shore up its straight protagonist's subjectivity and to map his evolution into a less selfish, less homophobic and transphobic person. By prioritizing a cisgender, heterosexual man's perspective over a trans woman's;

by making Rayon subordinate to Ron in on-screen authority, agency, and even lifespan; and by sidelining or excluding people of color, the film mirrors the hierarchies that govern relations between marginal groups and their alleged majoritarian allies. Laura Copier and Eliza Steinbock observe too that "Rayon is also positioned to be the educator of Ron, a mammy function to promote acceptance and dispense free expertise to cisgender people" (929). Just as in social reality, *Dallas Buyers Club* calls on marginalized people to perform discursive, emotional, and other labor to educate and nurture even well-meaning members of majority groups.

In film culture, status markers and measurements can often become blurred. Tracking intersections of screen representations, actors' labor in commercial cinema, professional recognition of that labor through industry awards, and trade-press and entertainment-news discourse, we find both entrenched systems of privilege and – particularly in independent cinema – incremental efforts to use that privilege to foster awareness, tolerance, and social and institutional change. Economic and reputational motivations underwrite performances of allyship but do not fundamentally devalue progressive efforts or the signifying power of screen representation and discourse. *Dallas Buyers Club* has inspired fierce debate over its avowed blind spots and its selective engagement with the history of the AIDS epidemic and those most impacted by it. As such, the film functions not only as a marker of 2010s independent-film practice and critical and industry taste but also as a focal point for discussions of cinema's social responsibilities and screen actors' obligations to the communities whose members they claim as supporters and allies.

Note

1 Scholars use "allyship" and "allydom" interchangeably, though allyship enjoys a longer linguistic history.

Works Cited

Copier, Laura, and Eliza Steinbock. "On Not Really Being There: Trans* Presence/Absence in *Dallas Buyers Club*." *Feminist Media Studies*, vol. 18, no. 5, 2018, pp. 923–941.

Edelstein, David. "Outlaw Pharmacology." *New York Magazine*, 24 Oct. 2013, nymag.com/movies/reviews/dallas-buyers-club-about-time-2013-11.

Galloway, Stephen, and Matthew Belloni. "Awards Roundtable: 6 Top Actors' Uncensored Tales, From Worst Auditions to Leg Waxing." *The Hollywood Reporter*, 30 Oct. 2013, www.hollywoodreporter.com/news/general-news/matthew-mcconaughey-jake-gyllenhaal-at-651358.

Gardner, Chris. "Matthew McConaughey Recalls 'Shirtless Rom-Coms' Phase and How Turning Down $14.5M Offer Led to Career Renaissance." *The Hollywood Reporter*, 16 June 2021, www.hollywoodreporter.com/movies/movie-news/matthew-mcconaughey-shirtless-romantic-comedies-1234969201.

Hadley, Bree. "Advocacy, Allies, and 'Allies of Convenience' in Performance and Performative Protest." *The Routledge Companion to Theatre and Politics*, edited by Peter Eckersall and Helena Grehan. Routledge, 2019, pp. 85–88.

Juhasz, Alexandra, and Ted Kerr. "Home Video Returns: Media Ecologies of the Past of HIV/AIDS." *Cineaste*, vol. 39, no. 3, Summer 2014, www.cineaste.com/summer2014/home-video-returns-media-ecologies-of-the-past-of-hiv-aids.

Leto, Jared [@JaredLeto]. "I just waxed my legs for this new role. Ladies, I feel your pain." *Twitter*, 14 Nov. 2012, twitter.com/jaredleto/status/268820634606383105.

Masters, Tim. "Matthew McConaughey on Dallas Buyers Club: 'I Became Almost Hyper'." *BBC News*, 5 Feb. 2014, www.bbc.com/news/entertainment-arts-25979138.

Scott, A.O. "Hiding From Trouble, Found by Innocents." *New York Times*, 25 Apr. 2013, www.nytimes.com/2013/04/26/movies/mud-stars-matthew-mcconaughey-and-reese-witherspoon.html.

Yuan, Jada. "Damn, Jared Leto Knows How to Be Charming." *Vulture (New York Magazine)*, 12 Sept. 2013, www.vulture.com/2013/09/jared-leto-charming-dallas-buyers-club.html.

46

JASON AND SHIRLEY (2015)

Alexandra Juhasz

> In the '90s the only film about Black gay men in the canon was *Portrait of Jason*. We aren't represented, we are angry.
> – Stephen Winter ("*Chocolate Babies* Q&A" [May 2021])

Anger

"I'm angry," playwright Jeremy O. Harris said in 2021, referring to Stephen Winter's 1996 film *Chocolate Babies*, "that I was robbed of this film canonically" ("*Chocolate Babies* Q&A"). But who robbed Harris? Why was this gay Black 31-year-old wunderkind – whose *Slave Play* enjoyed a reprisal on Broadway after receiving a record-breaking 12 nominations for the 74th Tony Awards, and no wins! – angry? And why is Stephen Winter, a gay Black male filmmaker from a previous generation, also incensed? Is it how Black and gay Jason Holliday was misrepresented as the subject of a 1967 documentary portrait bearing his name (*Portrait of Jason*), in a first and now canonical role on screen? Or that *Chocolate Babies* (1996) and Winter's homage to Holliday, *Jason and Shirley* (2015), are two of what is still too few? The answers are simple and also very hard, pointing to interlocked systems that create, perpetuate, or seek to change (or queer) taste, gates, and the canons that result.

A film being "in the canon," one in a list of celebrated greats, allows for more: more viewings, writing, money, community, more chances to make more, and more opportunities for someone who needs it to not be robbed. But as Harris, Winter, and I will soon attest, queering the canon proves to be not just tricky … but often infuriating.

Simply getting an independent film made is hard: you need an idea, and then a crew, equipment, and funding. Then you need to get it seen. Festivals, distributors, teachers, fans, funders, and scholars all play some part in creating visibility.

DOI: 10.4324/9781003246930-47

FIGURE 46.1 Jack Waters in *Jason and Shirley* (Photo by Ricardo Nelson, courtesy of JaShirl LLC).

Tougher still is how a film can stay readily available over time and platforms. Libraries, archives, distributors, and self-distribution can keep a film around, but this demands diligence over time. Then, how does a film accrue enough cultural capital to be remembered enough so that any Black gay man in need would know it existed?

Women, people of color, the disabled, queers, and others denied access to voice for most of film's history began making indie films in some numbers in the 1970s, 1980s, and 1990s aligned with opportunities connected to technological and social movements. It was not until the 1990s that New Queer Cinema (named as such in 1992 by B. Ruby Rich in *Sight and Sound*) heralded a relative deluge of narrative feature films where there had been zero, including *Chocolate Babies*, which Harris was glad to see at Queering the Canon: BIPOC NY, but still mad about because of all the earlier not-seeing. This a matter of canons, taste, and also of gates, and thus fundamentally of race. Many forces need to align for a film to end up "in the canon." As Geoff King explains in *Quality Hollywood,* prestige is awarded by gatekeepers like festival programmers, buyers, critics, and professors. Awards (like the ones #MostTonyNominatedOneHitWonders O. Harris did not get), reviews, and scholarly book chapters are interrelated symbols and practices of growing cultural valuation. And there is a "political dimension" to the traditions of giving value, itself producing a predictability and circularity to entry (King 19). Exasperation results when oppressive cycles of distinction stay stuck. Shyon Baumann identifies a "legitimation framework" that includes opportunity, resources, and "intellectualizing discourses" (18) like this one. And then, some artists are downright counter-cultural. More than wanting *in*, they seek to stay out and proud, so as to critique, change, or demolish the structures that produce legitimation. Some people do not want to be seen on others' terms. Many members of BIPOC queer New York scenes (like Winter, Jason, and Harris) live countercultural lives organized against hetero-patriarchy, cis-normativity, white privilege, racist capitalism, ableism, and the like, not to mention "straight" understandings of drugs, sex, work, family, and art.

Jason and Shirley (2015) is a film about the many costs of (not) being seen on others' terms and the related delights of living on your own. It is a creative remake of one of the only films "in the canon" made before the 1970s by a woman: Shirley Clarke's *Portrait of Jason*, discussed in this collection by James Morrison. Hers is a documentary about Shirley (and us) seeing Jason talk and talk. He is the first Black gay man to be willingly out on camera because this could (and does) lead to severe consequences (humiliation, violence, oppression), as he testifies to in the film. While Clarke also suffered the indignities of sexism and racism as a Jewish woman director who made critically acclaimed films, her *Portrait of Jason* has enjoyed countless honorific efforts (like Winter's, Morrison's, and mine here),[1] as well as its share of censorship given the salacious nature of Jason's act and identity.[2] *Jason and Shirley* (and *Portrait of Jason*), queer or bust the canon by making films about (and by) people who are not supposed to be seen, who are deemed distasteful or objectionable, or who make some squeamish or outraged. Anger defines the scene. In both films, and the intellectualizing discourses that buoy them, outbursts of emotions, both on and off camera, allow us to see the stakes for those who experience under- or misrepresentation, as well as those who choose to challenge this legacy. How are canons made or changed? According to Wyatt D. Phillips, "Independent cinema is generally seen as a space for those marginalized by the mainstream to find a 'way in' to the conversation, but as this chapter makes clear, even independent cinema itself engages such boundary-forming and canon-forming practices."[3]

The narrative film, *Jason and Shirley*, and the documentary it mirrors, *Portrait of Jason*, are self-reflexive works about formative hierarchies within American culture and its indie filmmaking. "I can't make it with you; you can't make it without me," says Shirley (Sarah Schulman) to Jason (Jack Waters) in *Jason and Shirley*, reflecting lines spoken by the real Jason to the actual Shirley: "It gets to be a joke sometime: who's using who." The significance of support and censorship, taste and anger, power and cruelty in the workings of independent cinema and American culture – and how these are imbricated by race, class, gender, ethnicity, and sexuality – affect us all. An aggravating obstacle to the queering of the independent film canon is white dominance. "Oppression by white people… There is a lot of material there," explains Jason to the camera, and to Shirley, always off screen, but in the picture even so.

Canon(s)

Jason and Shirley premiered at BAMcinemaFest in 2015 and went on to play on the queer film festival circuit. At the time of this chapter's initial writing, it was available on vimeo, distributed by the filmmaker.[4] Later, Winter gained a much-deserved career benchmark. In October 2021, his films became available on the Criterion Channel, albeit only for a limited time (Hereford, Williams). Hence, this mark of prestige and opening up of access was quickly closed down again, evidence of the churning, burning cycles of distinction that regulate visibility. Thus, while this tale of anger, taste, and action hits at one happy ending, it circles forward to consider what enabled (and then hindered) this newfound (and easily lost) attention. There has been little written about Winter.[5] Robert Mills, in a forthcoming piece about *Chocolate Babies*, reflects on these canon-troubles: "resisting an unproblematic alignment with either its cinematic or political contemporaries, *Chocolate Babies*' insurgent novelty here seems to have had the inadvertent consequence of obstructing its own entry into a periodized corpus" (3–4).

Jason and Shirley – like *Chocolate Babies* – is an insurgent and hard to align film made in Winter's signature style and unapologetic position, one built from a countercultural, avant-garde, and radical dismissal and attack on dominant culture. A hard-to-pigeonhole "drama fantasy comedy" (as Wikipedia labels it), *Jason and Shirley* blends narrative, performative, experimental, and documentary techniques to reconsider *Portrait of Jason*, itself a hard-to-categorize film. Winter, working in the canon form, albeit (borrowing from the musical definition of "canon") "at some other pitch," begins his version at a time unpictured in the original, before Jason arrives at the Chelsea Hotel. Behind the scenes, with the director and crew as they prepare for the shoot, we meet these characters, see the hard work of filmmaking, and become privy to the power relations that underwrite their scene, as the scene expands to include several rooms of Clarke's apartment and the roof of the Chelsea Hotel. These are narrative and visual motifs that challenge the stark, long-take, single-subject gaze of the original where Jason's face and one wall are all that we watch for more than two hours. Winter embellishes and extends Clarke's constricted frame, while also externalizing Jason's frame of mind, through the addition of trippy fantasy or perhaps hallucination sequences, fueled by what we did see, in the original, of Jason's drug and alcohol use, as well as his anger, sadness, and unrequited longing. We are made privy to some of the debauchery that Jason previously could only testify to as oft-told tales. In the remake, we watch Jason (remembering, fantasizing) having sex with an older white woman while working as her "houseboy" (played by Waters's real-life partner, Peter Cramer), and with a younger white male lover; in conversation with his dead mother; getting a heroin fix; and performing his much-talked-about "act" in a glittering, glamorous, empty club.

Outside of Winter's outré subjects and formal experimentation, there are other blocks on his long road to canon. The owners of Milestone Film and Video, Amy Heller and Dennis Doros, played their part. The distributors of *Portrait of Jason,* and the directors of Project Shirley – an "ongoing commitment to learn everything about Clarke as a director, an artist and a person" (Heller "*Jason and Shirley*") – also attest to seek canonical change:

> At Milestone Films, we sought out films that reflected the lives and work of African Americans, women, LGBTQ people, and Native Americans. Rather than smashing icons, we decided to work to radically reshape and enlarge the pantheon we believed in. [...] We are still at it. And we are amused to learn that many film programmers have adopted our Milestone motto: 'We like to fuck with the canon!'
>
> *(Heller et al., "How Can Film")*

As do *Portrait of Jason* and Shirley Clarke! Clarke's inclusion of her own directorial voice, as well as the beautiful roll-outs of film stock and blurs as the camera comes out and in to focus, are two of *her* milestones, indications of her mastery and her privilege and power in this interrogation of filmic control (Mekas). Winter makes this explicit through scripted interactions where Jason (Waters) and Shirley (Schulman) discuss the play of power between them. This is only another canonical move, mirroring the master:

JASON: I did underestimate you.
SHIRLEY: What a surprise: that happens every day of my life.
JASON: What happens to you when the tables are turned?
SHIRLEY: Now, I'm the director. There's enough movies about women not by women.

Even as Winter's film thoughtfully considers Shirley's position, Milestone took umbrage at his portrayal of Clarke. In a scathing and tarnishing turn, these bulwarks of independent cinema penned an opinion piece, "*Jason and Shirley*: The Cruelty and Irresponsibility of 'Satire,'" perhaps unselfconsciously taking up (again borrowing from the musical definition of "canon") a "retrograde mirror": "We feel we must go on the record about the film's inaccurate and simplistic portrayals of a brilliant filmmaker and her charismatic subject.... The filmmakers claim the right to re-imagine the events that took place in that Hotel Chelsea apartment, but they fail to understand something that Shirley Clarke knew and conveyed in all her films: the need for integrity."

Winter imagines lots of things, including (as did Clarke), the play with and movement of integrity between people joined and separated by artificial hierarchies. In this, we all play a part – as viewers, writers, distributors, students, canon-makers – although this is usually left off screen, and only some of us, it seems, are self-aware. Okay… I too quickly entered the fray, writing an opinion piece for *IndieWire*:

> I commend and support Milestone's project of unearthing and sharing materials for scholars, teachers, and fans of Clarke, and also acknowledge and salute their under-sung role as distributors of avant-garde, experimental, and independent cinema, including the work of female film directors, like Clarke and others whose voices and vision would otherwise fall outside the scope of accessible media culture.
>
> (Juhasz "In Defense")

I go on to explain that I too am a supporter of Winter's work. As the white, female, culturally Jewish, and queer producer of Cheryl Dunye's *The Watermelon Woman* (1996) – trying to gain traction for our tiny indie film, the first African American lesbian feature: "I knew about the glaring and damaging under-representation of Black queer Americans, about the obstacles to entry for films about and from this perspective, and perhaps as critically, the haunting burden for most artists in such a terrain to make and share 'positive images' of their under-represented community."

Back to Heller and Doros, in the name of Shirley: "Lazy filmmakers make bad movies and *Jason and Shirley* is false, flaccid and boring – unforgivable cinematic sins. Perhaps its most egregious and painful crime is taking the strong, brilliant woman that Shirley Clarke truly was and portraying her as a lumpy, platitude-spouting Jewish hausfrau." At this point, I will let their takedown skitter off this rondo. I do not want its ill-will to further saturate this consideration, even as I emphasize how their words did serve some role in muffling the film's opportunities. Elsewhere, I have written about the formative role of censorship in the history of AIDS cultural production. I note that the anger that it instills in those it tries to silence often produces the reverse, canon-like (Juhasz "AIDS Video"). And *Jason and Shirley* is an AIDS film. Schulman, Waters, and Winter are central players in the New York and international AIDS cultural scene. More on queer scenes soon.

In *Jason and Shirley*, Winter and his co-screenwriters and leads, the Jewish, lesbian Schulman and the Black, gay Waters, do perform as once-alive people with similar positions. And yes, some aspects of these portrayals are cruel, if also funny, sad, and complex. In their narrative re-rendering, these artists imagine what never made it to the documentary screen in Shirley's great work. But also, critically, Schulman and Waters perform an eerie doubling – canon-like – of the self-aware performances first enacted by Jason who played himself for a Shirley with her own need to stage power. "A man's world is a woman's world pretending to be a man's world," explains Jason (Waters) to Shirley (Schulman). Or as the real Jason puts it: "Sell a little tragedy; people like to see you suffer." Thus, if there is cruelty, irresponsibility, or satire (in all this, from films to criticism to screening series conversations), this is canonical in the musical sense: mirrors in the opposite direction. For Schulman is one of our period's rare white, Jewish, lesbian artists to (finally, deservedly) reach canonical attention as an author and playwright; and Waters is an infamous denizen and revered artist of this and previous periods' demimonde of BIPOC queer New York. People, films, and causes move into and out of the picture as canons are changed within and by communities or art scenes. Writes King, "An art world, for [Howard] Becker, is constituted not just by a body of work but also its accompaniment by a range of institutional and discursive practices through which claims to the status of art are made, legitimized or contested – processes central to the notions of quality" (17).

The idea that films are placed into canons based on meritocracy is challenged by any look at the inner workings of the organizations and individuals entitled to choose. But, of course, there are many canons: mainstream, indie, Black, queer, academic, and so on. These influence each other; some are widely known, others stay small. The shaming of the Hollywood Foreign Press Association (Barbaro) and the campaigns around #OscarsSoWhite (Ugwu) are contemporary efforts to reveal (and change) the longstanding obstructions and obfuscations behind mainstream film awards and the significant attention they allow. In a similar vein, Matt Brim's discipline-busting work, *Poor Queer Studies*, considers hierarchical support in another institutional setting: "To what extent does academic Queer Studies trade on the value – and therefore the values – of its wealthy institutions, thereby sustaining their commitment to structural inequality?" (10). His answer? "Queer Studies, like much of academia, construct[s] its identity around the myth of meritocracy that disguises the unqueer protocols of academic elitism" (195). How is this related to the queer BIPOC film canon that some of us need?

My back and forth over email about this chapter with the collection's editors reveals how even the most open-minded scholars can be hindered in our queer valuations by tastes and gates. As Winter does in *Jason and Shirley*, let's take a peek behind-those-scenes.

AJ: [Dear] Justin and Wyatt: I understood an essay I could write. On Stephen Winter's *Jason and Shirley* (2015). An essay about the film would put it into the Black queer canon, place it into American experimental documentary, think more about Winter's oeuvre, and would also talk about how it was black-listed by Shirley Clarke's distributor, Milestone Film and Video, and would, thus, of course, also need to be about *Portrait of Jason*. ("Re: An Invitation" 15 Dec. 2020)

In response a few days later, Justin Wyatt and Wyatt Phillips inform me that their editors have set forth some limiting pre-conditions for entry. "Routledge wants every film title to be accessible within both North America and Europe."

They ask, "Is *Jason and Shirley* readily available?" (Wyatt). I inform them that Stephen has affirmed that the film is available on his vimeo site, and that he is in negotiations for a broader distribution. They reach out again and I am informed that vimeo won't cut it. I respond from the angry space of canon-busting.

AJ: Might there be a way to be more creative and/or flexible about this? The film's lack of distribution is a sign and symptom and outcome of the very issues about voice, access, power, and legacy I'd want to consider in American Indie Cinema.... I believe this is telling us something about academic scholarship and publication and its place in promoting or maintaining power and visibility in light of race, gender, and sexuality, that I think we need to address head on. ("Re: An Invitation" 16 Jan. 2021)

The Wyatts listen, readjust, and play their part in expanding canons. This chapter results.

Excess, Rage, Legibility, and Legacy

In 1967, a white Jewish female filmmaker – in an act of cinematic bravura aligned with avant-garde techniques of her scene – invents an austere, minimalist style to clarify the power of documentary as it aligns with gender, race, class, and sexuality. Decades later, styles and scenes a-changing, Stephen Winter tells his version of one Black gay man's story. Winter's style, like that of the gender-non-conforming performance artists, activist lesbians, Black and radical faeries, who make up his community and the scenes he represents with them, is a narrative rendered in his cinematic language as he attempts to honor Jason's pain, courage, and over-the-top campy mess in the face of Shirley's control and the success it gains her. While both films represent embodiments of queer Blackness and white female creativity, one is stark and conceptual, the other excessive and trippy (if no less conceptual).

Matt Brim, working as do I to show the behind-the-scenes of academic field formation, considers the racism of our queer canons: "If counternarratives put narrative in the service of Blackness by writing Black and racialized non-histories back into the historical record, they also do so by countering some of the West's most familiar stories, revealing them to have been told in the service of whiteness" (170). Whiteness, like all unearned, institutionally sanctioned, and supported power, seeks to persist and dominate by staying unseen and unnamed. Shirley Clarke had the chutzpah to expose and examine whiteness by including her voice in an exposé of the life, style, and pain put into play by making Jason her film's visible subject. Stephen Winter puts white power and Black agency into "the service of Blackness," through psychedelic color, bravura countercultural showmanship, and the radical political agenda of self-representation.

Notes

1 The belatedness and other altered temporalities of the attention paid to women filmmakers in American indie cinema are discussed in Pamela Robertson Wojcik's entry on *Wanda* (1970) in this collection.
2 See Morrison here on Clarke's oeuvre and its reception, including the censorship of *Portrait of Jason* over several generations of viewership.
3 Editorial comments made during chapter revisions.
4 Eds.: As of June 2022, it was no longer available there, likely due to the licensing agreement with Criterion.
5 Michael Gillespie mentions Winter as part of his ongoing project to build an American and Black cinematic canon (see for example, Longo 115).

Works Cited

Barbaro, Michael, with Kyle Buchanan. "The Rise and Fall of the Golden Globes." *The Daily – New York Times*, 20 Jan. 2022, www.nytimes.com/2022/01/10/podcasts/the-daily/golden-globes-awards.html.
Baumann, Shyon. *Hollywood Highbrow: From Entertainment to Art*. Princeton University Press, 2018.
Brim, Matt. *Poor Queer Studies: Confronting Elitism in the University*. Duke University Press, 2020.
"Canon (music)" *Encyclopedia Britannica*, 1998, www.britannica.com/art/canon-music.
"*Chocolate Babies* Q&A Moderated by Jeremy O. Harris." YouTube, uploaded by NewFestNYC, 24 May 2021. www.youtube.com/watch?v=AK1ac0mT8FA. The discussion was recorded as part of the BAM NewFest film series Queering the Canon: BIPOC New York, which screened online 7–10 May 2021.
Heller, Amy [with Dennis Doros]. "*Jason and Shirley*: The Cruelty and Irresponsibility of 'Satire.'" *SydneysBuzz The Blog*, 23 June 2015, blogs.sydneysbuzz.com/jason-and-shirley-the-cruelty-and-irresponsibility-of-satire-9037ffc84459.
Heller, Amy, et al. "How Can Film Restoration Rewrite the Cinematic Canon?" *Walker Reader – Soundboard VIII*, 17 July 2019, walkerart.org/magazine/soundboard-film-restoration-amy-heller.
Hereford, André. "Stephen Winter's Audacious 'Chocolate Babies' and 'Jason and Shirley' Join Criterion's Classics." *MetroWeekly*, 20 Sept. 2021, www.metroweekly.com/2021/09/stephen-winters-audacious-chocolate-babies-and-jason-and-shirley-join-criterions-classics/.
"*Jason and Shirley*." *Wikipedia*, en.wikipedia.org/wiki/Jason_and_Shirley.
Juhasz, Alexandra. "AIDS Video: To Dream and Dance with the Censor." *Jump Cut* no. 52, 2010, www.ejumpcut.org/archive/jc52.2010/juhaszAIDS.
———. "In Defense of *Shirley and Jason*: A Lovely Incantation of a State We All Can Identify With, The State of Jason." *IndieWire*, 14 July 2015, www.indiewire.com/2015/07/in-defence-of-shirley-and-jason-a-lovely-incantation-of-a-state-we-all-can-identify-with-the-state-of-jason-214922/.
———. "Re: An Invitation." Received by Justin Wyatt and Wyatt Phillips. 15 Dec. 2020.
———. "Re: An Invitation." Received by Justin Wyatt. 16 Jan. 2021.
King, Geoff. *Quality Hollywood: Markers of Distinction in Contemporary Hollywood Film*. Bloomsbury Publishing, 2015.

Longo, Regina. "The Art of Film Blackness: A Conversation with Michael Boyce Gillespie on *Film Blackness and the Idea of Black Film* [sic]." *Film Quarterly* vol. 70, no. 1, 2016, pp. 112–117.

Mekas, Jonas. "An Interview with Shirley Clarke on *Portrait of Jason*." *Movie Journal: The Rise of a New American Cinema, 1959–1971*. Macmillan, 1972, pp. 289–291.

Mills, Robert. "Death in the Streets, Blood on Your Hands: *Chocolate Babies* and the 'End' of AIDS" [peer-evaluation manuscript]. *JCMS: Journal of Cinema and Media Studies*, forthcoming (2023), pp. 1–40.

Rich, B. Ruby. "New Queer Cinema." *Sight & Sound*, vol. 2, no. 5, 1992, pp. 30–34.

Ugwu, Reggie. "The Hashtag that Changed the Oscars: An Oral History." *New York Times*, 6 Feb. 2020, www.nytimes.com/2020/02/06/movies/oscarssowhite-history.html.

Williams, Conor. "For the Love of Black Queer Cinema: A Conversation with Stephen Winter [Interviews – 27 October 2021]." *Criterion.com*, www.criterion.com/current/posts/7582-for-the-love-of-black-queer-cinema-a-conversation-with-stephen-winter.

Winter, Stephen. "Stephen Winter." *vimeo*, vimeo.com/stephenwinter.

Wyatt, Justin. "Re: An Invitation." Received by Alexandra Juhasz and Wyatt Phillips. 10 Jan. 2021.

47
THE WITCH (2015)

Alex Brannan

The Witch premiered at Sundance on 27 January 2015 to much fanfare. To critics who reviewed it, it was a smart blend of supernatural horror and psychological drama (Chang; Smith; Kohn). The initial reviews heralded the film as an accomplished feature debut for writer-director Robert Eggers. This praise was affirmed when Sundance awarded Eggers its Directing Award, citing his work as "a consistent and excellently rendered vision … masterfully executed" ("Sundance Film Festival"). Even before its premiere at the prestigious festival, the independent studio A24 had entered a bidding war for the film which also included IFC Films and Magnolia (Kit), ultimately securing US distribution rights for the film for a reported $1.5 million (Lang and Setoodeh). As part of this deal, one of the "most-buzzed about" films of Sundance 2015 was to receive a sizeable theatrical release with a substantial marketing campaign behind it (Tallerico). While some critics predicted that the film would struggle to draw a mainstream audience (McCarthy; Chang; Smith), *The Witch* turned a healthy profit with a worldwide gross of $40.4 million ("The Witch (2016)"). This made it, at the time of its release, the highest grossing film A24 had distributed. This chapter examines the film's situation as part of multiple categories: *The Witch* is at once a member of the divisive genre of "elevated horror" and an independent film in A24's growing library of prestige titles. Through analyses of the genre makeup of the film and its connections to indie film aesthetics, as well as the marketing campaign behind the film as part of A24's brand-driven strategy, the chapter places *The Witch* within the broader contexts of American independent cinema.

Set against the backdrop of the emergent colonial New England of the 1630s, *The Witch* is a self-described "folktale" which depicts the ironic moral degradation of a Puritanical family at the hands of paranoia and accusations of witchcraft and devil worship. The film begins, appropriately, in a church, where a council

FIGURE 47.1 Thomasin (Anya Taylor-Joy) plays peek-a-boo with baby Samuel, moments before the child is kidnapped.

is being held to determine the fate of said family. William (Ralph Ineson), the family's patriarch, is accused of heresy to the Church. It is intimated from William's opening monologue that he believes the church has failed in its religious duties; he states to his adjudicators, "I cannot be judged by false contented Christians under an unseparated Church." As Brandon Grafius explains in his monograph on the film, the impetus for many English Puritans to leave for the colonies was the belief that, during the Protestant Reformation, "the split between the Church of England and the Catholic Church did not go nearly far enough" (15). William's dissent from the church, revealed later in the film to be fueled at least in part by pride, leads his family to be exiled from the settlement.[1]

William moves his family – his wife Katherine (Kate Dickey), eldest daughter Thomasin (Anya Taylor-Joy), eldest son Caleb (Harvey Scrimshaw), twin siblings Mercy (Ellie Grainger) and Jonas (Lucas Dawson), and the newborn baby Samuel – to a small home on the outskirts of an ominous woods. Not long after, Samuel, under Thomasin's watch, is stolen away by a witch and carried into the woods, never to be seen again. Quickly, relationships among members of the family are strained, and the homestead becomes the site of multiple accusations of foul play, mostly involving Thomasin. As tensions rise, violence ensues, and Thomasin is left the sole surviving member of the family.

The Witch: Elevated Folk Horror

The Witch belongs to more than one category of horror. As indicated by the film's full title, *The Witch: A New England Folktale,* it is an example of contemporary folk horror.[2] Folk horror finds its cinematic roots in three British films:

Witchfinder General (1968), *The Blood on Satan's Claws* (1971), and *The Wicker Man* (1973). The other genre to which *The Witch* belongs, so-called elevated horror, is similarly tied to late-1960s and 1970s genre cinema. Influenced by relatively less violent and more mood-driven horror films like *Rosemary's Baby* (1968) and *Don't Look Now* (1973), the contemporary cycle of elevated horror began in the mid-2010s as a response to the hyper-violent horror cycle of the 2000s.[3]

Elevated horror, which has been alternately labeled "post-horror," "art-house horror," and "prestige horror," can be loosely defined by the following common characteristics: an emphasis on shot composition and an atmospheric mood over the traditional "jump scare" mechanics common of mainstream horror; reliance on the depiction of psychological states instead of, or in conjunction with, the depiction of traditional horror monstrosity; deliberate pacing that gives way to a more rapidly paced (and oftentimes more violent) climax; a discordant musical score; and the use of visual symmetry and slow camera movement. Furthermore, David Church, in his book *Post-Horror: Art, Genre and Cultural Elevation*, establishes thematic commonalities within the elevated horror corpus (13). Three of these themes – trauma, gaslighting, and familial inheritance – are evident in *The Witch*.[4]

The elevated horror cycle that began in the 2010s was initiated in the independent sector, most visibly by A24. A24's prestige brand and theatrical distribution strategy set its elevated horror properties – films like *It Comes at Night* (2017), *Hereditary* (2018), *Midsommar* (2019), *The Lighthouse* (2019) (Eggers's next film), and *Men* (2022) – apart from their genre contemporaries. Other independents also adopted the elevated horror trend, including IFC Films (*The Babadook* [2014]), the now defunct RADiUS-TWC (*It Follows* [2015]), and Neon (*Titane* [2021]).

While major studios have occasionally forayed into the distribution of elevated horror, most notably in the case of Universal dealing with Blumhouse to distribute *Get Out* (2017), the conventions of elevated horror are more in line with those of independent cinema. Chiefly, the foregrounding of form and the undermining of genre conventions, which Geoff King identifies as two elements common of independent films (137-138, 165-167), connect elevated horror to indie style. *The Witch* exemplifies this connection quite clearly. An early scene in the film depicts the family's baby, Samuel, being stolen away into the woods. The scene relays plot information, but it does so in a way that emphasizes cinematic form over narrative function. It begins with an establishing shot that slowly pushes in toward the woods, an unsettling vocal chorus intruding on the soundtrack. The kidnapping itself is never shown, the absence of the child only revealed to the audience when Thomasin looks down to discover he is not there. This is followed by two slow tracking shots of the woods as a cloaked figure hurries away with Samuel, the framing of the action obscured by tangled branches in the foreground. These shots enhance the foreboding tone and prominently display the natural landscape, an element which is central to the folk horror genre.

The subsequent shots depicting Samuel's demise, with their low-key lighting and intermittent cuts to black, are stylized in such a way as to call attention to themselves. This scene, as with others in the film, asks the viewer to focus as much on film form as on the story.

The Witch also challenges generic conventions in the way independent films are wont to do. Elevated horror's restraint on violence undermines the Grand-Guignol spectacle found in most other horror cinema.[5] The violence of the aforementioned scene is obfuscated by lighting and elliptical editing, and the remainder of the film's violent content is reserved for the final minutes. Furthermore, the absence of jump scares presents a "denial of the usual pleasures" associated with the genre (King 190). The film is thus a departure from the mainstream horror fare produced by major Hollywood studios, revealing its status as an independent not only through its means of production and distribution but also its style and its genre.

A24: Branding Independence

Throughout the 1990s, independent cinema became increasingly institutionalized.[6] The Hollywood majors made moves to diversify their output, which had become increasingly hit-driven since the late-1970s. Their solution to distributing films "not broadly targeted to all moviegoers" was to establish subsidiary indie divisions (Perren 56). This period of consolidation brought with it, according to Michael Newman in *Indie: An American Film Culture*, a notion of independent cinema that "achieved a level of cultural circulation far greater than in earlier eras, making independence into a brand, a familiar idea that evokes in consumers a range of emotional and symbolic associations" (4). Branding independence in this way involved discourses of "alternativeness" and opposition, even as films identified as independent were being created under the umbrella of massive media conglomerates (Newman, "Indie Culture" 17). These conglomerates were also responsible for the mainstream cinema against which independent film was positioned as an alternative. The subsidiary independents operating during this Indiewood period (c. 1996–2008) used this discursive construction of "indie" and their position within the major studios to their advantage. They endeavored to make crossover "indie blockbusters" by "calculatingly nudging some indie films toward the mainstream" (Newman, *Indie* 5). Even after the Indiewood wave started to wane in the late-2000s, with most conglomerate-owned indie divisions closed or restructured between 2006 and 2008 (Schatz 137-138), this concept of indie branding remained a critical part of the independent film scene.

For independents that launched in the 2010s, most prominently A24 (2012) and Neon (2017), establishing the brand was a top priority. A24's branding strategy involved a careful negotiation of the tensions between "indie" and "mainstream." According to a *Los Angeles Times* profile, one of A24's driving goals was "to rewrite the indie-movie playbook by erasing the divide between art-house cinema and the multiplex" (Lee). Speaking of the "art-house ghetto," the piece illustrated the indie space as one where creativity was being suffocated by a lack of visibility (Lee). With conglomerate Hollywood's Indiewood period giving way to an even greater emphasis on franchise blockbusters, there was a perception that independent cinema had stagnated. The *LA Times* profile celebrated A24 as a company which could free films from indie stigma by providing them with "hard-won cultural exposure" (Lee). A24 was framed here as similar to the biggest indie brand of the 1990s, Miramax, and it positioned A24 as a beacon of hope in the desolate desert of independence.

This portrayed the company's theatrical goal as a noble pursuit. However, I would argue that the theatrical distribution of A24's products served a goal beyond this rose-colored narrative of "saving" indie cinema. "Erasing the divide" by bringing art-house cinema to multiplexes was a means of cultivating brand recognition. By claiming its films as art-house fare with mainstream appeal, A24 situated itself as an alternative to both the art-house theater environment and the big-budget blockbuster product that dominated the multiplexes. In doing so, the company branded itself as part of an indie taste culture – a niche within which it could fight for cultural prestige – while nevertheless capitalizing on theatrical distribution and the lucrativeness of its library in the streaming space as a means of reaching for mainstream recognition.[7]

A24 seeks both to differentiate itself from the homogenized mainstream of Hollywood and to embrace the commercialism of the entertainment industries. There are parallels between this model and those of the conglomerate-owned indie divisions of Indiewood. Namely, A24 is emulative of the market strategies New Line and Miramax employed to make crossover hits out of indie content. As was the case with New Line's classics division, Fine Line, A24's films are distributed under the presumption that they have "more crossover potential" than competing indie product (Tzioumakis 33). As the next section will outline, the company's marketing tactics share ties with Miramax's, albeit without Miramax's emphasis on selling controversy.[8] While A24 has not found the same level of blockbuster success as Miramax and New Line did in their heyday – 2022 marked the first year that the studio's annual market share at the domestic box office crossed 1% ("Box Office History") – it distributes and markets its films with crossover success in mind. Of course, A24's current autonomy from the major studios presents a divergence from the structures of Indiewood, where the formerly fully independent Miramax and New Line were purchased in the 1990s by media conglomerates Disney and Turner Broadcasting System, respectively. In addition, A24 has not separated its branding across multiple labels, as New Line did in isolating its art-house films to its Fine Line imprint and as Miramax did with its genre label Dimension. However, the brand-driven, crossover strategy of Miramax and New Line is maintained in the contemporary independent landscape by studios like A24.

Marketing *The Witch*

In line with its branding strategy, A24 markets its films to both casual moviegoers and a cinephile audience consisting primarily of Gen Z and young millennial cinephiles. The youth market, which took concrete shape as a lucrative demographic in the 1950s (Osgerby 15–16), is increasingly engaging with media through digital and online technologies (Wee 135). Appropriately, A24 markets directly to these young audiences through targeted social media campaigns, viral marketing gimmicks, and an online shop catering to cinephiles and brand loyalists. The company also works to entice the casual moviegoer by marketing its films in a more traditional manner. A24's genre films are decidedly not conventional genre fare with broad market appeal. However, the theatrical trailers produced for these films depict them as such. These trailers are not without appeals to cinephile audiences who recognize the A24 brand, but they are constructed in such a way that the films appear more akin to mainstream product. By reconfiguring the generic elements of these films within its marketing, A24 works to sell most of its genre properties as something with which a casual filmgoer would be more familiar.

The Witch was an early success in the deployment of this two-pronged strategy. Prior to its screening at Sundance in 2015, A24 purchased domestic distribution rights for Eggers's film alongside DirecTV (Kit). The plan was to release the film as part of the two companies' deal to jointly acquire films and release them exclusively on DirecTV's VOD (Video on Demand) platform. Following critical praise and growing buzz over the film, A24 decided instead to give the film a wide release. In February 2016, the film debuted in 2,046 theaters domestically (McClintock), where it grossed a total of $25.1 million (growing to $40.4 million worldwide) over a 14-week theatrical run ("The Witch (2016)"). This made it, at the time, the company's most profitable release.

A24 took a variety of approaches in its marketing for *The Witch*. For the cinephile demographic, it created a viral social media campaign which played out on Facebook, Twitter, and Instagram accounts for the company (@a24) and the film (@TheWitchMovie), as well as a Twitter account with posts "authored" by Black Phillip (@BlackPhillip), the goat in the film through which the devil speaks to characters.[9] Embracing internet meme culture and an ironic tone, @BlackPhillip and the rest of the social media campaign targeted young, film savvy moviegoers. This campaign was complemented by an endorsement of the film by the Satanic Temple, which A24 leveraged through special screenings of the film hosted by representatives of the Temple and additional online marketing touting the endorsement (Lang). Reporting on the endorsement in *Variety*, Brent Lang claimed A24 prioritized this social media campaign over traditional television advertising as a cost-cutting measure.

For the more casual audience, A24 cut trailers for *The Witch* which sold it as something of a mainstream folk horror film. Rather than depict the film's less-mainstream elevated horror elements – slow pacing, atmosphere over scare tactics, a relative restraint on violent content – the main theatrical trailer presented the folk horror elements using propulsive editing which made the film appear as a more conventional horror product.[10] The trailer foregrounds the landscape and the physical isolation of the film's characters, while also focusing on the supernatural presence of the witch and the "horrific fallout" which it will incite – all characteristics of the folk horror genre (Scovell 17–18). But the trailer also frames these elements as part of a more conventional "cabin in the woods" style horror film, showing imagery that presents the external threat of witchcraft rather than the more internal, psychological conflict that lies at the heart of the film.

This marketing strategy is similar to how Miramax sold a casual moviegoing audience films which appeared mainstream, regardless of whether the films actually resembled that marketing. Miramax's successful *The Crying Game* (1992) campaign, as Alisa Perren notes, "pulled seemingly every explosion, act of violence, and chase scene out of the film and assembled them into a rapidly paced trailer, thus effectively transforming a methodical, relatively slow-paced film that had a limited number of such sequences" (66). Justin Wyatt's analysis of the company's *Pulp Fiction* (1994) trailer concurs that Miramax's marketing broadened the film's appeal by foregrounding action and sexuality while also selling to the art-house crowd by touting the film's Palme d'Or win (81). *The Witch*, similarly, was marketed to both the cinephile niche and mainstream audiences. The trailer's editing downplays the film's slow pacing and instead gives the appearance of exciting action and violence. The advertisement features images of weapons and bloodshed, such as the images of William prying Caleb's lockjawed mouth open with a knife and of Thomasin disrobing with blood across her chest. But it also proves its art-house bona-fides by calling attention to Eggers's Best Director award win from Sundance.

Conclusion

The marketing strategies behind *The Witch* are illustrative of continuities present between Indiewood and A24. A24 may be economically autonomous from the Hollywood majors, but its corporate aims intersect in key ways with strategies and practices that leading Indiewood production companies like Miramax and New Line had utilized since the 1990s. By employing both a targeted online campaign and traditional theatrical trailers, *The Witch* was presented to audiences as both a lauded art-house product and a familiar genre product. The actual aesthetics of the film, meanwhile, adhere to formal characteristics which appear in prior independent cinema. Drawing attention to style and subverting genre conventions are elements which situate *The Witch*, and its umbrella subgenre of elevated horror, as part of a broader indie style which challenges the "norms of the dominant Hollywood style" (King 106). These elements of economics, marketing, form, and genre situate *The Witch* as part of a broader history of independence.

Notes

1. Grafius also relates William's exile to that of Anne Hutchinson, a member of the Massachusetts Bay Colony who dissented through the belief that one's personal relationship with God superseded the authority of Church doctrine (18–19).
2. The film's association with folk horror is analyzed in greater detail in: Grafius 44–60; Walton.
3. Wharton describes that 2000s cycle as the "neo-grindhouse," which included so-called "torture porn," a trend launched by the popularity of *Saw* (2004), and films which adopted the sensibilities of 1970s exploitation (e.g., *House of 1000 Corpses* [2003] and *Grindhouse* [2007]).
4. For detailed analyses of the themes of trauma, gaslighting, and family ties in *The Witch*, see Olivetti 244–246, 252–253; Church 155; and Carroll, respectively.
5. Agnès Pierron's account of the Grand-Guignol theater describes the "range of tortures" performed on the lead actress (98–99), shades of which carry over into a range of horror subgenres such as splatter, slasher, and torture porn. Incidentally, the Grand-Guignol, under new direction, shifted away from violent spectacle to psychological drama in a move not dissimilar to elevated horror's turn away from the hyper-violence of the neo-grindhouse (100).
6. The introduction of film festivals, most prominently the US Film Festival (later known as Sundance), the creation of "small-scale distributors," and the rapid growth of the home video market in the 1980s all contributed to the success of independent cinema (King 19–23).
7. For a detailed definition of indie taste culture, see Newman, "Indie Culture."
8. For more on Miramax's marketing practices, see Wyatt 79–84.
9. According to Kevin Lincoln at *Vulture*, A24 at the time would "neither confirm nor deny" its ownership of the @BlackPhillip account. Lincoln is quick to point out that the similarity in posting activity on @BlackPhillip and @A24 showed signs of the goat's account being an in-house marketing gimmick.
10. This theatrical trailer was also made available on YouTube: https://www.youtube.com/watch?v=iQXmlf3Sefg.

Works Cited

"Box Office History for A24." *The Numbers*, https://www.the-numbers.com/market/distributor/A24. Accessed 6 Mar. 2023.

Carroll, Chloe. "'Wouldst Thou Like to Live Deliciously?': Female Persecution and Redemption in *The Witch*." *Frames Cinema Journal*, no. 16, 2019, https://framescinemajournal.com/article/wouldst-thou-like-to-live-deliciously-female-persecution-and-redemption-in-the-witch/.

Chang, Justin. "Film Review: 'The Witch'." *Variety*, 23 Jan. 2015, https://variety.com/2015/film/reviews/sundance-film-review-the-witch-1201411310/.

Church, David. *Post-horror: Art, Genre, and Cultural Elevation*. Edinburgh University Press, 2021.

Grafius, Brandon. *The Witch*. Liverpool University Press, 2020.

King, Geoff. *American Independent Cinema*. Indiana University Press, 2005.

King, Geoff, Claire Molloy, and Yannis Tzioumakis, editors. *American Independent Cinema: indie, indiewood and beyond*. Routledge, 2013.

Kit, Borys. "Sundance: A24 Acquires Hot Horror Title 'The Witch' (Exclusive)." *Hollywood Reporter*, 24 Jan. 2015, https://www.hollywoodreporter.com/news/sundance-a24-acquires-hot-horror-762174.

Kohn, Eric. "Review: 'The Witch' Is a Uniquely Spooky Discovery." *IndieWire,* 23 Jan. 2015, https://www.indiewire.com/2015/01/review-the-witch-is-a-uniquely-spooky-discovery-65958/.

Lang, Brent. "How 'The Witch' Scored the Satanic Temple's Endorsement." *Variety,* 21 Feb. 2016, https://variety.com/2016/film/box-office/the-witch-satanic-temple-1201711408/.

Lang, Brent, and Ramin Setoodeh. "Sundance: A24 to Buy 'The Witch' for $1.5 Million (Updated)." *Variety,* 24 Jan. 2015, https://variety.com/2015/film/news/sundance-radius-twc-a24-circling-the-witch-exclusive-1201414043/.

Lee, Chris. "A24: The Brains Behind 'The Bling Ring' Zing." *Los Angeles Times,* 14 June 2013, https://www.latimes.com/entertainment/movies/moviesnow/la-et-mn-bling-ring-brains-20130614-story.html.

Lincoln, Kevin. "The Goat from Horror Movie *The Witch* Has a Twitter Feed: An Investigation." *Vulture,* 9 Sept. 2015, https://www.vulture.com/2015/09/the-witch-goat-black-phillip-twitter.html.

McCarthy, Todd. "'The Witch': Sundance Review." *The Hollywood Reporter,* 23 Jan. 2015, https://www.hollywoodreporter.com/review/witch-sundance-review-766073.

McClintock, Pamela. "Box Office: 'Deadpool' bedevils 'Risen', 'The Witch' with $55M." *The Hollywood Reporter,* 21 Feb. 2016, https://www.cnn.com/2016/02/21/entertainment/deadpool-the-witch-risen-box-office-thr-feat/index.html.

Newman, Michael Z. "Indie Culture: In Pursuit of the Authentic Autonomous Alternative." *Cinema Journal,* vol. 48, no. 3, 2009, pp. 16–34.

———. *Indie: An American Film Culture.* Columbia University Press, 2011.

Olivetti, Kerry A. "Lost without Breadcrumbs; Family, Scapegoating, and the Rationalization of Abuse in Robert Eggers' *The Witch.*" *Marvels & Tales,* vol. 24, no. 2, 2020, pp. 239–255.

Osgerby, Bill. "'A Caste, a Culture, a Market': Youth, Marketing, and Lifestyle in Postwar America." *Growing Up Postmodern: Neoliberalism and the War on the Young,* edited by Ronald Strickland. Rowman and Littlefield Publishers, 2002, pp. 15–33.

Perren, Alisa. *Indie, Inc.: Miramax and the Transformation of Hollywood in the 1990s.* University of Texas Press, 2012.

Pierron, Agnès. "The House of Horrors." *Grand Street,* no. 57, 1996, pp. 87–100.

Schatz, Thomas. "Conglomerate Hollywood and American Independent Film." King et al., pp. 127–139.

Scovell, Adam. *Folk Horror: Hours Dreadful and Things Strange.* Liverpool University Press, 2017.

Smith, Kyle. "The Eerie 'Witch' Leaves Plenty of Haunts and Chills." *New York Post,* 23 Jan. 2015, https://nypost.com/2015/01/23/the-eerie-witch-leaves-plenty-of-haunts-and-chills/.

"Sundance Film Festival." *IMDb,* https://www.imdb.com/event/ev0000631/2015/1?ref_=ttawd_ev_48. Accessed 11 May 2022.

Tallerico, Brian "Cinematic Exorcism: Director Robert Eggers on 'The Witch'." *RogerEbert.com,* 17 Feb. 2016, https://www.rogerebert.com/interviews/cinematic-exorcism-director-robert-eggers-on-the-witch.

Tzioumakis, Yannis. "'Independent', 'Indie' and 'Indiewood': Towards a Periodisation of Contemporary (Post-1980) American Independent Cinema." King et al., pp. 28–40.

Walton, Saige. "Air, Atmosphere, Environment: Film Mood, Folk Horror, and *The Witch.*" *Screening the Past,* no. 43, 2018, http://www.screeningthepast.com/2018/02/air-atmosphere-environment-film-mood-folk-horror-andthe-vvitch/.

Wee, Valerie. "Youth Audiences and the Media in the Digital Era: The Intensifications of Multimedia Engagement and Interaction." *Cinema Journal*, vol. 57, no. 1, 2017, pp. 133–139.

Wharton, Sarah. "Welcome to the (Neo) Grindhouse! Sex, Violence, and the Indie Film." King et al., pp. 198–209.

"The Witch (2016)." *The Numbers*, https://www.the-numbers.com/movie/Witch-The#tab=summary. Accessed 11 May 2022.

"The Witch | Official Trailer HD | A24." *YouTube*, uploaded by A24, 19 Aug. 2015, https://www.youtube.com/watch?v=iQXmlf3Sefg.

Wyatt, Justin. "The Formation of the 'Major Independent': Miramax, New Line and the New Hollywood." *Contemporary Hollywood Cinema*, edited by Steve Neale and Murray Smith. Routledge, 1998, pp. 74–91.

48
1985 (2018)

Daniel Humphrey

Introduction

Historiographers posit many origins for American Independent Cinema, from avant-gardists in the late 1920s to the founding of the Independent Feature Project (IFP) in 1979 and the Sundance Institute in 1981, respectively. One often sees accounts beginning somewhere between, with exploitation filmmakers such as Russ Meyer (*Faster, Pussycat! Kill! Kill!*, 1965) or George A. Romero (*Night of the Living Dead*, 1968) or post–World War II directors inspired by European art cinema like John Cassavetes (*Shadows*, 1958) and Adolfas Mekas (*Hallelujah the Hills*, 1963).

However, as a movement defined by a community of artists responding to specific historical circumstances, what we think of as American Independent Cinema's first chapter must surely begin at the moment that saw the decline of New Hollywood: the late 1970s and early 1980s as demarcated by the founding of the IFP and Sundance. In terms of LGBTQ cinema's place of pride in that movement, a schism is often identified between two recognizably different modes of filmmaking, between what one might call the liberal LGBT Indies of the 1980s and the more formally radical and politically angry New Queer Cinema that exploded in the 1990s. Decades later, Yen Tan's modestly budgeted drama *1985*, which emerged with strong reviews but little fanfare in 2018, represents a stellar example of current American Independent Cinema, one combining the modesty of the LGBT Indies with the infernal fire of New Queer Cinema.

1985 focuses on Adrian Lester (Cory Michael Smith), a young HIV-positive gay man from Fort Worth, Texas, who has managed to escape his conservative origins and create a new life in New York City. The film follows his brief, grim return to the Lone Star State for a Christmas reunion during which he plans to come out to his family as both gay and a person with AIDS. Upon his return,

FIGURE 48.1 Visually referencing an early work of LGBT American independent cinema: *Parting Glances* (1986, left) and *1985* (2018, right).

he realizes his adolescent brother, Andrew (Aidan Langford), is also gay and will have to face the plague-ravaged, homophobic world himself. Meanwhile, Adrian's parents – angry, self-righteous Vietnam veteran, Dale (Michael Chiklis), and nurturing, browbeaten housewife, Eileen (Virginia Madsen) – preside over a home with Christian kitsch on the walls and hateful right-wing talk shows on the radio. Adrian's resolve to assert his identity ultimately dissolves in the presence of his ill-tempered father, who, it turns out, already knows he is gay, and who warns his son in no uncertain terms not to tell his mother. Although Adrian is able to offer some support and love to his kid brother, he begins to sink into despair about ever becoming truly close to his family or even fully accepting himself.

Due to its understated esthetics, thematic concerns, and setting, *1985* commemorates the early years of the American Independent Film movement that it all but exemplifies and to which it implicitly refers. It functions as a conscious invocation of late-1970s and 1980s independent film in a number of its overlapping incarnations, including regional film, family drama, critical illness "social-problem" film, and of course LGBT features, while serving as an authentic representation of and memorial to a lost generation of gay Americans. More politically, if more subtly, Tan's film implicitly connects a certain stoic sensibility in American life to the ultimate failure of that sensibility to create change. This insight would not be out of place in the corpus of the New Queer Cinema of the 1990s.

The moniker New Queer Cinema was given to a number of American independent films by critic and scholar B. Ruby Rich in 1992, films directed by LGBTQ survivors of the first decade of the AIDS catastrophe and whose work, among other things, reflected a deep outrage at the homophobic, AIDSphobic, and monstrously indifferent culture at large (*The New Queer Cinema*, 16–32).

They include *Edward II* (1991), *Poison* (1991), *Swoon* (1992), *The Living End* (1992), *Totally F★★★ed Up* (1993), *Go Fish* (1994), and *Postcards from America* (1994). These were in sharp contrast to gentler AIDS-themed LGBT Indies made by those who came a few years before, most of whom died young: *Buddies* (1985), *Parting Glances* (1986), and *Longtime Companion* (1989), films that might seem to suggest an acceptance of a history that, as Fredric Jameson says, "hurts," that "refuses desire and sets inexorable limits to individual as well as collective praxis" (102). One of *1985*'s many strengths all these years later is that it pays tribute to those more politely political dramas of the pre-New Queer Cinema era to which it harkens while ultimately revealing a modulated, acute sense of moral and social outrage that rivals anything one might find in the early work of Haynes, Kalin, Araki, and McLean. Above and beyond its specific concerns with the impact of AIDS on a generation of gay men, *1985* stands as a new classic within American Independent Cinema.

A Cinema of Outsiders

For many who live in Texas, including this author, the origins of the American Independent Cinema are close at hand, in Austin, Dallas, and the Brazos Valley. It began with Eagle Pennell, son of a Texas A&M professor, whose $30,000 black and white film, *The Whole Shootin' Match* (1978), follows a pair of under-educated, underemployed men struggling to adapt to a then-new information economy. Shot in and around Austin, it premiered at the USA Film Festival in Dallas, having been programmed by film scholar and *Hollywood Reporter* columnist Arthur Knight, who championed it as a shining example of what he called a new "regional cinema." *The Whole Shootin' Match* was, he said, "one of the first truly 'regional cinema' feature films with enough humor and serendipity to appeal to nationwide audiences" (qtd. in Macor 57).

Mary P. Erickson defines regional cinema as:

> filmmaking… that comes from regions… grouped according to similarities in geography, culture, and so on…. For some… they represent something closer to the "true" character and fabric of American cinema, not because they are similar to one another but because they revel in creating an impression of uniqueness, with what are presented as honest portrayals of live experiences.
>
> *(310)*

Initial proponents of this regional cinema touted its origins far from LA and New York, pointing to an impressive canon including *Northern Lights* (John Hanson and Rob Nilsson, North Dakota, 1978), *Gal Young 'Un* (Victor Nunez, Florida, 1979), and *Return of the Secaucus 7* (John Sayles, New Jersey, 1980). Nevertheless, many films laying claim to the regional cinema project come from urban centers. Charles Burnett's *Killer of Sheep* (Los Angeles, 1978), Claudia Weill's *Girlfriends*

(New York, 1978), and Arthur J. Bressan Jr.'s *Abuse* (New York, 1983) have been recognized alongside their rural counterparts. They tend to feature rough-hewn, often black and white, cinematography, appropriated locations, and the kind of uneven acting that results from being unable to afford multiple takes or long rehearsal periods, but which can give the films their own awkward form of verisimilitude. Of course, the urban films within this movement focused on subjects somewhat different from their country cousins: African Americans, "career women," and LGBTQ individuals.

Following its Dallas premiere, Robert Redford saw *The Whole Shootin' Match* at what was then called the Utah-US Film Festival, which had as its *raison d'être* a "Regional Cinema" competition as well as a first-year theme, "American Landscapes: Cycles of Hope and Despair" ("Utah-US Film Festival Set"). As Redford remarked later, "I got to thinking, No one else is going to see this little gem. It seemed a crime to me.... I decided, There is an inequity. This guy needs some help" (Callan 284). The result was The Sundance Institute, which, with its directors', screenwriters', and producers' workshops served an increasing number of filmmakers newly drawn behind the camera.

As Independent Cinema developed during the early and mid-1980s and the Utah-US Film Festival changed its name (repeatedly), moved from Salt Lake to Park City, and was absorbed into Redford's now-thriving organization (where it was eventually rechristened the Sundance Film Festival), Hollywood took note. Studios began developing their own more authentic rural-set films. Waxahachie, Texas-born Robert Benton helmed small-town chronicle *Places in the Heart* (1984), loosely based on his childhood, for Tri-Star Pictures that is prototypical in this regard. Meanwhile, female filmmakers and those from other groups long shut out of Hollywood's corridors of power continued working on personal, low-budget films. Claudia Weill's feminist *Girlfriends* led to other chronicles of female subjectivity like Marisa Silver's *Old Enough* (1984) and Joyce Chopra's *Smooth Talk* (1985). African American Charles Burnett followed his *Killer of Sheep* with *My Brother's Wedding* in 1984. For his part, gay Arthur J. Bressan Jr.'s *Abuse*, which provocatively presents a sexual relationship between a 32-year-old filmmaker and the 14-year-old boy he is trying to protect from physically abusive parents, was followed by *Buddies,* a micro-budget feature exploring a friendship between two gay men: a bedbound AIDS patient and the emotional support volunteer who visits him in his hospital room.

Buddies proclaimed itself the first feature film to focus in any significant way on AIDS, appearing just weeks before the highly publicized, predictably heteronormative, TV movie *An Early Frost* (1985). But the next Sundance-managed film festival – called the United States Film Festival that year – had a particularly diverse, for its time, program, including Wayne Wang's *Dim Sum* (1985), Donna Deitch's lesbian romance *Desert Hearts* (1985), and the first gay directed, AIDS-themed film that broke through in a significant way, Bill Sherwood's *Parting Glances*. The latter follows a couple, Robert (John Bolger) and Michael (Richard Ganoung), during the 24 hours before Robert leaves New York for a job in

Africa. In the hours prior to Robert's departure, we see that the pair's relationship is foundering, which seems to be the reason Robert accepted the overseas job in the first place. Later, a more sobering reason is mentioned. The departing partner wants to be gone while Nick (Steve Buscemi), a friend of the couple who turns out to have been the love of Michael's life, succumbs to HIV.

Yen Tan has spoken of *Parting Glances*'s influence, something *1985* acknowledges by giving its protagonist the same haircut as Nick in Sherwood's film (Tan). Like *1985* and the regional films that appeared in the late-1970s, *Parting Glances* was made by people who knew the milieu they were chronicling, in this case gay New York. Filmed in crowded apartments where dinner parties and party parties take place, as well as on the streets connecting them (with a final excursion to Fire Island), the film is as much a time capsule/anthropological look at struggling mid-80s queer bohemians in the Big Apple as *The Whole Shootin' Match* is of the white, heterosexual poor in 1970s Austin. And, like the best examples of regional filmmaking, *Parting Glances* offers a sense of lived-in authenticity and generosity toward its characters that, in some moments, evokes the spirit of Jean Renoir, who, in 1939's *The Rules of the Game*, has a character, played by the director himself, acknowledge "there is one thing which is terrible, and that is that everyone has their own, good reasons."

Act Up Fight Back Fight AIDS

The year after *Parting Glances* debuted, the AIDS Coalition to Unleash Power was formed, and the membership of this direct-action collective was unwilling to entertain homophobic society's "good reasons" for ignoring the pandemic. Almost immediately, the word "queer" was reappropriated within the now LGBTQ community, which turned it from moniker of derision to signifier of defiance. Three events happened in quick succession: the formation of another direct-action group, Queer Nation, and the coining of the term Queer Theory by scholar Teresa de Lauretis, both in 1990; and, finally, the emergence of New Queer Cinema, in 1992.

Around this time, the larger arena of American Independent Cinema had entered a stagnant period, exhibiting what one critic called a penchant for "earnest adaptation, thematic plod, and boob-tube aesthetics" (Powers 4). As a result, Sundance programmers Tony Safford and Alberto Garcia began encouraging a more politically modernist form of cinema, printing remarks in the 1989 program taken from one of the previous year's panels, during which theorist and experimental filmmaker Peter Wollen made observations that would prove useful for emerging independent filmmakers:

> The concept of 'independence'... goes back to nineteenth-century art and the idea of the 'salon of the independents' in France. This was the beginning of a breaking away from academic painting and the introduction of the modernist breakthrough.... I see the idea of an independent cinema

> really within that kind of framework. The salon of the independents... developed out of the salon of the rejected, the refusal [to be part of the mainstream].... Independence comes from a working through of rejection rather than a search for acceptance. In that sense... American independent filmmaking still has a great deal to contribute...: is [Independent Cinema] meant to be some kind of training ground for Hollywood... or is it a cinema of the rejected?
>
> *(62, 64)*

One year later, Sundance programmers formally embraced Wollen's argument with a manifesto by Garcia and Safford titled "Optimistically, Toward a 'Cinema of the Rejected'" in which they castigated "the failure of regurgitated derivative works of the dominant cinema." Explicitly evoking Marxist playwright Bertolt Brecht and radical filmmakers Jean-Luc Godard and Jean-Pierre Gorin, they asserted that "theories around a Brechtian or 'counter' cinema abounded in the late sixties and early seventies, and now form a viable critical core to be explored by the independent community" (10, 13).

The following year, as if to end 1990's Sundance festival with a defiant assertion, the jury awarded *Chameleon Street* (1989), Wendell B. Harris's infernal drama of African American poverty and alienation, the Grand Prize over safer possibilities, including a final genteel LGBT community AIDS drama, *Longtime Companion*, which, like *Parting Glances*, showcased a great deal of sadness but little rage. With *Poison*, in a surprise, winning Sundance's 1991 Grand Prize and the first full wave of explicitly defined New Queer Cinema coalescing in 1992, an undeniable sea change occurred. Henceforth, few observers would use regional cinema and American Independent Cinema as anything close to analogous terms. Indeed, for a while, few would talk about the former movement at all.

The newer "queer" films of the rejected often lacked any a lived-in, regional specificity, but they made up for that with political acuteness. They owed more to the European art cinema of Godard, Pier Paolo Pasolini, Rainer Werner Fassbinder, and Chantal Akerman than to figures like John Ford, Jean Renoir, and Vittorio De Sica, who had all been evoked as models for the earlier regional films. In these later works, the suffering caused by AIDS-era homophobia and national neglect were rather differently presented: metaphorized in a harrowing horror film allegory in the "Horror" section of *Poison* and posited as the cause of a righteous crime spree by a pair of HIV-positive lovers in Gregg Araki's *The Living End*. In these films, Brechtian distanciation and other formalist interventions express an intelligent rage about a willfully ignorant general public and the unconcerned political establishment that served it. As B. Ruby Rich put it in an essay that appeared in 1992's Sundance program,

> the nineties already show every indication of ushering in a whole new level of image making for a queer sensibility – or, to be more exact, a range of

new modern and postmodern queer sensibilities that respond to this difficult, unimaginable, but unavoidable decade.

(Rich, "The Gay Nineties" 60)

The queer film and film-studies communities celebrated the New Queer Cinema as something like its own *Nouvelle vague*, with its auteur filmmakers, from Araki to Haynes, heralded as something like queer Godards and Rivettes. The pride this movement engendered remains, with New Queer Cinema and its descendants taught in universities and identified on streaming platforms like the Criterion Channel. The previous generation of LGBT filmmakers, many of which died before they could become as angry as, perhaps, they would have, are often overlooked. When they have been remembered, they are often framed as a necessary prologue to New Queer Cinema, and gently dismissed along with the "plod[ding]" "earnestness" and "boob tube aesthetics" of so many of the worst (non-queer) features of the regional cinema of the 1970s and 1980s. This is hardly fair to micro-budget, deeply felt passion projects like *Buddies* and *Parting Glances*. While naturalistic and straightforward, they have a sincerity and authenticity that comes from artists making near-biographical work on shoestring budgets. This had become a rarity in many of the most derided regional films of the mid- to late-1980s, which gradually became Hollywood products or calling-card films in rural-American disguise.

Synthesis

In addition to its regional cinema roots, *1985,* draws on influences from beyond the United States, just as New Queer Cinema did, particularly Taiwanese "New Cinema" directors like Edward Yang and Hou Hsiao-Hsien and British filmmaker Ken Loach, whose *Looks and Smiles* (1981) provided acknowledged inspiration for *1985*'s high grain, high key monochrome cinematography ("Last Christmas"; Kornits). *Looks and Smiles* is a fitting reference to Tan's film in that it was itself a homage to an earlier era in cinema history, the 1950s' Kitchen Sink realism movement ushered in by (largely queer) directors including Tony Richardson, John Schlesinger, and Lindsay Anderson, much as *1985* is a recreation of the 1980s channeled through that decade's American Independent Cinema. Both *Looks and Smiles* and *1985* harken to a seemingly simpler era with a seemingly simple style. For their part, Yang and Hou, the filmmakers most associated with the Taiwan New Cinema (itself a movement of the early/mid-1980s), seem to have inspired Tan's confidence in, and felicity with what Guo-Juin Hong calls Taiwan New Cinema's propensity for "long shots and long takes that insist on looking from a distance, over time" (97). These strategies allow Tan to stress situational cause-and-effect dynamics and the oscillations between strength and weakness, deception and honesty, fear and yearning, as they appear in ordinary lives. One is sobered by and impressed with the sense of true hatred and fear that Adrian's subtle facial expressions betray toward his paterfamilias. In others moments, a conflicted longing to bond with his father is visible.

An exemplary scene on the Lester's patio, in which Dale tells Adrian he's known about his son's sexuality for some time, begins with a six-minute shot that almost imperceptibly tracks forward. It becomes electric with tension, as the father shifts from supportive – "you know you can always count on me, right?" – to condemnatory, even menacing – "don't lie to me," "don't you even think about telling your mother." The deliberate pacing, in concert with the monochrome image, allows for eerie, poetic effects, such as moments when one notices Adrian's eyes occulted behind deep shadows that give his face something like the appearance of a skull. In concert with the black shadows in Adrien's eye sockets, the gray skin on all the film's characters subtly implies a past tense to a film that functions as a manifestation of ghosts and as a memento mori requiring no mention of mortality rates or visibly ill individuals to break the heart of the spectator. Adrian represents a generation of ghosts who should haunt us more today than they do. Tan succeeds in making us feel haunted. These close-ups, along with the long shots and long takes, as in Taiwan New Cinema, hasten a historical consciousness within the viewer that becomes quietly overpowering.

Where Tan's film shows the greatest connection to Taiwan New Cinema is in the moral and psychological complexities of its characters. Dale, Adrian's father (both men interestingly have names used as often for girls as for boys, something that resonates in different ways with each), carries around the scars of Vietnam (a friend he served with seems to have committed suicide) and the shame of a downwardly mobile lower middle-class life. Eileen, at first seen as little more than a typical housewife, is shown to harbor her own doubts regarding the conservative Christian life she lives, but it seems unlikely she will ever challenge her husband's homophobia, although we are left yearning for her to do so, if only for her younger son. Perhaps the most painful aspects of the film involve Adrian's decision to remain dishonest to his mother, after having been bullied to do so by his father. The patriarchy wins out over the mother/son bond: Adrian's response to Dale's gag order is a firm "yes sir." In what can be interpreted as an act of tragic self-delusion near the end of the film, Adrian essentially thanks his father for getting him a new bible, promising to reassess his life based, one can only conclude, upon what's to be found in that book. Tan gives us a painful and unresolved ending.

Despite the allusions to *Parting Glances*, Tan has said "[t]here's unquestionably a New Queer Cinema vibe" to be felt in his film (Kornits). Clearly, the anger and cinematic complexity, as well as its deeply painful account of those rejected by a dominant cinema that values strength, optimism, and uncomplicated nostalgia earn *1985*'s status as a worthy descendant of the original New Queer Cinema, as itself a contemporary instance of the Cinema of the Rejected. But Tan's film adds another layer of meaning and mourning beyond its New Queer Cinema felicities, with its affiliations with, and loyalty to, earlier films like *Buddies*, *Parting Glances*, and *Longtime Companion*, films that were themselves all but rejected by the newly emboldened "queer movement" of the 1990s with the latter's efficacious anger and formalist esthetics. *1985* replicates a kind of seemingly impassive sensitivity that marked *Buddies, Parting Glances,* and *Longtime Companion*. However, while paying tribute to those films, it also shows the tolls of the behavior it exhibits, a failure to inspire change or effect progress.

The fact that this modest, only seemingly simple film still has not received the accolades it deserves, seems sadly predictable, and in some ways an ironic sign of its core truth. With the dominant cinema even more narrowly configured than it was in the 1980s and 1990s, with 100 million dollar fantasy franchises showcasing limited visions ironically described as "extended universes," a film like this seems like the smallest and most delicate of flowers growing in a crack in the vastest of asphalt parking lots. For those who haven't taken the opportunity to watch it, understand it, and embrace it in all its true complexity, the loss is finally their own.

Works Cited

Callan, Michael Feeney. *Robert Redford: The Biography*. Knopf, 2011.
Erickson, Mary P. "The Pull of Place." *A Companion to American Indie Film*, edited by Geoff King. Wiley-Blackwell, 2016, pp. 303–324.
Garcia, Alberto, and Tony Safford. "Optimistically, Toward a 'Cinema of the Rejected.'" *Sundance United States Film Festival* Program 1990, pp. 10, 13.
Hong, Guo-Juin. *Taiwan Cinema: A Contested Nation on Screen*. Palgrave Macmillan, 2011.
Jameson, Fredric. *The Political Unconscious: Narrative as a Socially Symbolic Act*. Cornell University Press, 1981.
Kornits, Dov. "Yen Tan: Bittersweet Nostalgia." 27 Dec. 2020, https://www.filmink.com.au/yen-tan-bittersweet-nostalgia/. Accessed 10 Oct. 2021.
"Last Christmas, 1985: An Interview with Yen Tan." *Curzon*, 20 Dec. 2018, https://www.curzonblog.com/all-posts/interview-with-yen-tan-director-of-1985.
Levy, Emanuel. "The New Gay and Lesbian Cinema." *Cinema of Outsiders: The Rise of American Independent Film*. NYU Press, 1999, pp. 442–493.
Macor, Alison. *Chainsaws, Slackers, and Spy Kids: 30 Years of Filmmaking in Austin, Texas*. University of Texas Press, 2010.
Powers, John. "Journals: Taking Shots: Downhill at Park City." *Film Comment*, vol. 22, no. 2, Mar.–Apr. 1987, pp. 4–5.
Rich, B. Ruby. "The Gay Nineties." *Sundance Film Festival* Program 1992, pp. 56–66.
———. *The New Queer Cinema: The Director's Cut*. Duke University Press, 2013.
Tan, Yen. Personal interview. 10 Feb. 2019.
"Utah-US Film Festival Set," *Orem-Geneva Times* (Orem, UT), 7 Sept. 1978, p. 8.
Wollen, Peter. "Peter Wollen: Five Points/John Powers: Three Words." *United States Film Festival* Program 1989, pp. 60–65.

49

FIRST COW (2020)

J.J. Murphy

Kelly Reichardt's films have been discussed by a number of scholars, such as Elena Gorfinkel and Catherine Putnam, in terms of "slow cinema," seeing them as countering the hyperkinetic pace of Hollywood cinema. In *Indie 2.0,* Geoff King relates Reichardt's films to social realism, while Fusco and Seymour, in their monograph on the director, employ the twin concepts of "emergency" and the "everyday." Temporality and realism are certainly valid approaches to Reichardt's work. Yet, despite being slow-paced, *First Cow* (2020) seems the least tied to realism of all her films, largely due to its more theatrical style of acting. Strictly auteur approaches, however, ignore a fundamental fact about Reichardt's most successful films, namely the role that screenwriter Jon Raymond plays in her work. As a result, another productive avenue is to view *First Cow* through the lens of screenwriting studies and collaboration.

The collaboration between filmmaker Kelly Reichardt and writer Jon Raymond, which now extends to five critically acclaimed features – *Old Joy* (2006), *Wendy and Lucy* (2008), *Meek's Cutoff* (2010), *Night Moves* (2013), and *First Cow* – remains unique in the history of American independent cinema. In this chapter, I explore their collaboration on *First Cow,* while suggesting its implications for the art of film and, in particular, for American indie cinema. How does their achievement highlight some widespread conceptions of how indie film directors employ screenplays? How does their collaboration point out different roles that screenwriting plays within the independent film community? Does this joint effort suggest a model for how screenwriters and directors can work together more fruitfully?

Many independent directors – Jim Jarmusch, Todd Solondz, Miranda July, and Eliza Hittman, to cite several examples – write their own screenplays. This allows an indie director the ability to maintain greater artistic control over a project than is possible within the studio system. It also reflects the firm

DOI: 10.4324/9781003246930-50

FIGURE 49.1 Cookie and King-Lu selling oily cakes at market.

grip that auteurism continues to hold on indie cinema. When independent directors do collaborate, they seldom work consistently with a single screenwriter. Cinema is at once a narrative and a visual art, so a skillful fiction writer and a gifted film director ought to be able to merge their skills. Yet it has not happened very often in film history, and rarely with such commitment and consistency.

Kelly Reichardt began her career by working as a crew member on Todd Haynes's debut dramatic feature, *Poison* (1991), which won the Grand Jury Prize at the Sundance Film Festival and helped to inaugurate New Queer Cinema. Reichardt, who grew up in Florida, made her own low-budget feature, *River of Grass* (1994), a regional and feminist genre piece set in the area between Miami and the Everglades. Reichardt's film brought her attention within independent film circles, but received only limited theatrical distribution. Her career stalled, which she attributes to sexism in the industry at the time. As she observes, "Independent filmmaking, or any kind of filming, was really not open and generous to women in any way. It was really like beating your head against a brick wall" (Paiella). It was her collaboration with Portland-based fiction writer Jon Raymond that rekindled her feature-film career.

Raymond had been influenced by other artists in the Portland, Oregon, area who were making more experimental films, including Matt McCormick and Miranda July. He also made his own cable-access feature, *Crock* (1996), based on a comic strip by Bill Rechin and Brant Parker about the French Foreign Legion. By Raymond's own account, the film was a humiliating failure. He subsequently served as a personal assistant to Todd Haynes on *Far from Heaven* (2002). Haynes later introduced Raymond to Reichardt, who was looking for material to adapt into a film. Raymond's short story, "Old Joy," became the basis for her new film of the same title. Following its critical success, Raymond and Reichardt jointly developed another of his short stories "Train Choir" into *Wendy and Lucy*, which became a much bigger box office success.

Their backgrounds are significantly different, but Raymond and Reichardt both exemplify the "new regionalism" in modern American fiction and film. Raymond grew up in Oregon and his stories and novels all take place there. Raymond's model for his first short story collection, *Livability* (2008), was Sherwood Anderson's *Winesburg, Ohio* (1919) – a benchmark of regional writing from an earlier era. Before she met Raymond, Reichardt had exemplified the regional bent of much indie film. Her characters in *River of Grass* are very much shaped by the Florida landscape they inhabit. Raymond wrote the short story "Train Choir," on which *Wendy and Lucy* is based, using locations in his own Portland neighborhood. In filming *Wendy and Lucy*, Reichardt scouted locations all around the country before finally deciding to shoot the film exactly where the short story had been set (Sholis). In fact, Raymond's strong sense of place furnishes a basis for Reichardt to present specific landscapes and their shaping effects on the story action.

Reichardt offers insight into the nature of her relationship with Raymond and a sense of the perspective they share:

> Jon Raymond and I are in each other's worlds, and we have a similar political point of view and interest in people. Jon always says that our writing sessions are more like gossip sessions because we are always trying to understand everyone and figure everyone out for character reasons.
>
> *(Kubincanek)*

As is the case of what Vera John-Steiner terms "complementary collaboration," the screenwriter and director also bring different skills to the projects. As John-Steiner suggests, "Differences in modalities – the translation of one's thoughts into a new language of expression or into the developed mode of expression of one's partner – are part of this rewarding process" (198).

Raymond sees a big distinction between writing fiction – short stories and novels – and writing screenplays. He views screenplays as much more schematic. In *The Secret Language of Film*, Jean-Claude Carrière famously observes, "The screenwriter must bear in mind at all times, and with almost obsessive insistence, that what he is writing is fated to disappear, that a necessary metamorphosis awaits it" (151). Like Carrière, Raymond clearly understands that his written words ultimately will be transformed into an entirely different medium during production. Raymond notes, "To write a screenplay is such an abbreviated form of writing. It's just providing a kind of template for a lot of other people to [add] their own creative life and creative contributions." In contrast, he views writing fiction as having to perform all the roles. He continues,

> Writing a story or a book – it's much more akin to being the writer, director, stage manager, cameraman, costume designer: you kinda have to do all

of it. And you have to create a flow from sentence to sentence and a logic from paragraph to paragraph.

(Macaulay)

Raymond's self-identity as a fiction writer (where he has complete artistic control) rather than as a screenwriter has no doubt helped him to partner so successfully with a visual film stylist like Reichardt.

Reichardt generally prefers to work from short stories as source material because they give her a deeper sense of the interiority of the characters, as well as more space to apply her strong visual skills. Her interest in making a film based on the novel *The Half-Life* represented a departure. According to Reichardt:

> Mostly I've been working just from novellas and short stories, like the Maile Meloy stories for *Certain Women* [2016], or the stories I've gotten from Jon. Or we start with an idea and we make it a screenplay. It's always been things that are smaller that I can extend, and get inside of them, and do. And this was a novel.
>
> *(Rubinstein)*

Raymond's novel presented a number of major obstacles for the director. It consisted of two different storylines covering a very large time span, as well as a voyage to China and back – an impracticality for a low-budget indie film.

Reichardt had no idea how the novel could possibly be reduced in scope until another feature project fell through and she and Raymond brainstormed on making *The Half-Life* workable. It was only after Raymond came up with the idea of introducing a cow into the "Cookie" storyline that everything began to fall into place (Rubinstein). They made two crucial decisions. One was to focus on the single earlier timeline set in the Oregon Territory; the other involved the idea of the cow as a way to deal with the issue of burgeoning international trade. A number of elements were retained from the novel, most notably the basic character of "Cookie," the male friendship he develops with King-Lu (who represents a combination of two characters in the novel), and the pair of skeletons that are found many years later. Adaptation into a screenplay and film involved completely reworking it. The screenplay ended up being 78 pages long, while the running time of the film is 122 minutes. If, as screenwriting manual writers such as Syd Field argue, one page equals one minute of screen time (22), the discrepancy suggests slower pacing, as well as Reichardt's predilection for visual storytelling over dialogue.

Although *First Cow* could be considered a heist film, it is, at heart, more a character study about male friendship. Like the book, the film begins with an epigraph from William Blake's *Proverbs of Hell*: "The bird a nest, the spider a web, man friendship." *First Cow* is not heavily dialogue-based. Otis Figowitz, aka "Cookie" (John Magaro), a chef for a rowdy group of early Northwest fur traders, and King-Lu (Orion Lee), a Chinese fugitive he initially discovers hiding in the forest, hardly speak to each other. After they come together a second time at the tavern, the relationship is manifest through their behavior – the way that they engage in domestic chores. There is an immediate shared understanding between them, but it remains, for the most part, unspoken. Reichardt acknowledges,

> Their friendship has nothing to do with anything that's coming out of either of their mouths. It's just totally not in the dialogue with them. We actually get to see them starting to spend time with each other and to cook and to sew, and to be in the fire light together.
>
> (Rubenstein)

The men do actually share some personal details about themselves. Cookie lost his mother at birth and his father soon afterward. King-Lu grew up in northern China and claims that he has been roaming the world ever since the age of nine. Cookie is not at all appreciated by the fur trappers who employ him. The frontier depicted in the film is a hostile and violent environment, where fistfights constantly break out. In describing Cookie's band of fur trappers, Raymond's novel makes this very explicit:

> After four months on the trail together, the trappers in Cookie's hunting party had come to hate each other. The way someone picked his teeth, the way the saddlebags were packed, anything was a good enough reason to come to blows. They hated each other simply for being alive, for breathing too loudly or not loudly enough, depending on what would allow them to hate each other more.
>
> (Raymond 9)

This attitude is epitomized in the film not only by the constant fighting, but by the character with a raven (played by René Auberjonois) who actively resents any newcomers and angrily sweeps the dust and leaves toward Cookie and King-Lu as they pass his shack.

Not only is King-Lu a different race, but, when the men first meet, he is being pursued by a band of Russians. The initial bond that he and Cookie share is one between outcasts. When the two men arrive at King-Lu's cabin, there is an initial awkwardness. After King-Lu pours Cookie a drink, he awkwardly toasts, "Here's to…something." When King-Lu goes outside to chop wood to make a fire, Cookie instinctively begins to tidy up the place – he sweeps the floor with a broom, shakes out a pelt that is used as a mat, and even picks wildflowers to put in a vase. Although there is no discussion about it, from this point on, Cookie and King-Lu begin to live together.

Utilizing what David Bordwell refers to as "restricted narration" (57–58), Reichardt buries the motivation of her characters. As the filmmaker puts it, "My films are just glimpses of people passing through" (Brooks). Cookie is a sad-sack character. He speaks very softly and wears his grief on his face. He often averts his eyes rather than engage another person directly. When he is left to care for a man's baby during a barfight, Cookie attempts to soothe the baby by making cooing sounds. He also has a sensitive and respectful attitude toward nature: righting a helpless salamander on its back in the forest and conversing and empathizing with the cow when he milks her. Cookie exhibits a passivity that is out of step with the new frontier of the Oregon Territory, which is better embodied by the more assertive and entrepreneurial King-Lu, who sees America as a land of "riches," a place that is still "new" – a place of unlimited resources and vast untapped potential. King-Lu, however, laments that a person needs capital to get a business started and even suggests the possibility of committing a crime as a means to obtain it. It seems to be a throwaway line at the time, but one that foreshadows the eventual scheme to steal the milk to make the oily cakes to sell at market.

Raymond has indicated a preference for characters who hide their feelings: "I think I feel more empathy for a character (and for that matter, a person), when I see them holding their worries, fears, loves, inside, out of view" (Colford). There are several instances where viewers have to guess at the motivation of characters. One puzzling incident occurs when Cookie and King-Lu run into each other in the tavern. As a fistfight breaks out, Cookie has been left to watch after Brilliant William's baby, but, at King-Lu's instigation, he abandons the cradle on the bar. Why? Although it seems out of character, we surmise that, seemingly very lonely, Cookie desperately welcomes the company of King-Lu who generously offers to share a bottle of liquor with him at his place.

The ending of the film proves important to understanding the characters, especially King-Lu. Once Chief Factor discovers the theft of cow milk, Cookie and King-Lu are forced to flee. To avoid being caught, King-Lu dives off a cliff into the river, but fear keeps Cookie from following suit. King-Lu does not look back to see what has happened to his friend but only seems intent on saving himself. When the two later reconnect at the cabin, Cookie's head wound becomes a serious liability, especially once King-Lu gets his hands on the bag of money they have hidden. The viewer knows that the young guard with the rifle, Thomas, has Cookie in his sights, but the two pursued men are unaware of this. As Cookie falls asleep, King-Lu fondles the money bag, before using it as a pillow. He grabs hold of Cookie's hand and remarks, "I've got you," before dozing off. The abrupt, caesura-like ending brings us full circle to the human skeletons that the dog helps to uncover at the film's opening.

The connection between the film's ending and the discovery of the buried skeletons exemplifies the propensity for Reichardt and Raymond to employ understatement and ambiguity and to leave gaps in the story for the viewer to fill. Like an imagist poem, crucial events occur off screen – essentially in the viewer's mind. The viewer must associate to the opening and then to the fact that Thomas has a rifle and has managed to track down Cookie. Once King-Lu retrieves the money that he and Cookie hid in the hollow of the tree, he has a choice to make.

Should he abandon Cookie and abscond with the money, or risk staying with his wounded comrade? The script makes this point more obvious:

> EXT. WOOD/CLEARING – NIGHT
>
> King-Lu stares at the trees, keeping watch. He strains to hear the world outside their spot.
>
> In the far distance, he hears the faintest calls. Or does he? He can't tell. He sees a bird. It's only a bird. They are alone.
>
> King-Lu looks at Cookie sleeping.
> He looks at trees, feeling the money sack in his hand, weighing his options.
>
> At last, King-Lu puts the money bag on the ground like a pillow. He lies down beside Cookie.
>
> KING-LU
> We'll go soon. I've got you.
>
> They clasp hands.
> King-Lu closes his eyes. In a moment, he's asleep.
> An owl calls.
> (Raymond and Reichardt 77–78)

The spare, minimal script reads like a poem, but the most telling aspect is the actual acknowledgment, as King-Lu holds the money bag in his hands, that he is "weighing his options." His decision to stay with his wounded pal Cookie over fleeing with the money makes the film a poignant tale about male friendship.

Raymond and Reichardt dealt with a male friendship undergoing change in *Old Joy*, the first film they made together, which had homoerotic overtones. The fur trappers in *First Cow* seem to sublimate their sexuality into fisticuffs. Any sort of sexual aspect to the relationship between Cookie and King-Lu is avoided because, if the nature of their relationship were complicated by sexuality, it would detract from the subject of male friendship. When King-Lu washes up outside, for instance, Reichardt chastely frames him behind the wooden slats of the cabin. In discussing the film's take on male camaraderie, popular culture critic Andy Crump suggests that Raymond and Reichardt provide a rare antidote to the toxicity of masculinity, which is manifest in the constant fighting, bullying, the pushing ahead of others, and the downright abuse of those perceived as weaker. He writes, "The message isn't that it's okay for men to be friends; it's that it's okay for male friendship to have deep roots that last and that endure beyond the span of years and decades."

The theft of the milk is hardly a crime worthy of death, but on the frontier, brute power is the only law, as we learn from a discussion between Chief Factor and the Captain. Factor discusses the punishment of mutineers by advising,

"Sometimes a properly rendered death is even useful in the ultimate accounting. It can be a vastly motivating spectacle for the indolent, let alone the mutinous." When Factor realizes the theft of his milk, he calls for Cookie and King-Lu to be killed. Yet there is irony in his valuing property over human life. Reichardt offers her own commentary about the protagonists' crime in *First Cow*:

> And I guess also there's resonance with a film like *Wendy and Lucy*, with the stealing of the dog food; in this film, there are these guys that are stealing a basket of milk, which is like the big crime in the film, as opposed to seeing the legitimate beaver trade, that's going to wipe out the beaver and wipe out the indigenous people who've lived there forever, as the real crime. So, it looks at those sort of power structures and ideas of justice, but also friendship, which has been a theme in a lot of my films, as well.
>
> (Reed)

It is the notion of "friendship" more than politics that Reichardt has emphasized in interviews about the film. In terms of their collaboration, it is a theme that both Reichardt and Raymond appear to share.

John-Steiner suggests that collaboration, as opposed to individualism, represents a major paradigm shift in the arts and sciences. As such, it complicates traditional notions of authorship. Film and the fine arts, for instance, seem to entertain different but equally imbalanced ideas of how collaboration works. There is a long tradition of collective creation in painting and sculpture, in which artists have employed assistants to make their work. Yet the creator of the work, the artist, is identified as the person who came up with the concept – not the person who executed it. Commercial feature filmmaking works on exactly the opposite idea. Primarily due to its reliance on a crew of technicians and production companies, cinema from its beginnings has been recognized as a collective art form – at least in principle, if not in actual practice, largely due to its hierarchical structure.

In his book *The Screenplay*, Steven Price notes the traditional separation that exists between the screenwriter and director within the studio system, "in which the writer is almost invariably a worker for hire, contractually obligated to relinquish control over the text on submission to the studio, which customarily subjects a 'final draft' to ongoing revisions from many different writers" (x). In the Hollywood film industry, studio heads, producers, and gradually directors came to be recognized as the most powerful creators, while the screenwriter occupied a significantly lower status. The cult of the director was reinforced by the auteur theory of the late 1950s and early 1960s, promulgated by the French New Wave critics and popularized by the influential New York critic Andrew Sarris. In cinema, unlike fine art, it is not the person who comes up with the idea who receives authorial credit, but rather the person – the director – who executes it.

Both tendencies are decidedly off-balance. Because American indie cinema is often auteur-driven, most directors try to recover balance by writing their own screenplays. But there might be another way to achieve equilibrium – a way that Raymond and Reichardt are pointing toward. As a result, their unique complementary collaboration illuminates a somewhat alternative view toward the screenplay and the role of screenwriter and director. In fact, it has been key to Reichardt's success as a director that she has been willing and open to working so closely with a talented fiction writer like Jon Raymond. In the process, they have been able to maintain their separate identities, and their close working relationship in no way detracts from Kelly Reichardt's achievement as one of American indie cinema's most critically acclaimed filmmakers.

Works Cited

Bordwell, David. *Narration in the Fiction Film*. University of Wisconsin Press, 1985.
Brooks, Xan. "Kelly Reichardt: 'My Films Are Just Glimpses of People Passing Through.'" *Guardian*, 21 Aug. 2014, http://www.theguardian.com/film/2014/aug/21/-sp-kelly-reichardt-my-films-are-just-glimpses-of-people-passing-through.
Carrière, Jean-Claude. *The Secret Language of Film*. Translated by Jeremy Leggatt, Pantheon, 1994.
Colford, Caitlin. "An Interview with Jon Raymond." *The Rumpus*, 29 Apr. 2011, https://therumpus.net/2011/04/an-interview-with-jon-raymond/.
Crump, Andy. "*First Cow* is a Necessary Portrait of Male Platonic Affection." *The Week*, 6 Mar. 2020, https://theweek.com/articles/898300/first-cow-necessary-portrait-platonic-male-affection.
Field, Syd. *Screenplay: The Foundations of Screenwriting*. Revised ed., Delta, 2005.
Fusco, Katherine, and Nicole Seymour. *Kelly Reichardt*. University of Illinois Press, 2017.
Gorfinkel, Elena. "Exhausted Drift: Austerity, Dispossession and the Politics of Slow in Kelly Reichardt's *Meek's Cutoff*." *Slow Cinema*, edited by Tiago De Luca and Nuno Barradas Jorge. Edinburgh University Press, 2016, pp. 123–136.
John-Steiner, Vera. *Creative Collaboration*. Oxford University Press, 2006.
King, Geoff. "Social Realism in Art Cinema: The Films of Kelly Reichardt and Ramin Bahrani." *Indie 2.0: Change and Continuity in Contemporary Indie Film*. Columbia University Press, 2014, pp. 169–215.
Kubincanek, Emily. "Kelly Reichardt on How 'First Cow' Questions the Myth of America's Roots." *Film School Rejects*, 4 Mar. 2020, https://filmschoolrejects.com/kelly-reichardt-first-cow/.
Macaulay, Scott. "The Independent Screenwriter: Jon Raymond." *Filmmaker*, 31 May 2014, https://filmmakermagazine.com/71594-the-independent-screenwriter-jon-raymond/#.YEuzrNxOlaQ.
Paiella, Gabriella. "*First Cow* Director Kelly Reichardt on Making Quiet Art and the Failure of American Individualism." *GQ*, 21 July 2020, https://www.gq.com/story/first-cow-kelly-reichardt-interview.
Price, Steven. *The Screenplay: Authorship, Theory, and Criticism*. Palgrave MacMillan, 2010.
Putnam, Catherine. "Countering Dominant Cinema: Temporality in *Meek's Cutoff*." *Senses of Cinema*, no. 96, Oct. 2020, https://www.sensesofcinema.com/2020/feature-articles/countering-dominant-cinema-temporality-in-meeks-cutoff/.
Raymond, Jonathan. *The Half-Life: A Novel*. Bloomsbury, 2004.
Raymond, Jon, and Kelly Reichardt. Screenplay: *First Cow*, n.d. *Deadline*, Feb. 2021, https://deadline.com/wp-content/uploads/2021/02/FIRST-COW-screenplay.pdf.

Reed, Christopher. "Interview: A Conversation with Kelly Reichardt." *Hammer to Nail*, 13 Mar. 2020, https://www.hammertonail.com/interviews/kelly-reichardt/.

Rubinstein, Bessie. "With *First Cow*, Kelly Reichardt Gives Us Friendship, Clafouti, and Udders." *Interview*, 19 Mar. 2020, https://www.interviewmagazine.com/film/kelly-reichardt-first-cow-a24.

Sholis, Brian. "Online Only: Interview with Kelly Reichardt." *Artforum*, Oct. 2008, https://www.artforum.com/print/200808/online-only-interview-with-kelly-reichardt-21124.

50
THE FORTY-YEAR-OLD VERSION (2020)

Sarah E.S. Sinwell

In 2020, filmmaker Radha Blank made her directorial debut with *The Forty-Year-Old Version*, receiving the US Dramatic Competition Directing Award at the Sundance Film Festival (the second Black[1] woman to win this award after Ava DuVernay won the award for *Middle of Nowhere* in 2012). Blank's work traverses multiple art forms, including playwriting, filmmaking, television, and music as a means of sharing both her own voice, and commenting on the need for the voices of Black women to be heard within American culture.

Blank was celebrated and honored during Sundance's Vanguard Award event in 2020, which also included Lulu Wang, Julie Dash (director of *Daughters of the Dust*, 1991), and Octavia Spencer. An award which "honors artists whose work and vision represent the highest level of breakthrough innovation, originality, and independent spirit" (Vanguard Awards), the Vanguard Award had previously been given to directors such as Dee Rees (*Pariah*, 2011 and *Mudbound*, 2017), Boots Riley (*Sorry to Bother You*, 2018), and Lulu Wang (*The Farewell*, 2019). At this event, Blank was heralded for "challenging what we think New York is," and creating creative independent and inclusive storytelling with "a distinctive point of view." Lulu Wang called the film "an instant classic" and *The Forty-Year-Old Version* was called "a mix tape about the forty-year-old woman's point of view." In an interview with Wang at that event, Blank considered the ways in which women "take up space in the storytelling" of her film, as well as how "what seems like mundanity is really about turning up the volume on our humanity," especially for people of color.

Throughout this chapter, I will be focusing on two primary aspects of *The Forty-Year-Old Version*. First, I will be discussing Radha Blank's role as a Black female filmmaker and how that impacts understandings of *The Forty-Year-Old Version*, as well as how the film functions within the context of contemporary American independent cinema, "Black women's filmmaking," and New African

FIGURE 50.1 Radha Blank in her directorial debut, *The Forty-Year-Old Version*.

American Cinema. Then, I will analyze the narrative, cinematic style, and aesthetics of the film itself, drawing attention to its representation of Black female identity and aging femininity and focusing on how it creates a space for Black women's voices to be both seen and heard on screen.

Revisiting New African American Cinema and Black Women's Independent Filmmaking

In his book *Cinema of Outsiders: The Rise of American Independent Film* (1999), Emanuel Levy defines the New African American Cinema as (a) focusing on the everyday experiences of African Americans, (b) questioning stereotypes about blackness (as poor, criminals, maids, prostitutes, etc.), (c) often focusing on the Afro-American oral tradition, (d) addressing social issues such as violence, class, racism, and civil rights, and (e) connecting with Black music (for example, spirituals, jazz, soul, blues, rap, and hip-hop). At the time of his writing in 1999, he argued that New African American Cinema included such directors as Charles Burnett (*Killer of Sheep*, 1978), Spike Lee (*She's Gotta Have It*, 1986), Robert Townsend (*Hollywood Shuffle*, 1987), John Singleton (*Boyz in the Hood*, 1991), and Julie Dash (*Daughters of the Dust*, 1991). Since the 1990s, the New African American Cinema has expanded to include the stories of Black women, LGBTQIA+ communities, and a rebirth of Black horror cinema, including filmmakers such as Gina Prince-Bythewood (*Love & Basketball*, 2000), Lee Daniels (*Precious*, 2009), Dee Rees (*Pariah*, 2011), Ava DuVernay (*Middle of Nowhere*, 2012), Ryan Coogler (*Fruitvale Station*, 2014), Justin Simien (*Dear White People*, 2014), Barry Jenkins (*Moonlight*, 2016), Jordan Peele (*Get Out*, 2017), and Channing Godfrey Peoples (*Miss Juneteenth*, 2020), among others.

Focusing on the everyday experiences of African Americans, these films and filmmakers draw particular attention to the structural inequities associated with race and racism within the United States and reimagine the place of Black voices within American culture. Since the advent of Black Lives Matter in 2013 (following the acquittal of George Zimmerman after the death of Trayvon Martin), the Ferguson protests in 2014, the death of Breonna Taylor in 2015, and the death of George Floyd in 2020, there have been even more films that have addressed police violence and brutality against people of color (including not only *Fruitvale Station*, but also Ava DuVernay's *13th* (2016), Chinonye Chukwu's *Clemency* (2019), and Shaka King's *Judas and the Black Messiah* (2021)). Following these events, there has been a resurgence of independent films that address the racial injustice and systemic racism that plague both the United States and the globe.

Until relatively recently, Black women's voices and Black women filmmakers have rarely been included within this history. In their discussions of Black female filmmakers such as Sanaa Hamri, Dee Rees, Kasi Lemmons, and Ava DuVernay, Shelley Cobb and Cynthia Baron argue for the need to discuss how African-American women have been involved in filmmaking not just as directors but also as writers, producers, cinematographers, and in both above-the-line and below-the-line roles. In this way, Blank's role as producer, director, writer, and star of *The Forty-Year-Old Version* is especially significant. As Jacqueline Bobo writes of Black female filmmakers' histories, "Black women's films are corrective narratives, a form of "representational reparations" featuring aspects of Black women's lives, histories, and experiences different from those evident in mainstream films" ("Black Women Filmmakers" 248).

Speaking of Leslie Harris, director of *Just Another Girl on The I.R.T.* (1992), Samantha Sheppard writes that she is

> one of a small cadre of African American female directors, including Julie Dash, Darnell Martin, Cheryl Dunye, Kasi Lemmons, and Cauleen Smith, who expanded and critiqued black independent cinema with feminist, girl-centric, urban, and rural narratives that were acclaimed and profitable but did not lead to robust cinematic careers.
>
> (29)

In fact, these directors made very few films and their careers often stalled after their auspicious debuts. Instead, some of these filmmakers turned to television or became involved in other filmmaker's work as a means of making ends meet and creating a space to fund their own future films. In the case of Cheryl Dunye, for instance, though she has been attempting to get her next feature *Black Is Blue* funded, in the meantime, she has been working as a director on television series such as *Queen Sugar* (Oprah Winfrey Network, 2016-present), *The Chi* (Showtime, 2018-present), and *Lovecraft Country* (HBO, 2020) (Sinwell). For *Queen Sugar*, Ava DuVernay worked with Winfrey with an expressed goal of employing women directors and focusing on filmmakers who had made "successful" independent films but had largely been blocked from moving to Hollywood-financed films, including hiring directors such as Dunye, Julie Dash, and So Yong Kim.

In an attempt to foster more inclusive storytelling at the Sundance Film Festival, in 2021, Sundance announced that it was its most inclusive festival yet. As noted on the Sundance blog,

> Across 139 films and projects, 50%, or 69, were directed by one or more women; 4% or 6, were directed by one or more non-binary individuals; 50%, or 70, were directed by one or more artists of color; 15% or 21 by one or more people who identify as LGBTQ+.
>
> *(Anon. 2020)*

However, as Samantha Sheppard writes "how the very idea of black film circulates in the current moment of presumed breakthrough, crossover, and arrival" and "the visibility and viability of a few diverse voices do not necessarily translate into greater opportunities for either new or old faces" (26).

Though many of these films focus on the Black women's experience, it is rarer to see stories that do not center around coming-of-age narratives, crime and violence, or familial strife. Stories of single Black 40-year-old hip-hop artists are almost unheard of. In this way, *The Forty-Year-Old Version* is drawing upon and contesting these histories of New African American Cinema to create a place for (aging) Black women's voices to be seen and heard on screen.

Analyzing *The Forty-Year-Old Version*

The semi-autobiographical tale of Radha Blank herself, *The Forty-Year-Old Version* tells the story of a teacher, playwright, and rapper as she approaches her 40th birthday. The film begins with Blank in bed alone as she listens to her neighbors having sex through the thin walls of her cheap apartment. Bringing in elements of New York City, gentrification, hip-hop, and homelessness, the film (both figuratively and literally) asks the question, "What do you think of a girl turning forty?" Like the interviews in Spike Lee's *She's Gotta Have It*, the film includes "man on the street" interviews with a local shopkeeper, neighbors, and students as they respond to the question.

Written, directed, and produced by Blank, *The Forty-Year-Old Version* was shot on 35mm black and white film stock. In an interview with Mary Harron (director of *I Shot Andy Warhol* (1996) and *American Psycho* (2000)), Blank discussed the six year back story to her film, saying,

> A lot of people – financiers, potential producers who were a part of my six-year journey of getting the film made – were just like, "Why don't you just shoot it in digital? What is the big deal?" And I was like, "The people who influenced me didn't have that format." I just wanted to make it the way that they did.
>
> *(Harron)*

Blank worked on *The Forty-Year-Old Version* in the Sundance Director's Lab, where she also worked with her co-star Peter Kim (who plays her agent and her Korean queer best friend in the film). Blank even used the location of her own apartment and cast her own brother Ravi as her brother. She also used her mother's art, her father's music, and her own family photos to create the film, mixing in her own family legacy.

When making *The Forty-Year-Old Version*, Blank said she was especially influenced by Spike Lee's first feature film, *She's Gotta Have It*, which debuted at the San Francisco Film Festival in 1986 (Harron). Shot in 12 days with a budget of $175,000, along with Jim Jarmusch's *Stranger than Paradise* (1984), *She's Gotta Have It* ushered in the 1980s independent film movement and won Best First Feature Award at the Indie Spirit Awards in 1987. In 2017, the film became a television series on Netflix (which Blank wrote for). Incorporating formal experimentation with the authorial female voice, as well as comedic first-person interviews from local characters to add humor and authenticity to the storytelling, Blank's authorial style draws upon not only the work of Spike Lee's *She's Gotta Have It* but also Cheryl Dunye's *The Watermelon Woman* (1996) (Juhasz and Zimmer). In an interview at Sundance, Blank said she was also inspired by Steve McQueen's *Lover's Rock* (2020) and Lena Dunham's *Tiny Furniture* (2010), in so far as those works focused on real-life locations, actors, and characters that elicit authentic and emotional responses (Fleming).

The black and white aesthetic of the film is also reminiscent of American independent filmmakers such as Woody Allen (*Manhattan*, 1979) and New African American Cinema filmmakers such as Charles Burnett (*Killer of Sheep*, 1978). In fact, in her interview with Lulu Wang, Blank stated that her film addresses questions such as "Who gets to make a black and white movie?" and "Who gets to make a two-hour movie?" These questions also draw attention to how *The Forty-Year-Old Version* fits into ideas of "quality" cinema as a marker of distinction that is associated with both cinematic aesthetics as well as film festivals such as Sundance, Cannes, and Toronto. In her discussion of aesthetics in "quality" and "prestige" cinema such as Barry Jenkins's *Moonlight* (2016), Racquel Gates writes,

> Film and television have created an aesthetic (via lighting, coloring, framing, etc.) that is designed to beautify and humanize whiteness while simultaneously masking the process of that beautification and humanization. That aesthetic has become the visual marker of "quality" or "prestige," and, for the most part, black images have been excluded from that aesthetic representation.
>
> *(40)*

Blank's film, on the other hand, draws attention to the presence of Black and female voices and these aesthetics as it insists upon putting those stories at the center of both the narrative and the visual and aural storytelling.

In her famous discussion of the "oppositional gaze" in *Black Looks*, bell hooks argues, "Critical black female spectatorship emerges as a site of resistance only when individual black women actively resist the imposition of dominant ways of knowing and looking" (128).

As Blank said in her interview with Mary Harron, "But I'm in love with a culture that hasn't always been loving to women, namely Black women. We're often seen through a very hypersexualized lens." In the film, Blank resists the traditional representation of Black women as hypersexualized or as mammies to complicate conventional understandings of aging Black women's identities and subjectivities since Blank is defined neither by her sexuality nor her motherhood, but rather by her desire to be a playwright, musician, and artist.

The film also self-reflexively comments on more traditional Black narratives as one of Blank's students says "She ain't no Tyler Perry" and Blank herself responds by saying, "This isn't *Dangerous Minds*." These short hands for how Black stories are traditionally told, as audience-pleasing comedies and soap operas, or as dramas featuring young Black children being taught by heroic white (female) saviors, also point out the limitations and restrictions of these narratives. As Blank laments that she is unable to produce her own plays because of her Blackness, she insists that she "just wants to make art," while she also draws attention to how Black theater spaces are often underfunded and under-resourced.

As Jacqueline Bobo writes, "centering Black women as subjects recognizable as human beings is paramount in Black Women's films" ("Black Women's Films" 8). In the film, Blank is trying to find a way to get her play about gentrification in Harlem (*Harlem Ave.*) made. However, when she is approached by a middle-aged white man who wishes to produce her play, he insists upon her lack of authenticity, asking "Did a Black person really write this?" Blank facetiously suggests that perhaps the play should include teen moms and drugs, while the producer refers to the need to spice it up with "a little rap number," as well as his need for a writer for his "Harriet Tubman musical." Blank refuses the offer since she believes she cannot make the art she wishes to make under these constraints and instead decides that she's going to make a hip-hop mix tape about the 40-year-old woman's point of view. Singing lyrics such as, "This is 40," "A white man with a Black woman's butt," and "You Regular Blacks Are Such a Yawn," she finds a DJ Producer on Instagram and she sings (as RadhaMUSprime) about the white gaze's eroticization of Black pain in "Poverty Porn."

When Blank fails at her public debut as a rapper, her DJ brings her to see a rap battle among women (played by themselves) in the boroughs of New York and Blank is once again encouraged to continue with her rapping as she sings about her dead mother in "Mommy, May I." Throughout the film, Blank uses jazz music to add to the mood and to continue to create an aural black aesthetic in the film that echoes the work of Spike Lee and John Cassavetes, even using the music of her own father, who was a jazz musician. The lyrics of her rap, "FYOV," "Find Your Own Voice, Forty-Year-Old Version, Fund Your Own Vision, Fill Your Own Void" also draw attention to the need to create a space for Black women and artists in art, music, and playwriting, as well as the notable absence of those voices from women of a certain age within those fields.

When the white producer again insists that he is willing to produce her play *Harlem Ave.* "pending some changes in length and tone," she asks, "Do I want to compromise my play for some arrogant asshole?" but agrees to do it since her desire to be a playwright overrides these misgivings. Though she insists on a black director for her play, the producer can only manage to find a white female director, the director of the all-male version of *Steel Magnolias*. In addition, the producer and director insist on including a white female character within the play to serve as a means of connecting with the presumably mostly white (and privileged) audience for the play. In this way, Black stories are undermined and revised to meet white expectations. In turn, Blank becomes more and more disappointed in the final production of her play and even almost misses its debut on stage since she is no longer proud of her work. At the same time, her refusal to accept the mediocre quality of her play once it had been rehashed through the white eyes of her producer and director is also a reminder of her refusal to sell out on her vision as well as her desire to create art that builds upon her own voice and point of view.

As another means of centering around these stories of Blackness and Black femininity, Blank also explicitly pays attention to the notion of Black hair and the beauty of Black hair. Throughout the film, she wears multiple head scarves and head wraps and the film draws attention to the aesthetics of these hairstyles both visually and narratively. At one point in the film, her DJ and lover D (played by Oswin Benjamin) even asks why she always covers her hair. In response, she notes that it makes her feel safe. But, later in the film, when she attends the opening of her play *Harlem Ave.*, she reveals her hair for the first time on screen. Though she may not be proud of the final version of her play, she is proud of her hair and body, and she owns her own aging Black femininity on screen. As Christina Baker notes in *Contemporary Black Women Filmmakers and the Art of Resistance*,

> Black women's reasons for choosing a particular hairstyle are varied and complex, ranging from racial ideology, to personal aesthetics, to convenience. Choosing a hairstyle can be one of the ways in which Black women reject externally defined ideas and practices and claim self-definition and empowerment.
>
> *(140)*

For Blank, this attention to the significance of Black women's hair and her choice to hide it and reveal it throughout the film functions as a means of resisting and challenging traditional ideas of female beauty, while at the same time emphasizing the complexities and contradictions that define both Black femininity and Black beauty.

The final few minutes of the film end with the color imagery of a New York City street as she walks with her DJ, rap producer, and lover D. The credits also include more fictional interviews with her community, as well as actual footage of her rapping as RadhaMUSprime. These stylistic choices also call attention to the intertwining of authenticity and fiction as the fictionalized interviews interact with the authentic documentary footage of her own rap career and musical performances. At the same time, this self-reflexivity also draws upon the ways in which Blank's own personal (and cinematic) style is rooted in the work of other independent storytellers. However, unlike the representation of Nola Darling in *She's Gotta Have It*, Blank is allowed to own her own identity and sexuality (Foote). Rather than being defined by the white men and women that surround her, she instead creates a space for her own voice and her own style of storytelling.

Conclusion

In Blank's film, the representation of not only Black women, but also gay men, Asian men, and Black men moves beyond what Kristen Warner calls "plastic representation" and toward what Mary Beltrán calls more "meaningful" diversity. As Kristen Warner notes in "In the Time of Plastic Representation," "To many men and women of color, as well as many white women, meaningful diversity occurs when the actual presence of different-looking bodies appear on screen" (33). By including the stories of people of color and the LGBTQIA+ community, and representing these characters as multi-dimensional, complex, and layered, Blank reconstructs and resists traditional and stereotypical representations of these marginalized identities. At the same time, the film also draws attention to the ways in which the cinematic aesthetics, multi-dimensional characters, and complex storytelling within independent filmmaking enables these representations of "meaningful diversity."

Thus, at the time of this writing, though Blank has plans to make another film, it is still unknown whether or not she will be able to secure funding and financial support for her next film. Blank responds to this concern over who the gatekeepers of this storytelling are, saying,

> "I had to get this story out….As an artist in New York, I've had my share of troubles and noticed these trends in terms of who decides who gets to tell what story to what audience – and that really frustrated me….Oftentimes the gatekeepers doubt your ability to tell a story or be an artist because you don't fit the mold of what they want to present," she continued. "It was a way to confront my frustrations – and celebrate the city that informs my way of telling stories."
>
> *(Ramos)*

Nevertheless, when asked about POC (People of Color) creators in her interview with Lulu Wang, she stated "Once we create the content, the possibilities are endless, the audience is right there." Thus, it also remains to be seen how audiences will continue to respond to these stories of Black female identity and resistance.

Note

1 I use the term Black and capitalize it here and throughout this chapter not only to follow the formatting changes of the *New York Times* and Associated Press in 2020, but also to acknowledge, as Lori Kido Lopez notes in *Race and Media: Critical Approaches* (NYU Press, 2020), that Black is capitalized "in order to deliberately center those who have historically been marginalized" (ix).

Works Cited

"2021 Sundance Film Festival Announces Audience Attendance." Sundance Blog. 8 Feb. 2021, https://www.sundance.org/blogs/news/2021-sundance-film-festival-announces-audience-attendance.

Baker, Christina. *Contemporary Black Women Filmmakers and the Art of Resistance*. The Ohio State University Press, 2018.

Baron, Cynthia. "Not Just Indie: A Look at Films by Dee Rees, Ava DuVernay, and Kasi Lemmons." *Indie Reframed: Women's Filmmaking and Contemporary American Independent Cinema*, edited by Linda Badley et al. Edinburgh University Press, 2016, pp. 204–220.

Beltrán, Mary. "Meaningful Diversity: Exploring Questions of Equitable Representations on Diverse Ensemble Cast Shows." *Flow*, vol. 12, no. 7, 2010, http://flowtv.org/2010/08/meaningful-diversity/.

Bobo, Jacqueline. "Black Women's Films: Genesis of a Tradition." *Black Women Film and Video Artists*, edited by Jacqueline Bobo. Routledge, 1998, pp. 3–20.

———. "Black Women Filmmakers: A Brief History." *The Routledge Companion to Cinema and Gender*, edited by Kristin Hole et al. Routledge, 2016, pp. 247–255.

Cobb, Shelley. "Black Women, Romance and the Indiewood Rom Coms of Sanaa Hamri." *Indie Reframed: Women's Filmmaking and Contemporary American Independent Cinema*, edited by Linda Badley et al. Edinburgh University Press, 2016, pp. 154–168.

Fleming, Mike. "'The 40-Year-Old Version's [sic] Radha Blank Is No Flash In The Pan: Sundance Q&A." *Deadline*, Jan. 25, 2020, https://deadline.com/2020/01/the-40-year-old-version-radha-blank-is-no-flash-in-the-pan-sundance-qa-1202841384/.

Foote, Thelma Wills. "Happy Birthday, Nola Darling," *Women's Studies Quarterly*, no. 35, 2007, pp. 212–233.

Gates, Racquel. "The Last Shall Be First: Aesthetics and Politics in Black Film and Media." *Film Quarterly*, vol. 71, no. 2, 2017, pp. 38–45.

Harron, Mary. "Flipping the Script: Mary Harron Interviews Radha Blank About Her Spirited and Wise New York Comedy *The Forty-Year-Old Version*." *Filmmaker Magazine*, 28 Oct. 2020, https://filmmakermagazine.com/110543-flipping-the-script/?fbclid=IwAR0myat5DeDFzsToCS5LZ6WIyOpBbGnDCcVoWjb3Ind6fe5lCx1Rmi116xA#.YTZmvmZKi3J.

hooks, bell. *Black Looks: Race and Representation*. South End Press, 1992.

Juhasz, Alexandra. "A Stake in the Future: Transforming Queer Cinema, Staying Dissident." *Coming Out to The Mainstream: New Queer Cinema in the 21st Century*, edited by JoAnne C. Juett and David Jones. Cambridge Scholars Publishing, 2010, pp. 257–275.

Levy, Emanuel. *Cinema of Outsiders: The Rise of American Independent Film*. NYU Press, 1999.

Ramos, Dido-Ray. "Radha Blank's 'The Forty-Year-Old Version' 'Confronts Frustrations' About Gatekeepers of Storytelling – Sundance Studio." *Deadline*, 28 Jan. 2020, https://deadline.com/video/40-year-old-version-radha-blanks-reed-birney-oswin-benjamin-peter-y-kim-sundance/.

Sheppard, Samantha. "I Love Cinema: Black Film and Speculative Practice in the Era of Online Crowdfunding." *Film Quarterly*, vol. 71, no. 2, 2017, pp. 25–31.

Sinwell, Sarah E. S. "Interview with Cheryl Dunye." *Independent Female Filmmakers: A Chronicle Through Interviews, Profiles and Manifestos*, edited by Michele Meek. Routledge, 2019, pp. 102–116.

"Vanguard Awards." Sundance Film Festival. https://www.sundance.org/festivals/nextfest/vanguard-awards.

Warner, Kristen. "In the Time of Plastic Representation." *Film Quarterly*, vol. 71, no. 2, 2017, pp. 32–37.

Zimmer, Catherine. "Histories of the Watermelon Woman." *Camera Obscura*, no. 68, 2008, pp. 41–67.

51

NOMADLAND (2020)

Geoff King

Critical opinion on *Nomadland* was divided even before the Oscar success that considerably upped the profile and reputational stakes surrounding Chloé Zhao's adaptation of the Jessica Bruder book about van-dwelling communities living and working on the margins of contemporary American life. The film, and Frances McDormand's central performance, was widely praised and the recipient of numerous awards. But it also faced criticism from some commentators for offering what was seen as a depoliticized and excessively rose-tinted portrayal of its world, particularly its treatment of the central character's employment at an Amazon depot at a time when the company's poor treatment of workers was in the spotlight.

The film seems somewhat radical by mainstream standards in certain dimensions, such as its depiction of an unvarnished older-woman central character, while less so in others. Rather than contributing directly to such evaluative debate, my aim in this chapter is to situate the stance of the film as more broadly characteristic of the tendencies of American indie films that engage in territory of this kind. If in several ways *Nomadland* represents a distinct alternative to the kind of material likely to be found in the Hollywood mainstream, it also manifests limits to how far this goes that are typical of this part of the contemporary film landscape rather than any exception to the rule.

A key focus of debate around the film was on its socio-political context but this also extends to the formal dimension, in which it was judged either to be exquisitely poetical – or some such terms – or to risk overly aestheticizing its subject matter.[1] Central to understanding the film also is the process through which it was conceived and produced, from the role of McDormand as producer to that of Zhao and former collaborators in the shaping of a distinctive blend of fictional and real-life narrative material. "Authenticity" is a key term in the discourse surrounding *Nomadland*, one that resonates at the socio-political, formal,

FIGURE 51.1 On the road in the frontier landscape in *Nomadland*.

and production levels and that marks another dimension in which it fits into prevailing indie tendencies and debates. This chapter engages in all three of the dimensions in which I argue elsewhere (King, *American*) that various degrees of the independence of indie cinema are marked: the socio-cultural-political, the formal, and the industrial/institutional.

Narrative

Nomadland is focused around the experiences of Fern (McDormand), a widow in her 60s who takes to the road, living in a van, after the evacuation of an entire settlement following the closure of the gypsum plant around which its existence was based. She joins a colony of itinerant workers who travel in pursuit of short-term work for employers including Amazon warehouses and campgrounds. The film charts the establishment of relationships of mutual support, if sometimes passing, between Fern and two other women, each played by real-life figures from Bruder's book, Linda (Linda May) and Swankie (Charlene Swankie).

In narrative terms, the format is driven chiefly by the rhythms of such movements and connections. A relatively more mainstream-conventional dimension comprises a series of intertwined meetings between Fern and another member of the nomadic community, Dave (played by the established indie performer, David Strathairn), which might be expected to develop into a romance. They first meet some 26 minutes into the film. He invites her to dance at a social event in a bar a few minutes later. Dave turns up again around the 47-minute mark, after Fern has moved to work as a host at a South Dakota Badlands campsite. Trying to help Fern soon afterward, he accidentally breaks precious items of crockery she has kept that were a gift from her father, provoking a briefly sharp response. She subsequently provides support when he is hospitalized, after which she joins him at his next place of employment, the nearby Wall Drug tourist attraction. Dave eventually moves in with the family of his son. Fern visits him during the latter stages of the film but leaves early one morning, after he asks her to stay, the film ending with a return visit to the shell of her former home in Nevada.

This can be viewed as a broadly characteristic indie treatment of such material. The narrative as a whole is low-key and undramatic, in contrast with Hollywood norms and in keeping with one established indie strand (for more on this, see King, *American*). It is driven primarily by responding to a sense of the realities of the life Fern has joined, lacking much in the way of classical-Hollywood-style development. Mixing this with what might be a romantic strand is a move of the kind more likely to be found in a Hollywood production. This dimension is also played down, however. It never moves into any clearly "romantic" modality, in what is implied about the relationship between the two figures. Moments that might have been developed in this manner, such as their dance together or Fern's response to the breaking of crockery, are passed over swiftly. And the relationship does not end with any more conventional "happy ever after" form of coupling, even if Fern's return to the road – and to the big wilderness landscape within which her former home is situated – constitutes what can be seen as a conventional gesture in its own right. The role of the "freedom" and "frontier" rhetoric drawn upon in the latter material is a significant aspect of the sociopolitical dimension of the film.

The Frontier, "Freedom," and Exploitation

A key nexus in politically focused debate about *Nomadland* occurs between notions of "freedom", particularly as associated with the longstanding American frontier-myth tradition, and freedom to be exploited by a variety of minimum-wage employers, most prominently but not only Amazon. The first workplace at which Fern is seen is Amazon, which is depicted quite positively in the film. Fern generally appears happy when shown at work and, when asked if she likes it, replies "Uh, yeah, great money." This contrasts with attitudes toward the company expressed by some of the subjects of Bruder's book, or by Bruder herself, for the grueling nature of the labor required of a primarily aging workforce (for example 55, 99, 101–104). While we might ask whether a soft line on Amazon was a condition of the company giving permission to film in one of its warehouses – a significant resource for the relevant part of the film – the issue is a broader one than just a matter of such practicalities. Bruder also questions the practices of other employers such as those who hire campsite hosts (23–26). She links the underlying situation of the inhabitants of her *Nomadland* to fundamentals of the economy that created a situation in which the costs of wages and housing have diverged to a point at which growing numbers can do longer achieve the dream of a middle-class life (7). This is especially the case for older people, she suggests, many of whose hopes for restful retirement have been undermined by such factors, along with shortcomings in social security and pensions.

A less specific form of criticism is voiced in the film, although not by the central protagonist. Another real-life figure from the book is Bob Wells, who offers support services and advice to van dwellers such as Fern, declaring that: "We gladly throw the yoke of the tyranny of the dollar on and live by it our whole lives" and suggesting also the analogy of workhorses that are being put out to pasture that need to gather together and take care of themselves. His offer of solidarity is matched by some of the small-scale acts of mutual support witnessed during the film but these exist in tension with an underlying evocation of notions of freedom and independence conventionally associated with American frontier heritage (that is, the longstanding and culturally deeply embedded notion that America embodies a particular variety of individual freedom, once guaranteed by a frontier point of contact with a supposedly "empty" wilderness).

Fern is painted as a strongly independent-minded, sometimes irascible figure. An exchange with her suburban-dwelling sister at one point makes clear that she left home as soon as she could, was seen as eccentric when growing up but was, in her sibling's words, "braver and more honest" than anyone else. It is the sister who spells out what the film seems often to imply: that "what nomads are doing is not that different from what the pioneers did. I think Fern's part of an American tradition. I think it's great."

If the film can be viewed as politically progressive in some ways, as part of the socially liberal or radical tradition within the American independent tradition – particularly in its sympathetic focus on what are presented as "ordinary people" living close to the margins, especially older women, whose representation is usually very limited in mainstream cinema – this seems to be compromised through its reliance on such discourse. American frontier mythology is enmeshed in many deeply exploitative, including near-genocidal, historical complexes, and remains a wellspring of reactionary tropes (too many to list here). The reliance on frontier tropes – both explicit and implicit – can be seen as not just evading political-economic reality but providing a form of ideological justification for the dubious practices exhibited by employers such as Amazon and others that feature in both film and book. As Wilfred Chan puts it, in a widely cited piece in *Vulture*, the film "plays into platform capitalists' favorite talking point: that temporary gig work, shorn of all rights and benefits, is what the workers want, *because freedom! because flexibility!*" By ignoring the mistreatment of such workers, he suggests, "the film misses the core insight that made Bruder's book so heart-wrenching: that there is no escape from the American economic system, and it preys upon the nomads continuously."

Ultimately, despite situating its protagonist within a real community, the film remains individual-centered and focused on a figure presented firmly as an individualist. In this respect, it shares a limitation of perspective characteristic of a great deal of even the relatively more socially/liberally oriented varieties of American indie film, a point I have made more generally elsewhere (King, *American*, 250). Fern is not presented as an individual who has any specific concerns about the nature of her labor. It is often presented as somewhat unappealing, including cleaning toilets at the campground and hard work on a beet farm. The film fits with established tradition, even for most indie films that touch on socio-political territory, in sharing and/or evoking this kind of individualized and depoliticized experience. It has, in this sense, something in common with the work of John Sayles, one of the most social issues-oriented stalwarts of the indie sector, a connection underlined by the presence in the cast of Sayles's regular Strathairn.

Style, Music, and Subtle Expressiveness

The audiovisual style of *Nomadland* can also be situated within broader indie tendencies. If American indie film in general varies considerably in its formal qualities, this example draws on two approaches that can be identified in such work: that which makes claims to the status of realism and that which is more expressive in effect, two tendencies I have examined at length elsewhere (King, *American*). *Nomadland* uses both in what can be characterized as a subtle and underplayed manner, closely related to the approach to narrative outlined above.

The impression of authenticity created by the film through its low-key narrative focus and its employment of very "ordinary" seeming characters is enhanced through the frequent use of hand-held camerawork, especially in following the movements of characters. This is not pronounced but sufficient to create a subliminal sense of verité footage that captures rather than constructs the on-screen material. A somewhat more expressive potential is found in some of the footage of real-world characters relating their stories, usually framed full-face, in cases where this occurs around a campfire, the visages glowing warmly against a background of dark sky. More clearly expressive sequences serve to chart some of the emotional valences of Fern's experiences. These also play an important role in how the film comes to embody aspects of the frontier discourse examined above.

Much of the film eschews the use of nondiegetic music that might, more mainstream-conventionally, offer an orchestration of how it is intended to be read at an emotional level. This can be seen as part of a commitment to a plainer, realist aesthetic. But music plays an important role in a number of more expressive sequences, starting with quiet and often quite minimal piano themes. One such sequence begins after Dave's departure from the Badlands campsite. The piano creates a sad, contemplative impression as Fern looks out at the landscape, through a hole in a distinctively shaped stone left by Dave, continuing over images of the protagonist in various parts of this location – including working, wandering a night-time street, and sitting out in the landscape. It persists under the noise of a beet farm, indicating her next destination, while at a laundromat, standing outside a cinema, in a diner, and receiving a video on her phone from Swankie. At this point, a violin enters, marking a more overtly emotional note, in tune with the material: the video contains footage of a special encounter Swankie talked about earlier with swallows, one of the experiences she said had made her life already complete.

Another such sequence leads Fern to her visit to Dave at the home of his son's family. This begins in a more literally poetic mode. Fern quotes lines from

Shakespeare's sonnet, "Shall I compare thee to a summer's day?," presenting this as her wedding vow in a conversation with a young drifter. The lines continue as the man is seen walking away and afterward while Fern looks at slides from her past. The piano theme then begins, the music continuing over shots of her in a big Redwood-style forest and then on the road. The mood seems mournful and elegiac, as before, but also evokes a sense of space, place, light, and "the road," building as before, with added violin, to accompany more images of driving, a sunset, and then her arrival at the family house. The impression here is perhaps evocative of the unspoken emotions that lead her to take up Dave's offer, if only briefly. But these sequences also embed emotionally in the film an elegiac sense of more broadly romantic frontier-freedom mythology expressed elsewhere, either in some of the comments of characters or the prevalence of other images of spacious/spectacular open western landscapes.

Production and Conception

The processes of conception and production of *Nomadland* also embody a mix of resonances from the domains of distinctively indie (or art cinema) social realism and the involvement of what can be seen as more conventional industrial practices. Zhao's preferred mode of production offers a romantically alternative (although demanding) "grass-roots" development process of going into communities and developing narratives from a basis in real-life material, although the initial conception of the film came from more established industry figures such as agents and the involvement of the star, McDormand, the latter's input also shaping the finished form.

Zhao's creative process in her first two films, *Songs My Brothers Taught Me* (2015) and *The Rider* (2017), was akin almost to a form of ethnographic research, an approach likely to be celebrated for its authenticity within broader indie discourse. For the former, she spent four years visiting the Pine Ridge Lakota reservation in North Dakota, writing multiple drafts of what became a screenplay that explores the relationship between two teenagers (Macaulay; Brooks). *The Rider* is focused on a real-life figure, Brady Jandreau, from the same community, who Zhao met after the completion of *Songs*, a young rodeo rider for whom she decided to write a script in which he plays a version of himself. This was before Jandreau suffered the head injury that subsequently became a central part of the narrative (Ponsoldt). Many of the characters in these films are playing versions of themselves, with much of the low-key narrative material set against real-world background activity, a production process aided by the filmmaker's establishment of trusting relations within the community.

Nomadland retains some aspects of this approach, including the involvement of central members of her production team, although with material not primarily originated by Zhao. The narrative is a combination of background and characters from Bruder's book, Zhao's research (conducted in her own campervan travels) and the story of Fern, the latter inspired at least partly by McDormand. As in Zhao's earlier films, many of those who appear are playing versions of themselves and telling of their real-world experiences, including central secondary figures such as Linda May, Swankie, and Bob Wells. Like *Songs* and *The Rider*, *Nomadland* can be interpreted as semi-documentary in status. Zhao describes the former as about 60 percent narrative and 40 percent documentary (Macaulay). A more overt process of fictional imposition is found in *Nomadland*, in that the story of Fern is not rooted in an actual individual experience. This central fictional focalization is key to the element of controversy surrounding the film. A treatment more thoroughly rooted in the perspectives of the individuals who feature in the book might have included some critique of the employment conditions they face. This would not necessarily be the case, however, as not all express such criticisms. A relatively more documentary-oriented approach might also have highlighted the broader socioeconomic context within which these are situated by Bruder. The film can be understood here within a long tradition of controversy about the mixing of elements of fact and fiction, in what is sometimes known as "docudrama," especially in the treatment of potentially contentious material (for a classic discussion, see Caughie).

The source of the fictional character of Fern appears to have been McDormand herself, in an anecdote often cited in discussion of the film. During her 40s, she apparently declared that when she was 65 she planned to change her name to Fern, get an RV (recreational vehicle), and hit the road. From this starting point, Zhao is reported to have filled in the rest of the character, including stories and photographs from McDormand's life (Aguirre). The star features in the discourse of authenticity surrounding the film, being hailed by Zhao as "so authentically herself" and apparently not having been recognizable as a professional performer by some of those with whom she engages in the film (Buchanan).

McDormand also played a central role in the initiation of the production, the involvement of a figure of her status creating an easier route to funding than had characterized Zhao's previous very-low-budget productions. An important part was also played by agents in this case, giving the initiation of the film something more in common with a Hollywood-style mode of business, even if at a smaller scale. Bruder received an offer to represent the book from one of Hollywood's leading agencies, one of the largest in the world, United Talent Agency.[2] The agency also represented McDormand, who was considered ideal for the lead role, then expected to be that of Linda May (this and the following detail are from Jolin). The book was optioned by McDormand with actor-turned-producer Peter Spears, the partner of the agent who represented McDormand. McDormand and Spears had met, particularly during the 2017 awards circuit, where they also encountered Zhao, which led to her agreement to make the film.

If the festival circuit played a role in bringing together the principals involved in the production, this is also a marker of the typically indie status of the film at the institutional level, such events playing a key role in the infrastructure of the sector. While industrially more marginal in status, Zhao's preceding films achieved high-profile festival screenings, *Songs* showing at Sundance and then Cannes, among others, and *The Rider* premiering at Cannes. *Nomadland* premiered at another of the elite festivals, Venice, where it won the Golden Lion. Its awards successes culminated with Oscar wins for best picture, director, and actress. These and its six nominations gained the film a much wider, Hollywood-style profile than that constituted by appearances at festivals. A match can also be seen between the textual blend offered by the film, including being star led and not overtly political in its orientation, and its domestic theatrical distribution by Searchlight Pictures, the speciality division renamed (losing the original "Fox") after the acquisition of 21st Century Fox by Disney. This is an achievement usually limited to relatively more mainstream-oriented independent productions in the crossover territory often known as Indiewood (for more on this, see King, *Indiewood*).

Conclusion

Although distinctively independent in various ways, *Nomadland* can be seen to manifest a range of both textual and extratextual qualities that demonstrate broader tendencies within the indie field that have persisted, from the boom of the late 1980s and early 1990s until the early 2020s. It is one of many examples, including the striking earlier films of Zhao, that counter any suggestion that indie/independent cinema of this kind died or disappeared at any point in between (see, for example, Tzioumakis). It is characteristic of many indie films both in offering a vision of the world alternative to that usually found in the commercial mainstream and in being limited in how far that goes, especially in terms of any translation into more overtly socio-political terms. It employs a low-key narrative design, embodying a major strand of indie film, but one that retains certain relatively conventional dynamics, principally the focus on a doughtily appealing central character. The film also mixes realist and quietly more expressive audiovisual style in a manner that fits into the longer tradition of both American indie and broader art-house approaches. Its mode of production and circulation is also a combination of that which is more independently distinctive, particularly the element of continuity with the community-rooted approach of Zhao, and some more established film-institutionalized processes such as the role of an agency and star in the initiation of the production and that of major festivals and a studio division in the gaining of reputation and distribution.

Notes

1 For an example of the latter, see Brody.
2 For background on the agency, see Katz.

Works Cited

Aguirre, Abby. "The World According to Frances McDormand." *Vogue*, 10 Dec. 2020, https://www.vogue.com/article/frances-mcdormand-cover-january-2021.

Brody, Richard. "'Nomadland' Reviewed: Chloé Zhao's Nostalgic Portrait of Itinerant America." *New Yorker*, 19 Feb. 2020, https://www.newyorker.com/culture/the-front-row/nomadland-reviewed-chloe-zhaos-nostalgic-portrait-of-itinerant-america.

Brooks, Xan. "Chloé Zhao: Film Director Poised to Make History Tomorrow." *Guardian*, 24 Apr. 2021.

Bruder, Jessica. *Nomadland*. 2017. Swift Press, 2021.

Buchanan, Kyle. "What Frances McDormand Would (and Wouldn't) Give to 'Nomadland.'" *New York Times*, 22 Feb. 2021, https://www.nytimes.com/2021/02/22/movies/frances-mcdormand-nomadland.html.

Caughie, John. "Progressive Television and Documentary Drama." *Screen*, vol. 21, no. 3, 1980, pp. 9–35.

Chan, Wilfred. "What *Nomadland* Gets Wrong About Gig Labor." *Vulture*, 22 Feb. 2021, https://www.vulture.com/article/nomadland-amazon-warehouse-chloe-zhao.html.

Jolin, Dan. "'Nomadland' Producers Explain How the Unorthodox Project Came Together." *Screen Daily*, 6 Apr. 2021, https://www.screendaily.com/features/nomadland-producers-explain-how-the-unorthodox-project-came-together/5158545.article.

Katz, Brandon. "Content Kings: Hollywood's 7 Most Powerful Talent Agencies." *Observer*, 11 July 2017, https://observer.com/2017/11/hollywood-talent-agencies-wme-uta-apa-icm-info-details/.

King, Geoff. *American Independent Cinema*. I.B. Tauris, 2005.

———. *Indiewood, USA: Where Hollywood Meets Independent Cinema*. I.B. Tauris, 2009.

Macaulay, Scott. "Parting Shot: Chloé Zhao." *Filmmaker*, 20 Jan. 2016, https://filmmakermagazine.com/96999-parting-shot-chloe-zhao/#.YN7feRNKj1I.

Ponsoldt, James. "Rodeo Dream: Chloé Zhao on *The Rider*." *Filmmaker*, 8 Mar. 2018, https://filmmakermagazine.com/104938-rodeo-dream/#.YN7eoxNKj1I.

Tzioumakis, Yannis. "'Independent', 'Indie' and 'Indiewood': Towards a Periodisation of Contemporary (Post-1980) American Independent Cinema." *American Independent Cinema: Indie, Indiewood and Beyond*, edited by Geoff King et al. Routledge, 2013, pp. 28–40.

INDEX

Note: *Italic* page numbers refer to figures and page numbers followed by "n" denote endnotes.

Adams, John 405
aesthetics/aesthetic style 1, 78, 98–99; aesthetics-in-action 351, 353–354, 356, 358–359; amateur 389, 392–393; of American independent cinema 247; avant-garde 113–116; of black and white 137, 470; cinematic 275, 392, 470, 473; conventions 46, 292; elements 292; experimental 305; film's 88, 141–142, 146–147, 215–216, 247, 287, 292, 384, 437, 443; Hollywood's relationship with 75, 126, 138, 254; independent filmmaking 215, 245, 266; industrial context of film 6, 22; influences 205, 207; innovation 3, 355; interactive 391; low budget 51–56, 392; naturalism 190; new scheme 210; noir 82, 199; personal 472; political 353; popular 305; priorities 136, 211; in quality and prestige cinema 42, 470; of science fiction 177, 180, 335; sensibilities in film 72–73, 254; and social distinctions 25; virtues 49; visual 138
"A" film: actors 51; *The Black Cat* (1934) 52; budget 43, 47n6, 51; directors 51; Hollywood film companies 6–7; rental rates 52; in rural markets 44; *The Strange Woman* (1946) 52
a-ha: "Take On Me" (1985) 289
Akerman, Chantal 452
Algren, Nelson 68

Ali, Muhammad 159
'all-colored comedies' 18
Allenberg, Bert 91, 92
Allen, Woody 470
Allied Artists Pictures Corp. 78
Almodóvar, Pedro 305
Altman, Robert 223–225, 228, 231, 301
American independent film/American independent cinema: aesthetics of 247; *American Beauty* (1999) 339; The American Independent Intervention (1989–1994) 8–9; analytical areas of 1930s 46; The "B" Film & Poverty Row (1938–1945) 6–7; chronological survey of 5; creation of 5–6; critical characteristics 3; critics' views 244–245; definition of "indie" 390; design of collection 4–5; *Edward Scissorhands* (1990) 339; exploitation filmmaking 292; filmmakers 253, 262–264, 306; history of 3, 12, 223, 291, 447, 456; institutionalization of 246; *Kiss of the Spider Woman* (1985) 244; LGBT 448, 449, 452–453; minority perspectives 205; outsider perspective and social engagement 351; periodization of 380; *Pleasantville* (1998) 339; purpose and premise 1, 3; social change & new markets (1969–1974) 7–8; social inequality & rethinking distribution

(2020) 9–10; *The Trip to Bountiful* (1985) 244, 245; *The Watermelon Woman* (1996) 323–324, 351, 363, 366, 432
American International Pictures (AIP) 78, 151–152; *The Born Losers* (1967) 152
American Splendor (2003) 379–387, *380*; comix movement 380–385; HBO Films 379; voice-over narration 383–384
America, Paul *105*, 107
Amirpour, Ana Lily 311
Anderson, Laurie 405
Anderson, Lindsay 453
Anderson, Sherwood 458; *Winesburg, Ohio* (1919) 458
Anderson, Wes 246, 342–347, 349; *Bottle Rocket* (1996) 344; *The Grand Budapest Hotel* (2014) 344; *The Life Aquatic with Steve Zissou* (2004) 344
Andrew, Geoff 243
Andrews, Michael 337
Anger, Kenneth 114, 170
Anthology Film Archives 115–116
Appalshop: *Buffalo Creek Flood: An Act of Man* (1975) 404
appropriation 280, 284, 363, 401, 406
Araki, Gregg 211, 449, 452, 453
Arbuckle, Roscoe "Fatty" 31, 34, 36
archives 356, 428; canonical 366; censorship and erasure 400; effect 400; of feelings 366; films 323–324, 367; gay cinematic *362*, 362–365; queer Hollywood 367; sparse or nonexistent 353; UCLA film 146
Arnold, Matthew 129
Arnold, Steven 190; *Luminous Procuress* (1971) 190
art cinema 110, 144, 227, 292, 345, 481; European 126, 128, 214, 225, 229, 447, 452; independent 254, 290; international 264, 290; tradition of 228
art-house horror *see* elevated horror
Artisan 376
Arzner, Dorothy 366
A24's brand-driven strategy: *Hereditary* (2018) 439; *It Comes at Night* (2017) 439; *The Lighthouse* (2019) 439; *Men* (2022) 439; *Midsommar* (2019) 439; *The Witch* (2015) 437, 440–441
Ashley, Christopher: *Jeffrey* (1995) 193
Asian CineVision (ACV) 208–209
Asinof, Eliot 264
Attack of the 50 Foot Woman (1958) 77–84, *78*; generic convergences 82–84; generic dependencies 79–82;

grotesque monstrosity 77; independent/ exploitation 78–79; melodrama 79–81; noir 81–82
audience/viewership: alternative viewership 46, 172; crossover audiences 236; spectatorial expectation 167; underserved audiences 7
auteur 150, 197, 202, 299–301, 317–318, 345; Hollywood 214, 220–222; indie auteur 135, 221–222, 333–335, 342–344, 349
authenticity 63, 119, 451, 453, 470, 473, 476, 480–482; of film 389, 391; heterosexual 384; with indie film movement 408; narratives of 409–411, 413, 415; of ordinary people 205; performance art's 210; street 71; underground 102
authorship/authorial voice 3, 8, 314, 325, 383; in collaboration 61; directors' 334; filmmaking model 313–314; intertextual canon 363; traditional notions 463
Autry, Gene 40, 42, 45, 46
avant-garde film 3, 101, 106–107, 113–114, 168, 207, 209–210, 304–305, 310, 430, 432, 434
Azoulay, Ariella 400

Babb, Kroger 98
Backman Rogers, Anna 147
Badalamenti, Angelo 305
Báez, Jillian 370
Baillie, Bruce 209
Baker, Christina: *Contemporary Black Women Filmmakers and the Art of Resistance* 472
BAMcinemaFest 430
Barenholtz, Ben 170, 172
Barker, Clive 100
Barkin, Ellen 245
Baron, Cynthia 468
Baron, Jaimie 400
Barron, Steve 289
Barrymore, Drew 299
Bass, Saul 70, 72–74
Bastién, Angelica Jade 325
Bauchau, Patrick 226
Baugh, Scott L. 375
Baumann, Shyon 428
Bean, Henry 334
Bechdel, Alison 381
Before Midnight (2013) 408–415, *409*; authenticity and autonomy 411; definition of independent film 408–409; gender dynamics 413–414; Generation

X youth culture 409–411; naturalistic approach 412; sense of naturalism 408; smart cinema 413
Belafonte, Harry 70
Beltran, Mary 473
Bender, Lawrence 320
Benigni, Roberto 245; *Life is Beautiful* (1997) 245
Benjamin, Robert 68, 69
Benjamin, Walter 395
Bennett, Tony 127
Berlin, Brigid 106
Berlin International Film Festival 10, 208
Bernstein, Armyan 215
Bernstein, Elmer 70, 72–74, 361; *Blues and Brass* 73
Bernstein, Matthew 91
Bertolucci, Bernardo 305
"B" film 5, 43; 1938–1945 6–7; *Billy the Kid Returns* (1938) 40–46, *41*; characteristic of 41, 49, 53, 56; economy 51, 57; filmmakers 52, 55; performers/personas 45; *Raw Deal* (1948) 52; rise of 50–51; in 1930s 6; *T-Men* (1947) 52
Billy Jack (1971) 149–156, *150*; American International Pictures (AIP) 151; Hollywood cinema 149–151; independent biker exploitation film cycle 152; *Jaws* (1975) 155; *Jaws 2* (1978) 156; narrative works 151; plot and cinematic style 150; Warner Bros. 155
Billy the Kid Returns (1938) 40–46, *41*; "B" film 40, 43; Roy Rogers 40–41, *41*, 45–46
Bingham, Dennis 90
Black filmmaking 5
Blank, Radha 466, 467, 469
Blockbuster films: big-budget blockbuster 441; *Billy Jack* (1971) 149–156, *150*; *Days of Thunder* (1990) 290; found-footage horror 392; franchise blockbusters 441; indie blockbuster 391–394, 440; *Paranormal Activity* (2007) 389–396, *390*; *Pulp Fiction* (1994) 313–321, *314*; *Teenage Mutant Ninja Turtles* (1990) 286–293, *287*
Blumenthal, Ralph 158
Bob & Carol & Ted & Alice (1969) 8, 122–129, *123*; content and style 124; Mazursky's characters 128–129; Natalie Wood 122–123, *123*; sexual curiosities and contingencies 124–128
Bobo, Jacqueline 468, 471
Bonello, Bertrand 311
Bong Joon Ho 311

Borden, Lizzie: *Blood Simple* (1984) 207; *Born in Flames* (1983) 207
Bordwell, David 110, 217, 460
Boultenhouse, Charles 115, 117
box office: A-films 45, 51; anarchistic comedies 37; *Billy Jack* (1971) 155–156; *Bob & Carol & Ted & Alice* (1969) 122; Buster Keaton Productions 32, 35–36; *Deep Throat* (1972) 159; *The Devil in Miss Jones* (1973) 160; *Donnie Darko* (2001) 333, 336, 340; *Down by Law* (1986) 245; *Easy Rider* (1969) 142, 152; flops 38; *The Graduate* (1967) 152; *The Killing of a Chinese Bookie* (1976) 199; *Kiss of the Spider Woman* (1985) 244–245; *Lone Star* (1996) 263; *Marty* (1955) 92; *My Big Fat Greek Wedding* (2002) 376; receipts 75, 87; record breaking 15, 29, 74; *Stranger than Paradise* (1984) 244; *Wendy and Lucy* (2008) 456, 458
Boyd, William 40
Brakhage, Stan 115–117
branding 353, 390, 440–442
Brando, Marlon 70, 71, 422
Brasell, R. Bruce 110
Bressan, J Arthur Jr. 450; *Abuse* 450
Brim, Matt 433, 434
Brokaw, Cary 245
Brown, Garrett 216
Brown, Helen Gurley 127
Bruce Lee 206, 289; *Enter the Dragon* (1973) 289
Bruder, Jessica 476–479, 481–482
Buñuel, Luis 311
Burke, Tarana 258
Burnett, Charles 209, 449, 450, 467; *Killer of Sheep* (1978) 449; *My Brother's Wedding* (1984) 450
Burton, Tim 97, 289; *Batman* (1989) 97
Buscemi, Steve 317
business practices and strategies 3, 6–7
Buster Keaton Productions: *Back Stage* (1919) 34; *Battling Butler* (1926) 33; *The Boat* (1921) 34; *College* (1927) 32, 34, 35; *The General* (1927) 32, 33; *The Navigator* (1924) 34; *One Week* (1920) 34; *The Saphead* (1920) 36–37; *Sherlock Jr.* (1924) 33, 35; *Steamboat Bill, Jr.* (1928) 31–38
Butler, Judith 277, 278, 283, 284

Cagle, Chris 89
Callender, Colin 373, 376
Camacho Xtravaganza, Luis 280
Campbell, Joe 107

Campion, Jane 305
Canby, Vincent 145, 146, 201, 225, 301
Cannes Film Festival 245, 304; *Pulp Fiction* (1994) 8; *sex, lies, and videotape* (1989) 8, 269
Cannon, Dyan 122, 123, 128
canon 113, 115–116, 142, 180, 284, 363, 366–367, 427–434, 449
Capra, Frank 304
Carpenter, John 7, 177–184, 308; *Assault on Precinct 13* (1976) 178; *Dark Star* (1974) 7, 178
Carson, Diane 262
Cassavetes, John 115–117, 137, 195–202, 447, 471; *Faces* (1968) 195, 200; *Husbands* (1970) 195; *The Killing of a Chinese Bookie* (1976) 195–202, *196*; *Minnie and Moskowitz* (1971) 195; *Shadows* (1959) 200; *A Woman Under the Influence* (1975) 195
Catherine, Putnam 456
censorship: film ratings 151, 165n1; Production Code 68, 70–71, 73–75, 104, 151, 171; X as a film rating 171
Chan is Missing (1982) 204–212, *205*; cinema vérité approach 206–207; Icon of 1980s Independent Cinema 205–207; and independent filmmaking 206, 211–212; independent film's cultural and institutional context 208–209; independent performances 209–211; independent production and distribution journey 207–208
Channing, Stockard 235
Chan, Wilfred 479
Chaplin, Charlie 23, 31, 36, 68, 69, 137, 138
Chion, Michel 305
Choose Me (1984) 223–231, *224*; art cinema 229–230; Coda 230–231; Hollywood 226–228; independent filmmaking 228–229; story 225–226
Chopra, Joyce: *Smooth Talk* (1985) 450
Choy, Christine: *Who Killed Vincent Chin?* (1987) 211
Christian, Barbara 353
Christie, Julie 223
Christina, Frank 150
Chubb, Caldecot 324
Church, David: *Post-Horror: Art, Genre and Cultural Elevation* 439
Cieutat, Michel 128
Cinecom Pictures 298
Cinema 16 209
cinematography: camera angles 28, 345; camera movement 108, 216, 225, 229, 275, 307, 329, 342, 350n3, 412, 439; close-up 26, 37, 54, 71, 89, 106, 126, 128, 249, 272–273, 299, 308, 313, 325, 347, 379, 403, 418, 454; color 132–133; compositions 100, 126–127, 133, 161, 219, 230, 244, 246–247, 250, 262, 353, 439; continuity 261, 343, 346–347, 381, 483; cutting 63, 109, 128, 142, 217; lighting *50*, 56, *60*, 62, 64, 82, 126, 143, 199, 310, 470; long shot 28, 34, 37, 144, 169, 308, 338, 453–454; medium shot 37, 417; monochrome 453; reverse shots 37, 108, 274, 317; shadowy 199
Claremont, Chris 288; *X-Men* 288
Clarke, Shirley 113, 115–117, 119, 120, 143, 429–434; *The Connection* (1961) 115, 117; *The Cool World* (1964) 117; *Portrait of Jason* (1967) 113, *114*, 429
class 263, 277, 283, 404, 429, 434, 467; real 71; social 420; of theater patrons 18; working 24, 40, 44, 71, 89, 109, 137, 372, 375, 377, 381, 404, 420
Classical Hollywood: aesthetics 62, 78, 88, 90; genres 62; industry/industrial structure 104, 110, 214, 344, 361, 365, 478; narrative/storytelling 78
Clayton, Alex 27
Cobb, Ron 468
Cobb, Shelley 468
Coen brothers: *Barton Fink* (1991) 8
Collins, Eddie 266
Collins, Patricia Hill 352
Color Me Blood Red (1965) 96–102, *97*; "Blood Trilogy" 97; Herschell Gordon Lewis 96–102
Comics Code Authority (CAA) 380–381
Comique Film Corporation 36
commentary 342–343, 346, 422; authorial 264, 267; comic 124; cultural 3; direct 217; Director's 235–236; meta 28, 30; narrational 348; off-screen 423; political 183; social 7, 117, 311, 364
Conner, Bruce 401; *A Movie* (1958) 401
controversy 61, 68, 70, 73–75, 138, 234, 253, 290, 317, 319, 321n2, 376, 386, 482
Coogler, Ryan 467
Cooper, Chris 263
Cooper, Natalie 238
Copier, Laura 425
Coppola, Francis Ford 179, 200, 214–222, 229; *Apocalypse Now* (1979) 220; *The Conversation* (1974) 220; *The Godfather* (1972) 155, 200, 220; *The Godfather Part II* (1974) 200, 220

Coppola, Sofia 308; *The Virgin Suicides* (1999) 308
Corey, Dorian 277, 279, 280
Corliss, Richard 124
Corman, Roger 79, 101, 263; *A Bucket of Blood* (1959) 97; *War of the Satellites* (1958) 79
Cornell, Joseph 401; *Rose Hobart* (1936) 401
counterculture 154, 181, 379, 387
Crenshaw, Kimberlé 283
Crimp, Douglas 110
critical reception 17–19
Crittenden. John 144, 145
Cromin, Christopher 143
Cronenberg, David 100, 311
Crosby, Bing 70
Crow, Jim 134
Cruise, Tom 290
Crumb, Robert 381
cult movies 340n7, 362
cultural criticism/critical 8, 115
cultural studies 4, 361
cultural visibility 160
Cvetkovich, Ann 363, 365, 366

Dalí, Salvador 311
Dallas Buyers Club (2013) 417–425, *418*; character and story elements 420–422; critiques of film 418–419; film style 420; formation of alliances and pseudo-alliances 424–425; gay or trans characters 423–424; professional challenges and opportunities 424; reviews and commentaries 422–423; 1980s AIDS epidemic 417–418; US film industry 419–420
Damiano, Gerard 158–164; *The Devil in Miss Jones* (1973) 160
Daniels, Lee 467
Dark Star (1974) 176–184, *177*; cult film 177–178; Dan O'Bannon 177–183; genre 178–180; John Carpenter 177–183; political commentary 182–183
Dash, Julie 209, 323, 331, 466–468
Davis, Angela 356
Davis, Blair 81
Davis, Glyn 362, 363
Davis, Hope 385
Davis, Kimberly Chabot 282
Day, Doris 70
Dean, James 317, 422
Deep Throat (1972) 8, 158–165, *159*; big screen appeal 161–163; comedic and cinematic 163–165; phenomenal box office 159; studio system 159; US independent cinema 158
Defender: critique of Ebony 18–20
De Havilland v. Warner Bros. (1944) 87
Deitch, Donna 233–238, 240, 450
Delpeut, Peter 401
Delpy, Julie 408, 410
Demme, Jonathan 356
DePalma, Brian: *Blow Out* (1981) 214, 222
Deren, Maya 114, 116, 310
Desert Hearts (1986) 233–240, *234*; audience reactions to landmark lesbian romance 237–239; Gay New Wave 239–240; independent filmmaking 235; low-budget film 235; overcoming production and distribution hurdles 235–237
DeShannon, Jackie 128
Desjardins, Mary R. 363
Desser, David 125, 129
Detour (1945) 49–57, *50*; Independent Filmmaking in studio era 50–51, 57; low budget aesthetic 51–56; Poverty Row filmmakers 49; rise of B-Film 50–51, 56–57
Detweiler, Robert 125, 128, 129
Deutchman, Ira 298, 301
digital cinema 218
Dillon, Matt 296
directors 31, 36, 60, 87, 91, 219, 311n1, 458, 463; A-directors 51; commentary 235–236; European 214, 221; female 145, 164, 323, 429, 432; festival's 298; fictional 356; first-time 277, 323; indie *auteurs* 333, 361, 456–457; inexperienced 136; New Hollywood 214, 344, 366; North American independent 311; queer 453; statements 300; Taiwanese "New Cinema" 453
DirecTV's VOD (Video on Demand) platform 442
Dire Straits: "Money For Nothing" (1985) 289
Disney 289, 291, 441, 483; *Dick Tracy* (1990) 290; purchase of Miramax 318, 320
distribution: four-walling 149, 155–156; platform release 10, 299; saturation release 155; self-distribution 375, 428
distribution companies 24, 31, 115, 129n2, 254, 320, 371, 376
distributors 7, 75, 427–428, 431; AIP 151; Allied Artists 81; Columbia 200; four-wall 153; independent 8–9, 36, 38, 69, 190, 237, 245, 289–291, 298, 319, 334; Miramax 269, 319; New Line Cinema

190, 289–290; UA 93; Universal 200; VHS-era 321
Doan, Brian 379, 382
Doane, Mary Ann 81
documentary film 12, 125, 281
Doherty, Thomas 79
Donnie Darko (2001) 333–340, *334*; *Back to the Future* (1985) 336, 337; blank style, concept of 337–338; coming-of-age story 338; events of 9/11 340; genre 335–337; Indie Auteur 334–335; smart cinema 333, 337–339
Doren, Mamie. Van 317
Doros, Dennis 431, 432
Douglas, Kirk 88
Down by Law (1986) 243–250, *244*; from relative failure to slow critical recuperation 244–246; "reworking" of *Stranger than Paradise* 243–244, 250; symmetry, rhythm, and narrative time 246–250
DreamWorks 390, 393
Dunham, Lena 470
Dunye, Cheryl 323, 351–356, 358, 359, 363, 365–367, 432, 468, 470; *The Watermelon Woman* (1996) 323–324, 351, 363, 366, 432
DuVernay, Ava 467, 468
Dyer, Richard 187, 366

Eastman, Kevin 288, 289, 293
Ebert, Roger 99, 204, 252, 329, 330
Ebony productions: *A Busted Romance* (1917) 19; *Dat Blackhand Waitah Man* (1917) 19; *Shine Johnson and the Rabbit's Foot* (1917) 19
Edelstein, David 422
editing: long take 34, 37, 107, 109, 126, 142, 243, 250, 261, 321, 327, 403, 412–413, 454; rhythmic editing 244, 246, 249–250
Egoyan, Atom 311
Ehrenstein, David 222
Eight Men Out (1988) 261–268, *262*; and class in 1980s America 265–267; critical analyses of 264–265; independent from baseball film 267–268
Eisenstein, Sergei 208, 401
elevated horror 427, 439, 440, 442
Elgin Cinema 170, 172–173
Elias, Robert 265
Elliot, Wild Bill 40
Erickson, Mary P. 387, 449
E.T. (1982) 337
Eve's Bayou (1997) 323–331, *324*; experimental black-and-white exposition 326–327; power and responsibility of looking 325–326; production and power 324–325; reception and legacy 329–331; ways of seeing 327–329
The Evil Dead (1981) 337
exhibition practices 167, 392, 394
exhibition venues/spaces 3, 17
The Exorcist (1973) 155
experimentation 49, 113, 124, 156, 250, 304, 310, 333, 380, 387, 392, 396, 431, 470
exploitation films 78, 81, 97–99, 152, 156n1, 290–292; *Freaks* (1932) 98; *Maniac* (1934) 98; *Reefer Madness* (1936) 98, 290

Fairbanks, Douglas 31, 68
Fairbanks, Harold 188, 189
Far From Heaven (2002) 361–367, *362*; "archival" filmmaking 362–363; from Hudson to Heaven 363–365; queering Hollywood's racialized gazes 365–367
Fassbinder, Rainer Werner 361, 362, 365, 366, 452; *Ali: Fear Eats the Soul* (1974) 361, 362
femininity 358, 420, 424, 467, 472
Field, Todd 334
Figowitz, Otis 459
film; acquisitions/negative pickup 61, 371, 394, 396n1; critics/film reviewers 124, 155, 182, 192, 287, 334, 343; distribution 105, 171, 200, 289, 394; exhibition 10, 24, 118, 159, 171, 173, 191; history 4, 78–79, 204, 313, 354, 362, 367; movements 5–6, 144, 170, 239, 408, 448, 470; production 12, 14, 24–25, 49, 51, 55–56, 81, 220, 376–377; reception 13, 68, 142, 151, 191, 196, 214–220, 329–330; reviews 144–145, 182, 186, 192, 201, 238, 280
filmmakers of color 352
Fine Line Features 298
Finney, Albert 223
First Cow (2020) 9, 456–464, *457*; complementary collaboration 458; protagonists' crime 463; restricted narration 460–461; slow cinema 456
fiscal practices/budget: grassroots fundraising 235; low-budget/low-budget filmmaking 8, 40, 43, 49, 51–57, 59, 61, 70, 98, 101–102, 137, 152, 154, 167–168, 179, 193, 206–207, 214, 235, 286, 290, 292, 297, 390, 393, 450, 459; micro-budget 204, 211, 450, 453

Flanagan, Matthew 142
Flatley, Jonathan 111
Flower Drum Song (1961) 211
Flynn, Charles 101
folk horror: *The Blood on Satan's Claws* (1971) 439; *The Wicker Man* (1973) 439; *The Witch* (2015) 438–440; *Witchfinder General* (1968) 439
Foner, Eric 263, 265
Foote, Thelma Willis 253
Ford, Enfield 135, 136
Ford, John 452
Forgács, Péter 401
The Forty-Year-Old Version (2020) 9, 10, 466–474, *467*; American independent cinema 466; analyzing 469–473; Black women's filmmaking 466, 467–469; New African American Cinema 466–469; Sundance Film Festival 466
Foster, William 12, 13
found-footage films: *Black Door* (2001) 391; *The Blair Witch Project* (1999) 290, 389, 391–393; *909 Experiment* (2000) 391; *FeardotCom* (2002) 391; *Suicide Club* (2002) 391
Fox Movietone Newsfilm Library 401
Francis, Terri 131, 354
Frankovich, Mike 122, 123
Frankovich Productions 122
Frank, Robert 115; *Pull My Daisy* (1959) 116
Frank, T. C. 150
Freeman, Joel 137
Freud, Sigmund 161
Friedan, Betty 125; *The Feminine Mystique* (1963) 125
Friedlander, Judah 385
Friedman, David F. 97, 98
Friedman, Lester D. 124, 125, 129
Frisell, Bill 398, 402, 405, 406
Fulci, Lucio 99
Fuller, Samuel 116
Fullerton, Hugh 267

Gaines, Jane 142
Gaines, Sam 17
Gandil, Chick 266
Garcia, Alberto 451, 452
Gates, Racquel 470
Gayle, Crystal 217, 218, 220
gender norms 59, 67, 279
gender representation 78–79
genre/film genre: action 141, 201–202; animation 37, 181, 321; biography 353, 380, 384; comedy 8, 13–20, 22–23, 27, 32–34, 137, 161, 163–164, 178–179, 222, 244, 246, 299, 307, 377, 430; crime film 52–53, 55, 196–198, 201; disaster 33, 35, 253, 398–399, 402–406; epic 201, 207, 220, 222, 405; fantasies 77, 79, 127, 179, 216, 240, 413, 430; gangster 195, 198–202, 207, 315–316, 320; horror 80–81, 83, 90, 96–97, 101, 178, 290, 336, 389, 392, 393, 395, 439, 442, 452; hybridity 59, 79; melodrama 59, 62–64, 71–72, 78–85, 98, 132, 141–142, 198, 305, 308, 324, 326, 329, 354–358, 361, 364–365; mystery 155, 173, 207, 212, 305, 307, 310–311; neo-noir 196–197, 199, 207; noir 59, 64, 72, 81, 197–199, 206, 305; revision 179, 198, 320, 361; romcom (romantic comedy) 8, 320, 365; science fiction (sci-fi) 77, 79–81, 84, 161, 178–180, 207, 335–336, 339; slapstick 15, 22, 37, 164, 178; superhero 288–289, 292, 381–382; thriller 59, 80, 223; war 59–60, 69, 321, 437; western 42, 46, 151
Gerima, Haile 209
Giamatti, Paul 382, 383, 385, 386
Gianikian, Yervant 401
Gill, John 365
Ginsberg, Allen 117
Giorno, John 106
Godard, Jean-Luc 99, 221, 452, 453
Godfrey, Channing 467
Goldfarb, Harry 419
Goldsby, Jackie 282
Gordon, Michael 405
Gordon, Stuart 100
Gorfinkel, Elena 141, 145, 146, 456
Gorin, Jean-Pierre 452
Graham, Barbara 87–91, 270–275, 339
Grandrieux, Philippe 311
Grant, Barry Keith 79
The Great Flood (2012) 398–406, *399*; compilation films 399–402; filmmaker and musician as historiographers 405–406; identifying structure 400, 402–403; national exceptionalism 398–399; reevaluating history 403–405
Griffith, D.W. 31, 68, 212
Guerrero, Ed. 252

Halberstam, Jack 277, 283, 284, 356, 366
Hamri, Sanaa 468
Harris, Jack H. 181
Harris, Jeremy O. 427, 428

Harris, Leslie 468; *Just Another Girl on The I.R.T.* (1992) 468
Harris, Wendell B. 452
Harron, Mary 471; *American Psycho* (2000) 419, 469
Hawke, Ethan 408, 410
Hawks, Howard 179
Hayek, Salma 373
Haynes, Todd 308, 361–367, 449, 453, 457; *Safe* (1995) 308
Haysbert, Dennis 364
Hayward, Susan 87–93
HBO Films 370, 372–373, 376, 379, 386
Hedman, Lars 143
Heller, Amy 431, 432
Hemphill, Essex 280, 282
Hendershot, Cyndy 80
Henreid, Paul 61
Henson, Jim: *The Story Teller* (1987) 289
Hertz, Nathan 79
Hesford, Victoria 144
Higgins, Michael 143
Higson, Andrew 210
Hillberg, Gary 401; *Lip* (1999) 401
Hillier, Jim 291
Hirsch, Foster 128
Hitchcock, Alfred 73, 78, 116, 316; *Psycho* (1960) 316; *Strangers on a Train* (1951) 316; *Topaz* (1969) 116; *Vertigo* (1958) 73, 78
The Hitch-Hiker (1953) 59–67, *60*; genre and form 62–65; industrial context 59–62; Nicholas Musuraca *60*; themes 65–67
Hittman, Eliza 456
Hoberman, J. 171
Holliday, Jason 113, 427
Hollywood film companies 6
Hollywood/Hollywood studios 7, 12, 45, 50, 69, 214, 221, 234, 269, 371, 440
Hollywood's Production Code 68
Holt, Tim 40
hooks, bell 254, 256, 257, 277, 281–283, 325, 331, 471; *Black Looks: Race and Representation* (1992) 281
Horne, Philip 404, 406
Hou Hsiao-Hsien 453
Hubbard, Jim 118
Hyman, Kenneth 137, 138

I Married a Monster from Outer Space (1958) 80
I Want to Live! (1958) 87–94, *88*; Figaro, Inc. 91–93; traditional Hollywood style 88–91

identity politics 321n2, 363–364, 367
ideological positions/ideology 1, 146, 372, 472
Iger, Vijay 405
Independent Cinema Moments, creation of 5–6
Independent Feature Project (IFP) 447
independent film companies 7, 24
Indiana, Robert 106
indie cinema/indies 28–29, 228, 237, 246, 275, 295–296, 301, 314, 317, 319, 344–345, 441, 447, 449, 456, 463–464
Indiewood 9, 313–314, 316–318, 320–321, 371, 373, 380, 401, 440–441, 443, 483
industrial structures and mechanisms 3, 40, 215
innovation: aesthetic 3, 355; design 180; in four-walling 149; in genre 197; technological 219
institutional structures 41, 46, 182–183, 358, 425, 433, 482
intersectionality 283–284, 363
Ivens, Joris 402; *Regen* (1929) 402

Jackie Chan 289; *The Big Brawl* (1980) 289
Jackson, Joe 267
Jackson, Michael 289
Jackson, Samuel L. 315, 324
Jacobs, Ken 115
Jacobs, Lea 43
James, Bill 266
Jancovich, Mark 101
Jarmusch, Jim 189, 243, *244*, 245, 246, 249, 250, 262, 300, 456, 470; *Stranger than Paradise* 243–246, 250, 261, 270
Jason and Shirley (2015) 427–434, *428*; canon(s) 430–434; marginalized voices 428–429
Jason-Leigh, Jennifer 223
jazz music 405–406
Jeffries, Herb 14
Jenkins, Barry 467, 470
Jenkins, Bruce 106
Jenkins, Henry 37, 343, 344
Jodorowsky, Alejandro 178
Johansson, Johann 405
Johnson, Ban 266
John-Steiner, Vera. 458, 463
Jones, Kent 178, 214
Jones, Quincy 125
Jones, Rhodessa 356
José Gutierez Xtravaganza 280
Joyrich, Lynne 364
Juhasz, Alexandra 417, 423

Jules, Gary 337
Julien, Isaac 365; *Looking for Langston* (1989) 365–366
July, Miranda 456, 457
Juran, Nathan 79

Kael, Pauline 145, 304
Kalin, Tom 107, 290, 449; *Swoon* (1992) 290, 295
Kane, Joseph 43
Kaufman, Charlie 311
Kazan, Elia 123, 143, 145; *Splendor in the Grass* (1961) 143; *Wild River* (1960) 143
Keaton, Buster 23, 31–33, 35–38
Kelly, Richard 311, 333–338
Kelman, Ken 115
Kenehan, Joe 263
Kerr, Ben 417
The Killing of a Chinese Bookie (1976) 195–202, *196*; Cosmo ventures 196, 199; genre expectations 199–200; intellectual experiment 195–196; as "post-noir masterpiece" 197; prioritization of "white events" 197–198
Kim, So Yong 468
King, Geoff 80, 81, 122, 198, 200, 286, 306, 373, 428, 433, 439, 456
King J.J. 33–35
King, Martin Luther Jr. 131
Klein, Martin 17
Koch, Stephen 108
Kramer, Stanley 87–88
Krim, Arthur B. 68, 69
Krzywinska, Tanya 80
Kubo, Duane 209
Kubrick, Stanley: *Dr. Strangelove or: How I Learned to Stop Worrying and Love the Bomb* (1964) 179; *2001: A Space Odyssey* (1968) 179
Kunka, Andrew J. 383
Kusturica, Emir 305

Laird, Peter 288, 289, 293
Lancaster, Burt 88
Landis, John 73
Lang, Brent 442
Lang, Charles 122
Lang, David 405
Langston, Tony 18, 19
Lantz, Robert 91, 92
Lardner, Ring 267
La Rue, Lash 40
Laughlin-Taylor Productions 153

Laughlin, Tom 8, 149–156; *Billy Jack Goes to Washington* (1977) 155; *The Born Losers* (1967) 152; *The Master Gunfighter* (1975) 155
LaVoo, George 370–373, 375
Leacock, Richard 143
The Learning Tree (1969) 131–138, *132*; "auteurism" 134; "Black film" 131–132; film about race 131–138; W7 contract 131, 134–135, 137
Lee, Ang: *Pushing Hands* (1991) 211; *The Wedding Banquet* (1993) 211
Lee, Carl 117, 120
Lee, Christina 410
Lee, Spike 189, 352, 404, 467, 469–471; *BlacKkKlansman* (2018) 258; *Crooklyn* (1994) 253; *Do the Right Thing* (1989) 253; *Girl 6* (1996) 258; *Malcolm X* (1992) 253, 258; *She's Gotta Have It* (1986) 252–259, *253*, 469; *When the Levees Broke: A Requiem in Four Acts* (2006) 404
Léger, Nathalie 145
Leigh, Mike 305
Lemmons, Kasi 323–325, 327, 329–331, 468
Lennard, Dominic 124
Lennon, John 145
Leone, Sergio 116; *Once Upon a Time in the West* (1969) 116
Leslie, Alfred: *Pull My Daisy* (1959) 116
Leto, Jared 417–424, *418*
Levy, Emanuel 167, 168, 268, 390, 394, 467
Lewis, Herschell Gordon 96–102; *Bell, Bare and Beautiful* (1962) 97; *Blood Flesh 2: All U Can Eat* (2002) 102; *Goldilocks and the Three Bares* (1963) 97; *The Gore Gore Girls* (1972) 102; *Jimmy the Boy Wonder* (1966) 98; *Multiple Maniacs* (1970) 102; *Two Thousand Maniacs!* (1964) 102
Lierow, Lars 131
The Lincoln Lawyer (2011) 417
Linklater, Richard 52, 408–413; *Boyhood* (2014) 408; *Slacker* (1990) 409
Livingston, Jennie 8, 9, 277, 280–283; *Paris Is Burning* (1990) 8
Lloyd, Harold 22–25, *23*, 28–30
Loach, Ken 453; *Looks and Smiles* (1981) 453
Lochary, David 172
Loden, Barbara 7, 140, 142–146; *Ernie Kovacs Show* (1952–1956) 143; *Wanda* (1970) 7
Lombardo, Patrizia 250
Lopez, Jennifer 373
López, Josefina 370–373

Lorentz, Pare 402, 403; *The Plow That Broke the Plains* (1936) 403; *The River* (1937) 402
Los Angeles Gay & Lesbian Film/Video Festival 298
Lott, Tommy L. 131
Lovecraft, H.P. 180
Lucas, George 178–180, 184; *Star Wars* (1977) 155, 178; *THX 1138 4EB* (1967) 179–180
Lucchi, Angela Ricci 401
Lulu Wang 261, 466, 470, 473
Lurie, John 245
Lynch, David 8, 53, 300, 304–311; *Blue Velvet* (1986) 245, 304; *Eraserhead* (1977) 170, 304; *Inland Empire* (2006) 305; *Lost Highway* (1997) 305; *Mulholland Drive* (2001) 305; *Twin Peaks: Fire Walk with Me* (1992) 304–311, *305*; *Wild at Heart* (1990) 8

Mabry, Tina 331
Macdonald, Dwight 115
Maharg, Billy 267
mainstream film/media 9–10, 12, 14, 27, 30, 46, 50, 161, 204, 214, 254, 270, 344–345, 347, 370, 373, 375, 433, 468
Mandel, Johnny 89, 90
Maneri, Joe 382
Mankiewicz, Joseph L. 87, 88, 91–94; *The Barefoot Contessa* (1954) 88, 93
Mann, Anthony 52
Mann, Denise 94
Manne, Shelly 72
The Man with the Golden Arm (1955) 68–75, *69*; aesthetics and style 72–73; censorship: challenges and creative constraints 73–74; Otto Preminger 68–70; Sinatra's Stardom and Performance *69*, 70–72; United Artists (UA) 68–70
marginalized communities 4, 209, 419, 425
marginalized filmmakers: Black filmmakers 138, 209, 258; female filmmakers 434, 450, 466, 468; Latinx filmmakers 8, 277, 280; queer/LGBTQ+ filmmakers 8, 240n2
marginalized voices 9
marketing: advertising 8, 93, 98, 105, 118, 153–154, 172–173, 201, 298; promotion 153, 319–320, 393, 422
Markopoulos, Gregory 115–117
Marquette, Jacques 79
Marshall, Jimmy 17; *Aladdin Jones* (c. 1914) 17, 18; *Money Talks in Darktown* (c. 1914) 17, 18; *The Shooting Star* (c. 1914) 17; *Two Knights of Vaudeville* (1915) 12–20
Martin, Alan R. 135–137
Martin, Darnell 468
masculinity: American 27, 29; Black 256; female 356; heterosexual 120, 363; white 23–24, 26
Mathijs, Ernest 79
Mayne, Judith 366
Mayshark, Jesse Fox 410
Mazursky, Paul 122–129
McCarthy, Todd 101
McClain, Florence 15–17, 19
McConaughey, Matthew 417–424, *418*
McCormick, Matt 457
McGowan, Todd 252
McLaughlin, Tom 8; *Billy Jack* (1971) 8
McMillon, Joi 331; *Moonlight* (2017) 331
McQueen, Steve 470
media: comic books 182, 286–290, 335, 382–385; journals 115, 173, 192; magazines 61, 73, 119, 134, 158, 160, 164, 181–182, 299, 314; mass media 318; news 73, 336, 400, 405; print ads 155, 299; radio 72, 219, 268, 448; social media 393, 409, 442; television 8, 45–46, 69, 153–154, 167, 171, 209, 271, 306, 316, 371, 466; video games 293
media conglomerates 9, 291, 371, 440–441
media industries studies 408
Mekas, Adolfas 447
Mekas, Jonas 105, 107, 114, 115–117, 119, 120, 143
Méliès, Georges 16
Mendik, Xavier 79
Menken, Marie 116
Menne, Jeff 91
Merande, Doro 72
Mercer, Kobena 366
merger/acquisition 68, 123, 152, 291, 319, 371, 394, 420, 483
Metz, Christian 342
Meyer, Russ 98, 99, 164, 192, 447; *The Immoral Mr. Teas* (1959) 98, 164
Michael Jackson: "Billie Jean" (1983) 289
Micheaux, Oscar 13, 14, 19
Michel, Frann 358
Mickwitz, Nina 384
midnight movies 7, 167, 170–174
Miles, Ron 405
Milk, Harvey 107
Miller, Arthur 143
Miller, Frank 288; *Daredevil* 288
Milne, Tom 229

Miramax Films 9, 277, 291, 376, 390
Mitchell, David Robert 311
Mitchell, John Cameron 334
Moffatt, Tracey 401
Monogram Pictures 51
Monroe, Marilyn 317
Montgomery, Edward 87
Montgomery, Frank 15–17, 19
Montgomery, Robert 61
Moore, Alan 381
Morrison, Bill 398, 400, 402, 403, 405; *Dawson City: Frozen Time* (2016) 405; *Decasia: The State of Decay* (2002) 402; *The Film of Her* (1997) 405; *The Miners Hymns* (2011) 405
Morrison, James 429
Motion Picture Association of America (MPAA) 255; rating system 7
Motion Pictures Patents Company (MPPC) 3
Murphy, Jack 181
museum/museum showings 208, 313, 317, 321, 405
Musser, Charles 14, 16
My Big Fat Greek Wedding (2002) 372, 376
My Hustler (1965) 104–111, *105*; Andy Warhol's film 104–105; Hollywood cinema 104; overview 105–107; queerness of 107–111
My Own Private Idaho (1991) 295–302, *296*; Fine Line Features 298–299, 301; Gus Van Sant 296–300; New Queer Cinema 295–296; promotional discourse 299–301

NAACP 12
Nair, Mira: *Salaam Bombay* (1988) 211
Nakamura, Robert A. 209
Namaste, Viviane K. 283, 284; *Invisible Lives* 283–284
Nance, Terence 354
Naremore, James 55, 81
narrative temporality 357, 456
Nathan, Daniel 265, 267
National Archives 401
National Film Registry 376
The Natural (1984) 265
naturalism 63, 90, 190, 225, 227, 408
Nava, Gregory 209: *El Norte* (1983) 207
Nelson, Ricky 317
New American Cinema 105, 113–117
New Hollywood (Hollywood Renaissance) 7, 26, 78, 88, 94, 115, 124, 126, 150–151, 178–179, 214, 220–222, 318, 393, 447

New Line Cinema 8, 291, 293; *Austin Powers* (1997–2002) 291; *Boogie Nights* (1997) 291; *House Party* (1990–1994) 290; *Lord of the Rings* (2001–2003) 291; *Nightmare on Elm Street* (1984–1994) 290; *Rush Hour* (1998–2007) 291; *Wag the Dog* (1997) 291
Newman, Michael Z. 23, 26, 264, 343, 344, 409, 440; *Indie: An American Film Culture* 440
New Queer Cinema (NQC) 9, 295, 366; *Edward II* (1991) 449; *Go Fish* (1994) 449; *The Living End* (1992) 449; *Longtime Companion* (1989) 449; *Parting Glances* (1986) 449; *Poison* (1991) 449; *Postcards from America* (1994) 449; *Swoon* (1992) 449; *Totally F***ed Up* (1993) 449
New York Film Fest 10
New York's Lesbian and Gay Experimental Film Festival 118
Nichols, Bill 399
Nichols, Mike 123; *The Graduate* (1967) 123
1985 (2018) 447–455, *448*; AIDS Coalition 451; American Independent Film movement 448; cinema of outsiders 449–451; Independent Feature Project (IFP) 447; LGBTQ cinema 447; New Queer Cinema 448–449
Nixon, Richard M. 158
Nochimson, Martha P. 305, 307, 309
Noé, Gaspar 311
Nolan, Christopher 333; *Memento* (2000) 333
Nomadland (2020) 9–10, 476–483, *477*; critical opinion on 476; debate around film 476–477; frontier, freedom, and exploitation 478–480; narrative 477–478; production and conception 481–483; style, music, and subtle expressiveness 480–481
non-theatrical film 12
Norman, Richard E. 13
Novak, Kim 68, 71–74

O'Bannon, Dan 177–184; *Alien* (1979) 178; *Heavy Metal* (1981) 178; *The Return of the Living Dead* (1985) 178
Ohashi, Alan 209
Oishi, Eve 281
One from the Heart (1982) 214–222, *215*; dawn of electronic cinema 218–220; Independent Filmmaking 220–222; New Hollywood Auteur 214, 220–222; theatrical realism 216–218; theatrical

realism & cinematic style 215–218; Zoetrope Studios 214–215
Ono, Yoko 145
oppositional strategies 42, 152, 325, 336–337, 471
Orion Pictures 291
Orlovsky, Peter 117
Ortiz, Raphael Montanez 401
Oscars: *Dances with Wolves* (1990) 291; *The Silence of the Lambs* (1991) 291
Osco, Bill: *Mona, The Virgin Nymph* (1970) 160

Pacific Film Archive 208
Palmer, Laura 304, 307, 308
Palmer, Leland 306
Palmer, R. Barton 124
Paradin, Joe: *The Gay Alternative* 191
Paramount 40
Paranormal Activity (2007) 389–396, *390*; budget of film 389–390; definition of "indie" 390, 394–395; demon and loss of aura 395–396; found-footage horror 391–392, 396; history of genre 390–391; post-9/11 "torture porn" 392; reframing "independent blockbuster" 392–394
Paris is Burning (1990) 277–284, *278*; "realness" and representation in 278–280; trans lives and intersectionality in 283–284
Parker, Brant 457
Parker, Eleanor 71, 72
Parker, Honey 79
Parks, Gordon 7, 89, 131–138; *The Learning Tree* (1969) 7
Pasolini, Pier Paolo 452
Payne, Aaron 117, 118
Peary, Danny 98, 101
Peckinpah, Sam 116; *The Wild Bunch* (1969) 116
Peele, Jordan 467
Pekar, Harvey 379–387
Peli, Oren 389, 390, 393, 394
Penn, Arthur: *The Family Rico* (1972) 200; *Mickey One* (1965) 200
Pennell, Eagle 449
Peoples, Channing Godfrey 467
performance/performance style 13–17, 20, 27, 37–38, 70–75, 90, 92, 127, 199, 209–211, 283–284, 300, 321, 417, 420–424
Perren, Alisa 297, 318, 371, 372, 376, 409, 443
Perry, Frank: *David and Lisa* (1962) 116
Perry, Troy 191, 471

Pfeiffer, Carolyn 230, 231
Phillips, McCandlish 145
Phillips, Wyatt D. 429, 433
Pickford, Mary 31, 68, 69
Pierson, John 244, 252, 254, 269; *Spike, Mike, Slackers & Dykes* 254
Pink Flamingos (1972) 167–174, *168*, 190; advertisements for 172–173; bad taste 170; independent film 167–168; midnight movie exhibition 167, 170; narrative of film 168–169; rating system 171, 173
Polanski, Roman 212, 221; *Chinatown* (1974) 212
political film 3, 78, 447, 449, 478
Pollard, Luther J. 17
Pomerance, Murray 124
Poole, Wakefield 160; *Boys in the Sand* (1971) 160
Portrait of Jason (1967) 113–121, *114*; exhibition of 118–119; New American Cinema 114–117; Shirley Clarke 113; spiritualized reality 115
Poster, Steven 338
post-horror *see* elevated horror
post-1978 "indie" film 23, 26
post-studio Hollywood 419
Poverty Row: *Billy the Kid Returns* (Republic, 1938) 6–7; *Detour* (PRC, 1945) 6–7; Monogram Pictures 51; Producer's Releasing Corporation (PRC) 51; Republic Pictures 51
Powell, Dick 61
Powell, Michael 220
Powell, Ryan 187
Preminger, Otto 68–70, 72–74, 87
Presley, Elvis 70
press coverage 8, 221, 299
prestige horror *see* elevated horror
Price, Steven 463; *The Screenplay* 463
Prince-Blythewood, Gina 331, 467
producer/producing 13, 17, 69, 75, 468; creative 93; entertainment 26; independent 25, 50, 60, 68, 87, 93, 94, 136, 152, 181, 334, 370–371; low-budget 61; queer 432
Producer's Releasing Corporation (PRC) 51
production companies 6, 35, 36, 42, 49, 51, 60, 69, 87, 377, 443, 463
production location 7
Proferes, Nicolas 143, 144
promotional discourse 393, 410
Puente, Henry 376; *The Promotion and Distribution of U.S. Latino Films* 376

Pulcini, Robert 379–381, 383–387
Pulp Fiction (1994) 313–321, *314*; and the auteur 317–318; as entertainment 320–321; "cinema of cool" 318; production 318–320; retrospection 313–314; story 314–317
Pyramid Theater 173

queer cinema 5; LGBTQ films/filmmaking 188, 192, 237, 239; New Queer Cinema (NQC) 9, 295, 366, 449

race 253, 263, 277, 283, 355, 402, 404, 406, 409, 429, 434
Rae, Issa 354
Raimi, Sam 100
Rain Dogs (1985) 246
Rainer, Yvonne 116
Rappaport, Mark 361, 363; *Rock Hudson's Home Movies* (1992) 361, 363
Raymond, Jon 456–464
Ray, Nicholas 123
Reagan, Ronald 263, 266
realism: documentary 64, 90, 384; social 29, 137, 456, 481; theatrical 215–218
Real Women Have Curves (2002) 370–377, *371*; adaptation 372–375; Chicana feminist perspective 371; independent production 372; recognizing 375–377
reception discourse 419, 422
reception practices 13, 17–19, 142, 191, 220, 329–331
Rechin, Bill 457
Rees, Dee 466–468
Reeves, Keanu 295, 297, 299, 300
reflexivity/reflexive 124, 129, 342–349, 383
regional cinema 449; *Gal Young 'Un* (1979) 449; *Northern Lights* (1978) 449; *Return of the Secaucus 7* (1980) 449
Reichardt, Kelly 456–464; *Meek's Cutoff* (2010) 456; *Night Moves* (2013) 456; *Old Joy* (2006) 456; *River of Grass* (1994) 457
Reisz, Karel 343
René, Norman: *Longtime Companion* (1989) 193
Renoir, Jean 451, 452; *The Rules of the Game* (1939) 451
Republic Pictures 51
re-release 10, 17–18, 153, 156, 178–179, 181, 200, 202, 245, 282, 290
Reynaud, Bérénice 143, 144, 146
Richardson, Tony 453
Rich, B. Ruby 9, 295, 298, 419, 428, 448
Rickey, Carrie 216

Riley, Boots 466
risk-taking 70, 75
Ritter, Tex 40
Roberts, Jean 149
Robeson, Paul 70
Robson, Mark 308; *Peyton Place* (1957) 308
Rodriguez, Robert 102, 318
Roeg, Nicolas 221
Roemer, Michael: *Nothing but a Man* (1964) 116
Rogers, Maureen 154, 155
Rogers, Roy 40, 41, 43–46
Rogers, Shorty 72
Romero, George A. 447
Rosenbaum, Jonathan 171, 197
Rosenbaum, Richard 292, 293
Rother, Larry 253
Rothman, Tom 245
Rothstein, Arnold 267
The Royal Tenenbaums (2001) 342–349, *343*; familial themes and reflexive use of style 344–346; Indie auteur 343–344; reflection and commentary 342–343; reflexive use of storytelling 346–349; voice-over (VO) 348
Rudolph, Alan 223–231
Rule, Jane 234
Rybin, Steven 230
Ryder, Winona 299

Safety Last! (1923) 22–30, *23*; Harold Lloyd 22–25, 28–30; three-act structure 24–30
Safford, Tony 451, 452
Salloum, Jacqueline: *Planet of the Arabs* (2005) 401
Sarris, Andrew 117, 330, 343, 463
Sayles, John 235, 262–268, 480; *Baby It's You* (1983) 262, 263; *The Brother from Another Planet* (1984) 207, 263; *City of Hope* (1991) 263; *Eight Men Out* (1988) 263; *Lianna* (1983) 263; *Lone Star* (1996) 263; *Men with Guns* (1997) 263; *Matewan* (1987) 263, 265; *The Return of the Secaucus 7* (1980) 263; *Sunshine State* (2002) 263
Scherr, Tony 405
Schlesinger, John 453
Schub, Esfir: *The Fall of the Romanov Dynasty* (1927) 401
Schulman, Sarah 118, 432, 433
Schwartz, Russell 245
Schwarzenegger, Arnold 290
Sciamma, Céline 311
Sconce, Jeffrey 79, 101, 413

score/music 142, 181, 198, 403, 439
Scorsese, Martin 73, 179, 214, 222; *The King of Comedy* (1982) 222
Scott, A.O. 421
screenwriter/screenwriting 59, 61, 188, 227, 238, 262, 356, 410, 423, 450, 456–459
Sedgwick, Edie 106
sex, lies, and videotape (1989) 246, 269–276, 270; classic *indie* 269–270; media production and consumption 270–271
Sexton, Jared 358
sexuality 277–278, 355; Black 254–258; female 80, 162, 164, 256–258; lesbian 263; male 255; queer 295–296
Shakespeare, William 9, 295, 411, 481; *Henry IV* 9
Sheen, Martin 220
Sheppard, Samantha 468, 469
Sherman, Henry 344, 347
Sherwood, Bill: *Parting Glances* (1986) 193, 450–451
She's Gotta Have It (1986) 245, 252–259, 253, 270; black feminist critiques 255–258; black representation and sexuality in film 254–255; Spike Lee 252–253
Shropshire, Terilyn A. 331
Shub, Esfir 401
Shumway, David 262, 264, 265
Shuster, Harry 143
Sica, Vittorio. De 452
Silvera, Darrell 74
Silver, Marisa 450; *Old Enough* (1984) 450
Sim, Dave 288
Simien, Justin 467
Siminoski, Ted 156
Simpson, Don 381
Sinatra, Frank 58, 70–75; *Frank Sinatra Conducts Tone Poems of Color* 73; *From Here to Eternity* (1953) 70–71; *The Man with the Golden Arm* (1955) *69*, 70–72; *On the Town* (1949) 70; *On the Waterfront* (1954) 70
Singer, Jack 221
Singer, Leslie: *Taking Back the Dolls* (1994) 365; *Valley of the Dolls* (1967) 365
Singleton, John 323
Sirk, Douglas: *All That Heaven Allows* (1955) 80, 361, 362; *Imitation of Life* (1959) 362; *Written on the Wind* (1956) 362
Slater, Christian 299
Smith, Andrew Brodie 44
Smith, Cauleen 468
Smith, Harry 115
Smith, Jack 115; *Flaming Creatures* (1963) 115

Smith, Kevin 318
Smith, Murray 124
Smith, Valerie 353
social impact 8, 356
Soderbergh, Steven 8, 9, 269, 287, 362, 409; *sex, lies, and videotape* (1989) 8, 409
Soldier Blue (1970) 151
Solondz, Todd 456
Sontag, Susan 115
Sorg, Adam 97, 100–102
sound 14, 37, 42, 162–163, 366
Spadoni, Robert 310
specialty divisions (of the Hollywood studios) 297
Spencer, Octavia 466
Sperb, Jason 383, 385
Spielberg, Steven 184, 214, 222, 254, 390, 393; *The Color Purple* (1985) 254; *1941* (1979) 222
Spivak, Gayatri Chakravorty 281
Springer Berman, Shari 379, 381, 383–387
Stacey, Jackie 238
Stang, Arnold 72
Starrett, Charles 40
Starrett, Jack 321; *The Losers* (1970) 321
star text/star persona 299, 421
Steamboat Bill, Jr. (1928) 31–38, *32*; Buster Keaton Productions 31–33, 35–38; classic of silent cinema 31; long-shot long takes 34, 37; United Artists (UA) 31–32, 35–36
Steckler, Ray Dennis 98
Steele, Bob 40
Steinbock, Eliza 425
Steinem, Gloria 145, 235
stereotypes 12, 55, 120, 145, 205, 226, 254, 257, 279
Stewart, Jacqueline Najuma 14
Stranger Inside (2001) 351–359, *352*; Dunyementaries 352–354; ins and outs 358–359; women-in-prison (WIP) film 351, 355
Sullivan, Ed 317
Sundance Film Festival 457
Sweeten, Madylin 385

Taiwan New Cinema 453–454
Tajima, Renee: *Who Killed Vincent Chin?* (1987) 211
Tarantino, Quentin 9, 102, 246, 313, 317–320, 362; *Pulp Fiction* (1994) 9, 246; *Reservoir Dogs* (1992) 246
taste cultures 46, 337, 441
Tavel, Ronald 106
Taylor, Delores 149, 150, 152–156

technology: distribution 220; exhibition/ projection 200, 329; production 62, 106, 219, 275, 379, 386, 389, 393, 401
Teenage Mutant Ninja Turtles (1990) 8, 286–293, *287*; as independent film 286–287
Teenage Mutant Ninja Turtles III (1993) 290
Teenage Mutant Ninja Turtles II: The Secret of the Ooze (1991) 290
Telluride 10, 329
20th Century Fox 40; *All About Eve* (1950) 87; *The House on 92nd Street* (1945) 62; *A Letter to Three Wives* (1948) 87; *The Naked City* (1948) 62
Thomas, Emma 333
Thompson, Kristin 110, 216
Thonen, John 183
Thurman, Uma 315, 317
Till, Emmett 331
Till-Mobley, Mamie 331
Tinkcom, Matthew 168
Tomlin, Lily 235
Toronto Film Festivals 329
Townsend, Robert 467
transsexual 282, 284
Travolta, John 315
The Trial of Billy Jack (1974) 155
Trier, Joachim 311
Tri-Star Pictures 450
Trouble in Mind (1985) 224
Tucker, Larry 122, 128
Turner Broadcasting System 291
Twin Peaks: Fire Walk with Me (1992) 8, 304–311, *305*; Laura's Voyage 307–310; lineages, missing pieces, and returns 311; primacy of atmosphere 310
Two Knights of Vaudeville (1915) 12–20, *13*; Bert Murphy *13*, 15; critical reception of 17–19; Ebony Film Co. 16–17; Florence McClain *13*, 15; Frank Montgomery *13*, 15; Historical Feature Film Company 13–14, 16–17; historically grounded analysis 14–15; performers 15–16
Tyler, Joel 164, 165
Tyler, Parker 115
Tynan, Tracy 228, 229
Tzioumakis, Yannis 43, 214, 286, 291, 316, 318, 380

Underground movies 170–171
United States v. Paramount (1948) 87
US Library of Congress's National Film Registry 401
Utah-US Film Festival 450

Vanderbeek, Stan 115
Van Sant, Gus 9, 290, 295–301; *Drugstore Cowboy* (1989) 246, 295, 296; *Mala Noche* (1986) 296, 298; *My Own Private Idaho* (1991) 9, 290, 295–302, 296
A Very Natural Thing (1974) 7, 186–193, *187*, 298; production of 188–189; scholarship on 187–188; vision of sexuality 189
Villeneuve, Denis 311
Vincent, Amy 326, 329, 331
Visual Communications (VC) 209
VOD (Video-on-Demand) 9
Vogel, Amos 209
Von Praunheim, Rosa 170

Wagner, Karyn 331
Waits, Tom 215, 217, 218, 220, 245–247
Walken, Christopher 321
Walsh, Keri 90
Walsh, Raoul 59; *High Sierra* (1941) 59; *They Drive by Night* (1940) 59
Wanda (1970) 140–147, *141*; beginnings 143–144; belated recognition 142–143; generic framework 141–142; returns 146–147; and Women's Liberation 144–146
Wanger, Walter 50, 87, 88, 90–92; *Foreign Correspondent* (1940) 91; *The Quiet American* (1958) 92; *Riot in Cell Block 13* (1953) 90; *Scarlet Street* (1945) 91; *Stagecoach* (1939) 91
Wang, Wayne: *Bean Sprouts* (1977) 207–208; *Dim Sum* (1985) 450; *Dim Sum: A Little Bit of Heart* (1985) 208, 211; *Fire Over Water* (1981) 208; *The Joy Luck Club* (1993) 211; *New Relationships* (1977) 207; *Wah Kue: The Chinese in America* 207
Warhol, Andy 104–108, 110, 111, 115, 117, 119, 143, 173
Warner Bros. 40; *Bonnie and Clyde* (1967) 142; *Crazy Rich Asians* (2018) 211
Warner, Kristen 473
Wasser, Frederick 153, 155
Waters, Jack 432, 433
Waters, John 7, 8, 102, 167–174, 190, 290, 298, 300, 311; *Hairspray* (1988) 174; *Pink Flamingos* (1972) 7, 290; *Serial Mom* (1994) 174
Wayne Wang 204, 450
W7 contract 131, 134–135, 137
Weaver, Buck 267
Weill, Claudia 449, 450; *Girlfriends* (1978) 449–450

Welles, Orson 137, 138, 295; *Chimes at Midnight* (1965) 295; *Citizen Kane* (1941) 138, 326, 328
Wenders, Wim 221, 305
Wexler, Haskell 190, 263
Wilder, Billy 81, 82; *Love in the Afternoon* (1957) 81
Wilinsky, Barbara 169
Williams, Linda 141, 161
Williams, Spencer 14
Williams, Tennessee 330
Willis, Bruce 223, 315
Willis, Ellen 165
Willis, Sharon. 363, 364
Winger, Newt 132, 134, 138
Winter, Stephen 427, 430–434; *Chocolate Babies* (1996) 427–428, 430
Wise, Robert 88–90, 92
Wishman, Doris 99, 164
The Witch (2015) 437–443, *438*; A24's brand-driven strategy 437, 440–441; elevated folk horror 438–440; marketing 442–443
Wolfe, Julia 405
Wollesen, Kenny 405
Women of the Movement (2022) 331

Wong, Eddie 209
Wood, Edward D. Jr. 98
Wood, Natalie: *Rebel Without a Cause* (1955) 123; *Splendor in the Grass* (1961) 123
Woodroof, Ron 417–419, 421–423
Woolner, Bernard 79
Workman, Chuck 401; *Precious Images* (1986) 401
Wright, Joseph C. 74
writer-director 131, 133, 190, 196, 269, 325, 327, 330, 333, 366, 437
Wyatt, Justin 156, 171, 190, 290, 291, 320, 433, 443

Xtravaganza, Angie 277
Xtravaganza, Venus 279, 282

Yang, Edward 453
Yasui, Lise: *Family Gathering* (1988) 211

Zanuck, Richard 152
Zhao, Chloé: *The Rider* (2017) 481, 482; *Songs My Brothers Taught Me* (2015) 481, 482
Zinoman, Jason 183

For Product Safety Concerns and Information please contact our EU
representative GPSR@taylorandfrancis.com
Taylor & Francis Verlag GmbH, Kaufingerstraße 24, 80331 München, Germany

www.ingramcontent.com/pod-product-compliance
Lightning Source LLC
Chambersburg PA
CBHW050300010526
44108CB00040B/1905